A HISTORY OF THE BLACK WATCH [ROYAL HIGHLANDERS] IN THE GREAT WAR, 1914-1918

VOLUME ONE

VOLUME ONE: REGULAR ARMY
1st, 2nd and 3rd Battalions

VOLUME TWO: TERRITORIAL FORCE
4th, 5th, 4/5th, 6th and 7th Battalions
and Allied Regiment
The Royal Highlanders of Canada

VOLUME THREE: NEW ARMY
8th, 9th, 10th, 11th, 12th, 13th and 14th Battalions

A SOLDIER OF THE BLACK WATCH ON THE ROAD TO ARRAS, 1916
After the drawing by Sir William Orpen

Vol. I

Frontispiece

A HISTORY OF THE BLACK WATCH
[ROYAL HIGHLANDERS]
IN THE GREAT WAR, 1914–1918

EDITED BY

MAJOR-GENERAL A. G. WAUCHOPE, C.B.

Author of
"The Black Watch, 1725–1907"

AM FREICEADAN DUBH

LONDON
THE MEDICI SOCIETY LIMITED
MCMXXV

Printed and bound by Antony Rowe Ltd, Eastbourne

TO
THE MEMORY OF
THE EIGHT THOUSAND MEN
OF THE
REGULAR, TERRITORIAL AND SERVICE BATTALIONS
OF
THE BLACK WATCH
WHO GAVE THEIR LIVES IN THE GREAT WAR
THIS HISTORY IS DEDICATED

" Without labour there is no coming to rest, nor without fighting can the victory be obtained."

PREFACE

THIS record of The Black Watch during the Great War shows how some thirty thousand men served in the Regiment in France, Belgium and Salonica, in Palestine and Mesopotamia, of whom eight thousand were killed and over twenty thousand were wounded.

The long days in the trenches encouraged a very close understanding between officers and men, and many hours were spent talking over what might best be done for the good of the Regiment after the war. Serving in the earlier part of the war as a company officer, I gathered from these discussions that there were three schemes which great numbers of our men hoped might, one day, be realized.

The first of these schemes entailed the reorganization of the Regimental Association, in order that help might be given to the large number of men, who, it was feared, would find themselves in difficulties or in distress after the war. This first object has been achieved through the labours of many officers of The Black Watch, among whom I must mention the names of the Earl of Mansfield, Colonel S. A. Innes and Major L. Gibson.

The second scheme often spoken of was that of a War Memorial, which should not only be a visible monument to those who fell, but, at the same time, be of help to those who had suffered through the war, and to all widows and children.

This object has also been achieved by the establishment of the Dunalistair Home, the successful foundation of which was so largely due to the labours of the late Brigadier-General W. McL. Campbell and of Colonel H. H. Sutherland.

The third object which I found so many of our men were anxious to see fulfilled was that a history of The Black Watch during the war should be written and published at such a price as would render its purchase possible by all ranks and their relatives. It was hoped that this history would form a true record of the main achievements of our Regular, Territorial and Service Battalions, that is to say, a record of the gallantry of all those men who bore the Red Hackle and crossed the seas in the service of the Regiment; and further, that this account, written by those who shared equally in the hardships and in the fighting, might also furnish a picture of the life led by our men in various lands and campaigns throughout these years of trial and danger.

It has been, therefore, in the endeavour to realize this last object that this history has been written. In these volumes the work of each separate battalion is described mainly by officers who took part in the actual actions and scenes here set out; and the thanks of the Regiment are due to those who have given so much time and labour to this end. But as these accounts have

PREFACE

been revised, and in many parts re-written by me, I accept full responsibility for the whole.

Our Territorial Battalions, direct descendants of The Black Watch Volunteer Battalions, had long held a fine reputation in Scotland for discipline and soldierly bearing. The conduct of their contingents which served as reinforcements to the Second Battalion during the South African War, served but to enhance this reputation and to knit all units of the Regiment yet more firmly together. It was no surprise therefore that our four Territorial Battalions were among the earliest ready to take the field, and among those who earned the highest praise for gallant deeds and unstinted good work.

Unlike the Territorial Battalions, the Service Battalions had no organization and no history, yet from the first day that they went into battle till the end of the war they nobly upheld the traditions of The Black Watch. This was partly due to their well-trained officers, to the splendid quality of the recruits who came so very largely from our 42nd Regimental District, and, above all, to the fine spirit—of which the Red Hackle is the symbol—that enheartened every man and, though unseen, was felt by every man to be the link that binds together each platoon, company and battalion of The Black Watch.

The task of editorship has at times seemed almost beyond my powers. As editor I am conscious of many defects, both of omission and commission. None the less I believe that this history, which describes the many gallant deeds and cites the names of those who fell in action, gives a faithful record of all those Battalions whose spirit and achievement have brought yet more honour and glory to The Black Watch. I believe also that this history shows that the same spirit of trust and good fellowship which has united all ranks of the Regiment since its earliest days still flourishes: that this spirit which inspired The Black Watch in the great victories of the Peninsula, Waterloo and Seringapatam, and sustained the heroes of Fontenoy and Ticonderoga, is the same spirit which filled the hearts and strengthened the resolve of those who in this last war gave their lives in the service of their King, their Country and their Regiment.

It is impossible for me to thank all those officers, non-commissioned officers and men who have given their help in the writing of this history, but I well know that they gave their help willingly and for the good of the Regiment. I must, however, take this opportunity to thank Colonel John Stewart and Colonel A. P. Wavell for their assistance in revising proofs and arranging the appendices of these volumes.

It is therefore with the hope that the great deeds described

PREFACE

in these pages will serve as an example and an encouragement to all those who in future years join The Black Watch and wear the Red Hackle that I am emboldened to publish this history.

I ask all readers who detect errors in the text, or who are in possession of additional material or facts dealing with the history of the Regiment in the Great War, to send any information or corrections to the Officer Commanding, The Black Watch Depot, Perth.

A. G. W.

BERLIN,
November, 1925.

CONTENTS OF VOLUME ONE

	PAGE
EDITOR'S PREFACE.	vii
FOREWORD BY GENERAL THE RIGHT HON. SIR JOHN G. MAXWELL, G.C.B., K.C.M.G., C.V.O., D.S.O.	xvii
BATTLE HONOURS OF THE BLACK WATCH.	xvi

THE FIRST BATTALION

CHAPTER I—1914.
1. Mobilization and Allied Concentration in France. — 1
2. Mons and the Retreat. — 4
3. The Battle of the Marne. — 9
4. The Battle of the Aisne. — 11
5. The Battle of Ypres. — 15

CHAPTER II—From December 20th, 1914, to May 9th, 1915.
1. The Attack of the 1st Brigade at Givenchy. — 27
2. The Battle of Aubers Ridge, May 9th, 1915. — 34

CHAPTER III—From May 9th, 1915, to July 5th, 1916.
1. The Summer of 1915. — 40
2. The Battle of Loos and the Action of Hohenzollern Redoubt. — 43
3. The Autumn of 1915 and the Loos Salient. — 48
4. The Spring of 1916. — 51

CHAPTER IV—July 6th, 1916, to May, 1917.
1. The Battle of the Somme. — 56

CHAPTER V—May, 1917, to November, 1917.
1. The Battle of Messines. — 64
2. The Attack on Vox Farm, November 18th, 1917. — 71

CHAPTER VI—November 17th to March 31st, 1918.
1. The Houthulst Forest Front. — 72

CHAPTER VII—April, 1918, to the Armistice.
1. The Defence of Givenchy. — 81
2. Storming the Hindenburg Line. — 93
3. The Capture of Wassigny. — 97

CONCLUSION. — 101

LIST OF APPENDICES—
I. Record of Officers' Service. — 104
II. Summary of Casualties. — 130

CONTENTS

LIST OF APPENDICES (*cont.*)—

		PAGE
III.	Casualties—Officers.	131
IV.	Nominal Roll of Warrant Officers, Non-Commissioned Officers and Men Killed in Action or Died of Wounds or Disease in the Great War, 1914–18.	134
V.	Honours and Awards.	149
VI.	List of Actions and Operations.	154
VII.	Roll of "Other Ranks" appointed to Commissions during the Great War.	156

THE SECOND BATTALION

PART I

FRANCE, 1914–15

CHAPTER I—1914.
1. Mobilization and voyage to France. 161
2. The fighting of 1914. 165
3. Conditions in the trenches, 1914. 172

CHAPTER II—1915.
1. Neuve Chapelle. 176
2. Aubers Ridge, May 9th, 1915. 180
3. The Battle of Loos. 184
4. Givenchy and the departure to Mesopotamia. 195
   Note on Dress, 1914–15. 200

PART II

MESOPOTAMIA, 1916–17

CHAPTER III.—JANUARY, 1916.
1. Arrival in Mesopotamia and Battle of Shaikh Sa'ad. 203
2. Battle of the Wadi. 214
3. First Assault on Hanna. 216

CHAPTER IV—FEBRUARY TO APRIL, 1916.
1. Formation of the Highland Battalion. 222
2. First and Second Assaults on Sannaiyat. 224
3. Third Assault on Sannaiyat and Fall of Kut. 227

CHAPTER V—FROM THE FALL OF KUT TO THE END OF 1916.
1. Breaking up of the Highland Battalion and reorganization. 232
2. Description of life in Mesopotamia. 234

CONTENTS

CHAPTER VI—1917.

		PAGE
1.	The Advance on Baghdad.	243
2.	The Battle of Mushaidie.	251
3.	The Battle of Istabulat.	258
4.	Samarrah, and the departure from Mesopotamia.	267
	Note on the Wauchope Medallion.	269
	Note on Dress, 1916–17.	269

PART III

PALESTINE, 1918

CHAPTER VII—JANUARY TO SEPTEMBER, 1918.

1.	Arrival on Palestine Front.	271
2.	Arsuf, June 8th, 1918.	275

CHAPTER VIII—SEPTEMBER, 1918, TO END OF WAR.

1.	Battle of Megiddo, September 19th, 1918.	281
2.	Advance to Beirut and Tripoli.	288
3.	After the War.	290

LIST OF APPENDICES—

I.	Record of Officers' Services.	295
II.	Summary of Casualties.	322
III.	Casualties—Officers.	323
IV.	Nominal Roll of Warrant Officers, Non-Commissioned Officers and Men Killed in Action or Died of Wounds or Disease in the Great War, 1914–18.	325
V.	Honours and Awards.	336
VI.	List of Actions and Operations.	340
VII.	Roll of "Other Ranks" appointed to Commissions during the Great War.	342

THE THIRD BATTALION

AUGUST, 1914—AUGUST, 1919.	345
APPENDIX. Casualty List.	356
INDEX.	357

ILLUSTRATIONS TO VOLUME ONE

A SOLDIER OF THE BLACK WATCH ON THE ROAD TO ARRAS, 1916. AFTER THE DRAWING BY SIR WILLIAM ORPEN. *Frontispiece*

THE FIRST BATTALION.

Facing page

OFFICERS BEFORE EMBARKING FOR FRANCE, 1914.   2

COLONEL GRANT-DUFF, C.B.   13

THE BATTALION CHRISTMAS CARD, 1917, "THE TWA BINGS."   56

ROLL CALL AT NOEUX-LES-MINES, OUTSIDE BILLETS, APRIL, 1918.   90

"JOCK, 1914." AFTER THE DRAWING BY "SNAFFLES."   158

THE SECOND BATTALION.

"HIELAN' LADDIE." AFTER THE DRAWING BY "SNAFFLES."   183

A COMPANY UNDER MAJOR THE HON. T. G. F. COCHRANE CROSSING THE TIGRIS TO OCCUPY SAMARRAH, 1917.   265

CROSSING THE PONTOON BRIDGE AT SAMARRAH, 1917.   265

BEIT-AL-KHALIFA: BATTALION HEADQUARTERS, SUMMER, 1917.   267

BLACK WATCH SOLDIERS IN TEKRIT, NOVEMBER, 1917.   267

A HALT AT KEFR ZIBAD, PALESTINE, SEPTEMBER, 1918.   271

MEDALLION PRESENTED BY COLONEL A. G. WAUCHOPE TO MEN OF THE BATTALION FOR GALLANTRY AT THE BATTLE OF LOOS, 1915, AND THE BATTLE BEYOND BAGHDAD, 1917.   271

MARCHING THROUGH BEIRUT, OCTOBER, 1918.   289

THE BLACK WATCH MEMORIAL HOME, DUNALISTAIR HOUSE, NEAR DUNDEE.   345

LIST OF MAPS TO VOLUME ONE

THE FIRST BATTALION.

Facing page

THE RETREAT FROM MONS AND SUBSEQUENT ADVANCE.	14
THE BATTLES OF YPRES, 1914–17.	22
ACTIONS NEAR GIVENCHY, FESTUBERT, NEUVE CHAPELLE AND LOOS, AND LINE HELD BY INDIAN CORPS, 1914–15.	38
THE BATTLE OF LOOS, SEPTEMBER 25TH, 1915.	44
BATTLE OF THE SOMME, 1916.	62
THE STORMING OF THE HINDENBURG LINE.	94
CAPTURE OF WASSIGNY AND FORCING OF THE OISE-SAMBRE CANAL, 1918.	100

THE SECOND BATTALION.

BATTLE OF NEUVE CHAPELLE.	176
BATTLE OF SEPTEMBER 25TH, 1915.	192
BATTLE OF SHAIKH SA'AD.	210
ACTION OF THE WADI.	214
FIRST ATTACK ON HANNA.	216
OPERATIONS FOR RELIEF OF KUT, JANUARY–APRIL, 1916.	230
BATTLE OF MUSHAIDIE.	252
BATTLE OF ISTABULAT.	261
OPERATIONS IN MESOPOTAMIA, 1914–18.	268
ACTION OF ARSUF.	276
ASSAULT OF TABSOR DEFENCES—SEPTEMBER 19TH, 1918.	286
PALESTINE AND SYRIA.	290

GENERAL MAP OF FRANCE.   *End of Volume*

BATTLE HONOURS OF THE BLACK WATCH

The Royal Cypher within the Garter. The badge and motto of the Order of the Thistle. In each of the four corners the Royal Cypher ensigned with the Imperial Crown. The Sphinx, superscribed " Egypt."

" GUADALOUPE, 1759," " MARTINIQUE, 1762," " HAVANNAH," " NORTH AMERICA, 1763-64," " MANGALORE," " MYSORE," " SERINGAPATAM," " CORUNNA," " BUSACO," " FUENTES D'ONOR," " PYRENEES," " NIVELLE," " NIVE," " ORTHES," " TOULOUSE," " PENINSULA," " WATERLOO," " SOUTH AFRICA, 1846-7, 1851-2-3," " ALMA," " SEVASTOPOL," " LUCKNOW," " ASHANTEE, 1873-4," " TEL-EL-KEBIR," " EGYPT, 1882-4," " KIRBEKAN," " NILE, 1884-5," " PAARDEBERG," " SOUTH AFRICA, 1899-1902."

The Great War—25 Battalions.—" Retreat from Mons," " MARNE, 1914, '18," " Aisne, 1914," " La Bassée, 1914," " YPRES, 1914, '17, '18," " Langemarck, 1914," " Gheluvelt," " Nonne Bosschen," " Givenchy, 1914," " Neuve Chapelle," " Aubers," " Festubert, 1915," " LOOS," " SOMME, 1916, '18," " Albert, 1916," " Bazentin," " Delville Wood," " Pozières," " Flers-Courcelette," " Morval," " Thiepval," " Le Transloy," " Ancre Heights," " Ancre, 1916," " ARRAS, 1917, '18," " Vimy, 1917," " Scarpe, 1917, '18," " Arleux," " Pilkem," " Menin Road," " Polygon Wood," " Poelcappelle," " Passchendaele," " Cambrai, 1917, '18," " St. Quentin," " Bapaume, 1918," " Rosières," " LYS," " Estaires," " Messines, 1918," " Hazebrouck," " Kemmel," " Béthune," " Scherpenberg," " Soissonnais-Ourcq," " Tardenois," " Drocourt-Quéant," " HINDENBURG LINE," " Épéhy," " St. Quentin Canal," " Beaurevoir," " Courtrai," " Selle," " Sambre," " France and Flanders, 1914-18." " DOIRAN, 1917," " Macedonia, 1915-18." " Egypt, 1916." " Gaza," " Jerusalem," " Tell 'Asur," " MEGIDDO," " Sharon," " Damascus," " Palestine, 1917-18," " Tigris, 1916," " KUT AL AMARA, 1917," " Baghdad," " Mesopotamia, 1915-17."

The list of Honours given above shows that The Black Watch had won 28 Battle Honours before 1914, and gained 69 Battle Honours during the Great War. As it was impossible to emblazon all these Honours on the King's or Regimental Colours, the Army Council decided that only ten Great War Honours selected by the Regiment should be emblazoned on the King's Colour. A committee therefore was appointed, under the Chairmanship of Sir John Maxwell, Colonel of the Regiment, which selected the following ten Honours to be borne on the King's Colour :—

(1) MARNE, 1914, '18
(2) YPRES, 1914, '17, '18
(3) LOOS
(4) SOMME, 1916, '18
(5) ARRAS, 1917, '18
(6) LYS
(7) HINDENBURG LINE
(8) DOIRAN, 1917
(9) MEGIDDO
(10) KUT AL AMARA, 1917

These 10 Honours were chosen as being the most representative of the various Campaigns in which the twelve Battalions of the Regiment who fought overseas took part.

The Regimental Colour still bears the 28 Honours won before the Great War, and the 10 Honours chosen by the committee are emblazoned on the King's Colour.

FOREWORD

BY

GENERAL THE RIGHT HON. SIR JOHN G. MAXWELL,

G.C.B., K.C.M.G., C.V.O., D.S.O., COLONEL—THE BLACK WATCH

THIS year, 1925, is the 200th Anniversary of the formation of the Independent Companies from which, in 1725, The Black Watch originated. The commissions of the six Captains of these Independent Companies are dated 1725, therefore it seems very appropriate to publish this year *The History of The Black Watch in the Great War*.

I, as its Colonel, have been asked to write this " Foreword," a task rendered no easier by the admirable Preface of Major-General A. G. Wauchope, the editor of this history.

In no part of the Empire was there a more hearty response to the call for men than in Scotland. We, of The Black Watch, are not given to boasting unduly of our deeds: we prefer to rest assured that every man who had the honour of wearing the Red Hackle acted up to and, collectively, enhanced the glorious traditions of our Regiment. No less than twenty-five Battalions served in the Great War, and eight thousand men of The Black Watch laid down their lives for their King and Country.

The official record of the battles and engagements in which these Battalions served shows that in whatever theatre of war the Regiment was represented, the traditions of The Black Watch were most worthily upheld. It is therefore right and proper that, as far as possible, a complete and true story of the exploits of each Battalion, in the various theatres of war, is recorded and incorporated in this history.

I desire to emphasize what General Wauchope has said, that no matter its shortcomings, if there be any, this history is written by the Regiment for the Regiment and for the countless friends of The Black Watch all the world over. No outside aid has been evoked. Every endeavour has been made, consistent with the design of the work, to keep within certain limits, so that the history can be published at such a price to bring it within the reach of all. One would like to know that a copy is in the hands of all past and present Black Watch men, as well as the relatives of those whose loss we mourn.

We are proud of our Regiment, and of the fact that His Majesty the King is our Colonel-in-Chief. We are justly proud of our records, both of the past and of the Great War. We hope that this history will be kept as a treasured heirloom and handed down to future generations of Black Watch men in order that they may emulate the valour and devotion of their predecessors.

FOREWORD

Our thanks are indeed due—and I offer them in the name of the Regiment—to Major-General Wauchope, and all who have assisted him in the compilation of this history. It has been an onerous task, though one of love and pride, and we congratulate them on having accomplished so successfully that which they set out to do.

J.G. Maxwell

COLONEL, THE BLACK WATCH.

THE FIRST
BATTALION

CHAPTER I

1914

1.—*Mobilization and Allied Concentration in France*

THE outbreak of the Great War found the 1st Battalion The Black Watch at Aldershot, where it formed part of the 1st Brigade, 1st Division.[1] The Battalion had been in this station since February, 1913, and was under the command of Lieutenant Colonel A. Grant-Duff, C.B. The Battalion thus took the field with the advantage of having spent the previous eighteen months at the principal training station of the army, under a Brigadier with a high reputation as a practical instructor of troops. It was also fortunate in having as Commanding Officer one of the most gifted soldiers in the army. The Battalion was in a high state of efficiency and well up to its peace strength of about seven hundred. On mobilization, however, about two hundred of these men were left behind under the regulation debarring soldiers under twenty years of age from proceeding on active service. Their places were taken and the Battalion completed to its war establishment by the arrival from the regimental depot of five hundred reservists, almost all of whom had served seven years in either the 1st or 2nd Battalions of the Regiment.

The " precautionary period," which involved the recall of all officers and men on leave, had been declared on July 29th. The order for mobilization was issued on the afternoon of August 4th. The mobilization of the Battalion proceeded smoothly, even keeping ahead of the official time-table. The excellent organization of the quartermaster and his staff was testified by the manner in which within the short time available, such difficulties as changing the boots issued to the reservists from the mobilization store at Perth, the closing of accounts and ledgers, the returning of surplus stores and the holding of the required boards of audit were all overcome.

By the 8th of August all reservists had arrived, and the Battalion was ready to take the field; but, as departure was delayed, the next five days were spent in training the reservists and improving their musketry. On the 11th of August, His Majesty the King inspected the 1st Brigade, and as Colonel-in-Chief of the Regiment, bade the Battalion farewell, and gave his best wishes for its good fortune in war.

On August 13th the Battalion marched out of Oudenarde

[1] The 1st (Guards) Brigade, commanded by Brigadier General F. I. Maxse, C.B., C.V.O., D.S.O., was composed of—1st Coldstream Guards, 1st Scots Guards, 1st Black Watch, and 2nd Royal Munster Fusiliers.

THE FIRST BATTALION THE BLACK WATCH

Barracks, with a strength of 28 officers and 1031 other ranks. At Farnborough it entrained in two trains, and, on arrival at Southampton, embarked on the *Italian Prince*, and landed at Havre about midday, August 14th. All the way to the rest-camp at Harfleur, about five miles distant, the French people of the district were most enthusiastic in their welcome.

The following was the organization of the Battalion on embarkation for France:—

Headquarters

Lieutenant Colonel A. Grant-Duff, C.B. (killed 14.9.14).
Major J. T. C. Murray, Second-in-Command (d. of w. 16. 2. 15).
Lieutenant G. B. Rowan Hamilton, Adjutant.
Lieutenant F. G. Chalmer, Machine Gun Officer.
Lieutenant F. Anderson, Transport Officer.
Lieutenant W. Fowler, Quartermaster.
Captain C. J. Coppinger, M.B., Medical Officer.
Regimental Sergeant Major A. Smart.
Regimental Quartermaster Sergeant A. S. Lawson (killed as Second Lieutenant 11.11.14).

A Company

Major Lord George Stewart-Murray (killed 14.9.14).
Lieutenant V. M. Fortune.
Lieutenant R. C. Anderson (d. of w. 27. 9. 15).
Second Lieutenant J. E. H. Rollo.
Second Lieutenant R. G. Don (killed 14.9.14).
Company Sergeant Major A. Wanliss (killed as Lieutenant 9.5.15)
Company Quartermaster Sergeant J. Millar.

B Company

Captain the Hon. M. C. A. Drummond.
Captain C. A. de G. Dalglish (d. of w. 9.9.14).
Lieutenant E. H. H. J. Wilson (killed 8.9.14).
Lieutenant L. R. Cumming (killed 14.9.14).
Second Lieutenant J. L. Rennie.
Second Lieutenant P. E. A. Blair (killed 29. 10. 14).
Company Sergeant Major C. Scott.
Company Quartermaster Sergeant A. McAndrew (killed as Second Lieutenant 24.12.14).

C Company

Captain W. Green.
Lieutenant W. D. Allan.
Second Lieutenant P. K. Campbell.
Second Lieutenant N. J. L. Boyd (d. of w. 12.10.14).

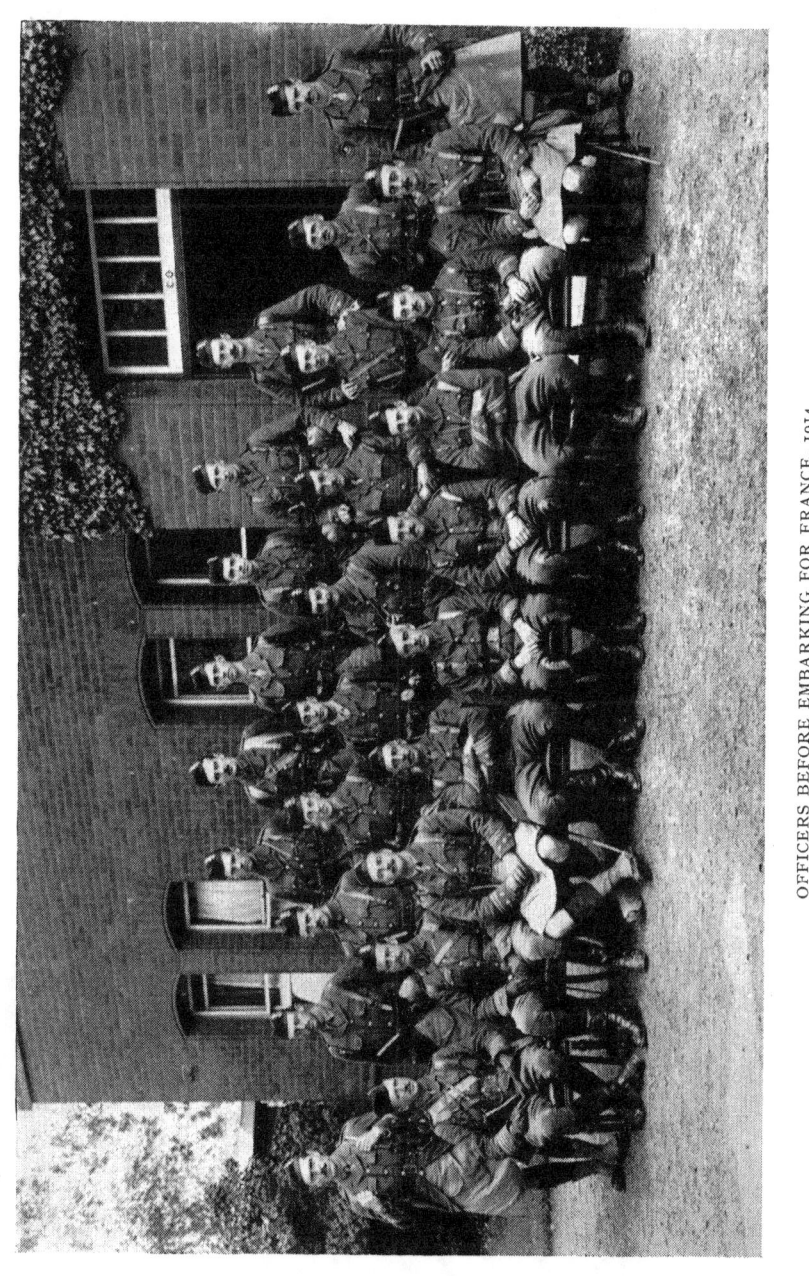

OFFICERS BEFORE EMBARKING FOR FRANCE, 1914

Back Row: 2nd Lt. R. G. Don, 2nd Lt. P. E. A. Blair, Lt. L. R. Cumming, 2nd Lt. N. J. L. Boyd, 2nd Lt. K. S. MacRae, 2nd Lt. G. W. Polson
Centre Row: Lt. V. M. Fortune, Lt. R. C. Anderson, 2nd Lt. J. E. H. Rollo, Lt. E. H. H. J. Wilson, 2nd Lt. J. L. Rennie, Lt. F. G. Chalmer, Lt. F. Anderson, 2nd Lt. P. K Campbell, Lt. W. D. Allan, Lt. R. E. Anstruther.
Front Row: Major Lord George Stewart-Murray, Capt. Hon. M. C. A. Drummond, Capt. C. A. de G. Dalglish, Major J. T. C. Murray, Lt-Col. A. Grant-Duff, C.B., Lt. and Adjt. G. B. Rowan-Hamilton, Capt. W. Green, Capt. H. F. S. Amery, Capt. A. D. C. Krook.
Capt. N. G. B. Henderson, Lt. J. N. O. Rycroft, and Lt. and Qmr. W. Fowler, were also present with the Battalion.

Vol. I

ARRIVAL IN FRANCE, AUGUST, 1914

Company Sergeant Major A. Burns.
Company Quartermaster Sergeant R. Lindsay.

D Company

Captain H. F. S. Amery (d. of w. 24.11.15).
Captain A. D. C. Krook.
Lieutenant R. E. Anstruther.
Second Lieutenant K. S. MacRae.
Second Lieutenant G. W. Polson (killed 15.9.14).
Company Sergeant Major A. Gray (killed as Second Lieutenant 9.5.15).
Company Quartermaster Sergeant J. R. Renton.

Of the officers and men 92 per cent were Scottish. The average height of the officers was 5 ft. 9¾ in. and of the rank and file 5 ft. 7⅛ in.

The next day was spent under canvas in the rest-camp, and everyone took the opportunity to write farewells to those whom they had left behind. Officers experienced the new and not very pleasant duty of having to read carefully through these letters, to see that the censor's rules were in no way broken.

Early on the morning of the 16th the Battalion marched to Havre railway station, and there entrained for an unknown destination. At every stopping-place a warm welcome was given, the people cheering heartily and bringing fruit, cigarettes and other gifts. The arrival of the British Army had been eagerly awaited and the appearance of the Highlanders excited the greatest enthusiasm. At Arras the inhabitants not only came out in large numbers to see what they called " the famous Waterloo Black Watch," but had provided a Guard of Honour on the platform, which, to the strains of " God Save the King " and the " Marseillaise," presented arms to The Black Watch, as the train moved out. The townspeople distributed flowers, wine and all kinds of food; in return they were given many souvenirs, such as cap badges or officers' buttons.

At 1 a.m. on the 17th the Battalion arrived at Le Nouvion, where it detrained, and rested in a field for a few hours; about 6 a.m. it marched to the village of Boué, its allotted place in the concentration scheme, where it remained until August 21st. While at Boué the Battalion carried out route marches and tactical exercises, and the men learned something of the type of country over which they would have to fight. It was at this village that the mess-cart and the old white horse, both well known to all who served with the Battalion, were purchased. " Allez-vous-en," as the horse was nicknamed, went through the whole war (earning three wound stripes), and came

THE FIRST BATTALION THE BLACK WATCH

home at the end with the cadre. The billets were comfortable, and the French peasants at every turn wished to show some kindness; all this, combined with the training, the glorious August weather, and frequent bathing in a large reservoir, heightened the good spirits of the men and kept them fit for the hard work which was soon to follow.

On August 21st the British Army began its forward movement on the left of the French Fifth Army. This was in accordance with the general plan in course of execution by General Joffre, by which the French Third and Fourth Armies through Luxembourg were to carry out the main offensive, while the French Fifth Army, the British Expeditionary Force and the Belgians were to hold up the German advance through Belgium, of the overwhelming strength of which advance General Joffre was completely unaware.

Accordingly the Battalion marched on the 21st to Cartignies, where it spent the night in billets. Just before dawn on the 22nd, the advance was recommenced, and the Battalion marched by way of Dompierre, Doulers and Maubeuge to Grand Reng, in Belgium, arriving at 1 a.m. on the 23rd. The Battalion marched for the first time on *pavé* roads; but the discomfort of these was more than balanced by the expectation of fighting, aroused by what seemed to be the sound of gunfire. In the end it was found that General Fournier, the commander of the fortress of Maubeuge, was clearing away, by blowing them up, woods and buildings which obstructed the field of fire. This was a long and trying march, the men being under arms for twenty-two hours: the original intention was for the I Corps to halt for the night on the positions reached in the early afternoon; but the requirements of the strategical situation necessitated the march being prolonged, so that the I Corps might fill the gap between the II Corps and French XVIII Corps.

2.—*Mons and the Retreat*

At Grand Reng the Battalion billeted in the town, covered by day by an outpost line which was held successively by a platoon of A company and one of B company. At night an entrenched position was taken up along the Beaumont-Mons road, between the nineteenth and seventeenth kilometre stones, with B company on the right, C company in the centre, D company on the left, and A company in reserve. A section of artillery from the 26th Brigade, R.F.A., and half a troop of cavalry (15th Hussars) were attached to the Battalion. This position was the right flank of the 1st Brigade, which was now the right brigade of the Expeditionary Force. About five miles to the right of The Black Watch was the French XVIII Corps.

RETIREMENT FROM MONS, AUGUST, 1914

From the position of The Black Watch to Harmignies, the line of the I Corps followed the Beaumont–Mons road; from Harmignies the II Corps curved westward through Obourg and the Nimy Salient, and, covering Mons, extended along the canal as far as Pommereuil. Further to the west the newly arrived 19th Brigade gained touch with a French Territorial Division which arrived at Condé during the 23rd. But no possible disposition of the two corps could have availed against the six or more German corps who, unknown to our forces, were streaming south-westwards from Brussels. On the morning of Sunday, August 23rd, the full force of the attack broke against the II Corps, who held their positions for twenty-four strenuous hours. No serious breach was made in the British line, and the subsequent retirement was only made in consequence of the retreat of the French forces on the right of the British Army.

During the whole of the 23rd the fighting in progress could be seen from our position; the Battalion was not engaged, but it fully expected to be attacked during the night of the 23rd or at dawn on the 24th. Meanwhile, Sir John French, realizing on the night of the 23rd the strength of the forces opposing him, and the exposed and perilous position of the British Army, ordered a retirement.

Orders to retire were received at daybreak on the 24th, just as the Battalion had completed an entrenched position in a more advanced line. The retirement began at once and, passing through rear-guards, the Battalion marched direct to Villers Sire Nicole, where the whole Division was halted and concentrated in expectation of an attack. The Scots Guards were on the right of the 1st Brigade, and the Royal Munster Fusiliers on the left; the Coldstream Guards and The Black Watch were held in reserve for counter-attack. Positions were reconnoitred and prepared, and the artillery deployed for action; but before the enemy came to close quarters, a retirement was again ordered, and the Battalion marched to La Longueville, where it billeted. The reason for the retirement was not disclosed, and it was difficult for troops who were keen for action, to appreciate why it was ordered; however, all ranks, having the greatest confidence in their commanders, recognized that it was necessary to enable some decisive battle to be brought about later on. The civilian population, on the other hand, had good reason to be mystified and alarmed by the absence of opposition to the enemy's advance; and in La Longueville British officers and men were more than once greeted with the cry of "*Perfides.*"

Under cover of the fortress of Maubeuge, the retirement was continued on the 25th, through Hautmont and Limont-Fontaine to Dompierre. Here the Battalion went into billets,

THE FIRST BATTALION THE BLACK WATCH

taking the usual defensive precautions. During the night very heavy firing was heard; this turned out to be an unsuccessful attack on the 4th Guards Brigade at Landrecies.

At daybreak on the 26th the Battalion left Dompierre, and marched through Marbaux to Le Grand Fayt, where the 1st Brigade relieved the 6th in a defensive position. On the march being resumed, B company formed the left flank guard to the Brigade, and marched through Le Petit Fayt to Prisches, later rejoining the Battalion at Erruart. The whole then marched to La Laurette Farm, about two miles north-west of Oisy, and billeted there.

The next day was made eventful for the 1st Brigade by the tragic loss of the 2nd Battalion Royal Munster Fusiliers. The march was resumed at dawn, the 1st Brigade and the 26th Brigade R.F.A. being rear-guard to the Corps. The 2nd Royal Munster Fusiliers were in a position on the right of the Brigade, a little north-east of Oisy and east of the Sambre Canal; with them was one section of the 118th Battery, R.F.A. The Coldstream Guards held the centre position with the Scots Guards on their left, and The Black Watch, kept in reserve with one section of artillery, entrenched themselves astride the Landrecies-Guise road just north of Etreux. As the retirement proceeded, the Scots Guards and Coldstream Guards passed through the Battalion, but there was no sign of the Munster Fusiliers. Only a few Uhlans, who were driven rapidly back, approached from the direction of Oisy; but to the south-east heavy rifle and artillery fire was heard, and the villages were seen burning about Boué and Bergues. This made it obvious that some German troops had broken through and were now on the right rear.

Orders to retire were received, and the Battalion fell back through Etreux and Iron. On the high ground between the two places, considerable rifle and artillery fire was opened on the Battalion, as it was marching in fours.[1] The bank of the road was quickly lined, and the attack driven off by rapid fire. Owing to the very bad German shooting the losses of the Battalion were small, only 3 missing and 7 wounded. The 117th Battery, commanded by Major Packard, had come rapidly into action, and now covered the withdrawal to Iron.

Marching through Guise, the Battalion finally arrived and bivouacked at Jonqueuse Farm, about two miles south-west of Guise. The fate of the Royal Munster Fusiliers now became known. In the early morning they had taken up a rear-guard position just east of the Sambre-Oise Canal, which made communi-

---

[1] The attackers were part of the Guard Cavalry Division of Richthofen's Corps of Von Bulow's Army.

RETIREMENT FROM MONS, AUGUST, 1914

cation with the rest of the Brigade very difficult; there they were attacked, and, after a most gallant fight, surrounded by a greatly superior force. Only one platoon, supported and brought out of its perilous position by the help of two troops of the 15th Hussars, returned to the 1st Brigade to tell the story.

On the 28th the Battalion left its bivouac in the dark, and continued the march through La Fère to the Forest of St. Gobain. During the day, the Corps Commander, Sir Douglas Haig, spoke to the Battalion, as it passed him on the march, and complimented it by saying that it had done splendidly, and that it looked very fine.

The Battalion reached St. Gobain on the 28th, and on the 29th had a much needed day of rest. Though it had not yet been seriously engaged, the Battalion had been on the move almost continuously since the 21st, and had performed long marches on hard, dusty and crowded roads under a blazing sun. But the chief trial had been lack of rest; so close had been the contact with the enemy that the short halts at night had been continually disturbed. Thus, although the men were still very fit and in high spirits, they were very weary. On the march at each ten minutes' halt everyone, who was not on duty, fell asleep. On the 28th a man reported himself to the medical officer as unable to march. When his shoe was taken off, a bullet fell out of it. He had been shot through the foot on the previous day, but owing to weariness he had not noticed it, and it was only when his foot refused to perform the work required of it that he had reported to the medical officer.

All this time the men were carrying full equipment, including the pack. At St. Gobain the Commanding Officer, in order to lighten the load, gave permission for greatcoats to be handed in. Some five hundred men availed themselves of the permission; but the coats could not be transported and had to be burnt. Their want was soon badly felt.

The transport had a particularly hard time, since during the short halts for the night rations had to be brought up and distributed and the horses watered and fed. The men of the transport, under Lieutenant F. Anderson and Sergeant McVey, gave a splendid response to the heavy call made on them.

The 29th of August was the day on which, according to current newspaper reports, The Black Watch repeated a story of Waterloo by going into action hanging on to the stirrup leathers of the Scots Greys and the 12th Lancers. The story was, however, entirely untrue. An action was fought on this day by the Scots Greys and the 12th Lancers; but the only connection between these regiments and The Black Watch is that their patrols passed through the billets of the Battalion during the day.

THE FIRST BATTALION THE BLACK WATCH

The general retreat was continued on the 30th and lasted for another seven days before the moment came when the Allies were able to take advantage of the situation caused by Von Kluck's wheel to the east of Paris. On the 30th the Battalion continued its march through Septvaux and Brancourt, both in the Forest of St. Gobain, and bivouacked at Allement Château, where were also the Coldstream Guards. B company had left St. Gobain on the evening of the 29th as escort to a convoy, and rejoined the Battalion at Allement.

The line of march of the next day was through Soissons, and ended at Missy aux Bois. Before dawn on September 1st the Battalion had left Missy and was marching through the Foret Dominiale de Retz. At Villers-Cottérêts heavy firing was heard, which proved to be an attack on the 4th Guards Brigade and the 6th Brigade by Von Kluck's III Corps with a Cavalry Division.

Since The Black Watch formed the rear-guard to the 1st Brigade, they halted and, supported by the Brigade machine guns and a battery of the 26th Brigade, R.F.A., held the ground covering Villers-Cottérêts and the exits to the forest until the 4th Guards Brigade had passed safely through; then, in turn passing through the 2nd Infantry Brigade, crossed the Ourcq and bivouacked on the high ground just west of La Ferté Milon. On this day extra wagons were for the first time available, and the packs of each company were carried in a wagon. This made a great difference to the marching and fighting power of the men.

At 2 a.m. on the 2nd, the march continued for some time along a very bad track; passing through Varreddes, the Battalion reached the high ground at Chambry, and went into bivouac. On the 3rd the Marne was crossed, and the Battalion, passing through Bois de Meause, billeted at La Ferté sous Jouarre. On the 4th Coulommiers was reached, and the Battalion, after resting on the canal bank, found outposts for the Brigade. During the night of the 4th/5th a party of the enemy approached B company, to which were attached the machine guns of the Scots Guards, but was driven off. A patrol of six Uhlans galloped into a picquet of A company; one was killed, and the remainder, including an officer, were captured. One of the captured horses served with the Battalion transport for the rest of the war, and answered to the name of " German Jimmy "; at the time of writing he is still interned, and leads a comfortable life somewhere in Scotland.

The 5th was the last day of the retreat, and the last stage of the march lay through Mauperthuis to Nesles. Here the first reinforcements, under Lieutenant Macnaughton, of the 3rd

THE BATTLE OF THE MARNE, SEPTEMBER, 1914

Battalion, were waiting. At Nesles the 1st Battalion Cameron Highlanders joined the 1st Brigade in the place of the Royal Munster Fusiliers.

3.—*The Battle of the Marne*

On September 4th, Marshal Joffre ordered a general attack of the left or Western Allied Armies for the 6th, to take advantage of the dangerous situation in which the German First Army had placed itself. The final day's march of the British Army, which thus appears unnecessary, was made in conformity with the original plan of withdrawing it until in line with the French Armies.

The French Sixth Army of Maunoury had been assembled near Compiègne, and thus, after the move southwards of Von Kluck's force, threatened the right flank of the German Armies. Maunoury's Army was ordered to cross the Ourcq, while simultaneously the British and French Fifth Armies were to close in towards Montmirail, the British marching east from Coulommiers, and the French north from the Seine Valley. On the right of the French Fifth Army was the French Ninth Army of Foch, whose duty it was to hold the enemy and cover the general offensive.

So it was with great enthusiasm that the Battalion received on the 6th September the order to move eastwards. The Coldstream Guards, with the Brigade machine guns and Brigade cyclists, were the advanced guard to the 1st Brigade, and reached the objective allotted to them, against heavy opposition; but were afterwards withdrawn, to prevent their being too heavily involved. Their withdrawal was covered by The Black Watch, who later entrenched themselves just west of Violaines, troops of the 2nd Division being on their left. The enemy made no attempt to follow up the withdrawal, and the only rifle targets to be seen were some Uhlans at a long range. On the other hand, artillery fire was heavy throughout the whole day, and the Battalion was fortunate in having only five men wounded. Later in the day the Battalion moved forward as advanced guard to the Brigade, driving back small parties of Uhlans, and at nightfall bivouacked at Gloise Farm, about two miles south of La Plessie.

On the 7th the Cameron Highlanders furnished the advanced guard, and met with only slight resistance. The Battalion passed through Amillis, Chevru and Choisy, and bivouacked in a field near Le Temple, to the south of La Ferté-Gaucher.

On the morning of the 8th the Battalion, with the 117th Battery R.F.A. as vanguard, furnished the advanced guard to the 1st Brigade, and with B company marched through Jouy and Montigny. Champ Martin proved to be empty, but near

THE FIRST BATTALION THE BLACK WATCH

Bellot the Battalion met the 4th French Cavalry Division, which had recently been under artillery fire from the north.

The 3rd French Cavalry Brigade, with a battery of artillery, supported the advance of the Battalion into Bellot, and there reported having found the enemy in strength in the woods to the north-west. At the same time, about 9.30 a.m., artillery fire was opened on the Battalion from the wooded heights across the Petit Morin river.

C company was left to hold a lesser ridge to the east of Bellot, and thus safeguard the flank of the Brigade, while A, B and D companies pushed through the village and crossed the Petit Morin. Here a road runs north-west along the valley to Sablonnières village, the whole length of it dominated by a wooded ridge, some three hundred feet high, lying half a mile to the north. A and D companies began to climb this ridge, with a section of the 15th Hussars to keep connection, whilst B company moved along the road. The 117th Battery R.F.A. remained in Bellot.

The woods along the ridge were so dense that the progress of A and D companies was slow; but B company, after marching about a mile, heard heavy rifle fire on the left, which was answered from the direction of Sablonnières. This was apparently a fight between the 1st Cavalry Brigade, which had advanced from Rebais, and a German rear-guard.

The leading platoon of B company, under Second Lieutenant Rennie, extending on both sides of the road, pushed on and quickly came into action. Later, the rest of B company and the Scots Guards machine guns reinforced the platoon on the right, while two companies of the Cameron Highlanders and The Black Watch machine gun section, under Lieutenant Chalmer, advancing on the left, caught the enemy at Sablonnières in enfilade. C company arrived shortly afterwards, and Lieutenant Colonel Grant-Duff ordered a general advance. About sixty prisoners were collected from the houses and hedges, and the locality was completely cleared. B company lost Lieutenant Wilson killed and Captains Drummond and Dalglish wounded. The latter died on the following day. Of the rank and file 25 were killed or wounded. The enemy were the Pomeranian Jäger Battalion, who had come from Von Bulow's Army. Their orders were to hold their position to the last, and this they did as their Battalion was entirely destroyed in this day's action.

In the meantime, the Brigade closed up, and the Coldstream Guards went forward as a fresh advanced guard. The operation had been very successful, and Lieutenant Colonel Grant-Duff was commended for the way he handled the advanced guard. At Hondevilliers, three miles further north, the Battalion bivouacked

THE BATTLE OF THE AISNE, SEPTEMBER, 1914

and the second batch of reinforcements arrived, under the charge of Lieutenant A. V. Holt.

On learning that the British were across the Petit Morin, the enemy made an attempt to destroy the bridges of the Marne, but only at La Ferté sous Jouarre had they time to complete the destruction. The Battalion crossed the Marne next day at Nogent, and bivouacked at La Nouette Farm and on the high ground above Charly-sur-Marne.

September 9th marked the end of the Battle of the Marne, which may well be regarded as one of the decisive battles of the war ; the advance of the Allies, particularly of the British Army, into the gap between Von Kluck's and Von Bulow's Armies had compelled their hasty retreat, and they were already on the march, the former for the Aisne. The German hopes of a quick and victorious end to the war were over; for in a speedy victory had lain their chief hope of winning the war.

On September 10th the Battalion marched through La Thiolet, Lucy and Torcy to Courchamps. A little beyond this place, the 2nd Brigade was sharply and heavily engaged by the German rear-guard. The 1st Brigade was brought up in artillery formation to support the 2nd, but although it advanced beyond Priez to Latilly, it met with only slight opposition.

The Battalion billeted in Latilly on the night of the 10th, and on the next day acted as advanced guard and marched to Trugny, where two companies went on outpost duty. On the 12th the advance continued through Fère-en-Tardenois and Mont Notre-Dame to Bazoches.

4.—*The Battle of the Aisne*

The march the next day was by Vauxcère and Longueval to Bourg, where the Aisne was crossed. The German line of resistance was now close at hand, and the 2nd Brigade, who were leading, were strongly opposed. The Black Watch was sent forward to support them by occupying the ridge of Paissy. On the way up they came under shell fire, but suffered only five casualties. Paissy was found to possess caves, where the Battalion was sheltered in safety, until it was relieved in the outpost line by the 2nd Brigade. The passage of the I Corps across the river was, however, not completed until the 14th.

To the north lay the Craonne plateau, a long ridge of chalk hills, where artillery positions commanded the whole river valley. Along these hills the old and famous Roman road, the Chemin des Dames, followed the crest, an obvious position for a German stand to be made. It was not known, however, on the morning of the 14th whether the crest of the ridge was held merely by rear-guards to a retreating force or by a

German army in position. Orders were issued on the former supposition, whereas the latter proved to be correct. Thus it happened that the British divisions went into action piecemeal with no concerted plan of attack, and found an enemy entrenched, not only with no intention of retreating further, but with every intention of driving the British back across the river. The thick mist which covered the battlefield all the morning obscured the situation; and so September 14th was a day of close, furious, and extremely confused fighting.

The 2nd Brigade, which had been ordered to occupy the ridge by Cerny to cover the advance of the remainder of the 1st Division, was heavily engaged before 6 a.m. By 7 a.m. the 1st Brigade, forming the advanced guard, had reached Vendresse, and was ordered into action on the left of the 2nd Brigade. The sugar factory near Sucrerie on the top of the ridge, between Troyon and Cerny, was a conspicuous feature, round which much of the fighting took place. The original order of march of the 1st Brigade was Coldstream Guards, Camerons, The Black Watch, Scots Guards. At Vendresse the Coldstream Guards moved straight up the road leading direct to Sucrerie, while the remainder of the Brigade moved by a cart track to the south end of the Vendresse spur. As soon as the plateau of the crest was reached the Battalions came under very heavy fire and could make little progress, and the supports were soon called up.

Owing to the heavy mists, the confused nature of the fighting, and to the fact that the Battalion became split up to support different portions of the line, it is difficult to give a connected account of its action as a whole. The fortunes of individual companies are here related in such detail as it has been possible to ascertain.

A and C companies were ordered to move to the right. They appear to have become split up, but about half of each company, under Captains Green and Fortune, eventually reached a point well forward on the Chemin des Dames itself to the east of the sugar factory.

Here were part of the Coldstream Guards and some units of the 2nd Brigade, Northamptonshire Regiment and K.R.R.C.; and in conjunction with these, the greater portion of A and C companies remained for the rest of the day, facing the Germans at short range. Of the remainder of these two companies, part penetrated far into the German line with some of the Coldstream Guards, and part seems to have joined D company on the left of the 1st Brigade.

The details of the action of D company, which was sent to support the Camerons on the left of the 1st Brigade, will never be known, since they lost all their officers on this day. Other

COLONEL GRANT-DUFF, C.B.
Killed at the Battle of the Aisne, when in command of the First Battalion

THE BATTLE OF THE AISNE, SEPTEMBER, 1914

officers of the Brigade saw them moving up the Chivy Valley with the Camerons to counter-attack the enemy; they were in turn heavily counter-attacked, and the observers from whom this information is obtained had the pain of seeing them borne down by superior numbers, far forward in the distance, without being able to give them help in time. It is believed that Major Lord George Murray, commanding A company, was killed with D company in this fight.

B company acted as escort to the 116th Battery, R.F.A., which, under heavy fire, came forward up the track from Vendresse to the sugar factory and unlimbered where the track reaches the plateau. Later, part of this company reinforced D company with the Cameron Highlanders.

The Battalion machine gun section was ordered to move in a westerly direction in order to meet a German counter-attack from the projecting Beaulne Ridge. Later on the machine gun section was engaged in helping the Gloucestershire Regiment to repel a German attack made down the Chivy Valley on the 3rd Brigade.

About an hour before noon a strong counter-attack was made by the enemy, who for a moment drove back the three leading battalions of the 1st Brigade, and made our hold on the plateau precarious. The risk of disaster, however, was averted, largely by the action of Lieutenant Colonel Grant-Duff, who successfully rallied and reorganized some troops of the Brigade, and personally led them forward. In doing so he was mortally wounded.

The rest of the day's action could only be defensive, since there were no reserves. The reorganized troops occupied the position originally held by B company, and a new line was linked up from the south end of Vendresse plateau to the Troyon road. The 2nd Brigade lay forward near Troyon, and from their left the whole of the Corps was echeloned back, further and further from the plateau, until its left touched the II Corps near Vailly, down in the Aisne Valley.

At nightfall the survivors of the companies closed in on the reorganized position, D and the machine guns from Chivy on the left, and A and C under the command of Captain W. Green, from near Troyon on the right. These two companies had, as related above, been holding the line of the Chemin des Dames all day, and only fell back after dark to conform with the general line. Lieutenant MacNaughton and a few men had, with part of the Coldstream Guards under Colonel Ponsonby, penetrated the German lines still further towards Cerny, but were able to work their way back by night. In pouring rain the Battalion began to entrench, and threw up some of the first spadefuls of that long line which was soon to stretch from Switzerland across France to the sea. It was a sad night, for the Battalion had suffered many casualties, and had lost its commander, Lieutenant Colonel Grant-Duff, a gallant and able officer beloved and respected by all.

Besides their Colonel, the Battalion had lost Major Lord George Stewart-Murray and Lieutenants Don and Cumming killed; and Captain Amery, Lieutenants Holt, Anderson and Anstruther, and Second Lieutenants Rennie, Boyd and Campbell wounded.

Major Lord George Murray joined The Black Watch in 1893. He served through the Boer War, being attached to the Gordon Highlanders during the siege of Ladysmith and later with the Scottish Horse. He had been a most capable and popular Adjutant to the Battalion, and was deeply imbued with the spirit and traditions of the Regiment. His fate was uncertain for some time after the action; and it was with the deepest sorrow that the Regiment was eventually forced to realize that there was no hope of his return.

On the 15th, Major J. T. C. Murray assumed command of the Battalion. At daybreak a reconnaissance was made to see whether the ridge was still occupied, and C company, reinforced by D, advanced to the crest and engaged the enemy with rifle fire; but they were heavily fired on by artillery, and compelled to withdraw. Lieutenant Polson was killed and Captain Green wounded. The Brigade now spent four days, the 15th, 16th, 17th and 18th, in " digging in," the first of which marked the opening of stabilized warfare in France. The 2nd Brigade, lying exposed on the right of the line, was attacked several times, and more than once the Battalion was able to enfilade the attacking Germans at a range of about 1200 yards.

Platoons and companies, commanders and men had now, within a few hundred yards of the enemy, to learn and grow used to the life and normal routine of trench warfare—tours of duty, reliefs, rests behind the line, defence against artillery fire and patrolling towards the enemy lines.

These were busy days for the Battalion Commander, but Major J. T. C. Murray found time to write to Colonel Campbell, commanding the 2nd Battalion, who arrived in France this month from India, giving valuable advice from the experiences gained by the 1st Battalion during the retreat and on the Aisne. This help was of real value to the officers of the 2nd Battalion, and is typical of the strong feeling of comradeship that united all battalions of The Black Watch throughout the war.

On the 19th the Battalion was relieved by troops of the 18th Brigade, and for two days was in billets at Œuilly. On the 21st it marched to Verneuil and took over the line on the heights on

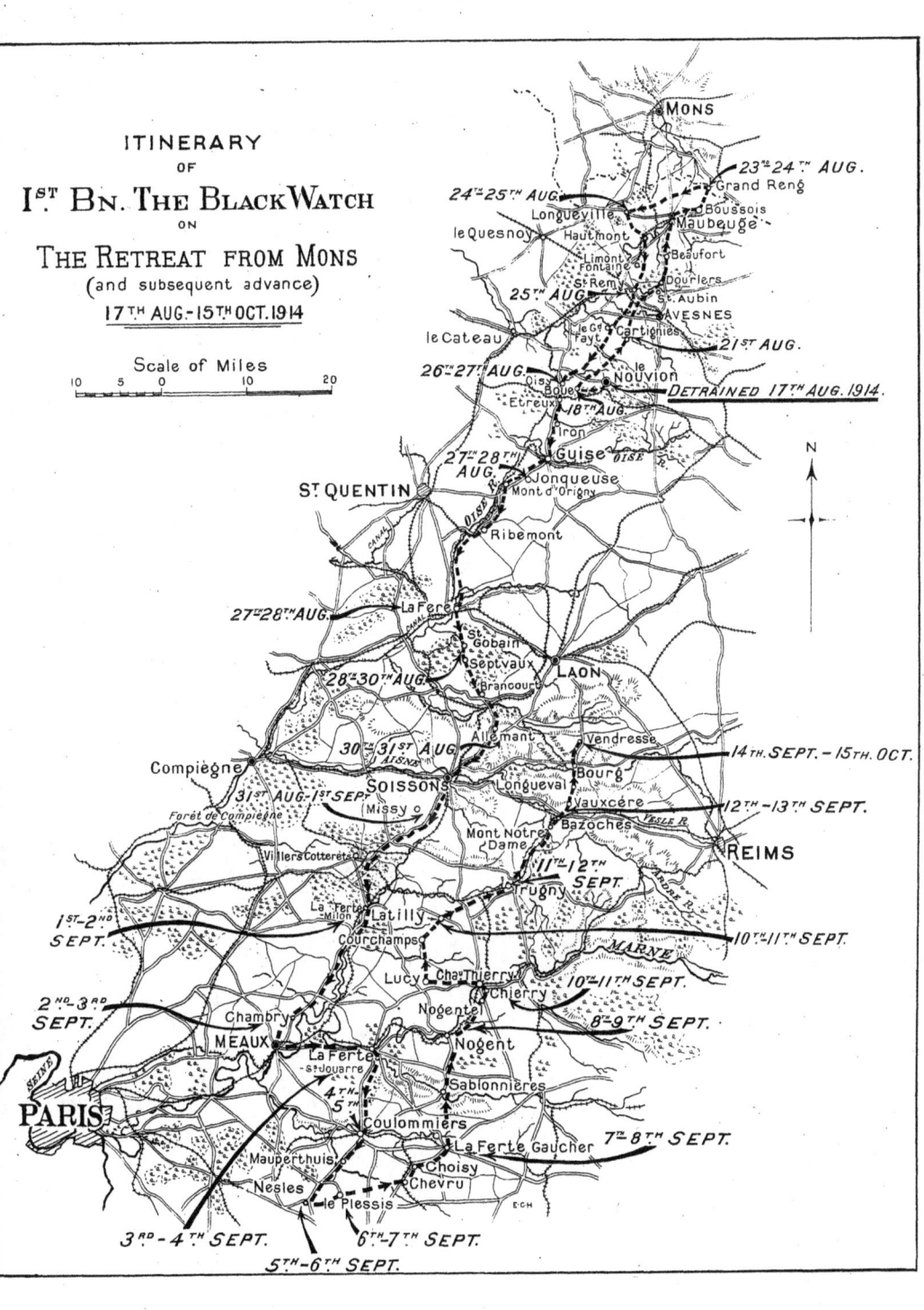

THE BATTLE OF YPRES, OCTOBER, 1914

both sides of the Chivy Valley. After three days it was relieved by the Cameron Highlanders, and moved back to Cretonne Farm, in the woods behind Verneuil. Finally, on the 28th it was sent to reoccupy its original position on the Vendresse plateau, receiving reinforcements as it went up.

The following, amongst others, joined the Battalion on the Aisne: Captains Urquhart, Hore-Ruthven, West, Sir E. Stewart Richardson, Mowbray, Nolan and Lieutenant Hay.

During the first long spell in a fixed position, little or no change was made in the dispositions of companies—a curious contrast to the regular inter-company reliefs of later days. A company (Captain Urquhart) was on the right, C company (Captain Mowbray) in the centre, D company (Captain West) on the left, and B company (Captain Ruthven) in support. The support company, Battalion Headquarters and Brigade Headquarters were all within two hundred yards of the front line. No serious attack was made by the enemy, but the trenches were regularly shelled, and a weapon of the nature of a trench mortar was used against the Battalion. In spite of this losses were few, the only officer casualty being Lieutenant C. Bowes-Lyon, who was wounded on the 6th of October. It is perhaps worth remarking that this portion of the line remained unchanged till 1917.

On the 16th of October, French infantry relieved the Battalion, which marched through Bourg to Blanzy, where it billeted for the night. On the next day, the Battalion marched to Fismes, and there entrained about 6 p.m., reaching Hazebrouck, its destination, at 6 a.m. on the 19th.

5.—*The Battle of Ypres*, 1914[1]

During the three weeks that the Battalion lay entrenched in the Aisne Valley, the centre of gravity of the fighting gradually shifted to the north, each opponent " racing to the sea " in an endeavour to turn the flank of the long line of trenches. The French moved corps after corps northwards, until they had created a new Tenth Army in the Arras-Albert area. At the end of September, Marshal Joffre agreed with Sir John French's suggestion that the British forces should be moved to the left of the Allied line, so as to shorten their line of communications and give them their natural task of defending the Channel ports.

The 2nd Cavalry Division, followed by the II Army Corps, moved early in October to the Aire district, and linking on to the left of the French Tenth Army attempted, by a turning movement to the south, to outflank the German line, an attempt which ended in a stalemate situation like that of the Aisne, the

[1] The Battalion War Diary for the latter half of September and the whole of October is missing, having been lost in the fighting at Ypres.

15

THE FIRST BATTALION THE BLACK WATCH

new trench line stretching from La Bassée to opposite Aubers. Two days after the II Corps went into action, the III Corps came up from the south, detrained about St. Omer and Hazebrouck, and assisted the II Corps by taking Bailleul and establishing a position across the River Lys about Armentières.

The fall of the fortress of Antwerp, on October 10th, had freed the path of the German Army across northern Belgium. The Royal Naval Division had been evacuated, and General Rawlinson's IV Corps, too late to save Antwerp, stood unsupported and in great danger between Ghent and Ypres, with five German Army Corps advancing against the British front. Between October 3rd and October 19th, however, the transference of British troops was continuous, until by the latter date some semblance of a defensive line covered the Channel ports.

On the left of the French Tenth Army at La Bassée, the II and III Corps held a front of about twenty miles, from La Bassée Canal to Neuve Eglise; a gap of a mile between them was filled by the French Cavalry Division of General Conneau. From Messines to Hollebeke ran the line of the Cavalry Corps; and from Zandvoorde through Kruiseecke and Gheluvelt to Zonnebeke, the IV Corps guarded, rather than held, the roads that led into Ypres. French and Belgian cavalry continued the line to Dixmude, whilst the last section towards the sea, the Yser Canal, was manned by French Marines and Belgians. In rear, at Hazebrouck, was the I Corps; and around St. Omer lay the Lahore Division of the Indian Corps, two Yeomanry regiments, and two Territorial battalions.

On the 19th of October, Sir John French ordered a general advance of the British forces, in accordance with the general Allied plan, and in ignorance of the greatly superior German forces already in motion towards Ypres. The I Corps was ordered to advance on Bruges, with Thourout as a first objective, the IV Corps and the French conforming to this movement. On the 20th, the day before the I Corps moved forward, the Germans launched their attack from Gheluvelt to the sea.

On the 21st the 2nd Division advanced on Passchendaele, and the 1st Division on Poelcappelle. The German strength on the two divisional fronts was far from equally distributed; while the 2nd Division was advancing steadily on its objective, although with frequent fighting at close quarters, the 1st Division was compelled to be more cautious, since the French on its left were in danger of giving way before the heavy attacks launched on them from the north. It was this fact which modified the advance so as to create, on this day, the curious line afterward called " the Ypres Salient." As will be seen, the 1st Brigade, who joined up with the French, was unable to advance and had,

THE BATTLE OF YPRES, OCTOBER, 1914

indeed, a hard task to maintain its ground against the heavy German attacks.

The Battalion rested in Hazebrouck during the day and night of the 19th, and on the 20th marched to Poperinghe, with one company on outpost duty. On the 21st it marched through Elverdinghe and Boesinghe to Pilkem, where it remained in Brigade Reserve during the following night.

On this day the Cameron Highlanders, guarding the French flank, had sited a strong post at Kortekeer Cabaret, an inn about a mile north of Pilkem. On the afternoon of the 22nd, this important post, and the line of the Coldstream Guards on the right of it, were heavily attacked by picked German volunteers, and both positions were overrun. A, B and D companies of the Battalion were sent forward to restore the situation, and, advancing with some French cyclists, reached the line of the Steenbeek about 6 p.m. and prevented any further advance of the enemy. During the next three or four hours the machine guns of the 1st Black Watch, under Lieutenant F. G. Chalmer, inflicted heavy losses on the attackers by firing from a windmill on the Langemarck-Bixschoote road. C company and the machine guns remained at Pilkem on the night of the 22nd, and Captain Ruthven and Lieutenant Hay were wounded.

During the 23rd the 2nd Brigade recaptured the Cabaret, releasing sixty Cameron Highlanders, and gained touch with the left of the Battalion line. In the evening the rest of the Battalion moved up to Remi Farm, and established connexion with the Coldstream Guards on the right, so that by midnight the position was restored and reorganized. Another attack was made on the Cabaret during this night, the Germans advancing in mass formation, singing " Die Wacht am Rhein " and " Heil dir im Siegerkranz "; they were beaten off, but all through the 24th heavy attacks were made on the Camerons, and on D company on the left of the Battalion. Captain Urquhart and Lieutenant Bowes-Lyon were killed on the 24th and Lieutenant K. G. Macrae badly wounded. Large reinforcements of the French were expected from the south, but it was not until the early morning of the 25th that our Allies were able to take over part of the line of the I Corps. At 5 a.m. on the 25th French Territorials relieved the Battalion, which had been constantly engaged for two days and two nights. There was no opportunity for rest; on relief, the Battalion moved to another threatened sector, marching through St. Jean and the outskirts of Ypres to Verbrandenmolen.

During the last few days the numbers of the 7th Division had grown dangerously few for the defence of the Menin road, the main thoroughfare into Ypres from the east, and the 1st Brigade was ordered to shorten its line. On October 26th the 20th

THE FIRST BATTALION THE BLACK WATCH

Brigade, 7th Division, was driven from Kruiseecke Village, which overlooked and commanded the furthest point in the general advance, namely the important cross-roads a mile east of Gheluvelt.

The Battalion was sent up to hold the Zandvoorde-Gheluvelt road on the left of the 20th Brigade. B company moved on the right of the road, and C company on the left of it; A was in support of B, and D in support of C. This advance restored the line, and for the remainder of the day the Battalion held its position, which it entrenched at nightfall. Lieutenant Chalmer, the Battalion machine gun officer, was wounded this day. In a month's fighting all the officers who originally left Aldershot with the Battalion had become casualties, with the exception of seven.

In the early hours of the 27th the enemy bombarded the trenches of A company, by which three officers were wounded, and more than three quarters of the company became casualties. In the evening the Battalion was relieved by the 2nd Bedfordshire Regiment, and was split up to relieve two separate sections of the line which needed reinforcement. Headquarters, A and D companies moved back through Gheluvelt, and relieved the 2nd Grenadier Guards, 2nd Division, about one and a half miles to the north, while B and C companies, isolated from the rest of the Battalion and from each other, were sandwiched in among three separate battalions. Such dispositions are bad at any time, more especially when heavy fighting is in progress, but in this case they were unavoidable, for the need was urgent and of reserves there were none.

The 28th passed without incident except for the steady shelling of our lines. On the evening of the 28th the front of the 1st Brigade and neighbouring troops was as follows : On the south of the Menin road lay the left battalion of the 7th Division, the 1st Grenadier Guards, 20th Brigade; on the road and just north of it—at a road junction called at the time the Gheluvelt cross-roads—was B company, under Captain Moubray, 1st Black Watch; then in succession the 1st Coldstream Guards, only 350 strong; C company, under Captain Campbell Krook, 1st Black Watch; 1st Scots Guards; 1st Cameron Highlanders; A and D companies 1st Black Watch; then the 4th Guards Brigade, 2nd Division.

The line was not continuous and there were some wide gaps; between the left of C company, for instance, in a thick wood, and the nearest post of the Scots Guards there was an interval of 200 yards.

On the early morning of the 29th, which was foggy, the Germans in great strength attacked down the Menin road and just north of it. Although B company made a determined resistance, some Germans broke through near the road and then turning northwards rolled up B company and the two right companies of the Coldstream Guards, party by party, from the flank and rear. Some two or three hours later the same fate overtook the two left companies of the Coldstream Guards and C company, who had previously repulsed several frontal attacks. A and D companies, meanwhile, had driven off a frontal attack against the left of the 1st Brigade. Only a few men of B and C companies, and these men were mostly wounded, were able to rejoin Battalion Headquarters near Polderhoek Château; the Battalion's losses for the day amounted to 5 officers and 250 men.

The line was eventually restored after heavy fighting, but the lost trenches at the cross-roads were not recovered. The enemy had now brought up three fresh Army Corps for a decisive break through against troops already weary and much reduced in numbers, but with no chance of relief; and the fighting continued on the 30th and culminated on the 31st—the crisis of the first battle of Ypres.

On the 30th the 1st Brigade had a comparatively quiet day; shelling was continuous, but the attacks of the German infantry were only half-hearted and were easily repulsed. Further south, however, Zandvoorde and Hollebeke were lost.

On the morning of the 31st the enemy broke through at Gheluvelt. The 1st Scots Guards on the right of the 1st Brigade became involved in the fighting round Gheluvelt Château, but the rest of the Brigade, with the Battalion on its left, continued to hold its original position. A few men of the Battalion who were in reserve were sent up to protect the flank of the 1st Brigade. Gheluvelt was retaken later in the day by the 2nd Worcestershire Regiment and the line restored. But at nightfall the line was withdrawn and reorganized more compactly to the west of Gheluvelt. The line of the 1st Brigade—from south to north, Coldstream Guards, Scots Guards, Cameron Highlanders and The Black Watch—now ran from the eastern houses of Veldhoek, a small hamlet half-way between Gheluvelt and Hooge, to Polygon Wood.

On the 1st of November, while Battalion Headquarters were at breakfast in a cottage, a shell struck the building and wounded Major Murray, the commanding officer. Twelve hours later, Lieutenant Colonel C. E. Stewart arrived from the 2nd Battalion to take command in succession to Lieutenant Colonel A. Grant-Duff. On November 1st, Captain Amery, Lieutenant Rennie and sixty men, who had been wounded during previous fighting, rejoined from the base.

On the 2nd the British line on the Menin road was again

broken. The Battalion played a very considerable part in restoring the line by a brilliant counter-attack, in which A company under Captain V. M. Fortune, B company under Lieutenant J. L. Rennie and C company under Captain H. Amery took part. These companies, which thus stopped the forward German movement on the Menin road and helped to fill the gap, were only 120 strong and were reduced to 75 in the course of the attack. Lieutenant Nolan was killed, Captain Amery so severely wounded that he died some months afterwards, and Lieutenant Rennie was also wounded. Of the rank and file 5 were killed, 21 missing, almost all of whom were killed, and 34 wounded. Corporals Culpin and Redpath greatly distinguished themselves by their gallant leading in this attack.

From the 3rd until the 11th the Battalion was in position on the left of the 1st Brigade. Its portion of the line was normally held by D company, with Lieutenant McNeill's platoon of A Company attached, the whole under the command of Captain West. On the left lay the 5th Infantry Brigade of the 2nd Division, and on the right, in succession, the Camerons, the Scots Guards and the Coldstream Guards. Battalion Headquarters were at Vorbeek Farm, six hundred yards in rear; two platoons of A and B companies, in reserve, were entrenched in the paddocks of the farm, while C, in a wired post to the north-east of the farm, acted as support.

The enemy artillery fire was incessant and heavy from the 3rd onwards, and the losses sustained from shell fire during the previous few days were far greater than the reinforcements of thirty-two men which arrived on the 7th under Lieutenant Sprot.

On the 8th a heavy bombardment proved to be the usual prelude to an attack down the Menin road. Since the 2nd the sector south-east of Ypres had been held by a mixture of French and British. The line was pierced just north of the Menin road, about 2.30 p.m. and the Zouaves and the 1st Loyal North Lancashire Regiment were driven back into the wooded grounds of the Château immediately west of Veldhoek Village and north of the Menin road. This locality was afterwards known as "Inverness Copse."

B company, under Lieutenant Sprot, and two platoons of A company, under Lieutenant Lawson, the whole only ninety strong, were sent, under Captain Fortune, by General FitzClarence, commanding the 1st Infantry Brigade, to assist in re-establishing this part of the line. Meanwhile the North Lancashire Regiment had reoccupied the greater part of the ground which had been lost; so on arrival B company and the two platoons of A company strengthened their line and helped to fill

THE BATTLE OF YPRES, NOVEMBER, 1914

up gaps caused by the losses suffered in the earlier attack. Behind this part of the line a platoon of the 1st Northamptonshire Regiment, under Captain Crow, was established as a supporting point, and the second line of defence was completed by several isolated bodies of Zouaves. During the night of 8th/9th Captain Prince, North Lancashire Regiment, was killed in attempting to reoccupy part of the trench originally held by the North Lancashire Regiment, which was then discovered to be strongly held by the enemy. The Battalion machine gunners during the night crawled out and enfiladed this portion of the enemy's line and a large number of dead Germans were seen next morning outside the trench. Corporal Dewar and Privates Roy and Mitchell were very conspicuous during this hazardous operation.

Next day, the 9th, Captain Crow, in charge of the supporting point in rear, was killed. During the next two days the greater portion of B company and the two platoons of A company, under Lieutenant Sprot, returned to Battalion Headquarters at Verbeek Farm and went again into their reserve position.

Captain Fortune and Lieutenant Lawson, with a few men, remained with the North Lancashire Regiment until they were relieved on the 10th/11th; they only rejoined 1st Brigade Headquarters in Nonne Boschen, Glencorse Wood, during the attack by the enemy on the morning of the 11th. In spite of the proximity of the enemy during the 9th and 10th, the contingent of the North Lancashire Regiment and of The Black Watch had a comparatively quiet time, but the troops had little rest by night as alarms were frequent and the German guns were never silent.

Two episodes will help to show the conditions prevailing in this part of the line, when men were still unused to trench warfare, and many found the close presence of the enemy somewhat trying. On one occasion during the night, a wild figure rushed towards the trench held by our men, and miraculously escaping the fire that was opened on him, jumped into the trench, and luckily avoided being transfixed by the bayonets of the defenders. He proved to be a Zouave who had been buried in his trench in the enemy's attack against the North Lancashire Regiment–Zouave line on the 8th. The British are apt to call all French soldiers who wear baggy trousers, " Zouaves," but he belonged to the " Tirailleurs Algériens "; and anyone who has seen these excitable colonials can picture the scene in the trench on his unexpected and hasty arrival.

On another occasion a German soldier carrying rations mistook the Battalion trench for that held by his comrades, and appeared silently out of the darkness. To repeated challenges he

THE FIRST BATTALION THE BLACK WATCH

only answered, " Ssh———"; and at a yard's distance he was recognized and shot.

Between 6.30 and 9 a.m. on the 11th of November, the heaviest bombardment so far experienced by the British forces broke out; as it ended, a Division of the Prussian Guard, with orders from their Emperor to break the line at all costs, attacked the front of the 1st and 2nd Divisions. Under cover of the bombardment, a strong force drove back D company and the two platoons of A company entrenched at the south-west corner of Polygon Wood, and broke through the line. Second Lieutenant M. McNeill, commanding this portion of A company, was last seen on the parapet of his trench, revolver in hand, fighting right gallantly to the end with all his men.

The supporting point of C company, under Lieutenant F. Anderson, held out firmly, and split the attack into small parties of twenty or thirty men, many of whom were soon lost in the woods behind. It is interesting to note that Lieutenant Anderson's post was the first instance in the war of the "strong point," or wired-in locality, which later became a salient feature of defensive warfare. This particular post was sited and constructed by a great friend of the regiment, Major C. Russell-Brown, R.E., commanding the 23rd Field Company.

B company and the two platoons of A company, under Lieutenant Sprot, who were in reserve in the paddocks of Verbeek Farm, were overwhelmed by the first onrush of the enemy; Lieutenant Sprot and most of his men were killed. A few men, among whom were Privates Jackson and Gardner, were taken prisoner; but when their captors took cover from a chance shell, they slipped away and escaped into the Nonne Boschen Wood.

Verbeek Farm, the joint Headquarters of The Black Watch and the Cameron Highlanders, was temporarily occupied by the enemy; the actual Headquarters dug-out, a primitive brushwood lean-to against the farmhouse was, however, kept safe by the spirited defence of the two commanding officers, Lieutenant Colonels C. E. Stewart and D. McEwan, and of Sergeant D. Redpath, The Black Watch signalling sergeant. Lieutenant Colonel Stewart was wounded in the head at point-blank range by a German who was, in his turn, despatched by Sergeant Redpath.

Lieutenant Rowan Hamilton and Captain Brodie of the Camerons, the two adjutants, had previously, when the attack commenced, gone to 1st Brigade Headquarters in Nonne Boschen Wood to report the situation. Lieutenant Rowan Hamilton, in returning to report to Colonel Stewart at Verbeek Farm, was wounded.

Meanwhile, Nonne Boschen Wood, in which the 1st Brigade

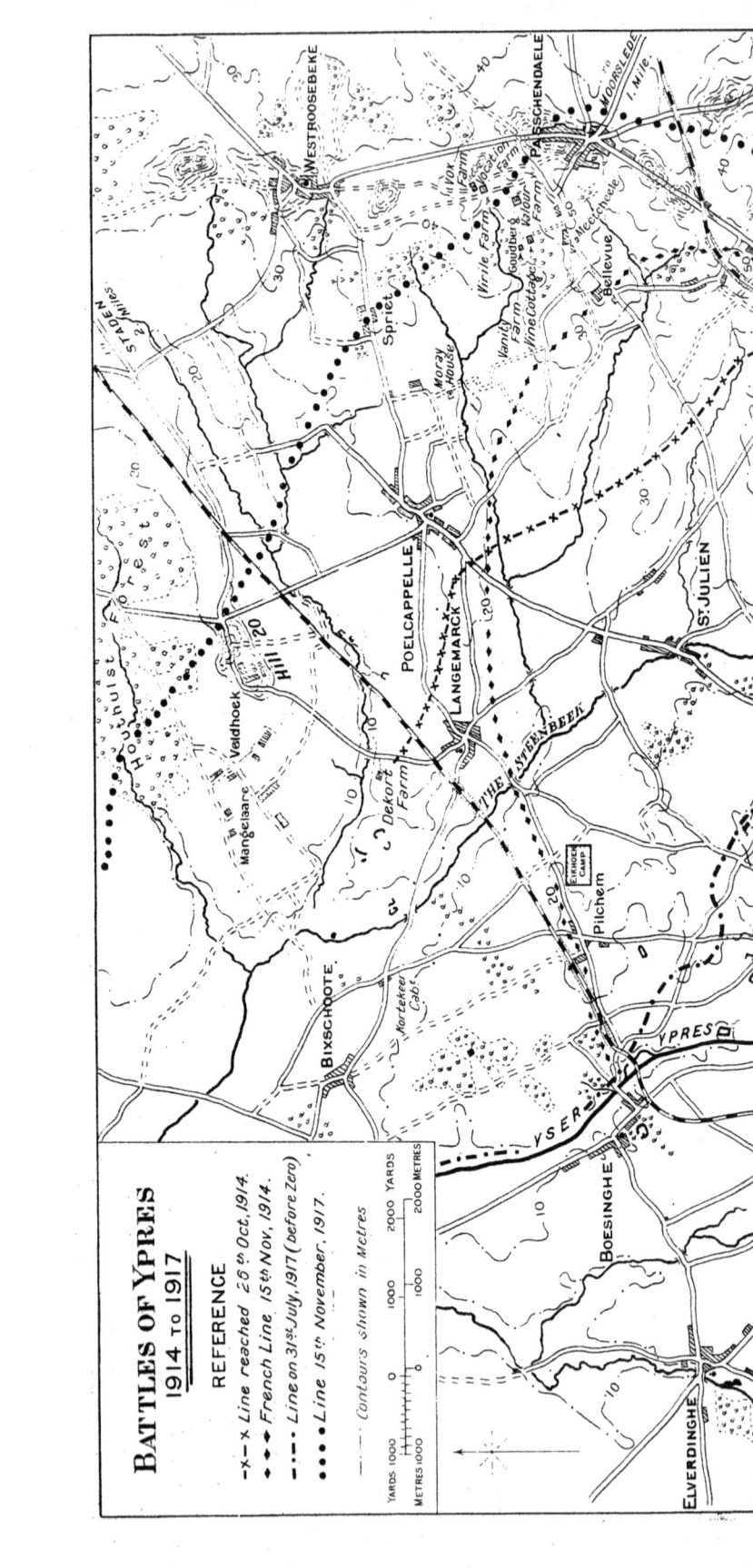

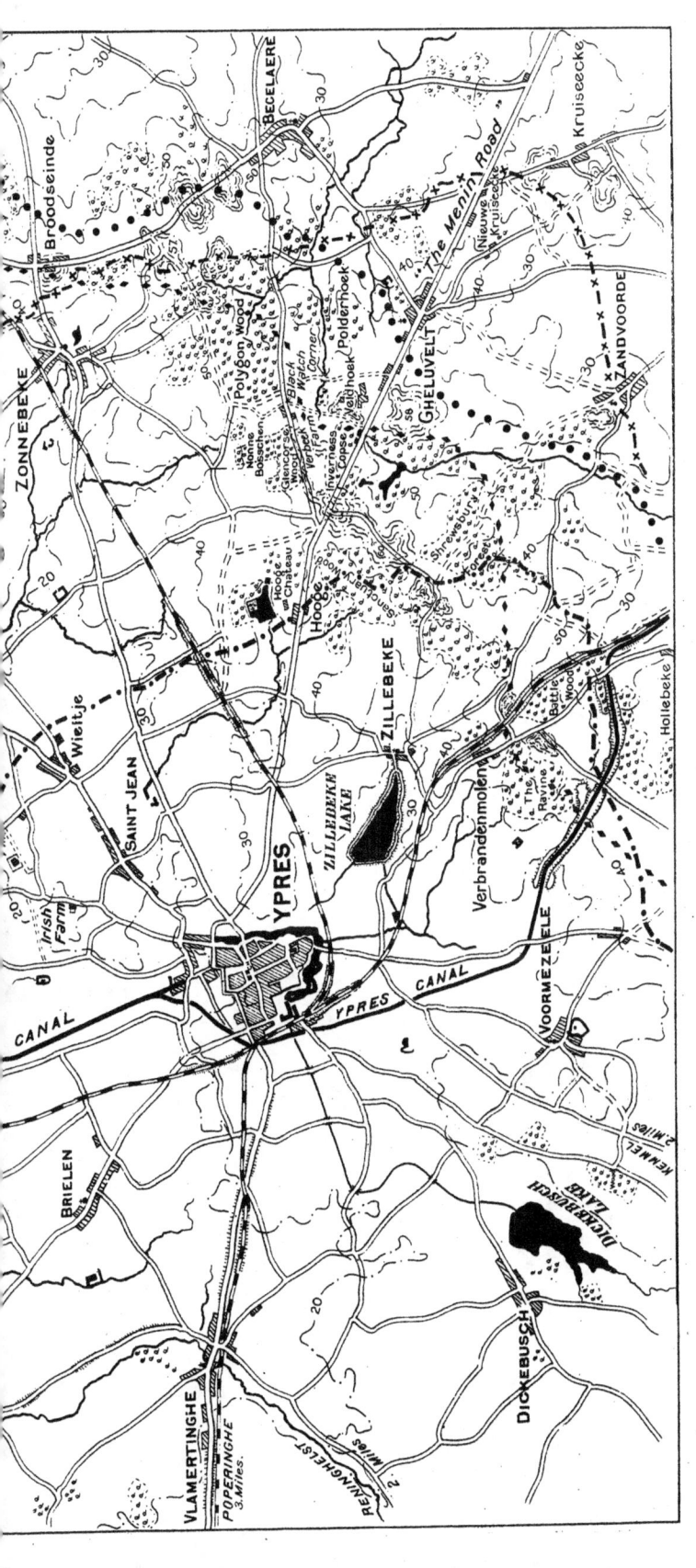

THE BATTLE OF YPRES, NOVEMBER, 1914

Headquarters was situated, was held by 1st Brigade Signal Section, The Black Watch party that had been with the North Lancashire Regiment for the past three days and had reported at 1st Brigade Headquarters during the preliminary bombardment, and a few men who had got away from the front line. Several small parties of the enemy had broken past Lieutenant Anderson's Post and Verbeek Farm and had attempted to enter the wood or passed along its eastern edge, but they were successfully dealt with. During this fighting Captain Brodie of the Cameron Highlanders and Lieutenant Lawson were killed. Lieutenant Lawson had recently been granted a commission, having come out to France with the Battalion as Regimental Quartermaster Sergeant—a most gallant officer, who fell fighting, having served the Regiment loyally for over nineteen years.

About 3.30 p.m. three companies of the 1st Northamptonshire Regiment, assisted by a party of The Black Watch and Camerons, advanced from Nonne Boschen Wood and regained the line Verbeek Farm–Lieutenant Anderson's Post, south-west corner of Polygon Wood, this corner being known on all later maps as " Black Watch Corner." Lieutenant Anderson was most severely wounded and his garrison suffered many losses; but they had accounted for a large number of the enemy—Lieutenant Anderson having himself shot several—and had broken up the main German attack in this area.

The net result of the German effort was to drive back the British line about five hundred yards on a front of a mile. Only one officer, Captain V. M. Fortune, remained unwounded at the end of this day. The casualties were: killed, Lieutenant Lawson and 18 other ranks; missing (nearly all subsequently ascertained to have been killed), Lieutenants Sprot and McNeil and 49 other ranks; wounded, Lieutenant Colonel Stewart, Captains West and Rowan-Hamilton, Lieutenant Anderson and 52 other ranks.

Those Germans who had advanced into the woods were held up by our artillery, who defended their batteries with an improvised firing line until the evening. The first Battle of Ypres had been won, since the Germans had failed in their single objective of piercing the British line. The trenches lost this day might have been retaken, had not the Brigadier of the 1st Brigade, General FitzClarence,[1] been killed as he led the 2nd Grenadiers and the 1st Irish Guards to counter-attack on the early morning of the 12th. Captain Fortune, Company Sergeant Major Gray and 2341 Private Mitchell were acting as guides to this counter-

---

[1] Brigadier General FitzClarence had succeeded to the command of the 1st Brigade at the end of September, on the promotion of General Maxse to command a Division.

THE FIRST BATTALION THE BLACK WATCH

attack, which was counter-ordered on the death of General FitzClarence.

On November 13th the Battalion was withdrawn from the line after eighteen days of almost continuous and hard fighting. Sanctuary Wood was the first halting-place, Hooge Château the second. Here, the next day, Captain Thompson, Argyll and Sutherland Highlanders, Lieutenant Buist and thirty reinforcements joined. Buist and his thirty men had landed in France with the 2nd Battalion The Black Watch from India and were sent to reinforce the 1st Battalion owing to its heavy losses. But now the task of the Expeditionary Force was lightening; the 8th Infantry Division, the Indian Corps and many Territorial regiments were arriving in France, and the Battalion, with other units of the Division was now, for the first time, given a considerable period in reserve areas to allow units to refit and reorganize.

On the 15th the Battalion marched to Westoutre, passing to the south of Ypres, where some of its old and beautiful buildings were still burning. On the 16th it moved on to Borre, and there stayed in reserve until the 20th of December.

Two hundred and eighty reinforcements now arrived from home, and the Battalion was re-equipped and reorganized. The peace and quiet of a small French village was very pleasant after this severe fighting, but the first leave given during the war was none the less welcome. A few officers were granted ninety-six hours, and two non-commissioned officers one hundred and twenty hours' leave. The number may seem small, but the first and all-important work of the railways and Channel steamers was to cope with the increasing volume of supplies and stores.

On December 3rd the Battalion had the honour of a visit from its Colonel-in-Chief, His Majesty the King.

On December 28th, Sir John French, the Commander-in-Chief, inspected and addressed the Battalion. " Black Watch," he said, " you have suffered great losses, on which I condole with " you; you have suffered great hardships. I condole with you on " the loss of your gallant Colonel, Colonel Grant-Duff, who fell, " as I am certain he would have wished to have fallen, in the " forefront of battle.

" The Black Watch—a name we know so well—has always " played a distinguished part in the battles of our country. You " have honours on your colours of which you are proud; but you " will feel as proud of the honours which will be added to your " colours after this campaign. At the Battle of the Marne you " distinguished yourselves. They say that the Jäger of the Ger- " man Guard ceased to exist after that battle—I expect they did. " You have followed your officers and stuck to the line against

IN RESERVE, DECEMBER, 1914

" treble your numbers, in a manner deserving the highest praise.
" I, as Commander-in-Chief of this force, thank you, but that is
" a small matter; your country thanks you and is proud of you."

This speech had an unexpected sequel; the Commander-in-Chief had ended with these words: " We have just received news
" of another victory; but you, by holding back the Germans,
" have won great victories as well, since if you had not done so
" the Russians could not have achieved their successes." An officer on leave mentioned these words to his friends at the depot; the news filtered through Perth, and within a few days a local newspaper produced an edition with the headlines and newsbills running: " HOW THE BLACK WATCH SAVED THE RUSSIAN ARMY ! "

During this month in reserve, training allowed very little time for sport, but there were some recreations, of which the most interesting was an officer's paper-chase (mounted), organized by the 1st Division on December 4th. The Kaiser was presumed to have been dropped from an aeroplane on his way to Calais.

" Special Idea; the 1st Division takes up the pursuit. The
" Kaiser endeavours to tear up his manifestoes as he flees, and
" thus makes a trail; he will be mounted on his well-known pie-
" bald charger."

But the 1st Division was haunted by the demon " Efficiency," and its amusements were never carried to extremes; the notice bore a stern footnote. " This is not a race. Any officer who in-
" capacitates for service either himself or his horse will be liable
" for trial under Section 18, Army Act."

NOTE

It is not out of place to give a short account of Lieutenant Colonel Grant-Duff's career, so unfortunately cut short on the Aisne.

Lieutenant Colonel A. Grant-Duff was the son of the Right Hon. Sir Mountstuart Elphinstone Grant-Duff, G.C.S.I., and was born on the 29th September, 1869. Educated at Wellington College and the R.M.C., Sandhurst, he was gazetted to The Black Watch in 1889. In 1897–98 he was in charge of the Base Depot of the Tirah Expedition, in Peshawar, and received for his services the thanks of the highest military authorities in India, and the Tirah medal with clasp.

He served in the South African War from January, 1902, until the end, being present at operations in the Orange River Colony, for which he received the Queen's medal with two clasps. In 1904 he graduated at the Staff College, and from 1905–9 was employed at the War Office.

THE FIRST BATTALION THE BLACK WATCH

From 1910 to 1913 he was Assistant Military Secretary to the Committee of Imperial Defence, being awarded the C.B. in the latter year. In May, 1914, he succeeded to the command of the 1st Battalion The Black Watch and took it to France on the outbreak of the Great War. He was killed at the Battle of he Aisne on the 14th September, 1914.

The award of the C.B. to Lieutenant Colonel Grant Duff was in recognition of his designing and editing *The War Book*. Before 1912 there was practically no co-ordination between the various Government Departments in case of war. But in January of that year a sub-committee on co-ordination was appointed under the Imperial Defence Committee, and in August of the same year the risk of war with Germany revealed our unpreparedness in this matter. Colonel Grant-Duff was secretary of the sub-committee and it was he who designed the framework of *The War Book*, namely, the full instructions to each Government Department for the action to be taken by it on the outbreak of war.

The death of Adrian Grant-Duff was a severe loss, not only to the Battalion and the Regiment, but also to the country which he had served so well.

CHAPTER II

FROM DECEMBER 20TH, 1914, TO MAY 9TH, 1915

1.—*The Attack of the 1st Brigade at Givenchy*

THE Battle of Ypres had drawn the British reserves in a steady flow northwards to such an extent that the German High Command was justified in assuming that the line held by the Indian Corps and the III Corps was weak and attenuated. An attack made on the Indian Corps on the 20th of December resulted in the loss of considerable portions of the trench line in front of Festubert and Givenchy, in spite of a resolute stand by some units of the Indian Corps, in which the 2nd Battalion The Black Watch was, amongst others, conspicuous. Several local counter-attacks met with little success, and it became obvious that large reinforcements were needed before the lost ground could be regained. All three Brigades of the 1st Division were ordered into the line in this area, the 1st Brigade reinforcing the sector from the Aire-La Bassée Canal to the north of Givenchy Village.

The Battalion, with the remainder of the 1st Guards Brigade, had been at an hour's notice to move. The order to move came on the afternoon of the 20th, and at 5 p.m. the Battalion left Borre for Merville, and then received orders to march straight on to Béthune, which was reached at 2.30 a.m. on the 21st. The march of 23 miles was very trying, since a much-needed issue of new boots had been made the day before; in addition, many of the men were in the state of weakness that follows immediately after innoculation. A tobacco factory provided a temporary billet, but before noon the Battalion was roused and ordered to move out of Bethune eastwards towards the front line.

The 1st Brigade had been placed at the disposal of the Commander of the Lahore Division, and had been ordered to retake the lost trenches north of La Bassée. The 1st Coldstream Guards, 1st Scots Guards, and 1st Cameron Highlanders carried out the attack, and made good all the ground lost. The Battalion, with the London Scottish (now attached to the Brigade), remained in reserve, and was not called upon.

The fighting in the village of Givenchy was most determined on both sides; time and again the Germans forced their way in, but were unable to maintain their ground. Mention ought to be made of a company of French Territorials, brought up to counter-attack on the 20th, who held with the greatest gallantry an isolated farm, afterwards known as "French Farm," until relieved by troops of the 1st Brigade. The Manchester Regiment, belonging to the Indian Corps, had also earlier in the

THE FIRST BATTALION THE BLACK WATCH

day regained most of the village of Givenchy by a very fine counter-attack carried out under Lieutenant Colonel E. P. Strickland, later commanding the 1st Division. Although sent into action with the expectation and promise of immediate support by the 1st Brigade, which did not materialize, the Manchester Regiment remained the only complete unit in Givenchy, and were not driven out.

On the morning of the 22nd the efforts of the Germans slackened, and infantry attacks ceased. In the evening the Battalion relieved the Coldstream Guards, the Camerons, and the French Territorials, and held the northern part of Givenchy and the trenches to the north of the village. These latter were some way in rear of the general line, and during the 23rd, the companies holding them were occupied in pushing the line forward. Snipers were active on both sides, and the Battalion trenches were frequently shelled with sudden and heavy bursts of fire.

On the night of the 25th the Battalion was relieved and spent three days at Cuinchy, a support position south of the canal. The remainder of the 1st Brigade moved back to Béthune, but The Black Watch and the London Scottish returned to the line at Givenchy, under the orders of the 2nd Brigade. The weather had for some time been fine and clear, but on the 27th it changed, and heavy rain and high wind flooded the newly dug trenches with water, so that they were constantly falling in. In such conditions as these, the Battalion saw in the New Year to the strains of "The Garb of Old Gaul," played on the pipes by Lance Corporal D. McLeod.[1]

Three companies occupied the front line, with the fourth billeted in close support. The return of the 1st Brigade, who came back to the line on New Year's Day, did not alter these dispositions, and for a fortnight there was nothing to record, except continual sniping and bursts of artillery fire by both sides. On January 14th the Battalion was relieved by the 2nd South Wales Borderers, under Major A. J. Reddie, D.S.O., who afterwards commanded the 1st Infantry Brigade. Billets in Beuvry were found for that night, and on the next day a short march was made to new billets in Béthune.

Casualties had been light over the period since the Battalion marched south, but several men had their feet swollen and paralysed by exposure to water and mud. The term "trench feet" was then unknown, and the careful medical arrangements, which later prevented this form of sickness, had not yet been organized.

Since the Battalion was destined to fight in many hard en-

[1] Afterwards Pipe Major McLeod; he was killed by an aeroplane bomb when the Battalion was at Albert in the summer of 1916.

GIVENCHY, JANUARY, 1915

counters in this district, before the enemy was finally driven from it, it will be useful to describe the La Bassée front. Its main importance lies in its nearness to the valuable coalfields of the Lens area. When the line was stabilized by the efforts of the French in October, 1914, the eastern half of these coalfields was left in enemy hands; both portions were now reorganized for production, and the capture or retention of either portion would make a great difference to the total production of munitions.

The roads, railways and canals of the district converged on the two " county towns," Béthune and Lens. East and north of Béthune, the country was flat and open. A network of ditches and canals failed to change the marshy nature of the soil; on the other hand, they formed an effective barrier to rapid advance. Most of the fields and orchards were enclosed by stiff hedges, and infantry combats were often localized to one field at a time. Occasionally a hillock of twenty or thirty feet high provided a site for a village, and incidentally a point of tactical importance. These small ridges, hardly noticed at first glance, were sufficient to gain or deny observation and a clear field of fire over a wide area. To this fact was due the importance attached to the village of Givenchy, and a little later to the village of Cambrin. It followed that the best defensive system for this front was to organize the villages as " strong points," permanently garrisoned, and organized for all-round defence. A thinly held trench line connected these garrisons, and mobile reserves were held in rear. An occasional farmhouse in or near the line was similarly fortified, and will be found on the war maps of the area as a " keep," " fort," or " castle," according to the fancy of the first occupier.

To the south of Béthune, rounded slopes of chalk (part of the same beds that underlie Southern England) allowed a more continuous and better-drained line of trenches. Dug-outs were habitable at any depth, and about this time the Tunnelling Companies were introducing the system of underground tunnels which later allowed whole battalions to be billeted, secure from shell fire, in the very front line. Ten or twelve pit-heads, with high towers for the winding-gear, and spoil-banks higher than most of the hills of Northern France, lay on either side of the line. Observation, therefore, was equally easy for both sides; in addition, a pit-head usually served to conceal machine guns, and a very strong defensive position could be constructed round it.

During the whole of the war, no part of the British front changed so little as this. The brick-stacks of Auchy, shortly to be contested by the Battalion, lay within a stone's-throw of the point where the 15th Infantry Brigade, coming north from the Aisne, first met the enemy; and from this spot the Germans

THE FIRST BATTALION THE BLACK WATCH

began their retirement in the early autumn of 1918. The whole area was ideal for the engineer constructing defences, and a perpetual problem to the infantry. In all ages it would have been found difficult to attack over such ground, where the attackers were exposed without a vestige of cover.

After inspection by the Commanders of the I Corps and the 1st Division, the Battalion began to make its way back to the line on the 21st of January, and first marched to Beuvry, where it was held in Brigade reserve. The front of the 1st Division was held by two Brigades, the 3rd Brigade holding the left or Givenchy sector, and the 1st Brigade, in touch with the French on the right, the right or Cuinchy sector. It was now obvious that the German attack, foiled at Ypres in November, would break out again before the Divisions of the New Army were in a fit state to be added to the Expeditionary Force. Work was vigorously put in hand to strengthen the Divisional front, and the Battalion was called upon to send one company to the 3rd Brigade for this purpose.

C company, under Captain W. Green, was detailed for this duty, and on reaching Givenchy, was attached to the 2nd Battalion the Welch Regiment. Two platoons, under Lieutenant W. H. C. Edwards, remained in cellars in the village, where they worked in the daytime, while Company Headquarters and the other two platoons were billeted in cottages about 300 yards south of the Pont Fixe, over which "Harley Street" crosses the canal. In the event of an attack, the whole was destined to form part of the garrison of Givenchy.

On the morning of January 25th, the expected attack began. A deserter had given warning of the enemy's intentions in the early hours of the morning, and his story was confirmed by a fierce bombardment, which opened about 7.30 a.m. Fifteen minutes later, Captain Green, seeing that the attack was imminent, marched his detachment from the Pont Fixe to Givenchy, a reserve platoon of the Welch Regiment following. The forward platoons of C company had been shelled out of their cover, and the whole company came together at the Keep. Meanwhile the enemy had entered the front line in several places, and was in the village itself.

After consulting the Officer Commanding the 2nd Welch Regiment, Major H. C. Rees, Captain Green moved round in rear of the Keep to the south part of the village, and from there attacked the enemy, with three platoons of The Black Watch, and the reserve platoon of the Welch Regiment, under Lieutenant James. The attack was successful, the enemy were driven out of the village, and the original line was restored. Lieutenant Edwards distinguished himself by the gallant and skilful way in

GERMAN ATTACK ON GIVENCHY, JANUARY, 1915

which he led his men forward, and his prompt action had much to do with the saving of the village.

One incident of the day's fighting will never be forgotten by those who witnessed it. Lance Corporal Swan of C company was shot in the close-range fighting that went on among the houses; his brother, Sergeant Swan, marking down the German who had fired the shot, stalked him and chased him from house to house for some ten minutes, until he finally closed with him and killed him.

C company now took over 200 yards of trench on the left of the Welch Regiment, and remained in the line until, on relief, they joined the Battalion at Béthune on the 27th. On the way back, the company was stopped at Brigade Headquarters, and Brigadier General R. Butler, Commanding the 3rd Brigade, congratulated Captain Green and his men on the part they had played in the defence of Givenchy. It afterwards became known that the prompt counter-attack of C company made unnecessary the use of two battalions of the 2nd Division, who were detailed to retake the village.

Meanwhile, the rest of the Battalion had been in heavy fighting. At 8.45 a.m. on the 25th the Battalion had received orders to march from Beuvry to Cambrin, and a little later was ordered to go straight on to Cuinchy. The enemy had mined and blown in the trenches of the Scots and Coldstream Guards, east of this village, and had broken the forward defences of the 1st Brigade. The *point d'appui* was a brick-field about 500 yards east of Cuinchy church, where a maze of trenches marked the heavy fighting that had already taken place around the brick-stacks.

The Guards, fired into from three sides, were unable to hold their ground, and fell back to the Keep at the western edge of the brick-fields. Here they made a stubborn stand, but the Germans came forward on both the north and south sides of the Keep, and again the defenders were enfiladed from both sides, and attacked from the front. This was the situation when the Battalion arrived at Cuinchy at 11.30 a.m.

Lieutenant Colonel Stewart was given command of the 2nd Battalion K.R.R.C. (from Divisional Reserve), and of six platoons of the Cameron Highlanders; with these and his own battalion, he was ordered to attack and re-establish the original line. At 1 p.m. the attack was launched; the Battalion advanced in the centre, with the 2nd K.R.R.C. on its right, and the detachment of Camerons moving along the canal bank on its left. B and D companies found the firing line and supports, and A company was held in reserve.

The canal on the north hemmed the attackers in, so that only a frontal attack was possible. In addition, the strong position

31

held amongst the brick-stacks, and the high embankments bordering La Bassée railway station, gave the Germans an extremely good field of fire in all directions, and casualties, especially among officers, were heavy. A continuous advance was impossible, and by 5 p.m. the attacking force had not got beyond a line running north and south through the brick-stacks, about 300 yards behind the original front line.

The 2nd Battalion Royal Sussex Regiment, from the 2nd Brigade, was now placed at Lieutenant Colonel Stewart's disposal, and another attempt was made to push forward. As before, the enemy poured in a heavy enfilade fire from the railway station, and at 3.45 a.m., when the Battalion was withdrawn from the line, the Royal Sussex were no further forward. Although no success attended the efforts of the Battalion, the casualties sustained, 6 officers and 205 other ranks, indicate the formidable nature of the task attempted. In particular, the energy and bravery shown by Lieutenant Anstruther in leading on his company after he was wounded, deserve to be mentioned. Similarly, Captain P. G. M. Skene and Lieutenant G. M. Richmond, who were both wounded in the attack, refused to leave their men, and carried on until the Battalion was relieved.

The Battalion moved into billets on the evening of the 26th January, and from then until the 4th February, it was alternately under the command of the 2nd and the 1st Brigades. During this time, it moved between Béthune, Beuvry and Annequin, and finally, on the 4th February, marched via Chocques to Burbure, for training and reorganization.

At Burbure the depleted Battalion was made up to strength by a number of drafts from the base. The time was fully taken up in organizing these, in refitting, and in continuous training at drill, musketry and bombing. At this period bombing was becoming, for the first time, seriously organized—that is, so far as the nature of make-shift bombs available would allow of organization. On February 16th, during experimental bomb practice, a premature explosion caused the death of Major J. T. C. Murray, D.S.O., and of Sergeant P. Hart.

Major Murray's death was keenly felt by his many friends, and his loss to the regiment was irreparable. He had joined The Black Watch in 1893, and served in the Tirah Campaign and in the South African War. He then exchanged to the 2nd Battalion and remained for some years in India. His valuable services when in command of the 1st Battalion on the Aisne have been already mentioned. It was well said of him that among soldiers and sportsmen no man was more honoured and loved than Crockatt Murray.

On the 27th February the Battalion, greatly increased in

IN THE TRENCHES, FEBRUARY–APRIL, 1915

efficiency after some rest and training, marched to Les Choquaux, and on the following day relieved the 2/3rd Gurkhas (Garhwal Brigade, Meerut Division) in a sector of the line south-east of the Rue de Bois, and just north of Festubert. The Divisional front extended over 4000 yards, from the northern outskirts of Givenchy exclusive on the south, to Chocolat Menier Corner[1] on the north, with inter-Brigade boundary to the north of Festubert.

In this area the ground was so marshy that it had been found most difficult to dig trenches, and impossible to keep them free of water. Both sides had therefore constructed breastworks about four feet six inches high, with a shallow trench running behind them. On the right half of the Battalion's line the breastworks were continuous, but on the left, where the ground was worst, only small circular posts could be constructed. " The Grouse Butts," as they were called, held a platoon each, and were so exposed that they could only be reached in safety after dark. The weather was bitterly cold, with occasional falls of snow, but it improved as time passed.

Until the 15th of April the Battalion occupied various parts of the northern half of this line, with one period of rest at Hinges, from the 23rd to the 30th of March. The enemy was harassed by rifle fire whenever an opportunity could be found, but nothing of importance happened. In this comparative lull, the first of the trench mortars appeared—stove-pipes almost as dangerous to their users as to the enemy. Lieutenant J. B. S. Haldane was the first "Bombing Officer" of the Battalion, and with his detachment moved about the line, firing his stove-pipes from different positions. The bombers were not popular in the line, since their action invariably drew artillery fire from the enemy, by way of retaliation, by which time, of course, the mortar detachment had disappeared. There is a well-authenticated story that Lieutenant Haldane was remonstrated with for walking about, "deficient of" a glengarry; he gave as his excuse the fact that the men of a neighbouring regiment had pushed him into a ditch for having fired mortars from their trenches!

On April 15th the Battalion was relieved by the 4th Royal Welch Fusiliers, and with the 1st Brigade went into reserve at Mesplaux, moving to Long Cornet on the 19th, and to Allouagne on the 23rd. As the weather improved, and the ground dried, offensive action by the Allies was certain, and so at Allouagne

---

[1] "Chocolat Menier Corner" was so called from an advertisement that was nailed on the wall of a house; it is the road junction on the south side of the Rue de Bois, about a mile south-west of Richebourg l'Avoué. It was a well-known name to the Regiment, for to the immediate front of this house the 1st, 2nd and 4th Battalions had some hard fighting in 1915; and round "Chocolat Menier Corner" the transport of these battalions had often come under severe shell fire when bringing up rations after nightfall.

THE FIRST BATTALION THE BLACK WATCH

training in attack was carried out. On the 2nd of May the Battalion marched via Le Casan to Richebourg St. Vaast, and relieved the 9th Battalion the Liverpool Regiment in billets and dug-outs, and two days later relieved the 1st Cameron Highlanders in the line.

2.—*The Battle of Aubers Ridge, May 9th, 1915.*

It has been mentioned that a British offensive was considered certain. Sir John French selected the early spring as the opportune time, and the Aubers Ridge, " which guarded La Bassée to the south-west and Lille to the north-east as the objective. The German line there formed a marked salient, and an attack on the ridge, if completely successful, would shake the security of Lille, and if but moderately successful would cut off La Bassée."

This was the Battle of Neuve Chapelle, 10th–13th March, in which the Battalion took no part; it was fought on a narrow front, with a limited objective, and was comparatively successful, although the enemy defences had not been completely destroyed by our artillery. At the second attempt on the 9th of May the front was extended, and the I Corps on the right of the First Army co-operated with the previous attackers, the VII Corps and the Indian Corps.

On the 7th of May orders were received that an attack would be carried out on the front of the First Army, with the object of breaking the enemy's line, occupying the line of the La Bassée–Lille road, and afterwards advancing to the line Beauvin–Don. The 1st Division was on the right of the attack—but before describing this action, it is necessary to give a short description of the position.

The main feature of the front is the Rue de Bois, connecting Béthune and Lille. Near the line, two smaller roads ran north-west from the Rue de Bois, one to Rue des Berceaux, and one about half a mile to the east of it; these were known as Albert and Edward roads respectively. A few hundred yards further west along the Rue de Bois, and nearer to Béthune, a road known as Princes Road left the main road and ran south-east in the direction of La Quinque Rue. It was the junction of Princes road and the Rue de Bois that has been referred to as Chocolat Menier Corner.

From Richebourg l'Avoué the line kept parallel with the Rue de Bois, and to the south of it, until at Chocolat Menier Corner, it took a right-angled turn to the south-east. It then ran parallel to Princes Road for about threequarters of a mile, took another right-angled turn to the south-west, crossed Princes Road and ran east of " Indian Village." The Battalion, with Headquarters

BATTLE OF AUBERS RIDGE, MAY 9TH, 1915

at the Rue des Berceaux, had, on moving into the line on the 4th, occupied the sector from Chocolat Menier Corner to Richebourg l'Avoué; these two points were the Divisional boundaries for the attack.

The immediate objective of the 1st Division was a line from Rue de Marais to Lorgies, about two miles in rear of the enemy's front line. The 2nd and 3rd Brigades were detailed to carry out the attack, the inter-Brigade boundary being a cinder-track running from the Rue de Bois to Ferme du Bois and Ferme de Toulotte.

On the south there was no co-operation, the ground east of La Bassée being impassable. To the north the Meerut Division (in which were the 2nd and 4th Battalions The Black Watch) was to attack La Tourelle. After the first objective had been gained, it was intended that the 1st Brigade should pass through the 2nd and 3rd Brigades and advance on an objective to be given later. In the meantime the 1st Brigade was held in Divisional Reserve, the Battalion being held in readiness to move first.

These orders were received on the 7th; but at 7 p.m. on that day the Battalion was informed that the attack had been postponed; and it was not until the evening of the 8th that the attacking troops of the 2nd Brigade took over the breastworks. On relief, the Battalion went into bivouac in an orchard a hundred yards west of Chocolat Menier Corner.

The infantry assault was preceded by a continuous bombardment which lasted for forty minutes. It is interesting to compare this preparation with the days and weeks of bombardment which preceded the later and more successful assaults of the war. The Allies had not yet learnt the lesson that where the enemy's defences consisted of entrenched positions, nothing short of absolute destruction could break them.

The bombardment opened at 5 a.m. and at 5.40 a.m. the 2nd and 3rd Brigades advanced. The enemy replied to our bombardment with an artillery fire that could not be called very severe, and the Battalion crossed Albert Road and occupied the rear lines of breastworks, intending to go forward to each line as the Brigades in front vacated it.

These Brigades, when they advanced, were met by a heavy rifle and machine gun fire from the German breastworks. Their start was difficult; they had to surmount the breastworks themselves, cross a dyke about ten feet wide, over which wooden bridges had been placed during the night, and then make their way across No Man's Land, which was rough and pitted with shell-holes. At the German line they found that the wire was uncut, and in face of the opposition offered they were unable to reach the enemy breastworks.

THE FIRST BATTALION THE BLACK WATCH

The failure of this attack was known about 6.15 a.m., and the 1st Brigade was at once ordered to occupy the front-line breastworks and be ready to meet any counter-attack launched by the enemy. It may be mentioned that in no part of the Army front did the attack meet with any greater success than here on the front of the 1st Division.

In this action of May 9th there is ample evidence that the Germans were well informed as to the impending movement, and were well prepared for it Their trenches were very deep, and more vulnerable to high explosives, in which the British artillery were deficient, than to shrapnel. In addition, the arrangements for cutting the wire proved inadequate.

The Battalion now occupied the front breastworks from Albert road on the right to the cinder track on the left, with three companies in the line and C company in reserve in the second line. At 7 a.m. the 2nd and 3rd Brigades attempted a second assault, but this was also unsuccessful, through the heavy machine gun fire and the difficulty of passing the still uncut wire. At 8 a.m., therefore, artillery began deliberate wire-cutting, and at 9.20 a.m. orders were issued that the 2nd and 3rd Brigades should assault again at 12 noon; this was later cancelled, then postponed until 2.40 p.m., and again until 4 p.m.

For this attack the objective was limited to the enemy's first system of trenches, and the 1st Brigade was ordered to take the place of the shattered 2nd Brigade. Two battalions carried out the assault, The Black Watch on the right, and the Camerons on the left. At the outset the communication trenches and breastworks were crowded with troops, and so great was the congestion that both battalions found it difficult to reach their jumping-off positions. The Camerons, in fact, could not reach their position by the time the attack opened; but such few men as came up in time attacked most bravely on the left of The Black Watch.

After an artillery bombardment of twenty minutes the Battalion advanced to the attack, and made one of the finest assaults it delivered during the war, distinguished by skilful leadership of officers and section commanders under the most adverse conditions, and great gallantry on the part of the men. Throughout the war the Special Reserve officers attached to the Battalion did well, and especially so on this day. Many were professional men who in peace time had worked hard, under various difficulties, to make themselves efficient soldiers; they had not the same training as their Regular brother officers, yet they displayed, even from the outset, fine soldierly qualities.

As in the original assault, the wire had not been sufficiently cut, nor had the German breastworks and machine guns been

BATTLE OF AUBERS RIDGE, MAY 9TH, 1915

much damaged. Against them, A and B companies advanced over the open, followed by two platoons each from C and D companies. The reserve, consisting of the remainder of C and D companies, and the four battalion machine guns, remained in the breastworks where was also Lieutenant Colonel C. E. Stewart and Headquarters.

The companies advanced to the sound of the pipes—for the last time—since gas helmets were shortly to muffle the pipers. It was not possible to recognize "Highland Laddie" in the noise of gunfire, but the pipes themselves could not be silenced, and there is no doubt that they raised the spirit of the attackers. As soon as our men topped the breastworks, they were met by a terrific rifle and machine gun fire, which seemed to come from every direction; machine guns were not only firing from the breastworks, but from tunnels cut underneath them.

The distance between the lines was about 300 yards, so that it did not take more than two minutes for the leading troops to reach the enemy wire. A few gaps existed, and into these the attacking platoons converged; then, forcing their way into the German line, they began to clear the trenches by hand-to-hand fighting. The advantage lay with the enemy from the first, since the platoons could only enter the breastworks on narrow fronts where the gaps existed; and though the Battalion established itself at various points, it was attacked from three sides, being bombed from both flanks, and fired into from the enemy's rear line.

Casualties amongst the officers were especially heavy. Major F. M. B. Robertson, who had made many attempts to join the Battalion since the outbreak of war, and who had only arrived from home the night before, was hit soon after the assault started, while advancing at the head of his men. Four former non-commissioned officers of the Battalion who had served the regiment loyally for many years died fighting bravely: Second Lieutenants A. Gray, A. Wanliss and J. Wallace, led their platoons into the German front line, and never returned; Second Lieutenant A. Shand was killed while leading an attack on two enemy machine guns. On the right of A company, Second Lieutenant T. B. Lyle, with his platoon, reached the second German line, but all lost their lives in a bombing encounter; similarly on the left, Lieutenant J. G. Scott of C company appears to have broken through the first German line, but was killed, with all his command, in the enemy's rear positions.

As the Camerons on the left had been stopped by machine-gun fire, the two remaining platoons of C company were sent forward in support of the Battalion left, but were met in their turn by an intense fire; casualties were heavy, and only a few men

THE FIRST BATTALION THE BLACK WATCH

succeeded in reaching the German breastworks. At Chocolat Menier Corner there was a right-angled turn in the line which has been already described; this allowed machine guns from the left to enfilade the Camerons and The Black Watch; moreover, the 3rd Brigade on the left appeared to have been unable to make any advance.

By this time the Germans had been reinforced; and though the Battalion machine guns had caused some casualties to their reinforcements as they came up the communication trenches, the position of our troops in the front line was precarious, and repeated requests for reinforcements reached Battalion Headquarters.

When the information that The Black Watch had entered the enemy's front line was received at Brigade Headquarters, the 1st Battalion Loyal North Lancashire Regiment was sent up in support; but before its companies had left the front line, the order was cancelled, and instructions were issued that the attacking troops were to be withdrawn from the German lines, presumably on account of the difficulties in which the 3rd Brigade found themselves. The Battalion was therefore withdrawn, although many had to be left in the German lines and in No Man's Land, and marched to Hinges, which was reached just before midnight.

Two of the many gallant deeds of the day may be mentioned here, though they are in no danger of being forgotten in the Regiment. Corporal Ripley displayed great bravery in leading a platoon up to the enemy's trenches and was awarded the Victoria Cross. The following is the official description of Corporal Ripley's conduct on this occasion.

" For most conspicuous bravery at Rue du Bois on 9/5/1915.
" When leading his section on the right of the right platoon in
" the assault, he was the first man of the Battalion to ascend the
" enemy's parapet and from there he directed those following
" him to the gaps in the German wire entanglements; he then
" led his section through a break in the parapet to a second line
" of trench which had previously been decided upon as the final
" objective in this part of the line. In that position Corporal
" Ripley, with seven or eight men established himself, blocking
" both flanks and arranging a fire position until all his men had
" fallen and he himself been badly wounded in the head."

Private Anderson of C company asked for permission to remain behind, after the relief, and went out at dusk to find his company commander, Captain W. Green, whom he had seen fall in the attack. He found Captain Green severely wounded and brought him back.

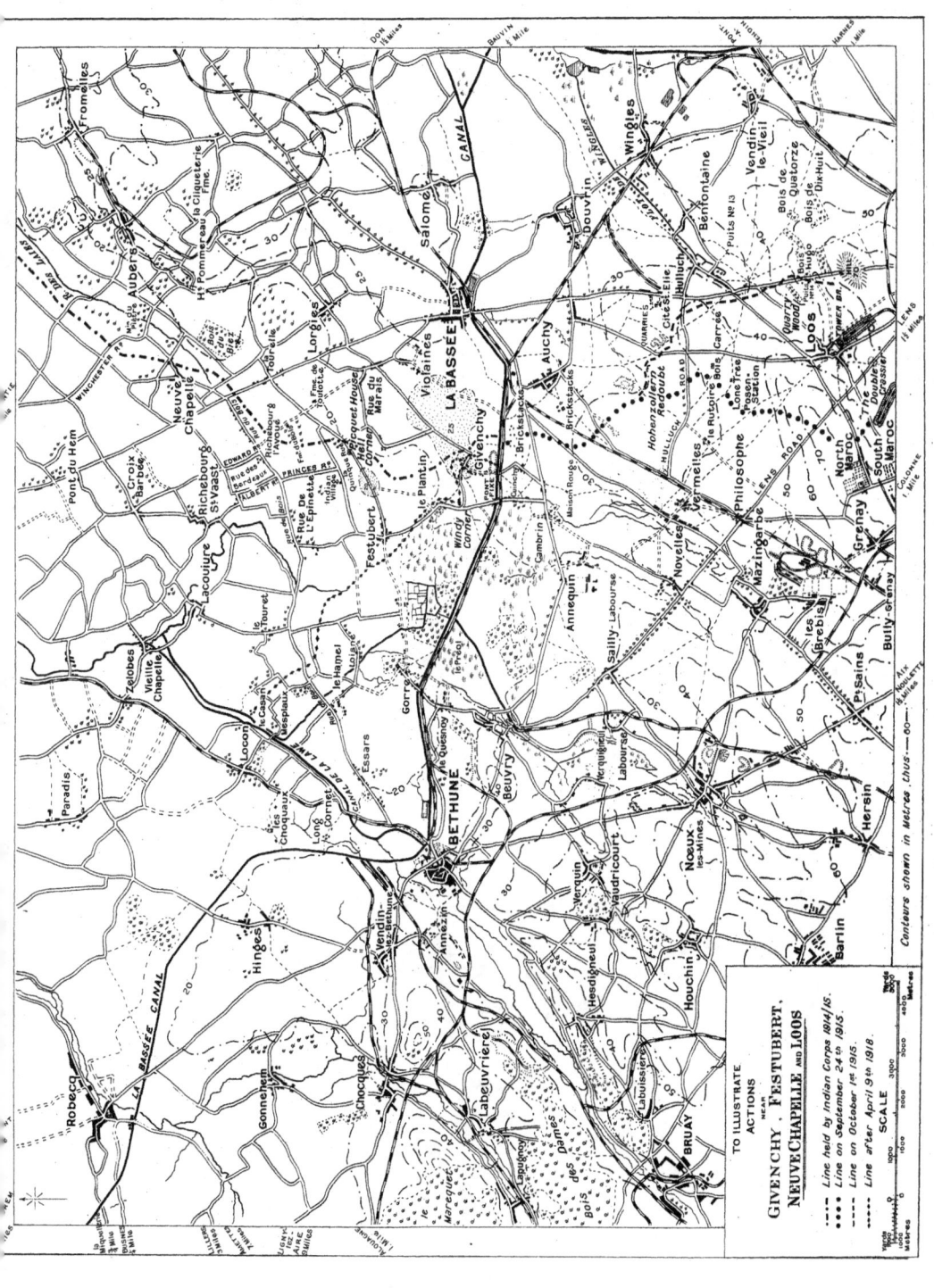

BATTLE OF AUBERS RIDGE, MAY 9TH, 1915

The gallant conduct of the Battalion, which alone in the Division attained its objective, brought messages of thanks and admiration from the 2nd Battalion the Royal Sussex Regiment, and the 2nd Battalion the King's Royal Rifle Corps; and a further proof of the difficulties of the attack, and of the bravery with which they were faced, is the number of killed, wounded and missing in the Battalion—14 officers and 461 other ranks.

CHAPTER III

FROM MAY 9TH, 1915, TO JULY 5TH, 1916

1.—*The Summer of* 1915

ONLY 8 officers and 354 other ranks could be assembled to march back on the 9th of May, and the next two days were needed for the reorganization of the Battalion, which was carried out in Divisional Reserve at Beuvry and Béthune. On both these days H.R.H. the Prince of Wales paid a visit to the Battalion, and interviewed several non-commissioned officers and men who had actually been in the German trenches on the 9th.

Major General R. Haking, C.B., came over to carry congratulations on the Battalion's gallantry from the Commanders of the I Corps and the First Army (Lieutenant General Sir Charles Monro and General Sir Douglas Haig); Sir Charles Monro also inspected the Battalion on the 12th May, and referred to its "fine behaviour." In spite of their heavy losses the men were in good spirits; they sang lustily as they entered Béthune, and bystanders were heard to say, "Those cannot be the men who were so badly cut up three days ago!"

The 13th and 14th of May were spent at Beuvry, and on the 15th a march was made to Sailly Labourse, the reserve position for the Vermelles sector, in which the 1st Brigade, on this day, relieved the 18th French Division. The sector, which consisted of old French trenches in quite good order, was officially known as "Y.2." After the previous weeks, this sector seemed comparatively quiet, and there is nothing to record except the regular incidence of reliefs. On the 19th of May the Battalion relieved the 1st Cameron Highlanders in the line, and were in turn relieved by them on the 23rd, moving into Brigade Reserve at Noyelles and digging a reserve line there. On the 27th it again relieved the Camerons in the line, and was finally relieved by them on the 31st, when it moved back to Sailly.

On the 1st of June, the Battalion, by this time up to a strength of 26 officers and 835 other ranks, marched to billets in the Faubourg d'Arras, Béthune; here it remained in Corps Reserve for ten days. The 1st Brigade had now moved northwards into the Cuinchy sector ("Y.3."), the left of which rested on the La Bassée Canal. In this portion of the line, the 1st Battalion The Black Watch relieved the 2nd Battalion the Royal Munster Fusiliers[1] on the evening of the 10th of June.

Owing to the increasing supply of munitions, and partly

---

[1] The 2nd R. Munster Fusiliers, whose complete destruction on August 27th, 1914, was mentioned in Chapter I, had been reformed, and had joined the 3rd Brigade.

IN THE TRENCHES, JUNE–SEPTEMBER, 1915

owing to an attack made by the Canadians, who lay north of the canal, on the 15th, this tour was marked by a greater volume of artillery fire on both sides, and the Battalion lost 6 men killed and 27 wounded through shell fire. Captain R. E. Forrester, commanding D company, was killed by a sniper during the progress of the Canadians' attack on the 15th. In Captain Forrester the Regiment lost a very gallant and much-loved officer. In the South African War he had served in the Yeomanry and gained a D.C.M. and a commission in The Black Watch. He landed in France with the 2nd Battalion in 1914, and was severely wounded when gallantly leading a raid into the enemy trenches. A true sportsman and most zealous soldier, all ranks in the Regiment knew that no heart was more loyal, no sense of right more sure, no devotion more true than that which died with R. E. Forrester on this day.

On the 16th of June, the 1st Northamptonshire Regiment relieved the Battalion, which marched back to billets in Béthune. For various reasons a series of moves was made in the reserve area, and on the 19th the Battalion billeted in Lapugnoy, moving to Burbure on the 23rd, to Hurionville on the 24th, and to Labeuvrière on the 29th. At Burbure the 8th (Service) Battalion of the Regiment, commanded by Lieutenant Colonel Lord Sempill, was in billets, and all ranks enjoyed the pleasure of meeting old friends from home.

On the 5th of July a move was made from Labeuvrière up to Noyelles again, and the Battalion took over billets from the 2nd Royal Munster Fusiliers; on the 9th it relieved the Camerons in its old trenches in " Y.2." at Vermelles. On the 12th dispositions were slightly altered, and the Battalion " side-stepped " northwards into " Y.3.", handing over " Y.2." to the London Scottish.

From now until the autumn offensive, the story is a dull record of moves and reliefs which are most easily shown by the accompanying table. It represents a monotonous summer, characterized by the growing number of casualties from shell fire, and varied chiefly by such amusements as the British soldier can be trusted to provide for himself, whether in or out of the line. On the 24th July, for instance, a Brigade Horse Show was held at Annezin, which was a great success. There were many entries, and the Battalion took several prizes, and did especially well in the heavy draught class.

On the anniversary of the outbreak of war, the 4th of August, the Battalion was in the line at Cambrin, with the 1st Coldstream Guards on the left. The evening of this day was celebrated by a picnic, the Guards providing an amateur orchestra of cornets, which serenaded the Germans to the tune of " Die Wacht am

THE FIRST BATTALION THE BLACK WATCH

Rhein." At midnight the music changed to "God Save the King," and every trench mortar in the sector fired a salvo. Lightheartedness of this kind was disconcerting to the enemy, who chose to take it seriously; and three hours of artillery retaliation passed before their indignation cooled.

Two changes remain to be noticed: on July 13th, Lieutenant Colonel C. E. Stewart, returning to England sick, handed over command of the Battalion to Major J. G. H. Hamilton, D.S.O.

TABLE OF MOVES DURING THE SUMMER OF 1915

Date	From	To	
July 13th	Y.3 Sector (Vermelles)	Noyelles	To Bde. Reserve. Relieved by 1st Camerons
July 16th	Noyelles	Y.3	Relieving 1st Camerons.
July 19th	Y.3	Annezin	Relieved by 2nd R. Sussex Regt.
July 25th	Annezin	Annequin	To Bde. Reserve.
July 27th	Annequin	Z.1 Sector (Cambrin)	Relieving 1st Camerons.
July 31st	Z.1	Annequin	Relieved by 1st Camerons.
Aug. 3rd	Annquin	Z.1	Relieving 1st Camerons.
Aug. 6th.	Z.1	Annezin	To Div. Reserve. Relieved by 1st Loyal N. Lancs.
Aug. 12th	Annezin	Noyelles	To Bde. Reserve. Relieving 2nd R. Munster Fusiliers.
Aug. 15th	Noyelles	Y.3	Relieving 1st Camerons.
Aug. 18th	Y.3	Noyelles	To Bde. Reserve.
Aug. 21st	Noyelles	Y.1	Relieving 1st Scots Guards.
Aug. 24th	Y.1	Annezin	To Div. Reserve.
Aug. 31st	Annezin	Ferfay	For rest and training.

The formation of the Guards Division about this time removed the 1st Coldstream and 1st Scots Guards from the 1st Infantry Brigade; their places were taken by the 8th Royal Berkshire Regiment and the 10th Gloucestershire Regiment. The Guards, with whom the Battalion had fought side by side since the beginning of the war, and from whom it was sorry to part, were played out of the area by the band and pipers of The Black Watch.

From September 1st to September 20th the Battalion re-

BATTLE OF LOOS, SEPTEMBER 25TH, 1915

mained in Brigade Reserve at Ferfay; this period of rest was the longest from the line that the Battalion had known since the beginning of the war. Rigorous training was relieved by sport and games, and some good concerts were given at nights. On September 21st the Battalion marched to bivouacs in Le Marquet Wood; the weather was fine, the band played at night, and men thoroughly enjoyed life. Dining by lantern light, to the sound of music, the officers were tempted to make a comparison with the evenings that had preceded the battle of Waterloo, a comparison that in some ways events proved true.

In the evening of the 23rd the Battalion marched to billets at Verquin, in pouring rain, and at 6.45 p.m. on the 24th, moved up to battle stations in " Y " section, east of Vermelles. For four days there had been an intense bombardment of the enemy's lines; but on this night there was an absolute stillness, only an occasional Véry light revealed the fact that a trench system stretched across the silent plain of Loos.

2.—*The Battle of Loos and the Action of Hohenzollern Redoubt*

Sir John French had decided that the I and IV Corps, in conjunction with the French on the right, were to attack the enemy from a point opposite the village of Grenay to the La Bassée Canal; the Vermelles–Hulluch road divided the two Corps, the IV Corps (in which was the 1st Division) being on the right. " Opposite the front of the main line of attack, the dis-
" tance between the enemy's trenches and our own varied from
" about 100 to 500 yards. . . . The country over which the
" advance took place is open, and overgrown with long grass and
" self-sown crops. . . . From the Vermelles–Hulluch road south-
" wards the advantage of height is on the enemy's side, as far as
" the Bethune–Lens road." [1]

Over this open, slightly uphill ground, the 1st Division was to attack; on its right the 15th (Scottish) Division had been ordered to take Loos Village and Hill 70; on its left, the 7th Division had been allotted the task of capturing Cité St. Elie and the northern half of Hulluch Village. The objectives were to be reached in two stages; for the 1st Division, the first was a line running through the pit-head Puits 14 bis–Bois Hugo–Chalk Pit–the south-west edge of Hulluch Village; the second a support line of trenches running from east of Bois Hugo to the south-east of Hulluch, together with Puits 13 bis. The 1st Brigade on the right and the 2nd Brigade on the left were to carry out this assault, with the 3rd in support; but as the more important points of the objective were on the outer flanks of the attack, which would thus possibly

[1] Sir John French's despatch.

THE FIRST BATTALION THE BLACK WATCH

diverge, an independent force ("Green's Force"), consisting of the London Scottish and the 9th Liverpool Regiment, under Lieutenant Colonel W. E. Green, D.S.O., was ordered to follow the attacking brigades, seize, and consolidate the intermediate ground between Posen Alley and Vendin Alley.

The orders issued by the 1st Brigade, summarized, were as follows: The enemy front system was to be attacked by the 8th Royal Berkshire Regiment on the left and 10th Gloucester Regiment on the right, Bois Carrée being the dividing line between them. After the front line had been carried, the Berkshire Regiment, reinforced by the Camerons from support, were to advance on the southern half of Hulluch, followed by A company of the 1st Black Watch, two sections R.E., and a Brigade "wiring" party, who were to consolidate positions in the German support lines 700 yards west of Hulluch Village. The remainder of The Black Watch were ordered to move into the front line trenches as soon as the assault began, and there await orders. Brigade Headquarters moved forward from Le Rutoire Farm to Daly's Passage.

On the morning of September 25th, gas was released from the British trenches at 6 o'clock, and a heavy bombardment of the German lines began. Half an hour later the attack opened, and the Gloucester and Berkshire men disappeared into the smoke in front. At the outset several men were obviously affected by the gas, and many of the remainder were unable to keep the direction. At 7.20 a.m. a message came through to the Brigade that some men of the Cameron and Gloucester battalions were in the enemy front line; and by eight o'clock parties of all three attacking battalions, mixed with various troops of the 7th Division, were only 500 yards west of Hulluch, having captured two field guns on the way.

But no more good news of this sort came through; and it was soon evident that the 2nd Brigade on the right had fared badly, since the trenches round Lone Tree were almost intact and strongly wired; the Gloucesters, too, on the right of the 1st Brigade, were losing their men fast. At 9.10 a.m., therefore, B company of The Black Watch was ordered to push forward with its right on Bois Carrée, gain the first trench, and then swing to its right. The Germans, however, had now recovered portions of their front line, and only about thirty men of B company reached the German lines, the remainder falling under enfilade fire; none the less, the company was able to establish itself and form a protective flank.

It was obvious that stronger measures than these were necessary, and at 2 p.m. two battalions of the 3rd Brigade pushed through between the Hulluch road and the Bois Carrée. A and

BATTLE OF LOOS, SEPTEMBER 25TH, 1915

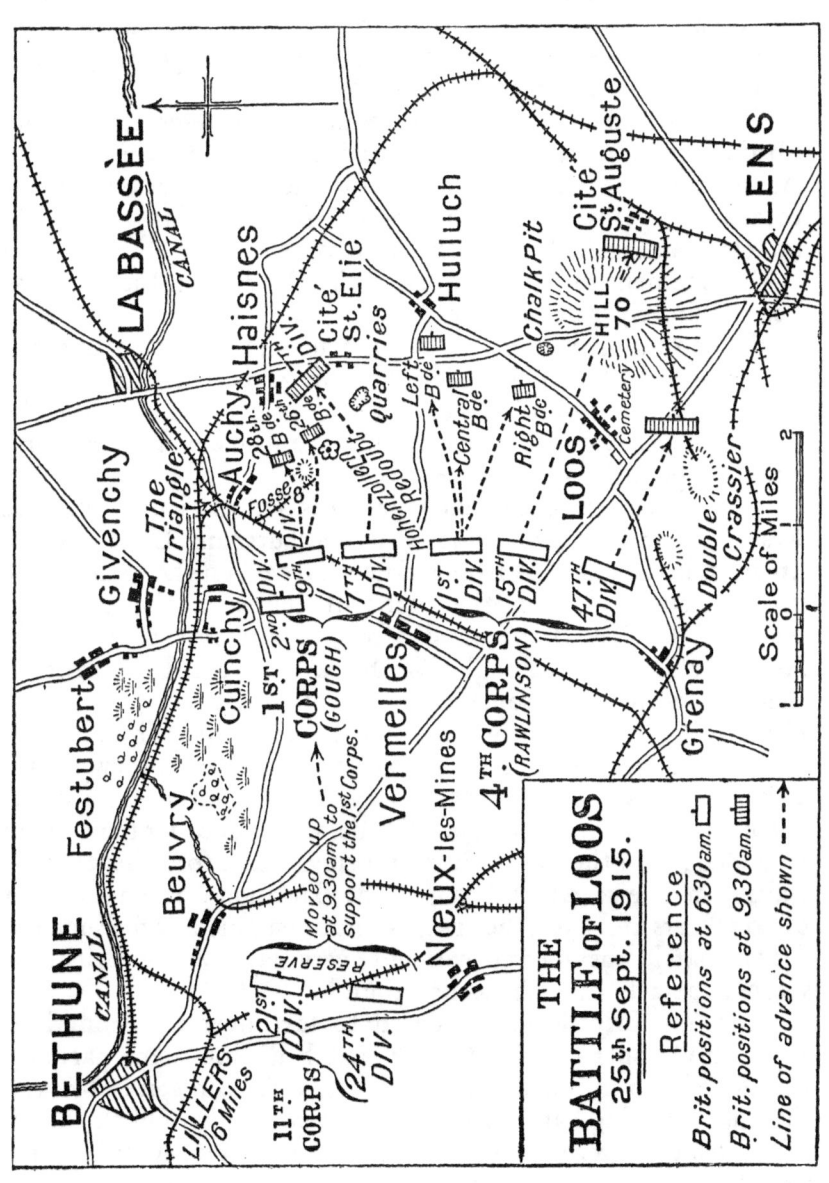

THE FIRST BATTALION THE BLACK WATCH

C companies of The Black Watch followed them. A continuous line was made, but no unit could advance, and when night fell, the front of the 1st Division ran parallel with, and about twenty yards west of, the La Bassée–Lens road. The night passed in comparative quiet, but rain began as the darkness came down, and the wet appeared to bring the gas out of the ground, adding much to the discomfort of the troops.

The morning of the 26th broke fine, and as reserves had come up during the night it was determined to renew the advance. At 10 a.m. the Battalion received orders to attack with two companies against the south edge of Hulluch. At 12 noon the attack was cancelled, since the units on the right and left were at that moment losing ground, and the Division on the right had been definitely forced to retire.

In the meantime, the two companies in the front line had gone forward; but they achieved nothing more than the capture of an advanced T-head trench. The divisions in Loos were also losing heavily in counter-attacks, and the whole of the two corps were temporarily on the defensive.

During the 27th the Battalion was withdrawn to Brigade Reserve in the old front line, where Lieutenant Colonel C. E. Stewart, now recovered from sickness, arrived on the 28th to take up his command. On the night of the 30th the Battalion marched to Les Brebis, and after a short rest to billets in Nœux-les-Mines. Although The Black Watch had not suffered such great losses as some other units casualties were heavy. Captain R. C. Anderson, Second Lieutenants Whyte, Moir and W. Fraser were killed, together with 60 other ranks; Captains Cooke, Campbell and Hay, Lieutenant Erskine-Bolst, Second Lieutenants Gunn and Ritchie, with 151 other ranks, were wounded; 61 other ranks were missing. Reinforcements were waiting at Nœux, which brought the Battalion up to a strength of 20 officers and 836 other ranks—indispensable reinforcements, for the battle was not yet over and every day saw new British or German attacks over the same ground.

The 1st Brigade was ordered to take over the front line again on October 5th, The Black Watch holding some partially completed trenches near the Chalk Pit, where, in spite of heavy shelling, they dug hard during the next two days. On the night of the 7th they were relieved, and spent two more days in digging near Lone Tree, taking over the line west of Hulluch on the night of the 10th. The situation had changed very little since the 27th of September; but a heavy German attack on October 3rd had recaptured a large part of the Hohenzollern Redoubt. To remedy this loss the 46th (Midland) Division were ordered up to attack on October 13th; and on their right the 1st Division,

HOHENZOLLERN REDOUBT, OCTOBER 5TH, 1915

with a smoke and gas screen, were to assist by attacking the German front line south-west of Hulluch.

On this day B and C companies of the Battalion were holding the front line, with A and D in a new assembly trench sixty yards behind; 14 officers and 536 other ranks went into action. At 2 p.m. two platoons each of B and C went forward to take the two cross-roads that lie west of the southern part of Hulluch on the Lens–La Bassée road. The ground was flat and open, and they reached the German trenches in three minutes; but the wire was thick and uncut, and both the attackers and the supporting platoons of B company, who followed on behind with picks and shovels, lost many men from the fire of machine guns on either flank.

In Fortescue's *History of the Army* there is one poignant sentence that sums up the charge of the 42nd Highlanders at Ticonderoga. "Not once only, but thrice more, the British, and " the Americans with them, hurled themselves desperately " against the French stronghold, only to be beaten back time " after time, until the inner abattis was hung with wisps of " scarlet, like poppies that grow through a hedge of thorn." Here was another Ticonderoga; but here were no sunlit overhanging woods nor ranks of scarlet—only rows of drab figures that ran a little way into a cloud of green gas and sulphurous smoke, and after fifty yards were lost to view. Let the War Diary tell what happened to them.

" 2.45 p.m.—A and D companies sent up supporting platoons " to assist with fire, and at 3.15 p.m. D company sent up other " two platoons, who were much harried by machine gun fire. " A sent forward a second, and, after, a third platoon. 4 p.m.— " Again the right platoon of B was reported to have got in. More " bombs were sent up. The report was incorrect; the bombs " never reached the front companies.

" 4.45 p.m.—Lieutenant Mercer collected some bombers of " the Northamptonshire Regiment, who assisted our party on " the right flank. (The 'party' now consisted of only one man.) " The left platoon of C company was reported to have got into " the trench near here, but had only got into the wire. 7.25 p.m. " —Instructions received to hold present position until further " orders. Every officer of the Battalion who had left our trench " had become a casualty.

" 8.50 p.m.—A patrol of men, under Lieutenant Mercer, " reconnoitred the sunken road leading to the right of our " objective, as it was rumoured that the Berkshires had reached " the cross-roads. The rumour was unfounded, and everyone in " the patrol was either killed or wounded. 12.20 a.m., 14th

THE FIRST BATTALION THE BLACK WATCH

" October.—The Battalion reorganized, holding the British
" front line."

It was only on the morning of the 14th that the events of the attack were known and the situation understood. On the left the battalions of the 46th Division had taken about half of the Hohenzollern Redoubt, though with very heavy losses; but the 1st Division, suffering almost equal losses, had hardly made any headway. The Black Watch, throughout the afternoon and evening, had made one attempt after another to penetrate the belts of wire; they had never been able to close with the enemy, but the list of casualties reveals the courage of their efforts, in the face of unlocated bombing saps and machine guns. Six officers, Second Lieutenants Paton, A. Fraser, Ballantyne, Hutchison, Hayes and Mercer, and 33 other ranks had been killed; Lieutenant Merrylees, Second Lieutenants Home, Lamb and Young, and 163 other ranks had been wounded, and 33 other ranks were missing.

Few actions aroused more criticism at the time than the battle of Loos, but it is certain that The Black Watch, with other units of its Division, had once more given the enemy a proof of their spirit. General Capper of the 7th Division, who was killed at Loos, used to say: "We are here to do the "impossible." In that temper the Battalion had gone into battle; it came out of action with spirit unsubdued.

3.—*The Autumn of 1915 and the Loos Salient*

On the afternoon of the 14th of October the Battalion was relieved in the line by the 15th County of London Regiment, and marched back through Le Rutoire and Sailly Labourse to Nœux-les-Mines railway station. Entraining was completed about midnight, and everyone settled down to sleep until the arrival in Lillers, about noon on the 15th. The next fortnight was spent here in refitting and training, varied by boxing tournaments, organized both by the Brigade and Battalion.

After a train journey back to Nœux-les-Mines on the 28th, a march was made to Houchin; it is worth noting that the inhabitants were far from friendly, and only with difficulty were any billets found. The sequel is that when, a few weeks later, The Black Watch again visited Houchin, they were very warmly received—which goes to prove, if proof were needed, that the men of the Regiment had a way of endearing themselves to the French inhabitants of their billets. On this day A company [1]

---

[1] A company consisted of Captain W. D. McL. Stewart, Lieut. Murray Menzies, Second Lieutenants I. D. Brown, J. C. Murray and R. Alexander, and 204 other ranks.

IN DIVISIONAL RESERVE, NOVEMBER, 1915

marched over to Labuissière, where representatives of the 1st Division were inspected by H.M. the King. (It was just after this inspection that His Majesty was injured by his horse falling.)

The 29th and 30th were spent in training, and on the 31st the Battalion marched back to Lillers; the daily strength return for this day showed 25 officers and 627 other ranks, and the Battalion was strong enough to profit by the fortnight of training that followed. Throughout 1915 the use, both by the Allies and Germans, of the hand grenade became more and more general; every company formed selected parties of bombers who were specially trained for the attack on enemy trenches. In some corps in 1916 so much reliance was placed on the hand grenade that the training with rifle and bayonet suffered considerably. The rifle grenade was also freely used by both sides, but this weapon was never so much used or so highly developed as were the various forms of trench mortars. The only incident of note is the inspection of the 1st Brigade by the Commander of the IV Corps, Lieutenant General Sir Henry Rawlinson, on the 10th of November. Addressing The Black Watch, he congratulated it on the gallantry shown on the 25th of September. Otherwise the days were spent in the ordinary training of drill and musketry, with football in the afternoon (the London Scottish were favourite opponents), and a concert or boxing in the evening.

A long spell of existence in trenches on the Loos front was to follow, and on the 14th of November the Battalion moved back by train to Nœux, and on the same night marched up to the trenches in "A.1.," west of Loos, relieving the 8th London Regiment in the line. The 8th Royal Berkshire Regiment was in the line on the left, and the French 77th Regiment on the right. After the past fighting it was to be expected that the trenches in this district would be in poor condition, and continuous work was needed to prevent wet weather and the enemy's shelling from making them impassable.

The 10th Gloucester Regiment relieved the Battalion on the 17th of November, and it moved back into Divisional Reserve at Houchin, where, as has been said, it was well received. On the 24th it was inspected, with the rest of the 1st Brigade, by the Commander-in-Chief, Field Marshal Sir John French. After referring to the previous successes of the Brigade in the campaign, the Commander-in-Chief praised the fine work of the Brigade at Loos; speaking afterwards of The Black Watch, and referring to the great record of the 42nd, he said that in his opinion the honour "Loos" was as splendid as any borne on their colours. He also commented to the Commanding Officer on the good appearance of the Battalion.

After a week the Battalion marched up to Philosophe in

THE FIRST BATTALION THE BLACK WATCH

Brigade Reserve, and on the 29th took over the right half of the Brigade sector (B.1) from the 8th Royal Berks Regiment. This was the trench system facing the corner of Hulluch Village. The village lies at the bottom of a badly drained chalk valley; the front line was at the foot of a slope which rose westward to higher ground and was overlooked by the high pit-heads of Cité St. Élie in the German front line. From all directions the natural drainage fell towards the British line, and between shell fire and weather the trenches were mere pools of chalky mud. So difficult were the communication trenches that occasionally a ration party would be out all night, and yet not have gained the front line by daybreak.

The 8th Royal Berkshire Regiment relieved the Battalion on the 2nd of December, and was in turn relieved by it on the 5th; the three days in support had been spent at Lone Tree, the old German front line north of Loos, and large working parties of The Black Watch had been repairing the trenches in that area. The employment of the rifle grenade grew much more general about this time. The Germans had made considerable use of this weapon all the summer, and now men in every platoon were trained as rifle grenadiers. In spite of continuous work on communication trenches and rear approaches, when the Battalion was relieved, on the 8th of December, by the 6th Welch Regiment, it took three and a half hours to complete the move from the support positions to Mazingarbe, a distance of under four miles.

On the 14th of December the Battalion relieved the Loyal North Lancashire Regiment, in trenches east of Loos (A.1 sector). Here similar conditions existed, with the additional fact that Hill 70, on the right, overlooked the trenches, and helped the enemy's shelling to be as accurate as it was heavy. The Camerons took over this sector on the 17th, the Battalion marching back to Brigade Reserve in Philosophe, and going up again on the 20th to relieve the Camerons, who again relieved the Battalion on the 23rd.

The second Christmas in France was spent in support in Gun Alley, poor trenches full of mud and water, which the Battalion willingly handed over to the South Wales Borderers on the 26th of December. The signallers, as was the custom, were relieved in daylight, and on this occasion the amount of movement round Battalion Headquarters resulted in heavy shelling on this position. One shell burst in a cellar, in which the runners and signallers lived; 3 were killed and 3 wounded, but 7 others, though buried, were rescued uninjured.

Buses were waiting at Philosophe, and by 10 p.m. the Battalion was in billets at Nœux-les-Mines, where it remained

AT REST, DECEMBER, 1915–JANUARY, 1916

until the 1st of January. In order to make sure that the men should have their New Year's dinners while the Battalion was "at rest," New Year's Day was this year celebrated on December 30th.

The evening of New Year's Day found the Battalion relieving the King's Royal Rifle Corps in front of Hulluch; the tour in the line was now in most places standardized to three days, and on the 4th the Battalion was relieved by the Cameron Highlanders. On this day Lieutenant Colonel C. E. Stewart, who had commanded the 1st Black Watch since November 1st, 1914, left to take command of the 154th Brigade in the 51st (Highland) Division, and handed over command of the Battalion to Major J. G. H. Hamilton, D.S.O.

It was the last time the Regiment was to see Colonel Stewart. His high qualities as a leader had long been recognized, and he was given command of the 154th Brigade in January, 1916, which he commanded until September, 1916. He was unfortunately killed by a stray shell when going round the forward trenches.

After three days in reserve at Philosophe, the Battalion moved up to relieve the Camerons, and on the 10th was again relieved by them, and went into the support trenches, the old German front line. This was the last visit of the 1st Black Watch to the Hulluch trenches, which were left without regret. On the 13th of January troops of the 15th Division took over the sector, the Battalion marching back to billets in Nœux-les-Mines. Next morning a move was made by train to Lillers; from there the Battalion marched to its billets at Allouagne, in the corps reserve and training area.

4.—*The Spring of* 1916

The Battalion spent a quiet month at Allouagne. General Joffre visited the town on the 20th when Captain Lumsden and a hundred men formed a Guard of Honour at Ferfay, and the Battalion lined the streets of Allouagne. On the 17th of February the Battalion again moved forward by train from Lillers to Nœux, and thence by march to billets in Mazingarbe. The comment in the War Diary of the day reads: " The weather is horribly rough " and very wet." On the 20th the Battalion relieved the 1st Northamptonshire Regiment in the left half of the Maroc sector.

The striking landmark of this front was the well-known " Double Crassier," always known in the Regiment as the " Twa Bings." The Bings were two parallel slag-heaps which had been captured by the 47th Division at the Battle of Loos. By this time, however, the line had been driven back a little, and only the western ends were held by the British. The tops of the Bings were about twenty yards apart, and the hollow between them was filled with wire.

The southern Bing was occupied for about fifty yards, the trench ending in a T-head, which was almost within bombing distance of the German T-head that faced it. A similar trench, T-headed, ran out about 140 yards along the northern Bing, and a communication trench, linking the Bings up with the system of trenches near Loos, went obliquely down the northern slope of this Bing.

The end of the Crassiers always received a good deal of attention from the enemy's artillery, but the good dug-outs which existed there prevented heavy casualties. On the top of the Bings there was a good deal of sniping; the pithead spoilbanks and winding towers made observation easy in all directions, and it was hard to know whether trench sentries were not exposed to enemy observation. The trenches running up the west end were continually blown in by shell fire, and in spite of being observed, parties of men would zig-zag over the open to the top. Indeed, to an observer from Maroc, the Bings often seemed like great ant-heaps, with khaki-coloured ants running up and down, occasionally being dispersed by a puff of smoke, burrowing for a while, and then running off again.

The first tour in this sector lasted until the 23rd, and though there was some snow there was also hard frost, and the trenches could be kept comparatively comfortable and in good order. On the 23rd the Camerons came up to take over the line, and the Battalion went back to South Maroc in support. After three days here, the Battalion relieved the Camerons on the 26th, and were again relieved by them on the 29th, going back to Les Brebis in Brigade Reserve. The last few days had been trying, as a thaw and rain set in, and all fire trenches and communication trenches gradually collapsed as the frost came out of the ground.

Until the 8th of March, the Battalion stayed in Les Brebis, providing each night large working parties for the forward defences. It was bitterly cold all the time, and snow fell almost daily. At Les Brebis, on the 7th of March, Captain J. W. C. Stubbs, M.C., the Medical Officer, left the Battalion to fill a higher appointment at Divisional Headquarters. Captain Stubbs had joined the Battalion on a very dark and busy night on the Menin road in November, 1914. Since then, besides being indefatigable in his care of wounded and sick, he had also been largely responsible for organizing the brass band which for over a year now had been a great asset in billets and on the march. " Stubbo " had deservedly earned the affection of all ranks, and

TABLE OF MOVES, SPRING AND SUMMER, 1916

Date	From	To	
March 9th	Les Brebis	Line (Right Loos Sector)	Relieving R. Sussex Regt.
March 12th	Line	N. Maroc	To Bde. Reserve. Relieved by Camerons.
March 15th	N. Maroc	Line	Relieving 1st Camerons.
March 18th	Line	Old German front line	To support. Relieved by Camerons.
March 21st	Support	Les Brebis	To Bde. Reserve.
March 27th	Les Brebis	Line (Right Maroc Sector)	Relieving K.R.R.C.
March 30th	Line	S. Maroc	To support. Relieved by Camerons.
April 2nd	Support	Line	Relieving Camerons.
April 5th	Line	Support	Relieved by Camerons.
April 8th	Support	Petit Sains	To Div. Reserve.
April 14th	Petit Sains	Line (Left Loos Sector)	Relieving K.R.R.C.
April 17th	Line	O.G. Line	To support. Relieved by Camerons.
April 20th	Support	Line	Relieving Camerons.
April 23rd	Line	Support	Relieved by Camerons.
April 26th	Support	Les Brebis	To Div. Reserve.
May 2nd	Les Brebis	Line (Right Maroc Sector)	Relieving Loyal N. Lancs. (3rd Bde.).
May 8th	Line	S. Maroc	To support. Relieved by Camerons.
May 13th	S. Maroc	Les Brebis	To Div. Reserve.
May 18th	Les Brebis	Line (Calonne Sector)	Relieving King's Regt. (3rd Bde.).
May 22nd	Line	Calonne village	To support. Relieved by Camerons.
May 26th	Support	Line	Relieving Camerons.
May 30th	Line	Bully Grenay	To Bde. Reserve.
June 2nd	Bully Grenay	Les Brebis	To Div. Reserve. Relieved by 3rd Bde.
June 10th	Les Brebis	Line (Left Maroc Sector)	Relieving R. Sussex Regt. (3rd Bde.).
June 14th	Line	N. Maroc	To support. Relieved by Camerons.
June 18th	Maroc	Les Brebis	To Div. Reserve. Relieved by Loyal N. Lancs.
June 22nd	Les Brebis	Line (Calonne Sector)	Relieving 1st Gloucesters.
June 25th	Line	Support	Relieved by Camerons.
June 29th	Support	Line	Relieving Camerons.

the news of his leaving the Battalion was received with genuine regret.

Between the beginning of March and the opening of the Somme battle, the 1st Division rang all the possible changes of dispositions and reliefs in the four miles of line that faced Lens from the north-east. The various moves of the Battalion are shown on the accompanying table. The area in which the Division lay was divided into five battalion fronts.

On the right, the Calonne sector, whose support positions were the cellars of Calonne Village, had recently been taken over. Those at Calonne had been largely built up of palisade work, with narrow communication trenches: excellent in a quiet sector, but useless against much artillery or trench mortar fire. Trenches were continually blown in, and, as can be imagined, there are few materials harder to dig through than a mixture of woodwork, revetting wire and earth. One section of the front line, being blown in, could not be repaired, and had to be abandoned.

In the left half of this sector was the "Burning Bing," a slag-heap which had either caught fire or been purposely fired. It smoked continuously, and at times burst into flames, which the troops had to smother with earth. This locality was always hot, and excessively dirty, and the men looked like coal miners when coming away from it. The sector, as a whole, was an active one, with a great deal of artillery, heavy trench mortar and rifle grenade fire; and in one ordinary tour of four days the Battalion lost 4 officers wounded, 9 other ranks killed, and 38 other ranks wounded.

The right Maroc sector, immediately to the south of the "Twa Bings," was a marked contrast. Here the trenches were good, and the line usually quiet. For example, between the 2nd and 8th of May, when the Battalion was holding the line, only one man was wounded. The left Maroc sector contained the "Double Crassier," and has already been described.

Next on the left lay the right Loos sector, through the front line of which the main Lens–Béthune road ran at an angle; near the road two large mine craters, "Hart's" and "Harrison's," had been blown and occupied by our troops. The German line lay along higher ground, as high as Hill 70, to the north; hence the sector was tactically important and was steadily shelled and battered by trench mortars. From this area the line turned eastwards, and the left Loos sector ran from the south-east of Loos Village, by the Loos Crassier, in the direction of Quarry Wood. It was quieter than the "right Loos," but many mines were dug at this time, and in consequence the Battalion had to find heavy working parties.

The Brigade Reserve positions along this front were Bully

IN THE TRENCHES, FEBRUARY–APRIL, 1916

Grenay and Les Brebis, mining villages built round pit-heads; Petit Sains, a similar village less than four miles from the line, held the Divisional Reserve. These areas were being increasingly shelled by high-velocity guns, and the Battalion's transport, which began by billeting about two miles from the line, was driven back, with that of other units, into quarters near Petit Sains.

The Battalion, it will be remembered, had encountered bad weather at the "Twa Bings" in February; this persisted during March, and snow fell almost daily. At the beginning of April, however, it changed, and for the most part the spring was fine and warm. In such conditions, good, comfortable trenches were built, but heavy thunder showers in June spoilt much of the work, and at the last relief the Battalion handed over trenches that were in very poor condition. During this last tour of all, a "Bantam" battalion was attached for instruction. To suit their few inches the height of the parapet had to be lowered, which may have helped the "Bantams" considerably, but was dangerous for men of The Black Watch.

CHAPTER IV

JULY 6TH, 1916, TO MAY, 1917

1.—*The Battle of the Somme*

BEFORE the summer of 1916 the strength of the British Army in France had been increased by a number of new divisions. But the German effort had also grown, and for some months the group of armies under the Crown Prince had continued to attack the French positions round Verdun in great strength. Brilliant as was their defence, the French had not been able to drive back the Germans to their original positions, and Verdun remained in some danger.

It was decided therefore to lighten the pressure on the French armies by launching a strong offensive on the Somme front. For this attack new railheads were built, and the necessary supplies of guns, ammunition and stores were collected.

Such preparations, followed by a heavy bombardment, necessarily gave warning to the enemy where the blow was to fall; the initial attack was only in part successful, and after a few weeks, heavy rain had covered the whole valley of the Somme with a layer of chalky mud which greatly impeded the movement of troops and rendered the success of subsequent attacks all the more difficult. The heavy shell fire of these attacks broke up the drainage system of the entire area, and prevented any improvement in these conditions from taking place.

No battalion, nor even division, can boast of large captures of ground or prisoners during the Battle of the Somme. But every tactical objective that was proposed was gained, sooner or later, and the constant attacks, repeated week after week until the late winter, shook the confidence of the German Army and began that decline of its moral, which continued until the end of the war. It added to the general feeling of elation when the hard-pressed soldiers in any British trench realized that opposite them some enemy trench was being shelled even more heavily than their own. British tanks were here employed for the first time, and though not wholly successful on their first trial, they were to the British soldier a symbol that the Allies had now begun to surpass the enemy in material strength and mechanical invention.

On the 6th July, 1916, the Battalion entrained at Béthune for the Somme. Arriving at Doullens that evening, it marched to Naours, north of Amiens, and billeted for the night. The route from Doullens passed through scenes of great activity; motor convoys, in an endless file, were taking fresh formations to the battlefield, and on the return journey, bringing out all that was left of the divisions which had been in the line since

FIRST BATTALION XMAS CARD, 1917. "THE TWA BINGS"
After a sketch by the late Lieutenant D. Murray Menzies, M.C.

CONTALMAISON, JULY, 1916

the first attack a week before. In the villages by the roadside, troops fresh from the fighting turned out to greet The Black Watch, and many were the friendly jokes and words of advice on the best ways of dealing with the Hun. One homely and well-meaning corporal, with his pipe in his mouth and his coat unbuttoned, walked into the middle of the road as the Pipe Band and Headquarters were passing, and delivered a long harangue of tactical advice. This was too much for Sergeant Major Scott, who ordered him to " take his pipe out of his mouth, button " up his coat, stand to attention, and salute the old Army."

After four days of marching in very bad weather, the Battalion reached the battle area, by way of Molliens aux Bois, Baizieux and Albert; and on July 10th took over a position (Scott's Redoubt) in the old British front line in front of Becourt. On the same day, troops of the 23rd Division attacked and took Contalmaison, in which they were relieved on the night of the 11/12th by the Battalion and the 8th Royal Berkshires. The fighting was continuous in this part of the line, and within an hour or two of the relief, the Germans were making a strong counter-attack against the village; but they were driven back, and with heavy losses. Later in the day, this success was followed up by an advance that brought our line in front of Contalmaison Wood, where four enemy guns were captured by the Battalion.

For one day there was a comparative lull; then on the 14th two platoons, approaching under cover of darkness from opposite directions, captured the fortification known as Contalmaison Villa. As was natural when the advance had been so indirect, there was a difficulty in organizing a new line; and two officers attached to Battalion Headquarters, Lieutenants Marcus Gunn and Duncan Murray-Menzies, who had exceeded their instructions by joining the fighting, behaved very gallantly in helping the reorganization. Lieutenant Gunn returned to report the new line; but his night's work was not yet over; in an old dug-out he discovered twelve Germans who had taken refuge on the failure of their counter-attack of the 12th. Except for a clasp-knife, he was unarmed; but he threatened them vigorously with the knife, which they took to be a revolver, and brought them in as prisoners.

The casualties of the night were not heavy; but among others, one gallant soldier, who had served the regiment faithfully in many a fight, was killed—Private George, runner to Lieutenant Gunn.

On the night of the 14th, The Black Watch was relieved and moved back to Divisional Reserve at Albert; on the 20th and 25th the Battalion was in the line for very short periods, which call for no comment. The whole Division went back to rest in the

THE FIRST BATTALION THE BLACK WATCH

Baizieux area on the 25th July, and here the Battalion held their regimental games, and welcomed many officers of the Regiment from other formations.

On August 14th the Battalion moved forward to Bécourt, near Albert, and on the next day held support positions in Bazentin-le-Petit. The Battalion now held the old German line which ran south of Bazentin-le-Petit Wood, and the enemy were defending the ridge north and west of High Wood. Between the two positions ran an old communication trench, known as the "Intermediate Trench." The eastern end was held by the Battalion, the western end by the enemy, and strong barricades defined the two spheres. Before the next ridge could be taken, this trench had to be captured. The 34th Division, whom the 1st Division had relieved, had tried several times to gain the small portion of the "Intermediate Trench" that still held out, but with no success. On the 16th, three platoons of D company launched a surprise attack from the Battalion's section of the trench, bombing their way down, while patrols tried to envelop the enemy's barricade from both flanks. This, too, was unsuccessful; Lieutenant Urquhart, one of the many gallant men who left the Scottish Ministry to fight for their country, and one other soldier was killed; Lieutenant Templeton and 14 other ranks were wounded, and 5 others missing.

While relieving the Camerons on the night of the 17th, the Battalion lost a good many men from shell fire, but none the less, all four companies attacked the "Intermediate Trench" on the following morning. At 4.15 a.m., after a two minutes' intense bombardment, A company on the left, and B on the right, followed a creeping barrage; behind them C company advanced on the left and D company on the right. The left met with no great resistance, but the right could not push forward, so great was the enemy's volume of fire, and the operation proved a failure. Lieutenant J. M. Scott and 12 other ranks were killed; Lieutenants D. A. Miller, R. S. Macpherson, D. L. Munro, and 75 other ranks were wounded; and Lieutenants Skey and Macdougall, with 40 other ranks, were missing.

Once again the 1st Brigade attacked this trench, and once again failed; it was never taken by direct assault, but a few days later the 15th (Scottish) Division encircled it by night, and at daylight the garrison found themselves completely surrounded, and surrendered after an hour. It was then found that the position of the enemy barricades, taken from the Corps map, was 270 yards further to the east than had appeared. The contours of the ground had hidden the barricades from direct observation, and heavy shelling made air photography difficult, so that 270 yards of the enemy's trench had never been

ATTACK ON HIGH WOOD, SEPTEMBER 3RD, 1916

dealt with, and the companies had been outflanked as they attacked.

On the 19th the Battalion moved back into support at Mametz Wood, the whole Brigade marching back to Divisional Reserve on the 20th. Until the 27th the Battalion was billeted in trenches in the Quadrangle Wood area; accommodation, where it existed, was very bad, but fortunately the weather was fine. A draft of 3 officers and 361 other ranks was very welcome, as the Battalion was feeling the constant drain made on its strength by these small attacks.

On August 27th, The Black Watch relieved the 2nd Welch Regiment in the line in front of High Wood, returning to Quadrangle Wood on the 31st. The weather had broken, and the tour was wet, muddy and full of discomfort, apart from the heavy shelling. For only one hour in the four days did the rain cease, an event so remarkable that Colonel Bartlett, Commanding the 8th Berkshire Regiment, sent the Battalion a message by carrier-pigeon through the Corps loft: "Floods subsiding; herewith dove!"

After only one day in support, the Battalion returned to the High Wood trenches on September 2nd. On September 3rd, The Black Watch, together with the Camerons on the right, attacked High Wood and the ground to the east of it; A, C and D companies were in the line, with B company in reserve. At 12 noon, which was fixed for Zero, a mine was successfully blown in the enemy front line, and flammenwerfers and oil-can projectors added to the efficiency of the barrage. On the right, everything went well, the right company Black Watch and the Camerons occupying the lip of the crater; but the whole advance was checked by an unfortunate occurrence on the left, where our trench mortar shells were falling very short. A company alone lost 75 per cent of its strength through this cause. Had the Divisions on the flanks been advancing in line, the mishap might have been remedied; but the attack was on a narrow front and isolated. Forty prisoners, however, were taken. The Battalion's losses were heavy; Lieutenants Marcus Gunn and Dixon died of wounds, Lieutenants Wells, Preston and Godfrey were missing; 37 other ranks had been killed, 123 wounded, and 36 were missing. By the death of Lieutenant Gunn the Battalion lost an officer who had for eighteen months displayed all the qualities of a leader of men, and who had shown a wonderful example of coolness and great courage in many critical periods.

Gradually the 1st Division was withdrawn from the line to Army Reserve, the Battalion passing by stages through Bazentin-le-Grand (September 4th), Black Wood, near Albert (September 5th), and via Millencourt to La Houssoye (September 10th). Meanwhile two drafts had arrived from home, the one 70, the

THE FIRST BATTALION THE BLACK WATCH

other over 300 strong. Six days were spent at La Houssoye, and then the Battalion, on the 16th of September, marched to Bresle, where the billets were very indifferent; but even the worst billet was a pleasant change from the muddy trenches of the Somme front, and the Battalion was thoroughly rested and re-equipped.

On the 17th came the sad news of the death of Brigadier General C. E. Stewart, Commanding the 154th Brigade 51st Division. Charles Edward Stewart had joined the 2nd Battalion in 1889. In Matabeleland he had commanded The Black Watch Section of the Highland Company of Mounted Infantry; during the South African War he first commanded a company of the 2nd Battalion, and later was appointed Signalling Officer to the Highland Brigade. From 1904 to 1908 he had been Adjutant to the 6th Volunteer Battalion of The Black Watch. The outbreak of war found him acting in command of the 2nd Battalion in India during the absence of Colonel Campbell, and Stewart was responsible for the rapid mobilization and excellent organization which preceded the embarkation of the 2nd Battalion for France. In September, 1914, he succeeded to the command of the 1st Battalion on the death of Lieutenant Colonel Grant Duff on the Aisne. He was mentioned three times in despatches and awarded the C.M.G. A man of the highest ideals, no soldier had served the Regiment more faithfully, and none had rendered better service. His death was keenly felt among all ranks in all battalions of The Black Watch.

Lieutenant Colonel J. G. H. Hamilton, D.S.O., now left the Battalion to take over the Brigade lately commanded by General Stewart, and was succeeded in command of the Battalion by Major V. M. Fortune, D.S.O.

During the absence of the 1st Division from the line, the 47th (London) Division had taken Mametz Wood, and were holding the line about threequarters of a mile to the north of High Wood. The Battalion moved forward to Albert on the 18th, and took over from the 47th Division, on the night of the 19th, a portion of the line opposite Flers. During the relief, a most important part of the trench, which connected the line of the 1st Division with that held by the New Zealand Division on the right, was retaken by the enemy. Within an hour or two, " Drop Alley," or the " Cough Drop," as it was called from its curious shape, had been captured by B company. Altogether the Battalion only spent forty-eight hours on this tour of duty, but in that short time it lost Second Lieutenant J. E. Denniston, died of wounds, 6 other ranks killed, and 32 other ranks wounded.

On relief, the Battalion spent two days in Mametz Wood, and on the 24th, owing to the tactical situation, was ordered forward in two detachments. Headquarters with A and B companies

ATTACK ON THE FLERS LINE, SEPTEMBER, 1916

went in support of the 3rd Brigade in the Flers line, and C and D companies relieved the 2nd Munster Fusiliers in the front line of the sector. This sector sloped downwards from Flers on the right, through a narrow and shallow valley, to Eaucourt l'Abbaye on the Albert–Bapaume road; the " Flers line " was the old front and support system of the enemy, and much of it, on the left, was still in enemy hands.

On this day, the New Zealand Division was ordered to attack a switch trench called " Goose Alley," which ran to the right, away from the right bombing post; C and D companies were to assist by attacking down the Flers trenches, front and support in the direction of Eaucourt l'Abbaye, thus helping to prevent counter-attacks. Before seven o'clock D company was established in the old front line, C company in the old support line; each had a bombing post where the enemy's section of the trench began. Within an hour of arrival the enemy made a determined bombing attack up the Flers front line, drove in the D company bombing post, and turned down the communication trench into C company's area. Here, fortunately, they encountered Captain W. D. McL. Stewart sitting down to his breakfast; he was quite equal to the emergency, and with Sergeant Barclay drove them back with bombs, the few survivors escaping by the way they had come. In a short time he had re-established D company's front post, but in the moment of his success fell shot through the head; it is certain that but for the bravery and vigour he showed, the main attack later could not have been launched.

The loss of so popular an officer as Captain McL. Stewart was keenly felt. He had served with distinction in the 2nd Battalion in 1915 until wounded in the orchard near Chocolat Menier Corner. After a short period at Nigg he returned to France, joined the 1st Battalion and distinguished himself throughout the fighting on the Somme by his coolness and daring.

Captain Feiling, Intelligence Officer of the Battalion, at once took over command of C company in the line.

In spite of all difficulties the attack was carried out exactly at twelve noon, and regardless of heavy resistance met with in the Flers support line, ten prisoners were taken and about 40 enemy killed; the Battalion casualties were Captain McL. Stewart, Second Lieutenant Husband, and 35 other ranks killed; Second Lieutenant Macfarlane-Grieve and 74 other ranks wounded; and 7 other ranks missing. One company of the South Wales Borderers did invaluable work by bringing up bombs. Mention must be made of Corporal Hay, who, although severely wounded, pulled himself to the top of a barricade, where in full view of the enemy he continued to direct his platoon; for this he was recommended for the Victoria Cross, and was awarded the D.C.M. Private

King, a noted figure in the Brigade, and most popular in the Battalion, was shot through the head as he served his Vickers gun over the bombing post of C company.

Often had the gallantry and efficiency of the New Zealand Division been praised, and as in this attack they started slightly in rear of the Battalion, their advance could be plainly seen; in the judgment of many officers, no finer exhibition of steadiness under fire could have been given.

That night the Battalion was relieved, and marched back to Mametz Wood, and from there, on the 27th, to Bresle. On October 3rd the Brigade moved by bus to Mianny, between Abbeville and the sea, where all enjoyed the first real rest since the beginning of the war, in a town where the sound of guns could hardly be heard. An unfortunate accident marred this rest period, for Lieutenant MacMillan, when instructing at the Divisional School, was killed by the premature explosion of a bomb.

On October 31st, the Battalion moved back by bus to a camp in Hennacourt Wood. Close at hand was the III Corps Headquarters, where a former Commanding Officer, Lieutenant Colonel Hugh Rose, of Kilravock, was camp commandant; he paid several visits to the Battalion, and all ranks were delighted to see their old friend again.

The winter of 1916 was uneventful; so terribly had the Somme valley been devastated by shell fire that movement on a large scale was impossible, and the Battalion, in common with many others, went monotonously in and out of the line, wiring, working and training in the muddy back areas. On the very first day in the line, the 20th November, Captains Feiling and Anderson were killed; and from then to the end of December there was a small but constant flow of casualties. The Battalion's movements during this period are summarized in the table below:

Moves in the Somme Area ; Winter of 1916/1917

1916		1917	
Nov. 5th.	Bécourt.	Jan. 10th.	Albert.
,, 16th.	High Wood.	,, 23rd.	Warloy.
,, 20th.	In line, Eaucourt l'Abbaye.	Feb. 4th.	Hamel.
		,, 7th.	Marley.
,, 22nd.	Mametz Wood.	,, 8th.	Chuignes.
,, 27th.	Bazentin-le-Petit.	,, 14th.	In line, Barleux.
Dec. 5th.	In line, Eaucourt.	,, 27th.	Assevillers.
,, 9th.	Bazentin-le-Petit.	Mar. 3rd.	Chuignolles.
,, 17th.	Mametz Wood.	,, 12th.	In line, Barleux.
,, 21st.	In line, Eaucourt.	,, 15th.	Becquincourt.
,, 25th.	Bazentin-le-Petit.	,, 16th.	Enemy retirement began.
,, 29th.	Road-making near Fricourt.		

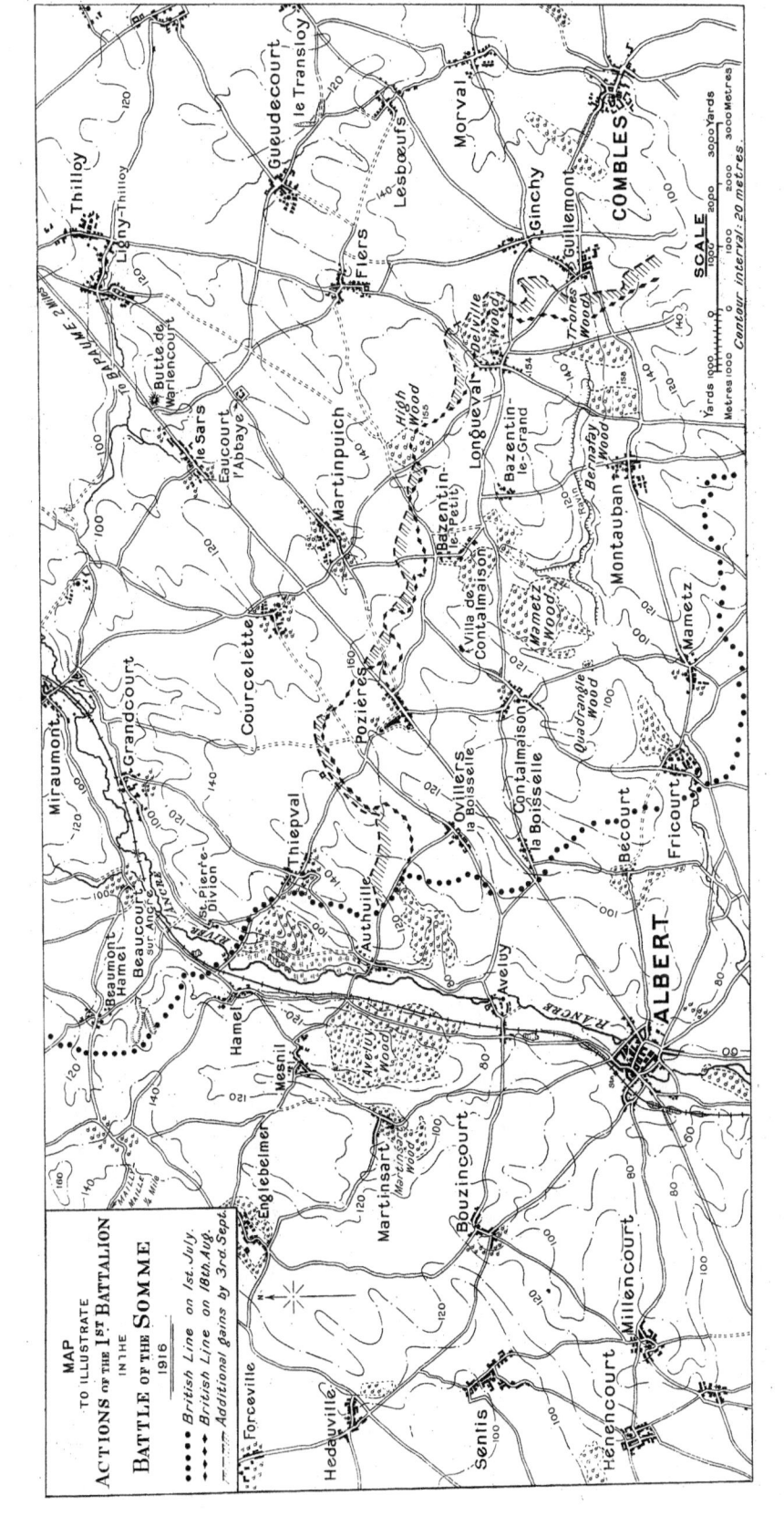

GERMAN RETIREMENT, MARCH, 1917

On March 16th, 1917, the German Army began the retirement that was to take it back to the shorter, stronger, and well-prepared positions of the Hindenburg Line, leaving to the British the task of evolving communications out of the muddy area which they evacuated. Such a move was the logical outcome of the determined Allied attacks in the summer of 1916; the enemy was no longer able to maintain his position on so wide a front, and while he had yet time, broke away from the impending battle.

Infantry pursuit was impossible, and The Black Watch only moved forward to the banks of the Somme, where the Cavalry Corps and Cyclists, followed by two fresh Divisions, passed through, and the 1st Division was withdrawn to the area round Rosières. The Commander-in-Chief, Sir Douglas Haig, moved up to advanced Headquarters at Caix, and during his stay, the Battalion had the honour of providing his guard. The Commander-in-Chief afterwards wrote congratulating the Battalion on the smartness of the guard, and the excellence of the piper, adding he had not forgotten the work of the 1st Black Watch in the I Corps during the retreat.

Between March 29th and April 26th, the Battalion moved from place to place, carrying out salvage work, and reconstructing roads and railheads which had been destroyed in the German retreat; the names of Curchy, Nesle, Chuignes, Fay and Marcelcave may bring back to some readers pleasant memories of this time.

CHAPTER V

MAY, 1917, TO NOVEMBER, 1917

ON May 19th, 1917, the Battalion left the Somme area, and moved northwards with other units of the 1st Division, entraining at Marcelcave (where it had been stationed for about a month), and detraining at Flêtre, about 14 miles to the south-west of Ypres. On arrival in this area, the Division became part of Lord Cavan's XIV Corps, at this time the Reserve Corps of the Second Army.

1.—*The Battle of Messines*

The Battle of Messines was close at hand, an operation whose success was in part due to the strictly limited objective imposed by the presence of the Warneton Canal to the east of the Messines Ridge. The Reserve Corps, therefore, had not to play its usual part of preparing for a " break-through," and the action of the Battalion was limited to a reconnaissance of the front areas, since the Corps would have supported the attacking Divisions had they been heavily counter-attacked during the battle. On the 7th of June the Messines Ridge was stormed with striking success; the ground won was immediately and firmly consolidated, and the 1st Division was now free to be used for other purposes.

The Battalion left Flêtre on June 11th, and marched northwards through Bavinchove, so avoiding the steep gradient of Cassel, Wormhoudt, where the 8th Battalion, under Lieutenant Colonel R. W. Hadow, was resting, and Bergues. On the 20th of June the Battalion spent the night at the seaside village of Zuydcoote, which lies a few miles to the east of Dunkerque. Since September, 1914, The Black Watch had looked on no other scenery than the coalfields of Lens and the rolling chalk downs of the Somme; and it requires little imagination to picture how welcome was the first sight of the sea and the sandhills. On the next day a move was made by train to Coxyde, a village about five miles west of the line in the Nieuport sector; from Coxyde the Battalion marched to Rinck Hutment Camp, near Oost Dunkerque. The route from Flêtre seemed circuitous; but it was probably designed to defeat the enemy's observation balloons, which had a remarkable range of vision in this perfectly flat country.

The part of the line nearest the sea had, since 1914, been held by French Fusiliers Marins, who at this moment were in process of being relieved by General Du Cane's XV Corps consisting of the 1st and 32nd Divisions. The sector was handed over by the French as a quiet one, but the arrival of British troops materially increased the amount of enemy shelling. Throughout this month

NIEUPORT SECTOR, JUNE, 1917

the cafés at Oost Dunkerque were open and carrying on their usual custom, only 1800 yards from the front line.

The front was just over three miles in width, and from a point immediately to the south of Nieuport the Belgian Army carried on the line southwards. On both sides of the line the type of country is the same; in this area the North Sea washes against a ridge of low sandhills, which extend inland for any distance between 300 yards and a mile. The "coast towns" had originally depended upon a belt of cultivable ground, and are in consequence a mile or two inland; in modern times, however, each has developed a watering-place on the seashore, called by the name of the parent town, with the addition of "Les-Bains." Thus, Coxyde lies to the south of Coxyde-Les-Bains, and Oost Dunkerque has a seaside suburb, Oost Dunkerque-Les-Bains.

Roughly speaking, the area of the 32nd Division included the three towns of Nieuport, Oost Dunkerque and Coxyde, and the area of the 1st Division comprised the watering-places of these names. In the latter sector the three Brigades were distributed in depth, the Support Brigade being in hutments between Oost Dunkerque-Les-Bains and Coxyde-Les-Bains, and the Reserve Brigade in billets and huts to the west of Coxyde-Les-Bains. Two battalions held the line to the east of Nieuport-Les-Bains, separated from the support battalions by the River Yser—dispositions which later caused an unfortunate episode.

On June 23rd the Battalion, with three companies in the line and one in support, relieved the 15th Lancashire Fusiliers of the 32nd Division (which had temporarily taken over the whole Corps front) in the left battalion sector, that is, with its left on the sea. There were no trenches, since the sand was constantly shifting its levels; breastworks had been built, and concrete "pill-boxes," in the dunes, took the place of dug-outs. In the end, rain and wind had shifted the sand from most of the pill-boxes, so that they stood out bare and very visible. The surroundings, as has been said, appealed to all ranks, for it was a novel experience to look out of the firing-line over the open sea and a wide expanse of sands; though the latter, it must be owned, was somewhat spoiled for most purposes by the acres of barbed wire which prevented enterprising patrols from coming round the left flank.

During the six days that the Battalion occupied the line, nothing of importance happened; yet in spite of the quite reputation of the locality, everyone was convinced that some kind of offensive was to take place in this sector. The evidence was that an Australian Tunnelling Company, specially trained to mining in sandy soil, was allocated to the sector; more convincing was the fact that Staff officers of the Corps and

THE FIRST BATTALION THE BLACK WATCH

of various Divisions were frequently to be seen reconnoitring the line.

On June 29th the Battalion was relieved by the 1st Camerons,[1] and went into support at Nieuport-Les-Bains, being billeted in cellars, connected up by passages, and in dug-outs on the edge of the town. Nieuport-Les-Bains is merely one long street running parallel with the sea; consequently, since all the houses except the eastern ones were defiladed from the enemy's artillery, many were in good condition.

While in this town the Battalion received orders to carry out a raid in the sector recently held, with the object of identifying the enemy unit holding the line. The choice of an objective gave some difficulty, since it was essential to raid a post that would certainly be occupied by night. Two places fulfilled this condition, and in both—the post nearest the sea, and the "Black Dune," a post about the middle of the sector—the distance of a hundred or two hundred yards between the lines narrowed down to twenty yards. After much reconnaissance, the former was chosen. This post formed a prominent salient in the enemy's line, and at a point a few yards in rear of the post, on the landward side, the wire appeared to consist of only one length of *chevaux-de-frise*.

Second Lieutenant G. W. Ferguson and 16 men of A company were selected to carry out the raid; all arrangements were left in the hands of Captain Colquhoun, commanding A company. Sergeant J. Bain was to have been the sergeant of the raiding party, but in consideration of his continuous service since 1914, and the many actions in which he had fought, his place was taken, much against his will, by Sergeant Forsyth.

On the evening of July 3rd the raiding party, armed with pistols and knob-kerries, and with faces blackened, moved up to the centre company of the Camerons. A temporary quarter was established in Company Headquarters, and points of exit and entry were fixed in this company's line; the retaliation, it was expected, would fall more heavily on the Cameron's left company, opposite whose front the enemy post lay. After a short bombardment of the Black Dune as a blind and of the post to be raided, the raiders entered the enemy's line without difficulty, and a stiff hand-to-hand fight took place. One of the enemy was captured, but was killed in a struggle to get him through the wire surrounding the post; another was immediately seized and brought back, but he, too, had been mortally wounded, and died shortly after arriving at Battalion Head-

---

[1] The reason for the continual inter-reliefs of the Camerons and The Black Watch was that the enemy should not realise the changes of units by noting kilted troops in the line one day and "trousered" troops the next day.

ON THE BELGIAN COAST, JULY, 1917

quarters, at Nieuport-Les-Bains. The raiding party escaped that night with only two wounded, but one of these two, Corporal Hanlon, unfortunately died of his wounds a few days later at La Panne Hospital. An important identification had been secured, and at least ten or twelve of the enemy had been killed.

On the night of the 3rd of July the Battalion was relieved by the 2nd King's Royal Rifle Corps, and moved back to camp at St. Idesbald, Battalion Headquarters being in the hotel. St. Idesbald has a beautiful beach, and as the weather was warm, sea-bathing was the recreation of all ranks—an amusement, however, liable to interruption, as the Germans, with their odd sense of humour, never lost an opportunity of giving a few salvos, once all were stripped and in the water. This, however, proved a source of innocent merriment to the civilian population, who watched the scene through their telescopes. At St. Idesbald the Battalion also enjoyed a pleasant afternoon's racing on the sands. Between this camp and La Panne, where the King and Queen of the Belgians had made their Headquarters, a good open training area was available, and much time was spent in battalion training.

On July 10th the 1st Brigade, without being able to help, witnessed from a distance one of the most tragic incidents of the war. The Germans, using to the full their local superiority in aircraft and artillery, severely bombarded the 2nd K.R.R.C. and the 1st Northamptonshire Regiment, the battalions holding the line to the east of the Yser river. Towards the end of the day few men of either of these battalions were left alive, and when at 7 p.m. a division of German Marines attacked, most of these survivors, and the few Australian tunnellers working in the area, were overwhelmed. The four floating bridges behind them were broken by shell fire, but a few men escaped by swimming; only 3 officers and 52 men of the K.R.R.C. rejoined the 3rd Brigade, and few survivors of the Northamptonshire Regiment lived to return.

During the bombardment the Battalion's transport lines had suffered considerably. " Dolly," the chestnut mare captured in 1914, who had been wounded at Les Brebis in 1916, received a second wound. Under a special arrangement she was ordered to be sent back as a mascot to Scotland in 1919, but died under an anæsthetic while being operated on at Calais.

On the 17th of July, the Battalion marched to a Hut Camp at Bray Dunes, further west along the coast, and on the 18th marched through Dunkerque to Le Clipon Camp. This ended the connection of the 1st Division with the Nieuport area; the Battalion had made one tour in the trenches of six days, and had carried out a successful raid. The casualties for the period were 6 killed, 10 missing, 2 officers and 27 other ranks wounded.

As early as 1915 a combined naval and military plan was formed to land three Divisions at Ostend in co-operation with an attack from Ypres northwards, and from Nieuport along the seacoast. This operation, after due deliberation by both naval and military authorities, was cancelled. From that moment, however, Admiral Sir Reginald Bacon, commanding at Dover, set himself to evolve another scheme. The result was the plan to land the 1st Division, in three brigade columns, between Westende Bains and Middelkerke Bains, in August, 1917, in conjunction with the attacks on the Fifth and Second Armies near Ypres and with attacks along the sea-coast from Nieuport.

By the beginning of 1917 the Germans had over eighty guns of 6-inch calibre and above, on a stretch of coast 25 miles long, which showed the importance they attached to retaining every inch of the Belgian coast. A large number of these guns outranged those of the British monitors, and the British shore guns could not get close enough to deal with Zeebrugge Harbour and Lock, and with the Bruges Docks. These two Belgian towns were becoming a serious menace to the naval authorities responsible for the transport of men and materials to France, and once they could be brought under fire of the British heavy guns, the most dangerous German submarine base would be destroyed. The chief object, then, in view, was to seize a portion of the Belgian coast, which would enable us to mount heavy guns within easy range of Zeebrugge and Bruges, and at the same time, capture a large proportion of the German troops in occupation of that area.

The details of the naval side of the operation are graphically told in Admiral Sir Reginald Bacon's book, *The Dover Patrol*.

The 1st Division, under Major General E. P. Strickland, was selected to carry out the landing, and assembled in Le Clipon Camp, on the shore about eight miles to the west of Dunkerque. The proposed landing force was composed of Divisional Headquarters and three columns, Right, Centre and Left, the Battalion forming part of the first-named.

The chief difficulties of the landing force and the methods of overcoming them were :—

(1) How could the landing be made an effective surprise? To ensure this a feint attack was planned east of Ostend, and the real landing was arranged to take place under the protection of a dense cloud of phosphorus smoke.

(2) How could the slope and the height of the beach at the landing place be calculated? At high and low water aerial photographs of the coast were made, with additional photographs

LE CLIPON CAMP, JULY–OCTOBER, 1917

when the tide was known to have fallen one foot. The various water lines, plotted on a map, gave a series of one-foot contours.

(3) How could a division of troops with tanks be put ashore with the maximum speed? The craft selected to convey the columns was a floating pier or pontoon, 550 feet in length, with tapering draught. Each column was to be transported on one pontoon, propelled by two monitors lashed together.

By the end of July the complete force was assembled and every precaution to ensure secrecy was taken. The camp was surrounded by sentries; the rations were driven into barbed-wire locks and dumped under military police supervision, and, in a word, no communication between those inside the camp and those outside was allowed.

In the Battalion, training chiefly consisted in keeping the men fit—daily practice on the sea wall, debouching on to the sand dunes from the road inland, forming bridge-heads, and advancing along the coast against a flagged enemy.

The operation was originally to have taken place in the first fortnight of August, but was postponed owing to the slow advance of the Fifth and Second Armies, who were hampered by heavy rainfall, the ground east of Ypres becoming practically useless for operations. From week to week the postponement was renewed, the authorities always hoping that they would have an opportunity of launching the expedition before the winter came on. At the end of October the operation was finally cancelled, and the 1st Division moved to the Ypres area to take part in the battle for the Passchendaele Ridge.

On October 21st, 1917, the Battalion marched out of Le Clipon Camp, and, passing through Zeggerscapelle on the 21st and Ledringhem from the 22nd to 25th, reached Herzeele on the 26th, staying in this town until the 5th of November. As it was common knowledge that the Division was about to join in the fight for the Passchendaele Ridge, the time of the officers was spent in learning the experiences of other units who had gone through the fighting of the past month.

The attack was usually launched at dawn after a night march. To ensure accuracy of direction during the advance, the Battalion was formed up on a tape line. As almost every natural feature had been blown off the face of the countryside, the difficulties can be imagined. These manœuvres, therefore, were practised regularly at Herzeele. On November 5th the Battalion marched to Schools Camp, between Watou and Poperinghe, and on the 7th to Dambre Camp, near Vlamertinghe. The area near the battle-zone was congested with troops, and moves forward became much slower in consequence. The 13th saw

THE FIRST BATTALION THE BLACK WATCH

the Battalion in dug-outs in the canal bank, just north of Ypres, from which on the 15th it moved a mile eastward to a hut camp at Irish Farm.

The 3rd Infantry Brigade was in the line at this moment. Although the "Second Battle of Passchendaele" ends, in the official accounts, on November 10th, a series of minor attempts was made later to carry the line forward, so as to cover the whole ridge, since the main battle had left the northern portion, between Passchendaele and Westroosebeke, still in enemy hands. The 3rd Brigade, attacking on the 12th, were successful at the outset, but were shelled away from their objective later in the day. Owing to the sodden state of the ground, the fighting was confined to the actual ridge, a width of perhaps half a mile; it was impossible to move bodies of troops of any size along the lower slopes. Thus the Germans had an unmistakable line along which to lay an intensive barrage whenever an attack opened, so the new ground, when won, soon became untenable.

On November 15th, the Cameron Highlanders and the 8th Royal Berkshire Regiment relieved the troops of the 3rd Brigade in the line; and in a minor attack on the 16th the Camerons took Vocation Farm, with a few prisoners. The 1st Black Watch relieved the Camerons in the line on the 17th, taking over from Vanity Farm to Virtue Farm, and at the same time the 10th Gloucester Regiment relieved the 8th Royal Berkshire Regiment on the left of the brigade sector. By a coincidence the 42nd Battalion Canadian Infantry (the Royal Highlanders of Canada), on the immediate right, were being relieved on this night by troops of the 8th Division. The Black Watch and Cameron relief was hindered by boggy ground and shell fire, and was not completed until 8 a.m. on the 18th. The 42nd Canadian Battalion gave their hearty assistance to The Black Watch; the roads near Passchendaele were naturally very crowded, and the good spirit with which the Canadians assisted the incoming battalions was much appreciated. Sergeant Stewart, of the 42nd Canadian Battalion, was responsible for leading C company into its place after all the guides had been killed—although, much to their alarm, he took them down No Man's Land to the Camerons' sector.

Four days later the Royal Highlanders of Canada were given the honour of the right to wear the Red Hackle in recognition of their gallantry in action when serving beside The Black Watch. All ranks were glad to see the Red Hackle worn by their comrades of the affiliated regiment.

C company took over the salient formed by the newly captured Vocation Farm; A company lay in support about Vine Cottage and Valour Farm; and B and D companies remained in

SECOND BATTLE OF PASSCHENDAELE, 1917

reserve, the former near Meetcheele, the latter near Bellevue. Battalion Headquarters were established at Meetcheele cross-roads.

2—*The Attack on Vox Farm, November 18th, 1917*

Captain H. L. F. Boyd, commanding C company, was killed by a sniper after his company had been only a few hours in the line. In Captain Boyd the regiment lost an officer of extraordinary promise. He had joined The Black Watch at Nigg and commanded a company in the 2nd Battalion in France in 1915, and was wounded when serving with the 1st Battalion in 1917. His power of leadership was exceptional, and his gift of ever seeing the bright side of life, even under the most adverse conditions, had rightly endeared him to all officers and men. His fine character gave him at all times and in all places the confidence of his commanders and the trust of those whom he led.

As the Battalion had come into the line with orders to advance and take Vox and Virile Farms when opportunity arose, Captain P. H. Colquhoun, commanding A company, was put in command of C company. But in the meantime Lieutenant Ramage, of C company, had moved forward on his own initiative and seized Virile Farm, which he found empty. The remainder of the company attempted to capture Vox Farm on the night of the 18/19th, but the enemy was encountered in strength, and the attempt failed. The casualties for the two days, 18th and 19th, in which this was the only operation, were: killed and died of wounds, 2 officers and 22 other ranks; wounded, 2 officers and 58 other ranks; missing, 6 other ranks.

On the night of the 19th the 1st Loyal North Lancashire Regiment relieved the Battalion; no casualties occurred during the relief, which was a very unusual happening on this front. The roads were either impassable or in use by guns and transport, and the troops had seven miles of duck-board track to cross before they reached the canal bank, so that it was morning before all were reported present in the canal dug-outs. It had been a short, but arduous tour in the line. The ground was water-logged to a degree that made even infantry movement almost impossible; and too much praise could not be given to the work of the Divisional Pioneers (the 1/6th Welch Regiment), who laid duck-board tracks under heavy fire, and so made it possible to organize the line. The bearers of the Royal Army Medical Corps worked night and day over this deep mud, carrying the wounded between Battalion Aid Post and "Waterloo," the advanced dressing station.

On the 22nd November the Battalion moved to Road Camp, between Poperinghe and Watou, and on the 27th to Pidgeon Camp, near Proven.

CHAPTER VI

NOVEMBER, 1917, TO MARCH 31ST, 1918

THE persistence of rain and bad weather in the autumn of 1917, which has been frequently referred to, was only one of several causes that had prevented a decisive success being achieved on the Flanders front. The withdrawal of Bolshevik Russia from the war, added to the disastrous defeat of the Italian Army at Caporetto, left the Central Empires free to concentrate their main forces against the French and British, both of whom had suffered severe losses in the offensives of the past year. On the Western Front arrangements had to be made to meet a greater counter-offensive by the Germans, which was expected to take place in the coming spring.

One necessary adjustment was the concentration of troops by nationalities; and so the French Corps which had fought on the left of the British Fifth Army all through " The Battle of Ypres, 1917," was now transferred to the French main sector in the south, part of its line being taken over by the 1st Division. On the first two days of December, officers of the Battalion made reconnaissances of the French area, into which the Battalion moved by train on the 3rd, billeting at Dekort Farm.

On December 4th the 1st Brigade relieved the 8th and 20th French Regiments on the Houthulst Forest front. Reliefs at this period were carried out in small stages, owing to the long distances traversed in single file over duck-board tracks; the Cameron Highlanders, therefore, going into the line, took over the support position first, and handed it over to The Black Watch, when they themselves went forward to the relief of the line. The support battalion occupied the area round Kortekeer Cabaret, the ground on which the Battalion had supported the Camerons during the German attack on October 21st, 1914. The boundary between the front and support positions was the Steenbeek, the largest of the many little streams that received the drainage from the Pilkem and Passchendaele Ridges.

At one time these " Beeks " were slow-moving muddy streams, their course through rich meadows clearly defined by lines of willows. They were now represented by wide stretches of slime, only the remnants of the willows tracing in places the original line of the stream. The French had numerous light bridges across this boggy stretch, but how the first attack had passed this obstacle defied imagination.

1.—*The Houthulst Forest Front*

On the night of December 8th the Battalion relieved the Camerons in the right battalion sector, about a mile north of the

HOUTHULST FOREST, DECEMBER, 1917

Ypres-Staden railway. This new front merits a short description, though no operations took place for some time.

The two forward companies occupied positions in the low ground on the outskirts of Houthulst Forest, as wet and unprepossessing a place as any on the Western Front. The actual "line" consisted of isolated sentry posts, each of about three men under a non-commissioned officer. In some places these posts were several hundred yards apart; in others, where there was some natural or artificial feature worth fighting for, or which offered special facilities for defence, the posts were concentrated in little platoon groups at about 50 yards interval. Whatever the distances, all posts were based on a Platoon Headquarters somewhere in the vicinity.

The enemy's facilities for observation in the front line were hardly as good as those of the British, but with the help of the trees in the forest, and with excellent artillery observation from the high ground beyond it, he appeared to see quite enough. On both sides, supervision of the line was limited to night visiting, except in foggy weather. This was unfortunate, for human nature is weak and optimistic in regard to possible dangers, and so, now and again, a post belonging to either side would quietly and mysteriously disappear. Such a fate never befell a post of The Black Watch, but in such conditions it did happen to several battalions.

Again, the post might be almost impossible to discover by night. On one occasion the commanding officer of a certain battalion failed to discover a sentry post, nor could the company commander and platoon commander do any better. A second night's search was fruitless, but he decided not to report the fact to the Brigade, on the principle of being hung for a sheep as soon as for a lamb. By this time the men of the sentry group had consumed all their rations, including the dry tea, which they had taken forward; and on the third night, during an inter-company relief, they took very good care that they remained lost no longer.

The remaining two companies, under similar conditions, held a series of posts along the ridge, Hill 20–Veldhœk–Mangalære; this was the Battalion's main line of resistance. The ridge ran at a distance of from 500 to 1000 yards from the front posts, and afforded excellent observation, and it was also a little less boggy than the low ground on either side.

From this month it became more and more important to identify the enemy in all parts of the line, in order to obtain early and definite information of the divisions arriving from the Balkan and Russian fronts, and to calculate the total strength and order of battle of the German forces. This demanded frequent raids, consequently when a Polish deserter of the German 35th Division gave himself up on the 9th of December to the Gloucesters, on the left of the Battalion, his arrival was very welcome, as his surrender did away with the need for a raid on this difficult front.

The next need was to locate the enemy's forward positions. Nothing moved by day, so this became the task of patrols at night. This, however, was far from easy; the personnel of the patrol, labouring through the clinging mud, and occasionally soaked by stumbling into a water logged shell-hole, soon ceased to be the active scouts the work demanded. "A scout should hear, and not be heard"; but not even a trained scout should precipitate himself into a deep shell-hole without splashing, nor could he always repress a loud and pithy exclamation. Above all, his rifle was as often as not clogged with mud, and useless as a firearm. The Divisional War Diary records that on two successive nights no patrol on the whole Divisional front gained touch with the enemy at any point.

On the night of December 8th, the 1st South Wales Borderers relieved the Battalion, which went back to Dekort Farm, resting there until the 15th, when it marched to Eikhœk Camp in the reserve brigade area. After six days of training the 1st Brigade moved forward again, and on the 21st the Battalion found itself back at Dekort Farm. Every available hour was now devoted either to training or to working on the defences. Christmas Day, however, was observed as a holiday. But on the 26th, double shifts turned out in falling snow, to make up for the lost day. The remainder of the year was spent in the support battalion area, near Kortekeer Cabaret, and with frost and some snow the year 1917 ended.

At the beginning of 1918 weather conditions were as bad as those of the three previous years, but the arrangements for the care and comfort of the troops were infinitely better. The Battalion was a cheerful community this winter; the 1st Division had come lightly through the offensives of 1917, and the casualties were small by comparison with those of many units. The Battalion had not failed to profit by this, and the time had been well spent by both officers and men, not only in training, but also in making many firm friendships which were to stand them in good stead during the hard fighting of the coming months.

Lieutenant Colonel V. M. Fortune commanded the Battalion; Major L. G. Gartside of the 2nd Highland Light Infantry was Second-in-Command, and Lieutenant J. S. Young was Adjutant. Captain W. Fowler still combined his many duties as Quartermaster with those of officer in charge of the First Line Transport. His unfailing care for detail and a readiness to accept responsibility had added greatly to the comfort and well-being of all ranks. His fund of happy stories and his willingness to help all

IN THE TRENCHES, JANUARY, 1918

in need made his nightly visits, when he brought the daily rations to the trenches, as welcome as they had been during the first year of the war. Scott, the Regimental Sergeant Major, had also come out with the Battalion in 1914, and his personality and influence were second only to those of Captain Fowler.

The company commanders were Lieutenant (A/Captain) J. G. Sinclair (A); Captain Dennis Cooke (B); Captain A. G. Duncan (C); and Captain J. W. H. Robertson (D). The junior officers were excellent; of the non-commissioned officers all were well trained, and a fair number were experienced men accustomed to command. About 140 men were entitled by their war services to wear the Mons Star. Unquestionably the Battalion was highly efficient.

The fine spirit that animated the Battalion was born of the old regimental tradition; it was strengthened by the results of recent training and the feeling of good comradeship and confidence that inspired equally both officers and men. Though the Colours were no longer carried into action, the spirit which had so often brought victory in the past, the spirit of which the Red Hackle is the glorious emblem, the spirit of the old 42nd, still lived and united every man of The Black Watch in his determination to uphold the good name of his regiment.

The 1st Division, under Major General E. P. Strickland, was now with the 32nd and 35th Divisions, in Sir Claude Jacob's II Corps, and held the left of the British line at Houthulst Forest. Ordinarily a Divisional front was held by two brigades, but here the three brigades were distributed in depth. The 1st Brigade began the New Year in the line, with a support and reserve brigade behind it. This meant that two-thirds of the time was spent out of the line, and that the brigades could concentrate respectively on holding the line, repairing the defences, and training. There was much to recommend this system, but obviously it was not feasible at all times.

On the night of the 1st of January the Battalion relieved the Camerons in the line, and the New Year dinner was accordingly postponed. The tour was uneventful, wiring of the outposts being the first consideration. After four days the Battalion was relieved by the 1st South Wales Borderers, and marched to Eikhœk Camp in the reserve brigade area. From the 7th to the 12th training took place around Eikhœk, and on the 13th the 1st Brigade moved forward into the support brigade area, the Battalion occupying Dekort Farm, as before. Between the 16th and 20th of January the 1st Brigade found large working parties daily for work on the Corps defence line, and in addition had to repair the ravages of weather on its own camps.

Lieutenant Colonel V. M. Fortune, D.S.O., after a period of

sixteen months in command of the Battalion, was transferred to organize and command the Fourth Army Musketry School. Colonel Fortune had come to France with the Battalion as a platoon commander, and, with the exception of ten months spent as Brigade Major of the 1st Brigade, had served with the Battalion throughout the war. None surpassed him in devotion to the regiment; he had few equals in gift for leadership; his departure was felt to be a heavy loss to the Battalion.

The appointment of Major (A/Lieutenant Colonel) L. P. Evans, V.C., D.S.O., to succeed Colonel Fortune was welcomed. Colonel Evans had fought with the 2nd Battalion in the Boer War and had served in the Royal Air Force in 1915 in France, and afterwards on the Staff. He had earned the V.C. when in command of the 1st Lincolnshire Regiment at Passchendaele, in 1917.

The next tour in the line was the last in this sector; but before this history passes on to another front, it is necessary to give a short account of the conditions in the front line during this winter. In the first place, frontages were very long in relation to the number of men employed, consequently the posts were widely separated; movement by day was inadvisable, as it disclosed our dispositions to the enemy. Concealment was therefore the principal consideration for the isolated sentry groups, and concealment is hard to combine with comfort.

Breastworks were out of the question; even in 1914 water lay very near the surface on all this Flanders front; in 1918, when the drainage system had been destroyed by constant bombardment, the whole countryside was waterlogged. Sentry groups, therefore, lay in shallow trenches or shell-holes, and vainly tried to drain the water away. A part of the hole was usually covered by a sheet of corrugated iron, and in the more luxurious posts a semicircular piece of corrugated metal formed a low roof; this looked like the back of an elephant seen through long grass, and was in consequence known as an " elephant shelter."

Hidden away in these holes, visited only by night, cramped for space, and without an adequate supply of hot food, the men were almost exhausted at the end of twenty-four hours of cold or wet weather; yet it was difficult to reduce the tour to less than forty-eight hours. Hot food could only be supplied after dark. It was brought to Battalion Headquarters on limbered waggons or by pack transport; thence, in gigantic thermos flasks, it was carried by hand to the headquarters of companies, under the supervision of company quartermaster sergeants. Up to this point there was usually a duck-board track, but beyond it the mud and water had to be faced. If any misfortune befell a carrier several posts had to rest content with the dry tea and tinned

SUPPORT TRENCHES NEAR YPRES, JANUARY, 1918

rations they had carried into the line; these were not battle conditions, but only too frequently the ordinary routine.

There was also the same marked contrast between the British and German lines near Ypres as had been noticed in the Somme fighting. Every foot of ground which the British occupied in this sector had been won by hard fighting. The country had been devasted by shell-fire to a depth of many miles behind the actual front line, and even in Corps Reserve the horizon was bounded by wastes of mud and water, in which there was neither house nor tree to relieve the dull monotony. Yet the enemy was living in a land where houses, villages and good roads were still existing. But distance lends enchantment to the view, and in a different way the plight of the Germans was no more happy than our own. The rations of the German soldier had greatly deteriorated, and the British supply of ammunition had increased in a far higher proportion than had the German; our shells went singing overhead to the enemy's lines, whilst the enemy guns were often silent. When a company commander demanded artillery retaliation, the response was no longer a couple of rounds, as in 1915; German shelling was now returned at a high rate of interest. The men realized that good food and a plentiful supply of ammunition weighed the scales in their favour, in spite of the hardships and discomforts of their waterlogged lines.

The 1st Brigade now took their turn in the line, and on the 21st January the Battalion moved up into support in the forward area, later relieving the Camerons in the line on the 24th. The Houthulst front showed no change, except that dispositions tended more and more to the defensive; in this tour three companies held the outpost line and main line of defence, with one company in support. The three days in the line were quiet, and there was little shelling; but the aeroplanes on both sides were very active.

On the 27th of January the 1st Division was relieved by the 32nd, in order to take over new ground about a mile and a half to the south. The Black Watch were relieved by the 16th Highland Light Infantry and marched to Reninghof Camp. In the past month, although the Battalion had spent two weeks in the forward area, and held the line for seven days only two men were wounded.

From the 1st to the 8th of February, 1918, the 1st Brigade was in reserve in the Eikhœk area, training and building improved shelter against aeroplane bombing, which was a frequent cause of casualties in the salient. On the 4th of February, in answer to a challenge from the 18th Belgian Regiment, the Battalion went over to Oostvleteren to play a football match. The Black Watch, of course, had plenty of supporters; but the numbers of Belgian officers and other ranks who attended, and the enthusiasm they showed, were a surprise to everyone, and the game, which ended in a draw, was closely contested.

During this time in reserve, the 1st Brigade was reorganized and reduced from four battalions to three. The difficulty of keeping battalions up to strength had been acutely felt throughout 1917, and all measures taken had failed to maintain the necessary numbers during the progress of a battle. In many instances platoons fell below the minimum strength at which infantry weapons could be used in combination; consequently, the four-section system broke up, and the organization for battle became divorced from the actual practice of the battlefield. To end this situation infantry brigades in British formations were reduced from four battalions to three. The change was not made without considerable and violent criticism, since though the resisting power of the battalion was not altered, that of the brigade or division was appreciably lessened. The result in the 1st Brigade was that the 8th Royal Berkshire Regiment and the 10th Gloucestershire Regiment left the Brigade, the 1st Loyal North Lancashire Regiment taking their place.

On the 9th of February the 1st Division began to take over the right half of the Corps front from the 35th. The Black Watch moved from Reninghof Camp to Hill Top Farm on the Wieltje-Pilkem Ridge, from which the Germans had overlooked the northern part of the Salient for over two years. From the 11th to the 18th all four companies were employed daily in work on the defences of the Second Army battle zone—wiring, building earthworks, reconstructing old German machine gun posts, and making new ones. The last of these tasks involved the handling of concrete under the supervision of Royal Engineer officers, and being a novelty was highly popular.

At the same time, officers and non-commissioned officers reconnoitred the Battalion assembly positions and the various roads leading from them to the Corps defence line. In a new Divisional area the Battalion had to know the way round the whole of the Corps line, and know it thoroughly. A horse was useless on any ground devastated by battle, least of all in the Salient; thus the time was fully occupied by frequent reconnaissances on foot and constant work on the defences. But the mind was no longer overwhelmed by the labyrinth of deep trenches, natural features were quickly understood and remembered, and had the German offensive begun thus early, it would have been met on the Passchendaele front by a carefully planned system of defence.

On the 10th February the 1st Black Watch relieved a battalion of the 3rd Brigade in the forward area, between the Steenbeek and Poelcappelle village, and on the 22nd took over about a mile

POELCAPPELLE AREA, FEBRUARY, 1918

of the front, between the hamlet of Goudberg and the southeast edge of Poelcappelle. All cover had been blown away, and the ground was open and exposed; wide frontages and great depth were therefore the general custom. This had the effect of reducing casualties, and indeed the Battalion lost only 2 men killed and 5 wounded in the month of February. The mud was not quite so deep as in Houthulst Forest, but Company Headquarters had to be reached on duck-board tracks, and thenceforwards it was necessary to wade.

Between the 26th and 28th the Battalion was in support, and on the 28th went back into the line. The Staff were now pressing more urgently for "identifications," and The Black Watch accordingly prepared a raid near "Moray House." The raiding party, Lieutenant R. K. Arbuthnott, Second Lieutenant R. Ramsay and 63 other ranks of C company, rehearsed their plan in the support area, and on the night of 2nd March, Second Lieutenant Ramsay made a daring approach very close to the German sentries, and definitely located three posts. At 9 p.m. on the 3rd the barrage came down, and four minutes later the raiders entered the locality of the enemy posts. The men were keen, so keen indeed that the chief anxiety of the officers was to prevent them from advancing into the barrage. As our men advanced the enemy ran from their posts, leaving one man dead, from whose body unluckily no identification could be obtained. The raiders then waited in the enemy line until the customary "retaliation" had passed, and returned without suffering any loss.

A little later on, Second Lieutenant D. Smith, of D company, on his own initiative took eight men and attacked an enemy post on the left of the Battalion front. Creeping to within bombing distance, the patrol tried to surprise the post by a rush; but here, too, the Germans fled without leaving a trace of their identity. There is no reason to suppose that cowardice was the motive of these retirements, since it was essential to the German plan that their dispositions should be kept as secret as possible.

On the night of 4th March the 3rd Brigade took over the Poelcappelle–Goudberg line, and the Battalion, on relief, marched to Wieltje, and thence moved by light railway to Hospital Farm. The rest was not a long one. By this time the approximate date and locality of the big offensive was known to General Headquarters, and one of the three divisions in the Corps was ordered to concentrate in reserve, the front of the 1st Division being extened from Poelcappelle to the Ypres–Staden railway.

As the opening of the offensive came nearer, raids and artillery fire increased on most fronts, so that the attention of the Allied General Staff might be dispersed. The 1st Division was unsuccessfully raided on the 15th and 17th of March, and the Battalion, which took over part of the new front on the 17th, was raided before it had been more than a few hours in the line. At 4.15 a.m. on the 18th, two parties, estimated at thirty or forty each, attacked the right platoon of C company; the locality contained four section posts, widely dispersed, not formidably wired, and forming a salient to the rest of the line. One party was driven off by Lewis-gun fire, but the other, coming in from the rear, surprised a section post while it was engaged with the frontal attack, and took four of the seven men prisoners. One of these men, however, knocked down with his steel helmet the German soldier who was acting as his escort, and rejoined the Battalion before dawn.

On the 20th the Divisional front was again raided; and nightly at this time hostile shelling cut all forward telephone lines, so that linesmen and runners of the Battalion were working in the open. Their qualities highly impressed several American officers who were attached to the Battalion for a short experience in the front line.

Between the 22nd and the 25th of March the Battalion was in billets in the canal bank, and from the 25th to the 29th in support near Langemarck, continually wiring and strengthening the defences of its area. On the 29th it went up again to its last sector. The casualties for the month of March had been light—9 killed, 23 wounded, 3 missing—when the steady increase of artillery fire is considered; many casualties had been avoided by the system of wide extensions and greater depth, a system however which left the posts in the line open to such losses as had occurred on the 18th.

CHAPTER VII

APRIL, 1918, TO THE ARMISTICE

1.—*The Defence of Givenchy*

WHILE the 1st Division was holding the northernmost part of the Ypres Salient, the storm had broken in the south, where the Fifth Army was now bearing the shock of the main German offensive. Corps and Army Reserves were entrained to this area, and by the beginning of April the Second Army front was so thinly held that it could not have stood out against a determined attack. The policy of the Allied Command was to withdraw, if necessary, from the Ypres Salient to a shorter front, but to yield no ground voluntarily.

As the offensive in the south was gradually held, it became more important than ever to persist in identifying the enemy opposite the Battalion, and B company, under Captain Dennis Cooke, was hurriedly called to organize a raid. Opposite the company front was a concrete machine-gun post, known as Gravel Farm, and here the enemy might confidently be counted on to be found at home. The approaches had already been reconnoitred; but it was a difficult objective, since both wire and concrete were undamaged. With the help of an artillery barrage Lieut. Higginbotham and twenty men of B company forced their way through the wire on the night of April 1st; but as had happened before, the enemy fired until he had caused a few casualties in the raiding party, and then escaped in the darkness. On the next night the Battalion was relieved by the Loyal North Lancashire Regiment, and went back to the canal bank for a few days of training.

But the 1st Division was now being relieved by two much reduced divisions from the battle front, the 30th and 36th. On April 7th the Battalion moved to Elverdinghe Château, a building which had miraculously stood unharmed through three years of war, though within easy artillery range from the German position; local gossip said that the building belonged to an Austrian, or that the enemy were sparing it to be a headquarters in a future advance. However, the Château had been accidentally burnt down this winter, and its old walls no longer offered hospitality. On the 8th the Battalion moved to Peselhœk, where it entrained for Chocques; the destination was reached at 10 p.m., and by 4 a.m. all were settled in billets at Lapugnoy, a village about four miles west of Béthune, in the I Corps and First Army area.

Almost at the same hour the enemy attacked the front of the Portuguese Corps between Béthune and Armentières, a not unexpected movement. In consequence the Battalion was at half an hour's notice to move, until the afternoon, when the situation became clear, and the gallant resistance of the 55th Division was known to be holding the enemy east of Bethune. On the 10th the battle continued, the sound of gunfire to the north moving slowly westwards, and proving that the enemy was gaining ground in the neighbourhood of St. Venant.

While officers of The Black Watch were reconnoitring forward positions, the Battalion moved by bus to Vaudricourt on the 11th, and on the 12th marched into billets in Beuvry. The roads to the south of Béthune were being heavily shelled by the enemy, and the Battalion, which had so often stayed in the village when in reserve to the Givenchy and Cuinchy fronts, in 1915, now marched into their old billets round the Square, but were soon driven by shell fire into the cellars, the contents of which were very varied. One well-remembered cellar contained old vintage wines of every description, but, alas! the Provost-Marshal issued a stern decree that not even vintage wines were to be spared. Thus it became the painful duty of B company to shatter bottle after bottle of priceless wine, until the garden literally flowed with it. The shelling continued for some days; but thanks to the strength of the cellars there were few casualties.

Most of the civilians had fled by this time, and none remained a day or two later. One dear old lady, in leaving, bequeathed her pig to Battalion Headquarters, saying, " she would sooner they ate it than the Germans." Her wish, of course, was gratified; but she took the feminine privilege of changing her mind, though too late, and sent in a bill for the full value of her pet.

On the night of April 16th the Battalion moved forward to the line in Givenchy, relieving the 4th Loyal North Lancashire Regiment, 55th Division. In this new sector, the 1st Loyal North Lancashire Regiment held the front line on the right, as far as the La Bassée Canal, and the Camerons remained in reserve; Brigade Headquarters were at Le Preol. Another attack was expected on the 18th, and all three Brigades of the 1st Division were in the line, the 2nd Brigade to the south of the canal, and the 3rd Brigade to the north of the 1st Brigade, their line bending back westwards from Festubert, in the direction of Le Touret. It may be as well to describe the Givenchy position in greater detail, as the events of the next few days in this area were of importance to the whole First Army and of enduring memory to The Black Watch.

From the canal, on the right, the line ran due north for about 500 yards, and was held by A company, under Captain Sinclair; this company directly covered the approaches to Givenchy

IN THE TRENCHES, GIVENCHY, APRIL, 1918

Church and Keep. From sap K (inclusive), C company, under Captain Arbuthnott, held another 500 yards of line, which ran almost south-west, and so formed a salient with the line of A company. On the left, D company, commanded by Captain Robertson, had two platoons in some old disused trenches between C company and Le Plantin Village; Lieutenant Balmain and Sergeant J. Robertson commanded these platoons, which faced north-east. The remaining two platoons, under Lieutenants Stewart and Jacobs, were in Grenadier Trench, immediately east of the Le Plantin–Festubert road, and faced due east. Thus D company was spread over a front of 600 yards, and had no reserve.

B company garrisoned three strong points behind the line; Company Headquarters and two platoons were in Givenchy Keep, one platoon was in Moat Farm, and one in Herts Keep. South Moor House, which had been the Headquarters of Colonel Stewart in the winter of 1914–15, was once again the Headquarters of the Battalion.

At first sight the defences appeared much as when the Battalion left them in 1915; in reality they had been greatly strengthened. The little hill, which since 1914 had given such high tactical importance to Givenchy, had been tunnelled from an entrance in the slope facing Moat Farm to an exit in the front line. Half-way along the tunnel was another exit, which was used as Headquarters of C company. Both A and C company Headquarters, and half of these two companies, were accommodated in the long tunnel. Such a distribution was known to be risky, since in similar tunnels on the Somme front the Battalion had taken large numbers of German prisoners before they had been able to climb to the surface after a bombardment. And yet it was certain that a sufficient concentration of artillery could soon make the high ground untenable for men in open trenches. The risk had been accepted before, and in the attack on the foggy 9th of April the tunnels had fully justified their construction.

Since 1915 there had been continuous activity in mining, and the result was a line of craters of all sizes, which filled the narrow No Man's Land. From the British line T-heads ran forward fifty yards to the lip of the craters, and small posts looked across to where similar enemy posts were facing them on the opposite lip. Somewhere underground between the British line and the craters ran a deep gallery and an intricate system of defensive mines, but the details of this system were unknown to regimental officers. There was an excellent system of buried cable, which held good throughout the fighting. In rear, trench lines had given way to fortified posts, from which the garrison (B company) could not be moved without reference to higher authority. These small defended localities, a short distance behind the front line, had been proved by both sides to be the most effective organization by which limited numbers could hold up an advance, until the situation could be understood, and the necessary counter-attack organized and launched.

To sum up briefly, the position was in many ways stronger than before, but contained elements of weakness; there was no battalion reserve, owing to the width of front to be held; the northern part of the line had only been in existence for a week, and was not yet strongly wired; and there was the danger that the company reserves, resting in the tunnel, might be caught before they could come above ground.

The relief on the night of the 16th of April was highly complicated, and it was late before the Battalion had completed the taking over; none the less, some useful work was done in strengthening the wire on D company's front. At 10 a.m. on the 17th the enemy began a slow bombardment of the Keep system with shells of a very large calibre. By 1 a.m. on the 18th, the day of the expected assault, the bombardment had become intense. It ceased at 5 a.m., but not for long; between six and eight it grew heavier, until at 8.10 a.m. the enemy could be seen advancing in the plain to the north of Givenchy.

The telephone operator at C company Headquarters sent through a message that the enemy had secured the central exit of the tunnel, and Battalion Headquarters manned their battle positions, with the barrage still coming down. By half-past eight it was clear that the enemy had penetrated the positions of A and C companies, and that the greater portion of the two companies in the tunnel had been cut off. Meanwhile, the Keep, Moat Farm, and D company on the low ground, were all resisting stoutly. Only one or two of the enemy penetrated as far as Battalion Headquarters, where Lieutenant Valentine, the Lewis-gun officer, was firing a captured German machine gun, one of several that were captured on the 9th, and that were used with good effect on this day.

It is hard to unravel the details of any fiercely contested fight, and this account does not pretend to do justice to all who took part in the day's fighting; a few names are mentioned, in the hope that they illustrate the undoubted courage of the remainder. It is doubtful if anyone remained alive in the outpost positions of A and C companies, which were destroyed beyond recognition; the bombardment had been as intense as any known on the Western Front, and if a few had survived, they could not have made an effective resistance. The light trench mortars and machine guns were buried by the bombardment, and their teams destroyed. Captain Sinclair and a small band of devoted

GERMAN ATTACK ON GIVENCHY, APRIL, 1918

followers waited on the tunnel stairway that faced the front line; they must have come out to meet the attack, in spite of the shell fire concentrated on their only exit, and were overcome by superior numbers at close quarters. Two days later their bodies were found by the exit, where they fell.

The remainder of A company, under Lieutenant J. C. Stephen, were cut off underground, and in darkness; the pumps had been destroyed in the bombardment, and water began to pour into the tunnel. In such surroundings they stood against bombing attacks until 11 a.m., when the repeated threat of a flame projector induced them to surrender. It is certain that their resistance played a part in the enemy's failure to penetrate further into the Brigade area.

C company had fared no better; one platoon, No. 11, had mistaken a pause in the barrage for the final lift, and had rushed out to their battle positions, only to be driven in with casualties by a new burst of fire. Captain Arbuthnott was already lying wounded in the Company Headquarters; of the four Lewis guns in the forward posts, three were destroyed. The remaining gun was overrun by the first rush of the enemy, which brought them without a check as far as the tunnel exit. Here, in the cramped space of a narrow winding iron stair, the reserves were being brought to the surface; the wounded from the outposts were crawling in to their only hope of safety; and the congestion that resulted allowed the enemy to capture the exit, the exact position of which was well known to them.

With two of the tunnel mouths in his possession, the enemy swept on against the rear defences. The third exit ran horizontally out of the hillside, and its garrison were able to take up their positions in time. Here was No. 12 platoon, under Lieutenant Stewart Smith, who had just been joined by a hurriedly improvised "No. 17 platoon" of Lieutenant MacKay and 20 men from the "nucleus"[1] left at Brigade Headquarters. They were helped, no doubt, by the resistance at the other exits, but they, too, were overcome after a gallant fight. Before the reinforcements could come back from the other end of the tunnel, Lieutenant MacKay was wounded, Lieutenant Stewart Smith had been wounded three times, and the exit was captured. The enemy attempted to enter the tunnel at this point, but the men of The Black Watch, together with a small party of Royal Engineers, whose officer was severely wounded, drove them out again. A and C companies had sacrificed themselves, but not in vain.

In the Keep two platoons of B company, under Captain

---

[1] Since 1916 units going into action had left behind a proportion of officers and other ranks, so that if any unit were destroyed a "nucleus" might begin at once the task of reorganization and assimilating reinforcements.

THE FIRST BATTALION THE BLACK WATCH

Dennis Cooke and Lieutenant Kilgour, had been hammered by heavy guns and trench mortars by a bombardment that could hardly have been excelled, either for size or quantity of projectiles. Fortunately the Keep had been well sited on the reverse slope, and a large number of the shells and bombs overshot their mark by about fifty yards, while the deep dug-outs enabled the greater part of the garrison to be kept in safety. Great credit is due to Captain Cooke and Lieutenant Kilgour, in that they succeeded in manning their positions in time to beat off the attack; there was no time to spare, for the wire had been torn to shreds, and a number of the enemy were on the very ramparts before they were checked.

Then began a protracted fight at close quarters, in which the German infantry, sheltering in the shell-holes and battered trenches on three sides of the Keep, fired steadily on its conspicuous outline. Many a gallant soldier of the regiment, among them the two officers, fell at this time, shot through the head; the odds were all in favour of the enemy—but human valour has defied odds before now. It is half the strength of defence to keep on firing at close quarters, for if an attack is to succeed, some portion of the line must rise and charge; but if the first man to rise draws the fire of a Lewis or machine gun, the attack is apt to fail. As the minutes crawled by the enthusiasm of the enemy died away in the face of the watchful defence. Twice the attackers thought the barrage had deserted them, and the air was thick with Véry lights; trench mortars were called up, too, and a heavy barrage fell with little discrimination on British and Germans alike. Twice the attack was renewed, but the Keep was not carried. At some part of the morning, at a time not exactly recorded, Company Sergeant Major Bennett, now in command, sent a messenger to Battalion Headquarters, asking for reinforcements, since "there were only 8 unwounded"; in the early morning there had been 44 in the garrison. It was a pathetic request, and an important one, but Battalion Headquarters in battle, if it is to maintain control, can ill spare its personnel, and only 6 men, under Lieutenant Addison, the signalling officer, could be sent at this moment to reinforce the Keep.

Later, the garrison was joined by a party of the 1st Loyal North Lancashire Regiment, under an officer. By noon, the battle for the Keep was over; it will remain a marvel of human endurance, at least to those who saw the weight of explosive hurled at this little circular fort.

At Moat Farm there was a similar story to tell. The heavy concrete shelters lying underneath the ridge had been bombarded with a concentrated fire, but the guns seemed to have been worn a little by the continuous firing, and, although the lighter guns

GERMAN ATTACK ON GIVENCHY, APRIL, 1918

made continual hits, only two shells from the heavy calibres struck the building. The lift of the barrage was seen in the nick of time, and Lieutenant Burton and his platoon of "B company turned out whilst a stream of shells was still falling on the post. Around the farm ran a shallow moat, well wired, and beyond it was a good open field of fire. The enemy was still some forty yards from the moat, and one Lewis gun, with one Vickers (the others had been smashed in the bombardment), opened fire on the instant. Under the stream of lead the attack died away, and the most anxious moment for Moat Farm was soon past.

To the north, D company had been busily engaged; three of its platoons came out of the bombardment with few losses, whilst the fourth lost heavily; but the day before there had been only one man to every six yards of front, and the reduced numbers would not have been enough to meet the attack, had not the attached machine gunners left their concrete emplacements and fought their guns in the open. A few Germans here and there penetrated this front, but a withering fire compelled the greater part to take cover in the old trenches, with which the plain was covered. Little groups pressed on along these trenches, and engaged D company in fighting at short range; Lieutenant Balmain, of No. 13 platoon, fell shot through the head whilst dealing with one of these parties.

By 9.30 a.m. it was clear to Battalion Headquarters that the enemy had been held along the line of the Keep, Moat Farm and D company, and the moment for a counter-attack seemed to have come. The Brigade and Divisional Reserves had to be kept sufficiently in rear to be protected from the creeping barrage and from the watchful observers in aeroplanes, and for the same reasons could not be closely concentrated. Three companies of the battalion had been holding very wide fronts, and the fourth was tied down to fortified posts, so that there was no Battalion Reserve, other than "No. 17" platoon, formed mainly from the band and employed men.

The German bombardment had caused such heavy losses among our batteries and to the Cameron Highlanders in support, that it was impossible to organize an effective counter-attack.

A request, however, was sent to Brigade Headquarters for permission to counter-attack with the platoon from Herts Keep; but the situation was not yet clear on the flanks, and the request was not granted. Later, a platoon of Cameron Highlanders came up to Herts Keep to relieve Lieutenant Smith's platoon, which at once advanced up the trench leading to what had been C company's position. But the opportunity had passed; the trenches were battered to pieces, the men had to advance in the open, and in the end the platoon could do no more than fill the dangerous gap between Moat Farm and the right of D company.

By noon the situation had definitely improved, and the enemy were no longer in the mood for attack; but on the right they had overrun the two forward companies of the Loyal North Lancashire Regiment, and the whole of the salient formed by the high ground of Givenchy Ridge was in German hands. General Thornton, the Brigadier, placed a company of the Camerons at the disposal of The Black Watch, at about 2.30 p.m. There was the keenest anxiety to assist any of our comrades who might even now be holding their own in the tunnel, but it would have been worse than useless to attack without artillery preparation. All the afternoon enemy aeroplanes were flying low over the position, and there were occasional heavy bursts of fire.

A second company of Cameron Highlanders came up at 6.30 p.m. and was held in reserve; with this reinforcement the Battalion was able to counter-attack at 8.30 p.m. South of the Keep the company of Cameron Highlanders had as their objective the original front line of A company; in the centre a bombing party, organized from Battalion Headquarters and led by Major Raynes, of the British Columbia Regiment, advanced on the tunnel exit which had been C company's Headquarters; on the extreme left Lieutenant Smith's platoon of B company was to push on parallel with Ware Trench, and join up with the Cameron company. The artillery preparations were not heavy, for the guns had been hard at it since 1 a.m., and had answered every call; and with the possibility that our own wounded might still be on the ground, no attempt could be made at annihilating fire. The enemy proved, however, to be unshaken, and the advance of the Cameron company was, quite correctly, not pressed. On the left, Lieutenant Smith's platoon reached and drove in the enemy front posts, but could make no headway beyond this. The bombing party met with stiff opposition, and the attempt had to be given up; but not before Major Raynes had received wounds of which he afterwards died. In the end, therefore, the tunnel exits remained in German hands.

From the "nucleus," 20 men came up during the evening to reinforce the Keep, Lieut. Ferguson commanding them, and one of the companies of Cameron Highlanders was withdrawn to the support area. The Keep was still continually shelled, and Lieutenant Ferguson was the right man for this awkward corner; "Am being heavily trench-mortared—All O.K." is typical of the messages he sent in the next forty-eight hours.

By the early morning of the 19th the situation was perfectly quiet—so quiet that a German ration party of five men was captured in the Battalion lines by Lieutenant Smith's platoon.

IN SUPPORT, APRIL 21ST, 1918

Throughout the day arrangements were pushed forward for the 1st Northamptonshire Regiment to counter-attack and recover the lost ground of the ridge. The Battalion would willingly have undertaken this task, but there were good reasons against it; the relief of B and D companies would have been intricate, and the Battalion had already suffered very heavy losses. There were more battles ahead; and the Commanding Officer refrained from making a request that probably would not have been granted. The morning of the 19th furnished an extraordinary contrast to the turmoil and bombardment of the day before. During the night there had been a fall of snow, and the general calm was only broken by the cries of the German wounded, who had apparently been left untended where they fell.

At dawn on the 20th the two companies of the Northamptonshire Regiment recovered the whole of the front line originally held by The Black Watch, with the exception of the Crater Lips. By eleven o'clock the position was consolidated and the two companies of the Northamptonshire Regiment passed under the command of the Officer Commanding The Black Watch. A half-hearted attempt at counter-attack was made by the enemy in the course of the morning, but this was effectively dealt with by artillery fire.

On the night of the 21st the Battalion was relieved, and went back into support between Pont Fixe and Le Preol; the 55th Division took over the line on the 23rd, and the Battalion marched to Houchin, and on the 24th to Nœux-les-Mines, where it remained for a week in a hutted camp. The fighting of a single day has been recounted at some length in this narrative; but not since the 9th May, 1915, had the Battalion endured such a day; Major Raynes, Captains Cooke and Sinclair, Lieutenants Kilgour and Kimber, Second Lieutenants Glencross and Balmain had been killed; Capt. Arbuthnott, Lieutenant Stewart Smith, and Second Lieutenant MacKay were wounded and missing; and Lieutenants Jameson, Kirkcaldy, Stephen, Hume and Ramsay were missing; 42 other ranks had been killed, 66 wounded and 258 were missing; 15 officers and 366 other ranks had become casualties, but the enemy had been held. The Black Watch had once more shown themselves the fit guardians of their fine traditions.

On the 2nd of May the 1st Brigade went into the line again, in the Cambrin sector. No reinforcements had arrived since the late fighting; there remained but a remnant of A and C companies, and the Battalion was not strong enough to hold either of the fronts in this sector; so it was spread over both fronts, in support. Two platoons of B company went to Pont Fixe, and two to near Maison Rouge; D company, attached to the Cameron Highlanders, garrisoned the "village line" at Cuinchy, while

THE FIRST BATTALION THE BLACK WATCH

Battalion Headquarters were in the Red Château, Cambrin. The German attack had been transferred to another front, glorious spring weather prevailed, and there is little to record except persistent work on defences, and an occasional shelling with mustard gas.

On May 20th the 1st Brigade was relieved, and the Battalion returned to camp at Nœux-les-Mines. Reinforcements arrived, and A and C companies were reorganized. One day was set aside for Battalion sports, but the time was usually devoted to tactical training, specialist training and range practices; after such heavy losses in officers and men there was every reason to work hard before going again into the line. On the 28th the Battalion marched up the line to relieve the 2nd K.R.R.C. in the Hohenzollern Redoubt, and on the way incurred a loss which was doubly sad, since it did not happen in battle. As the newly formed C company was parading in a side street of the town, more than five miles from the line, a solitary shell burst immediately behind their rear rank. None of the usual warning noises was heard, and observers from a distance looked up for an aeroplane; but the sky was clear, and without doubt it was a projectile from a high-velocity gun. Six men were killed outright, 4 died of wounds, and the company suffered 59 casualties.

During the next six weeks the Battalion was three times in the line, from May 29th to June 5th, from June 9th to June 13th, and from June 21st to July 11th; the intervals of rest and training were spent at Nœux and Annequin. On June 10th, Lieutenant Colonel F. Anderson, D.S.O., took over command of the 1st Black Watch from Lieutenant Colonel L. P. Evans, V.C., D.S.O., who had been appointed to command the 14th Infantry Brigade.

There was no reason to fear another German offensive on this front, which was now as quiet as any part of line in all France and Belgium; the natural difficulties in the way of an advance were immense, and had been made more formidable by three years' work on the fortification of the Loos plain. To add to the comfort, there were many good billets, even now untouched by war, within 4000 yards of the front trenches. At Nœux-les-Mines several officers of the Regiment visited the Battalion, and on one night, about June 15th, Brigadier General W. Green, Lieutenant Colonel S. H. Eden, Lieutenant Colonel the Hon. M. Hore-Ruthven, Lieutenant Colonel Tarleton, and Major A. Sutherland all came to dine with the officers.

On June 21st the Battalion moved back to the line at Cambrin, and during this tour, on July 7th, D company carried out a raid, which reached the reserve line of the enemy, bringing back six prisoners. The casualties were heavier than had been expected, since the leading line went forward too close to the artillery bar-

ROLL CALL AT NOEUX-LES-MINES, OUTSIDE BATTALION BILLETS, APRIL, 1918

HOHENZOLLERN SECTOR, JUNE–AUGUST, 1918

rage; however, this was a proof that, in spite of its experiences during the German attack, the Battalion was in the keenest fighting form.

From the 11th to 21st of July the Battalion was in rest at Nœux-les-Mines, from which town a composite company was sent to represent the Regiment at the French National Fête on July 14th, the anniversary of the destruction of the Bastille. Five officers and 220 other ranks, under Captain W. H. Robertson, formed a company in a composite battalion representative of the British Army. They were inspected by President Poincaré and General Joffre in the Bois de Boulogne, and marched through the streets of Paris to the Champs Elysées, being greeted everywhere with enthusiasm.

During the next month the Battalion did two more tours in the Hohenzollern Redoubt area, and on August 19th moved back by bus to the Lisbourg training area. From near Lisbourg the 1st Brigade entrained for Arras on September 1st, in support to the justly famous attack of the Canadian Corps on the Drocourt–Quéant switch line, which began at dawn on September 2nd. The Battalion moved forward through assembly positions at Guémappes, prepared to reinforce the Canadians, but the attack was so successful that the 1st Division was not called upon to advance. On the night of the 2nd, the Battalion halted in a newly captured system of trenches that faced the village of Dury, just north of the Arras–Cambrai road; the enemy had been preparing " boobytraps," in the form of delay action mines; but the time had been short, and the leads were not properly connected. Here the Battalion was quartered; and though there were many anxious moments there were no losses.

The attack was continued on September 3rd, and in the evening the Battalion moved forward in artillery formation to take over ground near Récourt Wood, captured by the 2nd Seaforth Highlanders, of the 4th Division, who had attacked on the left of the Canadians. During the advance all companies were in full view of the enemy, who opened a lively fire from 77 mm. guns; but in spite of this the men advanced without a check, as if the operation had been a peace-time manœuvre. In consequence of this steady advance, only few men were wounded, of whom Captain R. Cook was one.

At dusk some officers were sent forward to reconnoitre outpost positions. The ideal outpost position, like the rainbow, is just a little way beyond where one stands, and the officers of one company went on for more than a mile, over ground that the attack had not reached in daylight, and came back very late, to find the outposts had already been posted by an anxious commanding officer. The valley of the Sensée river is broad and shallow, and overflows into marshes that might trap a force retreating in action; the enemy had therefore withdrawn without being pressed, and the Battalion was able to advance northwards and establish posts on the river bank. One patrol, indeed, found an unguarded bridge, crossed and came back with valuable information as to the enemy dispositions.

Further south, on the Fourth Army front, the German retreat was even more pronounced; and as on this front the distance to the prepared positions of the Hindenburg Line was greater than on the Third Army front, a number of troops were transferred southwards. The 1st Division moved back through Arras to Marœil, where, on the 9th of September, it entrained for Marcelcave, near Amiens. From this time until the armistice the 1st, 6th, 32nd and 46th Divisions formed the IX Corps of the Fourth Army, and took part in a continuous advance from the Somme to the frontiers of Belgium.

The enemy, whose resistance had stiffened as the reserve positions were approached, now held an outpost line from two to three miles west of the Hindenburg Line; a high ridge effectively denied observation of the main system of defence, sunk as it was in the valley of the St. Quentin Canal. On September 18th, therefore, a general attack was made along the whole Army front, with the intention of gaining a footing in the outer trenches of the Hindenburg system. The front of the 1st Brigade was to the north of Holnon Wood, the Cameron Highlanders and Loyal North Lancashire Regiment attacking, with The Black Watch in reserve. Along the Corps front the objectives were not reached; machine-gun fire was too strong and the enemy had sufficient strength left to deliver a counter-attack.

On this day, the 19th, the Battalion was ordered forward to capture the trenches known as Fourmoy Alley and Sampson Trench, on the high ground south of Pontruet; B company led the advance, but its gallant commander, Captain Colquhoun, M.C., was killed whilst explaining the plan of attack to his officers. All the conditions were unfavourable, the ground sloped uphill, and both trenches and open country were exposed to the enemy, who had found time to consolidate his position since the previous day's fighting; moreover, the Army had advanced at such a rate since the beginning of August, that artillery support had of necessity at times become very difficult to organise. Before the Battalion had moved very far along Fourmoy Trench, it was resolutely opposed, and the trench was bombed from a parallel trench on higher ground. Machine-gun fire stopped any attempt to advance over the open, and the rest of the day was spent in beating back counter-attacks from Muguet Wood. One company was caught in a communication trench eight feet deep, and was bombed from front and rear until saved by the Lewis-gun fire of another company. The wounded were brought in with the utmost difficulty, and it was when gallantly assisting in this duty that Second Lieutenant H. H. Smith was killed.

During the close fighting on this day, Lieutenant Baxter, a Territorial officer attached to the 1st Battalion, captured a trench filled with Germans, every one of whom wore the Red Cross badge. These men had been firing until the moment their trench was captured, when one of them threw something into a dug-out. Lieutenant Baxter ordered the German to produce it. It proved to be a machine gun, which was still hot. Such incidents were happily rare, but even so they inevitably added to the mistrust with which our troops viewed the German ideas of what is honourable in war.

The fighting had brought but little success, but for this no blame has ever been attributed to the Battalion; the Corps Commander now knew that the enemy was determined to hold these positions, and broke off the engagement. After a few quieter days the Battalion was relieved on September 23rd, and went back to Vermand. The 2nd Brigade attacked over the same ground on the 24th and met with more success, since on this occasion a dozen tanks were detailed to assist the infantry advance.

The Battalion returned to the line on the night of the 26th of September, and was so fortunate as to occupy at once the southern half of the village of Pontruet, which had been the scene of desperate attacks by both the 1st and 46th Divisions. An officer of the Battalion noticed enemy trench-mortar shells dropping in the village, and took it as an indication that the enemy had withdrawn; daylight patrols confirmed this, and the line was advanced by half a mile.

Now was to begin that series of actions in which our success was unbroken until the armistice. Along the British line one army or another was steadily pushing the enemy back to unfortified positions; the spirit of the German troops was fast waning, and in the last two or three days our First and Third Armies alone had captured over 10,000 prisoners. Even on the Yser, where the inundations had prevented either side from attacking since 1914, the British, French and Belgians were beginning a move of great strategic importance, the clearance of the Belgian coast. Everywhere on the Allied front confidence prevailed; everywhere were seen the most tangible and unmistakable signs of victory.

2.—*Storming of the Hindenburg Line*

On the Corps front the immediate task was the storming of the Hindenburg Line; on the left, the vast entrenchment of the St. Quentin Canal, strengthened by wire and machine-gun em-

THE FIRST BATTALION THE BLACK WATCH

placements on both banks; on the right, a system of trenches that ran from near Bellenglise, over the ridge of Thorigny, to St. Quentin. The crossing of the canal, and the exploitation of the ground to the east, was the objective of the 46th and 32nd Divisions; the work of the 1st Division was the capture of the Thorigny Ridge, as far as the canal bank at Le Tronquoy. The 1st and 3rd Brigades were employed for this attack, the position of The Black Watch being in the front line, the Loyal North Lancashire Regiment on the left, and the South Wales Borderers on the right.

Zero hour was fixed for 5.50 a.m. on September 29th, and at this hour, in a dense fog, the Battalion entered the enemy's front line. A company on the right, D in the centre, C on the left and B in support. An indescribably dense barrage of artillery and machine-gun fire was put down. It is hard to say how many guns covered the Brigade front, but in rear of the Battalion position it was impossible to walk fifty yards in any direction without falling over gun or machine-gun emplacements. The smoke mixed with the fog, and although the close fighting in the first line had been favourable, it was impossible to make great headway until the fog lifted—as it did about ten o'clock.

Then, to quote a few lines from General Montgomery's *Story of the Fourth Army*, ". . . The 1st Loyal North Lanca-
" shires and the 1st Black Watch . . .cleared the trenches west
" of the canal astride the Bellenglise–St. Heléne road.

". . . The 1st Black Watch, with the 1st Loyal North Lancs.
" in support, had swung round its left west of the canal, and was
" clearing the trenches in the area as far east as the main St.
" Quentin–Cambrai road. The clearing of this maze of trenches
" was no easy task, and the fighting was severe, but the 1st Black
" Watch, and the 1st South Wales Borderers, of the 3rd Brigade,
" were not to be denied, and early in the afternoon, the high
" ground . . . and the trenches between it and the canal were
" captured."

On this day and the next the Battalion captured 6 German officers, 420 other ranks, 9 field guns, 120 light and heavy machine guns, and 4 trench mortars; this brilliant success, however, was thrown into the shade by the national acclamation which rewarded the crossing of the canal by the 46th Division, and it is only fair to quote once more the opinion of General Montgomery, who had planned this operation for the Fourth Army. " Not so dramatic, perhaps, but almost equally difficult
" and important in its results, was the work of the 1st Division on
" this day, as the safety of the right flank of the Army depended
" on its advance, which the enemy opposed throughout the day
" with the greatest determination."

GERMAN RETIREMENT, SEPTEMBER, 1918

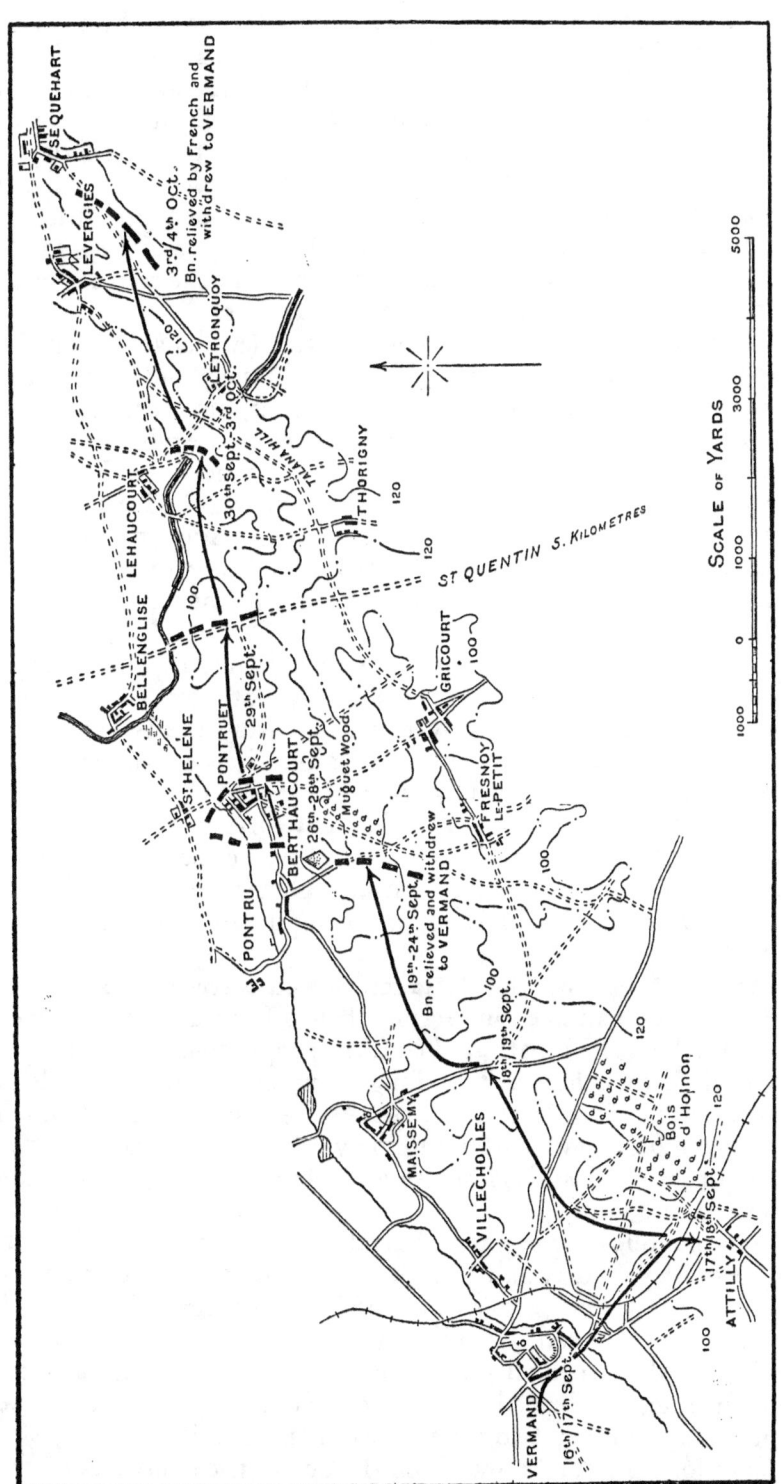

THE STORMING OF THE HINDENBURG LINE

THE FIRST BATTALION THE BLACK WATCH

At 5 p.m. a further advance was ordered; but the French, on the right of the Division, had not been able to keep up with the advance, and in consequence the right was enfiladed by German machine guns and could make no progress. But the attack was continued at 8 a.m. on the 30th, and while the 3rd Brigade captured Talana Hill on the right, the 1st Brigade cleared all the ground south of the canal, crossed it, and joined up with the remainder of the Corps between Le Tronquoy and Levergies; Battalion Headquarters was now established in the southern end of the tunnel through which the canal passes.

The German Infantry, in contrast to their behaviour on the previous day, made but the feeblest resistance, and during the night many of them attempted to surrender, but were unable to pass our standing barrage. A feature of the battle which deserves not to be forgotten, was the assistance which the Battalion received from a battery of field artillery, who had captured a number of German machine guns. Enthusiastic but inexperienced, the gunners followed the advance, firing these machine guns furiously, until every man in the front line was glad to lie down and take cover.

A few days were spent, and enjoyed, in Brigade Reserve. Then, on the night of October 3rd, the Battalion had the unusual experience of taking over the line from the Loyal North Lancashire Regiment, making a few alterations in the shape of the line, and being relieved by two regiments of Chasseurs Alpins, all in a few hours. The 6th Division now carried on the advance, and the 1st Division moved back to rest. At Vermand, on the 7th, the Battalion was addressed by Major General E. P. Strickland, commanding the 1st Division, and complimented on its success during the recent fighting.

On October 16th the Battalion moved eastwards to Bohain, a town which had been in German hands from the beginning of the war; here the repatriated country people could be seen coming back to their homes, trundling their few remaining goods in wheelbarrows or on carts; the old " lines " and " areas " which the Battalion knew so well had now been left behind, and the feeling that the last days of the war were in sight grew steadily in everyone's mind.

On the following night the Battalion assembled in the orchards of Becquigny, and at dawn on the 18th moved forward in a very dense fog to a rendezvous south of Vaux Andigny. The attack made on this day had two objectives: the first the capture of the La Vallée Mulatre, a village about a mile to the east; then, after reorganizing, the Brigade was under orders to advance and take Wassigny, a further two miles eastwards. The Battalion was in reserve for this attack; but from the outset the denseness of the

CAPTURE OF WASSIGNY, OCTOBER 19TH, 1918

fog caused the leading waves to pass, unnoticed, a good many machine-gun posts, and the Battalion was at once involved in the fighting. The progress was slow, and by the end of the day the first objective, La Vallée Mulâtre, had not been taken.

Little can be said about the fighting, which was of the most confused character; it showed, however, the need for constant training in marching by compass, and for working out compass bearings before the start of an attack. The type of country was beginning to change, and more hedges and wire were met with; this necessitated keeping to the roads, but on these, machine guns had been trained with deadly accuracy; every few minutes hedges were passed in which long gaps had been cut away by a stream of bullets, and the A echelon of transport often found itself under heavy indirect fire.

3.—*The Capture of Wassigny*

At a late hour on the 18th orders came through for an attack on Wassigny, the town where Sir Douglas Haig first established his Headquarters in 1914. Zero was postponed until several hours after daylight, so that the ground might be examined; but even with this allowance of time, it was only possible to issue verbal orders, and any success achieved was due to the quick appreciation shown by the officers, all of whom had experience of previous fighting in France. The town was attacked from the north-west, along its longest axis, a mile in depth; three companies were in the line: D on the right, B in the centre, A on the left and C in support. The advance from Angin Farm was covered by smoke, and since the leading troops never for a moment fell behind the barrage, the advance was completely successful, and the southern part of La Vallée Mulâtre, with the town of Wassigny, were occupied by The Black Watch. On the right, the French carried out a parallel operation, but did not join hands at Blocus d'en Bas till a late hour that night.

In the two days' fighting the Battalion captured 20 officers and 300 other ranks; and lost 3 officers (Lieutenant Jalland, Second Lieutenants Smith and Gyle) and 12 other ranks killed, 9 other ranks missing, and 4 officers (Captains Burton and Marshall, Second Lieutenants Wilson and Fyall) and 79 other ranks wounded. But the German moral was falling daily, and the number of prisoners had no longer the same relation to closeness of fighting as in earlier days. To give an example, 5 officers and 72 men surrendered to one of the Battalion Lewis gunners after he had fired a drum of ammunition down the steps of a dug-out.

All night long loud explosions were heard, and it was evident that the enemy was withdrawing to the east of the Oise–Sambre Canal. On the 19th the advance was resumed, and the Battalion

THE FIRST BATTALION THE BLACK WATCH

was allotted the task of capturing Arrouaise Farm, a mile to the east of Wassigny. At Zero Lieutenant Christie led his platoon forward; but they had not gone far when the barrage came down—behind, and not in front of them. There was nothing to be done but to make straight for the farm, which by good luck had been evacuated; and here they took shelter in the buildings while the barrage passed over them. The whole line of battle kept decreasing in length as the Belgian frontier was approached, and one Division after another was " pinched out "; this now happened to the 1st Brigade, and the Battalion returned to rest at Wassigny.

The officers had planned to celebrate the capture of Wassigny by marching the pipe band through the streets, but a stray, solitary gas shell fell on the billet occupied by Battalion Headquarters, and put so many pipers, runners, and scouts out of action that this and other projects were crippled. Four miles to the east lay the village of Boué, where the Battalion had first taken its place in the field with the Expeditionary Force in 1914; and for sentimental reasons everyone was anxious to pay it a second visit, and rid it of its German garrison. But the French took over more of the line, and the whole of the 1st Division was " pinched out." Very shortly, however, the 1st Division was posted to another part of the front, and from the 23rd to the 27th the Battalion held the line opposite to Catillon, about five miles further north.

By the beginning of November it was evident that the German campaign on the Western Front was doomed; Bulgaria and Turkey had already surrendered their forces, and Austria was on the point of yielding. The only hope that remained to the enemy was to make such a retirement as they had made in 1917, and bring the Allied forces to a check, perhaps on the very frontiers of Germany. Bearing this in mind the Commander-in-Chief decided to put even greater pressure on the German retreat, and the Fourth Army was instructed to force the Oise–Sambre Canal. For the 1st Black Watch, this action was the last contact with the enemy in the Great War.

On November 3rd the Battalion marched from La Vallée Mulâtre to assemble positions at La Louviére Farm, a little to the south of Catillon; at dawn on the next day the canal was to be crossed by the 1st and 2nd Brigades, and a deep bridge-head secured. Within the 1st Brigade, the Cameron Highlanders and the Loyal North Lancashire Regiment were detailed to make the crossing, and The Black Watch by leap-frogging through these two battalions, from support, was ordered to take the final objective for the day, some three miles beyond the canal.

The canal was a formidable obstacle, 70 feet from bank to bank, and the bridges were either destroyed or mined. For their crossing, therefore, the 1st Brigade took forward steel bridges,

CROSSING OF THE OISE-SAMBRE CANAL, 1918

carried on German steel floats that had been salved from a dump, and each fitted with a ladder for the scaling of the further bank. At 5.45 a.m. on the 4th of November, the 1st Brigade advanced towards the canal; and being protected by a heavy barrage were not heavily opposed. The Camerons and the Loyal North Lancashire Regiment had arranged to compete in a race across, in which the Camerons won by half a minute, in the very good time of six minutes. The enemy barrage was slow in coming down and fell behind, so that by 8 a.m. the leading battalions were able to secure the first objective, a temporary bridge-head.

The Loyal North Lancashire Regiment now fell back into support, and the Camerons on the right, and The Black Watch on the left, advanced in line. Across the canal, it was a country of thick orchards and high hedges, amongst which direction might easily have been lost; but the attack had been planned after a careful study of aeroplane photographs, and even at first sight the ground seemed strikingly familiar to the officers.

Large and complicated though the Fourth Army operations were, they went with the accuracy of clockwork. The Battalion was only once seriously held up, and very quickly a patrol of six aeroplanes came to its assistance and bombed a German post out of existence. D company met with some resistance at Grand Galop and Petit Galop farms; but the men pressed steadily forward, and the enemy attempted to break away. Thirty prisoners were captured, of whom 1 officer and 10 men wore the Iron Cross. At Mezières the left company of the Battalion had to fight its way into the village, which it finally captured, with 50 prisoners. Touch was established with the 32nd Division on the left, and the final objective was thus completely gained.

The fighting proved that the German troops were more than ever dispirited, badly fed, and badly clothed; and as their efficiency had decreased, that of the British army had risen. With the loss of three officers, Lieutenants Valentine and Wilson, Second Lieutenant Grant, 26 other ranks wounded, and 4 men killed, the Battalion had captured 5 officers, 128 other ranks, 5 field guns and 11 artillery horses, and had driven the enemy back 3000 yards.

In the evening the Battalion was relieved, and withdrew to Mazinghien; thence it marched to La Vallée Mulâtre on the 5th, and to Fresnoy-le-Grand on the 6th. The Army kept on advancing, and life in billets was uneventful until, on the morning of the 11th, the news came that the armistice had been signed. Very rightly General Strickland warned all ranks that cessation of hostilities did not necessarily mean peace. But when the news was received, there were few signs of any great outward rejoicing, such as were shown in cities at home; men's senses were, in some ways, dulled by the strain of marching, working, fighting

THE FIRST BATTALION THE BLACK WATCH

and marching again; in fact, if any effect were seen it was in the reaction to the strain of the last six months, the innate fatigue, both of mind and body, of gallant soldiers determined to show no sign of weariness until their task was achieved. There were serving with the Battalion on this day, 1 officer and 29 other ranks who had embarked on August 13th, 1914, and had served with it continuously throughout the Great War.

These were :—

Major and Quartermaster W. Fowler, M.C.

8466 R.S.M. C. Scott, M.C.
2035 Pte. G. Clarke
2496 Pte. W. Culross
 621 Pte. D. Dingwall
2179 L/Corpl. A. Duke
9299 Pte. R. Elliott
1954 Pte. J. Forbes
8059 Pte. J. Gardiner
2260 Corpl. L. Hobbs
7958 L/Corpl. D. Johnston
1838 Pte. W. Johnston, M.M.
1413 Pte. B. Jones
 277 Sgt. J. Keillor
1741 Pte. R. Low, M.M.
2236 Pte. R. Martin
7507 Pte. J. Mitchell
1073 S/Armr. Sgt. W. Mitchell, R.A.O.C. (attached)
 233 Pte. F. McCurrach
5629 Pte. J. McDiarmid
6194 Pte. J. McJade
2275 L/Corpl. F. McFarlane, M.S.M.
1197 Pte. A. McKinnon
6387 Sgt. J. Rennie
6867 Sgt. P. Rutherford, D.C.M.
1973 L/Corpl. H. Senior
2432 Pte. P. Spence, M.M.
 252 Pte. R. Thomson
1806 Corpl. W. Ure, M.M.
 119 Pte. T. Young

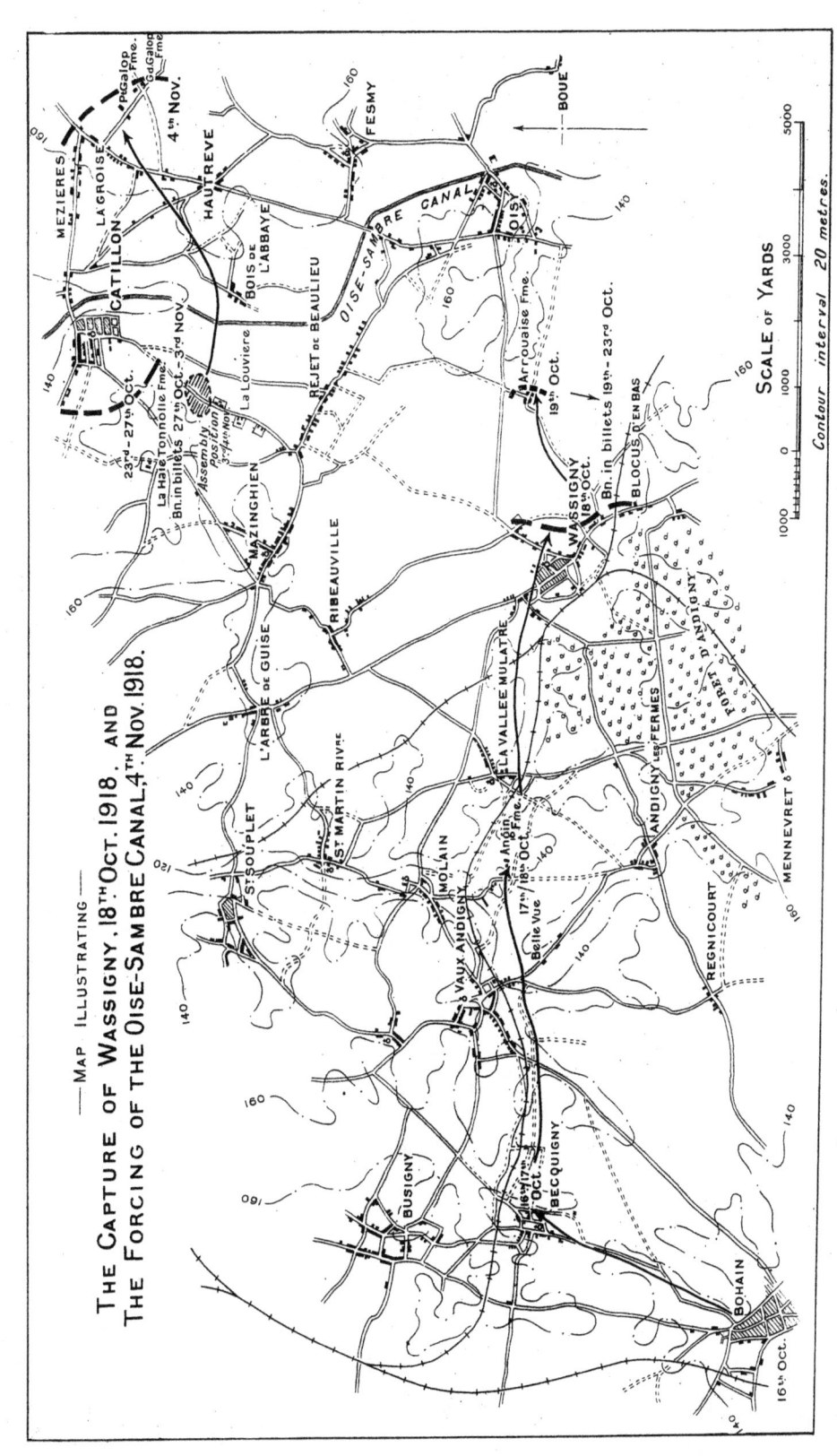

THE ADVANCE TO GERMANY, NOVEMBER, 1918

CONCLUSION

THE German retreat now became a rout, conducted at such a pace that our infantry lost touch with the enemy rearguards some days before the armistice. Delay action mines were constantly exploding on the railways, and communications depended on lorry convoys, driven on ever-increasing journeys over nightmare roads. Three of the five armies in France were now withdrawn from the line as it existed on armistice day, and from the further advance that followed shortly afterwards. To secure an orderly evacuation of Belgium, and to form a future Army of Occupation, the two remaining armies were reconstructed and ordered to advance to the Rhine.

The Battalion, now part of the Fifth Army, moved slowly across Belgium to the German frontier. Nothing was seen of the retiring German troops; but, by the terms of the armistice, all enemy aircraft had been parked in the fields, and the long deserted lines were a most satisfying sight. The weather proved fine and warm, and the scenery grew more beautiful as eastern Belgium was reached—" Awfu' like Scotland," someone was heard to say. The Battalion crossed the Meuse at Dinant, and saw broken walls of many fine buildings destroyed in the German advance of 1914.

Everywhere in the Ardennes the British troops were given a royal reception by the inhabitants; the march from Solres-le-Château to Dinant—40 kilometres in ten days—was no more than a saunter, and time was found to organize a party and hunt some wild boar in the neighbourhood. The whole Battalion was turned into a line of beaters, with fixed bayonets, and the order was given to "stick" the boar, if he broke away; the officers, as guns, were posted in the rides of a wood.

Three wild boars soon broke into the open, and some sportsman, unable to resist the temptation, opened fire on them. The boars turned back, the firing became general, and the real "guns," among whom bullets were passing freely, crouched on the ground behind any sort of cover. After much shouting and confusion, it turned out that no damage had been done to guns, beaters or boars.

The next day brought a strange contrast to this sport and a reminder that the tragedy of war persists long after victory. The Battalion passed while on the march a party of gaunt white-faced men, trudging wearily westwards; in spite of the torn remnants of uniform that these men wore, it was hard to recognize them as British soldiers. They were ex-prisoners of war, half-starved but determined in their sad plight to find their own way to their

THE FIRST BATTALION THE BLACK WATCH

comrades, rather than wait for the promised relief that might come too late.

The Regimental Colours were ceremoniously received on parade on the 8th of December, a party having brought them from the depot; and with colours uncased the Battalion crossed the frontier of Germany, and marched past the Divisional Commander on December 10th. The weather, which up to now had been good, turned cold and wet once the frontier was crossed, near St. Vith. Still no German troops were seen; the civilian population kept indoors, and the Battalion marched through long streets where every window blind was drawn—but round the corner of every blind a German face was peeping.

There was indeed something to look at, for the appearance of the Battalion was now very smart. Many days had been spent in painting steel helmets green, with red hackle showing; the transport was freshly painted, and all metal parts polished; the khaki apron was no longer worn. The men were in good marching form, and covered twenty miles a day for several days, during which time not a man fell out. The speed had to be kept up, for the high ground of the Eifel lay in front, and a fall of snow might have rendered the roads impassable for several weeks.

On December 23rd the Battalion arrived at Roisdorf, its allotted station, a small village six miles north of Bonn, where the band, now largely composed of boys, joined a few days later. The Battalion was never called upon for duty in the bridge-head, and only once crossed the Rhine, on a route march through Bonn, on the last day of 1918.

The following is the table of marches of the Battalion to the Rhine:—

Nov. 11th. Fresnoy-le-Grand.   Dec. 13th. Malempré.
   ,, 13th. La Basse Moroilles.   ,, 14th. Hebronval.
   ,, 15th. Sars Poteries.   ,, 15th. Beho.
   ,, 16th. Grandrieu.   ,, 16th. The Battalion
   ,, 17th. Silenrieux.   crossed the German
   ,, 18th. Hanzinelle.   frontier and marched
   ,, 23rd. Anthée.   to Neidingen.
   ,, 24th. Sommière.   ,, 17th. Manderfield.
Dec. 1st. Celles.   ,, 18th. Dahlen.
   ,, 2nd. Ronvaux.   ,, 19th. Blankenheim.
   ,, 9th. Heure.   ,, 21st. Iversheim.
   ,, 10th. Barvaux.   ,, 22nd. Esch.
   ,, 11th. Heyd.   ,, 23rd. Roisdorf.

During the first three months of 1919, the Battalion remained at Roisdorf. Training was carried out as in peace time, and opportunities were found for sports, of which football was the most

RETURN TO ENGLAND, APRIL, 1919

popular. A ground was laid out, many good matches were played, and many parties went over to the Bonn University ground to see the matches for the Rhine Army Cup. Educational classes were now organized and were well attended, for nearly all the officers and men had employment of one sort or another in civil life, in which they had suffered a complete loss of training during the war.

Demobilization began almost at once, some parties being posted straight to the depot, and others through transfer to the 8th and 10th Battalions of the Regiment. Major (A/Lieutenant Colonel) Francis Anderson gave up the command of the Battalion in order to take up an appointment at Sandhurst. A sound soldier and keen sportsman, his energy and unfailing good spirits had made him a commanding officer in whom everyone had the fullest confidence and trust. In February, Major Fowler, the Quartermaster, left the Regiment after thirty-five years of devoted service; he had served throughout the whole war with the Battalion, and there was no one whose loss was more keenly felt. Fortunately, however, his services were not lost to the Army.

On April 17th, 1919, the Battalion entrained for Dunkerque. The 8th Battalion, under Lieutenant Colonel V. M. Fortune, D.S.O., assembled with their colours and a guard of honour to bid all ranks farewell at Buir; at Duren the 6th Battalion, commanded by Lieutenant Colonel W. Green, D.S.O., were drawn up to greet the Battalion. Major-General A. H. Marindin also came to this station to wish his old Regiment " good-bye."

At Dunkerque the Battalion parted for a time from "Alley," the old mess cart-horse, which Lord George Stewart-Murray had bought at Boué, in August, 1914; after continuous good work all through the war, " Alley " had the honour conferred on him of being permitted to wear the Red Hackle. All ranks were glad to see him later at Aldershot.

After a day in Dunkerque the Battalion, on April 20th, embarked for England, landed at Dover, and went by train to Aldershot. Here it was met by General Sir Archibald Murray, Lieutenant Colonel J. G. H. Hamilton, who was appointed to command of the Battalion, and by many other officers. Officers and men could not help recalling other receptions that had been given the Battalion—the warm greetings of the villagers during the first march in France, the decorations at Arras in August, 1914, and the march through the streets of Paris in 1917. There the French nation had looked on the officers and men of the 1st Black Watch, and had seen them determined to rival the gallantry of their predecessors in the Regiment; now the British Army welcomed home a battalion that had not only kept its honours undimmed, but had added to them a new and imperishable lustre.

APPENDIX I

RECORD OF OFFICERS' SERVICES

THE FIRST BATTALION

Abbreviations.—"K."—Killed. "D. of W."—Died of Wounds. "W."—Wounded. "M."—Missing. "P. of W."—Prisoner of War. "S."—Evacuated Sick. "R."—Rejoined. "Reg."—Regular Army Commission. "M. in D."—Mentioned in Despatches.

Notes.—(a) For Officers commissioned from the Ranks, this record covers only the period of their service as Officers (b) Where exact dates are not available, the month, where possible, has been entered.

Name	Rank on joining or commencement of campaign	Record	Actions at which present	Promotions and Regimental Appointments
Adam, J. N.	2nd Lieut.	From 3rd B.W., 23.10.15. S., 2.10.16.	Somme, '16.	Nil.
Addison, W.	2nd Lieut.	From 4th B.W., 26.1.17. Demobilized, 7.3.19.	Hohenzollern Redoubt, '15.	T/Lt., 2.10.15.
Alexander, R.	2nd Lieut.	From Temp. List B.W., 12.10.15. To M.G. Corps, 23.1.16.	Nieuport, '17. Ypres, '17.	Nil.
Allan, J. G.	2nd Lieut.	From 4th B.W., 9.2.17. To R.E. Training Centre, 7.12.18.	Mons, '14. Marne, '14. Aisne, '14.	Nil.
Allan, W. D.	Lieut.	With Bn. to France, Aug., '14. S., 14.9.14.	Mons, '14. Marne, '14. Aisne, '14. Ypres, '14.	Nil.
Amery, H. F. S.	Captain	With Bn. to France, Aug., '14. W., 14.9.14. R., 1.11.14. W., 2.11.14. D. of W. in U.K., 24.11.15.		

Name	Rank	Service	Battles	Honours
Anderson, F.	Lieut.	With Bn. to France, Aug., '14. W., 11.11.14. R. as C.O., 10.6.18. To U.K. in Command of Cadre, April, '19.	Mons, '14. Marne, '14. Aisne, '14. Ypres, '14. Arras, '18. Selle, '18. Sambre, '18.	Bn. T.O. till 9.11.14. C.O., 10.6.18, to end of war.
Anderson, F. J.	2nd Lieut.	From U.K. (Reg.), 25.8.18.	Arras, '18. Hindenburg Line, '18. Selle, '18. Sambre, '18.	Nil.
Anderson, J.	2nd Lieut.	From U.K., Temp. commission in B.W., 8.5.16. W., 2.9.16.	Somme, '16.	Nil.
Anderson, R. C.	Lieut.	With Bn. to France, Aug., '14. W., 27.10.14. R., 18.5.15. W., 25.9.15. D. of W., 27.9.15.	Mons, '14. Marne, '14. Aisne, '14. Ypres, '14. Loos, '14.	Capt.
Anderson, T. B.	2nd Lieut.	From 8th B.W. on T/Com. from Ranks, 30.10.15. D. of W., 22.11.16.	Somme, '16.	Nil.
Anstruther, R. E.	Lieut.	With Bn. to France, Aug., '14. W., 14.9.14. R., 3.1.15. W., 25.1.15. Subsequently to 8th Bn.	Mons, '14. Marne, '14. Aisne, '14. Cuinchy, '15.	Nil.
Arbuthnott, R. K.	2nd Lieut.	From U.K. (Reg.), 22.9.16. P. of W., 18.4.18.	Somme, '16. Nieuport, '17. The Lys, '18.	Lt. A/Capt., 3.12.17 to 16.1.18 and 17.2.18
Armytage, E. O.	2nd Lieut.	From 3rd B.W., 23.6.16. W., 1.7.16.	Somme, '16.	Nil.
Baillie-Hamilton, N. A. B.	Major	From G. Staff (Reg., B.W.), 27.7.17. To 1st S.W.B., 31.7.17.	Ypres, '17.	Nil.
Ballantyne, A.	2nd Lieut.	From London Scottish on T/Com. to B.W., 25.9.15. K., 13.10.15.	Loos, '15. Hohenzollern Redoubt, '15.	Nil.
Balmain, W.	2nd Lieut	Com. from Ranks, 24.6.17, after 4 yrs. service. K., 18.4.18.	Nieuport, '17. Ypres, '17. The Lys, '18.	Nil.
Baxter, D.	2nd Lieut.	From 3rd B.W., 24.5.18.	Arras, '18. Hindenburg Line, '18. Selle, '18. Sambre, '18.	Nil.

Name	Rank on joining or commencement of campaign	Record	Actions at which present	Promotions and Regimental Appointments
Blair, P. E. A.	2nd Lieut.	With Bn. to France. K., 29.10.14.	Mons, '14. Marne, '14. Aisne, '14. Ypres, '14.	Nil.
Bone, G. D.	2nd Lieut.	Com. from Ranks, 28.2.15, after 9 yrs. 5 mths. service. K., 9.5.15.	Neuve Chapelle, '15. Aubers Ridge, '15.	Nil.
Bowes-Lyon, C. L. C.	Lieut.	From 3rd Bn., 21.9.14. W., 6.10.14. K., 23.10.14.	Aisne, '14. Ypres, '14.	Nil.
Boyd, H. L. F.	Lieut.	From U.K. (Reg.), 24.3.16. W., 27.5.16. R., 24.2.17. K., 18.11.17.	Nieuport, '17. Ypres, '17.	T/Capt., 19.5.16 to 27.5.16. Capt., 17.7.16.
Boyd, N. J. L.	2nd Lieut.	With Bn. to France. W., 14.9.14. Subsequently D. of W.	Mons, '14. Marne, '14. Aisne, '14.	Nil.
Brown, I. D.	2nd Lieut.	From U.K. (Reg.), 18.10.15. W., 15.4.16. R., 6.4.18. To H.Q. IV. Corps, 27.4.18.	The Lys, '18.	T/Lt., 10.5.15.
Brown, J.	2nd Lieut.	From 7th B.W., 15.1.17. To U.K., 2.8.18.	Nieuport, '17. Ypres, '17. The Lys, '17.	Nil.
Brown, O. S.	2nd Lieut.	From 3rd B.W., 23.10.15. K., 22.12.15.	Nil.	Nil.
Bucknall, W. R.	2nd Lieut.	From U.K. (Reg.), 17.5.16. W., 18.5.16.	Nil.	Nil.
Buist, K.	2nd Lieut.	From 2nd B.W., 14.11.14. K., 25.1.15.	Ypres, '14. Givenchy, '15. Cuinchy, '15.	Lt., 29.12.14.

Name	Rank	Service	Battles	Honours
Bulloch, R. A.	Major	From 23rd Inf. Bde. (Reg. B.W.), 14.4.16. To Bde.-Major 57th Inf. Bde., 17.4.16.	Nil.	Nil.
Burnett, G.	2nd Lieut.	Com. from Ranks, 30.4.17, after 3 yrs. 11 mths. service. To U.K., 8.3.18. R., 24.10.18.	Nieuport, '17. Ypres, '17. Selle, '18. Sambre, '18.	Nil.
Burton, G. S. M.	2nd Lieut.	From U.K. (Reg.), 13.11.16. W., 17.11.17. R., 8.1.18. W., 17.10.18.	Nieuport, '17. Ypres, '17. The Lys, '18. Arras, '18. Hindenburg Line, '18. Selle, '18. Sambre, '18.	Lt., 17.3.17. A/Capt. 3.5.18 to end of War.
Bushe, W. F.	Lieut.	From 3rd B.W., 1.11.18.	Nil.	Nil.
Campbell, J. A. S.	2nd Lieut.	From 6th Cameron Highrs. on T/Com. to B.W., 16.12.15. S., 3.2.16.	Nil.	Nil.
Campbell, P. K.	2nd Lieut.	With Bn. to France. W., 14.9.14. R., 27.2.15. S., 12.3.15. R., 23.7.15. W., 26.9.15. R., 13.1.17. S., 4.5.17.	Mons, '14. Marne, '14. Aisne, '14. Neuve Chapelle, '15. Loos, '15.	Lt. T/Capt., 13.8.15. Capt., 1.1.17.
Carthew-Yorstoun, M. A.	2nd Lieut.	From U.K. (Reg.), 1.11.16. To H.Q. 1st Div. as A.D.C., Feb., '17.	Nil.	Nil.
Chalmer, F. G.	Lieut.	With Bn. to France, Aug., '14. W., 26.10.14. R., 13.5.15. To Bde. H.Q., 25.5.15.	Mons, '14. Marne, '14. Aisne, '14. Ypres, '14.	Capt., 26.9.14. Bt. Major, 1.1.17.
Christie, D. C.	2nd Lieut.	From 10th B.W., 1.11.18. To U.K. with Cadre, April, '19.	Sambre, '18.	Nil.
Christie, J.	2nd Lieut.	Com. from Ranks, after 1 yr. 11 mths. service, 5.7.18.	Arras, '18. Hindenburg Line, '18. Selle, '18. Sambre, '18.	Nil.

Name	Rank on joining or commencement of campaign	Record	Actions at which present	Promotions and Regimental Appointments
Clark, A. B.	2nd Lieut.	From 3rd B.W., 18.4.16. To U.K. on duty, 1.1.17. R., 8.6.17. H.Q. R.F.C., 19.12.17, or subsequently K.	Somme, '16. Nieuport, '17. Ypres, '17.	A/Adjt., 8.6.17 to 19.12.17. T/Capt., 15.9.16 to 1.1.17.
Colquhoun, P. H. L. C.	2nd Lieut.	From 3rd B.W., 22.5.15. S., 4.9.15. R., 16.12.15. W., 18.5.16. R., Feb., '17. To Second Army School, 12.3.18. R., 6.8.18. K., 19.9.18.	Nieuport, '17. Ypres, '17. Arras, '18. Hindenburg Line, '18.	Lt, 18.10.15. T/Capt 22.1.16 to 19.5.16.
Cooke, D.	2nd Lieut.	From 3rd B.W., 12.5.15. W., 25.9.15. R. from Fifth Army as a Captain, 3.1.18. K., 18.4.18.	Loos, '15. The Lys, '18.	Lt. A/Capt.
Cook, R.	Lieut.	From 3rd B.W., 8.9.16. To U.K., 1.2.18. R., 13.7.18. W., 3.9.18.	Somme, '16. Nieuport, '17. Ypres, '17. Arras, '18.	A/Capt., 1918.
Cumming, L. R.	Lieut.	With Bn. to France, Aug., '14. K., 14.9.14.	Mons, '14. Marne, '14. Aisne, '14.	Scout Officer.
Daglish, C. A. de G.	Captain	With Bn. to France, Aug., '14. W., 8.9.14. D. of W., 9.9.14.	Mons, '14. Marne, '14.	Nil.
Daly, D. C.	2nd Lieut.	From U.K. (Reg.), 8.5.18. S., 19.6.18. R., 23.7.18. S., 29.7.18.	Nil.	Nil.
Davie, S. H.	2nd Lieut.	From U.K., 6.8.18.	Arras, '18. Hindenburg Line, '18. Selle, '18. Sambre, '18.	Nil.

Deas, J. C.	2nd Lieut.	From 3rd B.W., 19.9.16. S., 18.12.16.	Somme, '16.	Nil.
Dempster, A. J. H.	2nd Lieut.	From U.K. (Reg.), 25.8.18.	Arras, '18. Hindenburg Line, '18. Selle, '18. Sambre, '18.	Nil.
Denniston, J. E.	2nd Lieut.	From 10th B.W., 6.6.16. W., 19.7.16. R., 24.7.16. W., 20.9.16. D. of W., 20.9.16.	Somme, '16.	Nil.
Dickie, C. B.	2nd Lieut.	From 11th B.W., 26.8.16. S., 13.11.16. R., 9.2.17. To H.Q., R.F.C., 9.12.17.	Somme, '16. Nieuport, '17. Ypres, '17.	Lt., 15.2.17.
Dixon, F. J. C.	2nd Lieut.	From 6th Cameron Hrs. on Temporary Commission to B.W., 12.6.16. W. (slight), 18.6.16. W., 4.9.16. D. of W., 6.9.16.	Somme, '16.	Nil.
Don, R. G.	2nd Lieut.	With Bn. to France, Aug., '14. K., 14.9.14.	Mons, '14. Marne, '14. Aisne, '14.	Nil.
Drumlanrig, F.A.K.D., Viscount	Lieut.	From U.K. (Reg.), 24.3.16. S., 26.4.16.	Nil.	Nil.
Drummond, M. C. A., Hon.	Captain	With Bn. to France, Aug., '14. W., 8.9.14.	Mons, '14. Marne, '14.	Nil.
Duff, R. D.	2nd Lieut.	From 11th B.W., 26.8.16. S., 15.11.16. R., 23.11.16. W. (shell shock), 29.6.17.	Somme, '16.	Nil.
Duncan, A. G.	Captain	From London Scottish for attachment, Nov., '17. Transferred to B.W. (Reg.), 16.1.18.	Ypres, '17. The Lys, '18. Arras, '18. Hindenburg Line, '18. Selle, '18. Sambre, '18.	Nil.
Edwards, W. H. C.	Lieut.	From U.K. (Reg.), 22.11.14. K., 9.5.15.	Ypres, '14. Givenchy, '14. Cuinchy, '15. Neuve Chapelle, '15. Aubers Ridge, '15.	Nil.

Name	Rank on joining or commencement of campaign	Record	Actions at which present	Promotions and Regimental Appointments
Erskine-Bolst, C. C.	Lieut.	From 3rd B.W., 23.8.15. Gassed, 27.9.15.	Loos, '15.	Nil.
Evans, L. P.	Captain	From attachment to R.F.C., 22.12.14. To Bde.-Major 7th Inf. Bde., 1.5.15. R. as C.O. (A/Lt.-Col.), 17.1.18. To Command of 14th Inf. Bde., 10.6.18.	Givenchy, '14. Cuinchy, '15. Neuve Chapelle, '15. The Lys, '18.	C.O., 17.1.18 to 10.6.18.
Feiling, H. St. L.	2nd Lieut.	From 3rd B.W., 6.12.15. S., 5.3.16. R., 24.4.16. K., 20.11.16.	Somme, '16.	T/Capt., 25.10.16 to 1.11.16.
Ferguson, G. W.	2nd Lieut.	Commissioned from ranks, after 4 yrs. 6 mths. service, 1.5.17. S., 15.6.18.	Nieuport, '17. Ypres, '17. The Lys, '18.	Nil.
Ferrier-Kerr, A.	2nd Lieut.	From U.K. (Reg.), 13.10.16. S., 18.10.16.	Nil.	Nil.
Forman, G. E.	2nd Lieut.	From U.K. (Reg.), 25.5.15. S., 19.6.16.	Loos, '15. Hohenzollern Redoubt, '15.	Lt.
Forrester, R. E.	Captain	From U.K. (Reg.), 18.5.15. K., 16.6.15.	Nil.	Nil.
Fortune, V. M.	Lieut.	With Bn. to France, Aug., '14. To B.M. 1st Inf. Bde., 30.9.15. R. as C.O., 16.9.16. To Fourth Army Musketry School, 17.1.18.	Mons, '14. Marne, '14. Aisne, '14. Ypres, '14. Givenchy, '14. Cuinchy, '15. Neuve Chapelle, '15. Aubers Ridge, '15. Loos, '15. Somme, '16. Nieuport, '17. Ypres, '17.	Capt., 17.9.14. Adjt., 11.11.14 to 30.9.15. C.O., 16.9.16 to 17.1.18. A/Lt.-Col., 30.9.16.

Fowler, W.	Lt. & Qr.Mr.	With Bn. to France as Q.M., Aug., '14. To U.K. on posting to S.A. School as Adjt. and Q.M., Feb., '19.	Mons, '14. Marne, '14. Aisne, '14. Ypres, '14. Givenchy, '14. Cuinchy, '15. Neuve Chapelle, '15. Aubers Ridge, '15. Loos, '15. Hohenzollern Redoubt, '15. Somme, '16. Nieuport, '17. Ypres, '17. The Lys, '18. Arras, '18. Hindenburg Line, '18. The Selle, '18. Sambre, '18.	Q.M. to the Bn. for the whole period of the war.
Foxcroft, H. J.	2nd Lieut.	From 4th B.W., 30.11.17. To Labour Corps, 6.4.18.	Nil.	Nil.
Fraser, A.	2nd Lieut.	From 6th B.W. on Temporary Commission, 22.8.15. K., 13.10.15.	Loos, '15. Hohenzollern Redoubt, '15.	Nil.
Fraser, J. W.	2nd Lieut.	From 4th B.W., 9.2.17. To Base Depot, Etaples, 3.6.18.	Nieuport, '17. Ypres, '17. The Lys, '18.	Nil.
Fraser, W.	2nd Lieut.	From 6th B.W. on Temporary Commission, 22.8.15. W., 26.9.15. D. of W., 29.9.15.	Loos, '15.	Nil.
Fyall, R. K.	2nd Lieut.	From U.K., 8.5.18. S., May, '18. R., 8.6.18. W., 18.10.18.	Arras, '18. Hindenburg Line, '18. Selle, '18.	Nil.
Galbraith, R. G.	Lieut.	From Temporary List, 13.12.17. W., 19.9.18.	The Lys, '18. Arras, '18. Hindenburg Line, '18.	Nil.
Garden, J. W.	2nd Lieut.	From Temporary List B.W., 6.3.15. W., 11.3.15. R., 18.5.15. W. (accidentally), 19.7.15. R., 6.12.15. To M.G.C., 23.1.16.	Neuve Chapelle, '15.	T/Lt., 9.1.16.

Name	Rank on joining or commencement of campaign	Record	Actions at which present	Promotions and Regimental Appointments
Glencross, A.	2nd Lieut.	Commissioned from ranks, after 4 yrs. 11 mths. service, 24.6.17. K., 18.4.18.	Nieuport, '17. Ypres, '17. The Lys, '18.	Nil.
Godfrey, W.	2nd Lieut.	From U.K. (Reg.) B.W., 18.4.16. K. 3.9.16.	Somme, '16.	Nil.
Graham, N.	2nd Lieut.	From 3rd Bn, Oct., '14. W., 5.11.14.	Ypres, '14.	Nil.
Grant, P.	2nd Lieut.	From Temporary List B.W., 30.12.16. S., 14.3.17.	Nil	Nil.
Grant, W. H.	2nd Lieut.	From U.K. (Reg.), 12.8.18. W., 4.11.18.	Arras, '18. Hindenburg Line, '18. Selle, '18. Sambre, '18.	Nil.
Grant-Duff, A.	Lieut.-Col.	With Bn. to France, Aug., '14. K., 14.9.14.	Mons, '14. Marne, '14. Aisne, '14.	C.O.
Gray, A.	2nd Lieut.	Commissioned from ranks, after 20 yrs. 5 mths. service, 10.2.15. S., 14.1.15. R., 6.4.15. K., 9.5.15.	Neuve Chapelle, '15. Aubers Ridge, '15.	Nil.
Green, W.	Captain	With Bn. to France, Aug., '14. W., 15.9.14, and subsequently to Hospitsl, 25.9.14. R., 1.1.15. W., 9.5.15.	Mons, '14. Marne, '14. Aisne, '14. Cuinchy, '15. Neuve Chapelle, '15. Aubers Ridge, '15.	Major, 1.9.15. T/Lt.-Col., 15.6.16.
Gregory-Smith, H. G.	2nd Lieut.	From U.K. (Reg.), 8.8.18. W., 6.9.18.	Arras, '18.	Nil.

Name	Rank	From	Battles	Notes
Gunn, K.	2nd Lieut.	From 3rd B.W., 2.8.15. W., 25.9.15. R., 29.2.16. K., 4.4.16.	Loos, '15.	Lt., 18.10.15.
Gunn, M. S.	2nd Lieut.	From 3rd B.W., 22.5.15. W., 4.9.16. D. of W., 6.9.16.	Loos, '15. Hohenzollern Redoubt, '15. Somme, '16.	Lt., 18.10.15. M.G. Officer.
Guthrie, R. S.	2nd Lieut.	From 2nd Seaforth Hrs. on Temporary Commission from ranks to B.W., 1.11.15. To 1/1 T.M. Battery, 27.1.16.	Nil.	Nil.
Gyle, E. W.	2nd Lieut.	From U.K., 15.10.18. K., 18.10.18.	Selle, '18.	Nil.
Haldane, J. B. S.	2nd Lieut.	From 3rd B.W., 15.2.15. W., 9.5.15.	Neuve Chapelle, '15. Aubers Ridge, '15.	Bn. Bombing Officer.
Hamilton, A. K.	Lieut.	From U. K. (Reg.), 13.10.16. S., 28.6.17.	Nil.	Nil.
Hamilton, J. G. H.	Major	From Regimental Depot as Second-in-Command, 8.1.15. To Command of 154th Bde., 15.9.16.	Cuinchy, '15. Neuve Chapelle, '15. Aubers Ridge, '15. Loos, '15. Hohenzollern Redoubt, '15. Somme, '15.	2nd-in-C., 8.1.15 to 13.7.15. A/C.O., 13.7.15 to 24.9.15. 2nd-in-C., 24.9.15 to 2.1.16. C.O., 2.1.16 to 15.9.16. T/Lt.-Col., 13.8.15 to 24.9.15; 3.2.16 to 14.9.16. Lt.-Col., 15.9.16.
Hamilton, J. S.	2nd Lieut.	From Temporary List B.W., 8.9.16. S., 12.10.16.	Somme, '16.	Nil.
Harrop, W.	2nd Lieut.	From 11th B.W., 13.12.17.	The Lys, '18. Arras, '18. Hindenburg Line, '18. Selle, '18. Sambre, '18.	Lt.

Name	Rank on joining or commencement of campaign	Record	Actions at which present	Promotions and Regimental Appointments
Hart, P. N.	2nd Lieut.	Commissioned from ranks, after 5 yrs. 11 mths. service, 17.2.17 W., 3.3.17.	Nil.	Nil.
Hay, L. F.	2nd Lieut.	From U.K. (Reg.), 21.9.14. W., 22.10.14. R., 21.2.15. W., 25.9.15.	Aisne, '14. Ypres, '14. Neuve Chapelle, '15. Aubers Ridge, '15. Loos, '15.	T/Capt., 9.5.15.
Hayes, H. U.	2nd Lieut.	From U.K. (Reg.), 18.5.15. K., 13.10.15.	Loos, '15. Hohenzollern Redoubt, '15.	Nil.
Hepburn, P. B.	Captain	From 10th B.W., 15.10.18.	Selle, '18. Sambre, '18.	Nil.
Higginbotham, I. K.	2nd Lieut.	From U.K. (Reg.), 8.1.18. S., 21.4.18. R., 8.9.18. W., Nov., '18.	The Lys, '18. Hindenburg Line, '18. Selle, '18. Sambre, '18.	Nil.
Holt, A. V.	Lieut.	From Regimental Depot, 8.9.14. W., 14.9.14. Subsequently to 2nd Bn. and R.F.C.	Marne, '14. Aisne, '14.	Nil.
Home, R. G.	2nd Lieut.	From U.K. (Reg.), 18.5.15. W., 13.10.15. Subsequently to R.F.C.	Loos, '15. Hohenzollern Redoubt, '15.	Nil.
Honeyman, G. E. B.	2nd Lieut.	From U.K. (Reg.), 25.3.17.	Nieuport, '17. Ypres, '17. The Lys, '18. Arras, '18. Hindenburg Line, '18. Selle, '18. Sambre, '18.	Lt. Transport Officer.
Hore-Ruthven, C. M., Hon.	Captain	From U.K. (Reg.), 28.8.14. W., 23.10.14.	Mons, '14. Marne, '14. Aisne, '14. Ypres, '14.	Nil.

Huddleston, S. C.	2nd Lieut.	From 3rd B.W., 22.11.14. K., 25.1.15.	Ypres, '14. Givenchy, '14. Cuinchy, '15.	Nil.
Hume, R. M.	2nd Lieut.	From 5th B.W., Jan., '17. K., 18.4.18.	Nieuport, '17. Ypres, '17. The Lys, '18.	Nil.
Hunter-Gray, G. T.	Major	From 11th B.W., 4.8.16. To U.K. for C.O.'s Course, 7.4.17. R., 3.7.17. To command of 15th Lancs. Fus., 12.7.17.	Somme, '16. Nieuport, '17.	2nd-in-C., 4.8.16 to 12.7.17.
Husband, P. L.	2nd Lieut.	From U.K., 8.9.16. K., 25.9.16.	Somme, '16.	Nil.
Hutchison, R. H.	Lieut.	From 8th B.W., 29.9.15. K., 13.10.15.	Hohenzollern Redoubt, '15.	Nil.
Inglis, J. A.	2nd Lieut.	From 3rd B.W., 10.12.15. W., 2.7.16.	Somme, '16.	Nil.
Jacobs, T. C.	2nd Lieut.	From 11th B.W., 19.9.16. S., 21.1.17. R., 8.6.18. To 1st T.M. Battery, 15.7.18.	Somme, '16.	Nil.
Jalland, H. H.	Lieut.	From 3rd B.W., 15.10.18. K., 18.10.18.	Selle, '18.	
Johnson, S. M.	2nd Lieut.	From U.K. (Reg.), 8.4.17. S., 17.4.18. R., 9.6.18. S., 14.7.18.		
Johnson, T.	Lieut.	From U.K. (Reg.), 24.7.16. W. (slight), 18.8.16. K., 4.9.16.	Somme, '16.	Nil.
Johnstone, B. C.	2nd Lieut.	From 3rd B.W., 24.8.17. Demobilized, 7.3.19.		
Johnstone, N. G.	2nd Lieut.	From Temporary List B.W., 8.9.16. To 1st T.M. Battery, 11.11.16.	Somme, '16.	Nil.

Name	Rank on joining or commencement of campaign	Record	Actions at which present	Promotions and Regimental Appointments
Kedie, W. T.	Captain	From Base duties (Reg. B.W.), 19.11.14. W. (slight), 29.12.14. To Hospital, 20.1.15. R., 12.3.15. W., 9.4.15, and subsequently killed at the Dardanelles.	Ypres, '14. Givenchy, '14. Neuve Chapelle, '15.	Nil.
Kelly, J.	2nd Lieut.	From 11th Hussars on Temporary Commission to B.W., 29.10.15. S., 30.6.16.	Somme, '16.	Nil.
Kilgour, A.	2nd Lieut.	From 7th B.W., 30.11.17. K., 18.4.18.	The Lys, '18.	Nil.
Kimber, J. W.	2nd Lieut.	From 4th B.W., 10.1.17. K., 19.4.18.	Nieuport, '17. Ypres, '17. The Lys, '18.	Nil.
Kirk, D. K.	2nd Lieut.	From U.K. (Reg.), 28.9.14. W., 23.10.14. R. as Lieut., 6.1.16. S., 3.1.17.	Ypres, '14. Somme, '16.	Nil.
Kirkcaldy, G. I.	Lieut.	From R.A.S.C. for attachment, 2.11.17. Transferred to B.W. (Reg.), 19.2.18. P. of W., 18.4.18.	Ypres, '17. The Lys, '18.	Nil.
Krook, A. D. C.	Captain	With Bn. to France, Aug., '14. M. (P. of W.), 29.10.14.	Mons, '14. Marne, '14. Aisne, '14. Ypres, '14.	Nil.

Name	Rank	Service	Engagements	Staff
Lamb, C. W.	2nd Lieut.	From U.K. (Reg.) on Commission from Scots Guards, 22.5.15. W., 13.10.15. R., 1.5.17. To Army Gymnastic Staff, Aldershot, 3.12.17.	Loos, '15. Hohenzollern Redoubt, '15. Nieuport, '17. Ypres, '17.	Nil.
Lane, V. C. T.	2nd Lieut.	From 6th B.W., 28.1.17. To Indian Army, 31.10.17.	Nieuport, '17.	Nil.
Lang, D.	2nd Lieut.	From 7th B.W., 10.1.17. To R.E., 14.2.17.	Nil.	Nil.
Lawson, A.	2nd Lieut.	Commissioned from ranks, after 19 yrs. 6 mths. service, 1.10.14. K., 11.11.14.	Ypres, '14.	Nil.
Leishman, A.	2nd Lieut.	Commissioned from ranks, after 8 yrs. 9 mths. service, 11.3.17. To U.K., 1.3.18.	Nieuport, '17. Ypres, '17.	Nil.
Lindsay, D. C. M.	2nd Lieut.	From 3rd B.W., 13.3.16. W., 17.3.16.	Nil.	Nil.
Livingstone-Learmonth, L. R.	2nd Lieut.	From U.K. (Reg.), 6.12.16. S., 13.11.17.	Nieuport, '17. Ypres, '17.	Lt.
Lumsden, D.	2nd Lieut.	From 3rd Bn. 28.9.14. R., 28.8.15. S., 1.11.14. R., 28.10.15. S., 12.10.15. XIV Corps School, 8.6.17. To '16.	Ypres, '14. Loos, '15. Somme, '16.	A/Adjt., 13.4.17 to 7.6.17. Lt. T/Capt.
Lyle, T. B.	2nd Lieut.	From 3rd B.W., 15.3.15. K., 9.5.15.	Aubers Ridge, '15.	Nil.
Machin, B. W.	2nd Lieut.	From U.K. (Reg.), 24.7.16. S., 10.8.16.	Somme, '16.	Nil.
Makgill-Crichton, J. D. M.	2nd Lieut.	From U.K. (Reg.), 6.12.16. W., 13.12.16.	Nil.	Nil.

Name	Rank on joining or commencement of campaign	Record	Actions at which present	Promotions and Regimental Appointments
Marshall, A.	Lieut.	From U.K., 12.8.18. W., 18.10.18.	Arras, '18. Hindenburg Line, '18. Selle, '18.	Nil.
Masterton, R. J.	2nd Lieut.	From Temporary List B.W., 8.9.16. To 1st T.M. Battery, 20.11.16. R., 25.7.18. S., 30.7.18.	Somme, '16.	Nil.
Mather, A. W.	2nd Lieut.	From 3rd B.W., 19.9.16. To R.A.F., 6.2.17.	Somme, '16.	Nil.
Maxwell, R. S. S.	2nd Lieut.	From U.K. (Reg.), 29.9.14. W., 27.10.14.	Aisne, '14. Ypres, '14.	Nil.
Mercer, A.	2nd Lieut.	Commissioned from ranks, after 16 yrs. 8 mths. service, 17.9.15. W., 13.10.15. Subsequently D. of W. at Le Touquet, 22.10.15.	Loos, '15. Hohenzollern Redoubt, '15.	Nil.
Miles, L. G.	Captain	From U.K. (Reg.), 15.7.18.	Arras, '18. Hindenburg Line, '18. Selle, '18. Sambre, '18.	
Miller, D. A.	2nd Lieut.	From 3rd B.W., 13.2.16. W. (slight), 12.1.16. W., 18.8.16.	Somme, '16.	Nil.
Miller, J.	Lieut.	Commissioned from ranks, after 17 yrs. and 9 mths. service, 17.11.14. S., 7.8.15. R., 22.2.16. To Fourth Army School, 23.10.16.	Ypres, '14. Givenchy, '14. Cuinchy, '15. Neuve Chapelle, '15. Aubers Ridge, '15. Somme, '16.	1.10.15 to 10.11.15. A/Adjt. 1.6.16 to 19.7.16; —.8.16 to 28.9.16; Jan, '17 to 13.4.17. Lt. A/Capt., 26.9.15 to 26.3.17. Capt., 27.3.17.

			Bn. Bombing Officer.
Mitchell, G.	2nd Lieut.	From 3rd B.W., 22.5.15. K. (accidentally), 22.7.15, by explosion of a trench mortar.	Nil.	Nil.
Moffat, R.	2nd Lieut.	From 3rd B.W., 23.6.16. To Corps Area Commandant, 25.1.17. R., 11.4.17. To R.E. Training Centre, U.K., 1.6.17.	Somme, '16.	Nil.
Moir, J. M.	2nd Lieut.	From 9th H.L.I. on Temporary Commission to B.W., 31.7.15. K., 25.9.15.	Loos, '15.	Nil.
Monday, J. C.	2nd Lieut.	From 3rd B.W., 11.1.16. W., 25.4.15.	Nil.	Nil.
Moore, G. G.	2nd Lieut.	From 3rd B.W., 28.10.15. To R.F.C., 4.2.16.	Nil.	T/Lt, 2.10.15.
Moubray, P. L.	Captain	From 3rd B.W., 28.9.14. K., 29.10.14.	Ypres, '14.	Nil.
Muirhead, J.	2nd Lieut.	From U.K. on Temporary Commission to B.W., 6.3.15. W., 3.4.15.	Neuve Chapelle, '15.	Nil.
Munro, D. L.	2nd Lieut.	From 3rd B.W., 23.6.16. W., 18.8.16.	Somme, '16.	Nil.
Murdoch, J.	2nd Lieut.	From Special R. of O., 4.2.15. W., 9.5.15.	Neuve Chapelle, '15. Aubers Ridge, '15.	Nil.
Murdoch, S. I.	2nd Lieut.	From U.K., 1.6.16. W., 14.7.16.	Somme, '16.	Nil.
Murray, A. D., Hon.	Major	From 3rd B.W., 1.11.16. To H.Q. Fourth Army, 11.2.17. R., 10.3.17. To U.K., 30.10.17.	Nieuport, '17. Ypres, '17.	Nil.
Murray, J. C.	2nd Lieut.	From 11th B.W., 8.10.15. S., 4.5.16.	Nil.	Nil.

Name	Rank on joining or commencement of campaign	Record	Actions at which present	Promotions and Regimental Appointments
Murray, J. T. C.	Major	With Bn. to France, Aug., '14. W., 1.11.14. R., 4.2.15. K., (accidentally by hand grenade), 16.2.15.	Mons, '14. Marne, '14. Aisne, '14. Ypres, '14.	2nd-in-C, Aug., '14 to 13.9.14. C.O., 14.9.14 to 1.11.14.
Murray-Menzies, C.W.	2nd Lieut.	From U.K. (Reg.), 3.1.15. K., 25.1.15.	Cuinchy, '15	Nil.
Murray-Menzies, D. I.	2nd Lieut.	From U.K. (Reg.), 7.6.15. To Tank Corps, 4.2.17, and subsequently killed.	Loos, '15. Hohenzollern Redoubt, '15. Somme, '15.	T.O. T/Capt., 17.10.15.
McAndrew, A.	2nd Lieut.	Commissioned from ranks, after 19 yrs. 2 mths. service, 17.11.14. K., 24.12.14.	Ypres, '14. Givenchy, '14.	Nil.
McCall, D.	2nd Lieut.	From Temporary List to B.W., 8.9.16. S., 5.1.17.	Somme, '16.	Nil.
McDougall, F. N.	2nd Lieut.	From 3rd B.W., 23.10.15. W. (slight), 19.7.16. K., 18.8.16.	Somme, '16.	Nil.
Macfarlane, R.	2nd Lieut.	From 3rd B.W., 1.2.15. S., 18.6.15. Subsequently to 2nd Bn. K. in Mesopotamia, 21.4.17.	Neuve Chapelle, '15. Aubers Ridge, '15.	T/Lt, 12.6.15. M.G. Officer.
Macfarlane-Grieve, G. M.	2nd Lieut.	From 3rd B.W., 8.9.16. W., 25.9.16.	Somme, '16.	Nil.
McGregor, D. N. M.	2nd Lieut.	From U.K. (Reg.), 8.9.16. S. when on leave, 2.1.17. R., 1.5.17. To U.K., 15.2.18.	Somme, '16. Nieuport, '17. Ypres, '17.	Nil.

MacKay, P. W.	2nd Lieut.	From U.K. (Reg.), 19.9.16. W., 25.6.17. R., 16.8.17. P. of W., 18.4.18.	Somme, '16. Ypres, '17. The Lys, '18.	Nil.
McKenzie, D.	2nd Lieut.	Commissioned from ranks, 13.2.16. S., 23.4.16.	Nil.	Nil.
McKenzie, R. I.	2nd Lieut.	From U.K. (Reg.), 10.1.15. D. of W., 11.4.15.	Cuinchy, '15. Neuve Chapelle, '15.	Nil.
McKenzie, W.	2nd Lieut.	Commissioned from ranks, after 6 yrs. 3 mths. service, 18.6.16. W., 25.8.16. R., 1.5.17. S., 28.5.17.	Somme, '16.	Nil.
McLeod, N. D.	2nd Lieut.	From U.K. (Reg.), 25.5.15. S., 17.10.15. R., 4.11.15. To U.K. for 6 mths. tour of duty, —.9.17. R., 22.4.18.	Loos, '15. Hohenzollern Redoubt, '15. Somme, '16. Nieuport, '17. The Lys, '18. Arras, '18. Hindenburg Line, '18. Selle, '18. Sambre, '18.	Lt., A/Capt., 24.10.16.
McMicking, N.	Captain	From U.K. (Reg.), 21.3.17. To H.Q. 24th Div. as G.S.O., 31.5.17.	Nil.	Nil.
McMillan, N.	2nd Lieut.	From U.K., 11.6.16. K. (accidentally by hand grenade), 29.11.16.	Somme, '16.	Nil.
McNaughton, A. C. R. S.	Lieut.	From 3rd Bn., 3.9.14. K., 29.10.14.	Marne, '14. Aisne, '14. Ypres, '14.	Nil.
McNaughton, M. L.	2nd Lieut.	From U.K., 5.7.18. S., 20.10.18.	Arras, '18. Hindenburg Line, '18. Selle, '18.	Nil.
McNeil, J.	2nd Lieut.	From U.K., 29.9.18.	Hindenburg Line, '18. Selle, '18. Sambre, '18.	Nil.
McNeill, N.	2nd Lieut.	From 3rd B.W., 28.9.14. K., 11.11.14.	Ypres, '14.	Nil.

Name	Rank on joining or commencement of campaign	Record	Actions at which present	Promotions and Regimental Appointments
McPherson, R. S. L.	Lieut.	From 3rd B.W., 11.7.16. W., 18.8.16.	Somme, '16.	Nil.
MacRae, K. S.	2nd Lieut.	With Bn. to France, Aug., '14. W., 24.10.14.	Mons, '14. Marne, '14. Aisne, '14. Ypres, '14. Selle, '18. Sambre, '18.	Nil.
Noble, M. H. N. A.	Lieut.	From U.K. (Reg.), 15.10.18.	Aisne, '14. Ypres, '14.	Nil.
Nolan, R. P. D.	Lieut.	From 3rd Bn., 21.9.14. K., 2.11.14.		Nil.
Paton, J. L.	2nd Lieut.	From 3rd B.W., 25.5.15. S., 18.6.15. R., 24.7.15. K., 13.10.15.	Loos, '15. Hohenzollern Redoubt, '15.	Nil.
Pennington, J.	2nd Lieut.	From U.K., 22.7.18.	Arras, '18. Hindenburg Line, '18. Selle, '18. Sambre, '18.	Nil.
Polson, G. W.	2nd Lieut.	With Bn. to France, Aug., '14. K., 15.9.14.	Mons, '14. Marne, '14. Aisne, '14.	Nil.
Preston, H. S.	2nd Lieut.	From U.K., 29.4.16. W., 3.9.16. D. of W., 8.9.16.	Somme, '16.	Nil.
Purvis, R. M.	2nd Lieut.	From 3rd B.W., 12.3.15. S., 21.3.15. Subsequently to 2nd Bn. and D. of W., 14.3.17.	Neuve Chapelle, '15.	Nil.
Ramage, W.	2nd Lieut.	Commissioned from ranks, after 6 yrs. 8 mths. service, 13.11.16. To U.K. (M.G.C.), 10.12.17.	Nieuport, '17. Ypres, '17.	Nil.
Ramsay, R.	2nd Lieut.	From 3rd B.W., 8.1.18. M., 18.4.18.	The Lys, '18.	Nil.

Name	Rank	Service	Engagements	Remarks
Rennie, J. L.	2nd Lieut.	With Bn. to France, Aug., '14. W., 14.9.14. R., 1.11.14. W., 2.11.14.	Mons, '14. Marne, '14. Aisne, '14. Ypres, '14.	Lt., 9.9.14.
Richard, J. E. M.	2nd Lieut.	From U.K. (Reg.), Jan., '15. W., 9.5.15.	Cuinchy, '15. Neuve Chapelle, '15. Aubers Ridge, '15.	Lt., 21.4.15.
Richmond, G. M.	2nd Lieut.	From 3rd B.W., 20.11.14. W., 25.1.15. R., 23.10.15. W., 21.12.15.	Ypres, '14. Givenchy, '14. Cuinchy, '15.	Nil.
Ritchie, A. F.	2nd Lieut.	From 10th B.W. (Reg.), 1.11.18.	The Lys, '18. Arras, '18. Hindenburg Line, '18. Selle, '18. Sambre, '18.	Nil.
Ritchie, N. M.	2nd Lieut.	From U.K. (Reg.), 18.5.15. W., 26.9.15. Subsequently to 2nd Bn.	Loos, '15.	Nil.
Robertson, A. F. W.	2nd Lieut.	From U.K., 12.8.18.	Aubers Ridge, '15.	Nil.
Robertson, F. M. B.	Major	From U.K. (Reg.), 8.5.15. W., 9.5.15.		
Robertson, H. J. G.	2nd Lieut.	From 3rd B.W., 11.5.15. K., 25.9.15.	Loos, '15.	Nil.
Robertson, J. W. H.	Lieut.	From 4th B.W., 13.10.16. To First Army Musketry School, R., 17.6.18.	Somme, '16.	A/Capt., 1917, 1918.
Robson, J.	2nd Lieut.	From Temporary List B.W., 12.6.16. W., 27.8.16.	Somme, '16.	Nil.
Rollo, J. E. H.	2nd Lieut.	With Bn. to France, Aug., '14. S., 28.10.14.	Mons, '14. Marne, '14. Aisne, '14. Ypres, '14.	Nil.
Ross, W. E.	2nd Lieut.	From Temporary List B.W., 8.9.16. W., 25.9.16.	Somme, '16.	Nil.
Rowan-Hamilton, G. B.	Lieut.	With Bn. as Adjt. to France, Aug., '14. W., 11.11.14.	Mons, '14. Marne, '14. Aisne, '14. Ypres, '14.	Capt., 17.9.14. Adjt. to 11.11.14.

Name	Rank on joining or commencement of campaign	Record	Actions at which present	Promotions and Regimental Appointments
Rusk, G. A.	Lieut.	From 10th B.W. (Reg.), 1.11.18.	Sambre, '18.	Nil.
Rycroft, J. N. O.	2nd Lieut.	To France as A.D.C. to G.O.C. 1st Div. in Aug., '14. To Div. H.Q., 25.11.14. R. as Adjt., 4.11.15. W., 1.6.16. R., 19.7.16. S., 2.8.16. R., 28.9.16. To B.M. 106th Inf. Bde., 13.3.17.	Ypres, '14. Somme, '16.	T/Capt., 1918. Adjt., 11.11.15 to Jan., '17. T/Major, 7.2.16. to 2.6.16.
Sarjeant, L. J.	2nd Lieut.	From 3rd B.W., 22.9.16. To XIV Corps Inf. School, 8.6.17.	Somme, '16.	Nil.
Scott, J. G.	2nd Lieut.	From 3rd B.W., 25.1.15. K., 9.5.15.	Cuinchy, '15. Neuve Chapelle, '15. Aubers Ridge, '15.	Nil.
Scott, J. M.	2nd Lieut.	From 11th B.W., 8.10.15. K., 18.8.16.	Hohenzollern Redoubt, '15. Somme, '16.	Nil.
Shand, A.	2nd Lieut.	Commissioned from ranks, 24.12.14, after 8 yrs. 8 mths. service. K., 9.5.15.	Cuinchy, '15. Neuve Chapelle, '15. Aubers Ridge, '15.	Nil.
Sinclair, G. J.	2nd Lieut.	From U.K. (Reg.), 29.4.16. W., 26.7.16. R., 13.1.17. K., 18.4.18.	Somme, '16. Nieuport, '17. Ypres, '17. The Lys, '18.	Lt. A/Capt., 1918.
Skene, P. G. M.	Captain	From U.K. (Reg.), 8.1.15. W., 25.1.15.	Cuinchy, '15.	Nil.
Skey, C. H.	Lieut.	From 19th Bn. R. Fus. on transfer, 18.6.16. K., 18.8.16.	Somme, '16.	Nil.

Name	Rank	Service	Battles	Notes
Smith, C. A.	2nd Lieut.	From U.K., 15.5.18. W., 24.6.18. R., 29.6.18. S., 1.7.18. R., 27.7.18.	Arras, '18. Hindenburg Line, '18. Selle, '18. Sambre, '18.	Nil.
Smith, D.	2nd Lieut.	Commissioned from ranks after 9 yrs. 6 mths. service, 8.1.18. K., 18.10.18.	The Lys, '18. Arras, '18. Hindenburg Line, '18. Selle, '18.	Nil.
Smith, H. H.	2nd Lieut.	From U.K., 8.5.18. K., 19.9.18.	Arras, '18. Hindenburg Line, '18.	Nil.
Smith, J. A.	2nd Lieut.	From 5th B.W., 10.1.17. Demobilized, 10.2.19.		
Sprot, J. W. L.	Lieut.	From T. F. Adjutancy (Reg.) in U.K., 7.11.14. K., 11.11.14.	Ypres, '14.	Nil.
Stephen, J. C.	2nd Lieut.	From U.K. (Reg.), 13.10.16. S., 10.4.17. R., 30.11.17. P. of W., 18.4.18.	Somme, '16. The Lys, '18.	Nil.
Steuart, B. C. A.	Captain	From Base (R. of Officers B.W.), 29.6.17. S., 31.8.17.		
Stewart, C. E.	Lieut.-Col.	From 2nd Bn., 1.11.14. Command vice Lieut.-Col. A. Grant-Duff, C.B., K. W., 11.11.14. R., 18.11.14. S., 13.7.15. R., 24.9.15. To Command of 154th Bde., 3.1.16, and subsequently killed in action, 14.9.16.	Ypres, '14. Givenchy, '14. Cuinchy, '15. Neuve Chapelle, '15. Aubers Ridge '15 Loos, '15. Hohenzollern Redoubt, '15.	C.O., 1.11.14 to 13.7.15; 25.9.15 to 2.1.16.
Stewart, D. I.	2nd Lieut.	From U.K. (Reg.), 3.3.17.	Nieuport, '17. Ypres, '17. The Lys, '18. Arras, '18. Hindenburg Line, '18. Selle, '18. Sambre, '18.	Lt. A/Capt, 1918.

Name	Rank on joining or commencement of campaign	Record	Actions at which present	Promotions and Regimental Appointments
Stewart, J.	2nd Lieut.	From 11th B.W., 6.6.16. To No. 35 P. of W. Co., 11.3.17.	Somme, '16.	Nil.
Stewart, J. B.	2nd Lieut.	From U.K. (Reg.), 13.11.16. S., 7.12.16. R., 1.5.17. W., 29.9.18.	Nieuport, '17. Ypres, '17. The Lys, '18. Arras, '18. Hindenburg Line, '18.	T.O., May, '17, to October, '17.
Stewart, U.	2nd Lieut.	From U.K., 15.10.18.	Selle, '18. Sambre, '18.	Nil.
Stewart, W. D. McL.	2nd Lieut.	From U.K. (Reg.), 18.10.15. K., 25.9.16.	Somme, '16.	T/Lt., 2.11.14 to 29.1.15. Lt., 30.1.15. T/Capt., 20.10.15. Capt., 17.7.16.
Stewart-Murray, Lord G.	Major	With Bn. to France, Aug., '14. K., 19.9.14.	Mons, '14. Marne, '14. Aisne, '14. Ypres, '14.	Nil.
Stewart-Richardson, Sir Edward, Bt.	Captain	From 3rd B.W., 28.9.14. W., 27.10.14, and subsequently D. of W. in U.K.	Ypres, '14.	Nil.
Stewart-Smith, D. C. [D. S.	Lieut.	From 3rd B.W., 9.2.17. W. and P. of W., 18.4.18. [26.10.14.	Nieuport, '17. Ypres, '17. The Lys, '18.	Nil.
Stirling-Smurthwaite,	2nd Lieut.	From U.K. (Reg.), 28.9.14. K.,	Ypres, '14.	Nil.
Sutherland, H. H.	Major.	From U.K. (Reg.), 25.5.15. To Command of 10th Bn. Gloucester Regt., 30.9.15. Subsequently to Command of 7th B.W.	Loos, '15.	Nil.
Tarbutt, A. C.	2nd Lieut.	From 11th B.W, 9.9.16. S., 28.9.16. R., 5.10.16. To U.K., 15.2.18. R., 18.10.18.	Somme, '16. Nieuport, '17. Ypres, '17. Selle, '18. Sambre, '18.	Nil.

Name	Rank	Service	Engagements	Casualty
Taylor, W. S.	2nd Lieut.	From 7th B.W., 10.1.17. W., 27.6.17.	Nil.	Nil.
Templeton, A. A.	2nd Lieut.	From Temporary List B.W., 6.6.16. W., 17.8.16.	Somme, '16.	Lt, 15.2.17.
Thomson, G. E. C.	2nd Lieut.	From U.K., —.11.17. K., 17.11.17.	Ypres, '17.	Nil.
Thomson, R. J.	2nd Lieut.	From 3rd B.W., 8.10.15. S., 8.11.15. R., 18.11.15. To H.Q. 30th Div., 28.1.16.	Hohenzollern Redoubt, '15.	Nil.
Thomson, W. V.	2nd Lieut.	From 7th B.W., 13.8.17. Demobilized, 27.1.19.		Nil.
Thrupp, R. L.	2nd Lieut.	From U.K. (Reg.), 8.4.17. W., 19.12.17.	Nieuport, '17. Ypres, '17.	Nil.
Tod, M.	2nd Lieut.	From U.K. (Reg.), 13.11.16. To R.F.C., 8.2.17.	Nil.	Nil.
Urquhart, E. F. M.	Captain	From U.K. (Reg.), 28.9.14. K., 23.10.14.	Ypres, '14.	Nil.
Urquhart, P.	2nd Lieut.	From 3rd B.W., 21.9.16. To 1st Bde. H.Q. (Gas Officer), 5.10.18.	Somme, '16. Nieuport, '17. Ypres, '17. The Lys, '18.	
Urquhart, W.	2nd Lieut.	From Temporary List B.W., 8.10.15. W. (accidentally), 11.11.15. R., 28.1.16. K., 17.8.16.	Hohenzollern Redoubt, '15. Somme, '16.	Nil.
Valentine, B. G.	2nd Lieut.	From 4th B.W., 10.1.17. W., 4.11.18.	Nieuport, '17. Ypres, '17. The Lys, '18. Arras, '18. Hindenburg Line, '18. Selle, '18. Sambre, '18.	Lt.
Walker, J.	2nd Lieut.	From 3rd B.W., 15.10.18.	Selle, '18. Sambre, '18.	Nil.

Name	Rank on joining or commencement of campaign	Record	Actions at which present	Promotions and Regimental Appointments
Wallace, J.	2nd Lieut.	Commissioned from ranks, after 19 yrs. 9 mths. service, 7.3.15. K., 9.5.15.	Neuve Chapelle, '15. Aubers Ridge, '15.	Nil.
Wanliss, A.	2nd Lieut.	Commissioned from ranks, after 14 yrs. 7 mths. service, 1.10.14. W., 2.11.14. R., 12.3.15. K., 9.5.15.	Ypres, '14. Neuve Chapelle, '15. Aubers Ridge, '15.	Nil.
Wells, J. R.	2nd Lieut.	From Temporary List B.W., 12.6.16. W. (slight), 18.8.16. W., 3.9.16.	Somme, '16.	Nil.
West, C C..	Captain	From Regimental Depot (Reg.), 28.9.14. W., 11.11.14.	Ypres, '14.	Nil.
West, H.	2nd Lieut.	From H. A. C. on Temporary Commission to B.W., 29.4.15. K. 9.5.15.	Aubers Ridge, '15.	Nil.
Whyte, R. B.	2nd Lieut.	From 3rd B.W., 18.5.15. K., 25.9.15.	Loos, '15.	Nil.
Whyte, W. J.	Lieut.	From Scots Guards on Commission from ranks, 22.7.18. K., 28.9.18.	Arras, '18. Hindenburg Line, '18.	Nil.
Willcocks, J. L.	Lieut.	From H.Q. Indian Corps (Reg.), 28.10.15. To H.Q. First Army as G.S.O., 18.5.16.	Nil.	Nil

Willett, L. H.	2nd Lieut.	From 3rd B.W., 29.11.14. W., 25.1.15. Subsequently with 2nd B.W. in Mesopotamia.	Givenchy, '14. Cuinchy, '15.	Nil.
Wilson, E. H. H. J.	Lieut.	With Bn. to France, Aug., '14. K., 8.9.14.	Mons, '14. Marne, '14.	Nil.
Wilson, E. R.	Lieut. (T/Capt.)	From 10th B.W., 30.9.18. W., 17.10.18. R., 1.11.18.	Selle, '18. Sambre, '18.	Nil.
Wilson, E. W. D.	2nd Lieut.	From 3rd B.W., 19.9.16. S., 14.2.17.	Somme, '16.	Nil.
Wilson, W.	Lieut.	From 10th B.W. (Reg.), 1.11.18.	Sambre, '18.	Nil.
Webster, W. B.	2nd Lieut.	From U.K., 17.5.18. S., 21.11.18.		
Young, G. F.	2nd Lieut.	From H.L.I. on Temporary Commission to B.W., 5.9.15. W., 13.10.15.	Loos, '15. Hohenzollern Redoubt, '15.	Nil.
Young, J. S.	2nd Lieut.	From 11th B.W., 26.8.16.	Somme,' 16. Nieuport, '17. Ypres, '17. The Lys, '18. Arras, '18. Hindenburg Line, '18. Selle, '18. Sambre, '18.	A/Adjt., 20.12.17 to end of war.

APPENDIX II

Summary of Casualties. The First Battalion

The discrepancy between these figures and those given by the war diaries is accounted for by the fact that, save in the case of regular battalions, the diaries seldom give a record of casualties other than those suffered in main actions.

OFFICERS, 1914-18

Year.	Killed and Died of Wounds.	Wounded.	Missing.	Total.	Year.
1914	20	29	1	50	1914
1915	29	23	0	52	1915
1916	15	28	0	43	1916
1917	2	5	0	7	1917
1918	18	14	7	39	1918
Totals:	84	99	8	191	Officers.

OTHER RANKS, 1914-18

1914	344	457	148	949	1914
1915	627	930	236	1793	1915
1916	318	763	113	1194	1916
1917	61	120	16	197	1917
1918	199	616	282	1097	1918
Totals:	1549	2886	795	5230	Other ranks

Note.—(a) Of the missing only 301 were reported as prisoners, the remaining 494 may therefore be added to the number of dead.

TOTAL: ALL RANKS

1633 K.   2985 W.   803 M.   Total 5421

APPENDIX III

Casualties—Officers

THE FIRST BATTALION

Name.	Rank.	Where killed.
Amery, H. F. S.	Captain	D. of W., U.K., 24.11.15.
Anderson, R. C.	Captain	D. of W., Loos, 27.9.15.
Anderson, T. B.	2nd Lieut.	D. of W., the Somme, 22.11.16
Ballantyne, A.	2nd Lieut.	Hohenzollern Redoubt, 13.10.15.
Balmain, W.	2nd Lieut.	The Lys, 18.4.18.
Blair, P. E. A.	2nd Lieut.	Ypres, 29.10.14.
Bone, G.	2nd Lieut.	Aubers Ridge, 9.5.15.
Bowes-Lyon, C. L. C.	Lieut.	Ypres, 23.10.14.
Boyd, H. L. F.	Captain	Ypres, 18.11.17.
Boyd, N. J. L.	2nd Lieut.	D. of W., the Aisne, 14.9.14.
Brown, O. S.	2nd Lieut.	Trench warfare, 22.12.15.
Buist, K.	Lieut.	Cuinchy, 25.1.15.
Colquhoun, P. H. L. C.	Captain	Hindenburg Line, 19.9.18.
Cooke, D.	Captain	The Lys, 18.4.18.
Cumming, L. R.	Lieut.	The Aisne, 14.9.14.
Dalglish, G. A. de G.	Captain	D. of W., the Marne, 9.9.14.
Denniston, J. E.	2nd Lieut.	D. of W., the Somme, 20.9.16.
Dixon, F. J. C.	2nd Lieut.	D. of W., the Somme, 6.9.16.
Don, R. D.	2nd Lieut.	The Aisne, 14.9.14.
Edwards, W. H. C.	Lieut.	Aubers Ridge, 9.5.15.
Feiling, H. St. L.	T/Captain	Trench warfare, 20.11.16.
Forrester, R. E.	Captain	Trench warfare, 16.6.15.
Fraser, A.	2nd Lieut.	Hohenzollern Redoubt, 13.10.15.
Fraser, W.	2nd Lieut.	D. of W., Loos, 29.9.15.
Glencross, A.	2nd Lieut.	The Lys, 18.4.18.
Godfrey, W. J.	2nd Lieut.	The Somme, 3.9.16.
Grant-Duff, A.	Lieut.-Colonel	The Aisne, 14.9.14.
Gray, A.	2nd Lieut.	Aubers Ridge, 9.5.15.
Gunn, K.	Lieut.	Trench warfare, 4.4.16.
Gunn, M. S.	Lieut.	D. of W., the Somme, 6.9.16.
Gyle, E. W.	2nd Lieut.	Selle, 18.10.18.
Hayes, H. U.	2nd Lieut.	Hohenzollern Redoubt, 13.10.15.
Huddleston, S. C.	2nd Lieut.	Cuinchy, 25.1.15.
Hume, R. H.	2nd Lieut.	The Lys, 18.4.18.
Husband, P. L.	2nd Lieut.	The Somme, 25.9.16.
Hutchison, R. H.	Lieut.	Hohenzollern Redoubt, 13.10.15.
Jalland, H. H.	Lieut.	Selle, 18.10.18.
Johnson, T.	Lieut.	The Somme, 4.9.16.
Kilgour, A.	2nd Lieut.	The Lys, 18.4.18.
Kimber, J. W.	2nd Lieut.	The Lys, 19.4.18.

THE FIRST BATTALION THE BLACK WATCH

Name.	Rank.	Where killed.
Lawson, A.	2nd Lieut.	Ypres, 11.11.14.
Lyle, T. B.	2nd Lieut.	Aubers Ridge, 9.5.15.
Mercer, A.	2nd Lieut.	D. of W., Le Touquet, 22.10.15.
Mitchell, G.	2nd Lieut.	Accidentally, 22.7.15.
Moir, J.	2nd Lieut.	Loos, 25.9.15.
Moubray, P. L.	Captain	Ypres, 29.10.14.
Murray, J. T. C.	Major	Accidentally, 16.2.15.
Murray-Menzies, C. W.	2nd Lieut.	Cuinchy, 25.1.15.
McAndrew, A.	2nd Lieut.	Givenchy, 24.12.14.
McDoungall, F. N.	2nd Lieut.	The Somme, 18.8.16.
McKenzie, R. I.	2nd Lieut.	D. of W., Trench warfare, 11.4.15.
McMillan, N.	2nd Lieut.	Accidentally, 29.11.16.
McNaughton, A. C. R. S.	Lieut.	Ypres, 29.10.14.
McNeill, M.	2nd Lieut.	Ypres, 11.11.14.
Nolan, R. P. D.	Lieut.	Ypres, 2.11.14.
Paton, J. L.	2nd Lieut.	Hohenzollern Redoubt, 13.10.15.
Polson, G. W.	2nd Lieut.	The Aisne, 15.9.14.
Preston, H. S.	2nd Lieut.	D. of W., the Somme, 8.9.16.
Ramsey, R.	2nd Lieut.	Missing, 18.4.18.
Robertson, H. J. G.	2nd Lieut.	Loos, 25.9.15.
Scott, J. G.	2nd Lieut.	Aubers Ridge, 9.5.15.
Scott, J. H.	2nd Lieut.	The Somme, 18.8.16.
Shand, A.	2nd Lieut.	Aubers Ridge, 9.5.15.
Sinclair, G. J.	Lieut.	The Lys, 18.4.18.
Skey, C. H.	Lieut.	The Somme, 18.8.18.
Smith, D., D.C.M.	2nd Lieut.	Selle, 18.10.18.
Smith, H. H.	2nd Lieut.	Hindenburg Line, 19.9.18.
Sprot, J. W. L.	Lieut.	Ypres, 11. 11.14.
Stewart, W. D. McL.	Captain	The Somme, 25.9.16.
Stewart-Murray, G., Lord.	Major	Ypres, 19.9.14.
Stewart-Richardson, E., Sir., Bt.	Captain	D. of W. in U.K., 17.10.14.
Stirling-Smurthwaite, D. S.	2nd Lieut.	Ypres, 26.10.14.
Thomson, G. E. C.	2nd Lieut.	Ypres, 17.11.17.
Urquhart, E. F. M.	Captain	Ypres, 23.10.14.
Urquhart, W.	2nd Lieut.	The Somme, 17.8.16.
Wallace, J.	2nd Lieut.	Aubers Ridge, 9.5.15.
Wanliss, A.	2nd Lieut.	Aubers Ridge, 9.5.15.
West, H.	2nd Lieut.	Aubers Ridge, 9.5.15.
Whyte, R. B.	2nd Lieut.	Loos, 25.9.15.
Whyte, W. J.	2nd Lieut.	Hindenburg Line, 28.9.18.
Wilson, E. H. H. G.	Lieut.	The Marne, 8.9.14.

APPENDIX III

Name.	Rank.	Where killed.
Attached.		
Jamieson, H. S.	Lieut.	Missing, the Lys, 18.4.18.
Raynes, S. H.	Major	D. of W., the Lys, 20.4.18.
		Colonial R.
Taggart, H. R.	2nd Lieut. A. & S. Hrs.	D. of W., the Lys, 24.7.18.

APPENDIX IV

NOMINAL ROLL OF WARRANT OFFICERS, NON-COMMISSIONED OFFICERS AND MEN KILLED IN ACTION OR DIED OF WOUNDS OR DISEASE IN THE GREAT WAR, 1914-18

Abbreviations.—* Killed in action. † Died of wounds. § Died.
¶ Died at sea. ‡ Died at home.

THE FIRST BATTALION

Abel, A., Pte., 2283	*29.10.14	Armstrong, W., Pte., 9196	*29.10.14
Adam, A., A/Cpl., S/7567	*18.4.18	Arthur, W., Pte., 7395	§21.6.15
Adam, A., Pte., 6000	*18.8.16	Arthur, W., Pte., 3/9539	* 9.5.15
Adam, J., A/Cpl., 1824	*9.5.15	Atkinson, L., Pte., 935	*21.5.16
Adam, P., Pte., S/3933	*20.9.16		
Adams, W., Pte., 3/2714	*9.2.15	Bagan, P., Pte., 11079	† 7.3.16
Adamson, G., Pte., 9422	*9.5.15	Baillie, R., Pte., S/5695	* 9.5.15
Adamson, W., Pte., 3/4112	*9.5.15	Bain, A., Pte., S/10327	† 8.9.16
Ahern, P., Pte., 2255	*14.9.14	Bain, A., L/Cpl., 8370	*18.4.18
Aikman, A., Sgt., 7862	*29.10.14	Baird, J. D., L/Cpl., 1987	*15.9.14
Aird, T., Pte., S/6773	*3.3.17	Baird, N., A/Sgt., 143	*9.5.15
Aitchison, W., Pte., S/9346	*18.4.18	Baird, R., Pte., 292728	*18.4.18
Aitken, W., Pte., 548	†25.9.16	Balfour, D., Pte., 241049	*28.5.18
Alexander, G., A/Sgt., 3/2689	†29.10.14	Balfour, J., Pte., S/40038	†28.6.17
Alexander, G. C., Pte., S/3773		Ballantyne, J., Pte., 1009	†28.10.14
	†28.2.18	Ballingall, J., Pte., 2060	*15.11.14
Alexander, H., Pte., S/6976	*14.7.16	Band, J., L/Cpl., S/7611	*13.10.15
Alexander, J., Pte., 7297	* 5.11.14	Bannerman, R., Pte., 180	*14.9.14
Allan, A., Pte., S/18758	†26.4.18	Barnes, T. H., Pte., S/8277	*23.8.15
Allan, G., L/Sgt., 1662	*29.10.14	Barrowman, T., Pte., S/17573	†20.3.18
Allan, J., Pte., 9055	*18.4.18	Batchelor, W., Pte., 3/4063	*25.1.15
Allan, J., L/Cpl., 345830	*19.9.18	Baxter, W., Pte., 9550	*16.6.15
Allan, R., L/Cpl., S/40217	*25.9.16	Beatts, A., Pte., 2680	* 9.5.15
Anderson, A., Pte., S/4052	†25.10.15	Beaton, A., A/Sgt., 1168	†13.10.15
Anderson, A., Pte., S/14608	*17.11.17	Beaton, J., Pte., 8438	*10.11.14
Anderson, A., A/Cpl., 265	*25.1.15	Beattie, G., Pte., S/7124	*16.12.15
Anderson, D., Pte., 1176	† 9.5.15	Beattie, J., L/Cpl., 1657	† 1.7.15
Anderson, D., Pte., 2552	*29.10.14	Beattie, R., Pte., S/8344	*13.7.16
Anderson, G., Pte., 137	*25.9.15	Beattie, R. L., Pte., S/7495	*18.8.16
Anderson, G., Pte., 3/3463	*25.1.15	Beedie, J., Pte., 1867	*20.9.16
Anderson, H. H., Pte., S/3157		Begg, W., Pte., S/4303	†17.8.16
	*13.10.15	Bell, H. T., Pte., S/7737	*13.10.15
Anderson, J., Pte., 3/2283	†21.6.15	Bell, J. C., L/Cpl., S/11588	* 3.9.16
Anderson, J., Pte., 3/3072	* 9.5.15	Bell, J., Pte., S/8067	*25.9.15
Anderson, J., Pte., 3/3622	*25.1.15	Bell, T., Pte., S/3103	*11.11.14
Anderson, J., Pte., 7376	*30.10.14	Bell, W. A. E., Pte., 310048	§28.3.17
Anderson, R., Pte., S/10253	*13.10.15	Bennet, A., Pte., 9324	§21.6.15
Anderson, T., L/Cpl., 2199	*29.10.14	Bennett, A. A., Pte., S/10320	†28.12.15
Anderson, T., Pte., S/4046	* 9.5.15	Bennett, R., Pte., 7440	§21.6.15
Anderson, T., Pte., S/8506	*13.10.15	Bennison, D., L/Cpl., 3/2026	*11.11.14
Anderson, W., L/Cpl., 2374	* 8.9.14	Benson, J., Pte., 950	*13.10.15
Andrews, J., Pte., 87	§21.7.18	Benvie, W., Pte., 9232	*14.9.14
Angus, R., Pte., 2760	*26.9.15	Benvie, W., Pte., S/11334	*18.8.16
Angus, R., Pte., S/14362	*18.4.18	Bern, A., Pte., 3/3943	* 9.5.15
Angus, R., Pte., S/7370	* 9.5.15	Berry, J., Pte., 7941	*15.9.14
Appleby, T., Cpl., 789	*18.8.16	Berry, W., Pte., S/16924	† 4.11.18

APPENDIX IV

Beveridge, R., Pte., 401	†28.9.14	Brown, J., Pte., 3/2225	* 5.10.14
Beveridge, W., Pte., 9965	*29.10.14	Brown, J., Pte., 3/4178	*10.3.15
Billington, A., Cpl., S/40650	*18.4.18	Brown, R., Pte., 3/3939	* 9.5.15
Birse, W., Pte., S/3991	* 3.9.16	Brown, T., Pte., S/7529	* 2.10.18
Bishop, A., Pte., 2132	*23.10.14	Brown, T., Cpl., 3/9603	*13.10.15
Bishop, H., Pte., S/6796	*13.10.15	Brown, W., C.S.M., 32	*25.9.15
Bishop, S. H., Cpl., 2376	†21.8.16	Brown, W., Pte., 3/3637	* 9.5.15
Bissett, J., Pte., 2519	*15.9.14	Brown, W., Pte., S/40125	*20.4.18
Black, A., L/Cpl., S/7480	* 7.7.18	Brown, W. T., L/Cpl., 44	†16.6.15
Black, D., Pte., S/7519	*25.9.15	Brownlie, W., Pte., S/4047	† 3.2.15
Black, H., A/Cpl., 3/3969	* 9.5.15	Bruce, C., Pte., S/43391	*25.9.16
Black, J., Pte., 2090	* 9.5.15	Bryce, J., Pte., S/40210	*25.9.16
Black, R., Pte., 9239	*13.10.15	Byrne, H., Pte., 3/3446	*12.1.15
Black, W., Pte., 655	†21.12.15	Buchan, C., Pte., S/11963	†26.7.16
Black, W., Cpl., 9593	† 9.9.16	Buchanan, C., Pte., 3/2705	*15.11.14
Black, W., Pte., 2631	*27.10.14	Buist, R., A/Sgt., 3/2356	*25.1.15
Blackley, R., L/Cpl., 3/1122	*25.9.15	Burke, J., Pte., S/3345	*25.9.15
Blackwood, A., Pte., 31992	* 9.11.14	Burke, T., Pte., 2789	* 6.5.15
Bloomer, J., Pte., 8688	† 9.12.14	Burnet, A., Pte., 9638	§21.6.15
Bloomfield, W., Pte., 3/2575	* 9.5.17	Burns, J. M., A/Sgt., 8530	* 9.5.15
Booth, J., Pte., S/6165	‡31.10.18	Burns, J., Pte., 2044	* 9.5.15
Boland, J., Pte., S/3136	*24.8.15	Burns, R., Pte., 2605	* 9.5.15
Bon, A., Pte., S/5421	*25.9.15	Burns, W., A/Sgt., 717	*13.10.15
Booth, G., Pte., 2497	*22.10.14	Burton, A., A/Cpl., 8082	*11.11.14
Booth, J., Pte., S/7913	*17.4.16	Butchart, W., Pte., 352	‡11.4.16
Borland, J., Pte., 3/3547	†25.8.16	Butcher, J., Pte., 1163	*26.4.16
Boslem, T., Sgt., S/3309	* 3.9.16	Byrne, J., Pte., 10203	*10.3.16
Boyd, J., Pte., S/5046	*10.2.15		
Boyd, W., A/Sgt., 7243	*25.1.15	Caddle, A., Pte., S/8860	*18.4.16
Boyle, J., L/Cpl., 1768	*23.2.17	Cairney, M., Pte., 7343	*16.9.14
Bracken, P., Pte., 3/4094	*25.1.15	Cairns, A., Pte., 2257	*23.10.14
Brackstone, A. V., Pte., 10229	†10.7.17	Cairns, B., Pte., 3/3717	* 9.5.15
Brady, T., Pte., 3/1958	*11.11.14	Calderhead, J., Pte., 3/2776	† 4.4.15
Braid, G., Pte., 7215	*11.5.16	Callaghan, G., Pte., 3/4010	†15.9.16
Braid, J., Pte., 2656	*25.9.15	Callaghan, G., Pte., S/7087	* 9.5.15
Bray, H., Pte., S/10257	*13.10.15	Callaghan, H., Pte., 3396	§25.11.14
Breen, C., Pte., 9240	*12.11.14	Callender, D., Pte., 3/2256	† 3.10.14
Bremner, W., Pte., 1745	*25.9.16	Cam, P., Pte., 3/2922	* 9.5.15
Brett, E., Pte., 2382	§21.6.15	Cameron, D., Pte., S/12568	*20.3.18
Brewster, J., Pte., S/17456	§17.7.17	Cameron, J., Pte., 2370	*15.9.14
Brinelow, J., Pte., 2672	*11.11.14	Cameron, J., Pte., S/9298	*30.4.16
Brodie, C., Pte., 3/2905	*22.7.16	Cameron, R., L/Cpl., 8360	*12.11.14
Brodie, J., Pte., 7390	*21.4.18	Campbell, A., Cpl., 2242	†20.9.18
Brough, J. A., Pte., S/14309	*21.9.16	Campbell, D., Pte., S/10700	*19.3.18
Brown, A., Pte., 2263	*15.9.14	Campbell, D., Pte., S/40165	*25.9.16
Brown, A., Pte., S/8016	*25.9.15	Campbell, J., Pte., 171	†23.10.14
Brown, C., Pte., S/7735	*26.9.15	Campbell, J., Pte., 3/3023	* 9.4.15
Brown, D., L/Cpl., 3/3300	‡16.10.15	Campbell, J., Pte., 3/3437	*13.10.15
Brown, D. A., Pte., 187	§23.10.18	Campbell, J., Pte., 6569	* 9.5.15
Brown, E., Pte., 1904	‡ 1.4.16	Campbell, J., Pte., 7129	*25.9.15
Brown, G., Pte., 3/1474	†26.10.14	Campbell, R., Pte., 7873	†21.6.15
Brown, G., Pte., 3/4115	*25.1.15	Campbell, R., Pte., 3/4045	*25.9.15
Brown, J., Pte., 2463	*12.10.14	Campbell, T. M., Pte., S/17161	† 7.11.18
Brown, J., Pte., S/5912	†18.8.16		
Brown, J., A/Sgt., 1242	*25.9.15	Campbell, W., Pte., 9547	*27.10.14

THE FIRST BATTALION THE BLACK WATCH

Canavan, R., Pte., 3/1618	* 9.5.15	Cook, G., Pte., 8066	†22.9.16
Carmichael, A., Pte., 8593	*31.10.14	Cook, J., L/Cpl., 2444	*11.11.14
Carmichael, D., Pte., S/40159	*22.3.18	Cook, J., Pte., 6691	* 9.5.15
Carmichael, J., Pte., S/14363	†30.11.16	Cooper, D., Pte., 9599	*26.10.14
Carr, D., Sgt., 342	†21.6.15	Cooper, J., Pte., S/10332	* 3.9.16
Carr, W., Pte., 2268	†19.10.14	Cooper, J. H., Pte., S/10068	†20.4.18
Carroll, F., Pte., 3/3293	*29.12.14	Corrigan, T., Pte., S/43393	*25.9.16
Carson, B., Pte., S/9270	*18.4.18	Coull, G., Pte., 3/3992	* 9.5.15
Carson, J., Pte., 3/2757	* 9.5.15	Coull, T., Pte., 6945	*11.11.14
Carstairs, A. N., Sgt., 1394	†21.8.16	Coultate, C., L/Cpl., S/40299	*18.11.17
Carstairs, D., Pte., 1877	* 9.5.15	Cowie, A., Pte., 7459	*13.10.15
Cation, A., Pte., S/3900	†27.9.15	Cox, D., Pte., 3/2501	†19.5.15
Chalmers, J., Pte., 2641	* 9.5.15	Cox, J. M., A/Cpl., 3/3278	*13.10.15
Chapman, G. A., Sgt., 540	*31.10.14	Cox, J. N., Pte., 1681	* 9.5.15
Chapman, J., Pte., 3/3629	* 9.5.15	Cox, W., Pte., 8265	*31.10.14
Charles, R., Pte., 3/3567	†24.7.16	Coyle, G., Pte., 454	* 4.9.14
Cheape, T., Pte., 2584	*10.11.14	Craig, D., L/Sgt., 1706	*14.9.14
Chick, H., Pte., 268947	*18.10.18	Crake, W., Pte., 3/2756	*19.9.18
Christie, J., Pte., 7382	*25.9.15	Crawford, A., Pte., S/14469	*25.9.16
Christie, W., Pte., S/7041	* 9.5.15	Crawford, R., L/Cpl., S/17819	†24.9.18
Christison, D., Pte., 380	†11.11.14		
Clark, A., Pte., S/7716	* 9.5.15	Crawford, W., Pte., 3/2137	*18.4.18
Clark, D., L/Cpl., S/9825	*18.8.16	Craythorn, J. W., Pte., S/11636	* 4.9.16
Clark, E., Pte., 3/2702	†11.5.15		
Clark, G., Pte., S/7098	* 9.5.15	Crichton, P., Pte., 7443	*25.1.15
Clark, G., Pte., 9774	‡11.6.18	Crichton, T., Pte., 2280	*11.11.14
Clark, G. P., Pte., 265453	*24.10.18	Crighton, P., Pte., S/12008	*14.7.16
Clark, H., L/Cpl., 556	* 9.5.15	Croll, W., Pte., 3/3297	*25.1.15
Clark, J., Pte., 434	*23.10.14	Crombie, J., Pte., 11777	*25.5.16
Clark, J., Pte., 3/1572	*29.10.14	Crooks, F., Pte., 8370	* 9.5.15
Clark, J., Pte., S/4087	* 9.5.15	Cruickshank, J., Pte., 2764	§ 8.2.15
Clark, J. M., Pte., S/16626	*20.4.18	Culbert, J., Pte., 276	†21.6.15
Clark, R. S., Pte., S/14411	* 7.5.18	Cully, J., Pte., 3/1155	†30.10.14
Clark, R., A/Sgt., 6930	*25.9.15	Culpin, G. F., Sgt., 313	*11.11.14
Clark, R. S., Pte., 7154	*26.10.14	Cummings, R. J., Pte., 1812	* 9.5.16
Clark, S., Pte., 350504	†28.5.18	Cunningham, A., Pte., S/40097	‡29.1.17
Clark, W., L/Cpl., 2180	†19.4.16		
Clark, W., Pte., S/9216	*29.5.16	Cunningham, J., Pte., S/20127	* 7.7.18
Clark, W., Pte., S/14409	*15.3.17		
Clements, W., Pte., 155	* 8.9.14	Cunningham, T. Pte., S/19890	*17.11.17
Clink, J., Pte., 3/1899	*25.6.17		
Close, D., Pte., 2767	†20.8.16	Cunningham, W., Pte., S/9898	*18.8.16
Coats, D., Pte., S/9393	†15.10.18		
Cochrane, P., L/Cpl., 3/3603	*10.2.15	Cunnison, T., Pte., 2638	*11.11.14
Coggans, J., Pte., S/40213	†18.4.18	Cunnison, W., Pte., 3/2165	* 4.10.14
Coleman, J., Pte., 3/2186	* 9.11.14	Curphey, J. T., Pte., S/6718	†12.5.15
Collingwood, T., Pte., 2691	* 9.5.15	Curran, F., A/C.S.M., 1875	*18.8.16
Connelly, J., Pte., S/11674	† 6.9.16	Curran, P., Pte., 9449	†12.11.14
Connelly, J., Pte., 3/3613	*26.9.15	Curran, P., Pte., S/11483	* 3.9.16
Connelly, J., Pte., 3/9508	*11.11.14	Curran, R., Pte., 3/2392	* 9.5.15
Connelly, T., L/Cpl., 3/1980	*11.11.14	Currie, D., Pte., 8108	* 9.11.14
Connelly, T., Pte., S/8206	*26.9.15	Currie, H., Pte., 3/9487	* 3.9.16
Constable, E., Pte., S/6751	* 9.5.15	Currie, P., Pte., 3/271	*29.10.14
Cook, A. G., Pte., 2720	* 9.5.15	Currie, T., Pte., 8174	*16.9.14
Cook, A., Sgt., S/2830	*18.8.16	Curtis, A., Pte., 2814	* 9.5.15

APPENDIX IV

Dalgleish, F., L/Cpl., 98	*17.10.18	Douglas, P., Pte., 2753(M.M.)	*18.4.18
Dall, A., Pte., 3070	*17.2.15	Douglas, R., Pte., S/10810	*30.8.16
Dall, G., Pte., 39	†11.11.14	Douglas, W. H., A/Cpl., 1978	†26.9.15
Dall, R. G., Pte., 3/4108	*10.1.15	Dow, A. J., Pte., 9436	* 9.5.15
Daly, J., Pte., 2742	*29.10.14	Doyle, E., Pte., 3/1375	* 9.5.15
Dalziel, G., Pte., 2033	* 9.5.15	Drummond, D., Pte., 3/2666	*28.4.16
Darby, F., Pte., 3102	†20.5.15	Drummond, H., L/Cpl., 8361	* 3.9.16
Davidson, A., Pte., 2768	*25.1.15	Drummond, J., Pte., 512	*15.9.14
Davidson, J. H., Pte., S/11839	*14.7.16	Drummond, J., Pte., 3/2599	*12.6.15
Davidson, P., Pte., 8678	*23.10.14	Drummond, J., Pte., 3/2685	*29.10.14
Davidson, W., Pte., S/6725	†29.9.15	Drummond, P., Pte., 2002	* 9.5.15
Davie, E., Pte., 2183	*25.1.15	Drummond, T., Pte., 3/1538	*25.1.15
Davies, H., A/Cpl., 3/4056	* 9.5.15	Drummond, T., Pte., 7689	†13.11.14
Davies, J., Pte., 3/3955	* 9.5.15	Drysburgh, D., Pte., 9926	* 9.5.15
Dawson, G. F., Pte., S/40239	*25.9.16	Dryburgh, A. G., Pte., 7446	*13.10.15
Deans, J. H. G., A/Sgt., S/9511	*25.9.16	Duff, G., L/Cpl., 7387	*27.10.14
		Duff, J., Pte., S/14599	*17.11.17
Dearden, J., Pte., 8068	†21.6.15	Duff, J. M., Pte., S/21038	†18.10.18
Delaney, P., Pte., 2556	*15.9.14	Duffie, T., Pte., 636	* 9.5.15
Dempster, J., Pte., 3/2862	*25.1.15	Duffus, C., Pte., 2509	* 9.5.15
Devine, F. B., Pte., S/7178	*26.9.15	Duffy, T., Pte., 3/2298	*19.3.16
Devine, H., Pte., 3/1328	†14.2.15	Duffy, W., Pte., 3/2531	* 9.5.15
Devitt, J., Pte., S/3076	* 6.10.15	Dumphie, A., Pte., 3/2750	* 3.9.16
Devlin, R., Pte., 6637	§21.6.15	Duncan, C., Pte., 3/2249	* 9.5.15
Dewar, G., Pte., 9876	†21.6.15	Duncan, J., Pte., 1953	*11.11.14
Dewar, R., Pte., 3/1270	*11.11.14	Duncan, J., Pte., 3/2551	*19.2.17
Dick, R., Pte., 110	†21.6.16	Duncan, J., Pte., 7426	*13.7.16
Dickson, R., L/Cpl., S/5271	*16.12.15	Duncan, J., A/Cpl., 1079	* 9.5.15
Dickson, R., Pte., 3/3726	* 3.9.16	Duncan, J., Pte., S/9798	* 3.9.16
Dingwall, A., Pte., 8317	*16.9.14	Duncan, J., Pte., 293131	*12.6.18
Dingwall, J., Pte., S/16510	*28.5.18	Duncan, P., Pte., 9369	*16.9.14
Dixon, A., Pte., 7923	†22.9.14	Duncan, T., Pte., 2477	*20.5.15
Doak, J., Pte., S/5954	†12.6.15	Duncan, T., Sgt., 7312	*18.10.18
Dobinson, H., L/Cpl., 292611	*18.10.18	Duncan, W., Pte., S/3011	†29.6.15
Docherty, J., Sgt., 8566 (D.C.M., M.M.)	* 3.9.16	Duncan, W., Pte., 9964	*25.1.15
		Dunlop, J., Pte., 3/3729	* 9.5.15
Docherty, T., Pte., 3/2698	*28.5.18	Dunn, J. H., Pte., S/12626	* 3.9.16
Docherty, W., Sgt., 3/107	†13.11.14	Dunn, J. A., Pte., 3/1745	*18.8.16
Dodds, J., Pte., S/8739	* 3.9.16	Durham, A., L/Cpl., 3/3091	*25.1.15
Doig, D., Pte., 3/3141	*25.9.15		
Doig, W., Sgt., 9277	* 1.11.14	Easton, G., Pte., S/8272	*25.9.15
Dolan, D., A/Sgt., 474	*25.1.15	Edgar, G., Pte., 2081	†21.6.15
Dolan, J., Pte., 3/1850	* 9.5.15	Edgar, P., Pte., S/8373	*17.8.16
Dolan, J., Pte., 3/3185	† 5.9.18	Edmond, T., Pte., 9247	* 9.5.15
Dolan, T., Pte., 54	†16.5.15	Edward, D., Pte., 3/2375	*25.9.15
Donachie, H., Pte., 3/726	† 9.5.15	Edwards, A. J., Sgt., 448	*25.9.15
Donald, T., A/Cpl., 2161	*18.4.18	Edwards, D., Pte., 7468	*16.9.14
Donaldson, G., Pte., 7271	†11.11.14	Egan, M., Pte., 3/3332	* 9.5.15
Donaldson, J., L/Cpl., 7384	* 9.5.15	Eggington, A., Pte., S/12704	* 3.6.18
Donaldson, W., Pte., S/6669	†16.8.16	Elder, J., Pte., 3/2671	*29.10.14
Donnelly, T., Pte., 3/2594	* 9.5.15	Elder, S., Cpl., 1396	* 9.5.15
Dorans, H., Pte., 3/2773	*13.10.15	Ellam, A. J., A/Cpl., 7816	* 9.5.15
Dougan, J., Pte., S/7951	*18.8.16	Elliott, J., Cpl., 1574	†22.9.14
Dougherty, E. S. F., Dmr., 1762	* 9.5.15	Elliott, R., Pte., S/2890	*25.9.15
		Elliot, T. Y., L/Cpl., S/10149	*18.4.18

THE FIRST BATTALION THE BLACK WATCH

Elliss, A. C., Pte., S/11848 * 3.9.16
Elrich, J., Pte., S/5779 *18.10.18
Elrick, J. M., Cpl., 667 †18.11.15
Elsden, W. J., Pte., 10244 *14.7.16
Emslie, D., Pte., S/12685 *25.9.16
Entrican, C., Pte., 2746 *25.1.15
Evans, D., L/Cpl., 9845 †29.10.14
Evans, T. H., Pte., 3/3017 *14.8.16
Ewan, J., Pte., S/40138 *21.9.16

Fairley, G., Pte., 7006 † 8.10.14
Fairweather, D. B., Pte., S/8305
    * 3.9.16
Fairweather, D. S., L/Cpl., S/8183
    *13.10.15
Fanning, A., Pte., 2115 *16.8.16
Farley, J., Pte., 3/1577 * 9.5.15
Farmer, R., Pte., S/9071 * 3.9.16
Farrell, T., Pte., 7188 *29.10.14
Farrington, D., Pte., 7871 †27.10.14
Fearns, C., Pte., S/11128 *24.12.16
Ferguson, A., Pte., S/8143 †14.10.15
Ferguson, D., Pte., S/6956 * 9.5.15
Ferguson, D., Pte., 2488 * 9.5.15
Ferguson, J., Pte., S/11948 *22.7.16
Ferguson, T., L/Cpl., 7529 §21.6.15
Ferguson, W., Pte., 2072 * 9.5.15
Ferguson, W. J., A/Sgt., 9503 * 2.11.14
Ferns, C., Pte., 3/2581 † 3.9.16
Ferrie, J., Pte., 3/2985 *22.7.16
Ferries, W., Pte., S/5468 §23.10.18
Filmer, C., Pte., S/10096 † 6.12.16
Findlay, C., Pte., S/22890 *18.4.18
Findlay, D., Pte., S/8358 *13.10.15
Findlay, J., Pte., S/22221 §25.10.18
Findleton, R., Pte., S/40153 *22.9.16
Finlayson, J., A/Sgt., 9734 *25.5.16
Finnigan, T., Pte., 3/2956 *12.2.15
Firrall, M., Pte., 722 †25.7.16
Fisher, W., Pte., 8438 *13.10.15
Fitzgerald, T., Pte., S/40199 *25.9.16
Fitzpatrick, W., Pte., 3/1044 *29.5.15
Fitzsimmons, N., Pte., 7324 *25.7.16
Flannery, J., Pte., 2109 *10.11.14
Fleming, A. S., Sgt., 9585 * 9.11.14
Fleming, T., Pte., 912 *27.10.14
Fletcher, H., Pte., 9859 *26.10.14
Forbes, J., Pte., S/18311 *28.5.18
Forbes, W., Pte., 188 * 3.9.16
Ford, E., Sgt., 266 (D.C.M.) * 3.9.16
Ford, J., Pte., 2398 *15.9.14
Forrest, A., Pte., 3/2838 *10.2.15
Forrest, D., Pte., 9475 *27.10.14
Forrester, J., Pte., 9275 * 8.9.14
Forrester, R., Pte., 2723 * 9.5.15

Forsyth, G. M., Pte., 2041 *18.9.14
Forsyth, W., A/Cpl., 2358 *16.9.14
Forwell, E. S. W., Cpl., 268996
    *18.4.18
Foster, J., Pte., 1980 †29.10.14
Fotheringham, W., Pte., 1760 †10.5.15
Foulger, J., Pte., S/8580 *13.10.15
Fowler, H., Pte., 3/3561 †11.3.15
Fox, G., Pte., 9978 *16.9.14
Fox, J., A/Sgt., 2154 †26.1.15
Fox, J., Pte., 3/1264 † 9.5.15
Fox, J., Pte., 3/3353 †27.1.15
Fox, P., Pte., S/23894 *30.9.18
Foy, J., Pte., 9454 *23.10.14
Fraiel, C., Pte., S/6337 † 5.5.16
Frail, J., Pte., S/4034 * 9.5.15
Fraser, A., A/Sgt., 97 *17.10.15
Fraser, A., L/Cpl., 3/2465 * 9.5.15
Fraser, J., Pte., S/40030 *25.9.16
Fraser, M., Pte., 7900 * 9.5.15
Frew, A., Pte., S/3746 *26.5.16
Frith, H., Pte., 3/3953 * 9.5.15
Frizzell, J., L/Cpl., S/9418 * 3.9.16
Fulton, J., Cpl., S/7393 *19.11.17

Galbraith, D., Pte., 3/3929 * 9.5.15
Galbraith, J., Pte., 3298 *25.1.15
Gall, P., Pte., 2489 *17.4.16
Gallacher, J., Pte., S/40141 *18.4.18
Gallacher, J., Pte., 3/2523 *13.10.15
Galligan, L., Pte., 3/3290 *21.10.15
Galloway, A. J., L/Cpl., 7890 *29.10.14
Gandie, J. L., Pte., S/40219 *25.9.16
Garden, N. R., Pte., S/17702 *18.4.18
Gardiner, J., Pte., 3/1764 * 9.5.15
Gardner, P. E., Sgt., S/9852 †20.3.16
Garrod, F. G., L/Cpl., S/10352
    *13.10.15
Gavine, G., Pte., 8323 *13.10.15
Geary, R., L/Cpl., 884 *23.10.14
Geddes, J., Pte., S/3959 *19.4.18
Geekie, A., Pte., 2581 *15.9.14
Gemmell, D., Pte., 3/3800 *25.1.15
George, W., Pte., 8036
    (D.C.M.) *14.7.16
Gibb, D., Pte., 1914 * 9.5.15
Gibson, A., Pte, 3/3243 † 2.11.15
Gibson, A., Pte., S/40201 †26.9.16
Gibson, W., Pte., 1213 * 9.5.15
Gibson, W., Pte., S/43366 *28.9.16
Gilbert, J., Pte., 3/2600 * 9.5.15
Gilbert, V. W. H., Pte., 22533 †20.9.18
Gilchrist, R. M., L/Cpl., S/40327
    *18.4.18
Gilder, G., Pte., S/8699 *15.2.16

138

APPENDIX IV

Gill, F., L/Cpl., 240053	†28.5.18	Greig, E., Pte., S/9797	* 1.6.16
Gillan, T. A., Pte., S/40298	*25.9.16	Greig, R. C., Cpl., 1720	* 2.11.14
Gillespie, A. B., Pte., S/8433	*13.10.15	Greig, W., Pte., 3/2081	*11.11.14
Gillies, D., Pte., S/8199	*15.10.15	Grieve, J., Pte., 83	†29.10.14
Gillies, J., Pte., S/40558	† 2.4.18	Griffiths, C., Pte., S/4329	* 9.5.15
Gilmour, J. P., Pte., 2567	*16.9.14	Gruar, A., Pte., S/23874	†11.7.18
Girven, J., Pte., 3/1396	*22.9.16	Grubb, D., Pte., 3/1635	†21.6.15
Given, J. A., Pte., 2193	*11.11.14	Grubb, F. P., Pte., 3/3714	* 3.9.16
Glass, D. M., C/Sgt., 1461	§31.3.16	Grubb, R. S., Pte., 3/3866	* 9.5.15
Glen, J., L/Cpl., 3/1146	*31.10.14	Guthrie, R., Pte., 2607	* 9.5.15
Glenday, H., Pte., 2027	†21.6.15	Guyan, W. R., Pte., 3/2223	* 9.5.15
Glover, G., Pte., 9993	† 8.9.14		
Goldie, D., A/Cpl., 16	*16.6.15	Hadwin, D., L/Cpl., S/12290	*14.7.16
Gordon, J., Pte., 3/650	*28.10.14	Haggart, D., Pte., 9888	*28.10.14
Gordon, J., Pte., S/7724	*21.12.16	Halkett, W., Pte., 2707	*29.10.14
Goudie, R. A., Pte., S/10189	*14.7.16	Hall, D. R., Pte., 2220	* 3.9.16
Govan, D., Pte., 3/6977	* 9.5.15	Hamilton, A. G., Pte., S/8555	† 7.9.16
Gow, A., Pte., 3/1599	*29.10.15	Hamilton, D., Pte., 201279	*28.5.18
Gow, A., L/Cpl. 7028	*16.9.14	Hamilton, R., Pte., S/16945	‡23.2.18
Gowans, C., L/Cpl., 9601	* 9.5.15	Hamilton, R. G., L/Cpl., S/40225	
Gowans, F., Pte., 2609	* 9.5.15		*17.11.17
Goward, P. L., Pte., S/8287	* 9.5.15	Hamilton, W., Pte., S/2894	*23.10.14
Graham, A., Pte., S/10017	* 3.9.16	Hampton, J. S., Pte., 9973	*12.11.14
Graham, A., Pte., 9565	*31.10.14	Handy, B., Pte., S/3251	* 9.5.15
Graham, D., Pte., S/14576	*30.11.16	Handy, T., Pte., 3/2639	† 7.9.16
Graham, G., Pte., S/14395	§27.12.16	Hanlin, G., L/Cpl., S/40069	†10.7.17
Graham, H., Pte., 1563	*25.9.15	Hannay, P., Pte., S/9214	†20.4.18
Graham, H., Pte., S/8493	* 3.9.16	Hardie, D., Pte., 8133	*25.1.15
Graham, J., Pte., S/6736	*13.10.15	Harkus, G., Pte., 608	*29.10.14
Graham, J., Pte., 8017	†28.10.14	Harley, A., Pte., S/40191	†20.9.18
Graham, J. H., Pte., 2276	§11.7.18	Harley, R., Pte., S/3472	† 3.9.18
Graham, J., Pte., S/12618	*25.7.18	Harrison, H., Pte., 7508	*15.9.14
Graham, R. W., Pte., S/16788	†24.2.17	Harrison, J., Pte., 2371	*27.10.14
Graham, T., Pte., S/2774	*24.7.16	Harrow, C., Pte., S/3529	* 9.5.15
Graham, T., Pte., S/7361	*26.9.15	Harrow, R., Pte., 1690	†21.11.14
Grainger, H., Pte., S/12953	*27.10.18	Hart, J., L/Sgt., 407	§16.2.15
Grannon, J., Pte., 7117	*27.10.14	Hastings, F. H., Sgt., 118	* 3.9.16
Grant, A., Pte., S/40118	*25.9.16	Hauchie, W., Pte., 293081	* 4.11.18
Grant, A. W., Cpl., S/13466	†22.11.17	Hawkes, D., Pte., 21049	* 4.11.18
Grant, D., Pte., 3/3751	* 3.6.15	Hay, A., Cpl., S/4013	*17.8.16
Grant, J., L/Cpl., 1281	*25.9.15	Hay, A. P., Pte., S/8260	* 4.9.16
Grant, P., Pte., 9626	*29.10.14	Hay, D., Pte., S/15002	*18.4.18
Grant, R., Pte., S/6991	*25.9.15	Hayes, J., Cpl., S/9675	* 3.9.16
Grant, T., Pte., 570	*25.9.15	Healy, J., Pte., 3/1175	* 9.5.15
Grant, W., Pte., 202677	†31.5.18	Heap, S., Pte., 7830	†27.9.14
Gray, A., Pte., 3/3334	* 9.5.15	Hedges, F., Pte., S/10112	†10.9.16
Gray, C., L/Cpl., 3/2683	*18.11.17	Heggie, H., Pte., 9915	*31.10.14
Gray, G., Pte., S/8159	*25.9.15	Heggie, W., Pte., 8309	* 9.5.15
Gray, S., Pte., S/7051	* 9.5.15	Henderson, A., Pte., 7751	* 7.10.14
Green, E. T., L/Cpl., S/9982	*28.5.16	Henderson, A., Pte., 7764	*29.10.14
Green, J., Pte., 3/2473	* 9.5.15	Henderson, A., Pte., 8061	*16.9.14
Green, R., Pte., S/13330	*22.9.16	Henderson, C. L., L/Cpl., 2486	
Greer, J. A., L/Cpl., S/15754	* 3.9.16		*27.10.14
Greer, W., Pte., 3/2492	†14.10.15	Henderson, G., Pte., 696	†26.10.14
Gregory, F., Pte., S/12477	*28.6.17	Henderson, G., Cpl., 2158	* 2.11.14

THE FIRST BATTALION THE BLACK WATCH

Henderson, J., A/C.S.M., 1451 (D.C.M.)	* 9.5.15	Imrie, J., Pte., 3/3230	*22.9.16
Henderson, J., Pte., 3126	*24.4.15	Inglis, D., Pte., S/2984	† 4.11.18
Henderson, J., Pte., 3/8691	*16.3.15	Ingleson, A. S., L/Cpl., S/10136	*26.9.15
Henderson, J. J., Pte., 2373	*11.11.14	Innes, N., Pte., 2298	*29.10.14
Henderson, J. M., Cpl., S/15879	*27.10.18	Izzatt, A., ——., 5857	*31.10.14
Henderson, J., Pte., 2401	§21.6.15	Jack, D., Pte., S/7736	‡ 7.9.18
Henderson, N., L/Sgt., S/10335	* 3.9.16	Jack, D., Pte., S/22899	*17.4.18
		Jack, G., Pte., 3/2906	*25.1.15
Henderson, R., Pte., S/40316	*25.9.16	Jack, R., Pte., 3/3718	* 9.5.15
Henderson, W., Pte., 7759	*15.9.14	Jackson, A., Pte., 2731	* 1.11.14
Hendry, G., Pte., S/11086	§21.4.16	Jackson, J., Pte., S/10263	† 1.7.18
Hendry, W., Pte., S/4056	*28.5.16	Jackson, W., Pte., 3/2212	*27.10.14
Hendry, W. F., Pte., S/10744	*19.2.17	Jamieson, W., Pte., 3/9067	* 9.5.15
Herbert, A., L/Cpl., S/7414	* 3.9.16	Jeffery, R., Pte., 40325	*18.11.17
Herd, C. M., L/Cpl., 46	* 9.5.15	Jeffrey, C., Sgt., 1387	* 9.5.15
Herd, R., Pte., S/5085	* 9.5.15	Jeffrey, J., Pte., 3/1885	* 9.5.15
Heugh, J., Pte., 2704	†21.11.14	Jeffries, J., Cpl., 9796	†24.5.15
Hewitt, R., Pte., 292399	*19.9.18	Johnston, J., Pte., S/40323	*17.11.17
Hiddles, J., L/Sgt., 3/3619	* 9.5.15	Johnston, J., Pte., 2747	*19.5.17
Hillan, J., Pte., 3/2007	*29.10.14	Johnston, M., Pte., S/7599	*25.9.15
Hilton, A. R., Pte., S/10164	*13.10.15	Johnston, N., Pte., S/40284	*22.9.16
Hirst, J. W., Pte., 7504	*15.9.14	Johnston, R., Pte., 3/4219	*13.10.15
Hodge, J., Pte., 3/2080	*12.11.14	Johnstone, G., Pte., 3/6800	* 9.5.15
Hogg, J., Pte., S/5540	*25.9.15	Johnstone, G., L/Cpl., S/10315	† 6.10.15
Hogg, T., Pte., 386	*14.9.14		
Holloway, J. H., Pte., 2627	* 9.11.14	Johnstone, J., Pte., 3/3437	*11.3.15
Holmes, W., Pte., S/23882	†19.9.18	Johnstone, W. M., Pte., 7538	* 8.9.14
Hood, W., Pte., S/11511	†18.5.17	Jones, A. T., Pte., S/10738	*15.3.17
Hook, A., Pte., S/7576	* 9.5.15	Jones, J. H., Pte., S/23426	§ 7.7.18
Hook, W., Pte., S/7463	* 3.9.18	Jones, T., Pte., S/40147	*22.9.16
Hope, G., L/Cpl., 3726	*29.10.14	Jones, W. R. M., Pte., S/12700	*13.7.16
Hopper, J., Pte., 2146	* 6.10.15		
Horsburgh, R., Pte., 9564	*29.10.14	Joseph, G., L/Cpl., 660	†14.11.14
Howie, A., L/Cpl., S/8155	†25.7.16		
Howie, W. H. S., Pte., 2502	*15.11.14	Kane, C., Pte., 3/1785	*25.1.15
Huckerdy, H., L/Cpl., S/12413	*12.12.17	Kay, G., Pte., 3/3337	* 9.5.15
Hughes, T., Pte., 3/3391	* 9.5.15	Kay, W., L/Cpl., S/3777	* 9.5.15
Hughes, W., Pte., 2667	* 3.9.16	Kean, J., Pte., S/5538	*24.7.16
Hulse, J., Pte., S/9101	*12.3.16	Kelly, B., L/Cpl., 3/2082	†21.8.16
Hume, E., Pte., 3/1811	†12.5.15	Kelly, F., Pte., 8190	*25.7.15
Hume, R., Pte., S/24072	*28.5.18	Kelly, J., Pte., 3/2216	* 3.9.16
Hunter, D., Pte., 3/2615	* 9.5.15	Kelly, J., Pte., S/6988	†14.7.16
Hunter, D., Pte., 3/2669	†16.5.15	Kelly, P., L/Cpl., 9238	*11.11.14
Hunter, D., Pte., 266877	§28.8.18	Kelly, P., Pte., 1185	§21.6.15
Hunter, G., Pte., 3/2668	* 1.11.14	Kelly, W., Pte., S/13347	*18.10.18
Hunter, G., Pte., 8301	*16.9.14	Kemp, A., Pte., 267047	*18.10.18
Hunter, J., Pte., 11	†21.6.15	Kennedy, A., Pte., 2171	†16.9.14
Husband, D., Pte., 7191	* 9.5.15	Kennedy, J., Pte., S/3369	* 9.5.15
Hutchison, D., Pte., S/7584	†18.10.15	Kennedy, R. G., Pte., S/5048	*13.10.15
Hutton, A., Pte., 1304	†26.12.14	Kent, G., L/Cpl., S/16314	†22.9.16
Hutton, I., Pte., 3/2635	† 6.11.14	Kermack, W., Pte., 3/1833	* 9.5.15
Hutton, R., Pte., 2930	* 9.5.15	Kerr, G. A., Pte., S/15586	*18.4.18
Hutton, W., Pte., 241221	†28.10.18	Kerr, W., L/Cpl., 3/2069	†10.5.15

APPENDIX IV

Kerwin, M., Pte., 3/2777	†13.6.16	Lister, W., Pte., S/10822	* 3.9.16
Kerwin, R., Pte., 9878	†12.10.14	Lithgow, W., Pte., 3/3255	*25.9.15
Kidd, C., Pte., 3/3940	* 9.5.15	Livie, J., Pte., 283	*25.9.15
Keillor, E. B., Pte., S/12682	† 3.9.16	Livingstone, C., Pte., 1510	*11.11.14
King, C. W., Pte., 10262	*13.10.15	Livingstone, D., Pte., 3/2877	*25.1.15
King, H., Pte., 2629	*25.9.16	Livingston, T., Pte., 3/3941	* 9.5.15
Kirk, W. N., Pte., 2445	† 8.11.14	Lorimer, J., Cpl., 8075	‡ 5.11.14
Kitchen, P., Pte., 2461	*11.11.14	Love, H., Sgt., 7486	† 1.11.14
Knight, G., Pte., 490	† 9.5.15	Low, C., Pte., 7246	*12.2.15
Knight, J., Pte., 2535	†19.6.15	Low, J., Pte., 874	* 9.5.15
Knight, T. A., Pte., 3/3313	* 5.9.16	Louden, G., Pte., 3/2613	*18.5.15
		Lowe, T., Pte., S/10484	*18.11.17
Laidlaw, A., L/Cpl., 3/3506	* 9.5.15	Lowson, J. B., Pte., 3/3695	* 9.5.15
Laidlaw, W., Sgt., 8462	* 9.5.15	Luke, D., Pte., S/14210	*20.11.16
Laing, D., Pte., S/40178	§10.1.17	Lumsden, A., Pte., 3/2086	*29.10.14
Laing, J. S. B., Pte., 3/1976	* 9.5.15	Lumsden, J., Pte., 9246	*31.10.14
Laing, J., Pte., 7067	*11.4.15	Lumsden, R., Pte., 202286	*16.4.18
Laing, J. Y., Pte., 2472	‡19.11.14	Lyall, J., Pte., S/8469	*25.9.15
Laing, L. B., Pte., 3/2537	§17.8.18	Lyle, J., Pte., 310001	*28.6.17
Lang, A., Pte., S/40234	*25.9.16		
Lamond, J., Pte., 2191	* 9.5.15	Macaulay, J., L/Cpl., 2886	*14.7.16
Lamont, A., Pte., 2135	*31.10.15	Macdowall, H., L/Cpl., 2732	* 3.9.16
Langslow, W., Pte., 3/2121	†24.10.14	Macintosh, C., Pte., 591	*22.12.14
Larkins, W. G., L/Cpl., 1015	† 3.11.14	Macintosh, D., Pte., S/8207	†21.10.15
Latto, G. R., Pte., 2353	*15.9.14	Macintyre, W., Pte., S/3411	†20.3.16
Laverty, F. S., Pte., 2356	*26.9.15	Mackay, H., Pte., 3/3156	†20.7.16
Law, W., Pte., 2677	*14.4.15	Mackay, P. A., Pte., 2821	†31.1.15
Lawler, H., Pte., 8020	*25.1.15	Mackay, R., Pte., 9719	*11.11.14
Lawrie, J. W., Pte., 1156	§ 6.3.17	Mackie, A. S., Pte., 6916	§27.2.15
Lawrie, R., Pte., S/10516	* 3.9.16	Mackie, J., Pte., 3/2884	*25.1.15
Lawson, D., L/Cpl., S/40372	*18.10.18	Mackie, J., Pte., S/40120	*25.9.15
Lawson, F., Pte., 2711	†22.5.15	Mackie, R., A/Cpl., S/9452	†11.11.18
Lawson, J., A/Sgt., 734	*10.11.14	Mackinan, W. T., Pte., 3/3302	*12.3.15
Lawson, J., Pte., 9440	* 8.10.14	MacNaughton, G. J., Pte., S/11955	
Leal, J., Pte., 12	*27.10.14		*18.8.16
Ledlie, R., Sgt., S/4294	*18.4.18	Macneil, D. J., Sgt., 2534	*10.11.14
Lee, A., L/Cpl., 268694	†18.11.17	Macpherson, J., Pte., 7718	† 1.11.14
Lee, J., Pte., S/40039	*25.9.16	Macrae, J., Pte., S/43093	*19.3.18
Leishman, C., Pte., 3/2182	*25.1.15	McAdam, H., Pte., S/40248	*18.3.18
Leitch, A., Pte., 2900	* 9.5.15	McAlpine, J., Pte., 5573	*11.11.14
Leitch, J. R., Pte., 3/1862	*29.10.14	McAndrew, J., Cpl., 3901	*25.4.16
Leitch, J., L/Cpl., 2046	† 5.11.18	McAree, W., Pte., S/4055	* 9.5.15
Lennox, J., Cpl., S/6881	†18.10.18	McBain, J., Pte., S/40631	*18.4.18
Leslie, W., L/Cpl., 124	* 9.5.15	McBeath, C., Pte., 9228	‡ 1.12.14
Lewis, W., Pte., S/10157	*13.10.15	McBeath, E., L/Cpl., 10174	† 7.8.16
Leyland, J., Pte., 3/4091	* 9.5.15	McBurnie, C., Pte., S/9057	*18.4.18
Liles, J., Pte., S/8156	*26.9.15	McCabe, J., Pte., 3/2253	†15.7.16
Lindsay, A., Pte., 9655	*11.11.14	McCallum, J., Pte., 7458	* 3.9.16
Lindsay, C., Pte., 9279	*28.10.14	McCallum, J., Pte., S/16565	*18.11.17
Lindsay, C., Pte., 310031	*18.11.17	McCaskill, N., Pte., 3/3986	*25.1.15
Lindsay, E. F., Sgt., 831	*15.9.14	McClusky, J., Pte., 2524	*15.9.14
Lindsay, G., Pte., 3/3140	*25.1.15	McColl, A., Pte., 7275	*13.10.15
Lindsay, J., Pte., 520	*27.10.14	McColl, R., Pte., S/25236	*29.9.18
Lindsay, W. G., Pte., 2752	*25.9.15	McCormack, R., Pte., 3/2021	*25.1.15
Linkston, R., Pte., S/9102	*25.9.16	McCormack, W. G., Pte., 938	* 9.5.15

THE FIRST BATTALION THE BLACK WATCH

McCormick, J., Pte., 3/2215 *22.10.14
McCorrach, G., Pte., 9194 *29.10.14
McCreay, W., Pte., S/7082 * 9.5.15
McCulloch, G., Pte., 9741 * 9.2.15
McCulloch, J., Pte., 266517 †29.9.18
McCulloch, R., A/Cpl., 3/2101 †29.9.18
McCulloch, R., Pte., S/4452 (M.M.) †6.9.18
McCutchen, W. J., Pte., 244 †31.10.14
McDermott, F., Pte., S/5069 †10.5.15
McDairmid, J., Pte., 1254 * 7.10.15
McDairmid, J., Pte., 2461 *11.11.14
McDine, W. J., A/Cpl., 1834 *13.10.15
McDonald, A., Pte., 350643 † 6.12.17
McDonald, A., Pte., 2256 *12.11.14
McDonald, A., Pte., S/40267 †24.12.16
McDonald, C., Pte., 9665 † 7.11.14
McDonald, D., Pte., 8451 *16.9.14
McDonald, D., Pte., 2597 *27.10.14
McDonald, D., L/Cpl., 2770 §13.4.16
McDonald, E., Pte., 302 † 8.10.14
McDonald, H., Pte., 870, *24.10.14
McDonald, J., Pte., 1700 * 6.11.14
McDonald, J., Pte., S/7008 * 9.5.15
McDonald, J. A., Pte., 266719 *24.10.18
McDonald, N., A/Sgt., 2341 * 9.5.15
McDonald, P., Pte., 206 * 8.9.14
McDonald, W. J., Pte., S/4205 †30.3.16
McDougall, A., Pte., S/21731 *19.9.18
McDougall, A., Pte., S/13074 *25.9.16
McDougall, G., Pte., S/12183 *17.11.17
McDougall, J., A/Cpl., 9622 *25.9.15
McEachnie, A., Pte., 3/2630 *12.9.17
McEwan, A., Pte., S/40221 †29.9.16
McEwan, J. N., L/Cpl., 9615 *14.9.14
McEwan, T., L/Sgt., 513 * 3.9.16
McFadyen, J., Pte., S/10166 * 1.9.16
McFarlane, J., Pte., 3/980 * 9.5.15
McGann, P., Pte., 1983 †30.10.14
McGeary, J., Pte., 9884 * 9.5.15
McGhee, G., Pte., 3/3273 *18.2.15
McGhee, J. L., Pte., 3302 * 9.5.15
McGhee, T., Pte., S/6057 * 9.5.15
McGillivray, C., Pte., 8604 * 9.2.15
McGlashan, R., Pte., 9707 †10.11.14
McGowan, T., Pte., 3/2811 *25.1.15
McGrath, M., Pte., 3/1796 *31.10.14
McGrath, T., Pte., 3/2516 † 8.9.16
McGregor, A., Pte., 268553 *19.9.18
McGregor, D., Cpl., S/10817 *3.9.16
McGregor, J., Cpl., S/5726 †18.10.18
McGrouther, R., Cpl., S/3802 *18.8.16
McGuire, A., Sgt., 7655 *23.10.14
McGuire, J., A/Cpl., S/13329 * 6.12.16
McGuire, T., Pte., 21 *25.9.15
McHattie, A., Pte., 1775 †13.7.16
McIlwraith, W., L/Cpl., S/6655 * 9.5.15
McInnes, J., Pte., 1373 *15.9.14
McInnes, J. S., Pte., S/7037 †28.9.15
McInnes, J., L/Cpl., 120 *26.10.14
McInnes, J., Pte., 3/2730 *26.9.15
McInroy, J., Pte., 2413 (D.C.M.) *26.9.15
McIntosh, J., Pte., 2851 *25.1.15
McIntosh, R. J., Pte., S/11569 *18.8.16
McIntyre, D., Pte., S/8280 *25.9.15
McIntyre, D., Pte., 203214 †19.10.18
McIntyre, J., Pte., 8239 §21.6.15
McIntyre, R., Pte., 1956 *16.9.14
McKay, A., Pte., 3/2899 * 1.4.15
McKay, H., Pte., 257 *14.9.14
McKay, J., Pte., 3/3222 *25.1.15
McKay, J., Pte., 8654 *29.10.14
McKean, D., Pte., S/7541 †18.10.15
McKechnie, C., Pte., S/40168 *21.4.18
McKenzie, G. R., A/Sgt., 8108 *25.1.15
McKenzie, J., L/Cpl., 1032 * 3.9.16
McKenzie, J., Pte., 3/4174 *25.9.15
McKenzie, J., Pte., S/8315 * 9.5.15
McKenzie, J., Pte., 9823 * 9.5.15
McKenzie, W. B., L/Cpl., S/4885 †28.8.16
McKeown, W., Pte., 3/2510 *9.5.15
McKimmie, W., Pte., 772 * 9.5.15
McKinlay, P., Pte., 3/1326 *13.10.15
McKinnon, J., Pte., 3/1713 *29.10.14
McLagan, J., A/Sgt., 3/3775 † 7.9.16
McLaren, A., Pte., 9589 ‡25.2.15
McLaren, J., A/L/Sgt., 306 †25.9.15
McLauchlin, J., Pte., 40 *25.9.15
McLean, D., Pte., 8237 §21.6.15
McLean, G., Pte., S/17100 *18.4.18
McLean, J., Pte., S/7722 * 9.5.15
McLean, N., Pte., 3/2965 * 9.5.15
McLean, P., Pte., S/5038 *24.8.15
McLellan, R., Pte., 3/2495 *22.10.14
McLelland, J., Pte., 3/2743 *17.2.15
McLeod, D., Pte., 3/1226 †25.1.15
McLeod, D., A/Sgt., 9617 †21.8.16
McLeod, G. M., Pte., S/12961 * 8.9.16
McLeod, M., Pte., 5881 * 9.5.15
McLeod, N., Pte., S/40278 *25.9.16
McLuckie, D., Pte., S/7490 *25.9.15
McMorran, A. F., Pte., 3/3818 * 9.5.15
McMurchie, A., Pte., 3/2546 * 5.9.16
McNaughton, D., Pte., 2600 * 3.9.16
McNaughton, D., L/Cpl., 2270 *15.9.14

APPENDIX IV

McNaughton, J., Pte., 8094	§12.3.15	Menzies, J. D., Pte., 1182	*21.5.15
McNee, D., Pte., S/5420	†23.4.17	Merrilees, G., Sgt., 1248	†20.11.14
McNeil, J., A/Cpl., S/5599	†14.12.15	Methven, J., Pte., S/12647	*14.7.16
McNicol, D., Pte., S/12593	*18.11.17	Middleton, G., Pte., S/10162	*18.10.15
McQuade, H., Pte., 3/2622	* 6.3.15	Middleton, R., Pte., S/10086	*25.9.16
McQuattie, R., L/Cpl., 2453	*15.9.14	Mill, R., Pte., S/11842	* 3.9.16
McQueen, R., L/Cpl., 8371	* 3.9.16	Millar, A., Pte., 3/3416	*25.1.15
McRitchie, J., L/Cpl., 1071	* 9.5.15	Millar, J., Pte., S/10293	*13.10.15
McRobbie, G., Pte., 7438	*29.10.14	Millar, W., L/Cpl., 8035	† 2.11.14
McRobbie, W. J., Pte., S/41401	§14.11.18	Millar, A., Pte., S/1859	* 9.5.15
McSwain, A., Pte., 9243	* 9.5.15	Miller, D., Pte., S/8208	*13.10.15
McVicar, A., Pte., S/40302	*25.9.15	Miller, G., L/Cpl., 3/2031	*28.10.14
Mabe, H., Pte., 3/2577	†26.12.14	Miller, G. M., Pte., 2693	* 9.5.15
Main, J., Pte., S/10393	*13.10.15	Miller, G., Pte., 3/1984	* 9.5.15
Mair, W., Pte., 231	*25.1.15	Miller, J., Pte., S/7649	* 7.12.16
Malcolm, D. B., Pte., S/16320	* 4.8.18	Miller, J., Pte., 3324	*13.10.15
Malcolm, T., Pte., 3/1248	*25.9.15	Miller, J., Pte., 322	†22.7.15
Mands, F., Pte., 18308	*18.11.17	Millie, J., Pte., S/11896	*18.8.16
Marr, A., Sgt., S/8337	*18.4.18	Milne, G., Pte., 558	†21.11.14
Murray, J., Pte., S/40297	*25.9.16	Milne, G. N., Pte., S/6445	* 2.1.16
Marshall, C., Pte., 7456	*15.9.14	Milne, J., A/Cpl., 617	*13.10.15
Marshall, J. A., Pte., S/40306	*25.9.16	Milne, J., Pte., 2572	* 9.5.15
Marshall, L., Sgt., 9808	*15.9.14	Milne, W., L/Cpl., 3/2125 (M.M.)	*20.9.18
Martin, C., Pte., S/16570	*18.4.18	Milton, J., L/Cpl., S/3014	†10.5.15
Martin, D., Pte., 9571	*14.9.14	Milton, T., A/Sgt., 9729	* 9.5.15
Martin, D., L/Cpl., 3/1730	* 2.11.14	Mitchell, A., Pte., S/7069	* 9.5.15
Martin, J., Pte., S/12000	†21.9.16	Mitchell, J., Pte., S/43365	*25.9.16
Mason, A. H., Pte., S/12579	*14.7.16	Mitchell, J., Pte., 8117	* 9.5.15
Mason, R., L/Cpl., 2322	*14.7.16	Mitchell, J., L/Cpl., S/40186	† 5.3.17
Massie, A., Pte., S/24590	* 7.7.18	Mitchell, J., Dmr., 1967	*26.12.15
Masterson, W. J., Sgt., 3/1941	* 9.5.15	Mitchell, P., Pte., S/7505	* 9.5.15
Matear, S., Pte., S/8327	†14.10.15	Mitchell, R., Pte., 918	*15.11 14
Mather, J. P., Pte., S/12301	* 3.9.16	Mitchell, R., Pte., S/43343	*20.4.18
Matheson, J., Pte., 3/3488	†26.1.15	Mitchell, W. T., Pte., S/11900 (M.M.)	* 3.9.16
Mathieson, D., L/Cpl., 3/2331	*14.7.16		
Matthew, P., Pte., 3/1924	*11.11.14	Moffat, J., Pte., S/40059	*25.9.16
Matthewson, D. C., Pte., S/40740	† 6.9.18	Moir, D. H., L/Cpl., 7363	*25.9.15
Mattocks, H., A/Cpl., S/7937	*13.10.15	Monaghan, J., Dmr., 9967	†20.1.15
Maude, F. M., Pte., S/12584	*25.9.15	Montague, J., Pte., 1172	†14.10.15
Mears, J., Pte., S/14462	†20.11.16	Montgomery, J., L/Cpl., 7366	§21.6.15
Meek, R., Pte., 2342	* 9.5.15	Moodie, A., Pte., S/14120	† 1.6.18
Meikle, F., Pte., S/13899	*27.10.18	Moon, J., Pte., 9236	*15.9.14
Meikle, J. H., Pte., S/7689	† 1.10.15	Moore, E., Pte., S/3838	*25.1.15
Meiklejohn, A., Sgt., 1039	*14.9.14	Morgan, J., Pte., 9234	†31.1.15
Meldrum, R., Pte., S/40089	*25.9.16	Morgan, W., A/Cpl., 3/3412	*25.1.15
Mellon, P., Pte., 3/2608	* 9.5.15	Morley, J. B., Pte., S/11149	* 3.9.16
Mellon, W., Cpl., 3/1370	*25.1.15	Morrice, A., Pte., 2010	* 8.9.14
Melrose, J., Pte., S/10901	*14.7.16	Morris, A., Pte., 3/1058	* 9.5.15
Melville, E., Pte., 8157	*27.10.14	Morris, C., Pte., 7307	† 1.10.15
Melville, J., Pte., 3/961	*29.10.14	Morris, D., Pte., 3/1776	*20.10.14
Melville, J., Pte., 3/1619	* 9.5.15	Morris, J., Pte., S/7549	*25.9.15
Menzies, A., Pte., 9545	† 5.11.14	Morris, P., Pte., 2825	§28.5.15
Menzies, G., Pte., 3/2696	*25.1.15	Morris, R., Pte., 3/1972	*27.10.14
		Morrison, A., Pte., S/6740	* 5.9.16

THE FIRST BATTALION THE BLACK WATCH

Morrison, D., Pte., 3/2535	*13.10.15	Ormerod, J. W., Pte., 7773	*26.10.14
Morrison, D., Pte., 3/2573	†22.8.16	Orr, T., Pte., 7704	*22.9.14
Morrison, J., Pte., 2741	* 9.5.15	Oswald, D. D., Pte., 3/2553	*30.12.14
Morrison, J., Pte., 3/3237	‡30.5.16	Owens, J., Pte., 3/1849	†12.10.14
Morrison, J., Pte., S/3723	* 9.5.15	Oxley, T., Pte., 9831	*11.11.14
Morrison, J. B., Pte., S/16515	*18.11.17		
Morrison, J, L/Cpl, S/5181	*25.1.15		
Morrison, W., L/Cpl., S/7440	* 9.5.15	Page, A., L/Cpl., 3/2074	*11.11.14
Morton, D., Pte., S/6747	*27.7.16	Park, A., Pte., S/7933	*17.11.17
Morton, W. G., L/Sgt., 2346	*18.8.16	Parker, P., Pte., 3/903	* 9.5.15
Moulden, E. H., Pte., S/11810	* 3.9.16	Paterson, G., Pte., 3/1138	†26.1.15
Mullen, P., Pte., 3/3531	§19.12 14	Paterson, G., Pte., 2450	*23.10.14
Munro, A., Pte., 3/2992	* 9.5.15	Paterson, J., Pte., 2852	* 6.3.15
Munro, A., Pte., 3/2489	*11.11.14	Paterson, J. F., Pte., 3/4044	* 9.5.15
Munro, H., Pte., 10317	*13.10.15	Paterson, J., L/Cpl., S/43390	*19.9.18
Munro, J., Pte., S/8422	†28.9.15	Paterson, J., Pte., 268389	*18.10.18
Murchie, W., Pte., 984	*15.9.14	Paterson, R., Pte., 363	*27.10.14
Murdoch, J., Sgt., 8054	*16.9.14	Paterson, R., Pte., S/11296	*22.9.16
Munro, M., Pte., S/4130	* 9.5.15	Paton, A., Pte., 9894	* 9.5.15
Murray, J., Pte., 1659	†21.5.15	Paton, J., Pte., 2586	*29.9.18
Murray, T., Pte., 8649	*16.9.14	Paton, J. C., Pte., S/14459	*25.9.16
Myles, W. J., Pte., 2538	*26.12.15	Paton, W., Pte., 9308	*15.9.14
		Paton, W., Pte., S/18850	* 4.11.18
Naismith, J., L/Cpl., S/40095	*12.12.17	Patterson, N. L., Pte., S/40086	
Neave, C., Pte., 7062	*11.11.14		*25.9.16
Neil, C. E., Cpl., 425	*15.9.14	Patullo, A., Pte., 3/3776	† 6.10.15
Neilson, A., L/Cpl., S/10396	* 3.9.16	Paul, J. A., Pte., 6033	†19.4.15
Neilson, J., L/Cpl., 3/3379	*25.9.15	Pearson, A., Pte., 8686	*13.10.15
Neilson, J., Pte., 3475	*25.1.15	Pearson, J., Pte., 825	* 9.5.15
Nelson, J., Pte., 333	* 9.5.15	Peat, S., L/Cpl., 3/2924	† 4.6.16
Nelson, T. B., L/Cpl., 2387	*28.10.14	Peat, T., Pte., 3/2015	*16.5.15
Ness, G., Cpl., 1704	* 9.5.15	Peebles, R., Pte., S/7012	*13.7.16
Niblo, W., Pte., 2412	† 4.11.14	Penman, A., Pte., S/6639	*25.9.15
Nicholson, A., L/Cpl, 3/3912	* 9.5.15	Penman, G., Pte., 9410	*29.10.14
Nicholson, A., Pte., 310034	*18.4.18	Penman, W., Pte., S/10435	*18.4.18
Nicoll, C., Pte., S/4091	*13.10.15	Percival, A., Pte., 1411	†26.9.15
Nicoll, J., Cpl., S/23117	†28.5.18	Pert, W., Pte., 3/2908	*25.9.15
Nicoll, P., L/Cpl., S/11894	* 8.1.18	Petrie, D., Pte., 3/2543	† 3.7.17
Neil, R., Cpl., S/7662	† 7.9.16	Phair, J., Pte., 3/3024	* 9.5.15
Niven, A., Pte., 3/3417	* 3.9.16	Philip, W., Pte., 1849	*25.1.15
Niven, G., Pte., S/22904	†28.2.18	Philip, D., Pte., 2165	*29.10.14
Niven, R., Pte., S/9507	†24.9.16	Philip, T., Pte., 14	* 9.5.15
Niven, W., L/Cpl., 8104	*25.1.15	Plant, H., Pte., S/2854	*25.9.15
Nivison, W., Pte., 7851	†26.1.15	Poe, J. P., Pte., S/11634	*25.9.15
Nixon, T., Pte., S/40291	*25.9.16	Pollock, J. P., L/Cpl., 3/1250	*10.2.15
Noble, J., Pte., S/9730	*25.10.18	Ponton, J. G., Pte., S/17866	*27.9.18
Noble, W., Pte., 3/1098	*25.9.15	Porteous, J., Pte., 3/2715	*12.11.14
Norrie, A., Pte., S/8453		Prentice, W., Pte., S/4128	*14.7.16
(M.M.)	*18.8.16	Punch, W. I., Pte., S/7509	*29.9.15
Norrie, J., Pte., 2494	*10.11.14	Purvis, W. J., Pte., S/7483	*13.10.15
Nutt, W., L/Cpl., 9340	†11.4.15		
Nuttall, T. L., Pte., S/8331	*13.10.15		
		Quayle, G., Cpl., S/6376	*18.8.16
Ogilvie, B. L., Pte., 3/1513	*11.11.14	Quinn, P., Pte., 3/3339	*10.2.15
Ogilvie, G., Pte., 676	*11.11.14	Quinn, P., Pte., S/6595	* 9.5.15

APPENDIX IV

Ramsay, A., Sgt., 1291
    (M.M. and Bar) §18.10.18
Ramsay, D., Pte., S/8441   * 3.9.16
Ramsay, E., Cpl., 3/2967   *25.1.15
Rattray, J., Pte., S/8140   *15.2.16
Redpath, R., Sgt., 1008
    (D.C.M.) §20.6.17
Reekie, C., Pte., 8144   *10.11.14
Regan, E., Pte., 13280 (M.M.)   * 3.9.16
Regan, H., Pte., 9935   §21.6.15
Reid, A., Pte., S/8276   † 3.10.15
Reid, F., Pte., 3/4053   *25.1.15
Reid, G., Pte., 9838   †31.12.14
Reid, J., Pte., S/8545   †17.10.15
Reid, J., Pte., S/9217   *22.9.16
Reid, R. T., Pte., 3/2349   §15.4.16
Reid, W., Pte., 2670   *16.6.15
Reilly, H., Pte., 3/2120   *10.11.14
Reilly, J., Pte., 2009   † 4.11.14
Rennie, C., Pte., S/7911   †16.9.15
Rennie, F., Pte., 587   *11.11.14
Rennie, G., Pte., S/40143   *17.4.18
Rennie, H., Pte., S/8166   † 9.9.16
Rennie, R., Pte., 1463   * 9.5.15
Reoch, D., Pte., S/8541   *13.10.15
Reoch, J. S., Sgt., 9987   †14.11.14
Reston, J., Pte., S/3479   *25.5.16
Reynolds, A., Pte., 1037   *16.9.14
Richardson, J. C., Pte., S/9968 †19.11.17
Riddell, G., Pte., 200086   †28.5.18
Rielly, W., Pte., 3/3559   *21.5.15
Ring, W., Cpl., S/9934   * 3.9.16
Ritchie, D., Pte., 8410   *29.10.14
Ritchie, G., Pte., S/8351   *25.9.15
Ritchie, J., Pte., S/7728   *25.9.15
Ritchie, J., Pte., S/7481   † 5.10.16
Ritchie, J., Pte., 8400   *14.9.14
Ritchie, R., A/Sgt., 9694   *13.10.15
Ritchie, W., L/Cpl., 2281   †15.10.14
Robb, W., Pte., 3/2962   * 6.3.15
Robb, W., Pte., 3/3814   * 3.9.16
Roberts, A. S., Pte., 3/2610   *25.9.15
Roberts, T., Pte., 3/3479   * 9.5.15
Robertson, A. L., Pte., 2593   * 9.5.15
Robertson, A., Pte., S/40040   *25.9.16
Robertson, C., A/Sgt., 9582   §21.6.15
Robertson, D., Pte., S/14439   *25.9.16
Robertson, D., Pte., 3/2529   * 9.2.15
Robertson, F., Pte., 2722   * 9.5.15
Robertson, G., A/Sgt., 9684   †10.5.15
Robertson, G., Pte., S/41498   † 9.10.18
Robertson, H., Pte., 8340   *11.11.14
Robertson, J., L/Cpl., 311   †29.2.16
Robertson, J., Pte., 7670   *11.11.14
Robertson, J., Pte., S/16415   †27.11.17
Robertson, J., Pte., S/22886   *28.9.18
Robertson, J., Pte., 685   * 9.5.15
Robertson, J., Pte., 3/2291   *13.10.15
Robertson, J., Pte., S/8299   *25.9.15
Robertson, J., L/Cpl., 1746   †24.10.15
Robertson, P., Pte., S/4092   †24.9.16
Robertson, R., Pte., S/7526   *25.9.15
Robertson, R., A/Cpl., 9671   *26.9.15
Robertson, W., Pte., 2751   * 9.5.15
Robertson, W., Pte., 9932   *12.11.14
Robertson, W., L/Cpl., S/10866
     *13.7.16
Robertson, W. B., L/Cpl., 1779
     *15.10.15
Rodger, W., L/Cpl., 796   * 7.5.15
Rogers, D. K., Pte., 8581   ‡ 7.5.16
Ross, D., Pte., S/40310   *25.9.16
Ross, G., L/Sgt., 3/2863   * 9.5.15
Ross, J. B., Sgt., 1913   * 2.11.14
Ross, J., Pte., 260   *27.10.14
Ross, T., Pte., 2532   * 9.5.15
Ross, W., Pte., 3/3829   §31.12.14
Ross, W., L/Cpl., S/7749   *18.8.16
Rougvie, A., Pte., 3/1268   † 9.5.15
Rowan, J. H., L/Cpl., S/7659 † 1.1.16
Rowell, C. J., A/Cpl., S/10272
     †18.4.18
Rowell, P., A/Cpl., 7330   * 9.5.15
Rudd, W., Pte., 114   *26.9.15
Rue, D., Pte., 2202   * 9.5.15
Rushford, A., L/Cpl., S/7437 *13.10.15
Rushford, M., Pte., S/3902   *25.1.15
Russell, A., Pte., 2969   †27.8.16
Russell, D. J., L/Cpl., S/10944
     *18.8.16
Russell, D., Pte., 202443   * 2.10.18
Russell, R., Pte., S/7497   †29.9.15
Russell, W., Pte., 89   †15.10.14
Rutherford, R., Sgt., 3/3947   * 9.5.15
Ryce, J. P., L/Cpl., 457   ‡12.10.18

Salmond, J., Pte., S/5472   †19.9.18
Salt, E., Cpl., 9595   †18.10.14
Samson, J., Pte., 3/3349   * 9.5.15
Sandiford, J., Pte., 9592   *16.9.14
Sands, G. R., Sgt., 3/766   * 9.11.14
Savage, G., Pte., S/7557   *25.9.15
Sayle, H., Pte., S/12370   † 9.8.18
Scarratt, J., Pte., S/7412   †21.5.16
Schofield, J., Pte., 3/8986   †10.11.14
Scotland, W., Pte., 2695   *25.1.15
Scott, A., Pte., 266421   *20.8.18
Scott, A., Pte., 2562   †21.6.15
Scott, C., Pte., 2325   *13.10.15
Scott, C., Pte., S/5356   * 9.5.15

THE FIRST BATTALION THE BLACK WATCH

Scott, D., Pte., 2527	*23.9.14	Small, J., Pte., S/8107	*14.10.15
Scott, D., L/Cpl., 9441	†27.10.14	Small, T., Pte., 7524	*11.11.14
Scott, G. A., A/Cpl., 1892	*22.2.16	Small, W., Pte., S/6809	*25.1.15
Scott, J., Pte., 7411	* 6.10.15	Smith, A. M., L/Cpl., 2771	* 9.5.15
Scott, J. S., C.S.M., 2365	*16.6.15	Smith, A., L/Cpl., 378	*27.10.14
Scott, J., Pte., S/22874	*28.2.18	Smith, A. A., Pte., S/10145	*22.12.15
Scott, R. S., Pte., S/9983	* 4.9.16	Smith, C., Pte., S/8229	†14.10.15
Scott, T. M., Pte., S/8376	*25.9.15	Smith, C., Pte., S/16603	† 9.7.18
Scott, W., Cpl., 1101	*23.10.14	Smith, C., Pte., 2406	*29.10.14
Scott, W., L/Cpl., 2485	* 9.5.15	Smith, D. G., L/Cpl., 2402	*16.9.14
Scott, W., L/Cpl., S/7314	†21.3.18	Smith, D. M., A/Sgt., 9560	*15.11.14
Scott, W. M., Pte., 2506	*16.6.15	Smith, E., Pte., 3/1893	* 2.11.14
Scrimgeour, J. R., Pte., S/40218		Smith, E., Pte., S/4351	*23.9.18
	†28.5.18	Smith, F. J., Pte., 3/1757	*23.10.14
Scully, J., Pte., 3/3211	* 9.5.15	Smith, F., Cpl., S/14555	§24.10.18
Seery, J., Pte., S/6107	*25.1.15	Smith, J., Pte., 1	*31.10.14
Shand, D., Pte., 3374	‡14.3.16	Smith, J., Pte., 3/3001	* 9.5.15
Shand, J., Pte., 3/1653	†28.10.14	Smith, J., Pte., 3/3892	* 9.5.15
Sharp, A., Pte., S/12536	*24.2.18	Smith, J., Pte., 9822	* 9.5.15
Sharp, J., Pte., 9421	*29.10.14	Smith, J., Pte., 9853	* 9.5.15
Shaw, A. A., Pte., 1560	* 6.10.15	Smith, J., Pte., S/40071	† 6.12.16
Shaw, C., L/Cpl., 2587	*14.7.16	Smith, J., L/Cpl., S/40079	‡30.9.18
Shaw, J., Pte., 8804	*21.8.16	Smith, J., Pte., 1091	* 9.5.15
Shepherd, J., Pte., 550	*23.10.14	Smith, J., Pte., 7323	*15.9.14
Shepherd, J., Pte., S/8105	*26.12.15	Smith, J., Pte., 7465	†24.9.14
Shepherd, R., L/Cpl., 3/2039	* 2.11.14	Smith, J., Pte., S/12534	*30.6.16
Sherriden, E., Pte., 3/3096	‡ 7.7.15	Smith, J. R., Pte., S/8050	†27.9.15
Shilling, T. J., Pte., 7644	† 8.10.14	Smith, R., Pte., S/11402	*18.8.16
Shirrefs, R. M., Pte., S/43197	*19.10.16	Smith, R. T., L/Cpl., 2318	†19.6.15
Sidey, W., Pte., S/17758	†19.4.18	Smith, S., Pte., S/9261	†30.12.15
Silk, F., Pte., 9658	*16.9.14	Smith, S., Pte., S/14451	*17.4.18
Sim, D., Pte., S/3883	* 9.5.15	Smith, T., Pte., 230	†17.4.18
Sim, G., Pte., 2522	*29.10.14	Smith, T. R., A/Cpl., 1940	*9.5.15
Sim, J., Pte., S/8446	* 7.10.15	Smith, W., Pte., 7680	*29.10.14
Sime, R., Pte., S/24090	*18.4.18	Smith, W. B., Pte., 1273	*15.9.14
Sime, W., Sgt., S/40096	†27.9.16	Smitton, D., Pte., 7405	†29.10.14
Simmonite, G., Cpl., 9586	† 8.6.15	Sneddon, J., Pte., S/11962	* 3.9.16
Simmons, J., Cpl., 3/4019	*24.8.15	Sneddon, J., Pte., 285009	†18.4.18
Simpson, A., Cpl., 3/4019	*24.8.15	Snelling, G. J. W., Cpl., 663	‡25.9.14
Simpson, A., Pte., 10090	†14.10.14	Sone, S. I., Pte., 2729	* 9.5.15
Simpson, G., Pte., S/4974	†13.12.16	Sorley, A., Pte., 1540	*13.10.15
Simpson, J., Pte., S/6389	* 3.9.16	Sorley, J., Pte., 1385	* 9.5.15
Simpson, T., Pte., 3/3709	* 3.9.16	Spence, J. D. W., Pte., S/11907	
Simpson, T., Pte., S/11351	*21.4.16		* 1.9.16
Sinclair, A., Pte., 9905	§21.6.15	Spence, P., Pte., S/3769	* 9.5.15
Sinclair, D., Sgt., 7396	*25.9.15	Spittle, R. J., Pte., S/11186	*24.12.16
Sinclair, D., Pte., 11225	*13.7.16	Stanners, T., Cpl., 345381	*19.9.18
Sinclair, J., L/Cpl., 832	*25.9.15	Stark, G., Pte., 3/3029	*13.10.15
Sivewright, D., Pte., 1421	†27.1.15	Stark, H., Pte., S/40272	*22.9.16
Sladen, C. H. C., Bdsm., 1776		Starrs, J., Pte., S/7506	§29.4.18
	*21.4.18	Steel, A., Pte., 1705	*22.9.16
Slaven, J., Pte., 3/8653	*25.1.15	Steel, W. E., Pte., 292700	*24.10.18
Slinger, W., L/Cpl., S/7706	*13.10.15	Steele, H., Pte., S/8615	†14.4.16
Sloan, W., Pte., S/43065	*22.9.16	Stephen, D., L/Cpl., 1933	‡ 2.11.14
Slorance, W., Pte., S/15320	*18.4.18	Stevens, T., Pte., S/8022	§20.10.18

APPENDIX IV

Stevens, S., Cpl., S/9091	*19.9.18	Taylor, J., Pte., 3/3716	*18.8.16
Stevenson, T., Pte., 3/2751	†23.3.15	Taylor, J., Pte., 9502	*26.10.14
Stevenson, W., Pte., 3/4201	†13.6.15	Taylor, R., Pte., 3/1324	*13.10.15
Stewart, A., Pte., 3/2831	‡29.4.16	Taylor, R., Pte., S/22846	† 6.5.18
Stewart, A., Pte., S/8557	*13.10.15	Teasdale, A. H., Pte., S/11968	
Stewart, C., Pte., 2755	† 5.8.16		*21.5.16
Stewart, D., Pte., 3/1927	* 4.10.14	Thacker, N., Pte., S/10251	*13.10.15
Stewart, D., Pte., 3/3279	† 4.1.15	Thain, W., Pte., S/40203	*25.9.16
Stewart, D. M., Pte., 3/1477	*25.9.16	Thom, J., Pte., 9492	† 8.10.15
Stewart, D., Pte., 438	* 5.9.14	Thomas, A. H. T., Pte., 9875	*14.9.14
Stewart, H., Sgt., 877	*14.7.16	Thompson, A., Pte., S/9336	*17.11.17
Stewart, I., Pte., 3/2787	*25.12.14	Thompson, W. G., Pte., S/8579	
Stewart, R., Pte., 3/3985	* 9.5.15		*25.9.15
Stewart, W., Pte., 2530	†27.1.15	Thomson, A., Pte., 3/1213	†25.9.15
Stewart, W., Pte., S/40176	*21.9.16	Thomson, A., Pte., S/40060	*25.9.16
Stormouth, D. P., Pte., S/43119		Thomson, C., Cpl., S/8652	*12.10.17
	†16.4.18	Thomson, D., C.Q.M.S., 2140	
Stott, J. S., Cpl., 267161	*28.9.18		† 3.9.18
Strachan, H., Pte., 3/3472	*25.1.15	Thomson, D., L/Cpl., 2174	* 9.5.15
Strachan, J., Pte., 3/9658	* 1.11.14	Thomson, G., Pte., S/11832	*18.8.16
Strachan, P., Pte., S/8426	*13.10.15	Thomson, G., Pte., S/40112	*21.9.16
Strachan, T., Pte., 7220	*15.9.14	Thomson, J. C., Pte., S/13373	
Strachan, W., Pte., 8603	*16.9.14		†23.4.17
Strachan, W., Pte., S/43352	†21.9.16	Thomson, P., Pte., 3/2943	* 6.1.15
Strath, A., Pte., 3/670	†25.8.16	Thomson, R., Pte., S/3636	* 6.10.15
Strathdee, A., Pte., 2736	*25.9.15	Thomson, R. C., Pte., 3207	§16.12.15
Strathie, J., Pte., S/7489	* 7.5.15	Todd, A., Pte., 9827	*11.11.14
Stuart, C., Pte., 7244	† 9.5.15	Todd, A., Pte., 3/8203	*23.1.17
Stuart, D., Pte., S/3073	* 9.5.15	Todd, C., Pte., 3/2620	*10.1.15
Stuart, G., L/Cpl., S/40233	*17.11.17	Todd, E., Pte., 3/2343	*22.10.14
Stuart, W., L/Cpl., 9430	* 9.5.15	Todd, W., L/Cpl., 107	†21.6.15
Sturrock, E., L/Cpl., S/14445	†22.4.18	Trail, G., Pte., S/8707	*20.9.16
Sturrock, P., Pte., S/10517	†19.8.16	Traynor, F., A/Sgt., 9237	†14.10.15
Summers, C., Pte., 331	†16.9.14	Traynor, P., Pte., 3/2221	* 9.5.15
Summers, J., Pte., 8538	*21.5.15	Traynor, P., Pte., S/43094	* 9.9.18
Summers, J., Pte., S/5536	† 5.11.18	Trotter, A. M., L/Cpl., S/9404	
Sutherland, J., Pte., 9881	*29.10.14		*18.4.18
Sutherland, J., Pte., S/16299	† 6.3.17	Trotter, J., Pte., 2564	†21.6.15
Sutherland, J. C., Pte., S/8450		Tullis, D., Pte., 3/3105	* 9.5.15
	*13.10.15	Tulloch, J., Pte., 2754	*26.9.15
Sutherland, J., Pte., S/7018	*18.4.16	Tunnah, D., Pte., 998	*11.11.14
Sutherland, W., Pte., 268260	* 4.11.18	Turley, G., Pte., 3/6642	* 9.5.15
Swan, D., Pte., 3/3730	* 9.5.15	Turnbull, G., Pte., 2292	*25.2.16
Swan, J., Pte., S/4032	† 2.9.16	Turnbull, R., Pte., 9306	†15.9.14
Swan, J., A/Sgt., 9291	†10.5.15	Turner, J. J., Pte., S/23949	§28.10.18
Sweeny, W., Pte., S/4031	* 3.9.16	Tweddle, J., Cpl., S/7005	*17.4.18
Symans, J., Pte., S/14176	*24.2.17		
		Utley, J. E., Pte., S/43362	*23.12.16
Taggart, W., Pte., 3/471	†16.1.16		
Tait, J., Pte., 8064	* 9.5.15	Valentine, A., Pte., 3/3581	*25.1.15
Talkington, H., Pte., S/5884	* 4.9.16	Valentine, J., Pte., 3/2725	* 9.5.15
Tate, T., Pte., S/11814	*25.9.16	Valentine, J., L/Cpl., 693	*27.10.14
Tavendale, C., Pte., 241141	*18.4.18	Vickers, W., Pte., 6694	* 9.5.15
Taylor, A., Pte., 2561	*13.10.15	Vogan, H., Pte., 922	* 9.5.15
Taylor, A., Pte., 12146	†28.6.17		

THE FIRST BATTALION THE BLACK WATCH

Waddell, W. D., L/Sgt., 1777	*13.10.15	Whyte, A., L/Cpl., S/9746	* 3.9.16
Wagstaff, W. H., Pte., S/10101	* 3.10.15	Whyte, D., Pte., 807	* 9.5.18
		Whyte, D., Pte., 3989	* 9.5.15
Waldie, D., Pte., S/43331	*25.9.16	Whyte, M. M., Pte., 3/2261	*9 .5.15
Walinck, D., L/Cpl., S/10154	*18.8.16	Whyte, W., Pte., 3/3455	†26.1.15
Walker, A., Pte., 3/3441	§23.10.17	Whyte, W., Sgt., 9578	†22.11.14
Walker, J., Pte., 820	†16.9.14	Wilkie, A., Pte., 285013	*22.3.18
Wallace, I., L/Cpl., 2184	†20.11.14	Wilkie, T., Sgt., 2098	*30.4.16
Wanliss, J. J., Pte., 2613	* 9.5.15	Will, D. B., Cpl., 2224	†29.10.14
Ward, G., Pte., S/10134	*13.10.15	Williams, B., Pte., S/5979	†26.4.18
Wardlaw, P., Cpl., S/5876 (D.C.M.)	* 3.9.16	Williamson, J., Pte., S/6744	* 9.5.15
		Willmott, J., Pte., 3/3216	*18.8.16
		Wilson, A., Pte., 3/4127	* 9.5.15
Wardlaw, R., Pte., S/8535	*18.4.18	Wilson, D., Pte., S/4028	†18.6.15
Wasson, R., Pte., 7776	†30.10.14	Wilson, E., Pte., S/13077	*19.9.18
Watson, A., Pte., 7820	*31.10.14	Wilson, G., Pte., 462	§ 2.11.18
Watson, A., Pte., S/40066	*22.11.16	Wilson, G., Pte., S/7397	* 9.5.15
Watson, I., Pte., 3/1886	* 9.5.15	Wilson, J., Pte., 7779	*29.10.14
Watson, J., Pte., S/6968	* 9.2.15	Wilson, J., Pte., S/11126	*18.3.16
Watson, J., Pte., 9444	†30.10.14	Wilson, J. S., Pte., S/15467	*30.9.18
Watson, J., Pte., 9975	* 9.5.15	Wilson, J., Pte., 916	†20.9.14
Watson, J., Pte., 3/2825	* 1.3.15	Wilson, J., Pte., 3/3410	* 9.5.15
Watson, M., Pte., S/4694	* 3.9.16	Wilson, J., Pte., S/40212	*18.9.18
Watson, T., Pte., 3/2185	*29.10.14	Wilson, J. C., Pte., S/24066	*18.4.18
Watson, W., Pte., 3/2202	*25.9.15	Wilson, R., L/Cpl., S/40651	*21.3.18
Watson, W., Pte., 2469	*25.1.15	Wilson, S., Pte., S/8198	† 7.9.16
Watson, W., Pte., S/43184	*17.11.17	Wilson, T., Pte., 9982	†20.9.14
Watson, W. C., A/Cpl., 3/2162	* 9.5.15	Wilson, W., Pte., 9922	†31.10.14
Watt, D., Pte., 3/2536	*22.7.15	Winton, W., Pte., S/4153	*18.8.16
Watt, G., L/Cpl., S/9438	†26.4.18	Wishart, R., Pte., 3/4067	* 9.5.15
Watt, J., Pte., S/2829	* 3.9.16	Withinshaw, J. M., Pte., S/7415	*13.10.15
Watt, R., Cpl., 2198	*18.8.16		
Watters, R., Pte., 9204	§21.6.15	Wood, C., Pte., 3/3352	†13.6.15
Watters, S., Cpl., 2042	*22.10.14	Worledge, C., L/Cpl., S/4164	*17.11.17
Webster, A., Pte., S/43330	*25.9.16	Wright, A., L/Cpl., 2170	*29.10.14
Webster, J., Pte., 3/2325	* 9.5.15	Wright, J., Pte., 3/3110	* 8.5.15
Webster, T. D. B., Pte., 310027	*18.4.18	Wright, J., Pte., 7256	*24.10.14
		Wright, R., Pte., 3/3085	*25.1.15
Wehrle, S., Pte., 3/3546	†30.12.14	Wright, S., Pte., S/12911	* 4.6.18
Weir, E., Pte., 268750	†11.6.18	Wright, W., Pte., S/40090	*19.9.18
Weir, J., Pte., 3/3007	* 9.5.15	Wright, W. L., Cpl., S/7074	*17.8.16
Weir, P., Pte., S/11834	†25.8.16	Wynn, J., A/Cpl., 3/2134	*25.1.15
Welch, H., L/Cpl., S/10088	* 2.9.16		
Welsh, A., Pte., S/18119	*18.4.18	Yeaman, E., Pte., 3/2354	* 9.5.15
Wemyss, D., L/Cpl., S/9088	†30.4.18	Yorke, R., Pte., 3/2845	* 9.5.15
West, A., Pte., S/7568	*13.10.15	Young, A., Pte., 3/3577	*25.1.15
West, G., Pte., 1514	*13.10.15	Young, D., Pte., 9394	* 7.10.15
Westwater, J., Pte., S/40111	*18.4.18	Young, E., Pte., S/3491	* 9.2.15
Wheatley, T., Pte., S/9865 (M.M.)	*17.9.18	Young, G., Pte., S/12566	† 3.9.16
		Young, J., Pte., 3/3706	*13.10.15
Wheeler, A., Pte., 2748	*14.7.16	Young, P., Pte., 7742	*29.10.14
White, A., Pte., 3/3311	* 9.5.15	Young, T., Pte., S/8510	†12.7.16
Whitehead, T., Pte., S/3948	* 9.5.15	Young, W., Pte., 912	†12.6.16
Whitelaw, G., Pte., 3/2020	*11.11.14	Younger, J., Pte., S/40076	* 7.7.18
Whitmore, F., L/Cpl., S/7106	§28.5.15	Yule, A. W., Pte., 9225	† 9.10.14

APPENDIX V

HONOURS AND AWARDS

The First Battalion

PROMOTIONS
Brevet Lieut.-Colonel
Capt. and Brevet Major V. M. Fortune.
Major J. G. H. Hamilton, D.S.O.

Brevet Major
Captain V. M. Fortune.

Hon. Major
Captain and Q.M. W. Fowler, M.C.

Hon. Captain
Lieut. and Q.M. W. Fowler.

BRITISH DECORATIONS
Victoria Cross
Corpl. J. Ripley.

C.M.G.
Lieut.-Col. C. E. Stewart.

Bar to D.S.O.
Capt. (A/Lieut.-Col.) F. Anderson, D.S.O., M.C.
Lieut.-Col. L. P. Evans, V.C., D.S.O.

D.S.O.
Capt. and Brevet Major V. M. Fortune.
Major W. Green.
Major J. T. C. Murray.

Bar to M.C.
Capt. N. D. Macleod, M.C.   Lieut. J. W. H. Robertson, M.C.

M.C.
Lieut. W. Addison, D.C.M.
Lieut. F. Anderson.
Capt. R. E. Anstruther.
Lieut. R. K. Arbuthnott.
2nd Lieut. D. Baxter.
Lieut. G. S. M. Burton.
Lieut. W. F. Bushe.
Capt. A. B. Clark.
Capt. P. H. L. C. Colquhoun.
2nd Lieut. A. J. H. Dempster.
Lieut. W. H. C. Edwards.
Lieut. G. W. Ferguson.
Capt. and Q.M. W. Fowler.
Lieut. M. S. Gunn.
Capt. P. B. Hepburn.
Lieut. T. Johnstone.
Capt. D. Lumsden.
Capt. N. D. Macleod.

THE FIRST BATTALION THE BLACK WATCH

M.C. (contd.)

Major D. Macleod (Chaplain).
2nd Lieut. N. L. MacNaughton.
2nd Lieut. J. Millar.
Lieut. D. M. Moffat, R.A.M.C. (attached).
Lieut. D. I. Murray-Menzies.
Lieut. M. H. N. A. Noble.
Lieut. R. Ramsay.
Lieut. A. F. Ritchie.
Lieut. J. W. H. Robertson.
Lieut. G. B. Rowan-Hamilton.
Capt. J. N. O. Rycroft.
2nd Lieut. D. Smith, D.C.M.
Lieut. J. A. Smith.
Lieut. D. I. Stewart.
Capt. J. W. C. Stubbs, R.A.M.C. (attached).
2nd Lieut. C. I. Sutherland.
Lieut. B. G. Valentine.
Lieut. W. Wilson, D.C.M.
Lieut. J. S. Young.
R.S.M. C. Scott.

Mentioned in Despatches

Capt. H. F. S. Amery.
Capt. R. C. Anderson (2).
Lieut. R. E. Anstruther.
2nd Lieut. K. Buist.
Capt. A. B. Clark.
Capt. Hon. M. C. A. Drummond.
Lieut. W. H. C. Edwards.
Capt. L. P. Evans (2).
2nd Lieut. H. St. L. Feiling.
Lieut. V. M. Fortune (2).
Lieut. and Q.M. W. Fowler (3).
Capt. W. Green (2).
Major J. G. H. Hamilton.
Lieut. G. E. B. Honeyman.
Lieut. D. Lumsden.
Major D. MacLeod, Chaplain, (attached).
2nd Lieut. A. Mercer.
Lieut. D. I. Murray-Menzies.
2nd Lieut. R. Macfarlane.
Lieut. G. M. Richmond.
Lieut. G. B. Rowan-Hamilton.
Lieut. J. N. O. Rycroft.
Lieut.-Col. C. E. Stewart (2).
Capt. W. D. McL. Stewart.

L/Corpl. G. Clark.
Pte. J. Devlin.
L/Corpl. A. Dewar.
Pte. J. Fenton.
Sgt. G. Ferguson.
Sgt. P. Hitchman.
Corpl. P. McArthur.
Sgt./Dr. C. McIntosh.
Pte. J. McIntosh.
Sgt. J. McVey.
Pte. J. Morrison.
Pte. M. Peebles.
Pte. E. Regan.
C.Q.M.S. J. Renton.
Pte. J. Ritchie.
C.S.M. E. Robertson.
R.Q.M.S. A. Scott.
L/Corpl. G. Simmonite.
Pte. J. Smith.
Pte. W. Tabor.
L/Corpl. W. Ure.
L/Corpl. D. Wilson.

Bar to Distinguished Conduct Medal
Sgt. G. Burnett, D.C.M.

Distinguished Conduct Medal

Pte. G. Anderson.
L/Sgt. W. Banks.
Sgt. D. Barclay.
C.S.M. H. Bennett.
Sgt. J. Burnett.
Sgt. J. Culpin.
Sgt. J. Docherty.
Corpl. R. Dunbar.

APPENDIX V

DISTINGUISHED CONDUCT MEDAL (contd.)

Sgt. E. Ford.
Corpl. A. Fraser.
L/Corpl. W. Gavin.
Pte. W. George.
Pte. J. Hall.
Corpl. J. Hay.
Sgt. J. Henderson.
Corpl. W. Hutchinson.
Pte. A. Inglis.
Corpl. J. Kerr.
L/Corpl. S. Lovejoy.
C.S.M. W. McCubbin.
L/Corpl. J. McDougall.
Pte. A. McGregor.
Pte. J. McInroy.
Pte. J. McMurchie.
Sgt. P. McNulty.
C.S.M. E. Mascott.
Pte. A. Mitchell.
L/Corpl. G. Moir.
Sgt. T. Moran.
Sgt. R. Redpath.
C.S.M. W. Reid.
Corpl. R. Ritchie.
L/Sgt. P. Rutherford.
Sgt. H. Sharp.
Sgt. G. Sievewright.
Pte. R. Sneddon.
C.S.M. T. Spence.
Pte. J. Spink.
L/Corpl. W. Stewart.
Sgt. J. Storrance.
Pte. A. Taylor.
Corpl. W. Wardlaw.
Sgt. R. Wilkie.
Corpl. J. Yardley.

BAR TO MILITARY MEDAL

Sgt. J. Arundel.
Pte. R. Davidson.
L/Sgt. G. Ferguson.
Pte. A. Harvey.
Sgt. G. Hunter.
Pte. G. McLachlan.
L/Corpl. J. Nicholson.
Sgt. A. Ramsay.
Pte. J. Skea.

MILITARY MEDAL

L/Corpl. T. Allan.
Corpl. W. Alexander.
Sgt. R. Anderson.
Pte. W. Anderson.
Pte. J. Armit.
Sgt. J. Arundel.
L/Corpl. R. Bain.
Corpl. W. Balmain.
Pte. J. Beattie.
Pte. R. Beattie.
Sgt. L. Begg.
Sgt. G. Berry.
L/Corpl. M. Beverley.
Pte. W. Bremner.
L/Corpl. D. Bratchie.
Pte. D. Bricknell.
Pte. A. Brown.
Pte. W. H. Brown.
Pte. R. Cairnie.
Pte. R. Clark.
Sgt. J. Coughlan.
Pte. A. Cowan.
Pte. C. Cranford.
Pte. J. Currie.
Pte. R. Davidson.
Sgt. J. Davie.
Pte. A. Devine.
L/Sgt. A. Dewar.
Pte. L. Dixon.
Sgt. J. Docherty.
Pte. H. Dodds.
Pte. J. Donnelly.
Pte. P. Douglas.
Pte. R. Dowie.
Pte. A. Drennan.
Pte. D. Duff.
Pte. W. Duncan.
Pte. W. Duncan.
C.Q.M.S. L. Dunn.
L/Corpl. F. Easedale.

THE FIRST BATTALION THE BLACK WATCH

MILITARY MEDAL (*contd.*)

Pte. W. Fallon.
Corpl. G. Ferguson.
Pte. D. Fernie.
Sgt. G. Foote.
Sgt. J. Forsyth
Pte. J. Fulton.
Sgt. D. Gardiner.
Pte. R. Gardiner.
Pte. J. Gibson.
L/Corpl. R. Gibson.
Corpl. A. Glencross.
Sgt. J. Gray.
Pte. G. Greenlaw.
Pte. D. Grieve.
L/Corpl. W. Hanson.
Pte. A. Harley.
Corpl. D. Harris.
Pte. E. Harrow.
Pte. A. Hay.
Pte. W. Herd.
L/Corpl. W. Hill.
Sgt. J. Hislop.
Pte. J. Hope.
Corpl. E. L. Hunt.
Sgt. G. Hunter.
L/Corpl. W. Hutchinson.
L/Corpl. A. Ibbotson.
Pte. A. Inglis.
Pte. A. Innes.
L/Corpl. A. Jamieson.
Pte. W. Johnston.
Pte. J. Kane.
Pte. D. Kidd.
Pte. J. Kinnear.
L/Corpl. J. Kirkwood.
Corpl. W. Lawson.
Pte. R. Leggatt.
Corpl. T. Linder.
Pte. J. Lindsay.
Sgt. C. Logan.
Pte. W. Longmuir.
Sgt. T. Lumsden.
Pte. R. McAlister.
Sgt. P. McArthur.
Pte. A. McCreadie.
Pte. R. McCulloch.
Pte. C. McDonald.
L/Corpl. J. McDonald.

Pte. P. McEwan.
Pte. A. McFayden.
Pte. J. McGinn.
Pte. A. McGowan.
Pte. G. McLachlan.
Pte. J. MacMahon.
L/Corpl. J. McMurchie.
Sgt. J. McVey.
Pte. D. Marshall.
Pte. D. Martin.
Pte. G. Martin.
Pte. W. Meek.
Sgt. R. Miller.
Pte. J. Mills.
Pte. W. Milne.
Pte. W. Mitchel.
Pte. W. Morrison.
Corpl. J. Murdoch.
Pte. A. Norrie.
Pte. J. Norton.
Pte. T. O'Dea.
L/Corpl. R. Perkins.
Pte. J. Pirney.
Pte. J. Purdie.
Pte. J. Rae.
Corpl. A. Ramsay.
Pte. J. Reay.
L/Corpl. W. Reekie.
Pte. A. Reid.
Pte. J. Reilly.
Pte. A. Reynolds.
C.S.M. E. Robertson.
Sgt. J. Robertson.
Sgt. W. Robertson.
Pte. J. Robinson.
A/Sgt. A. Russell.
Pte. J. Samson.
L/Corpl. P. Seath.
Pte. F. Seaton.
Pte. H. Shewan.
Pte. S. Shone.
Corpl. J. Sim.
Corpl. L. Simmons.
Pte. J. Skea.
L/Corpl. G. Slace.
Pte. J. Smith.
L/Corpl. T. Smith
Pte. R. Sneddon.

APPENDIX V

Military Medal (contd.)

Pte. H. Spalding.
Pte. P. Spence.
Pte. C. Spratt.
Pte. A. Steeples.
Pte. W. Stephen.
Pte. D. Stewart.
L/Corpl. J. Sturrock.
Pte. A. Thomson.
Pte. A. Thomson.
Pte. G. Thomson.
Corpl. J. Thomson.
Sgt. J. Thomson.
Corpl. W. Ure.
Pte. G. West.
Pte. T. Wheatley.
Pte. D. Whitecross.
Pte. A. Williams.
Sgt. J. Williamson.
L/Corpl. D. Wilson.
Pte. J. Wilson.

Meritorious Service Medal

L/Corpl. W. Cockburn.
Sgt. J. Duncanson.
Sgt. P. Hitchman.
Sgt. L. Hobbs.
C.Q.M.S. J. R. Renton.

FOREIGN DECORATIONS

Russia.—Cross of St. George, 3rd Class

Sgt. G. Henderson.

Cross of St. George, 4th Class

Sgt. G. Burnett.
Sgt. R. Redpath.

France.—Médaille Militaire

C.Q.M.S. L. G. Dunn.
C.S.M. E. Robertson.
Pte. A. Thomson.

Légion d'Honneur

Capt. Hon. M. C. A. Drummond (Chevalier.)
Brevet Lieut.-Col. V. M. Fortune, D.S.O. (Croix d'Officier.)

Belgian Croix de Guerre

Lieut.-Col. L. P. Evans, V.C., D.S.O.
C.S.M. W. Reid.

Croix de Guerre

Capt. P. G. M. Skene.

APPENDIX VI

List of Actions and Operations

The First Battalion

1914. Landed in France. 14th August.

> RETREAT FROM MONS (and rearguard affairs of Le Grand Fayt and Etreux and rearguard actions of Villers Cottérêts). 23rd August–5th September.
>
> BATTLE OF THE MARNE, 1914. (Vioneles and Sablonnières.) 7th–10th September.
>
> BATTLE OF THE AISNE, 1914. (Paissy Ridge, Vendresse Ridge and Chemin des Dames.) 12th–18th September.
> Action on the Aisne Heights. (Verneuil.) 20th September.
> Action of Chivy. (Chivy Valley.) 26th September.
>
> BATTLE OF LANGEMARCK, 1914. (Battles of Ypres, 1914.) (Kortaker Cabaret.) 21st–24th October.
>
> BATTLE OF GHELUVELT, 1914. (Battles of Ypres, 1914.) (Menin Road and Polygon Wood.) 29th–31st October.
> Fighting round Veldhoek and on the Menin Road. 2nd–8th November.
>
> BATTLE OF NONNE BOSSCHEN, 1914. (Battles of Ypres, 1914.) (Black Watch Corner.) 11th November.
> Defence of Givenchy. (Cuinchy.) 20th–21st December.

1915. Trench warfare. (Givenchy.) January.
> First Action of Givenchy, 1915. (Cuinchy.) 25th January.
> Trench warfare. Rue du Bois, Rue de l'Epinette. February–April.
>
> BATTLE OF AUBERS RIDGE. (Attack at Rue du Bois.) (Chocolat Menier Corner.) 9th May.
> Trench warfare. Vermelles, Cuinchy, Vermelles. May–September.
>
> BATTLE OF LOOS. (Hulluch.) 25th September.
> Actions of the Hohenzollern Redoubt. 13th October.
> Trench warfare. Loos, Hulluch Sector. October–December.

1916. Trench warfare. Hulluch Sector. Maroc, Loos, Calonne. January–June.

> BATTLE OF THE SOMME, 1916. (Battle of Albert.) Capture of Contalmaison. 12th–14th July.
>
> BATTLE OF BAZENTIN RIDGE. (Attacks on High Wood.) 20th–25th July.
>
> BATTLE OF POZIERES RIDGE. (Attacks on the Intermediate Line.) 16th–18th August, and High Wood, 3rd September.)

APPENDIX VI

BATTLE OF FLERS-COURCELETTE. (Drop Alley.) 20th September.

BATTLE OF MORVAL. (Flers.) 25th September.
Trench warfare. Eaucourt l'Abbaye, Flers Line. October–December.

1917. Trench warfare. Barleux. January–March. Nieuport Area. May–July. "Hush Camp," Le Clipon, July–October.

SECOND BATTLE OF PASSCHENDAELE. (Watou Area.) 20th October–10th November.
Trench warfare. Vox Farm, Bixchoote Area, Veldhoek. November–December.

1918. Trench warfare. Veldhoek, Poelcappelle Sector, Hubner Farm, Ypres-Staden Railway. January–April.

BATTLE OF BETHUNE. (Battles of the Lys.) (Second defence of Givenchy.) 1918. (Givenchy Ridge and Moat Farm.) 18th–19th April.
Trench warfare. Cambrin, Hohenzollern. May–August.

BATTLE OF THE DROCOURT-QUÉANT LINE. (Second Battles of Arras, 1918.) (Guémappes.) 2nd–3rd September.

BATTLE OF EPEHY. (Battles of the Hindenburg Line.) 18th September.

BATTLE OF THE ST. QUENTIN CANAL. (Battles of the Hindenburg Line.) 28th–30th September.

BATTLE OF THE SELLE. (The Final Advance.) (Wassigny.) 18th–19th October.

BATTLE OF THE SAMBRE. (The Final Advance.) (La Louvière.) 4th November.

APPENDIX VII

Roll of "Other Ranks" appointed to Commissions during the Great War

The First Battalion

Regtl. No.	Rank and Name.	Date of Commission	Corps to which appointed.
5991	Q.M.S. Lawson, A. S.	1.10.14	The Black Watch
7738	C.S.M. Wanliss, A.	1.10.14	,, ,,
6137	Q.M.S. McClellan, C.	4.10.14	,, ,,
6573	C.Q.M.S. Millar, J.	17.11.14	,, ,,
5646	C.S.M. Gray, A.	10.2.15	,, ,,
357	L/Sgt. Bone, G. D.	28.2.15	,, ,,
6017	C.S.M. Wallace, J.	7.3.15	,, ,,
5541	Cr. Sgt. Arthur, S.	29.4.15	,, ,,
830	Sgt. Sprake, G. H.	9.9.15	,, ,,
9924	A/Sgt. Millar, H. H.	4.10.15	The Cameron Highlanders
1063	Sgt. Grassie, J. T.	18.12.15	The Black Watch
681	R.Q.M.S. Tinley, J.	30.1.16	,, ,,
526	Q.M.S. Wilson, A. M.	30.1.16	,, ,,
1778	A/Sgt. MacKenzie, W.	11.5.16	,, ,,
1814	Sgt. Ramage, W.	4.11.16	,, ,,
1417	A/R.S.M. Ritchie, A.	15.2.17	,, ,,
2536	C.S.M. Burnett, G.	27.4.17	,, ,,
2443	Sgt. Ferguson, G. W.	1.5.17	,, ,,
959	Sgt. Potter, R.	5.6.17	,, ,,
2546	Sgt. Balmain, W.	19.6.17	,, ,,
12441	Sgt. Glencross, A.	19.6.17	,, ,,
533	Cpl. Hammond, F.	19.6.17	The Manchester Regiment
769	C.S.M. Studley, T.	27.6.17	The Black Watch
15131	A/Sgt. Rough, J. W.	21.8.17	,, ,,
1361	C.S.M. Smith, D.	28.8.17	,, ,,
11065	Cpl. Ramsay, R.	19.10.17	,, ,,
7950	Sgt. Hamilton, D. L.	31.10.17	,, ,,
1231	Sgt. Thomson, J.	2.11.17	,, ,,
1698	A/Sgt. Cook, C. T.	15.11.17	Gordon Highlanders
1204	C.S.M. Buttifant, E.	19.1.18	K.R. Rifle Corps
1752	Cpl. Brown, D.	20.2.18	The Lancashire Fusiliers
1804	Sgt. Garvie, E. E.	16.3.18	The Black Watch
472	A/R.S.M. Christie, D. C.	24.3.18	,, ,,
1196	L/Sgt. Mackie, J.	26.6.18	3rd Staffordshire Regt.
1613	Sgt. Tanner, D.	21.7.18	4th Royal Fusiliers
1455	Sgt. Fraser, A.	24.9.18	3rd Manchester Regt.
S/8574	L/Cpl. Cargill, J.	28.1.16	
S/9998	Sgt. McKenzie, D.	13.2.16	
S/8996	Pte. Dorricott, A.	13.3.17	The Northumberland Fus.
S/8273	L/Cpl. Lovejoy, S. C. W.	27.3.17	York & Lancs. Regt.
S/11899	Pte. Gleave, G. E.	27.3.17	Loyal Lancs. Regt.
3/2771	Pte. Edgell, A. H.	25.4.17	Machine Gun Corps

APPENDIX VII

Regtl. No.	Rank and Name.	Date of Commission	Corps to which appointed.
S/10423	Pte. McLenan, J. E. S.	26.5.17	R.G.A.
S/40637	L/Cpl. Hyslop, W. D.	29.5.17	3rd Black Watch
S/16675	L/Cpl. Reid, J. D.	26.6.17	Seaforth Highlanders
S/9935	Cpl. Swanson, J. W.	31.8.17	Labour Corps
S/17407	L/Cpl. Griffen, L. C.	25.9.17	18th Royal Irish
S/40133	L/Cpl. Allison, C. L.	30.10.17	4th Black Watch
S/40238	Pte. Featherstone, L. W.	30.10.17	The Northumberland Fus.
3/4089	A/Sgt. Munro, J. P.	15.11.17	Labour Corps
S/16452	Pte. Lindsay, J. C.	17.12.17	6th Middlesex Regt.
3/3820	Cpl. Moffat, J. A.	18.1.18	Royal Engineers
S/40312	Cpl. Campbell, J.	29.1.18	3rd Black Watch
9760	A/Sgt. Whyte, J.	29.1.18	The Hants Regt.
S/15020	L/Cpl. Puttick, J. E.	29.1.18	3rd Bedford Regt.
S/40328	L/Cpl. Hyde, G. W.	2.3.18	Royal Engineers
S/40226	L/Cpl. Fearnley, A. F.	28.5.18	York & Lancs. Regt.
S/4395	Cpl. Nisbett, A. F.	29.5.18	5th Black Watch
S/40249	Cpl. Graham, J.	8.10.18	The Border Regt.
S/9812	A/Cpl. Thomas, E.	3.2.19	
S/22225	Pte. Stewart, G. S.	8.3.19	General List

THE SECOND
BATTALION

"JOCK, 1914"
After the drawing by "Snaffles"

PART I—FRANCE, 1914-15

CHAPTER I

1914

1.—*Mobilization and Voyage to France*

THE outbreak of war found the 2nd Battalion of The Black Watch nearing the completion of a tour of foreign service. It had been abroad since the commencement of the South African War in 1899; in India since October, 1902. In 1914 it was stationed at Bareilly.

The Indian Force despatched to France for service with the British Expeditionary Force consisted of the 3rd Lahore and 7th Meerut Divisions.[1] Of this latter Division (under the command of Lieutenant General C. A. Anderson, C.B.) the Bareilly Brigade formed a part; its original composition on mobilization was:—

>2nd Battalion The Black Watch.
>41st Dogras.
>58th (Vaughan's) Rifles, F.F.
>2/8th Gurkha Rifles.

The Brigade Commander was Major General F. Macbean, C.V.O., C.B., formerly of the Gordon Highlanders.[2]

The two other British battalions in the Meerut Division were the 1st Seaforth Highlanders and 2nd Leicestershire. They are mentioned here, as throughout the war a strong link of mutual esteem and comradeship united these three British battalions of the 7th Division. With the Seaforths especially, the bond of a common nationality and a friendship of long standing was strengthened by the fortune of war. As will be related, the shattered remnants of the two battalions were, at one period, united to form " The Highland Battalion," which earned itself an undying glory during the last heroic efforts to avert the fall of Kut.

The Battalion received the order to mobilize at 3 p.m. on August 9th. In India, August comes towards the end of the long hot weather, and falls in the leave season, when a large proportion of the British troops move to summer camps in the hills. The Battalion had at the time a detachment of three companies at the hill station of Ranikhet, and some details, mainly convalescents, at Kasauli, also in the hills. These were at once recalled.

British battalions in India had not yet adopted the four-

---

[1] These two Divisions served together throughout the war in three different theatres—France, Mesopotamia and Palestine.

[2] Major General Macbean was succeeded by Brigadier General W. M. Southey of the Indian Army in January, 1915. Brigadier General C. E. de M. Norie, also of the Indian Army, succeeded Brigadier General Southey in the summer of 1915.

THE SECOND BATTALION THE BLACK WATCH

company organization, introduced at home in 1913, and were still organized in eight companies. The Battalion reorganized during mobilization, B and C Companies forming No. 1 Company, A and D No. 2 Company, E and F No. 3 Company, and G and H No. 4 Company. Web equipment was issued to the Battalion for the first time on mobilization. The reorganization was very well carried out by Major Stewart, who was in temporary command, in the absence of Lieutenant Colonel Campbell on leave at home. Much hard work, which was most ably performed, fell during this period on the Adjutant, on the Quartermaster and his staff and on the Orderly Room Sergeant, Quartermaster Sergeant Niven.

The following was the organization of the Battalion when it embarked for France:—

Commanding Officer	Lieut.-Colonel W. Campbell, M.V.O.[1]
Second-in-Command	Major C. E. Stewart.
Adjutant	Captain C. R. B. Henderson.
Quartermaster	Lieut. J. Anderson.
Medical Officer	Captain Dawson, R. A. M. C.
Chaplain	Rev. A. Macfarlane.
Regimental Sergeant Major	J. Johnstone.[2]
Regimental Quartermaster Sergeant	—— [3]

No. 1 Company

Captain G. C. S. McLeod.
Captain C. E. Strahan.[4]
Lieut. A. C. Denison (Machine-gun Officer).
Lieut. D. C. Hamilton-Johnston (Transport Officer).

2nd Lieut. W. D. McL. Stewart.
C.S.M. George.
C.Q.M.S. McAra.

[1] On leave in United Kingdom. Joined Battalion at Port Said.

[2] Regimental Sergeant Major Johnstone was wounded and invalided to United Kingdom on 11/11/14. During his absence the following acted as Regimental Sergeant Major: Company Sergeant Major Kennedy 12/11/14 to 4/12/14 (when he received a commission); Company Sergeant Major Hobbs 4/12/14 to 22/1/15 (when he was appointed Regimental Quartermaster Sergeant); Company Sergeant Major Johnson 23/1/15 to 1/2/15; Company Sergeant Major Muir 1/2/15 to 28/3/15 (when Regimental Sergeant Major Johnstone returned from United Kingdom).

[3] The Regimental Quartermaster Sergeant, Parker, was left with the Depot in India, medically unfit. Hobbs, from Company Sergeant Major No. 2 Company, became Regimental Quartermaster Sergeant in January, 1915. Sergeant Watson assisted the Quartermaster until the appointment of Hobbs. On Hobbs becoming Regimental Quartermaster Sergeant, Burnett became Company Sergeant Major of No. 2 Company and Robertson Company Quartermaster Sergeant.

[4] Captain Strahan and Lieutenant Durie left India for France in advance of the Battalion for duty as Railway Transport officers. They rejoined the Battalion in Marseilles.

MOBILIZATION, AUGUST, 1914

No. 2 Company

Captain R. E. Forester.
Captain P. G. M. Skene.
Lieut. K. R. Gilroy.[1]

C.S.M. Hobbs.[3]
C.Q.M.S. Burnett.

No. 3 Company

Captain A. G. Wauchope, D.S.O.
Captain D. Campbell.
Lieut. J. N. Inglis.[1]

Lieut. J. A. Durie.[4]
Lieut. I. B. McLeod.
C.S.M. Kennedy.
C.Q.M.S. Proudfoot.

(See footnotes on previous page).

No. 4 Company

Major H. H. Sutherland.
Captain H F. F. Murray.
Lieut. A. H. C. Sutherland.
Lieut. K. Buist.

Lieut. N. McMicking.
C.S.M. Muir.
C.Q.M.S. Johnson.

The strength of the Battalion on leaving India was 24 officers,[1] 934 other ranks (including 81 as first reinforcement, i.e. 10 per cent of the strength). A small depot, under Lieutenant H. Orr-Ewing was left behind at Bareilly. The wives and families of the Battalion were also left at Bareilly, and did not reach the United Kingdom till January, 1915.

The fact that the Battalion could find 934 fit men at the worst period of the Indian hot weather, points to a high level of physical fitness.[2] It is also worthy of note that from the day mobilization was ordered till the arrival at Marseilles these 934 men between them incurred only one punishment involving a regimental entry.[3]

The 2nd Black Watch reported " ready to move " on August 18th. It left Bareilly on September 3rd, and reached Karachi on

[1] Of the 22 combatant officers who sailed with the Battalion to France, 13 were killed during the course of the war. All the others, except one, were wounded, several more than once.

[2] The normal mobilization strength in India was 816 other ranks. A few days after mobilization this figure was increased by 37, to allow replacement of the native servants and syces included in the normal scale, which was based on service within India. A first reinforcement of ten per cent was also added. The Battalion received 20 reservists, men of the Regiment who had taken their discharge in India and obtained employment there, usually in the jute trade. Thus the Battalion had to find 118 less 20, i.e. 98 men more than the normal mobilization establishment.

[3] The Black Watch have always been nearly wholly Scottish. The actual percentage of nationalities in the ranks in October, 1913, the last date before the outbreak of war for which the figures are available, was : Scotsmen 88½, English 8½, Others 3. If the Band, which is recruited from Kneller Hall boys and is entirely English, be excluded, the percentage of Scotsmen was over 95. The percentage was similar in the mobilisation for the Boer War in 1899.

THE SECOND BATTALION THE BLACK WATCH

September 6th. The transports for the force were, however, not ready; and it was not till the 16th that the Battalion embarked (together with two companies of the Leicestershires, and the Headquarters of the Bareilly Brigade), on the s.s. *Elephanta*, which sailed from Karachi on the 21st, in a convoy escorted by three cruisers. Three days out from Karachi, the ships containing the remainder of the Meerut Division, which had embarked at Bombay, joined to form a single convoy of over forty ships, under the escort of six warships. The *Emden* and the *Königsberg* were still at large; and this imposing but somewhat cumbrous array of ships, regulated by the pace of the slowest ship (a captured German merchantman, producing for its new owners a grudging eight knots an hour) was accordingly maintained till the Red Sea was reached, when ships were allowed to proceed independently. So keen were the men to reach France that many volunteered to act as extra hands in the stokehold, and actually did so all the way up the Red Sea. The *Elephanta* reached Suez on October 2nd, and Port Said on October 3rd; after lying outside Port Said till the 6th, it proceeded under escort of French warships to Marseilles,[1] where the troops on board disembarked on October 12th.

Lieutenant Colonel Campbell, who had been on leave in the United Kingdom, rejoined the Battalion at Port Said. On coming on board the *Elephanta* he received a tremendous and entirely spontaneous ovation from his men. Always a strict disciplinarian, he combined absolute justice with strictness; and the welcome showed how the men appreciated his unremitting labours for the comfort and efficiency of the Battalion he commanded.

Captain F. M. B. Robertson and Lieutenants J. N. Inglis and K. R. Gilroy also rejoined at Port Said; but the first-named, who had been on sick leave, was still unfit to accompany the Battalion to France and had to be left behind in Egypt. He later joined the 1st Battalion and was severely wounded on May 9th, 1915.

The Battalion remained a week at Marseilles in a wet and muddy camp at La Valentine, five miles east of the port. Here the first reinforcement of eighty men, under Lieutenant Buist, was left behind; it never rejoined, for the 1st Battalion of the Regiment, reduced a month later to a handful of men by its heroic stand in the first battle of Ypres, had a greater need of men at the time, and the 2nd Battalion's reinforcements were sent to build it up. Buist was killed with the 1st Battalion at Givenchy,

---

[1] The Battalion furnished four regimental signallers during this voyage to maintain communication between the French warships and the ships of the convoy. These signallers were accommodated on the French battleship *Bouvet* (afterwards sunk at the Dardanelles), and went on to Toulon in her, subsequently rejoining the Battalion in La Valentine camp.

ARRIVAL IN FRANCE, OCTOBER, 1914

in January, 1915. Major C. E. Stewart also left the Battalion at Marseilles, to take over command of the 1st Battalion, *vice* Lieutenant Colonel A. Grant Duff, who had been killed on the Aisne in August.

New rifles were issued to the Battalion at Marseilles, as those brought from India did not take the latest mark of ammunition. After all the long training in peace to teach men to know and trust their rifles, it was a blow to be parted from their tried weapons on the eve of going into action, but it could not be helped. The 42nd had had a similar experience at the beginning of the Crimean campaign.

The transport received by the Battalion was not of the best or latest pattern, as that originally reserved for the Indian Corps had been depleted in making good the losses of the retreat from Mons. A luckier "issue" was the two interpreters allotted to the Battalion, M. Bertrand and M. Gabriel Brezet; the former was soon claimed by the Brigade, the latter remained with the Battalion to the end of its stay in France and was always most helpful.

On the 20th the Battalion entrained for Orleans, where the Meerut Division was concentrating and completing its equipment.

2.—*The Fighting of* 1914

The Indian Corps (to the command of which Lieutenant General Sir James Willcocks had now been appointed) reached France just after the British Army had been transferred from its positions on the Aisne to the left of the Allied line, and had begun its forward movement, which was to be the last period of open warfare on the Western Front till the autumn of 1918, and was to end in the first battle of Ypres. By the time that the Lahore Division, the first to arrive, was ready to take its place in the fighting line, the situation was as follows: the advance of the II and III Corps had been definitely checked opposite La Bassée and in front of Armentières; the Cavalry Corps held the Messines–Wytschaete Ridge, between the III Corps and the I Corps, which was still advancing east of Ypres; but already the greatly superior German force intended to break through the Allied line and gain the Channel ports was in movement; and the month's struggle round Ypres, which was to test the original British Expeditionary Force so highly, had begun.

In these circumstances there was no time for the Indian Corps to assemble as a whole or to be given any period of preparation for the conditions in which it was to fight. It had to be employed to meet an emergency. And it can fairly be claimed for the units of the Indian Corps that their arrival and prompt entry into the firing line saved the British front, and thus the whole Allied cause at this crisis.

Portions of the Lahore Division were sent north to assist the III Corps and Cavalry Corps, while the Meerut Division was used to relieve a part of the II Corps, which had borne the brunt of the fighting during the retreat from Mons, had been heavily engaged on the Aisne and by La Bassée, and was sorely in need of a rest.

Thus the Battalion, leaving Orleans on October 26th, detrained north of Lillers, and marched at once up to the front line. On the night of the 29th the Bareilly Brigade took over the extreme right of the British line; and to the Battalion was allotted the post of honour on the right—" within shouting distance " (for the trenches were by no means continuous) of the left of the French line. Very curiously the 1st Battalion, on taking up its first position before the Battle of Mons, had also been " the right of the line " to the Expeditionary Force.

Of all the low-lying land of Flanders, where the British Army has at various periods made so much history under such adverse conditions, no portion is so little relieved from a dead dreary flatness as that which was to be the scene of the operations of the Indian Corps during its year in France.[1] The Aubers Ridge, the possession of which gave such an advantage in command and observation to the enemy, is under 150 feet above sea-level at its highest point; while such small rises as the spur on which stands the village of Givenchy or the railway embankments south of La Bassée, formed, by their elevation of even a few feet above the surrounding plain, points of considerable tactical importance.

Naturally, in such terrain, where the water level lies at most a foot or two below the soil, the construction and holding of trenches was a matter of unending struggle against water and mud. And the winter in those low lands of Flanders is peculiarly harsh and chilling. The cold and wet were sorely felt by men who had spent the summer in the plains of India.

The front taken over by the Meerut Division was in the rudimentary stage of a trench line. Trenches were not continuous and no communication trenches from front to rear existed as yet.

The night of October 29th was wet and stormy. The relief of the West Ridings was successfully accomplished, but the Battalion suffered its first casualties on the road to the trenches, two

[1] It is curious to remark that during the whole of its service in the war, in three different theatres, the Battalion was never stationed or engaged at much more than a hundred feet above sea-level.

FIRST DAYS IN THE TRENCHES, OCTOBER, 1914

men being wounded by shell fire.[1] The front line held by the Battalion consisted of a single trench, some 800 to 1000 yards east of the village of Le Plantin. Nos. 1 and 2 Companies held the firing line, No. 4 Company held reserve trenches round the east side of Le Plantin, while No. 3 Company was billeted in the village, which though so close to the front line had at this time suffered no damage from shell fire.

The first few days in the line passed without incident, so far as the Battalion was concerned; but a little further north, on the left of the Bareilly Brigade, the 2/8th Gurkhas were attacked almost immediately after the occupation of the trenches, and suffered severely, losing nine of their British officers. Owing to this, The Black Watch was, on November 2nd, called on to send its Headquarters and the two reserve companies (Nos. 1 and 2, which had been relieved in the front line by 3 and 4 on November 1st), to take over a part of the line further north; and for the remainder of its first tour in trenches, which lasted till the third week in November, the Battalion was split up, Headquarters and Nos. 1 and 2 Companies being in the left section of the Bareilly Brigade, while Nos. 3 and 4 remained in the original trenches north of Givenchy, on the right of the line. Major St. J. Harvey, who had now rejoined the Battalion from the Egyptian Army, commanded these two companies.

The attack on the Gurkhas referred to above brought out a weakness from which the Indian Army was to suffer throughout the war. The establishment of British officers to an Indian battalion was only fourteen, and there was no adequate reserve. The

---

[1] The following is a short description of the manner in which the Battalion first went into the line in the Great War:

"After marching from near Hazebrouck, the Brigade halted behind the village of Gorre at about 2.30 p.m. and teas were made. At 4.30 p.m. the Battalion formed up and moved off in the gathering darkness and drizzling rain. Sounds of an intermittent cannonade were heard in front, and after a mile or so had been covered occasional shells, directed at one of our field batteries which had been passed previously, began to burst overhead. One of these shells caused the first casualties. Eventually the Battalion halted in column of route in the street of a small village—Le Plantin—while some officers and scouts went forward to reconnoitre the route to the trenches. Presently Nos. 1 and 2 Companies left the village and, still maintaining column of route, wheeled to the left and advanced in the rain and darkness across mangold fields and over ditches for about an hour with occasional halts. During this time flares rising from the trenches marked the position of the line, and many bullets and occasional shells passed overhead. Then the Companies extended, No. 1 to the right, No. 2 to the left, with orders to halt in rear of the first occupied trench line. Then, on the orders of the company commanders, the trenches were entered, the West Ridings evacuating them simultaneously. Private McInroy of No. 2 Company was killed by a rifle bullet just as he was about to enter the trench, and was thus the first man of the Battalion to lay down his life in the war."

THE SECOND BATTALION THE BLACK WATCH

percentage of casualties amongst British officers was high, since they were, especially in a Gurkha regiment, easily distinguishable from their men, and consequently the target of enemy sharpshooters. These casualties were extremely difficult to replace; and it is no disparagement of the Indian battalions to state the obvious fact that, with the loss of the leaders known and trusted by them, their efficiency as units decreased.

In order, therefore, that Indian battalions weak in British officers might have a backing of British troops, the British battalions of the Indian Corps were called on for more frequent periods in the front and were often split up between different sectors. In this respect their position demanded a higher degree of endurance and firmness than in the case of British battalions in a purely British formation.

The chief incident in the left section was a night raid made on the German trenches by some twenty men of No. 2 Company under Captain Forrester, with the object of destroying a machine gun which was causing annoyance from a sap pushed up close to our line. The raid took place on November 9th. Captain Forrester was wounded through the lungs as the raid started, but continued to lead his men, who reached the German trenches and killed ten of the enemy in hand-to-hand fighting; the machine gun had, however, been removed. The party returned with Captain Forrester, Sergeant Wallace and one private wounded.

On the 17th the Left Section was taken over by the Seaforths, Battalion Headquarters and Nos. 1 and 2 Companies moving into Divisional reserve. Meanwhile Nos. 3 and 4 Companies remained on the right of the line, the two companies relieving one another in the front line trenches every forty-eight hours.

Conditions in the front line were severe, for the Germans were continually sapping forward to within bombing distance. Opposite Nos. 3 and 4 Companies they were kept at a respectful distance by several successful raids on the sap heads. One of these raiding parties under Lieutenants Inglis and Denison met two German parties double their strength, and yet after a fierce struggle in No Man's Land, reached and demolished the sap head, though with a loss of nearly a third of the raiding party. Elsewhere the German efforts to get within assaulting distance had been more successful, and on November 23rd Nos. 3 and 4 Companies became involved in the heaviest fighting which the Meerut Division had yet been called on to face; and in this, its first serious test, the fine fighting qualities of the Battalion were abundantly proved.

On the morning of the 23rd the Germans made a heavy attack along almost the whole front of the Indian Corps. The

GERMAN ATTACK ON NOVEMBER 23RD, 1914

58th Rifles, the unit immediately to the left of No. 4 Company (which was in the front line at the time, No. 3 Company being in local reserve), was forced from its trenches, together with the Indian units further to the left, thus exposing the left flank of No. 4 Company. A few of the 58th Rifles joined the company, and immediate steps were taken to organize a flank defence to protect the exposed left. The steadiness of the company contributed greatly to the success of the counter-attack made the same evening, which resulted in the recovery of all the trenches lost. No. 3 Company was not detailed as part of the counter-attacking troops, but a number accompanied the counter-attack of the 58th Rifles, led by Company Sergeant Major J. Kennedy, who was one of the first to re-enter the lost trenches.

The following is from the report of the Officer Commanding 58th Rifles on the counter-attack: " I was greatly assisted in this " advance by four men of The Black Watch, Privates Venters, " Boyd, McIntosh and Stewart; these men came with me in the " final rush from the road, and by their example gave a fine lead " to my Dogra Company, in front of whom we were. There being " nobody at hand when we reached the trenches, I placed them " to hold a sap, which had been cut right into our line; and " although bombed, they held on till I could get the men to- " gether, after which they helped me considerably, and by their " sang-froid and cheeriness impressed those around them most " favourably." These four men, in fact, though exposed to incessant bombing, which wounded one of them, held for a considerable time a gap of 300 yards between the 58th Rifles and the 8th Gurkhas. All four received the Distinguished Conduct Medal for their gallantry, as did also Company Sergeant Major Kennedy and Private Swan.

Major Wauchope, commanding No. 3 Company, had made his way, just before the counter-attack and while it was still light, across the open up to No. 4 Company, to ascertain the situation. After the reoccupation of the trenches he carried the war into the enemy's line by attacking a German sap with Second Lieutenant McMicking and ten men, the Germans in it bolting.

The good work done by No. 2 Battery of the 13th Brigade, R.F.A., under Major P. J. Paterson, a trusted friend of the Battalion, in covering the front of No. 4 Company during the critical hours when they were isolated and exposed, deserves mention.

An Indian Army Corps Order of the Day, dated December 7th, 1914, contained the following:—

" Now that the reports of the action of the 23rd and 24th " November are all to hand, the Corps Commander has learned " with great satisfaction of the conduct of the troops engaged. A

THE SECOND BATTALION THE BLACK WATCH

"considerable number of the troops of both Divisions were engaged, and under the circumstances, it is difficult to single out corps, but the steadiness of The Black Watch and the portion of the 58th Rifles next them, and the flank attack by the 1st Battalion Garhwal Rifles, which helped to regain the lost trenches, merit especial notice."

On the 24th Nos. 3 and 4 Companies were relieved by two companies of the Connaught Rangers, and rejoined the remainder of the Battalion in reserve at Zelobes, the Battalion being thus reunited after three weeks' separation. On the very next day, however, it was called on to reinforce the Centre Section in front of Festubert with 300 men; and on November 27th Captain Strahan was shot through the head while endeavouring to put out of action a German machine gun posted some twenty yards from his trench. In him, the first of its officers to be killed, the Battalion lost a fine and gallant leader.

From December the 1st to 12th the Battalion held the trenches in the Centre Section opposite Festubert. This section included the Picquet House and a part of the line known as "Hell Corner," which ran for a length of 300 yards parallel to and within a dozen yards of the German trench. One part ("The Glory Hole") was within four yards of a German sap head. Here continual bombing encounters took place; the enemy had all the advantage in numbers and appliances for bombing at this time, and to hold "The Glory Hole" against these odds was a severe test of courage, in which our men never failed. Company Sergeant Major Muir greatly distinguished himself here in repairing the destroyed parapet within a few yards of the German sap.

It was known that the enemy was mining under our trenches; and an attack was proposed, but afterward vetoed by Divisional Headquarters. A local raid was, however, carried out by No. 3 Company, by which the nearest enemy trenches were captured and a number of Germans bayoneted. This vigorous measure delayed the enemy offensive, but the days and nights of this period were as trying to the troops as any during the war. The companies in the front line could capture, but were not strong enough to hold, the enemy trenches which ran so close to their own. Consequently the fighting resolved itself in a great measure to fighting with grenades. In this the Germans were superior both in equipment and training.

During the war men would often argue which they most hated, high explosive shells, shrapnel, rifle bullets, minenwerfer or grenades. There is no question but that every man in the Battalion at this time would have given his vote for grenades. Numbers were severely wounded in this not very scientific form of fighting; one corporal in No. 3 Company received thirty-two

FIGHTING IN THE TRENCHES, DECEMBER, 1914

separate wounds from one German grenade; the company commander, both subalterns and many others were slightly wounded. A good parapet or a deep trench gives a sense of security against rifle and shrapnel bullets, but from hand-grenades there was no rest for the men in the trenches. "Bomb right" or "bomb left" was a constant cry by day and night, and woe to him who was slow to pay heed to that warning.

Extraordinary motives occasion extraordinary deeds. One day when No. 3 Company was being relieved by No. 4 Company, Sergeant Wilson was reported missing. A great commotion suddenly arose in the enemy trenches, and, a moment after, Sergeant Wilson, amid a shower of bullets and grenades, fell unwounded over our parapet into his own lines. He had climbed the parapet, crossed the few yards of No Man's Land, jumped into the enemy trench and discharged among the astonished enemy a few hand grenades and then returned in this precipitate manner, ready to march off his platoon. An extreme desire to find out whether it was a few very active or a hundred very discreet Germans who kept throwing the constant shower of grenades into our trench, had impelled Wilson, so he said, to make this unexpected reconnaissance. His fearless act, if not exactly " according to plan," had at least the effect of maintaining quiet in the German trench until the relief was completed.

A week later the same trenches, then held by the Highland Light Infantry, who relieved the Battalion on their arrival from Egypt, were with their garrison almost completely destroyed by a series of mines laid, at intervals of a hundred yards, from the Picquet House to the end of the line.

On December 1st, Lieutenant Colonel W. Campbell, who had been ill for some time, was admitted to hospital. He did not again rejoin the Battalion, and Major St. J. Harvey assumed the command. Not only in peace, but during the early and most trying weeks of the war Colonel Campbell's services had been of the highest value to the Battalion, and his breakdown in health was a severe loss.

On December 4th the first promotions from the ranks of the Battalion took place, Company Sergeant Majors J. Kennnedy and W. George being appointed Second Lieutenants in the Battalion. Two men of outstanding character and ability, the fortune of war dealt unequally with them, though gloriously with both. Second Lieutenant George was killed at Neuve Chapelle shortly afterwards, while exposing himself to post under cover some Indian soldiers who were bringing ammunition up to the front line. Kennedy served with great distinction throughout the war, and commanded a battalion during the last two years of it.

From December 13th to 17th the Battalion was in reserve,

but once again its rest was cut short by the activity of the enemy. The attack on the Highland Light Infantry by mines, which was mentioned above, was part of a general attack against practically the whole front of the Indian Corps, during which the enemy succeeded in establishing himself in many parts of our front line. The Battalion was ordered up to Rue de l'Epinette, in support of the Dehra Dun Brigade, on the night of the 17th/18th. In face of repeated attacks, and in spite of the prevailing confusion, the 1st Seaforths had stood firm, though the units on both sides of them had fallen back and left their flanks exposed. Nos. 3 and 4 Companies under Major Wauchope were now sent forward as a support to that part of the line near the Picquet House.

Receiving no further orders after midday, Major Wauchope pushed forward, and was able, with part of his force, to restore connection between the Highland Light Infantry and the right of the Seaforths. No. 4 Company was sent up to support the Seaforths on their left, and for forty-eight hours assisted them to hold their isolated and dangerous position, till a counter-attack by troops of the I Corps partially restored the situation. The companies were forty-eight hours without rations while in the line, and no rations reached the Seaforths for four days. Second Lieutenant W. E. Maitland, who had joined the Battalion only a few days previously, was mortally wounded just after No. 4 Company reached the line. Major Wauchope was also wounded. Lieutenant I. B. McLeod, in command of No. 3 Company, showed his fine soldierly instinct during this difficult fighting.

Nos. 1 and 2 Companies had meanwhile remained holding reserve trenches.

As a result of this attack a great portion of the I Corps had been brought up to the assistance of the Indian Corps; and it was now decided that the latter should be taken out of the line and given a rest. Accordingly, from the 25th December to the end of January, 1915, the Battalion formed part of the Army Reserve behind the line near Lillers (at Amettes and then at La Micquellerie), and had time to refit and train.

On December 29th the first party for home leave (three officers and two sergeants) left the Battalion. The two sergeants, Sinclair and Wilson, had gone to South Africa with the Battalion in 1899, and had not been home for fifteen years.

3.—*Conditions in the Trenches*

These first winter months of 1914 had been spent in extremely trying conditions. Apart from the physical discomforts of cold, wet and mud, the tactical circumstances were all in favour of the enemy; he was sooner and better equipped with hand and rifle

CONDITIONS IN THE TRENCHES, WINTER OF 1914

grenades, trench mortars and appliances for mining; he was the aggressor throughout this first period, and with his better equipment was able to adapt himself to the novelties and necessities of trench warfare with greater readiness than our men.

The enemy, greatly superior both in numbers and equipment, was in November, and again in December, preparing attacks on a large scale against the Indian Corps; and with this object was continually sapping forward. Opposite Givenchy our frequent raiding had enforced a breadth of a hundred yards between our trenches and the enemy's; elsewhere the lines were not a grenade throw apart, whilst near the Picquet House little more than the breadth of the parapet separated the trenches. Barbed wire in these early days was difficult to obtain, and only in a few places did a single strand give any protection to the defenders.

In addition to his superiority in artillery, the enemy's fire from snipers, hand and rifle bombers and trench mortars was so continuous that the men had little rest by day and night. In sniping his superior numbers and the better organization of his trenches gave him the advantage at first over troops new to trench conditions; and any target given above the parapet was usually quickly out of action. The men used to hold up shovels, wait for a shot and then signal the result; but this amusement was soon found to be too extravagant in shovels. The enemy's bombs were both better and more plentiful than ours (which were merely improvised from jam tins filled with explosive or slabs of gun cotton tied to pieces of wood),[1] but were not instantaneous, and were often picked up and thrown back. To his rifle grenades and trench mortars we had no reply; but the missiles hurled by the latter signalled their approach by a peculiar noise, and could be seen in the air and dodged by the alert and active, provided the mud was not too deep for rapid movement. The sentries were posted in pairs, one to look for enemy movement, and one to shout warning of bombs.

The sticky mud seriously interfered with the mechanism of the rifles, and until bolt covers were improvised out of old socks, many rifles, especially those of raiding parties, became clogged with mud and out of action.

On the 20th November a hard frost set in, and during the

[1] The first hand grenades used by the Battalion were of "home-made" construction. During the first tour in the trenches, a factory (complete with red danger signal) was installed on the outskirts of Le Plantin. Here, under the instructions of a Major Smith, R.F.A., Lance Corporal Stewart of No. 3 Company and a bombardier of the Gunners packed gun-cotton slabs into empty tobacco tins and affixed a substantial length of safety fuse. The normal method of ignition was for the would-be bomber to smoke a pipe and to light the fuse at the appropriate time from the glowing tobacco. It shows the spirit of the men of 1914 that so many were found eager to use these primitive missiles.

action of November 23rd the ground was covered with snow. From the beginning of December it rained continuously; and from then till " Grouse Butts " (i.e. breastworks) were started in January, the trenches were worse than words can describe. In many places they were half filled with mud and water, and several wounded men were half drowned before their comrades could reach them. Doors, windows and beams were nightly carried from houses near the line to try and make a firm footing at the bottom of the trenches; but they soon sank and only interfered with the clearing of trenches when it was possible to bail the water out. Proper sanitation was impossible, as refuse could not be buried; it soon floated to the surface again and the only way to dispose of it was to throw it over the parapet. There were no dugouts; an occasional piece of corrugated iron or a board let into the side of the trench formed the only shelter, so that men suffered severely from frost-bite.

The kilt in these days proved its value, as it has in many a past campaign; officers and men could wade through the trenches well over their knees and arrive in comparative dryness and comfort, unhampered by wet trousers or clinging knee-breeches. Certainly it got very heavy with mud and wet, but undoubtedly prevented much sickness. The kilt apron served at least one purpose in keeping the kilt clean in the trenches. The mud of Artois proved, however, that the Highland shoe was less serviceable than a boot. Often men lost their shoes in the mud while going into the line, and went in to stand for hours in the wet trenches in stockinged feet.

The wounded had to lie in the trenches till nightfall; and then it took eight men to carry one back to the first-aid post. In many places the road was too exposed, and often the defenders were too few to allow the dead to be carried back for burial. After dark, shallow graves were dug close behind the trenches, and in these were laid the bodies of those who had given their lives on that day. The low and broken parapet gave but little cover to the mourners; but a few comrades, kneeling for the sake of safety as well as for a feeling of reverence, listened to a short prayer said by an officer whilst the earth was shovelled back into the grave. No firing party was needed to give honour to the dead; bullets flew continuously, and at least on one occasion a gravedigger was himself wounded. As the days passed, the line of wooden crosses lengthened; but that line of little crosses was long remembered, and in some measure became a symbol in later days of the proud boast, that not in France, nor on the Tigris, nor in Palestine, did the Battalion ever yield a yard of trench entrusted to its care.

During the Battalion's rest in January both British and Ger-

CONDITIONS IN THE TRENCHES, WINTER OF 1914

mans had been completely flooded out of the trenches, and had built lines of breastworks at some distance from one another. This altered matters considerably; hand bombing as a daily practice ceased for some months and the improvised mortars had not sufficient range to be of much value. Both sides were now working at their trenches harder than ever before; the enemy was no longer aggressive; more material for trench improvement was available; comforts began to arrive; and the Battalion received large drafts. The awful conditions of 1914 were over.

CHAPTER II

1915

1.—*Neuve Chapelle*

THE time spent in trenches by the Battalion in February, 1915, was devoid of any particular incident. We may pass on to the part played by it at the battle of Neuve Chapelle.

Neuve Chapelle was the first of the series of actions in 1915 in which the British Army tested the German lines opposed to it, and found them strong. The Aubers Ridge, already mentioned, was always available as the objective of any attack in this part of the British front, and, in fact, remained so available till the final advance in 1918. If the Aubers Ridge seemed too unambitious an aim, a reference to Lille could always be included in Operation Orders.

Apart from the great strength of the enemy defences, the attack had other disadvantages to meet in this part of the line; there were the difficulties of artillery support and observation from the low-lying ground, the absence of any natural features for flank protection during an advance, and the numerous water ditches and streams, notably the Des Layes brook, which always hampered and broke up attacks.

The initial assault for this battle was to be made by the 8th Division of the IV Corps and the Lahore Division of the Indian Corps. Although the Battalion did not form part of the assaulting troops at Neuve Chapelle, it took a considerable and distinguished part in the battle. Prior to the attack it had much hard work in preparing trenches from which part of the assaulting troops issued, and in reconnoitring the German lines; it assisted in the attack by its fire, and a small party took part in the attack; in the later stages of the battle it repulsed a German counter-attack. The casualties of the Battalion in this action were over one hundred and fifty.

The Bareilly Brigade held the trenches from which the attack of the Lahore Division was made. Its orders were simple: the Brigade was definitely forbidden to advance; should the attack fail and a counter-attack be delivered it was at all costs to hold the original British line. The section held by the Battalion just opposite the Bois de Biez was under the command of Lieutenant Colonel St. J. Harvey, who had, besides the Battalion, portions of the 1/4th Black Watch[1] and certain other units.

[1] The 1/4th Black Watch (City of Dundee Battalion) was the second of the Territorial battalions of the Regiment to arrive in France. It was posted to the Bareilly Brigade, and thus served in close touch with the 2nd Battalion as long as the Indian Corps remained in France—an association helpful to and welcomed by both units.

NEUVE CHAPELLE, MARCH, 1915

It consisted of three subsections known as Port Arthur, Roomes Trench and the Crescent. While the Battalion was preparing the ground for the attack in the days and nights just previous to the battle, it suffered some forty casualties, a proportion of which were due to the ranging of our own artillery. Major H. H. Sutherland and Lieutenant Hamilton-Johnston were wounded. Sergeant Johnston, the machine-gun sergeant and a very able instructor, was killed.

The assault on the German lines commenced at 8.5 a.m. on the 10th March. The 1/39th Garhwal Rifles, the right battalion of the assault, advancing from the lines held by the Battalion, swung too far to the right, owing to a wide ditch which ran half-

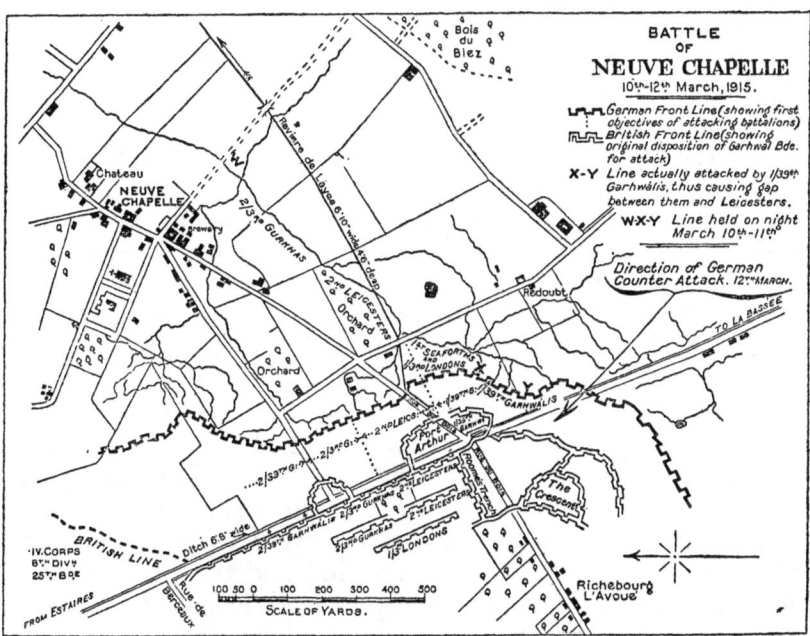

right across their front, and a gap grew between them and the 2nd Leicestershires, the next assaulting battalion to the left. The Commanding Officer of the Leicestershires sought assistance from the Battalion to close the gap, and ordered forward Lieutenant Holland with his platoon. But the gap was far too wide and too strongly held to be filled by so small a body; a proof of the unflinching courage with which this platoon attempted the task is that only one of them returned unwounded; their leader was killed. Eventually the greater part of two fresh battalions (Seaforths and 1/3rd Londons) had to be employed to close the gap.

Meanwhile, the 1/39th Garhwals had suffered very heavy loss; and though they had reached the German trenches, were practically isolated there, and had lost all their British officers. During the progress of this attack Lance Corporal V. Thompson performed an act of great gallantry in leaving the trenches under heavy fire to bring in the artillery officer who had been observing for the Garhwals and had fallen wounded. Lance Corporal Thompson was himself wounded while bringing him in. He received the Distinguished Conduct Medal for his courage.

Sergeant Drummond, in charge of the Telephone section of the Battalion signallers, also received the Distinguished Conduct Medal for repairing the telephone wires under fire.[1]

During the night of the 10th/11th, the Battalion sent out a working party to connect up our old trenches with the new line, but it was discovered by the enemy and driven in by heavy fire.

The battle continued on the 11th, and throughout the day the Battalion was under heavy and persistent shell fire, which caused some forty casualties. The operations of the 11th produced little change in this part of the field.

On the early morning of the 12th a German counter-attack was made, the left of which came up against the position held by the Battalion. The Battalion was forewarned owing to the good work of the scouts under Sergeant Fenton, who had reported considerable movement in the German trenches during the night of the 11th/12th, suggesting the possibility of a counter-attack.

Captain J. Inglis held the Crescent with his own (No. 2) Company and a platoon of the 1/4th Black Watch. He had with him two of the Battalion machine guns and two of the 4th Cavalry (Indian Army), also a trench mortar manned by men of the Battalion. The Crescent was a breastwork, and twenty or thirty yards in front ran the old Crescent trench, which had become waterlogged and had been abandoned in favour of the breastwork. There was a thick fog on this morning, and the Germans were close up to the old trench before they were seen. They were at once stopped by our rifle and machine-gun fire, but a number of them took cover in the old trench. Captain Inglis sent out a bombing party under 606 Lance Corporal J. Gordon, to work down an old communication trench towards the enemy, and covered their advance by rifle and machine-gun fire. Finding this communication trench blocked by water they had to get out and crawl across the open. After about five bombs had been thrown, the Germans, to the number of 71, surrendered—22 dead were also found in the trench. Another party of the German attacking

---

[1] The work of the regimental "buzzer" in trench warfare is arduous and dangerous. Whenever shelling is heavy, lines are likely to be cut and have to be repaired. The promptitude with which this is done, whatever risks it may entail, is the measure of the efficiency of a battalion's signallers. Throughout the war no unit can have been better served by its signallers than was The Black Watch.

NEUVE CHAPELLE, MARCH, 1915

line, which had gone to ground a little further back, was dislodged by a bomb gun, and nearly all shot down as they tried to regain their lines.

The enemy's shell fire was again heavy throughout the day; Second Lieutenant George was killed by shrapnel while placing some Gurkhas under cover, and Captain H. F. F. Murray was wounded by a shell. Lieutenant Gilroy was killed by a chance bullet while getting in the German prisoners mentioned above.[1]

On the 14th the Battalion was relieved. The next week was spent in reserve at Paradis.

The Lahore Division had acquitted itself gallantly in the attack at Neuve Chapelle, and that the success gained was not so great as had been hoped was not any fault of theirs.

The losses of the Battalion in the Neuve Chapelle operations were:—

Killed.—Lieutenant K. R. Gilroy; Second Lieutenants W. George, B. T. Holland; and 32 N.C.O.'s and men.

Wounded.—Major H. H. Sutherland; Captain H. F. F. Murray; Lieutenants D. C. Hamilton-Johnston, A. C. Denison, N. McMicking, C. D. Gilmour; and 126 N.C.O.'s and men.

On the 23rd the Battalion took over a trench line north of Neuve Chapelle. This was a new line reached as the result of the fighting of the 10th/12th, and much digging and wiring had to be done. This line was held till the 30th, when the Battalion returned to billets in the village of Paradis. Here it remained till April 11th, and then returned to trenches near Neuve Chapelle. This time the Battalion was split up between two sections; Nos. 3 and 4 Companies, under Major Wauchope, were attached to the 58th Rifles under Colonel Houston. This tour in the front line lasted till the 28th, the ordinary progress of reliefs being dislocated by the move of the Lahore Division northwards to the Second Battle of Ypres.

During these three weeks the Battalion scouts were reorganized and did some fine work, patrolling far in advance of our lines over ground not yet consolidated by the Germans after the Neuve Chapelle battle. Mixed parties of Highlanders and of the Pathans of the 58th Rifles formed, in the opinion of Major Wauchope (now in charge of the Battalion scouts), the best patrols he ever worked with. The Pathans were unequalled in " stalking " and gaining an enemy trench unseen, while the High-

---

[1] Although they held up their hands in token of surrender, the Germans refused to leave the cover of the trench and come in to our parapet till a man of The Black Watch, unarmed, ran out and seizing a German by the hand, led him in. The others then followed ; but at the other end of the trench a German who had surrendered picked up a rifle and shot one of Corporal Gordon's party. For this act of treachery he was subsequently tried by court martial and shot.

THE SECOND BATTALION THE BLACK WATCH

landers gave the necessary steadiness and feeling of security to the whole patrol. A firm alliance sprang up between the two battalions, and in November, on leaving France, the Indian officers of the 58th presented Major Wauchope with an address which stated that they looked on him as one of their own officers and on The Black Watch as their most trusted friends.

Except for the constant patrol work by day and night, these two periods in the front line passed quietly, though a good many casualties were suffered in a pronounced salient of our line known as the "Duck's Bill." On April 17th, Lieutenant I. B. McLeod, a most gallant officer was killed; and on the 19th Captain C. R. B. Henderson, the Adjutant, was wounded for the second time.

On April 15th, Company Sergeant Major T. Johnson and Sergeant Sinclair were promoted Second Lieutenants in the Battalion. Sinclair fell gallantly soon afterwards on May 9th; Johnson was killed with the 1st Battalion in 1916 on the Somme.

2.—*Aubers Ridge, May 9th, 1915*

The attacks on the British front which opened on May 9th, 1915, were undertaken to support a French attack between the right of the British line and Arras, on the Notre-Dame de Lorette Spur, opposite Vimy Ridge. Beyond affording a fresh proof of the astonishing gallantry of British and Indian troops in adverse conditions, the operations did not achieve any results. The British Army had not at this time a sufficient supply of guns or high explosive ammunition to carry out an attack on a wide front; and the failure was due to the strength of the German defences, which had been greatly improved since the action of Neuve Chapelle, and were insufficiently damaged by our artillery. In particular, the Germans had been at great pains to make their machine-gun positions as nearly proof as possible against destruction by bombardment; and in face of this machine-gun fire no attacks across the open could succeed; they could do no more than deserve success by their unflinching gallantry.

The Battalion had a particularly trying part to play on May 9th, as it had to relieve in the front line, in daylight and under continuous shell fire, a unit which with heavy loss had failed to advance; and it had to renew the attack against an enemy, not only unshaken by the previous attack, but obviously reinforced and ready to meet a second attempt. But the attempt was made with a determination and courage worthy of the Regiment which, one hundred and fifty years earlier, at Ticonderoga, had refused to acknowledge failure before an impregnable position till more than half their numbers had fallen.

The attack was made by the I Corps on the right, the Indian

ATTACK ON MAY 9TH, 1915

Corps in the centre and the IV Corps on the left. The assault of the Indian Corps was from the neighbourhood of Richebourg l'Avoué on a front of some 600 yards, with the Dehra Dun Brigade in the front line and the Bareilly Brigade in support.

At 5.40 a.m., after an artillery bombardment of forty minutes, the Dehra Dun Brigade advanced. The bombardment had been ineffective in damaging the enemy's defences, and the attack was at once met by a terrible fire from machine guns and rifles and was stopped dead in a few minutes. The bombardment was recommenced at 7.45 a.m. with a view to a further assault by the Dehra Dun Brigade: but in view of the equally complete failure of the 1st Division of the I Corps on the right, the attempt was postponed to the afternoon, to synchronize with a fresh attempt by the 1st Division. The Bareilly Brigade was ordered to relieve the Dehra Dun Brigade and to carry out the second attack.

About noon the Battalion received orders to relieve the 2nd Gurkhas on the right of the Dehra Dun Brigade. The Bareilly Brigade had been all the morning under heavy artillery fire, which increased as the Germans observed its forward movement to the front line; the communication trenches were partly destroyed, partly blocked with casualties; similar conditions prevailed in the front line. The relief was, however, carried out up to time without confusion.

The Battalion was formed for attack in two lines, No. 2 Company (Lieutenant A. H. C. Sutherland) and No. 4 Company (Captain G. C. S. McLeod) being in the front line. At 3.20 p.m. the bombardment recommenced; the assault was timed for 4 p.m. By about 3.55 p.m. the front lines issued from the trenches and lay down awaiting the signal to charge. Colonel Harvey remained on the right, and ordered Major Wauchope to watch and report progress on the left of our line. Large numbers of Germans could be seen issuing from communication trenches and filing along the front, unaffected by our very weak bombardment.

The attack was met by a very accurate and extremely heavy rifle and machine-gun fire from the moment it began. A wide stream full of water and mud ran across No Man's Land (which was about 200 yards wide), on the right within a few yards of our trench, on the left rather nearer the German than the British line. Some thirty bridges were supposed to have been constructed on our front, but few were existing when the Battalion made its attack. The greater number of the casualties fell close to or into this obstacle.

Major Wauchope reported that the attack of the battalion on our left was a complete failure and that no further progress could be made by No. 4 Company. Colonel Harvey had observed the same situation on the right, and with his usual promptness and

THE SECOND BATTALION THE BLACK WATCH

readiness to accept responsibility ordered the attack to cease, and No. 3 Company, which was to have followed the leading companies, not to cross the parapet; this action saved the Regiment many lives which would otherwise have been lost in continuing a hopeless attack.

In the brief period the assault lasted the losses of the Battalion were: killed, 3 officers (Lieutenants the Hon. K. A. Stewart, W. L. Brownlow and R. Sinclair) and 69 other ranks; wounded, 5 officers (of whom Captain G. C. S. MacLeod shortly died of his wounds) and 157 other ranks; missing (practically all killed close to the German trenches) 36 other ranks; total, 270 out of 450 engaged, or 60 per cent. The wounded and unwounded lay out in the open under fire till darkness enabled them to regain the trenches.[1]

Of the many examples of heroism displayed on this day, two may be recorded here. Lance Corporal David Findlay led a party of twelve bombers. Shortly after he left the trench he was knocked over by the explosion of a shell, but undaunted he led on his party till ten of his devoted twelve had fallen; he then ordered the two survivors to crawl back, and himself went to the rescue of a wounded man, whom he carried back into safety over 100 yards under a terrific fire. He was awarded the Victoria Cross, a distinction won on the same day by Corporal Ripley of the 1st Battalion, which was displaying equal gallantry in similar conditions in the assault of the 1st Division, a little further to the south.

Lieutenant Sinclair (promoted only a short time before from sergeant) gave a magnificent example of gallant leading and was killed on the right, close to the German parapet to which his determined valour had carried him—" None died with greater " glory that day." He had been granted leave to Scotland a day or two before, but had specially asked to be allowed to postpone it, so as to take part in the battle.

The Battalion was relieved during the night by the 3rd Londons, and retired to reserve trenches, where it remained from the

---

[1] The bodies of Lieutenant K. A. Stewart and about ten men of the platoon he had so gallantly led were not recovered on the night after the battle, and for months it was uncertain where they had fallen. But in July, when the grass had grown two or three feet long, Major Wauchope and Sergeant MacDonald proceeded on a search of No Man's Land, choosing the hour of 2 p.m. when German sentries were least watchful. Under the cover of the grass it was possible to go over the ground which the attacking troops had covered on the 9th of May. There were few bridges over the stream, and many bodies lay in its channel, about six feet deep, but at this time with little water in it. Lieutenant Stewart's body was found not far from the German trenches, with eight of his platoon beside him. A few articles were taken from the bodies for the relatives of the fallen men, and the patrol returned safely.

HIELAN' LADDIE
After the drawing by "Snaffles"

MAY 9TH, 1915

10th to the 15th. The battle continued till the 22nd. On the night of the 15th/16th the Garhwal Brigade made a third attack from the same ground, but met with no better success than the other two brigades of the Division. The Battalion was not called on to attack again, but held the front line trenches by the Rue de Bois from the 16th till the night of the 19th in very bad weather and under heavy shell fire. A very gallant officer, Captain D. Campbell, was killed on the 18th. The Battalion then held reserve trenches till the 24th, after which it was in billets near Vieille Chapelle till the 31st.

The following extracts from the reports of the commanders on the action of May 9th show the bravery with which a hopeless enterprise was executed: the G.O.C. Bareilly Brigade reported: " I wish to bring to the notice of the Lieutenant General Com" manding the gallant behaviour of all the regiments engaged. " They saw in front of them the hundreds of men of the Dehra " Dun Brigade lying out on our front wounded and dead. They " knew the enemy were unshaken, seeing them with their heads " over the parapet firing, and thoroughly realizing what had " happened to the Dehra Dun Brigade would in all probability " happen to them; but not a man faltered, and as they " boldly advanced over the parapet, only to be shot down, " British and Indian ranks alike did their level best to reach " the enemy's line. Even when the attack had failed, the moral " of the Brigade remained unshaken, and, had another attack " been ordered, they would have undertaken it in the same " spirit."

The G.O.C. Meerut Division wrote: " The gallantry with " which the various assaults were pressed by the infantry left " nothing to be desired. What human nature could do they did. " The successive attempts to reach the enemy trenches were " brought to a standstill by the disablement of all but a small per" centage of the assaulting lines by the German rifle and machine" gun fire. This fire started from the moment the men showed, " and numbers were put out of action within ten yards of our own " front line."

The G.O.C. Indian Corps wrote to the G.O.C. Meerut Division: " I have just read the report of the action of 9th May, " as far as the Bareilly Brigade is concerned. It is a stirring story " of disciplined valour. Please convey to Brigadier General " Southey and the commanding officers and all other ranks my " most sincere congratulations on the conduct and bearing of " the troops, which adds another bright page to the annals of " the Indian Corps in France."

THE SECOND BATTALION THE BLACK WATCH

3.—*The Battle of Loos, September 25th, 1915*
(See Map on Page 45.)

During June, July and August the Battalion spent sixty days in the trenches as against thirty-two out of the line. During July, Indian battalions were withdrawn to rest and reorganize, but the British battalions of the Indian Corps, concentrated in the Lahore Division, continued in the front line.

No events of any particular importance relieved the ordinary routine of trench warfare during these months.[1] It was the "interval" during which the stage was being prepared for the "star turn" of the Allies' 1915 programme, the autumn offensive in Champagne and at Loos.

During the first half of September, in addition to studying and rehearsing their parts in this coming attack, the troops were busily engaged in the rôle of stage carpenters, setting the preliminary scene; for no preparation was to be neglected to make this autumn production a success. The Battalion had to furnish numerous digging and carrying parties during this period. The overture, a four days' artillery bombardment, commenced on September 21st.

On September 6th, Lieutenant Colonel St. J. Harvey had been appointed to the temporary command of the Dehra Dun Brigade, in which he was confirmed ten days later.[2] Major A. G. Wauchope succeeded to the command of the Battalion.

On September 20th the Bareilly Brigade was inspected by Lord Kitchener.

The French attack in Champagne was the main effort of the Allies' autumn offensive; the other operations were subsidiary to it, and had as their chief object the holding of enemy troops from the Champagne battle, though important results were hoped from the subsidiary operations themselves. The scene of the principal of these was between La Bassée and Arras; the share of the British Army was the Battle of Loos.

The attack made by the Indian Corps on September 25th was one of a series of actions designed to prolong the front of attack to the north, and to hold or attract the enemy reserves to this part of the field. But this "holding attack" was not in any way limited in its scope; it was, on the contrary, given a practically unlimited forward objective. Briefly, the Indian Corps was to seize the Aubers Ridge and advance south-east to turn the defences of La Bassée from the north. It is important, in view of what

---

[1] On June 15, Company Sergeant Major Buchan and Acting Company Sergeant Major Wilson were gazetted to commissions in the Battalion and Sergeant Sladen to a commission in the Cameron Highlanders.

[2] He commanded this Brigade till killed in action with it in Mesopotamia in March, 1916. (See p.221.)

BATTLE OF LOOS, SEPTEMBER 25TH, 1915

occurred, to bear in mind this idea of a deep offensive, which was during the whole of the preparations continually impressed on all commanders taking part in the attack.

The attack was made by the Meerut Division, with the Garhwal Brigade on the right and the Bareilly Brigade on the left, the Dehra Dun Brigade being in Divisional reserve. Each of the assaulting brigades had three battalions in the front line and two in reserve.[1] The Bareilly Brigade was formed for attack with 1/4th Black Watch on the right, 69th Punjabis in the centre and 2nd Black Watch on the left. The 33rd Punjabis and 58th Rifles were in Brigade reserve.

The Battalion, being thus on the extreme left of the attack, was bound to have an exposed flank, if it was successful in advancing. This flank was to be protected by the right battalion of the brigade on its left (the 60th Brigade of the 20th Division), but in the absence of any good natural feature for flank protection, it was difficult to make detailed arrangements; as events happened the battalion of the 60th Brigade suffered severe losses in crossing No Man's Land, and their carrying parties with reserves of ammunition and grenades were never able to reach their forward platoons. Consequently, in spite of most gallant efforts, this battalion was unable to secure the left flank of The Black Watch against the enemy's vigorous counter-attacks.

The enemy line attacked by the Battalion formed a pronounced salient with two smaller salients at its apex. A road known as the Winchester road passed between these two small salients, which were the first objectives of the Battalion. Under the northern of the two salients a mine had been laid and was sprung shortly before the commencement of the attack.

Photography of the enemy's trenches from the air had only just been introduced; from the first photographs received by the Battalion, Major Wauchope ordered a plan of the enemy's trenches to be reconstructed on the ground behind our lines. Over this the Battalion practised. Such practice was, later in the war, the invariable preliminary to any attack. But at this time its value had not been generally realized; and to Major Wauchope's foresight the Battalion owed the advantage undoubtedly obtained in the attack from the previous rehearsals.

The Battalion strength and organization on the morning of September 25th was as follows:—

Commanding Officer   Major A. G. Wauchope, D.S.O.
Second-in-Command   Major C. W. E. Gordon (*wounded*).
Adjutant   Captain C. R. B. Henderson (*wounded*).
Medical Officer   Captain R. W. Duncan.

[1] Brigades consisted at this time of five battalions, each Brigade having a Territorial battalion added to it.

THE SECOND BATTALION THE BLACK WATCH

No. 1 Company : Strength 177
Captain W. Wilson (*wounded*). 2nd Lieut. Sotherby (*killed*).
2nd Lieut. Egerton (*wounded*). C.S.M. G. Davidson.
„   Hutchison

No. 2 Company : Strength 179
Captain M. E. Park.   Lieut. McConaghey (*wounded*).
Lieut. Balfour-Melville (*killed*). C.S.M. J. Robertson (*wounded*).
„   Barstow (*wounded*).

No. 3 Company : Strength 192
Captain A. C. Denison (*killed*). 2nd Lieut. C. Curdie.
2nd Lieut. Eglinton.   „   L. MacLeod (*wounded and prisoner of war*).
„ D. Stewart-Smith (*wounded*). C.S.M. B. Houston.

No. 4 Company : Strength 182
Captain J. I. Buchan (*wounded*). 2nd Lieut. McWilliams. (*wounded*).
2nd Lieut. N. Henderson (*killed*). C.S.M. R. Lawrie (*killed*).

Machine Gun Company : Strength 44
Captain T. G. F. Cochrane (*wounded*).

Brigade Bombing Company : Strength 22
2nd Lieut. H. A. T. Plunkett.

The total strength of the Battalion (excluding the depot left behind and those in Brigade and Divisional employment) was 21 officers and 796 other ranks.

The attack was made in four lines, Nos. 1 and 3 Companies forming the first two lines (each company with two platoons in each line), Nos. 2 and 4 Companies the third and fourth lines in similar formation. The Winchester road, already mentioned, was the dividing line between companies in the first phase of the attack. The Battalion's frontage was 250 yards.

September 25th was the first occasion on which gas was used by the British. Alternative programmes had been prepared, according to whether the wind was favourable or not on the morning of the attack. It was decided to use the gas; but a light and variable wind changed at the very moment when the cylinders were opened and blew it back into our trenches. It was turned off, but not before it had caused considerable casualties. The Black Watch, being on the leeward flank, suffered more severely from it than the remainder of the Brigade. No gas seems to have reached the enemy trenches. The smoke barrages used to protect the

BATTLE OF LOOS, SEPTEMBER 25TH, 1915

flanks were also, of course, affected by the change of wind; and though valuable in concealing the commencement of the attack from the enemy caused some confusion and loss of direction.

Before following the fortunes of the Battalion in the attack, it is necessary to describe briefly the results of the assault by the Garhwal Brigade on the right, as these had important consequences for the Battalion. The 2/3rd Gurkhas, the right battalion of this Brigade, and the Leicestershires, the centre battalion, were held up by uncut wire, and only one company of the latter reached the German front line. The 2/8th Gurkhas, on the left of the Leicestershires, carried the German lines opposite them, and eventually reached the German second line, opposite the Moulin de Piètre, but only in small numbers, and with only one surviving British officer. On the whole, then, the attack of the Garhwal Brigade failed; and this eventually forced the Bareilly Brigade to abandon the ground they gained.

The story of the Battalion's share in the day's fighting can best be given by quoting the report of the Commanding Officer, Major A. G. Wauchope :—

" In spite of the distress caused by the gas, the four leading
" platoons crossed the parapet and led towards the enemy line,
" vanishing into the smoke cloud. They were at once followed by
" the second and third lines, leaving only the four platoons of the
" fourth line, which followed in rear carrying extra tools,
" ammunition and bombs, etc.

" I led the third line and reached the enemy firing line in rear
" of our mine crater; the Germans were here still manning their
" parapet and I saw a number killed at this spot. I then made my
" way to the re-entrant at S., which I had declared to be my
" headquarters.

" The confusion was extreme. The gas had greatly upset
" everyone, though it ceased to trouble once the German line
" was gained. Half the officers and all my orderlies were casualties;
" the smoke cloud made it hard to recognize ground features, and
" bullets were flying thick.

" None the less much was achieved by 7 a.m. Part of No. 3
" and No. 2 Companies in organized parties under Captains
" Denison and Park drove the enemy back with bayonet and
" bomb on M, K, J. No. 1 Company had captured the enemy
" firing line from Elm Tree Salient to my headquarters at the
" re-entrant, and was now moving up towards Road Bend. Half
" No. 4 Company and some of No. 1 Company, under Captain
" Buchan, finding little resistance about the centre of our line,
" were following up the enemy towards the Moulin de Piètre.

" I informed the Brigade that this advance was taking place

THE SECOND BATTALION THE BLACK WATCH

" and asked for the 60th Brigade to hold our left flank. I got a
" reply that a battalion was being sent for this purpose.

" Meantime the 69th were coming on very well on our right,
" and the 58th soon appeared; part of one company went to our
" left flank about J, the bulk gallantly pushed forward towards
" the Moulin.

" Captain Buchan's party captured the enemy's reserve
" trench opposite and to the right of the Moulin, the other regi-
" ments following immediately afterwards on their right and
" later on their left.

" I now ordered the left to consolidate, and this was success-
" fully done in spite of a severe and continuous resistance, blocks
" being formed all well ahead of the line we were originally told
" to occupy.

" Seeing that Captain Buchan's party met with little resist-
" ance in their advance against the enemy second line in front of
" Moulin, and knowing the General's wish that this should be
" held, I collected my four reserve platoons and ordered them
" forward in support of Captain Buchan's party, who now rushed
" the enemy's second line opposite the Moulin.[1] These support-
" ing platoons I organized, together with many of the 58th and
" 69th, who came on very well indeed on our right; and though
" under considerable rifle fire from the Moulin and their right
" front, this body soon captured and held all the enemy second
" line to the right of the Moulin, linking up with Captain
" Buchan's party.

" I informed the Brigade of events, again asking for more
" troops to protect our left flank and also that our artillery should
" lift off the enemy's second line on to the Moulin itself. This
" last was promptly done.

" Though I had lost 12 officers out of 20 and many men, I

[1] The following quotations from the report of the Meerut Division on the plan of attack, and from Operation Orders of the Bareilly Brigade, show clearly that the front line troops were expected to push forward if possible.

Meerut Division Report.

" If the opposition was slight, the assaulting troops were not to stop at the
" enemy's support line, but were to advance to attack his second line, leaving
" sufficient troops to consolidate the lines gained."

Bareilly Brigade Operation Order.

" If the opposition of the enemy in his front system of trenches is slight, the
" leading lines of the assaulting battalions must be pushed on without delay to
" capture his second line, Moulin de Piètre–Point L, supporting companies being
" sent forward into the captured front trenches to support the leading companies
" closely.

The intention to push forward is also shown by the fact that the Dehra Dun Brigade, in Divisional reserve, was ordered at 9.20 a.m. to follow through the gap made by the Bareilly Brigade and advance on Haut Pommereau–La Cliqueterie.

BATTLE OF LOOS, SEPTEMBER 25TH, 1915

"felt things had gone very well provided our two flanks were
"secured. I pushed forward myself at once to our extreme left,
"and Captain Buchan established a block (under Second Lieu-
"tenant Noel Henderson) some 200 yards to the left of the
"Moulin. From there back to our left company consolidated at
"K² and J was a gap of about 600 yards.

"It was my main idea for the rest of the battle to close this.

"Finding no other officer of the 58th I ordered Subadar Tikla
"Khan to take his double company out of the second line, which
"was now being overcrowded with fresh arrivals, and form along
"the natural ditch which runs back from the enemy second line
"at Z. This he did in a most soldierly fashion. Later I informed
"Colonel Houston (O.C. 58th Rifles) and he added more men
"and closed about 150 yards of the gap.

"I then moved to the right and found Lieutenant Colonels
"Ridgeway (33rd Punjabis) and Walker (1/4th Black Watch).
"Part of the 4th Black Watch had charged the second line on
"our right, but Colonel Walker explained that his right was
"entirely exposed to attack. We both felt that if the Garhwal
"Brigade had not succeeded in pushing forward, the task of
"holding our right was too much for his battalion, but seeing
"some of the 2/8th Gurkhas on our right, at X, we hoped the
"right was secure. Colonel Walker agreed not to push on, but
"to do what he could to protect the right, and he kept his bat-
"talion mostly in the trench about G for that purpose. When
"I met Colonel Ridgeway I told him where Colonel Houston
"was, and begged him to keep the 33rd where they were, as a
"central reserve in case of the enemy attacking from either
"flank.[1]

"The 69th were now all in the enemy second line, about
"opposite the Chimney, so I also left Lieutenant Hutchison with
"about 50 men as a support, as I felt the enemy might push in
"from either flank. I then told Colonels Houston, Walker and
"Ridgeway[2] that I myself would go back to my left flank at K²
"and direct the 60th Brigade to move in and secure our left flank
"to the Moulin.

"The situation between 10 and 11 a.m. therefore was this:
"the 12th Rifle Brigade (of the 60th Brigade) was beginning to
"arrive about M. About a hundred men of the 2nd Black Watch

---

[1] The 33rd Punjabis, the other battalion of the Brigade Reserve, had been ordered forward to consolidate the lines originally gained. But they also, imbued with the offensive spirit, pressed on to the enemy second line, carrying with them a company left behind by the 69th Punjabis to consolidate the enemy's first line.

[2] Lieutenant Colonels Houston and Walker were killed later in the day and Lieutenant Colonel Ridgeway was wounded. The C.O. of the 69th Punjabis had already been killed.

THE SECOND BATTALION THE BLACK WATCH

"held M^2, M^3, K^2, J; Captain Buchan and some eighty men
"held enemy second line opposite Moulin; some 200 men of the
"58th Rifles held 200 yards from enemy second line towards Y;
"a mixture of 58th, 69th and 33rd in that order held enemy
"second line on right of Captain Buchan to about Q; some
"of the 2/8th Gurkhas held it about X; Lieutenant Hutchison
"was in support about Q, and most of the 1/4th Black
"Watch between Q and G. The enemy shell and rifle fire
"was severe.

"About 11 a.m. I got first contact with 12th Rifle Brigade;
"they had taken over correctly from Captain Park the blocks at
"M^2, M^3, K^2. I pointed out the Moulin to the officers with the
"12th and ordered them gradually to extend their men in that
"direction and to hold this flank to about Y, where they would
"join the 58th Rifles. I placed one company myself in the
"natural ditch that runs from J towards the Moulin, but the
"other companies never advanced as far as this before noon
"when the retirement began.

"Captain Park meanwhile withdrew without great difficulty
"and reorganized, preparatory to advancing to Road Bend. He
"reached the Electric Power Station about 12 noon. Here he
"saw three retirements of the Brigade from the trenches in front
"of Moulin. The first was chiefly 69th and 33rd rather from the
"right of the Moulin, the next included many of 4th Black
"Watch and 58th and some 2nd Black Watch; the last was wholly
"2nd Black Watch.

"This retirement was due to two distinct causes:

"(1) The left of the enemy's second line had been blocked by
"Captain Buchan, but on his rear there was no natural feature to
"give protection, and the Germans pressed through on his left
"rear just about noon.

"(2) The right of the Brigade was also unguarded, except for
"a few of the 2/8th Gurkhas who had most gallantly fought their
"way to a point to the right of the Moulin and to the right front
"of the 69th. A little after 11 a.m. they were forced out of this
"trench, and the 4th Black Watch and the 33rd then had their
"right exposed. Lack of officers made reorganization difficult,
"and rifle fire and bombing rendered the taking up of a new
"position immediately in rear almost impossible. Consequently
"about 11.30 this right flank gave way, the Germans constantly
"bombing and pressing in from the right.

"This flank giving way was the first of the three retirements
"seen by Captain Park from the Electric Power Station.

"Then the centre of our troops opposite the Moulin found
"the Germans on their right rear, and shortly afterwards the
"left section found both their right rear and left rear threatened;

BATTLE OF LOOS, SEPTEMBER 25TH, 1915

"and consequently each section was forced back, or there would
"have been no line of retreat left open. The final retirement
"from the left was due to the gap between Moulin and J never
"having been filled and a gap on our right having been created,
"as explained above.

"Both Captain Park and the party I had left under Lieu-
"tenant Hutchison found the men most ready to make a series
"of stands during the retirement, but whenever a stand was
"prolonged Germans came bombing up from trenches on either
"flank.

"Meanwhile my efforts at closing the gap about J were un-
"successful. I never found the Bareilly Brigade bombers or the
"half-company of 60th Brigade bombers. The two companies of
"the 12th Rifle Brigade apparently relied on their Brigade bomb-
"ers both for bombers and supplies of bombs, and when pressed
"by German bombers were unable to resist them, having few,
"if any, trained bombers or bombs. Consequently they were
"driven back from the blocks they had taken over at M^2, M^3 and
"K^2, and the Company I had placed in the natural ditch in the
"direction of Y was also forced back.[1]

"The situation about noon was that on the right of the
"German second line in front of the Moulin about X and Q no
"troops remained. They had been forced far back, if not into
"our own lines, at any rate out of the fighting zone. The troops
"in the centre opposite the Chimney were being forced back
"with their right rear threatened. The troops on the left oppo-
"site the Moulin, mostly 2nd Black Watch, were still holding on,
"but Germans were firing heavily from trenches on their left
"rear.

"By 12.30 they were forced back and to their right, both
"flanks being in the air and their direct retreat cut by the retire-
"ment of the 12th Rifle Brigade.

"By 1.30 they had effected their retirement under several
"officers; part of it I witnessed and it seemed orderly and steady,
"the men halting and firing at different places. They went past
"the Power Station and thence, mostly in the open, on both
"sides of the Winchester road.

"About half an hour after this six of the twelve men of The
"Black Watch I had with me (the other six being killed) followed
"the last few of the Rifle Brigade to A, pursued by bombs and
"heavy rifle fire from close range. At A we saw the Germans

[1] There is no doubt that a shortage of bombs, and in some cases of trained bombers, amongst our assaulting troops, was one of the main causes of the success of the German counter-attack. The Brigade bombers received no orders at all, and never left our original trenches. As they were all highly trained men, their presence in the fight would have been invaluable.

"about 5, and realizing that further delay was useless crossed
"to the British lines.¹

"Much confusion was caused from the start by the effects of
"the gas on all leaders. But the left flank was consolidated as
"ordered. That the second and third lines pressed on to the
"Moulin is hardly a matter for blame as they were told to keep
"pressing forward from one line to another if the resistance was
"not too severe.

"Had the Garhwal Brigade been able to make good the
"ground on our right, the initial retirement of the Bareilly Bri-
"gade would not have taken place, and more time and more men
"would have been available to fill up the gap on the left flank of
"the 2nd Black Watch.

"The 2nd Black Watch captured the enemy lines on a front-
"age of 550 yards, and advanced to within 80 yards of the Moulin
"(i.e. to a depth of 750 yards from our front line) over four lines
"of enemy trenches."

From careful enquiries and his own observation Major Wauchope estimated the total of enemy dead on the Battalion front
at 240.

The Germans fought very well, in most cases to a finish. One
of our sergeants with a bombing party captured a machine gun;
just as they captured it the two Germans left with it placed two
bombs under the gun and were themselves blown to pieces, the
gun being much damaged. Many other instances of the determination with which they resisted could be related. There seems
little doubt that many Germans in dug-outs were passed over
by the attacking troops, and some of these fired in the backs of
our men. This partly accounts for the very heavy loss in officers.

The fate that befell the attack of the Bareilly Brigade on September 25th was the almost inevitable fate of attacks in position
warfare, on a narrow front with an unlimited objective. The
creation of a deep salient with vulnerable flanks gave a resolute
enemy, such as the German always was, opportunities for counter-
attack of which he was seldom slow to avail himself. In open warfare such counter-attacks would have had to pass across the open,
and could have been dealt with by fire. In position warfare, the
trenches on the flanks gave covered approach to parties of bombers, and such a form of counter-attack could often be met only by
counter-bombing. Here the attack was always at a disadvantage,
owing to the difficulties of supply of bombs, and the attackers'
ignorance of the intricacies of a strange maze of trenches. The

¹ This party, consisting of Major Wauchope and the few unwounded men of
the Headquarter platoon under Lieutenant Curdie, were the last of the Brigade to
leave the enemy trenches.

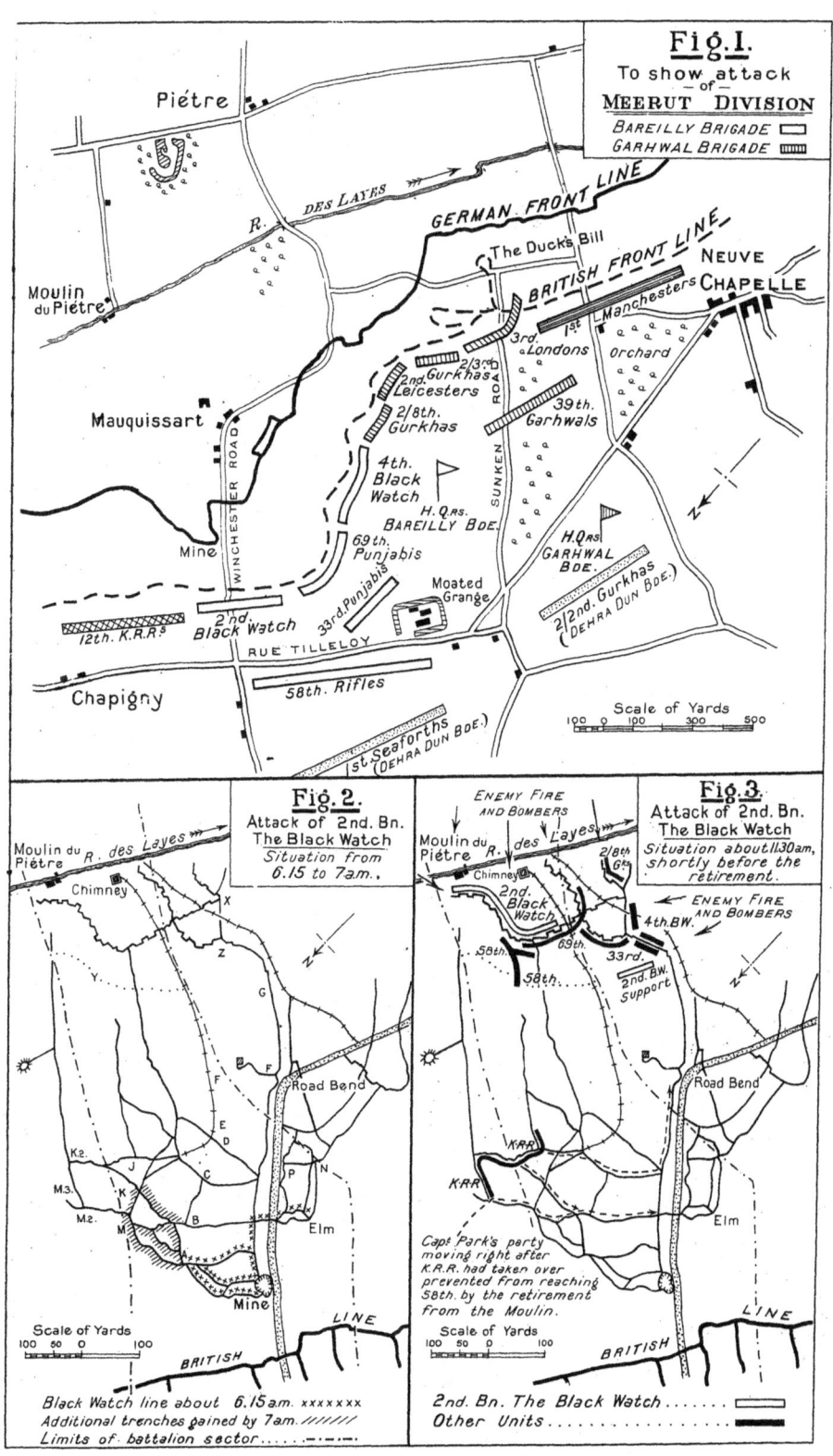

BATTLE OF SEPTEMBER 25TH. 1915.

BATTLE OF LOOS, SEPTEMBER 25TH, 1915

Battalion had always been at great pains to train its bombers and to practice methods of meeting such attack; and until the supply of bombs (supplemented by use of captured German bombs) gave out, they kept the enemy in check. But the uncut wire which prevented the advance of the Garhwal Brigade on the right caused so pronounced and narrow a salient that the infiltration of the enemy past the flanks and into the rear of the advanced troops could not be prevented. And the failure of the Garhwal Brigade was not known to the Bareilly Brigade till the great body of the assaulting troops had pressed on to the second line. In view of the orders received (see page 183) no blame can be attached to the troops for pressing on; and, in fact, they deserved and received the highest praise for the gallant way in which they carried out the intention of their higher commanders.

The Brigade Commander, Brigadier General Norie, paid the following tribute to the behaviour of the Battalion on this day:—

"Black Watch, in yesterday's battle you did splendidly. You did what was asked of you to do. That was to keep large German reserves from going down south, where our Allies the French are making great progress. You have therefore done a great service not only to them but to Great Britain. You fought magnificently; you fought like tigers. I saw you. You took trench after trench, but to have reached the Moulin Piètre will be an everlasting glory. And you would do it again."

The casualties of the Battalion were heavy—4 officers (Captain Denison, Second Lieutenants Balfour-Melville, Henderson and Sotherby) and 38 other ranks killed (to these must be added practically all the 49 reported missing); 10 officers (Major Gordon, Captains Henderson, Wilson, Buchan, Cochrane; Second Lieutenants Egerton, McConaghey, Stewart-Smith, Barstow, McWilliam) and 261 other ranks wounded; total, 363.

When so high a standard of collective gallantry has been displayed by a unit, it is difficult and invidious to single out for mention acts of individual gallantry. In a struggle such as that of September 25th the finest acts of courage and self-devotion may pass unnoticed. The number of those recorded was many, and the following are mentioned as typical of the spirit displayed by all.

Captain Denison gave a magnificent example to his company, exposing himself fearlessly at their head and inspiring by his gallantry the efforts of the bombing parties that drove the enemy 300 yards back and secured the flank of the first advance. He fell at the head of his company just as their task was completed.

THE SECOND BATTALION THE BLACK WATCH

Captain Park, Captain Buchan and Captain Wilson all led their companies finely. The two former received the D.S.O. for their gallant leading, a reward which had been well earned by all four company commanders. Captain Wilson fell badly wounded at the third line of enemy trenches; here he was found during the retreat, unable to move, by Private McHattie, who carried him under heavy fire back to our trenches, though the enemy were within twenty yards,

Second Lieutenants Henderson, Sotherby and Balfour-Melville were all killed in the enemy's trenches at the head of the platoons they had so bravely and skilfully led to success. Of the non-commissioned officers who led platoons as ably and fearlessly when their officers had been disabled may be mentioned Company Sergeant Major Houston, Sergeant Whytock, Sergeant Gant, Sergeant Lees, Corporal Strachan and Lance Corporal Martin. The last named in the retirement carried back to safety a British officer of an Indian regiment, and then continued the fight.

No. 1993 Sergeant John Mitchell, was three times during the war recommended for the Victoria Cross. On this, the second occasion, the recommendation was for his dauntless courage in leading bombing parties which drove the enemy back 250 yards and then held on, though the supply of grenades ran short and the enemy kept constantly attacking, for three hours until relieved by a party from another unit. He received a bar to the D.C.M. he had already won.

Similar gallantry was displayed by Sergeant John Easton, who also kept the enemy at bay for three hours and himself several times crossed the open under heavy fire to bring up more grenades. His clothes and equipment were half burnt by the explosion of an enemy grenade, but he was still hanging on grimly when another grenade killed him.

No. 1539 Piper A. McDonald, showed a courage typical of all the pipers of the Regiment in this action; he played the charge at the head of his platoon through the first and second lines of enemy trenches; and when they advanced bombing down the trenches to the third line continued to play at their head on the top of the parapet. Piper Armitt, after playing his platoon into battle, assisted the bombing parties to drive the enemy back. Piper D. Simpson of No. 1 Company fell gallantly at the head of his company while playing them into action.

As typical of the coolness and boldness with which the machine guns of the Battalion were handled throughout the battle, the examples of the commander, Captain Cochrane, and the sergeant, Sergeant Crowe, may be given. Both were conspicuous for their disregard of enemy fire when bringing forward and working the guns during the advance and when covering the withdrawal.

AFTER LOOS, SEPTEMBER, 1915

They were assisting to bring back a gun during the final retreat, under close range fire from the enemy, when Sergeant Crowe was killed.

No. 1543 Lance Corporal C. Easton, took charge of the Regimental stretcher bearers after the sergeant in charge had been disabled; under his cool leadership they did their work, as always, with complete disregard of their own safety.

Sergeant A. MacDonald, the scout sergeant, had done great work previous to the action in reconnoitring the enemy trenches; in the action he behaved with his usual skill and gallantry till wounded. Of the Regimental bombers, on whom so much desperate close fighting fell, may be mentioned Lance Corporal Pratt, Lance Corporal Clark, Lance Corporal Wynn, Private Pryde, Private W. McLaren and Private R. McDonald.

Private Crebar, Lance Corporal McLauchlan, Private Ogilvie and Private Menelaws distinguished themselves in bringing up ammunition and grenades to the front line under heavy fire.

Others whose names came to notice for their cool and determined fighting were Corporal Banks, Lance Corporal Robb, Privates Ferguson, Lynch, Clark, McKinnon, Stirton, Peacock, McGregor, Brown and Younger.

4.—*Givenchy and the Departure to Mesopotamia*

The Battalion was relieved by the 1st Seaforths on September 26th and marched to billets at La Gorgue.

The 1/4th Black Watch, which had lost 19 officers out of 20, and 230 men out of the 420 who actually took part in the attack, was now amalgamated temporarily with the 2nd Battalion. As their numbers were so few, Colonel Wauchope decided to organize the 4th Battalion as No. 5 and No. 6 Companies of a combined battalion, and this organization was maintained until November, when the 2nd Battalion left France with the Indian Corps and the 4th Battalion was again formed as an independent unit under the command of Lieutenant R. C. Cunningham, until the return of Major J. B. Muir. Two officers of the 4th Battalion, Lieutenants T. Stevenson and R. C. Cunningham, were given command of No. 5 and No. 6 Companies, and both showed the highest qualities of leadership and gallantry throughout the period of reconstruction and during the severe fighting round Givenchy Hill. Colonel Wauchope selected Lieutenant J. L. Pullar as Acting Adjutant to the combined Battalion until the arrival, early in October, of a strong draft under Captain Hamilton-Johnston, when that officer was appointed Adjutant, and Lieutenant Pullar, Assistant Adjutant.

Colonel Wauchope was able to report four days after the

battle that the reorganization of the two battalions was complete. This was a fine performance, especially on the part of the 4th Battalion, who had suffered such very severe losses on the 25th; but the spirit and traditions of Colonel H. Walker, their late commander, prevailed over every difficulty, and the six companies of the united Battalion were, on the last day of September, ready to undertake the new and arduous duty that was now demanded of them.

Givenchy had long been an important post in the British line. The hill, though a very low one, overlooked the flat marshy ground in front of the low-lying villages of Le Plantin and Festubert. The salient, though not very marked, was sufficient to protect by enfilade fire the British line both to the right and left. For the whole of the past year (and indeed for years to come) the struggle for the possession of this ruined village and battered mound proved terribly costly to both sides. During the fighting of 1914 both the 1st and 2nd Battalions had borne an honourable part in its defence. The place was now riddled with mines and counter-mines. The attacks made from the British lines near Givenchy on September 25th had not been very successful. Strong counter-attacks were now expected, and two British battalions from the Indian Corps were ordered to hold it. The Seaforth Highlanders and The Black Watch were selected to form this garrison. Lieutenant Colonel W. M. Thompson of the Seaforths commanded the garrison and, under him, Lieutenant Colonel A. G. Wauchope commanded the combined 2nd and 4th Black Watch, which took over the trenches in front of Givenchy on the first day of October.

The fighting was strenuous during the following week, and the losses severe. The hill had long been the centre of great mining activity and the line was now mixed up with the craters, large and small, of many exploded mines. Sometimes the forward edge and sometimes only the rear edge of a crater was held. In one night a new explosion would destroy the former dispositions, and a new line had to be selected, and, what was more difficult, seized, rebuilt and held. The regimental scouts had many exciting adventures in No Man's Land, for the space, though narrow, was covered with craters, some held by the Highlanders, some occupied by Germans, and others deserted. It was a form of warfare very trying to men whose nerves were at all overwrought, but which appealed strongly to the adventurous.

During the first two days after taking over the trenches at Givenchy, it was found that the German snipers altogether dominated the British line. Their look-out men were so well posted and so efficient that when a Highlander fired a single shot a dozen bullets immediately struck the loophole he had fired from.

GIVENCHY, OCTOBER, 1915

New arrangements for snipers were at once devised and a new system of look-out posts was planned, but a number of experienced snipers and workmen, including the Pioneer Sergeant,[1] were shot before these were put into working order.

Drafts, however, arrived, both for the 2nd and 4th Battalions, to replace the losses of the 25th. These drafts contained many men who had been wounded earlier in the war, and so had experience of trench fighting. From among these men each company commander selected new scouts and snipers; and before the Battalion left Givenchy the usual superiority in these two services, equally essential in trench as in open warfare, had been re-established.

It was soon evident that the Germans had determined to make a counter-attack on the hill, could they find a weak spot in the defence. During the first few days of October the enemy artillery bombardment was very severe, and on one afternoon the trenches of the right sector were nearly destroyed by the fire of some large minenwerfer. Heavy losses were only avoided by withdrawing men from the trenches during the bombardment, and holding strong supports in readiness to reoccupy the line at the first sign of an enemy attack.

On October 7th it was discovered that the enemy mines had reached up to the parapet. By vigorous counter-mining the Tunnelling Company succeeded in blowing up one of the mines, but a few hours later a second mine was exploded and part of the front parapet levelled. During the night the enemy bombardment increased, and the scouts reported unwonted activity in the German lines. Shortly before dawn on the morning of October 8th two more mines close in front of our parapet were exploded. Captain Park and about fifty men of No. 2 Company were half buried in the debris. Three were killed and many injured, but the remainder managed to extricate themselves and, with the local supports, rushed to the defence of the broken parapet.

It was a fine display of discipline and courage under most trying conditions, for of all the trials our men experienced in France none was more nerve shaking than to see their comrades killed in a mine explosion, and find themselves half buried in the ruins of their own trench. And it was a moment when both discipline and courage were needed. The Germans had opened a heavy rifle fire all along the front held by The Black Watch. Opposite Captain Park's company a strong party of Germans advanced across No Man's Land, and approached within bombing distance of our line where it had been broken by the mine explosions. The steady

[1] Sergeant Henderson. The original Pioneer Sergeant of the Battalion, Honeyman, had been killed a few days earlier while Company Sergeant Major of No. 2 Company.

fire from No. 2 Company drove them back, and the enemy realized the attempted attack had failed.[1] The next few days were passed in comparative quiet.

This was the last important incident of the Battalion's service in France. Givenchy was now considered secure, the Seaforth Highlanders and The Black Watch rejoined their respective brigades, and, during the next four weeks, took their share in holding that part of the line near the Rue de Bois, Chocolat Menier Corner and the Orchard, which they had known so well in the spring. Autumn rains were now setting in, and soon the mud of this October equalled the mud of November, 1914.

The conditions, however, were now very different. Parapets were bullet proof, trenches were deeper and well drained, dugouts were sufficient in number and gave shelter not only against rain and wind, but also against grenades and shrapnel. Reliefs were more frequent and more regular, and the comfort enjoyed during the periods of rest was infinitely greater.

When the Battalion first landed in France troops in reserve were kept very close to the front line trenches; officers seldom had a bed to lie on, men thought themselves lucky if they were given an empty barn for their billet, often with a little damp straw, alive with fleas, for their bedding. But after a year of position warfare great changes had been made. To troops coming from the front line trenches the new billets seemed almost perfect. The farms had been cleaned, the middens removed, the villages prepared for the arrival of troops. A good water supply, hot baths, and the regular cleaning of underclothing and uniform, not only saved the men from disease, but also added greatly to their comfort and well-being. Institutes such as the Y.M.C.A. were by this time established well forward and did much for the welfare of the men. Rations had always been excellent, but now accommodation was also improved and messes for officers were managed on a far more comfortable scale than in 1914. No one now acted as if the war would end in a month or two.

Nothing unusual disturbed the ordinary routine of these last few weeks. An attack was prepared, but had to be postponed as the mud rendered the crossing of No Man's Land impassable. Ten days' leave to Scotland was given to a large number of officers and men. Rumours of the departure of the Indian Corps enheartened our Indian comrades, who had fought right well in the Battle of Loos but had clearly no desire to spend another winter in the cold and wet trenches of Artois.

It was decided in October that the Indian Corps should be transferred to a theatre nearer its base; and on November 6th

[1] Sergeant Hutchison was later gazetted to the D.C.M. for his coolness and courage on this occasion.

DEPARTURE FROM FRANCE, NOVEMBER, 1915

the Battalion left the trenches of the Western Front for the last time.[1] From November 7th to 12th it was at Boesinghem, from the 13th to 17th at La Micquellerie, and from the 18th to 30th at Ligny-les-Aire. Orders for entraining were several times received and cancelled during this period. No. 2 Company (5 officers and 170 other ranks) entrained on November 23rd and eventually sailed separately from the remainder of the Battalion, which entrained on the 30th at Lillers, with a strength of 22 officers, 607 other ranks, and embarked on the *Royal George* on December 5th, at Marseilles.

The Battalion had had just over a year's hard fighting in France; how severe may be judged by the casualties (approximately 350 killed, 1080 wounded and 50 missing), and the record of those officers and men still remaining who had left India with the Battalion.[2] But they had worthily upheld the proud traditions of the Regiment and the honour of the Red Hackle. No higher praise can be given.

Throughout the war there was no single case of desertion in the Battalion; and when the Battalion left France only one man remained behind in prison. The few men who started the voyage from France as prisoners were soon released, and from now to the end of the campaign drunkenness and crime were almost unknown. It is doubtful if any other unit in the Army can point to a finer record of discipline than that of the Battalion in this war.

With memories of the winter mud of Flanders many welcomed the change to an eastern theatre, where there would always be sun and warmth, no mud, and an adversary who could be driven into the open and fought and beaten in the old style. Such optimists soon had a bitter disillusionment. In front of the Sannaiyat position they learnt that there was rain and mud even worse than in Flanders, that the Turk in an entrenched position was as determined and skilful a foe as the German, and, in the following summer, that the sun and heat could kill more surely than rain and cold. They learned, too, that the Indian Government, putting their trust in the old style, had made little or no preparation for the new. The number of guns was greatly reduced from the number allowed to the Indian Corps when in France; manœuvre was seldom attempted, and the enemy

[1] On its march from the front line the 2nd Battalion passed through Lillers, where the 1st Battalion of the Regiment was in billets. The last occasion on which the two battalions had met had been in Harrismith at the end of the South African War.

[2] The strength of the Battalion on leaving India was 23 officers and 934 other ranks. In France, reinforcements of 76 officers and 1628 other ranks joined during the year. The strength on leaving France was 29 officers and 846 other ranks. Thus the year's wastage was approximately 70 officers and 1700 other ranks. Of these 1500 were battle casualties.

strength often underestimated; mechanical transport was seldom seen in Mesopotamia until General Maude had reorganized the communications and supply services. Consequently the first months in Mesopotamia were to be as hard a trial as the first months in France. They were met with the same undaunted gallantry.

The voyage from France proved uneventful. The danger from submarines was considerable in the Mediterranean at this time; and all lights were kept turned down at night. But both officers and men welcomed the voyage as affording a degree of rest and comfort unknown during the past year.

Physical exercises and military training were carried on throughout the voyage. Under the tutorship of Company Sergeant Major Houston, at one time heavy-weight champion of India, every officer and man took part in boxing competitions; the zest for these competitions displayed by the officers was such as to cause Sergeant MacDonald, the privileged humorist of the Battalion, to remark that their faces, with black eyes and fiery noses, would alone be enough to drive the Turks in terror from their trenches.

There was need of haste to meet the situation in Mesopotamia; and after coaling at Aden the *Royal George* made no halt but steamed straight up the Persian Gulf, till on December 28th she reached the lightship at the bar which the Shatt-ul-Arab forms by deposits of silt at its mouth, some fifty miles below Basra. Here it was necessary to transfer all troops and equipment to smaller steamers. The weather was calm and this was done with little delay; and the Battalion reached Basrah in s.s. *Nizam* on the last day of 1915.

Note on Dress, 1914–15.

The Battalion, on arrival in France from India in October, 1914, was dressed and equipped in accordance with Indian Field Service scale: khaki drill jacket and Wolseley helmet (with *pagri* and Red Hackle).

During the period spent in La Valentine Camp, Marseilles, the Indian pattern clothing was replaced by khaki serge of home pattern. The "Coats, British Warm," brought from India, were replaced by great-coats, D.S., and the Wolseley helmet was replaced by Field Service caps (or, as the men termed them— "Cheese-cutters").

The latter were issued in order to render identification of units more difficult, the idea being that in trench warfare (which had just commenced) the enemy would be unable to distinguish a Scottish unit from any other. These F.S. caps, in which a small Red Hackle was worn, were highly unpopular with all ranks,

REGIMENTAL DRESS, 1914-15

and on arriving at the front they were speedily "lost" and replaced, temporarily, by the "Balaclava" (a knitted woollen head covering intended only for use at night).

Highland shoes and khaki gaiters were worn, but after the first few tours in the trenches it was found that the mud was of such consistency that numerous cases occurred of men pulling their feet clean out of their shoes, leaving the latter buried for all time in the mud, the unfortunate individual having to carry on his front line duties in his stockinged feet. During the month of December, 1914, the shoes and gaiters were finally discarded and were replaced by ankle boots and "half" or short puttees. This foot-gear withstood all further tests during the period of the war.

A type of "Bonnet" or "Tam o' Shanter" was introduced in the winter of 1914. This was of blue cloth and very small in circumference; a khaki cover was worn with it. By the month of May, 1915, the dress and equipment were as under:—

Dress

Balmoral bonnet: blue, with khaki cover and Red Hackle.
Jacket, Field Service: khaki serge.
Kilt: Black Watch tartan.
Kilt apron: full (instead of front half only, as worn on arrival from India).
Khaki (or Atholl) hose: instead of the diced hose.
Scarlet garters.
Half (or short) puttees: instead of khaki gaiters.
Ankle boots: instead of shoes, Highland.
Great-coat, D.S.: normally carried in the pack.

Equipment

Complete web equipment, 1908 pattern, with entrenching tool, ground sheet.

Arms

Rifle, S.M.L.E. Mk. III.*
Sword bayonet, pattern '07.
Scabbard, sword bayonet.
Oil bottle.
Pull-through.
S.A.A. Normally 120 rounds .303" ball, in chargers. During operations this was increased to 150 rounds on the man.
An "Iron Ration," consisting of 1 lb. biscuit, 1 tin preserved meat, 2 oz. sugar and $\frac{1}{4}$ oz. tea was carried at all times, in the haversack.

THE SECOND BATTALION THE BLACK WATCH

Full equipment—Marching Order—was carried in and out of the trenches. When actually in the trenches, however, the pack was discarded and placed on the fire-step or in the dug-out. (Few of the latter existed in the Battalion's area in 1915.)

The contents of the pack were normally:—

- Great-coat.
- Mess tin and cover.
- 1 shirt.
- Shaving kit.
- 1 towel.
- 1 piece of soap.
- Hair brush and comb.
- Holdall (less knife, fork and spoon—in haversack).
- Spare pair of laces.
- 1 pair of socks.
- Ground sheet—folded on top, and under the flap.
- Waistcoat—Cardigan, and cap comforter.

The following were carried in the haversack:—

- Iron ration.
- Unconsumed portion of day's ration (when necessary).
- Knife, fork and spoon.
- Oil, tin $\frac{1}{6}$th pint.
- Cleaning material for rifle.

Normally equipped and armed the private carried the following during an attack, in trench warfare:—

Rifle, S.M.L.E. III.*	8 lb.	$15\frac{3}{4}$ oz.
Sword bayonet and scabbard	1 ,,	$8\frac{3}{4}$,,
S.A.A. (150 rounds)	8 ,,	11 ,,
Equipment, with rations and water	10 ,,	2 ,,
Clothing and necessaries	16 ,,	10 ,,
	46 lb. approximately.[1]	

Specialists (signallers, bombers, etc.) carried a lesser scale of ammunition, but this loss of weight was more than balanced by the weight of telephones, telescopes, grenades, etc.

Bombers, when grenades were introduced, carried eighteen "Battye Pipe" or "Mills'" grenades (the latter were issued in August, 1915) in canvas buckets.

In addition to the above, a "Gas Mask" of impregnated cloth was carried in a satchel from about the end of April, 1915, until the service box respirator was introduced about October, 1915.

By the end of September, 1915, the blue Balmoral bonnet, with khaki cover had been replaced by a khaki Tam o' Shanter.

---

[1] This excludes the weight of the pack (12 lb. 4 oz.), as before an attack packs were discarded and collected under battalion arrangements.

PART II—MESOPOTAMIA, 1916-17

CHAPTER III

JANUARY, 1916

1.—*Arrival in Mesopotamia and Battle of Shaikh Sa'ad*

MESOPOTAMIA, the country in which the 2nd Battalion was called upon to serve for the next two years, is the land that lies between two rivers, the Tigris and Euphrates. During the whole of these two years the Battalion was never ten miles from the winding channel of the Tigris, and seldom out of sight of the river's banks. The land from Basrah to Amarah is for the most part a marsh, and from Amarah to Baghdad a desert, except where it has been drained or irrigated by the labour of the people.

In summer no country suffers from a greater heat. But in January, when the Battalion landed, the nights are cold and the rains and river floods change many miles of sandy desert into an endless waste of mud and water. To limit the extent of these floods, the Tigris is bounded by low embankments of mud; to keep these in repair proved later on a heavy labour to the overworked fighting troops.

Near the towns of Basrah, Amarah and Baghdad are countless groves of date palms, and from the deck of the small paddle steamer making its way slowly against the swift stream, the soldier can see from time to time small Arab villages with a few fields of maize and millet. The rest is desert, and all the country between Shaikh Sa'ad and Kut, where the Battalion was to spend the next twelve months, was almost without house, or tree, or inhabitant.

The Arabs are of two classes, the nomads of the desert, the men of the camel, a fine type whom The Black Watch never encountered, and those poorer tribes who live near the river, ploughing and sowing, reaping and stealing. These hated the Turk, but they hated far more this invasion of their country by British and Indian, by white men and infidels. After a battle, or round an unguarded convoy, they would suddenly appear, mounted on their swift ponies, with no desire to fight, but intent rather to steal than to murder. And when they had robbed the wounded and looted the carts, or had been beaten off by a few riflemen, they disappeared once more into the mirage. The Arab cultivator of these parts, General Maude said to Colonel Wauchope, is like a hornet, a poisonous fellow, but not so formidable as to hinder a man from completing the task he has set himself to do.

The force that was sent to Mesopotamia from India at the

THE SECOND BATTALION THE BLACK WATCH

end of 1914 was known as Force " D," and its original function was to protect the oil fields to the east of Basrah from which the British Navy drew a large part of its supplies. During 1915 part of this force, the 6th Division, under General Townshend achieved some notable victories. It was eventually decided to attempt the capture of Baghdad, and by November 1915 the 6th Division had advanced up the Tigris as far as Ctesiphon. Here it was met by a considerably superior Turkish force, hurried up to save Baghdad. In the battle that followed the 6th Division suffered a loss of 4500 men killed and wounded, and had to make a forced retirement down the Tigris to Kut. Here it was surrounded and besieged by an army of four or five Turkish divisions.

At the time when The Black Watch arrived in Mesopotamia it was believed that the situation of General Townshend's beleaguered force of about 12,000 soldiers at Kut admitted of no delay of any kind; and General Aylmer's relief force, which was concentrating at Ali-el-Gharbi, was expected to advance at once. Troops as they arrived were being pushed upstream as fast as the inadequate means of transport permitted.

Consequently, within a few hours of the *Nizam's* dropping anchor off Basrah, on December 31st, 1915, its contents were being poured into two paddle steamers, each with a straw-roofed barge on either side, while the Mesopotamian equipment of the Battalion was at the same time collected from the shore.

No 2 Company, under Captain Park, which had arrived a few days previously with the Seaforth Highlanders,[1] now rejoined Headquarters, bringing the strength up to 29 officers and 890 other ranks. Sir John Nixon, the Commander-in-Chief, came on board to wish the Regiment God-speed. By 9 p.m. the squat little ships were ploughing their way upstream; and the first dawn of the New Year of 1916 found them nearing Qurnah, where the Tigris and the Euphrates join to form the Shatt-ul-Arab.

Quartermaster Sergeant Niven and some twenty men were left at Basrah to form B echelon. The regimental transport, under Lieutenant Todd and Sergeant W. Anderson, were also left to proceed by march route and did not rejoin the Battalion till March.

The following was the state of the Battalion on arrival in Mesopotamia :—

Battalion Headquarters

Commanding Officer   Brevet Lieut.-Colonel A. G. Wauchope, D.S.O.
Adjutant   Captain D. C. Hamilton-Johnston.

[1] See page 199.

ORGANIZATION, JANUARY, 1916

Machine-gun Officer	Lieut. A. B. Cumming.
Quartermaster	Hon. Captain J. Anderson, D.C.M.
Medical Officer	Captain A. W. Duncan, R.A.M.C.
Chaplain	Rev. Andrew Macfarlane.
Regimental Sergeant Major	J. Johnstone.
,, Q.M.S.	E. Hobbs.
Orderly Room Sergeant	G. Morrison.
Pioneer Sergeant	A. Milligan.
Scout Sergeant	A. MacDonald.
,, Corporal	W. Cowie
Sergeant Cook	J. Crawford.
Signalling Sergeant	D. Yule.
Pipe Major	J. Keith.
,, Corporal	D. McMaster.
Sergeant Drummer	J. Simpson.

No. 1 Company

Officer Commanding — Captain T. Cochrane.
Second-in-Command — Lieut. I. O. Hutchison.

Platoon.	Officer.	Sergeant.
I	Lieut. Douglas.	Oswald.
II	,, Morrison.	Garritty.
III	,, Macfarlane-Grieve.	Allan.
IV	,, Dixon.	Smart.
	Company Sgt.-Major	Davidson.
	,, Q.M.S.	Cormack.
	,, Bombing Sgt.	Kiddie.
	,, ,, Corpl.	Pratt.

No. 2 Company

Officer Commanding — Captain M. E. Park, D.S.O.

Platoon.	Officer.	Sergeant.
V	Lieut. Soutar.	McNicholl.
VI	,, Stewart-Smith.	Lees.
VII	,, Plunkett.	Stuart.
VIII	,, Henderson.	Hutchison.
	Company Sgt.-Major	R. Proudfoot.
	,, Q.M.S.	A. Jessop.
	,, Bombing Sgt.	Findlay, V.C.
	,, ,, Corpl.	Rodman.

THE SECOND BATTALION THE BLACK WATCH

No. 3 Company

Officer Commanding	Lieut. T. Curdie.
Second-in-Command	Lieut. M. M. Thorburn.

Platoon.	Officer.	Sergeant.
IX	Lieut. Purvis.	Malcolm.
X	,, Cocks.	Whytock.
XI	,, Buchanan.	Wilson.
XII	,, Hunter.	Methven.
	Company Sgt.-Major.	B. Houston.
,,	Q.M.S.	Wallace.
,,	Bombing Sgt.	Maddill.
,,	,, Corpl.	L/Corpl. Brodie.

No. 4 Company

Officer Commanding	Lieut. H. Bowie.

Platoon.	Officer.	Sergeant.
XIII	Lieut. Paterson.	Henderson.
XIV	,, Young.	Hamilton.
XV	,, Broad.	Gant.
XVI	,, Dundas.	Palmer.
	Company Sgt.-Major.	Watson.
,,	Q.M.S.	Kinnear.
,,	Bombing Sgt.	Mitchell, D.C.M.
,,	,, Corpl.	Blyth.

With the exception of two officers, the six quartermaster sergeants and five other non-commissioned officers, every one of the above was killed or wounded within the following three weeks.

Every one of these men had proved his worth in France, and though men were held in readiness to take the place of every leader, the greater number of these "second strings" also fell in that fatal three weeks. Yet, however weak in numbers, the Battalion never grew weak in spirit.

The duties of the bombing sergeants and corporals and of the groups they led were not confined solely to bombing. They were picked men and became a great moral asset in every company. At all times of difficulty or danger, at Loos, Givenchy and in Mesopotamia, as the fight swayed between attack and defence, those groups, as ready with the rifle and bayonet as with the grenade, formed rallying points or gave impetus to a fresh attack.

Between Basrah and Amarah the Arabs had learned during

the past year that our forces were advancing to fight their hated master, the Turk, and that, unlike the Turk, the British and Indian troops were given neither to looting their cattle nor destroying their goods. So on the journey upstream our two paddle steamers passed many Arab craft; *mahailahs* laden with dates, or hired to carry stores for our troops, sailed swiftly with a favouring wind along one reach of the winding river, or in the next bend were pulled slowly along from the towpath; fishing boats were often seen with the owners casting their circular nets over some quiet back current; and canoes or round *gufahs*, paddled skilfully through the muddy water, brought fish and fowls to sell to our men on the crowded steamers.

The banks are low, and the river winds with so many deep bends that it sometimes seemed as though the leading steamer had missed her course and lay far behind the other. On either side nothing could be seen except the wide stretches of marsh land and the still wider expanses of desert, until the steamers drew near to Amarah, when the Pusht-i-Kuh, the range of hills on the Persian border, grew visible above the flickering mirage.

The voyage upstream seemed maddeningly slow to men who knew the danger that beset the garrison of Kut, and the quarters were extremely cramped. Yet much preparation was got through in carrying out the necessary changes of equipment, in discussing the tactics of the new campaign, and in taking every opportunity to land and exercise the troops. Advantage was thus taken of a halt at Amarah to carry out a practice attack, an exercise which was to bear fruit when only a few days later the Battalion was called on to attack in earnest with no time for preparation or orders. It is beyond question that the efforts made throughout the long voyage from France to keep the men fit and to lose no opportunity of training were of the greatest value in the days immediately following the arrival at river-head, when the Battalion was called on to show at once great powers of endurance and considerable handiness in manœuvre.

The Battalion landed on January 5th at Ali-el-Gharbi, a small village some fifty miles below Kut, where General Younghusband was endeavouring to organize the most forward troops of the Relief Force. It was to consist of the 3rd and 7th Indian Divisions from France with certain additional units. The original intention had been that these reinforcing divisions from France should reorganize in Egypt; but in view of the apparently immediate need of Kut, the transports had been passed straight through the canal independently, and the troops in a similar fashion up the Tigris from Basrah. This resulted in the arrival in the forward area of large numbers of infantry without their artillery, their hospitals, or even their own regimental transport.

THE SECOND BATTALION THE BLACK WATCH

In any case, the very limited number of river craft available at the time in Mesopotamia would have prevented formations being moved up complete from Basrah.

The only signalling equipment in the whole of the 21st Brigade was that brought by The Black Watch,[1] half of which was at once given to Brigade Headquarters. There was little medical equipment; there were no maps nor intelligence reports. It was an abnormal situation and regimental officers were actually found bemoaning the absence of the staff.

General Townshend had asked for relief before January 10th. By the New Year it was obvious that the Relief Force could not be ready to advance as an organized whole by this date, and General Aylmer stated his dislike of an advance before his force was complete. Apart, however, from General Townshend's urgent representations of the need for immediate relief, it is obvious from the general tenor of the telegrams between General Aylmer, Sir John Nixon (the Army Commander) and General Townshend that there was little anticipation of a serious stand by the Turks, downstream of Kut; in fact, as much attention was probably devoted to the plan of campaign subsequent to the Relief Force joining hands with the Kut force, as to the action to be taken to effect the junction. The brilliant series of successes of the original force had convinced its leaders that the Turk could not, even if he would, stand against the assault of British Indian divisions. This theory took no account of, or minimised, the importance of new factors, of which the chief was the arrival of divisions of superior troops from European Turkey, fresh from driving the British out of Gallipoli. It is at once the strength and the weakness of the British Army to despise its enemies; it is the key alike of its most brilliant victories and its most disastrous defeats.

The 3rd Division was later than expected; and the Relief Force was now organized into one division, the 7th, composed of the 19th, 21st and 28th Infantry Brigades, with one brigade of artillery, and Corps troops which included the 35th Infantry Brigade, two heavy batteries and the 6th Cavalry Brigade. The heavy losses of the Indian battalions in France had necessitated many changes in the composition of brigades, the units of which were consequently unaccustomed to work and manœuvre together.

The Turkish Army now south of Kut and opposed to this force, was variously estimated at from 20,000 to 36,000 men.

The advance commenced on January 4th, when General

[1] This had been obtained from Egypt, while the Battalion was passing through the Canal, by special application to General Sir John Maxwell, Colonel of the Regiment, who was commanding in Egypt at the time.

MARCH TO SHAIKH SA'AD, JANUARY 6TH, 1916

Younghusband, with all of the 7th Division available, moved forward from Ali-el-Gharbi. A week earlier the Turks had moved in force from their camp at Shumran, west of Kut, to Shaikh Sa'ad, some twenty-five miles south-east of Kut. Here General Younghusband found them astride of the river on January 6th, with two-thirds of their numbers on the left bank. Advancing slowly throughout the day he pushed the 28th Brigade up into battle outposts 400 yards short of the Turkish line on the right bank, while the 35th Brigade, on the left bank, engaged the Turkish centre, and had closed by the end of the day to within some 800 yards.

The landing of The Black Watch completed the 21st Brigade, which had not yet left Ali-el-Gharbi. The other units composing it were the 41st Dogras, which had been brigaded with the Battalion since the beginning of the war, the 6th Jats, which had joined the Brigade in 1915, and the 9th Bhopal Infantry, which had previously been in the Lahore Division. The Brigade Commander, Brigadier General Norie, who had commanded the Brigade in the latter months in France, was an experienced soldier who always had the confidence of The Black Watch.

The Brigade paraded at 7.30 a.m. on January 6th, but did not march till 9 a.m. owing to difficulties which the Indian battalions experienced with the untrained camel transport. The following day's march of some twenty miles, would, in any case, have been a trying one; after six weeks of inaction and ship life it called for an exhibition of endurance which was splendidly given. The bitter cold of the Mesopotamian winter night changed to the hot sun of the Mesopotamian day. The road was a rough track of dried and rutted mud; water was scarce. By the late afternoon the men were sticking grimly to their task, footsore, sweating, but refusing to give in. In the distance could be seen the bursts of shrapnel where the 35th Brigade was feeling for the Turk. About 5 p.m. the Battalion reached the bivouacs from which General Younghusband's force had advanced that morning. Every man came in with the Battalion, but some were too done to do more than drop down in their company lines without even unfastening their kits. A heavy shower of rain broke as they settled down for the night, amid a continuous roll of musketry from in front. The morning of January 7th broke cold and raw, with considerable mist which hung everywhere till about 10 a.m.

Strategically, the situation of the Turkish force was thoroughly unsound. About one third of their troops were on the right bank and the remainder on the left bank of the Tigris; and there was no bridge, ferry or ford for many miles, except the bridge of boats constructed near British Headquarters. The two portions of the enemy's force were thus exposed to defeat in detail. It was apparently the original intention to effect this by concentrating the bulk of our troops on the right bank, destroying that part of the Turkish force, and then using the bridge of boats to concentrate on the left bank and deal with the remainder of the enemy. But on the morning of the 7th it was decided to attack both portions of the Turkish army simultaneously.

On the left bank the enemy's trenches ran out at right angles to the river for some two miles, the extreme left thrown forward to enfilade the front,[1] while a refused left flank had been prepared in second line to enfilade any turning movement.

On the right bank the line was shorter, with no such strong flank protection. On this bank the Turkish position was carried at about 4 p.m. by the 28th Brigade, assaulting from their outpost trenches of the night before, with well-directed support from such artillery as was available.

Of the operations on the left bank, where the 19th, 21st and 35th Brigades were to attack, a different story has to be told. No line had been dug close up to the enemy; and the troops assaulted from the line of march, while the supporting artillery was unable to locate the enemy trenches, which were admirably sited and were concealed by the natural lie of the ground, artifice, and the effects of mirage.

Only two batteries were originally available on the left bank to support the attack of three infantry brigades. As by the change of plan mentioned above, the attack on the left bank was now the main attack, two out of the four batteries on the right bank were ordered at about noon to cross to the left bank; but owing to congestion of traffic on the pontoon bridge the battle was practically over before their fire could be made effective on the enemy.

The Battalion left its bivouac at 8 a.m. and moved slowly forward with the remainder of the 21st Brigade across the plain towards the Turkish lines. The 19th Brigade had orders to turn the Turkish left, while the 35th Brigade, the outposts of which had been in contact with the enemy during the previous night, attacked the centre and right. The 21st Brigade was to support the attack, moving in echelon on the right of the 35th Brigade. At 1.20 p.m. the Battalion halted while the 19th Brigade was taking ground to the right to turn the enemy's flank. The Brigadier sanctioned dinners being served. Officers and men threw off their equipment and settled in groups, glad of an hour's rest. Malcolm relates that just before one of the battles in the Pyrenees, soup was being cooked for the 42nd, when the Regiment

[1] The existence of this flanking trench on the extreme left of the Turkish front line does not seem to have been known to the Corps or Divisional staffs when the attack was ordered. It had a considerable influence on the course of the battle.

BATTLE OF SHAIKH SA'AD, JANUARY 7TH, 1916

was suddenly ordered into action. On this occasion the fires had scarcely been lit and the bully beef tins were not yet opened, when the Brigadier returned and ordered Colonel Wauchope to close at once a gap between the 35th Brigade and the 19th, which had, necessarily, moved rather far to the right.[1] Dinners could be

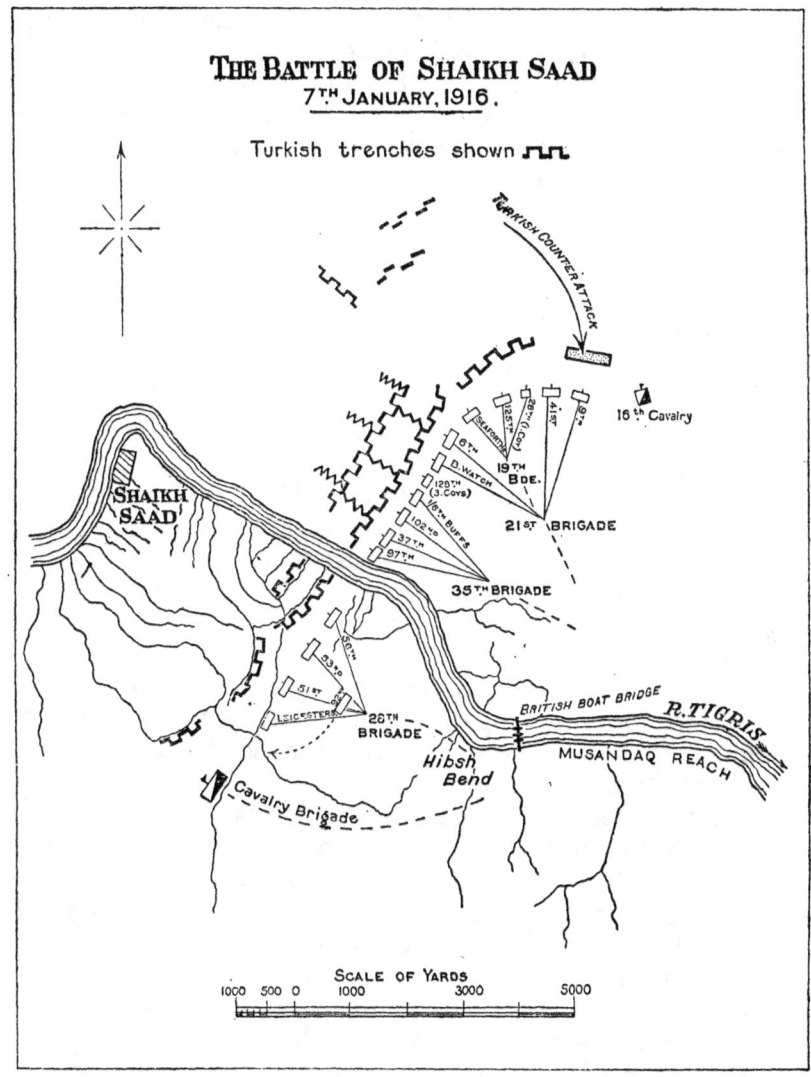

postponed; but Colonel Wauchope asked for time to issue instructions and to make the necessary arrangements for communi-

[1] The Brigade Commander of the 19th had by personal reconnaissance ascertained the position of the Turkish left flank and the existence of the flanking trench previously mentioned. He appears to have failed, however, to convince the Divisional staff of the accuracy of his observation.

cations, supply of ammunition and other matters during the attack, and also asked for a definite objective. The reply was that the attack must be made immediately and that " the objective was the enemy's trenches and the direction wherever the bullets were thickest."

There was certainly no time for dinners or delay. Turkish shells were already bursting and scattering some Indian transport that had rashly advanced under cover of the mirage into the battle zone. The Battalion therefore formed up and moved off at once in artillery formation, the Commanding Officer riding round to each company, detailing his orders on the move and indicating the direction as far as possible. A Territorial battalion of the Buffs, on the right of the 35th Brigade, was now advancing some 500 yards ahead of and immediately on the left of The Black Watch. The 6th Jats were also advancing a few hundred yards ahead and to the right. The two remaining battalions of the 21st Brigade were to support the attack, but shortly afterwards were sent far out on the right flank to ward off a counter-attack, which was threatening the British right and rear. Consequently the attack was delivered with little artillery and no infantry support.

The day was now bright and sunny. The Battalion advanced at great speed in four lines of platoons in fours, at forty paces interval, Nos. 2 and 4 Companies in front supported by 1 and 3. The Battalion covered about 600 yards' frontage and the same in depth, Battalion Headquarters moving with the third line. After advancing some 300 yards the Battalion came under long-range rifle fire, and the platoon columns broke up into section columns without checking the pace; later, as the Turkish fire became more effective, sections were extended into lines at about three paces interval.

Soon the rifle fire from both front and flank became extremely heavy, coupled with bursts of well-directed shrapnel. Cover in this flat open plain there was none, save one shallow drain, which soon became crowded with wounded, for men were falling fast. The attack was entirely unsupported by artillery fire, as the low parapets of the enemy's trenches were still concealed by the mirage. Still the lines carried on with unflinching determination, past the leading lines of the 35th Brigade, past the 6th Jats who had also advanced with the greatest gallantry and heavy loss, till a position was gained some 300 or 400 yards from the Turkish trenches.

The losses of all companies had been heavy, all supports had been absorbed and only one weak line remained, lying in the open maintaining a well-controlled fire. Without reserves, without artillery support, a further advance was impossible. Colonel

BATTLE OF SHAIKH SA'AD, JANUARY 7TH, 1916

Wauchope had been severely wounded early in the action, but lying in the shallow drain still tried to direct the fight; three out of four company commanders had fallen; only six unwounded officers and about 120 men were left with the Battalion. Captain Hamilton-Johnston then passed an order along the line that no further advance was to be attempted and that men should dig themselves in where they were. While this instruction was being carried out a message to the same effect arrived from the Brigadier.

On the right the Seaforths and the remainder of the 19th Brigade, turning west too soon, had come inside the Turkish flanking trench and had suffered the same cross-fire. The whole Brigade (which comprised two and a half battalions only) was deployed, had suffered almost as heavy losses as The Black Watch and Jats, and was unable to make progress, when some hostile force was seen advancing against the right flank. This proved to be a body of mounted Arabs, but they made no attack.

At dusk, the troops on the left having fallen back, Captain Hamilton-Johnston ordered the Battalion to retire 250 yards and dig in; it appeared later that orders from the Brigadier had been sent to retire 400 yards, but the messengers never reached the front line. Throughout the following day the two forces faced one another without movement. But on the morning of the 9th the Turks abandoned their position, and our troops, following up in the rain, occupied Shaikh Sa'ad at about 3 p.m.

Such was the battle of Shaikh Sa'ad. With no time given for organization and no clear objective, the attack of the Battalion was not only a most gallant affair, but from start to finish was carried out with perfect cohesion and thorough good order. The sun and mirage made all attempts at accurate location of the enemy's lines and fire effect against them almost impossible, and all ranks were animated by the one idea of locating the enemy by actually reaching his trenches. Everyone worked coolly and tirelessly under circumstances of the greatest difficulty. Second Lieutenant Cumming, although wounded early in the action, reached the advanced line with his machine guns. Signallers,[1] runners, ammunition carriers and stretcher bearers[2] all carried out their duties over the bullet swept plain with absolute steadiness. The pity was that so fine a Battalion should have been so reduced without an opportunity of striking back.

At a muster parade on January 10th, 10 officers and 352

---

[1] In the effort to maintain effective visual communication during the action the Battalion Signal Section lost 2 sergeants, 3 corporals and 5 men killed.

[2] Sergeant Humm, in charge of the Battalion stretcher bearers, won a D.C.M. this day. He was killed a fortnight later, doing his duty with the same quiet fearlessness, at Umm-el-Hanna.

other ranks were present, the casualties on the 7th having been 19 officers (including 2 killed and 1 died of wounds) and 378 other ranks (including 50 killed, 8 died of wounds and 19 missing). For tactical purposes Captain Hamilton-Johnston formed Nos. 1 and 2 Companies into A company and Nos. 3 and 4 into B company. On the 11th the Brigade advanced five miles and dug in near the river, The Black Watch with the 6th Jats being in reserve 400 yards behind the 9th Bhopals and 41st Dogras.

After the battle, even more than during it, the results of the confused haste with which the units from France had been brought up became apparent. In action, lack of men, of guns, of transport, might be made good by courage, skill, or the fortune of war. But after the battle none of these could lessen the needless suffering and waste of life caused by the lack of hospitals and medical necessaries. The Meerut Division went into action on the 6th; the Divisional Ambulances began to arrive on the 18th. The casualties at Shaikh Sa'ad numbered over 4000; the beds available were 250. One ambulance on the left bank which re-received 1900 patients consisted of two tents, three doctors and a supply of stretchers so limited that only one was available for each fifty cases. Dressings ran out; there were no arrangements for feeding the patients and only one over-crowded boat to take them downstream. The only land transport available was the springless, jolting, mule transport carts. But neither the knowledge of such condition nor the suffering entailed by them ever abated a jot of the fighting spirit of the Battalion.

2.—Battle of the Wadi

After Shaikh Sa'ad the Corps Commander's earliest information was that the Turks had retired on Kut; it was later found that they held the west bank of the Chubibat Canal, a wadi running down from the Pusht-i-Kuh hills to the Tigris, some seven or eight miles in rear of their late position. Some four miles behind them was the great Suwaikiya marsh, which at Umm-el-Hanna came within one mile of the Tigris.

It was decided that the 28th Brigade should make a frontal attack on January 13th, while the 21st, 19th and 35th Brigades, under General Younghusband, with the cavalry on the outer flank, should cross the Wadi by a ford to the north and attack the Turkish left flank and rear in the narrow space between marsh and river. It was hoped thus to cut off the whole Turkish force, estimated at some 15,000, which lay along and in rear of the Wadi.

General Younghusband started on his flanking march at 6.45 p.m. on the 12th. After marching throughout an intensely cold night the infantry waded across the ford in the early morn-

THE WADI, JANUARY 13TH, 1916

ing of the 13th. The guns, however, were not all across till 1 p.m. At about 10.30 a.m. the advanced troops came in contact with the enemy outposts, and the three brigades gradually took ground in succession to the right and attacked. It proved impossible, however, in face of the difficulties of unknown ground, the delay in getting the artillery across the ford, and the determination with

which the Turks held a series of hastily prepared positions in nullahs facing north, to press home the attack. At dusk the Turks steadily withdrew from the Wadi line to the bottle-neck at Umm-el-Hanna. The 28th Brigade lost heavily in their frontal attack. Thus the attempt, though it came near success, failed of its object.

The BlackWatch came under heavy rifle fire by about midday

THE SECOND BATTALION THE BLACK WATCH

and advanced in very open order by short rushes to within some 400 yards of the enemy. As the Battalion formed part of the holding attack it was not called on to assault and escaped, thanks to the skilful handling of Captain Hamilton-Johnston, with the loss of 5 other ranks killed, 1 other rank missing and 1 officer and 25 other ranks wounded. The officer, Second Lieutenant Douglas, unfortunately died subsequently of his wounds, in spite of a most skilful operation carried out immediately after the action in difficult conditions by Captain Duncan, the well-trusted medical officer of the Battalion.[1]

The Battalion remained in position during the night of the 13th/14th, suffering greatly, as in all these January operations, from bad weather and lack of food, the transport continually going astray in that featureless country. At 10 a.m. on the following morning the Brigade formed up and moved across the abandoned Turkish position to the river bank, where it remained for three days of piercing wind and soaking rain, bivouacked on ground which rapidly became a morass.

3.—*The First Assault on Hanna*

The failure of the Battle of the Wadi (as the operations of January 12th-14th are usually called) to win a decisive success, the stronger position the Turks now held, and the very heavy casualties the relieving force had already suffered, placed General Aylmer in an extremely difficult position. On the left bank, at Umm-el-Hanna, the Turkish position was exceptionally strong and was organized in considerable depth. Though the frontage of the position was less than a mile, it was impossible to turn either flank, for the right rested on the Tigris and the left stretched to the edge of the Suwaikiya marsh. Operations on the right bank were considered in combination with a suggested attempt by Townshend to cut his way out; but a combined plan could not be decided on; and the breaking of the bridge across the river on the 16th rendered major operations on the right bank temporarily impossible. The only alternative to awaiting reinforcements was therefore a direct assault on the Umm-el-Hanna lines to force a way through to Kut.

For the coming operation The Black Watch, together with the 41st Dogras and 6th Jats, was lent to the 35th Brigade, which was to deliver the initial assault. The 35th Brigade dispositions placed the Battalion on the left of the leading line, with the 41st Dogras on their right. The 6th Jats and 37th Dogras formed the second

[1] Captain Duncan was killed in March, 1916, while medical officer of the Leicestershire Regiment, to which he was transferred on the formation of the Highland Battalion.

216

ATTACK ON HANNA, JANUARY 21ST, 1916

line, and the 1/5th Buffs and 97th Infantry the third line. The 9th Brigade was in reserve.

On the 19th the Battalion moved forward into reserve trenches, unfortunately losing the Acting Adjutant, Lieutenant Curdie, who was wounded while taking over the position. On the 20th they advanced in extended order for 1000 yards to the advanced trenches, whence they pushed forward again the same night and dug in at their assaulting distance, some 200 to 300 yards from the enemy. Their second line was 150 yards in rear and the supporting regiments another 550 yards further back, with 1000

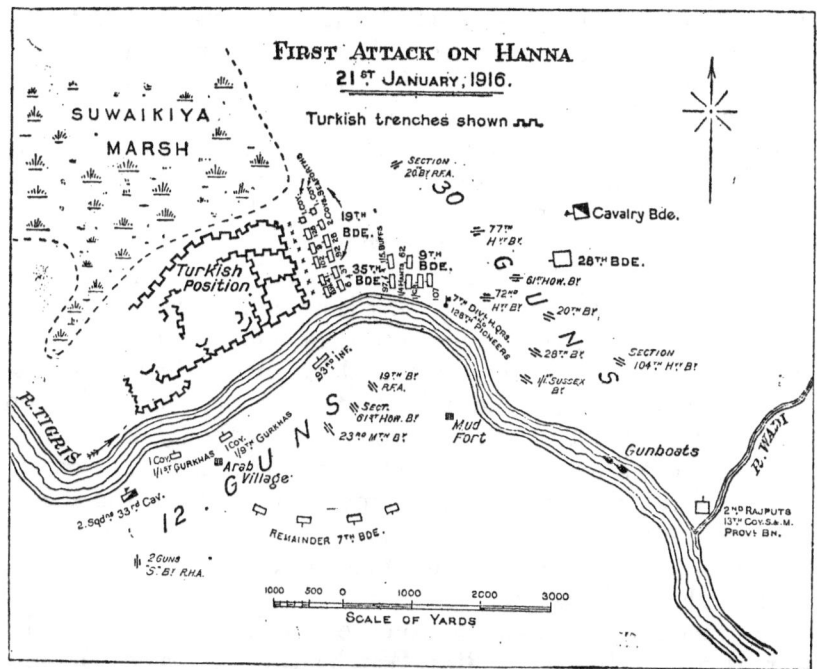

yards of deep mud between them and the enemy. There were no communication trenches from front to rear.

Owing to the severe losses of the earlier battles the Battalion had now under 250 bayonets available for the attack, and the frontage allotted to them was about 300 yards; the 41st Dogras had about 200 bayonets and a frontage of 200 yards; the 6th Jats supporting The Black Watch were reduced to about 120 rifles. Major Hamilton-Johnston [1] wrote to the Brigade Commander pointing out these facts and stating that while he was confident that The Black Watch would succeed in capturing the enemy's first line trench, other troops must be in close support to

[1] He had been granted the acting rank of Major while in temporary command of the Battalion.

ensure holding it. He suggested, therefore, that the supporting units should be moved closer up before the start of the attack. The Officer Commanding the 1/5th Buffs also asked to be allowed to move forward before daylight. These proposals were not, however, carried out. Further, only a few dozen grenades were available for each assaulting battalion.

During the 20th, and again before the assault next day, the Turks were bombarded with all available guns, some of which had been ferried across the river to fire in enfilade. Great reliance had been placed on this bombardment; but it was not continuous, even on the narrow front of assault, about 600 yards; and the heavy rifle fire with which the attack was met from the first proved its ineffectiveness. The contempt with which a Turkish officer from Gallipoli referred to it later during the truce showed that Indo-Mesopotamian ideas of what constituted an effective bombardment were at this period much behind the times,[1] and that the Turkish troops now on the front were of different quality from those over whom such a striking series of successes had been won in the previous year.

During the night of the 20th, Sergeant Mitchell led a reconnoitring patrol and, not for the first time in his career, succeeded in throwing one or two bombs into the enemy's trench. By this means he drew fire and located a machine gun on the right of the Turkish position near the head of their main communication trench. Sergeant Mitchell also reported that though the ground was muddy and heavy it was passable, and that a small irrigation channel offered a little cover a hundred yards from the enemy position. Orders were issued that each half-company should halt at this ditch, to allow the men to get their breath before making the final charge.

At seven minutes past eight on the morning of the 21st, as the bombardment lifted, The Black Watch advanced at a slow double, and were at once greeted by a storm of bullets. Despite the heavy mud, despite the losses, perfect order was kept, and after a momentary halt at the irrigation channel every man rose up simultaneously and swept forward into the Turkish trench. There for a few moments the Turks met them hand to hand. Lieutenant Thorburn, who was among the first in,[2] was bayoneted and clubbed to the ground, but recovered consciousness to hear the welcome sound of Piper Crichton playing along the captured trench.

On the right, the Dogras suffered heavily, lost all their British officers, and were unable to make good the right of the

---

[1] Two of the heavy guns employed were muzzle-loading 4-inch guns dating from 1873.

[2] He subsequently received the M.C. for his gallant leading.

ATTACK ON HANNA, JANUARY 21ST, 1916

objective. But a few small parties of them and of the 6th Jats gallantly pressed forward and joined the Regiment after the trench was captured. The Buffs started the attack nearly 1500 yards from the enemy's position and lost half their numbers in hopeless efforts to cross the bullet-swept mud flats. Two gallant young privates, however, eventually succeeded in joining The Black Watch, but were killed in the trench they helped to hold. Thus the flanks were exposed, and the Battalion was cut off from all support.

Immediately after the assault the Turks had fled across the open to their second line, losing heavily as they ran, for in spite of the exertions of the assault our men fired steadily and with good effect. Before long, however, the enemy was strongly reinforced, and soon discovered how few in numbers were the British who had penetrated his position. Two main counter-attacks now developed: one advanced along the communication trench on our left, and one from the uncaptured portion of the front line on our right. These attacks were checked for some time with the aid of one or two machine guns captured by the two flank companies.

The enemy bombing parties were also held in check by groups led by men such as Sergeants MacDonald and Mitchell, Findlay and Pratt, who equipped themselves with as many Turkish grenades as were found in the captured trench; our own few grenades refused to explode.

But force of numbers was bound to tell in time. Many of our men fell, and step by step the remainder were forced to give ground until they were gradually squeezed into the corner of the trenches nearest to the river bank. As Major Hamilton-Johnston had foreseen, bravery and discipline can make good lack of numbers in an assault, but it is impossible for a hundred men to hold a position indefinitely when attacked on three sides and with no supports forthcoming. He had found himself faced, after the first hour of battle in Mesopotamia, with the responsibility of leading the Battalion through one of the most trying periods of its history. And right well did he respond to the call of duty. Both as Adjutant, under Colonel Wauchope, and as Commanding Officer, he had complete faith in the Battalion as had the Battalion in him. He was first wounded and then killed in this assault, but he died with the knowledge that he had kept its fighting spirit unbroken to the end.

Of the remaining officers who took part in the attack Lieutenants Dundas, Thorburn, Dixon and Soutar were wounded, and one attached officer (Captain Simonet of the 1st Dorsets) killed. Second Lieutenant Henderson, the only unwounded officer, with but three months' service in the Battalion, was left in command.

THE SECOND BATTALION THE BLACK WATCH

For two hours a desperate resistance was put up against hopeless odds. Sergeant Finlay died fighting with the same cool courage that had won him his V.C. on the 9th of May in France. At last, about 10.15 a.m. when almost surrounded, the remnants of the shattered platoons, half of whom were wounded, fell back on the British lines, bringing with them one officer and about a dozen Turks as prisoners.

As in their capture of, and attempt to hold the Turkish trenches, so in their retirement they fought fiercely and with discipline, making for an advanced trench fifty yards nearer the Turks than the main line from which they had advanced. Here fell Sergeant MacDonald, most skilful and gallant of scouts and most cheery-hearted of men, keeping back the advancing enemy while the last of his men got back into safety. Here, too, fell Company Sergeant Major Proudfoot, doing his duty with the same intrepid coolness that he had shown at Shaikh Sa'ad and elsewhere.

Almost simultaneously with the retirement the rain descended in torrents, increasing the misery of the wounded, often half drowning in the mud and slime.

A second assault by other troops was ordered for the afternoon but did not develop. The remnants of the Battalion clung to their trench till dusk when they were relieved by the 9th Brigade, and taken out of the line by Second Lieutenant Henderson, who next day handed over the command of the Battalion to Second Lieutenant Stewart-Smith, the Transport Officer. Ninety-nine non-commissioned officers and men, wounded and unwounded, were present with The Black Watch on that evening. On the next day the numbers, increased by Battalion Headquarters, regimental transport and other employed men, amounted to 5 officers (including the Medical Officer and Chaplain) and 164 other ranks. The losses reported on the 21st were 6 officers (2 killed, 1 wounded and missing) and 175 other ranks (21 killed, 79 wounded and missing). Of those reported missing all were subsequently ascertained to have been killed, and at least one officer and many men who were wounded refused to report or go to hospital while the need of the Battalion was so great. The casualties in this action were approximately 60 per cent of the fighting strength of the Battalion.

Exclusive of the transport, 29 officers and nearly 900 men had landed at Basrah three weeks earlier. There now remained to report themselves fit for duty two combatant officers and 130 men, and of these not all were unwounded. They had met with defeat and extraordinary losses: they were without tents and suffered from a poor and insufficient ration and from every form of hardship. But the spirit of the Regiment remained unbroken and showed itself as true and fearless as of old, when fresh sacri-

ATTACK ON HANNA, JANUARY 21ST, 1916

fices were demanded in the further efforts to be made for the relief of Kut.

The following is an extract from the report of the General Officer Commanding 7th Division on this action: " I cannot " speak too highly of the splendid gallantry of The Black Watch, " aided by parties of officers and men of the 6th Jats, 97th Infan- " try and 41st Dogras, in storming and occupying the enemy's " trenches. Their advance had to be made across a perfectly open " bullet-swept area against sunken loopholed trenches in broad " daylight, and their noble achievement is one of the highest.

" The great and most admirable gallantry of all ranks is " worthy of the highest commendation. They showed the highest " qualities of endurance and courage under circumstances so " adverse as to be almost phenomenal."

On the 24th, Captain R. H. Crake, King's Own Scottish Borderers, temporarily assumed command, and on the 30th the details of the Norfolk Regiment (whose unit was part of the Kut garrison) were attached, 10 officers and 448 other ranks.

After the failure of the 21st the hopelessness of further attempts to storm the Umm-el-Hanna position without reinforcements became apparent. A six hours' truce was arranged to bury the dead and bring in the wounded on either side. General Townshend now announced that by putting his force on half-rations he could hold out for eighty-four days, and General Aylmer settled down to make preparations for a further attempt when fresh reinforcements should arrive.

Meanwhile the Battalion crossed on the 26th to the right bank and twice took part in supporting cavalry reconnaisances. On the 3rd of February it recrossed the river, as it had been decided to form The Black Watch, with the remnants of its old comrades, the 1st Seaforths, into a Highland battalion under the command of Lieutenant Colonel W. M. Thomson of the Seaforth Highlanders.

About this time The Black Watch suffered a severe loss in the death of Brigadier General St. John Harvey, who had commanded the Battalion in France from late in 1914 until September, 1915. A soldier of commanding personality and the broadest outlook, he was already making his influence felt as a Brigadier, when he was hit at extreme range, behind the Hanna lines. It is hard to say how deeply all ranks who had known him felt this loss of a true friend and well trusted former Commanding Officer.

CHAPTER IV

FEBRUARY TO APRIL, 1916

1.—*Formation of the Highland Battalion*

A RESPITE from the incessant marching and fighting, from the continual and heavy losses, and from the arduous conditions which had been their lot from the moment of their landing in Mesopotamia, was now granted to the shattered battalions of the 7th Division.

The Highland Battalion was formed on February 4th, 1916. The Black Watch, 5 officers (Lieutenant D. C. Stewart-Smith, Second Lieutenant T. A. Henderson, Lieutenant and Quartermaster J. Anderson, Captain R. H. Crake, K.O.S.B., and the Rev. A. MacFarlane) and 178 other ranks, formed Nos. 1 and 2 Companies, the remains of the 1st Seaforth Highlanders Nos. 3 and 4 Companies. Captain Macrae, of the Seaforths, became Adjutant, and Regimental Sergeant Major Johnstone of The Black Watch, Sergeant Major of the Battalion, which formed part of the 19th Brigade of the 7th Division. The Brigade Commander was Brigadier General Peebles.

Thus linked, The Black Watch and Seaforth Highlanders saw the remainder of the fighting for the relief of Kut. The union was a real one, in spirit as well as in name. There was never the slightest friction; and the keen *esprit de corps* and old traditions of the two regiments were merged in a Highland Battalion *esprit de corps*, which produced during the existence of the composite unit a tradition worthy of the spirit and fighting record of both regiments. This result was due not only to the long standing friendship between the two regiments, but also to the personality of the Commanding Officer, Lieutenant Colonel W. M. Thomson (now Major General Sir W. M. Thomson).

During February and March the Highland Battalion, except for three short periods in reserve, occupied front line trenches opposite the Hanna position. On February 9th Major C. R. B. Henderson, who, as Adjutant had been wounded at Mauquissart before The Black Watch left France, rejoined, and took command of The Black Watch wing, Captain R. H. Crake returning to his employment at General Headquarters. On March 1st a draft of 4 officers and 138 other ranks of The Black Watch arrived; on the 3rd Captain J. N. Inglis, M.C., took over command of The Black Watch wing from Major Henderson, who was evacuated sick.

Meanwhile reinforcements in large numbers had been ordered to Mesopotamia to take part in a final effort to relieve Kut. The 3rd Division of the Indian Corps and some much-needed batteries of artillery had arrived shortly after the failure of the

BEFORE KUT, FEBRUARY, 1916

attack made on January 21st. The 13th British Division and three Mixed Brigades from India were due to arrive early in March.

The decision not to await the arrival of reinforcements had undoubtedly been the chief cause of the failures of our attacks in January. After much discussion it was finally decided to make the next attack without waiting for the arrival of the 13th Division or assembly of the complete force. The river was rising daily, and the danger of the ground being flooded was a real one. General Lake's [1] force in Mesopotamia was already over 60,000 strong, and one of the main difficulties throughout the campaign was the supply and maintenance of the troops at the front. Only a small number of the many river steamers, subsequently collected from all parts of the Empire, had as yet reached the Tigris, and it would have been a hard problem, with the transport then available, to supply a larger force at the front. Also, it was desired to forestall the arrival of some fresh Turkish divisions which were now reported to be moving south from Baghdad.

Twenty-five miles still separated our force from the 6th Division in Kut. A slight advance was made on the right bank on the 22nd of February, and it was on the right bank, where manœuvre was still possible, that the next main effort was made.

Here the natural strength of the enemy's position was far less than on the direct road by the left bank, and the chief obstacle lay in the lack of adequate land transport. A night march completely surprised the enemy on the morning of the 8th of March; but mistakes, hesitations and misfortune rendered this initial success fruitless. The operation ended in retreat with a loss of 3500 men, and the Turk rapidly completed his defences on the right bank. Thereafter a direct assault on the left bank remained the one chance of relieving Kut. General Townshend now slaughtered most of his remaining animals, calculating by this means to hold out till April 15th, and thus to enable the Tigris Corps to wait for the arrival of all reinforcements then on their way.

The Highland Battalion took no part in this operation on the right bank (known as the Battle of the Dujailah Redoubt). It was employed during February and March in sapping nearer to the enemy and closing our forward line of trenches on the left bank to within assaulting distance of the Turk. The work was heavy and continuous; and the trenches were liable at all times

[1] General Lake had succeeded General Nixon as Commander-in-Chief on January 19th. General Gorringe succeeded General Aylmer in command of the Tigris Corps on March 11th.

to sudden flooding by the constant heavy rains and by the rising of the river on the one side or of the marsh on the other. Special sentries were posted to give warning of the rise of the water or of any break in the mud embankments built to protect the trenches from being flooded. For under a north wind the waters of the marsh rose with incredible swiftness; and the risk of being flooded out added greatly to the discomforts and dangers of the troops holding the trenches. On more than one occasion the embankments broke, the trenches filled with water, and the men had to rush across the open to higher ground in rear, offering an easy target to the enemy. Such a disaster occasionally also overtook the Turk. The strain on troops holding these trenches was exceptional, the labour continuous and the hours of rest few.

2.—*First and Second Assaults on Sannaiyat*

By the end of March the Highland Battalion, assisted in the later stages by Indian and Welch Pioneers, had made ready the assaulting position for the first stage of the last attempt to relieve Kut. Sixteen miles of trenches and redoubts had been dug, the front line was now within a hundred yards of the enemy, our guns were registered and the wire cut. On April 2nd the Highland Battalion went into reserve. On April 5th, at 4.55 a.m., the 13th Division assaulted, with the 19th Brigade in reserve, and without much difficulty captured the Hanna position, where were found a hundred Turkish riflemen, a few machine guns, and a notice which read "*Au revoir. A la prochaine bataille.*" The Turk knew well enough that time was growing short, and would not permit the infinite labour and care spent by us on preparations for assault at Hanna to be repeated against his lines in rear. In the narrow neck of land between the Tigris and the Suwaikiya marsh he had lines of trenches dug at Falahiyeh and Sannaiyat; and on these he had fallen back.

At 2.30 p.m. the advance was continued, the 19th Brigade still in reserve to the 13th Division. At 4.30 p.m. the advanced guard (40th Brigade) came under fire from the Falahiyeh trenches and dug in. At 7 p.m. a bombardment of the new position commenced; and three quarters of an hour later, the 38th and 39th Brigades carried the trenches with the bayonet. The Turks in the trenches stood to the last, and inflicted nearly two thousand casualties on the 13th Division; but Falahiyeh was merely a link between the Hanna and Sannaiyat positions and was not organized in depth. This, however, was not known to us; and it was at first thought that the Sannaiyat trenches were only an outpost line to the main Turkish position nearer Kut.

FIRST ATTACK ON SANNAIYAT, APRIL 7TH, 1916

The 13th Division, as the strongest and freshest formation, was accordingly reserved for the attack on the main position, and the 7th Division (less 21st Brigade) was passed through the 13th on the night of April 6th, to clear away the supposedly smaller obstacle at Sannaiyat.

The 19th and 28th Brigades moved forward in two columns, each in mass of platoons. At the head of the 19th Brigade, the Highland Battalion directed, with its left on a Turkish communication trench which ran from Hannah through Falahiyeh to Sannaiyat.

The force moved off at 1.30 a.m., and it was hoped to reach the enemy position before dawn, and to deliver the attack across the dead level plain in semi-darkness.

The Falahiyeh trenches were reached without incident at 2.30 a.m., but these were in several lines and were still occupied by parties of the 13th Division. The ground was unknown and had not been reconnoitred. As an inevitable result, the formations became dislocated. The consequent loss of time and direction was the main cause of the ensuing disaster; every effort was made to push on, but real control of the column had now been lost, and the troops found themselves long after dawn, still in close formation, with no very definite idea of their own position or that of the enemy.[1] The 19th Brigade was now ordered to open out into a less vulnerable formation. During the time taken to change formation the 28th Brigade got several hundred yards in advance. The attack had been timed for 4.30 a.m.; at 5.45 the force was advancing in broad daylight not yet deployed and without any idea of the enemy's position. Just as the leading platoons of the Highland Battalion regained alignment with the head of the 28th Brigade, and an order given by the leading platoon commander to open out into extended order had been carried out, fire was opened from the whole Turkish line 700 yards away. The leading platoon of The Black Watch and that of the Seaforths on its right continued to advance for a short distance in face of a pitiless hail of shrapnel, rifle and machine-gun bullets. Orders were then given to advance by short rushes, but when a position about 500 yards from the enemy had been reached, the advance was abandoned, only a handful of men having survived; and these few had considerable difficulty in loosening sufficient earth from the hard-baked ground to provide head cover for themselves. Some confusion occurred in the Indian battalion on the right of the Seaforths, for whom a long communication

[1] There was considerable uncertainty on the exact distance between the Falahiyeh and Sannaiyat trenches; neither the maps nor the staffs agreed on the point.

THE SECOND BATTALION THE BLACK WATCH

trench leading down from the Falahiyeh position right into the Turkish front line trenches proved a fatal attraction for the first few minutes. As the Turks had machine guns trained down it, not a few men lost their lives in this attempt to find cover. The steadiness of the Highlanders, however, in a very short time restored confidence.

But the effect of the fire on close formations at such a range had naturally been deadly. The losses of the 28th Brigade were 1100 and those of the 19th Brigade 700, the greater part of these men falling in the first few minutes. The Highland Battalion lost 11 officers and 187 other ranks. Second Lieutenant J. T. Grassie, who later received the D.S.O. for his gallantry in controlling one of the leading platoons when severely wounded, was the only Black Watch officer hit; but several Seaforth officers, who were serving with the Black Watch companies on this occasion, were also wounded.

In the evening both Brigades were withdrawn to some shallow trenches a few hundred yards in rear. Next day, the Battalion was held in reserve and lay in extended lines under long range fire, while the 125th Rifles and 92nd Punjabis advanced and dug themselves in 700 yards from the enemy, losing half their strength in so doing.

Two days later, on the morning of the 9th, at 4.30 a.m., the 13th Division assaulted Sannaiyat. The result was a complete and costly failure. At night, so heavy had been the losses, and so great the consequent disorganization of the 13th Division, that the 7th Division was ordered to take over the front line; this was a difficult task, as it had to be carried out at short notice, in the dark, amid the confusion consequent on the failure of the attack, and in face of an exultant enemy.

It must be remembered that not only on this night, but in every attack made from January to April, the Turk had the advantage of excellent intelligence. After the Battle of Shaiba in 1915, the Arab of Iraq had ceased to fight for his late masters, but he was still willing to sell to the Turk any information regarding the British Forces. The Riverine Arab is morally and physically far inferior to the Arab of the desert. Treacherous by nature, he had no love for the invader. The stories of his ill-treatment to our wounded were grossly exaggerated, but the intelligence he gave to the enemy of our every movement was a severe handicap to our operations, and more than once deprived us of the advantage of surprise.

The day following the attack, April 10th, was spent in improving the line, while parties of stretcher-bearers and volunteers showed great gallantry and self-sacrifice in bringing in the large number of wounded of the 13th Division still lying

SANNAIYAT, APRIL, 1916

out. During this time Sergeant Mitchell, seeing a hand raised one morning at some distance in front of an advanced trench, crawled out by daylight some 250 yards, under fire for twenty minutes from Turkish snipers, and found three wounded men of the 13th Division unable to move. These men were brought in when night fell, Sergeant Mitchell going straight to the spot without hesitation. If any of these three men is alive and ever reads this story, he may be assured that he owes his life to the bravery and devotion of one man. But for him they would never have been found, as it was thought that all the wounded had been brought in. Sergeant Mitchell was, for the third time, recommended for the Victoria Cross, and received a second bar to his D.C.M. Several of the regimental stretcher-bearers received the D.C.M.

During the night of the 10th/11th, working parties under a heavy fire dug a new line within 150 yards of the Turkish advanced posts. Captain Park and Lieutenant Purvis (the latter had rejoined that night from India, after being wounded at Shaikh Sa'ad) were hit, together with several other men of The Black Watch. The Seaforth companies also lost a number of officers and men.

3.—*Third Assault on Sannaiyat and Fall of Kut*

The position of the besieged force in Kut was now critical, and General Townshend reported April 24th as the last date to which he could ration his force. The weather had again become atrocious, and the river in flood and the marsh under wind were a constant menace to our positions. A brilliant success was almost within our grasp on the right bank on April 17th, when a Turkish position was captured and several counter-attacks repulsed with great slaughter, the Turks probably losing more heavily than in any other of the engagements fought for the relief of Kut; but in the end the Turks made a final and most determined counter-attack and succeeded in regaining a portion of their trenches and some guns they had lost.

Every condition was adverse. But our object was the relief of Kut, and it was held that it was right to give battle, right to accept any odds, while one chance remained to save the garrison and keep the flag flying over the walls of Kut. Therefore, in spite of the known strength of the Turkish position, it was decided to make one more attack; and a third and final assault on the Sannaiyat position was ordered for April 22nd.

It had been intended that the attack should be made on a frontage of two brigades, the 19th Brigade on the left and the 21st on the right. But before dawn on the 22nd the patrols

THE SECOND BATTALION THE BLACK WATCH

of the 21st Brigade reported that the ground on their front was waterlogged and impassable. Consequently the assault was delivered on a single brigade frontage, and the right flank of the 19th Brigade was left unprotected. The two Black Watch companies were drawn up on the left of the line, No. 1 Company leading and No. 2 Company in support; the two Seaforth companies were in the centre in the same formation, and the 92nd Punjabis on the right. The total frontage was little over three hundred yards, covered, except for a narrow strip, with water about four inches deep.

The number of available shells allowed for only a very moderate bombardment, and in view of this it was intended to give additional covering fire by posting a large number of machine guns on the right bank of the Tigris. From this position, however, observation was difficult, and at least one officer and a number of men of The Black Watch were wounded from the machine-gun fire of this post.

The bombardment started at 6.25 a.m. At 7 a.m. the signal was given, and the men of the leading lines clambered over the sodden parapets into the mud and water of No Man's Land. It had been calculated that the leading platoons would take seven minutes to cross the 400 yards which separated the two positions, but such was the dash of the Highland Battalion that four minutes had hardly elapsed when the leading platoons found themselves within twenty yards of the front line trench, on which our guns were still playing. The men flung themselves down in the mud, compelled to halt until our guns lifted their fire. Every second added to the numbers of killed and wounded, for the attackers were exposed to a heavy fire from the Turks third line, and were also being enfiladed by our machine guns on the right bank.

The moment the guns lifted, the attack went on over the enemy front trenches, so full of water that neither Turk nor Highlander could man them, and on to the second line about twenty yards in rear, men floundering through and over waterlogged machine-gun pits and communication trenches, exposed the whole time to the pitiless hail of bullets and shrapnel. This second line was likewise found empty. No. 1 Company in support, suffered, if anything, more severely than No. 2, and by the time the second line had been reached, only a remnant of the two companies was left.

At 7.35 a.m. the Composite English battalion of the 21st Brigade was seen issuing from its trenches over the ground previously reported impassable. It reached the Turkish front line just as a heavy Turkish counter-attack was in process of enveloping the depleted ranks of the Highlanders, who were

SANNAIYAT, APRIL 22ND, 1916

now approaching the enemy third line. One of the officers of the Composite English battalion, ignorant of the real situation, ordered a retirement, and his battalion fell back, losing heavily. The officer who ordered the retirement was himself killed.

Though thus deprived of all support and labouring under every disadvantage, the Highland Battalion still held what ground they had won. The supply of grenades, always meagre during these operations, had run out, and the majority of the rifles had become so clogged while the men were wading through the deep mud that the bolts jammed and the rifles could not be fired. Nearly all the officers had fallen, and it was evident that the impetus of the attack was at an end.

Yet two more examples were now added to the long roll of instances in the Regimental history of the unconquerable spirit that knows no defeat and fears no danger. Captain J. N. Inglis, M.C., one of the first officers in the Battalion to be rewarded for gallantry in France, and now the senior with The Black Watch, made a last effort to restore the fortunes of the day, but was killed as he advanced over the bullet-swept ground. Second Lieutenant H. F. Forrester, a name much honoured in the Regiment, collected the few men of his platoon who were still unwounded, and gallantly led a final charge against the third line, which was strongly held by the Turk. He and four survivors were seen to cross the open, climb the parapet and jump into the enemy trench, and were seen no more.

Unfortunately, the order to retire had reached the Indian regiments, and the Highland Battalion was now entirely unsupported. The 125th Rifles, sent in to reinforce the attack, suffered heavily, and were unable to cross No Man's Land in face of a heavy machine-gun fire. It was obvious that the attack had failed; and finally the survivors of the attackers were forced to fall back. The retirement was conducted with absolute steadiness to our original trenches, the water-logged ditches which formed the first and second Turkish lines being impossible to hold.

The following story illustrates how this attack of the Highland Battalion impressed onlookers. An officer of The Black Watch, when in hospital afterwards, was asked by an officer of the Royal Air Force, who had been flying over Sannaiyat on this morning of the 22nd, who were the troops on the extreme left of the British attack. When asked why, he said " I saw small " parties of men on three separate occasions make attempts to get "into the Turkish third line down a small nullah. In each case " all the men were knocked out and not one came back. To make " one attempt was all right, but for men to make two more, " knowing that almost for a certainty their efforts must fail,

THE SECOND BATTALION THE BLACK WATCH

"showed to my mind a bravery, a devotion to duty which must be considered by all who saw it as wonderful."

At 11.20 a.m. the Turks advanced showing the Crescent hospital flag; a Red Cross flag was sent to meet it, and about 150 wounded were brought in. This informal truce sought by the Turks freed a hundred unwounded men who had remained pinned down close to the trenches of the Turkish second and third lines, men unable to retire and unwilling to surrender.

It is worth recording that the Battalion had a similar experience seventeen years earlier after the battle of Magersfontein. On that evening the Boers came forward and spoke to our wounded (of whom Colonel A. G. Wauchope was one), and later gave permission to all who could walk to retire to our lines. This was done in good order under the command of Captain (afterwards Brigadier General) C. E. Stewart and Lieutenant F. G. Tait.

The Highland Battalion was now again reduced to a mere skeleton. The Black Watch companies had lost in this assault 10 officers and 321 other ranks, and the Seaforth companies 9 officers and 233 other ranks. Only one of The Black Watch officers who went into action on the 22nd escaped unhit, and five were killed, including Captain J. N. Inglis and Second Lieutenants D. H. and G. J. Anderson (twin brothers, Scotsmen who came together from Corsica to join the Regiment, and now fell side by side in their first fight). One, the young and gallant Forrester, was missing; and four were wounded, one of whom, Captain Gilmour, had but recently rejoined after being severely wounded at Neuve Chapelle, and was now wounded in four places. Of other ranks, 56 were killed, including Company Sergeant Major Wilkie, 76 missing and 181 wounded. The proportion of killed and missing (practically all of whom were killed) shows how deadly was that narrow patch of ground.

After the failure of the 22nd, the Tigris Corps was incapable of another effort. Many units were little stronger than the Highland Battalion; Indian regiments had few British officers left and practically none of any experience; the number of units represented in one composite English battalion ran into double figures. With decimated units and only a handful of officers to lead them, another assault across the waste of mud that still separated us from the Turkish positions was unthinkable. It was felt on all sides that the fate of Townshend and his men was sealed.

A last effort to push supplies into Kut on the river steamer *Julnar* failed; and on the 29th the garrison of Kut surrendered. The bitter disappointment of the men of the 6th Division at being forced by starvation into surrender after their gallant

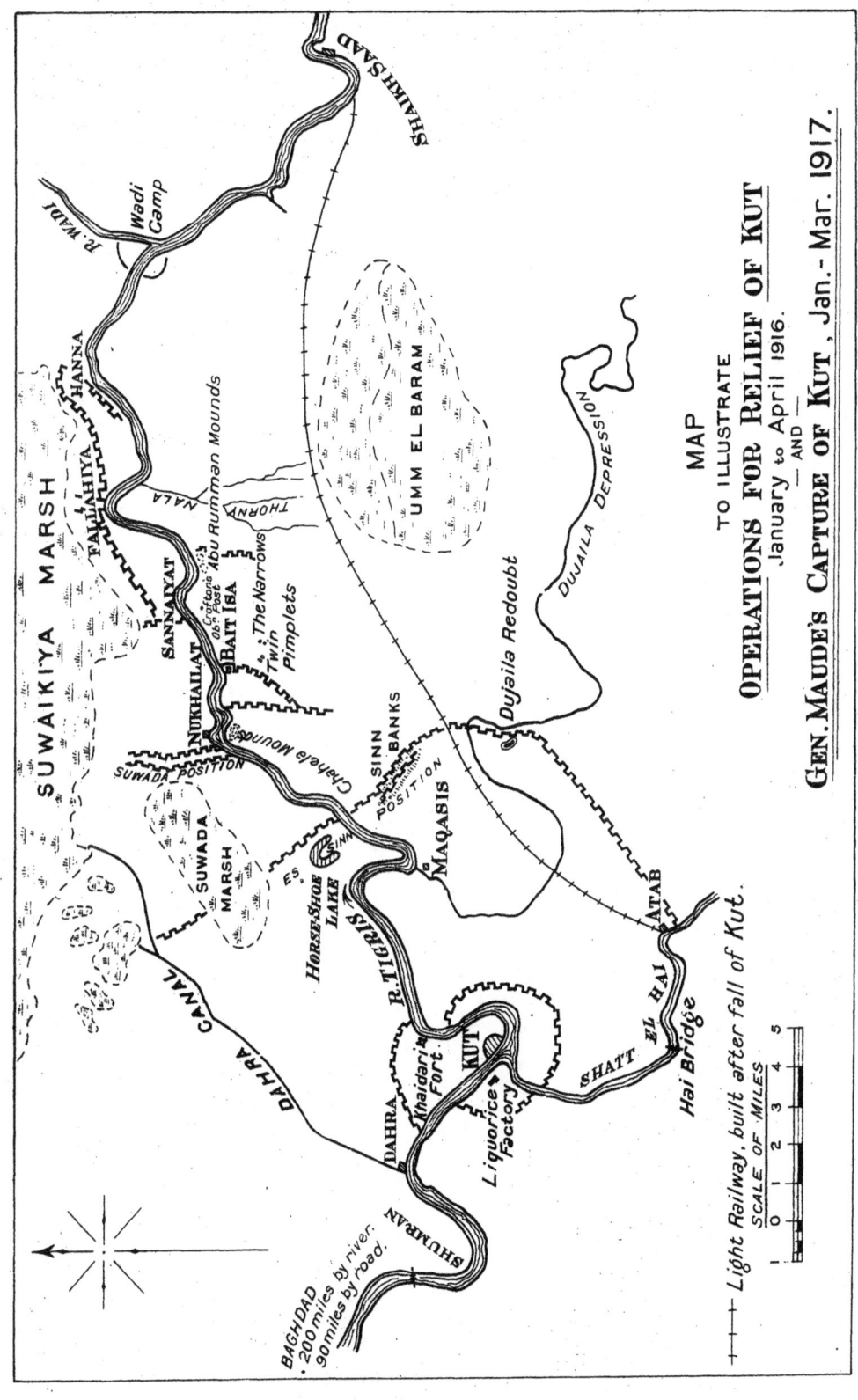

resistance cannot have been keener than the regret of the brigades before Sannaiyat and Es Sinn, who had failed to relieve them. For four months they had fought and marched and dug, in great heat or bitter cold, in high wind and blinding rain, across that great open plain where every advantage lay with the enemy in their prepared positions. Relief or rest they had not known; the sick and wounded had suffered pain and misery from the lack of medical preparations; some men had been hit two or even three times in the four months. Yet always the force had gone on, with the picture before them of their comrades waiting in Kut. And now they had failed; but they had failed magnificently. A Turkish officer during the truce after the fall of Kut said he had never seen such infantry. "My men are good in defence, but I have not seen men who "will advance repeatedly like yours over open ground under "such punishment. Only real devotion to duty will make men "do that."

The Black Watch has proud traditions of stubbornness and endurance in assaults against almost hopeless odds; and the men of Shaikh Sa'ad and Sannaiyat proved themselves no unworthy successors of those of Fontenoy and Ticonderoga.

CHAPTER V

FROM THE FALL OF KUT TO THE END OF 1916

1.—*Breaking up of the Highland Battalion and Reorganization*

WITH the fall of Kut our efforts to break through the Turkish lines ended. During the first week in May, in the part of the field held by the Highland Battalion, no shot was fired on either side, an informal truce being, for the time, observed.

Thereafter, both armies settled down to the routine of trench warfare, and to the endurance of a summer which was to prove exceptionally hot even for Mesopotamia.

On May 22nd, Colonel Thomson left the Highland Battalion on well-deserved promotion to command of a brigade, from which he rose later to the command of a division. A born leader of men in war, his inspiration will be remembered by all who served under him in the Highland Battalion. At the end of the month Colonel Wauchope, who had been wounded at Shaikh Sa'ad, returned from India and took over command. Under him, the Highland Battalion had, in June, its last tour in the trenches. Early in July, orders were received for the Battalion to be broken up again into Black Watch and Seaforth Highlanders, and on July 12th the Highland Battalion paraded for the last time. Yet the memory of that Battalion will live long in the annals of Highland regiments. Its career was marked by no victory, but by hard fighting, by terrible losses, and by defeat. But the hour of disaster is the test of true friendship, and during these months of trial no incident ever arose to mar the good feeling and good-will that existed among all ranks.

For many years the two Battalions had been united by common sympathies, keen rivalry in Highland games, and by many personal friendships. No two battalions held each other in higher esteem than did these two battalions of Highlanders. So, when they came to be joined outwardly by regulation, as they had long been inwardly in feeling, it was natural that the life and spirit which animated The Black Watch and Seaforth Highlanders were maintained and strengthened by the union.

The bond of sentiment holds when other bonds fail. To men of the Highland Battalion there was no sight like the swing of the kilt, no sound like the sound of the pipes. Men of both regiments might well recall how they had charged forward in France and in Mesopotamia, the pipers leading the way (and no body of men had shown greater gallantry or inspired others with their spirit more than the Regimental pipers). Yet, even

THE HIGHLAND BATTALION, MAY, 1916

in war, the days of battle are few and the days of trial many; and often at reveille and retreat, on the march and in camp did the sound of the massed pipers stir the memories and strengthen the spirit that inspired the men of the Highland Battalion to face all and every danger that lay before it.

During April and May, a proposal was on foot to send one of the two Highland battalions to India to rest and re-organize, since these battalions had suffered more severely than any others in the recent fighting. In this connection the Brigade Commander wrote: " I should like to point out that, when ordered " by the Divisional Commander to recommend which of the " Highland battalions under my command should be sent to India " to reorganize, I was at a loss to choose one before the other, " as in my opinion they were both thoroughly efficient, and their " moral and soldierly spirit had not suffered in any way, not- " withstanding the heavy fighting with the resultant numerous " casualties that they had experienced. . . . I have always " found The Black Watch a regiment that can be relied on in " any circumstances, however trying." Sir Percy Lake, the Army Commander, wrote: " I consider both battalions, which " make up the present Highland Battalion, to have given, in " the advance to relieve Kut, brilliant examples of cool courage " and hard and determined fighting which could hardly be " surpassed, and which have earned my unstinted admiration." Colonel Wauchope, when in Simla, was also asked by the Commander-in-Chief, whether he would recommend a temporary withdrawal of one battalion to India. Colonel Wauchope replied officially that unless a promise could be given that the Highland Battalion should return to Mesopotamia after the summer, he felt confident that both regiments would prefer to remain and re-organize at the front. All idea of the proposed relief was then given up.

Only with full confidence in the spirit of the Regiment could such a decision be justified. In the first four months of 1916 the Battalion had twice in succession been brought by losses in battle from full strength to a couple of hundred exhausted and underfed men. But though the individual dies, the spirit of the regiment remains. The spirit which had sustained the Regiment at Fontenoy and Ticonderoga, at Mangalore and Magersfontein, was now to revive the survivors of the Battalion, and lead what seemed a new regiment to the capture of Baghdad and the victories beyond.

The strength of The Black Watch on reorganization was only 15 officers and 226 men,[1] but the Battalion was gradually built

[1] The Battalion returned to its old Brigade, the 21st, the Seaforths remaining in the 19th Brigade. Both brigades belonged to the 7th Division.

up as the months passed, by the arrival of many drafts from home. These drafts had all undergone a period of training with the Reserve Battalion at Nigg; and with the mention of their training, it is only fitting to say that the thanks of the Regiment are due to Colonel Campbell Preston, who commanded that battalion, for his readiness to assist, in all matters of training and administration, the officers commanding battalions at the front.

2.—*Description of Life in Mesopotamia in* 1916

Throughout the summer and autumn of 1916, the 7th Division remained on the left bank of the Tigris. Each of the three brigades held in turn the Sannaiyat trenches for a tour of ten days, while the remaining two brigades were in rest camps along the river bank a few miles in rear. The 3rd Division was encamped some miles upstream on the right bank, in front of the Es Sinn Canal and Dujailah Redoubt, from which the Turk had withdrawn after the fall of Kut; on this bank the British were not in close contact with the enemy. The 13th Division was in reserve downstream at Amarah.

Thus, from August until the resumption of active operations in December, the normal monthly routine of the Battalion was a ten days' tour in the trenches, and twenty days out of the line in reserve. During the tour in the trenches, each Brigade kept one of the three Indian battalions in reserve; the British battalion usually held the section of the forward trenches nearest the river, as this flank was closest to the Turkish line, so close as to be well within range of the enemy rifle grenades.

Life in the trenches was very arduous. Men were few and the duties many. In the support trenches men were allowed to build up tent awnings in rear of the high parapets, and officers were given forty-pound tents; but in the front line there was no shelter, and the heat and glare at midday were hard to bear.

Shirt sleeves with spine pads was the ordinary dress; the Battalion always marched in the kilt, but khaki shorts were allowed in the trenches. Helmets were worn during the day even in the tents, but in the evening either glengarries or Balmoral bonnets were allowed.[1]

Even in France the heat, the lack of air, and all the smells inseparable from trench warfare were disagreeable enough on a hot summer's day. In Mesopotamia the sick returns show how severely these conditions re-acted on the health of men with

---

[1] See also note at the end of Chapter VI. An order forbidding men to remove the kilt for two hours after return to camp, when the kilt had been worn, undoubtedly averted much sickness by preventing the danger of chills to the lower part of the body.

MESOPOTAMIA, SUMMER OF 1916

no means of escape from the burning sun. British, Indian and Turkish troops all suffered from the unnatural environment.

Routine in the trenches began with an hour's " Stand To " an hour before dawn. After " Stand Down " was ordered, men had " gun-fire " tea before working for at least an hour digging and improving the trenches. After breakfast the daily inspection of lines, arms and kits was held. Weapon training was carried out before the light midday meal, after which as many men as possible were allowed to rest. Dinners were usually between four and five o'clock, and were followed by the hour's " Stand To " at dusk. Towards sundown a cool breeze often sprang up from over the Suwaikiya marshes, and in quiet times, men of the Reserve company were allowed to bathe in a deep bend formed by the Tigris to the rear of our position. Adventurous men who swam too far out into the stream were sometimes shot at by the Turkish snipers, but the plunge into the cool water was ever the best moment of these hot interminable days. Then in the cool came two or more hours' night work digging and repairing the trenches. Sentries were posted about every fifteen or twenty yards in the front line during the day, and were doubled by night. In addition there were selected posts for snipers, who fired a good number of rounds throughout the day whenever opportunity offered.

Throughout the summer the troops suffered from conditions that only a study of sick reports can help to realize. June was a quiet period in the trenches, but during that month 337 officers and men were admitted to hospital, of whom only 25 had been wounded. It was related that an officer was one day told he must go to hospital as his temperature was over 103 degrees. But that same evening he checked his batman, Private Thomson, for being slow at his work. The orderly acknowledged he was slow, but explained that the doctor had found his temperature to be 104 degrees. " But," he added, " I can carry on."

It was only the young soldier, on first arrival in Mesopotamia, who found it impossible to carry on, and often succumbed to fever before ever joining the Battalion. Out of one draft of over 350 men who landed at Basrah, less than a hundred reached the Battalion, all the remainder being fever-stricken, either at the port or on the river journey up the Tigris. The heat in a hospital tent was sometimes registered at over 125 degrees. Ice, soda water and fresh vegetables were unknown until the early autumn.

Many representations had been made regarding the poor quality of the ration issued to British troops in Mesopotamia. When Colonel Wauchope was in Simla, recovering from the wound he received at Shaikh Sa'ad, he used all possible means to obtain sanction that this ration should be increased, and he had the pleasure of reading in the last official letter he received before rejoining the Battalion, that " the ration of British troops will " be increased to the scale proposed by Colonel Wauchope." The cost of this new and varied ration was over 100 per cent more than that of the previous ration; but poor diet had been the indirect cause of much sickness and loss of stamina, and the action of the Commander-in-Chief was quickly justified.[1]

In many campaigns a poor ration can be supplemented by local purchases, but this was not possible till the Army reached Baghdad. No Arab was allowed in camp, and the few inhabitants had vanished into the desert, taking their sheep and their goats and their fowls with them.

The only Arab who visited camp was the thief who came by night; and he was seldom seen or heard. As a "*badmash*" the Arab rivals the Pathan; and he " lifted " this summer from one division many good boots, a number of rifles, and, a crowning achievement, the breechblock from an 18-pounder gun.

The desert yielded little but camel thorn and liquorice, which were no help to the hungry soldier; but one other shrub grew freely near the trenches, and as experiment proved, could be cooked to resemble a bitter spinach. This was a welcome discovery, for in May and June scurvy was common in the Indian battalions, and some form of fresh vegetable was much needed.

The Battalion was well served by Sergeant Crawford, the master-cook, and " Spud " Murphy, for many years cook to F company, was known and loved by everyone. A man of few words, yet his companions were always laughing. Nothing ever perturbed his good spirits. He entertained with equal cheerfulness Sir Victor Horsley on inspection duty, or a party of the Gurkhas who often came to visit their friends of the kilt. More than once the cookhouse was blown to pieces, but it was not till near the end of the war that Murphy stopped " getting ready the dinners," and, worn out by these long hot days, died, cheerful to the last, in hospital.

[1] The ration during the period from January to May, 1916, was normally two biscuits per man per day, a tin of bully beef and a liberal ration of tea, but with long intervals between issues of sugar or milk. Occasionally potatoes and onions were issued and at rare intervals bread (baked at the Base and usually hard and mouldy on reaching the front). Up to the fall of Kut all "comforts" (which term included at the time sugar and milk) were reserved for the garrison when relieved.

There were no war gifts, such as had come in such abundance in France, till June, 1916, when the people of Calcutta, under the presidency of Lady Carmichael, took the Battalion under their care and kept it well supplied with gifts of all kinds.

MESOPOTAMIA, SUMMER OF 1916

The crowded trenches, the swarms of flies and the heat made it necessary to give the closest attention to all forms of sanitation. Water was drawn by hand-pumps from the Tigris, stored in large tarpaulins and then chlorinated. Private W. Carrie, the oldest private in the Battalion, was entrusted with the duty of chlorinating the water supply, and worked unremittingly and successfully all summer. No Indian servants such as sweepers or cook-boys were available, but two or three *bhisties*, or water carriers, were attached to each British battalion. These Indians carried their *mussaks* along the trenches so that the men could keep their water bottles filled. Before the attack on February 17th, 1917, one was killed, but the others continued their work with the courage that has long distinguished their caste.

In the autumn, immense flocks of pintail sand-grouse flew from the desert to water at the Tigris, and large numbers of these were shot whenever cartridges could be obtained; at the same season numbers of so-called Tigris salmon (a kind of barbel) were caught, both in nets and on rod and line. On one occasion, at "Stand To," Lance Corporal Mackintosh shot a wild goose on the wing with his rifle—a feat which others tried in vain to emulate.

As the summer advanced, matters began to improve. It usually takes a disaster of the first magnitude to arouse the full capacity for organization of war latent in the British people. The surrender of Kut had suddenly quickened interest in the Mesopotamian campaign. The nation was roused, and the responsible minister declared that the resources of the Empire were at the disposal of the Army Commander in Mesopotamia. Something more tangible than this promise might have been preferred at the moment, but every month saw more river steamers on the Tigris; and as means of communication improved, more comforts, a little beer, and a more varied ration were issued. More tents became available, hospitals were enlarged, and the Field Force Canteen began to work. The Y.M.C.A. had not at first been encouraged in "Force D," but soon at Basrah, then at Amarah, and later on at the very front, the Y.M.C.A. tents were seen crowded every evening with soldiers "hungry, thirsty, weary, worn," but with spirit undaunted by danger or fatigue.

How great was the measure of this fatigue may perhaps be gauged when we read that it was necessary to publish a Divisional Order reminding officers that no man was to be posted as sentry unless he had had two hours' rest immediately before his tour of duty. Whatever the strength of the officers or men, the duties had to be performed. Time and again, men left their turn of sentry duty only to join one of the innumerable, but essential, working parties. Day after day men had to work during the cooler hours of the twenty-four, and pick up what rest they might in the heat and glare, amid the dust and flies, of midday. But, if there was much sickness there was no complaint, and the spirit of the Regiment remained undimmed and unshaken.

Better times came with the autumn; the great heat was ended, sick returns became lower, and drafts at last brought the Battalion up to fighting strength. On November 14th it was for the first time since February 4th sufficiently strong to be organized into four companies for tactical purposes.

Preparations for the coming winter campaign to revenge the disaster of Kut and reassert British supremacy in the Mesopotamian theatre occupied the periods of so-called rest, when the Brigade was not holding the trenches. The Battalion was fortunate indeed in having in Colonel Wauchope a commanding officer who had a genius for training troops for war, and who brought to the task an energy and driving power that allowed no opportunity to be wasted. Happy also was the Battalion in having in Captain Neil Ritchie an Adjutant whose " zealous and constant exertion," to quote the old Regimental Standing Orders, did so much to ensure that smartness in dress and in drill which is apt to deteriorate under conditions of active service. There was in him a rare union of strength of purpose and high standard of conduct which set a fine example to all ranks.

Once again was the Battalion fashioned into a fighting unit, complete in every detail; but unfortunately the considerable amount of sickness, in addition to the small but regular number of casualties, caused a constant change of command in companies and platoons. In November the four company commanders were Captain J. A. Barstow, Captain M. E. Park, Captain W. A. Young and Captain T. G. Cochrane. Later, Captain Cochrane became Second-in-Command; Captain MacFarlane on recovering from his wound took over command of No. 1 Company from Captain Barstow, and Captain Willett took over No. 3, and Captain Purvis No. 4 Company. These commanders were nearly all under two-and-twenty, but none the less worthy of their commands.

The Battalion was fortunate also in the Company Sergeant Majors: Muir, Gant, Houston and Kinnear. Regimental Sergeant Major Smart, who was up to September acting vice Regimental Sergeant Major Johnstone, whom he later succeeded, refused the offer of a commission, as he felt there was no position he could be so proud to hold as sergeant-major in The Black Watch. It would be impossible to praise his work too highly; he overlooked no fault and no folly, but lived laborious days; and never was discipline higher in the Battalion.

Lewis guns were not issued to the Indian Corps until August,

MESOPOTAMIA, SUMMER OF 1916

but men were quickly and thoroughly trained, and the number of teams gradually increased from one to four per company. The machine-gun platoon, at first under Captain Cochrane, and the signallers, under Sergeant Yule, had always remained efficient; riflemen, scouts, snipers and bombers were all well trained and exercised. After every battle the gallant work of the stretcher bearers, under Sergeant Easton, was deservedly praised, and the Battalion has seldom had a finer lot of pipers than those under Pipe Major Keith and Corporal McLeod, afterwards his worthy successor.

Pipers play an important part in the life of a Highland battalion. It is sometimes thought that their duties are confined to making a brave show, to playing at meals and at reveille. But that is far from the truth, for it is in the power of the pipers to touch the spirit of the Regiment. Even in peace time hundreds of men will turn out to see and listen to the pipes and drums, and in war their power is far more evident. Nothing scatters the gloom of a wet and cheerless billet so well as pipe music; on a long march they give fresh life to a weary column. Writing of the Görde campaign of 1813 Sergeant Morris says: "During our forced marches through " Germany the most serviceable man we had was our old piper, " Hugh Mackay, who when men were tired and straggling would " fall back to the rear and striking up some lively air he would " soon have the whole Regiment about him like a cluster of bees. " He would often go among the country people playing his " pipes to the delight of the inhabitants with whom he was an " especial favourite." Truly a serviceable man was Hugh Mackay.

In many battles men have followed where the pipers led, and great the service though heavy the toll our pipers rendered playing the way along the smoke-hidden trenches in France, or putting fresh life into men during the hard-fought battles near Kut and Baghdad. It was not luck, it was natural to the spirit of the Regiment to have such men as Keith, McMaster and McLeod to lead and to hand on the traditions of our pipers. Tradition and sentiment—how much is lost when they are neglected, how much is due to their magic; powerful factors towards victory, they are the essence of pipe music.

The Battalion was constantly practised in night exercises and made fit to endure long marches. It should be remembered that the successes and enhancement of its reputation won by the Battalion in the subsequent operations—no small successes and no little enhancement—were due chiefly to the thoroughness and knowledge with which this period of training was used.

The days spent in reserve were thus chiefly devoted to manœuvre and military exercises, but nothing was neglected that could relieve the monotony or lessen the discomfort of campaigning in a country so destitute of attraction or pleasure as is that most arid part of Mesopotamia. Highland games were held on several occasions, notably to celebrate the anniversary of the Battle of Loos, on the 25th of September, and on St. Andrew's Day, when our old friends the Seaforth Highlanders joined in every event. Officers and men of the Indian battalions were also always welcome in the camp of The Black Watch, and the goodwill thus encouraged did much to secure a feeling of mutual confidence within the Brigade.

Much of the success of these meetings was due to two men. The Rev. Andrew Macfarlane had now been Chaplain to the Battalion for nearly fifteen years, and his devotion to the Regiment, and the comfort he brought to all who were in sickness or distress, had won him the love equally of officers and of men. He laboured to bring faith, hope and charity into the spirit of the Regiment, and his task was well done. Through good days and evil he had served with the Battalion in France and Mesopotamia, and he marched from the trenches near Hanna to the palm groves round Baghdad. Then at last, worn out by constant fever, he was forced to leave the Regiment he loved so well and take up less arduous duties at Force Headquarters. Andrew Macfarlane sought no reward, but few earned the Distinguished Service Order better than he. No danger daunted him, and few of our killed were committed to earth, whether in No Man's Land or the appointed cemetery, without the padre conducting a service, however brief.

Captain J. Anderson, the Regimental Quartermaster, was an old soldier. He had joined before the Commanding Officer, and, like him, had served with the Regiment in the South African war and for many years in India. His experience, ability and goodwill were ever of the utmost service to the Battalion.

Nor did the training for future operations cease during the Battalion's tour in the line. The Sannaiyat system of trenches stretched from the left bank of the Tigris to the edge of the Suwaikiya marsh. Near the river the distance to the enemy's front trench was only 120 yards of bare and level ground. But as the summer passed the waters of the marsh receded, leaving the northern side of the trench system open to attack. British and Turk were therefore both compelled to refuse their outer flanks, which were held by a series of detached posts. There thus was formed a wide No Man's Land on the flank nearest the marshes, and across this stretch of country and against these detached posts Black Watch patrols moved every night.

A year earlier Colonel Wauchope had acted as Scout Officer to the Battalion in France; but of all those men who, as trained

MESOPOTAMIA, SUMMER OF 1916

scouts, had devoted their lives to the service of the Regiment, none had survived the fatal battles of January and March. Fresh scouts had, therefore, to be trained and new officers taught how to train them. In this work (and there is none more important in a soldier's training) Captain Park deserves the highest credit. To his knowledge, boldness and skill much of the vigour of our patrolling was due. Nor was the rapid progress made to be wondered at; the patrols were trained in the best of all schools, close up to or even behind the enemy's lines. Much of the work done was officially commended; Sergeants Logan and Anderson both received their Distinguished Conduct Medals for gallant leading, and several private soldiers the Military Medal for their good work on patrol. But the highest praise came with the Brigade Order which laid down that all work of reconnaissance in future was to be done by the patrols of The Black Watch.

In writing of the Regimental Scouts it is hard not to mention the name of Sergeant MacDonald. His career was extraordinary. Before the war he was perhaps the best-known private in the Battalion. As a "time-expired man" he went to Burmah, where his natural ability, good education and doubtless his ready wit, secured him well-paid employment. But adventures come to the adventurous. Having made his way overland into Central China, he obtained service on the staff of the Military Governor of some Chinese province, and it was here, in the autumn of 1914, that he learned of the outbreak of war in Europe. Secretly quitting the Chinese service, he managed to return to Burmah, and reached the 3rd Battalion of his old Regiment at Nigg, in the spring of 1915. By means not strictly in accordance with regulations, he soon afterwards joined the 2nd Battalion in France, where his many friends, some of whom had not been among his chief supporters with the Army Temperance Association in India, gladly celebrated his return. His qualities ensured rapid promotion in war. From corporal in the machine-gun platoon he soon became sergeant of the scouts, wearing the badges of rank in each case long before promotion. A commanding officer should have no favourites, but a love for MacDonald was justified, if not for that soft humorous voice of his, if not for his unfailing spirit, then for his brave deeds and the life he devoted to the service of his Regiment. In all manœuvres and in every battle he became the constant companion of Colonel Wauchope. When the latter was wounded at Shaikh Sa'ad, it was MacDonald who carried him from the firing line, and a fortnight later it was MacDonald and Sergeant Major Proudfoot who were among the last to leave the Turkish trenches. Great and unrewarded was the service that these two did that day, for neither lived to receive the commissions that had long been promised them. The last to quit the Turk's trench, both fell a

THE SECOND BATTALION THE BLACK WATCH

few yards short of ours. The fight, the struggle and their lives were ended, but not the spirit they did so much to strengthen, nor the example they set to all who wear the Red Hackle.

By the end of the year the Regiment was 29 officers and 877 other ranks strong, in excellent condition and in a high state of efficiency for the coming campaign. The temperature by day was now comparatively mild and the nights distinctly cool.

CHAPTER VI

1917

1.—*The Advance on Baghdad*

GENERAL MAUDE was given command of the Army in Mesopotamia in August, 1916. Few officers were blind to the many defects in organization that had gone far to sap the strength of the Army, but it required a highly trained mind like Maude's to realize the measures by which these defects might be put right. Few men were free from the depression due to the miseries and disasters of the spring of 1916, but it needed the great personality of Maude to inspire the Army with fresh life and a new spirit. For in the spring of 1916 the Tigris Force had been ill found, ill led, and was less used to victory than to defeat.

Maude realized the magnitude of his task, and devoted himself at first to the reorganization of the Lines of Communication and of the administrative services. His next care was the training of the troops for a vigorous offensive. His labours were ceaseless, but he found time to visit many battalions. Maude never left the lines of The Black Watch without making every man feel that no event could shake his faith in the resolution and leadership of the General.

By December, 1916, all preparations were complete, and in that month the brilliant series of operations, which culminated in the capture of Baghdad, began. To understand the Battalion's share in these operations an outline of the general plan of campaign is first necessary.

General Maude had organized his forces into two Army Corps. The I Corps, under Lieutenant General A. S. Cobbe, comprised the 3rd and 7th Divisions; the III Corps, under Major General W. R. Marshall, the 13th and 14th Divisions. The Battalion was in the 21st Brigade (Brigadier General C. N. Norie) of the 7th Division (Major General V. B. Fane). The other battalions of the 21st Brigade were the 9th Bhopal Infantry, the 20th Punjabis and the 1/8th Gurkha Rifles.[1]

General Maude, when he commanded the 13th Division during the operations to relieve Kut, had become convinced at an

---

[1] A great friendship was established between the Battalion and the 1/8th Gurkhas, who served in the same brigade for the remainder of the war. It was commemorated after the war by an exchange of gifts, the Gurkhas presenting the Battalion with a pair of kukris, while the Battalion gave the Gurkhas a set of bagpipes which had been carried during the war.

Colonel J. Alban Wilson of the Gurkhas also presented to the Battalion ("in remembrance of campaigning days together in 1916–17") a diary of Captain McGregor of the 73rd Regiment, which Colonel Wilson had found in a Hindu temple at Manipur during the expedition of 1891.

early stage that the true line of attack was by the right bank of the Tigris, where there was still room for manœuvre. Then, the all-important element of time had been the main factor that had compelled the costly, and in the end fruitless, efforts to advance on the left bank in the narrow neck of land between the river and the great Suwaikiya marsh. Now, the British commander was in a position to choose his time and place. Soon after taking over command Maude considered the possibility of turning the Turkish left by a movement *through* the now rapidly drying marsh, and had reconnaissances made to ascertain whether such a project was at all feasible. The results confirmed him in his opinion that it was on the right bank that the decision was to be sought.

The situation there was as follows: soon after the fall of Kut in May, 1916, the Turk had evacuated his advanced position on the right bank at Es Sinn, and had withdrawn to inner lines near Kut; here he had strongly entrenched positions on either side of the River Hai, which joins the Tigris at Kut just where that river forms a pronounced double bend; the bend east of the Hai was known as the Khaidiri bend, and that west of it as the Dahra bend; across these bends the Turkish entrenchments were constructed. The British held the Es Sinn positions, which they had occupied as soon as evacuated by the Turk, and had constructed for supply purposes a light railway from Shaikh Sa'ad to Dujailah.

On the left bank the Turks still clung to their trenches at Sannaiyat, and were thus in the curious position of having, across the river, an enemy nearly 11 miles in their rear, to whom their whole communications between Kut and Sannaiyat were exposed. To obviate this disadvantage a most elaborate series of entrenchments had been constructed in rear of the Sannaiyat position.

General Maude's plan is described in his despatch as follows: " First, to secure possession of the Hai; secondly, to clear the " Turkish trench systems still remaining on the right bank of the " Tigris; thirdly, to sap the enemy's strength by constant at-" tacks and give him no rest; fourthly, to compel him to give " up the Sannaiyat position, or in default of that to extend his " attenuated forces more and more to counter our strokes against " his communications; and lastly, to cross the Tigris at the weak-" est part of his line as far west as possible and to sever his com-" munications." Thus the main operations, at any rate for the first two phases, lay on the right bank. The rôle of the troops on the left bank was to keep the Turks at Sannaiyat in constant fear of attack and thus prevent any transfer to the right bank; or to take advantage of any weakening of the enemy opposite them and drive him from his positions.

Operations commenced on the 13th December with heavy

ATTACK ON KUT, JANUARY, 1917

bombardment of Sannaiyat and demonstrations intended to lead the enemy to expect an attack there. The Black Watch, which was in the front line trenches, took part in this demonstration by activity calculated to indicate an assault; and again on the 19th, from the reserve camp, formed up just before dark and marched with the remainder of the 21st Brigade towards the trenches, as though to fill them preparatory to attack, a movement observed, as was intended, by the Turkish airmen.

Meanwhile on the right bank the III Corps, after a night march, reached the Hai on the morning of the 14th, crossed it, and working forward on both sides of the Hai established themselves during the next few days within a mile of the Tigris near Kut, opposite the Turkish trenches in the Khaidiri and Dahra bends.

A pause now took place to enable the light railway to be continued to the Hai. From the 5th to the 18th of January severe fighting took place in the Khaidiri bend, which ended in the Turks abandoning this position; by February 4th the other Turkish positions east of the Hai had been similarly reduced, and on the 15th an attack on those in the Dahra bend resulted in a brilliant victory. All control of the right bank of the Tigris had now been practically wrested from the Turk, and the first part of General Maude's programme had been successfully carried out.

During this time the Battalion had, except for a period of duty on the right bank, presently to be described, remained in reserve opposite Sannaiyat. On January 1st Regimental sports and a concert were held. The sergeants received a pint of champagne each, and all other ranks a bottle of beer. On January 3rd, Regimental Sergeant Major J. Johnstone was admitted to hospital and eventually evacuated to India, where he was discharged after twenty-three years' most valuable and honourable service in the Battalion. He was later awarded the Military Cross. He was succeeded as Regimental Sergeant Major by A. Smart.

From January 21st to the 31st The Black Watch held the river picquet line on the right bank along the Narrows, a frontage of over four miles. The river here is 400 yards wide, and the Battalion found themselves looking across it into the rear of the line of trenches they had so long been facing on the other bank. The Turks had, of course, well covered their communications to the front lines of Sannaiyat by a series of works on the river bank; but the Battalion snipers under Captain J. B. S. Haldane did excellent work and took a considerable toll of the enemy across the water. So effective was their work that they were given a roving commission along the right bank as far as the Megasis bend.

General Maude was now maturing his final stroke, the crossing of the Tigris at the Shumran bend and the interception of the

Turkish line of retreat. It was essential that the attention of the Turk should be concentrated on the opposite end of his line at Sannaiyat, and orders were accordingly issued for the assault of this position at noon on February 17th.

The Battalion had recrossed to the left bank at the end of January and had been in the front line trenches since the 11th of February, but it was decided that the assault should be delivered by two Indian battalions of the 21st Brigade. One cause of failure in the earlier assaults on the Sannaiyat position had been lack of material. It was determined that this time there should be no lack. On the 16th, during the whole of the night of the 16th/17th and on the morning of the 17th, all available men of the Brigade, including those of the assaulting battalions, were employed in carrying up stores to the front line. This work should have been completed earlier, but unfortunately the rains broke on the 15th, and the trenches became almost impassable—first with mud and then with loads, which the carrier parties, unable to carry forward, had dropped on their way. The confusion was indescribable; the trenches, already deep in mud and water, were blocked by countless boxes of ammunition for rifles and trench mortars; boxes of bombs to destroy the Turks; boxes of bullet-proof waistcoats to protect the attackers; Véry lights and supplies of all sorts. Finally, many of the carriers themselves stuck fast in the mud and had to be dug out.

On the right bank also an attack had been ordered for the 17th, but owing to the weather was wisely postponed. Brigadier General Norie asked that the attack on Sannaiyat should also be postponed to the 18th, but was told that the situation demanded that it should be made not later than 2 p.m. on the 17th. At 10 a.m. the order was therefore issued that the assault should be made at 2 p.m. instead of at noon. But communication had so completely broken down that this order failed to reach certain platoons who started climbing over the parapet at noon.

The actual assault, however, was made at 2 p.m. and the Gurkhas and Punjabis captured the first two lines of enemy trenches. But an hour or so later a strong Turkish counter-attack drove both battalions back on our lines. No blame rests on the two Indian battalions for this failure. The men were exhausted before they started, and some actually fell asleep beside their wounded comrades in the enemy trenches. But their retirement made the confusion worse than ever in our front lines.

The Black Watch was ordered to rally the Indian troops, and Colonel Wauchope was asked if a second assault to reoccupy the enemy trenches could succeed. He reported that the Battalion was willing to assault, but that the confusion was so great that a well-organized attack was impossible. Further operations were

SANNAIYAT, FEBRUARY, 1917

therefore abandoned for the day. The Battalion stretcher bearers and others did fine work on this day and on the subsequent night, in bringing in wounded men and abandoned material from between the lines. Corporal Hutchison received the Distinguished Conduct Medal for bringing in a wounded Punjabi by daylight on the 18th, and Private Bogle the Military Medal for recovering a Lewis gun from close to the Turkish parapet.

Another gallant action which deserves to be recorded took place on the night of the 16th. It was important before the attack to locate enemy machine guns, and several patrols were sent out by the Battalion for that purpose. One of these, consisting of Second Lieutenant Cowie and two men, reached the enemy's barbed wire and located a machine gun with some Turks beside it. Into this group the patrol threw three bombs. Before they could escape the Turks opened fire, and Cowie and his orderly fell wounded. The third man was sent back, but some Turks jumped over their parapet and made the other two prisoners. They were well treated, and two days later, when the Turkish retreat began, were moved on to a river steamer. This steamer was captured during the retreat by one of our gunboats after a short but sharp engagement, during which Cowie, in the confusion of the fight, forced the pilot to run his vessel aground. Most of the Turks escaped, but Cowie and his orderly were rescued.

The 21st Brigade was relieved by the 19th Brigade on the night of the 17th, but the Battalion remained in the trenches, attached to the 19th Brigade, whose commander detailed them to lead the fresh attack to be made on the Turkish position. This order was, however, subsequently cancelled, it being desired to keep the 21st Brigade intact as a reserve. The Commanding Officer specially asked the Divisional commander that the original orders should stand and that The Black Watch be allowed the honour of leading a fresh attack on the lines that had already so often foiled the British assaults. General Fane replied as follows:
" Many thanks for sentiments which one expects from one of
" finest regiments in British Army. There are strategic and tacti-
" cal reasons against employment of the battalion in subsidiary
" operations, as one must keep one brigade in reserve at least.
" Corps commander vetoed me employing you as I wished, for
" very sound reasons. Please thank Battalion for all they did on
" 17th and subsequent night, helping in the gallant way The Black
" Watch always do."

The Battalion accordingly rejoined the 21st Brigade in reserve, the Seaforth Highlanders taking their place in the attacking line. The 19th Brigade assaulted on the 22nd and secured without heavy loss the enemy's first and second lines. Once again the Turk counter-attacked strongly, and The Black Watch was ordered

THE SECOND BATTALION THE BLACK WATCH

to move forward with all speed and hold our front line trenches. The Seaforth Highlanders yielded no ground, but part of the Indian battalions were forced to give way. Without waiting for orders, Colonel Wauchope sent two platoons into the enemy's second line and thus secured the left flank down to the river. In this movement only one officer, Captain Young, and one man were wounded. Colonel Wauchope then asked leave to push forward with the whole Battalion on the night of the 22nd. His judgment told him the Turk was on the run; but the situation was not clearly known at Divisional Headquarters and leave was refused. It was not till the 23rd that the enemy's third and fourth lines were secured by the 19th Brigade. The Battalion was now moved up about midnight of the 23rd/24th and relieved the Seaforths. Patrols were at once pushed forward and the enemy's fifth and sixth lines were occupied before dawn. The Turks had left a very weak rearguard, but sniping was continuous and the Indian battalion on our left met with considerable opposition.

None of our men will ever forget the scene on that clear morning, nor the feeling of freedom and elation as the companies gained trench after trench. The Sannaiyat position, which had held us back for ten long months, which had lost us Kut and before which so many lives had been given in vain, was now in our hands. The enemy had escaped with his guns, but many trenches were found to be filled with Turkish dead, rifles, boxes of ammunition and a few heavy trench mortars whose shells had caused so much trouble and loss during the past six months.

The Turk, in fact, was in full retreat. The crossing of the Shumran bend had been successfully accomplished by General Marshall's Corps on the 23rd and had placed the whole Turkish army in danger of being surrounded. The enemy's heavy losses and disorganization had rendered further resistance hopeless, and he was making for Baghdad with all possible speed and the remains of his force.

Orders were given to the 21st and 28th Brigades to push forward at once and capture the strong positions at Nakhailat and Suwada. So the advance was continued forthwith, The Black Watch leading in artillery formation. The patrols found the Nakhailat lines occupied only by a few Turks, whom they captured.

A halt was made to allow the 28th Brigade to come up into line on the right. The advance was then continued, and after a little sniping the Suwada position was also captured. A further rapid advance that day might have led to the capture of large numbers of the retreating enemy, and Colonel Wauchope reported that The Black Watch was ready and able for another ten miles. But it was held that enough had already been asked of the

ADVANCE ON BAGHDAD, MARCH, 1917

troops, and the two brigades bivouacked for the night. About 3 p.m., however, our cavalry reported some enemy in position at Horse Shoe Lake, six miles from Suwada. Two platoons were sent forward to dislodge them, but found the position vacated, and returned to Suwada at midnight without a man having fallen out. This was a fine performance, as the Battalion carried full trench warfare equipment, and had had no rest for twenty-four hours. These were no picked platoons, and the whole of the Battalion was capable of performing what the Colonel had offered earlier in the day.

On the 25th the 21st Brigade moved forward six miles to the Dahra Canal, on the next day another six, and on the 27th twelve miles to Shaikh Jaad. Here a halt was made till March 4th. The army had outrun the supply system, and could not march on Baghdad till reorganization of the administrative arrangements was completed.

On the 4th the whole Army moved on Baghdad, the cavalry leading, followed by General Marshall's Corps, with the I Corps in rear. The 7th Division marched eighteen miles to Azizieh, and the Battalion came in without dropping a man.[1] Next day the Division marched sixteen miles to Zeur, a trying day on account of a strong head wind and clouds of thick dust, and on the 7th, in similar conditions, fourteen miles to Bustan. The next morning the Division passed, on its way to Bawi, the great arch of Ctesiphon, where Townshend had fought the battle that eventually brought his force to retreat and captivity. Here too, many centuries earlier, the Emperor Julian, marching from Constantinople, had been forced to halt his army and had met with disaster and death.

On the 7th the III Corps had reached the line of the Diala river, and were held up by a strong Turkish rearguard. General Maude determined to turn the line of this obstacle by crossing to the right bank of the Tigris, and ordered a bridge to be thrown at Bawi. By this the I Corps was to cross on the night of the 8th/9th, leaving the III Corps to make good the passage of the Diala.

The Battalion had been rearguard to the Division on the 8th, when it marched to Bawi, and did not cross till 8 a.m. on the 9th. The Cavalry Division had crossed the Tigris during the night, but missed the way, and the Battalion, as advanced guard, had

---

[1] An old sergeant of the Battalion, who wore the Egyptian and South African medals, was this day offered by its occupant a lift in a Ford car. Indignant at the implied doubt of his powers of endurance, he replied in somewhat forcible language that he had been marching in the desert before Ford cars were thought of and would back himself to be marching still when that particular one was broken down.

THE SECOND BATTALION THE BLACK WATCH

exceedingly hard work crossing a series of irrigation ditches, each of which seemed to be wider and deeper than the last. The distances covered daily during this advance to Baghdad were not very great, but the troops had been in trenches for a long period, and only the constant efforts of leaders and men prevented the tartan of The Black Watch from being seen amongst the many stragglers along the hot and dusty road. That the transport of the Battalion kept up so well, under conditions which were possibly even more trying to animals than to men, reflects great credit on Lieutenant J. Todd and Sergeant Anderson.

The leading brigade of the 7th Division, the 28th, was this day engaged with the enemy near Shawa Khan, digging in opposite his position at nightfall. Next day, the 10th, was spent manœuvring to gain touch with the retreating enemy in the face of a thick and continuous dust storm. By the afternoon the troops reached the Euphrates–Baghdad railway and moved up it in face of fitful opposition till nightfall. No one in the Brigade had experienced, either in India or Iraq, a dust storm at all comparable to that which now blew continuously for two days in the faces of the troops marching doggedly along the endless plain. It was often impossible to see ten yards ahead. Men suffered an intolerable thirst, and for two days there was little water to be had.

On the morning of the 11th, at 3 a.m., the Battalion, in artillery formation, led the advance on Baghdad; two strong patrols under officers were pushed on ahead; one of these reached its objective, the iron bridge over the Masudiyah Canal, soon after 5 a.m. and found it intact. The second patrol was under Second Lieutenant B. Houston, who as Company Sergeant Major gained the D.C.M. in France and had lately been promoted to commissioned rank. It reached the outskirts of Baghdad before dawn. Hearing a regular fusillade near the railway station, Houston pushed forward, and after some firing cleared the Arabs from the neighbourhood and so saved the only railway station of Baghdad from destruction. This was at 6 a.m. and the men of this patrol were therefore, by some two hours, the first troops, British or Indian, to enter Baghdad. The report that a patrol of The Black Watch was in occupation of Baghdad railway station was at once communicated to the Army Commander. General Maude had foreseen the danger of part of the city being destroyed by looters, and this intelligence relieved him from much anxiety. Within a few minutes of receiving the message he ordered his own steamer to go full steam ahead up the river.

The Battalion followed its patrol to the railway station, and a few hours later moved to the northern outskirts of the town on the right bank, the defence of which had been entrusted to the

ADVANCE TO MUSHAIDIE, MARCH, 1917

21st Brigade. The Turks had evacuated Baghdad, but there was some firing from pillaging Arabs, before order was restored.[1]

The Battalion had had little actual hard fighting in the operations that led to the capture of Baghdad, but enough manœuvring and marching in trying conditions to show what a disciplined and handy machine for open warfare it had become as a result of its training in the summer. The hour was fast approaching when the value of this training, the fine quality of the unit it had produced, and the worth of the men who composed it were to be proved in a pitched battle.

2.—*The Battle beyond Baghdad–Mushaidie, March 14th, 1917*

The Battalion bivouacked on the night of the 11th on the banks of the Tigris, and rested the next day in the shade of a grove of date palms. This halt, after the rush of the 120 miles march from Sannaiyat, was almost as welcome as had been the change from the long period of trench warfare. For in the fighting of the last fourteen months the joy of lying under a tree, the hope of ever again seeing a human dwelling-place had almost faded from the mind. But now the city of Baghdad had been captured, and the minarets and golden dome of Kazimain were seen glittering in the sun. For a few hours some were ready to dream that the war was ended, and that the Regiment might rest in peace under those fig trees and date palms. But the task of the army in Mesopotamia was not yet achieved. The Turkish forces, though defeated and driven back, were far from being destroyed.

On the 12th of February a large enemy force was discovered by our airmen holding a strong position at Mushaidie, on the right bank of the Tigris, some twenty miles north of Baghdad. So on the 13th the 7th Division received orders to advance that night, and move so as to gain a position to attack the Turkish right flank next day. This meant moving away from the river over a waterless area, but it would place the force where the Turk least expected the main attack, for, as was learnt later, he had laid out the trace of most of his trenches between the river and the railway.

The whole of the afternoon of the 13th was spent in preparations for the move. Water bottles were filled, and enough water

---

[1] In the officers' mess there now hangs a picture presented by the 14th King's Hussars, which bears the following inscription :—" Surrender of Kazimain, 11th March, 1917. Presented to Colonel A. G. Wauchope and the officers of the 2nd Battalion Black Watch by the officers of the 14th King's Hussars to commemorate their comradeship in Mesopotamia, 1916–17, and with the British Army of the Rhine, 1920–22."

was carried on mules to refill them once on the next day. No more was given to man or animal till the morning of the 15th. This should be borne in mind when judging of the difficulties overcome by the troops in this action, for the shade temperature on the 14th was about 80 degrees, and there was no shade.

The Battalion marched off before sundown and formed up with the other units of the 21st Brigade in the centre of the Divisional column along the railway that leads to Samarrah. The column marched at 10 p.m. on a fine starlit night and by dawn had covered some fourteen miles, when a halt was made to gain news of the enemy, and to give the troops time to eat some biscuits and drink a few mouthfuls of the precious water. The leading brigade, the 28th, was then sent forward on the east side of the railway with orders to press back the Turk's advanced parties and assault his main position, which was some five miles north of the first halting place. Soon little puffs of white smoke showed that the Turk had opened the battle with salvos of shrapnel. Our batteries trotted forward and were quickly in action; the leading brigade deployed for attack. In the cool morning air the scene was clear in every detail, but as the sun rose our advanced troops were lost in a cloud of dust and smoke, and in the mirage of the sandy plain.

The battle was fought over ground typical of the Tigris Valley and the desert into which it merges. There were no hills, trees nor any distinguishing features; but the strip nearest the river, varying from one to several miles in breadth, was cultivated and intersected with irrigation channels, some six feet, some six inches in width and depth. It was here the enemy had expected attack and was holding numerous trenches between the river and the railway. But it was wisely decided to make the main attack on the enemy's right, west of the railway, some six miles from the river. The ground in this part is a wide open desert, bare and level except for a few low sandhills; but in the dips and hollows below the sandhills the desert changes into a thick growth of fresh green grass dotted with flowers.

During the morning the Battalion marched and manœuvred and then halted. Word came that the 28th Brigade was unable to make any further advance, and about noon orders were issued for the 21st Brigade to carry out an assault west of the railway against the right of the Turks' main position in conjunction with a renewed advance by troops of the 28th Brigade.

Some five miles beyond the place where the Battalion had halted preparatory to the final advance, after assisting to drive in the enemy's outposts, a definite ridge ran east and west across the railway, ending at the western extremity in a low sugar-loaf hill about forty feet high. It was this ridge, reported to be held

BATTLE OF MUSHAIDIE, MARCH 14TH, 1917

and entrenched by the Turk, which the 21st Brigade was now ordered to attack and capture.

The 28th Brigade had been held up mainly by enfilade artillery fire coming from positions nearer to the river than to the railway.

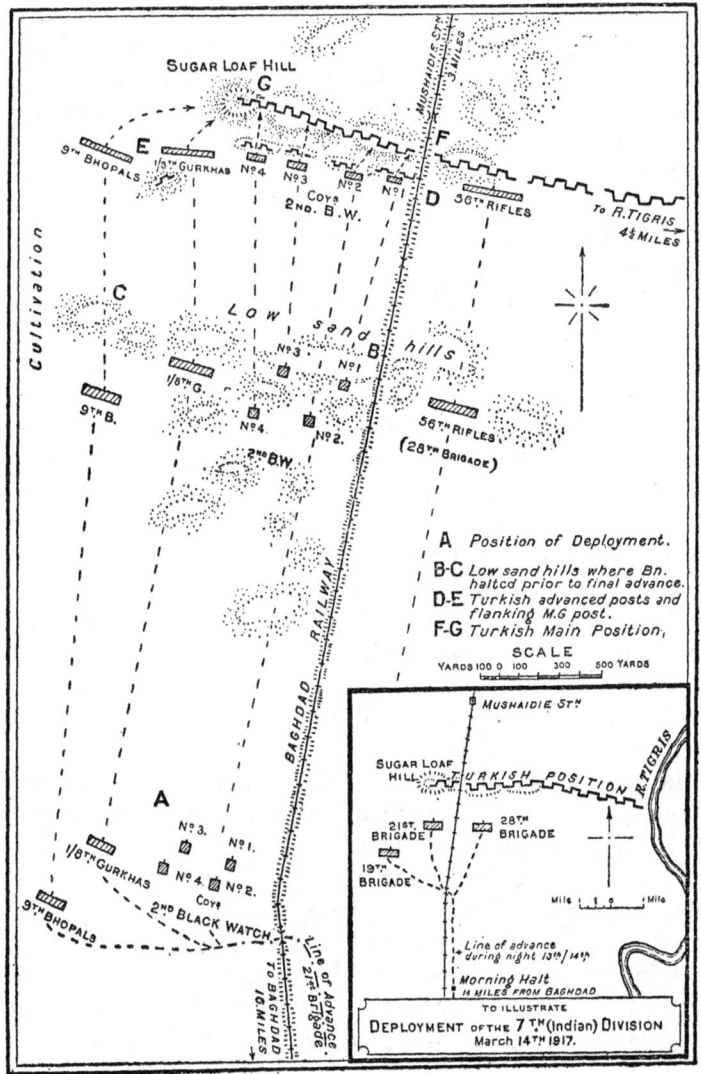

THE BATTLE OF MUSHAIDIE
MARCH 14TH, 1917

The whole Brigade was lying stretched out in extended order some 3000 yards ahead of the 21st Brigade, with the left regiment touching the railway embankment. The 21st Brigade, which had followed for some miles in their tracks, was now ordered to cross to the western side of the railway by a small culvert and form up

253

for the main attack some three or four miles south of the enemy's position. The third brigade of the Division, the 19th, was held in support on the left rear.

The Battalion was formed for attack in four lines, each of four platoons at irregular intervals of about 100 yards, with 100 to 200 yards distance between the lines. The Battalion thus covered a front of some 400 yards, and about 600 yards in depth. Nos. 1 and 3 Companies formed the first and second lines, Nos. 2 and 4 Companies the third and fourth lines. The right platoon, some eighty yards from the railway, was to direct. The 1/8th Gurkhas were on the left of the Battalion, and the 9th Bhopals in support, in echelon to the left rear of the Gurkhas.[1]

The first line transport, with the reserve ammunition, halted near the culvert through which the railway had been crossed, but both the reserve ammunition and the Aid Post were brought forward as the attack developed.

At 3.30 p.m. The Black Watch advanced, and soon had passed the two field batteries covering the front, and had come level with the lines of the 28th Brigade. About four o'clock the leading patrols reported that the enemy was holding not only the main ridge that joined Sugar Loaf Hill, with the railway embankment, but also a broken line of low sandhills a few hundred yards in front of the main position. At the same time some shrapnel burst over the leading platoons, and a party of Turks, directly on the left, opened long-range rifle fire. Advantage was now taken of the cover of some low sandhills to halt the Battalion and issue final orders. Half a company and two machine guns were sent to clear the Turks firing from the left flank. This party of the enemy retired at once when fired on.

The Battalion was now about 1000 yards from the enemy, and at about 4.30 p.m. continued the advance in perfect order; the small columns extending into line as the enemy's rifle fire grew more and more severe. The Turkish batteries also kept up a regular fire, happily without causing much loss. But the farther the troops advanced the more evident it became that Sugar Loaf Hill was the key of the position. It stood 700 or 800 yards west of the railway, and the enemy's riflemen from the entrenchments on top brought a deadly enfilade fire to bear on the advancing lines. The Gurkhas, moving in echelon on the left, escaped this, but to meet it and to dominate the enemy's fire The Black Watch was compelled to extend to the left, the supporting companies being used to fill the gap, the whole Battalion being thus in the front line. Two machine-gun sections also pressed gallantly forward, and in spite of continued and heavy losses from now onwards did much to help to gain superiority of fire over the enemy.

[1] The 21st Brigade had only three battalions available.

BATTLE OF MUSHAIDIE, MARCH 14TH, 1917

The enfilade fire from the left of the Turkish line was causing such losses that it seemed impossible to continue the advance without strong artillery support. Unfortunately this was not forthcoming at the time, because the covering batteries were now at extreme range, and were in the act of moving to a more forward position. The moment was critical, for if an attack wavers and halts within close range of an entrenched enemy, that attack is dead until supports come up and give it again an impetus. And there were few supports available.

Yet all along the front of the Battalion small sections still continued to rise up, make a rush forward and fling themselves down, weaker perhaps by two or three of their number, but another thirty yards nearer the enemy. Now the last supports pressed into the firing line, and as one leader fell another took his place. One platoon changed commanders six times in as many minutes, but a Lance Corporal led the remaining men with the same dash and judgment as his seniors.

It was during this advance of 500 yards that the Battalion met with its heaviest losses. No. 4 Company on the left had lost all four officers and half its numbers; the Lewis gunners had suffered particularly heavily; Lieutenant Gillespie, the officer in charge was killed while gallantly directing their fire. Company Sergeant Major J. Miller (who later received a commission) assumed command of the company. After the action he was found to have seven bullet holes in his kilt and several more in his equipment; but he himself was uninjured. No. 3 Company, next on the left, had fared but little better. But these two companies forced the enemy back, and occupied the low sandhills some 200 yards in advance of his main position, and there waited, by order, before making the final assault. These two companies lost six signallers killed or wounded in the act of calling for more ammunition; though many brave deeds were done, nothing was carried out with greater bravery, nothing contributed more to our success than the way in which communication was maintained throughout the battle.

Thus the left half-battalion, reduced to less than half its original numbers, was in need of help. This help it now gained from the action of Nos. 1 and 2 Companies on the right. Undismayed by the enemy shell and rifle fire, these two companies, gallantly assisted by the 56th Rifles on the east of the railway, pressed forward, and at five o'clock charged the enemy and drove him out of his advanced trenches at the point of the bayonet. The very quickness of the manœuvre had ensured its success, though it was only achieved with some loss to the attackers as well as to the Turk. But the gain was great. Small parties now crept forward among the sand dunes, two Lewis guns were taken

THE SECOND BATTALION THE BLACK WATCH

to the east side of the railway embankment, and a hot enfilade fire was brought to bear on the enemy main position. So effective was this that the Turks were forced to evacuate the ridge for some 400 yards nearest the railway; and even from Sugar Loaf Hill his fire weakened. The relief to the left half-battalion and to the Gurkhas was correspondingly great. Streams of wounded Turks were seen passing from the ridge to the rear; it was not only the British who suffered losses on this day of March 14th.

It now wanted only a final charge to complete the success. But this charge could not be made without either artillery support or the arrival of fresh troops to fill up the depleted and extended ranks. Orders were accordingly issued to all companies to wait in the positions they had gained, but to be ready to assault immediately after the batteries had bombarded the enemy trenches. The Commanding Officer was able to communicate by telephone with the Brigadier, who ordered up two companies of the Seaforths. It was also arranged that the batteries, as soon as they were in position, should bombard as heavily as possible the trenches on the east of Sugar Loaf Hill, the bombardment to begin at 6.25 and to last for six minutes.

During the next hour both sides remained on the defensive; rifle fire grew less and less, artillery firing ceased. Suddenly our batteries opened and with rare precision burst shrapnel all along the enemy trenches. At 6.30, as the shelling slackened in intensity, the Battalion rose as one man, and, their bayonets gleaming in the setting sun, rushed across the open, with the Gurkhas on their left. There was little work for the bayonet. The Turk fled as our men closed, and the position so long and hardly fought for was won.

The Black Watch had gained its objective, but had lost heavily in officers and men. The remainder were exhausted by the labours of the past twenty-four hours and by lack of water; but when orders came to push forward and capture Mushaidie Station, some four miles further north, there was no feeling either of doubt or hesitation. Some time was spent in reorganization, in bringing up and distributing reserve ammunition; the two left companies were amalgamated; and an officer was detailed to act with the right wing of the Gurkhas, since that battalion, though it had not suffered such heavy losses in men, had only two officers left unwounded. The two Seaforths companies now arrived and were ordered by Colonel Wauchope to act in immediate support of The Black Watch.

The 9th Bhopals had been operating far out on the left flank, and were now occupying Sugar Loaf Hill; the 56th Rifles, who had fought so well on our right flank through the earlier stages of the battle, had received orders to halt for the night. And so the

BATTLE OF MUSHAIDIE, MARCH 14TH, 1917

Battalion advanced alone; but though hungry, thirsty, weary, worn, all ranks were fully confident, and united in the determination to complete the rout of the enemy.

A mile ahead a strongly entrenched position was passed, luckily abandoned by the Turks. It was not for another two miles, when the advanced patrols came close to the station, that the enemy was reported in any numbers. At 11.30 p.m., close to the station, the companies deployed and charged with the bayonet. The enemy fired only a few shots; one of our men and a few Turks were killed, and a few more of the enemy made prisoners; but the rest fled and disappeared into the night, leaving piles of saddlery, ammunition and food behind them. The necessary piquets were posted, and the rest then forgot exhaustion, forgot even victory, in the most profound sleep.

The losses of the Battalion were 5 officers killed and 5 wounded out of 18, and 36 men killed and 184 wounded out of 525 who actually took part in the attack, a percentage of casualties of over 40. These are heavy losses, but small compared with the achievement. The men had been on the move for over thirty hours. Almost singlehanded the Regiment had captured a position that others had found too hard to assault; and by midnight, at Mushaidie, had accomplished the task the Divisional Commander had asked, but had hardly hoped that the Battalion could perform. Had regimental spirit been less strong, had trust in themselves and their leaders been less firm, the losses had been doubled and the day had ended in failure instead of success. The victory at Mushaidie stands out as the finest achievement of the Battalion in the war. The losses were heavy, but it was only due to their quickness in manœuvre and precision in fire that there remained at dusk three hundred dauntless men eager to charge and determined to capture the trenches which the Turk had held so long and so courageously. Even in this last war, where so much astonishing gallantry was shown, are there many instances recorded where men who had lost so many of their leaders, who had been without rest for twenty-four hours, charged with greater valour at the end of a long and arduous battle? The Corps Commander wrote to Colonel Wauchope: "I was indeed "pleased with the attack by your regiment on the 14th. It was "a fine determined attack and I think you can rank it as one of "the red-letter days in the diary of your regiment during the "war. You fairly routed the enemy."

The following day the Battalion remained at Mushaidie; a dust storm was blowing, and many reports came in of the enemy returning to make a counter-attack. But his defeat had been too severe, and he made no real resistance again till a month later at Istabulat, thirty miles further north.

THE SECOND BATTALION THE BLACK WATCH

Meanwhile the 21st Brigade was ordered to concentrate on the Tigris at the Babi bend, some six miles east of Mushaidie. A pleasant week of comparative rest was spent there, and then, there being no signs of the enemy, the Battalion, on March 25th, was withdrawn to its old camping ground in the palm groves north of Baghdad. Two companies were split up on outpost duty, but the remainder found time for military training and some visits to the city.

The following officers and warrant officers were present with the Battalion at the battle of Mushaidie:—

Commanding Officer	Colonel A. G. Wauchope, D.S.O.
Second-in-Command	Major T. G. F. Cochrane.
Adjutant	Captain N. M. Ritchie.
Captain and Quartermaster	J. Anderson, D.C.M.
Medical Officer	Captain J. MacQueen, R.A.M.C.
Chaplain	Rev. A. Macfarlane.
Regimental Sergeant Major	A. Smart.

Captains

M. E. Park, D.S.O.
R. Macfarlane (*wounded*).
J. A. Barstow, M.C.
R. M. Purvis (*died of wounds*).
L. H. Willett.

Lieutenants

A. E. Blair.
T. A. Henderson, M.C.
E. G. B. Miller-Stirling (*killed*).

Second Lieutenants

T. H. Cotterill (*died of wounds*).
T. Gant (*wounded*).
T. Gillespie (*killed*).
A. Gilroy.
B. S. Houston, M.C., D.C.M.
M. Jamieson.
J. Jeff.
D. Murray-Stewart.
G. B. Smart (*wounded*).
P. E. Smythe.
R. M. Smythe (*wounded*).
G. V. Stewart (*wounded*).
J. Todd.
A. A. Young (*killed*).

The Company Sergeant Majors were:—

No. 1 Co. A. Muir.   No. 3 Co. T. Bissett (*killed*).
  „ 2 „   D. Palmer.   „ 4 „   J. Miller.

3.—*The Battle of Istabulat*

In the evening of April 6th the Battalion left Baghdad and again marched northwards with the 7th Division. On the 9th Beled Station was reached, after an engagement in which the

BATTLE OF ISTABULAT, APRIL, 1917

21st Brigade took no part. Here a halt of some days was made, while the III Corps, on the left bank of the Tigris, cleared the Turks from the Shatt-el-Adhaim area. This made it possible to resume the advance on the right bank, till the Turks were found strongly entrenched beyond the Median Wall about Istabulat, covering the railhead at Samarrah, which was the objective of the British force.

The Median Wall, which once stretched unbroken from the Tigris to the Euphrates, is said to be the oldest fortification in the world. However that may be, it stands to-day the most prominent landmark in all this district of the Tigris Valley. Though broken tumble-down mounds represent the great wall towards the Euphrates, for many miles near the Tigris it stands without a break, fully thirty feet above the level of the plain. Behind this wall the 7th Division had for some days previous to April 21st been collecting for the attack on the Turkish position, which lay some three miles north of the wall and some twelve miles south of Samarrah.

The country here differs but little from the rest of the Tigris Valley, the same level plain of loam and mud, a strip of two or three miles nearest the river highly irrigated and at this season green with young corn and barley; further afield the bare, brown, featureless desert stretching out in every direction. Even in April the shade temperature runs to 110 degrees; and there is no shade from the sun, no escape from the heat.

Besides the Median Wall there remain two outward and visible signs of the old civilization. At frequent intervals, low flat mounds, composed of old sunbaked bricks, mark the sites of ancient cities; and occasionally walls of the canals that served to irrigate the country between the two rivers are seen stretching across the desert. The canals have for centuries past been dry and useless, but their walls, ten or twenty feet high and many miles in length, remain.

The Turkish position was very well selected, and a difficult one to attack. The left rested securely on a re-entrant bend of the Tigris. Thence the line ran west across the Dujail river, and continued for a mile along a dry canal, until it met the railway a little to the north of Istabulat Station. The right was refused and rested on the ruins of the ancient city of Istabulat. These ruins consisted of some low mounds and the high walls of an old canal that had run from the Tigris across the present line of the railway, four miles to the north of the station. The whole country was absolutely flat and bare except for the broken and uneven walls of the Dujail river and of the Istabulat canal.

The so-called Dujail river is a canal that takes off from the right bank of the Tigris some four miles north of the Median Wall.

THE SECOND BATTALION THE BLACK WATCH

Unlike the other old canals it still has water flowing in it. It has been dug and re-dug till it now flows below the level of the surrounding country, but its walls are fully twenty feet high, and so form the one dominant tactical feature of the level Tigris plain in this district.

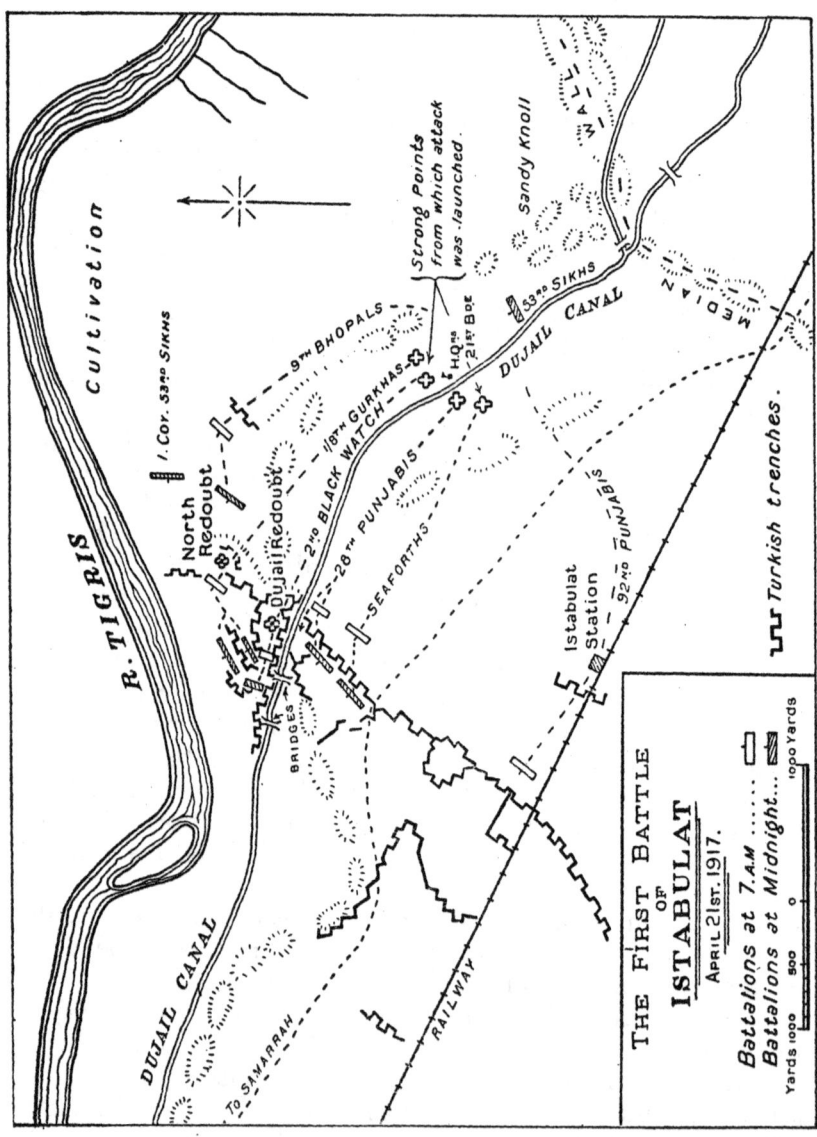

The key to the position was obviously this high double wall of the Dujail river. These walls were from 100 to 150 yards wide at the top, and being very broken and uneven gave some cover to skirmishers in attack or defence. A small ridge of sand-hills that had originally formed the walls of an old canal which

BATTLE OF ISTABULAT, APRIL, 1917

flowed in earlier centuries between the Tigris and the Dujail, also gave a little cover to attacking troops. The Turks had strengthened their line where it crossed the Dujail by building a strong redoubt on its eastern bank, some 300 yards long by 150 yards broad; here, too, were a number of machine-gun emplacements.

On the 18th of April, the Battalion pushed forward a strong patrol along the east bank of the Dujail, the 28th Punjabis doing the same on the west bank. The two patrols worked together and gave each other mutual support; both encountered the Turkish outposts within 600 yards, and after driving them some distance back, withdrew as night fell.

As an attack on the enemy position was decided on, Colonel Wauchope now suggested that a line of strong points should be constructed about a mile ahead of our line, and that when these had been made good, a second line 800 yards in advance of the first should be constructed, so that by this means the final assault might be made from a comparatively short distance to the enemy's main position; also artillery officers would be able to locate definitely the enemy's main trenches, and guns could be brought up within 2000 yards before the infantry assault. This idea was adopted.

On the 19th the Battalion, by some fine patrol work, drove the enemy advanced troops back with little loss. During the night three strong posts were built a mile in advance, two on the east and one on the west bank of the Dujail. From these posts both The Black Watch and the Punjabis skirmished further forward on the 20th, and the enemy's position was becoming seriously threatened with but little loss to ourselves.

One incident in this patrol fighting must not pass unnoted. An artillery officer had been sent forward in the morning to observe the ground and the enemy positions from our strong point on the east bank of the Dujail. He had crawled a little ahead of the strong point to an exposed position in order to observe more freely, when he was struck by a bullet which incapacitated him from coming back or escaping from his exposed position. Sergeant Easton had been sergeant of the Battalion stretcher bearers since his predecessor, Sergeant Humm, D.C.M., had been killed when recovering a wounded man; and had himself already won the D.C.M. for a fine piece of work in France. Easton now ran forward from the strong point without hesitation, and, though the enemy snipers were dropping bullets all round, roughly bandaged the officer, picked him up on his back, staggered down to the Dujail and got him across under the welcome shelter of the other bank, though the stream was over six feet deep. For this action Sergeant Easton received a bar to his D.C.M.

THE SECOND BATTALION THE BLACK WATCH

On the 20th, on the eve of battle, orders were received for Colonel Wauchope to take over command of the 8th Brigade. The loss to the Battalion was great. Colonel Wauchope was the only officer remaining, except the Quartermaster, who had left India with the Battalion; he had been continuously with it throughout the war up till now, except for two periods when incapacitated by wounds received in action. He had commanded the Battalion since September, 1915, and had led it at Loos, Shaikh Sa'ad, in the advance on Baghdad and at the victory of Mushaidie. His influence in this period, when the Battalion had twice been reduced by battle to a mere handful of men, had more than anything kept alive the spirit and traditions of the Regiment and seen to it that the same proud spirit and old fighting traditions of the Red Hackle should inspire all who came to build up the Battalion again.

Fortunately an able successor was available in Major J. Stewart, who now took over command. Within a few hours of doing so he was sent for to receive orders for attack. It had been definitely decided on the 20th that the situation demanded an immediate advance, and a direct frontal attack was ordered to take place at dawn on the following morning. The 21st Brigade was to lead the attack at 5 a.m. on the east of the Dujail. The Black Watch was to advance along the east bank of the river with one company of the 28th Punjabis covering their left flank on the west bank. On the right of The Black Watch the 1/8th Gurkhas were to advance from the right strong point with the 9th Bhopals in echelon on their right near the Tigris. The 20th Punjabis were held in reserve. When this attack had gained ground, the 19th Brigade was to advance over the bare plain on the west of the Dujail, and their right was to gain touch with the left of the company of the 28th Punjabis on the Dujail bank. The objectives of the main attack were the redoubt and the two bridges which crossed the Dujail immediately above it. The 28th Brigade formed the Divisional Reserve.

The orders were thus clear and the plan simple; the main difficulty was to ensure adequate artillery co-operation, since to come within effective range of the redoubt, our batteries would be forced to move forward over very open ground, and counter battery work would obviously be hard to arrange.

The width of broken ground available for the Battalion was but little over 150 yards; the Commanding Officer therefore wisely determined to attack on a narrow frontage of two platoons, rather than expose his men on the bare plain; and with the Dujail giving the direction to his left, to trust to the impetus of eight lines to force the enemy's position. Each company formed two lines, with two platoons in each line. Half-way between the

BATTLE OF ISTABULAT, APRIL 21ST, 1917

position of assembly and the objective the Dujail Canal bent sharply north, thus entailing a change of direction during the advance.

Precisely at 5 a.m. the covering batteries opened fire on the enemy outposts, the leading platoons advanced, and without pausing to fire moved forward at first at a steady walk. The necessary change in direction was carried out with the precision and accuracy of parade; and increasing the pace to a series of quick but equally steady rushes, our foremost lines drove back the Turkish advanced troops about a thousand yards from our strong points. A few Turks were bayoneted, a number more shot by the fire of a well-placed Lewis gun, but the surprise of the attack and the rapidity of its execution saved our men from any severe loss during this first advance. As the leading platoons drew near to the enemy main positions, they came under an enfilade fire from the west bank of the Dujail, and a number of men had to swing round to the left and, from the crest of the wall, reply to the enemy not 200 yards distant on the opposite bank. The succeeding lines, however, pressed forward, section after section rushing on to the help of their comrades. Every rise and every knoll along the river was held by snipers, and the battle developed into a fierce contest between skirmishers. But it was not of long duration. Shortly after six o'clock nearly two miles of country had been cleared of the enemy; our men were not to be denied, and the leading lines made a gallant charge and rushed the main redoubt and a small trench about sixty yards in front of it, killing a certain number of its defenders and driving out the remainder.

The success of the attack was greatly due to its rapidity, but this very rapidity had led to some loss of cohesion between the eight lines that had originally advanced to the assault. Some platoons had been forced to engage the enemy on the opposite bank, others with Lewis guns were keeping down the fire of the enemy who were holding several small trenches ahead, and a number of men had fallen never to rise again. Consequently for the first few minutes there were less than a hundred men in the redoubt, and these were subject to a heavy fire from their front, and enfilading fire from their left at very close range.

Now was the moment when artillery support was most needed. But, as explained above, this had been most difficult to arrange, owing to the nature of the ground. The batteries, posted under cover of the Median Wall, soon found themselves, as the enemy retired, at extreme range, and had been obliged in consequence to advance to new positions. This was done under great difficulties, for the enemy had established a strong barrage in rear of the assaulting troops. Many of the gunners were hit, especially of the telephone operators. Consequently just at this critical time there was little or no artillery support to be had.

The Turk is a stubborn fighter. His line on the west bank of the Dujail was some way behind the line now held by the Battalion, and the enemy was thus able to open a very galling fire from the commanding mounds on the west bank, at a range of only 200 to 400 yards. The redoubt had been taken at 6.15 a.m.; within ten minutes the Turks on the east bank had organized a strong body to make a counter-attack; and this body, headed by parties of bombers, rushed the redoubt, and after some few minutes of confused fighting drove the defenders back and re-occupied its front and side faces.[1] But our men were determined that what The Black Watch once had held, it should again hold and keep, and that the redoubt they had set forth to capture should be definitely theirs. The platoons which had originally formed the rear waves were now fast coming up, together with a reserve of bombers under Lieutenant J. C. Ritchie, and a fresh assault was immediately organized. But the losses were now very heavy. Within one minute one captain and two subalterns were killed, two captains and two subalterns wounded, and a large number of the rank and file also fell. The killed or disabled included all four company commanders. The smallest hesitation, the slightest wavering, and the Turks had made good their success. But there was no hesitation and, though only one unwounded officer remained, there was no wavering. The bombers dashed forward, every available man followed, and within fifteen minutes of its loss the entire redoubt was recaptured; its forward trenches were then rapidly consolidated. An artillery officer, who witnessed the assault wrote: " That day the Highlanders without " help won a victory that only those who saw it can realize was " among the most gallant gained in this war."

Many of the very men who charged forward had but ten minutes before been driven back; many of their comrades lay dead beside them; they had lost their accustomed leaders, shrapnel and heavy shell were bursting among them, and the fresh attack must have seemed to many a further and useless sacrifice. But the great stimulus of *esprit de corps*, pride in one's regiment and in oneself as a member of it, is the secret of success at such moments of crisis. To the leader and to the regiment which knows how to foster this spirit is given the knowledge of the one glory of war—the self-sacrifice of the individual for the good of all.

Of the gallantry of those who survived and of those who fell during that fierce struggle no complete tale can be written. But

[1] Portions of all four companies appear to have reached the redoubt or its near vicinity by this time.

A COMPANY, UNDER THE HON. MAJOR T. G. F. COCHRANE, CROSSING THE TIGRIS TO OCCUPY SAMARRAH, 1917

THE SECOND BATTALION CROSSING THE PONTOON BRIDGE AT SAMARRAH, 1917

BATTLE OF ISTABULAT, APRIL 21ST, 1917

one incident that was witnessed by several is worthy of record. The redoubt measured several hundred yards on its front and side faces, and the attackers were few in number. One of these, Private Melvin, of Kirriemuir, Forfarshire, had by some chance so damaged his bayonet that he could not fix it on his rifle. Throwhis rifle aside he rushed forward and encountered a group of Turks singlehanded. With bayonet and fist he brought three to the ground; the remaining six, stunned by the violence of his attack, surrendered, and were brought back by this brave old soldier in triumph to his company. For this deed Private Melvin was subsequently awarded the Victoria Cross.

Battalion Headquarters by this time had moved up close in rear of the redoubt, telephonic communication was established with the Brigade, and companies reorganized according to their losses. And fortunate it was that this was done with no loss of time, for the Turk had intended to hold this line of entrenchment, of which the redoubt was at once the key and the main defence of the two bridges, throughout the summer; and he was not going to surrender the position without further struggle. Two counter-attacks formed up and advanced against the front face of the redoubt; a few Turks got within fifty or a hundred yards, but each attack was broken up by steady rifle and Lewis gun fire and the position made more secure. A little nullah ran from the Turks' second position to within fifty yards of the redoubt, and up this channel from time to time he sent parties of bombers; but these were easily held in check. A group of machine guns from further up the Dujail swept the crest of the hard-won parapet, and the defenders of the redoubt were subject to a heavy bombardment of 5.9 shell from time to time throughout that long day. The nature of the ground and the skill with which the enemy had chosen his positions had prevented close artillery cooperation, in spite of every effort made by our artillery officers (five observers were killed in quick succession near Battalion Headquarters), and in spite of many casualties among our batteries. In consequence the enemy's batteries were never silenced, and kept up a heavy fire throughout the day, and our losses were heavy.

Meanwhile, on the right, the Gurkhas had advanced in gallant style, and in spite of a stubborn resistance had pushed the enemy back along the line of the old canal, keeping up with The Black Watch advance. Then when the salient bend of the Tigris narrowed their front, they swung round to their left in a most soldierly fashion and, despite heavy losses, joined the Battalion on the Dujail, sharing for the rest of the day the honours and the dangers of the defence of the redoubt and the trenches near it. The 9th Bhopals advancing still further on the right had met with misfortune, for, on reaching a small rise in the ground, their

THE SECOND BATTALION THE BLACK WATCH

lines had been suddenly swept with machine-gun fire at a range of 300 yards. Consequently no further advance was possible on this flank.

Nor on the west flank did the situation offer any greater promise. The 28th Punjabis on the immediate left of the Battalion had fought under great difficulties, but with such determination that they eventually dug themselves in opposite the redoubt on the west bank of the Dujail, though with heavy losses. On their left the Seaforths, of the 19th Brigade, had occupied some 800 yards of an old irrigation channel that ran westward from the Dujail towards the railway. Further to the west this dry channel remained in the hands of the Turks, the other battalions of the 19th Brigade not having advanced so far.

It was evident that without a renewed bombardment and strong reinforcements no further advance was possible on either side of the Dujail. The Battalion had advanced well over two miles, driven the enemy from his strongest positions and gained the immediate objectives. The final advance and capture of Samarrah had to be left till later. The Battalion had during this day's fighting lost over a third of its total strength in killed and wounded. The losses were 10 officers, of whom 4 were killed, and 173 other ranks, of whom 41 were killed.

The officers and warrant officers present with the Battalion at the Battle of Istabulat were:—

Commanding Officer	Lieut.-Colonel J. Stewart.
Second-in-Command	Major T. G. F. Cochrane.
Adjutant	Captain N. M. Ritchie.
Quartermaster	Captain J. Anderson, D.C.M.
Medical Officer	Captain W. Moore-Cameron, R.A.M.C.

Captains

J. A. Barstow, M.C. (*wounded*).   L. H. Willett (*wounded*).
R. Macfarlane, M.C. (*killed*).

Lieutenant   A. E. Blair.

Second Lieutenants

G. J. R. Brown (*died of wounds*).   A. H. Quine (*wounded and prisoner of war*).
A. Crombie.
A. Gilroy (*wounded*).   J. C. Ritchie.
K. Graham-Scott.   P. E. Smythe (*wounded*).
D. Haig.   G. V. Stewart.
J. Jeff.   J. Todd.
T. Loudon.   J. A. Byrom (A. and S.H.).
D. Murray-Stewart.   C. E. Gerard (Gordon H.).
D. McArthur (*died of wounds*). R. Walker (A. and S.H.) (*killed*).
T. Peel (*died of wounds*).

BEIT-AL-KHALIFA; HEADQUARTERS OF THE SECOND BATTALION IN THE SUMMER, 1917

BLACK WATCH SOLDIERS IN TEKRIT, NOVEMBER 2ND, 1917

SAMARRAH, APRIL, 1917

Regimental Sergeant Major A. Smart.
Company Sergeant Majors

No. 1 Co.	A. Muir.	No. 3 Co.	J. Hutchison.
„ 2 „	D. Palmer (*killed*).[1]	„ 4 „	J. Miller.

At 3.30 a.m. next morning, patrols reported the enemy trenches unoccupied. The Black Watch pushed forward strong patrols up the left bank of the Dujail to its junction with the Tigris, which was reached without opposition by 8.30 a.m. The Turk had, in fact, retired several miles on to the ruins of the ancient city of Istabulat. There he was attacked by the 28th and 19th Brigades, the 21st Brigade being this day in Divisional reserve. The Turk fought stubbornly and was only driven out of his position at nightfall.

On the third day the 21st Brigade was ordered to pass through the 19th and 28th Brigades and renew the advance on Samarrah. But the advanced patrols of The Black Watch, which was leading, found that the enemy had evacuated his forward positions; and the Brigade advanced in attack formation straight on Samarrah Station. Thus the Battalion was the first to enter Samarrah, as some six weeks earlier they had been the first to enter Baghdad. The Battalion was presented by the Brigade Commander, in recognition of this fact, with the Samarrah Station bell, on which the hours are now sounded, and it is hoped long will be, wherever the Headquarters of the Battalion stand. That bell is likely to have many wanderings and to see many places.

On the early morning of the 24th, Major Cochrane, with 100 men, embarked in *guffahs*, the circular Arab craft used in Mesopotamia, and crossed the Tigris to search the city of Samarrah.

4.—*Summer at Samarrah and the Departure from Mesopotamia*

With the capture of Samarrah the active winter campaign of 1916–17 came to an end. A position was chosen and fortified against attack, but the Turks had retired some distance and their most advanced troops were some five or six miles away. Both sides now settled down for the summer.

The summer was passed under much pleasanter conditions than in 1916. Leave to India for a month was granted to a number of officers and men. Tents, rations and comforts were plenti-

[1] Company Sergeant Major D. Palmer, who fell at Istabulat, was an old soldier who had left the Regiment with twenty-one years' service in 1912. On the outbreak of war he was employed as a storekeeper on a large cattle ranch in Patagonia, South America. He promptly left his employment, paid his own passage home and rejoined to do invaluable service with his old unit and to fall gallantly on the field of battle.

THE SECOND BATTALION THE BLACK WATCH

ful; and despite the great heat, which reached as much as 128 degrees, the Battalion maintained its health throughout the summer, thanks largely to the care and initiative of the medical officer, Captain Moore Cameron. It is worthy of record that while other battalions suffered severely from heat stroke The Black Watch, owing to Captain Cameron's measures, lost only one man (on Divisional employ) from this cause. Training was carried out continuously and the defences of the Samarrah position strengthened.

Nothing was seen of the enemy, except an occasional aeroplane, till towards the end of October, when a hostile force advanced from Tekrit, and after a few days' skirmishing in front of our line retired. It was decided to advance and attack this force.

In the first week of November the Battalion took part in these operations, which resulted in the capture of the Turkish positions at Tekrit. The Battalion was not, however, closely engaged with the enemy at any time during this advance. The force returned to Samarrah on November 12th. A few days later the 3rd Division relieved the 7th at Samarrah, and on the 15th the 21st Brigade marched for Akaab at the junction of the Adhaim and the Tigris, which was reached on the 17th. While halted here news was received of the death, on the 18th, of the Commander-in-Chief of the Mesopotamian Force, Sir Stanley Maude. Sir Stanley Maude had been a consistent friend to the Regiment since 1916 and had often visited the Battalion. His praise had been highly valued; his death was keenly felt.

On December 7th a sudden order was received for the move of the 21st Brigade to Baghdad, which was reached on December 10th.[1] This unexpected move caused great speculation. Though its actual destination was not known for some time, the 7th Division was, in fact, now leaving Mesopotamia. The Battalion entrained for Kut on the 14th and, travelling partly by river, partly by train, reached Basra on the 18th, where, after several delays, it was embarked on the s.s. *Palamacotta* on the 27th, and sailed on the same day. Next day, in Koweit Bay, the Battalion transhipped to the *Kinfauns Castle*, which sailed at early dawn on January 1st, 1918.

The Battalion had spent two years, almost to a day, in Mesopotamia. The contrast between those two years was striking. The first was a year of defeat, suffering and terrible losses; the second was marked by a series of great successes, the capture of Baghdad, the victories of Mushaidie and Istabulat; and the period of less active operations was spent in comparative comfort. But in suc-

[1] The return to Baghdad was accomplished in two marches, the second, from near Babi Bend to railhead at Hinadi, being over twenty-eight miles.

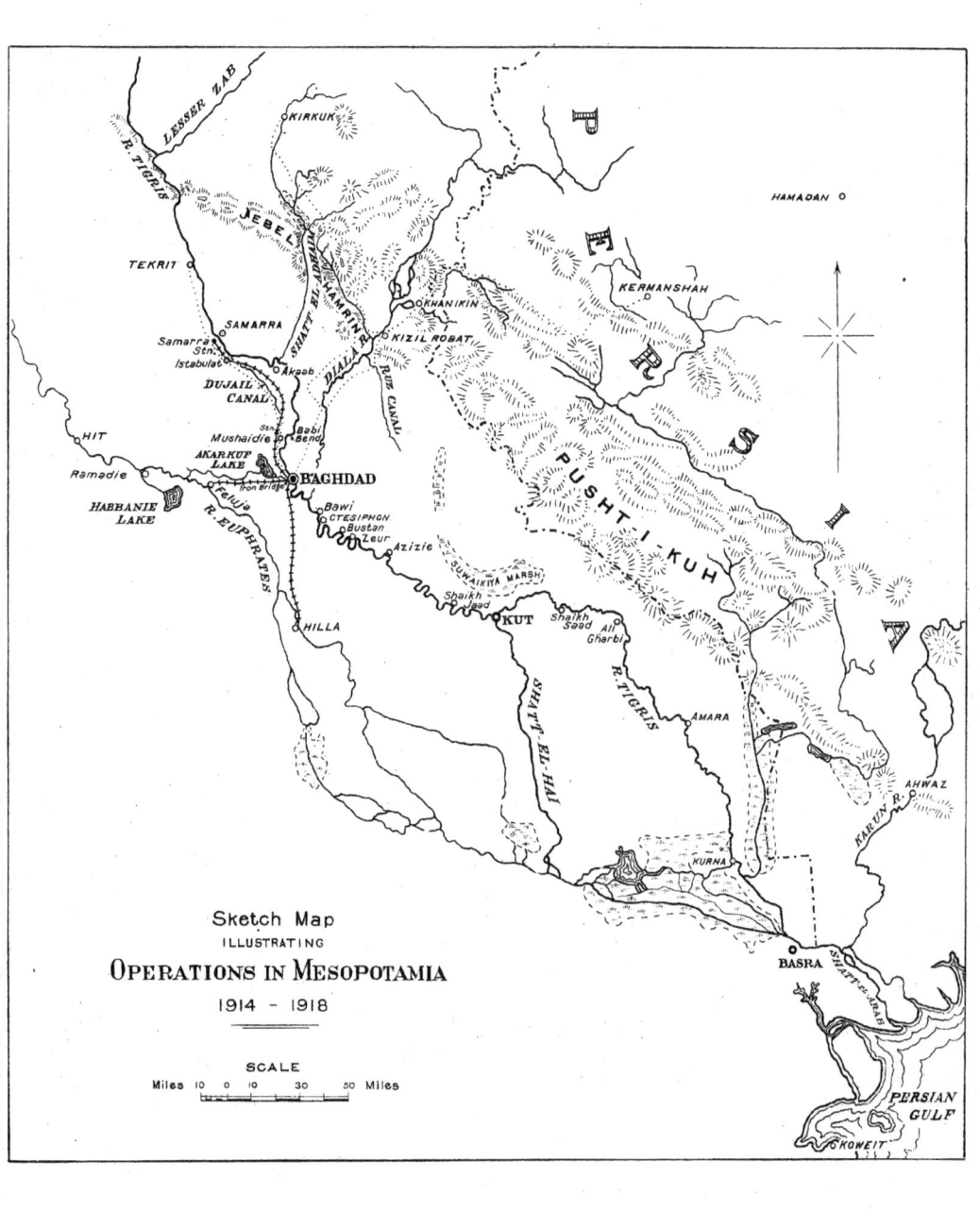

DEPARTURE FROM MESOPOTAMIA, DECEMBER, 1917

cess or failure, in heat or cold, in favourable or unfavourable conditions, the spirit of The Black Watch had ever remained the same; whatever failures there had been there was no failure of courage and endurance or in self-sacrifice for the common good. And these are the things that have counted in the history of the world, since the days when this land of Mesopotamia was the most fertile on earth, and the cradle of the earliest civilization, and will continue to count as long as man exists.

NOTES TO CHAPTER VI

The Wauchope Medallion

It is inevitable that in regiments such as The Black Watch, where every man seeks to distinguish himself when fighting for his country, there should be many whose gallant acts go unrewarded.

This fact was well understood by the men of the Battalion, but Colonel Wauchope was eager to give a mark of recognition to those who greatly distinguished themselves in battle. He therefore ordered a medallion to be specially struck, and gave this to non-commissioned officers and men who had led their sections with special distinction or had done some deed of marked gallantry in action. Colonel Wauchope gave sixty of these medals, mostly to men who had been recommended for gallantry after the battles of Loos and Mushaidie—the Battle beyond Baghdad —and ten others to men who had specially distinguished themselves scouting in No Man's Land.

The medallions became known as " The Wauchope Medal," and were highly prized by the men who gained them and by the platoons to which those men belonged; they are now, in all too many cases, treasured by widows as a symbol of the great deeds done by men of The Black Watch for their regiment and country.

The Dress of a Private of The Black Watch, during the summer of 1916

The Battalion arrived in Mesopotamia on 1st January, 1916, in the same dress as was worn in France, with the exception that the Balmoral bonnet was replaced by the Wolseley helmet.

By the month of March, 1916, khaki drill jackets, of Indian pattern, had replaced the field service jacket of khaki serge.

By June, 1916, spine-pads and sun-shades (to be worn over the helmet) had been issued to all ranks. Long khaki trousers were also issued about this time, as a precaution against sand-flies; and their wear was compulsory from sunset to sunrise, during trench warfare at Sannaiyat. Khaki shorts of Indian pattern were also issued, and, under normal conditions, worn by day in the front line, in place of the kilt.

By the end of June the dress of the private, in the trenches, was as follows :—

Wolseley helmet with Red Hackle and sun-shade.
Shirt-sleeves with spine-pad.
Khaki shorts (between sunset and sunrise, long khaki trousers with short puttees).
Khaki hose.
Scarlet garters.
Short puttees.
Ankle boots.

The khaki jacket was carried in the coat-carrier: the greatcoat being left behind in the Divisional area. During moves, or an attack, the kilt was worn in place of shorts.

Arms and Equipment, Mesopotamia, 1916

Rifle S.M.L.E. Mk. III*.
S.A.A. 150 rounds. 303" ball, Mk. vii.
Equipment—as for France in 1915.
The Battalion had two Vickers machine guns up till about the month of August, when the machine gun companies were formed. From that date machine guns were allotted to units as considered necessary by the Brigade Commander.
Eight Lewis guns per battalion were issued about the month of August, 1916.
No grenades of any sort were available in Mesopotamia until about the end of March, 1916, when Mills' grenades were issued.
These were carried by bombers in canvas buckets, as was done in France. A Belt-type grenade carrier was issued but seldom made use of.
In addition a Battalion Order made it compulsory for *every* officer, N.C.O. and man of the Battalion to carry two Mills' grenades, one in each breast pocket of his jacket, during an advance.
Rifle grenades were issued towards the end of 1916.
Several hundred bullet proof jackets were issued to the Battalion before the assault on Sannaiyat in 1917, but Colonel Wauchope did not have these issued, and they remained in store.

A HALT AT KEFR ZIBAD, PALESTINE, SEPTEMBER, 1918

MEDALLION PRESENTED BY COLONEL A. G. WAUCHOPE FOR GALLANTRY AT THE BATTLE OF LOOS, 1915, AND THE BATTLE BEYOND BAGHDAD, 1917

PART III—PALESTINE, 1918

CHAPTER VII

JANUARY TO SEPTEMBER, 1918

1.—*Arrival on the Palestine Front*

THE 7th Division was followed by the 3rd Division from Mesopotamia to Palestine a few months later. Thus these two, the original Divisions of the Indian Expeditionary Force, were once more to serve together in the same theatre of war. Their transfer to the Egyptian Expeditionary Force was a result of the change brought about in the strategical situation in the east by General Allenby's victories in Palestine at the end of 1917, and also of the general plan of the Allies for 1918.

General Allenby's crushing defeat of the Turks and capture of Jerusalem had compelled the Turks to reinforce the Palestine front with the army they had collected in the neighbourhood of Aleppo after the Russian collapse in 1917, with the avowed object of recapturing Baghdad. The threatened danger to our forces in Mesopotamia being thus removed, these two Indian Divisions were now added to the Egyptian Expeditionary Force; either to enable it to deal Turkey her knock-out blow (which could obviously be delivered with more effect from Palestine than from Mesopotamia), or to replace two British divisions which might be required to meet the impending German attack in France. At the time when the 7th Division left Mesopotamia, discussion was still taking place as to which of the two above policies should be adopted.

Thus it was that the Battalion sailed on New Year's Day, 1918, for its third theatre of war. Its composition as it embarked on the *Kinfauns Castle* at Koweit was as follows:—

Commanding Officer.	Lieut.-Colonel J. Stewart.
Second-in-Command.	Major T. G. F. Cochrane.
Adjutant.	Captain N. M. Ritchie, D.S.O.
Transport Officer.	Lieut. J. Todd.
Lewis-gun Officer.	2nd Lieut. J. C. R. Buchanan.
Quartermaster.	Captain J. Anderson, D.C.M.
Regimental Sergeant Major	A. Smart, M.C.
Regimental Quartermaster Sergeant	E. Hobbs.

THE SECOND BATTALION THE BLACK WATCH

No. 1 Company

Captain J. A. Barstow, M.C.
  ,,   W. D. McEwen, M.C.
Lieut. J. F. C. Dixon, M.C.
    (A. and S.H.).
2nd Lieut. J. C. Ritchie, M.C.

2nd Lieut. A. Scobie.
  ,,   T. Gant.
  ,,   A. Muir.
C.S.M. A. Milligan, D.C.M.
C.Q.M.S. S. Kelly.

No. 2 Company

Captain M. E. Park, D.S.O.
2nd Lieut. J. Jeff (Signalling Officer).
  ,,   K. Buchanan.
  ,,   G. B. Smart.

2nd Lieut. G. Ryrie.
  ,,   T. L. Smith.
C.S.M. A. Johnstone.
C.Q.M.S. G. Cormack.

No. 3 Company

Captain A. E. Blair.
2nd Lieut. R. M. Smythe.
  ,,   T. Loudon.
  ,,   T. Kinnear.

2nd Lieut. B. S. Houston, M.C., D.C.M.
C.S.M. J. Hutchison, D.C.M.
C.Q.M.S. J. Dormer.

No. 4 Company

Captain R. D. Robertson (Gordon H.).
Lieut. W. A. Young, M.C.
2nd Lieut. R. J. Haye.
  ,,   M. Jamieson (Bombing Officer).

2nd Lieut. A. E. Bairstow.
  ,,   J. MacGregor.
C.S.M. G. Wilson.
C.Q.M.S. D. Wilson.

Attached: Captain W. Moore-Cameron, R.A.M.C. (Medical Officer).
Rev. A Silver (Chaplain).
Strength: 30 officers, 1001 other ranks.

The voyage was uneventful. On January 3rd, at Muscat, the *Kinfauns Castle* joined a convoy of six ships escorted by H.M.S. *Sapphire*. The *Kinfauns Castle*, which proceeded independently of the remainder of the convoy, entered the Red Sea and anchored at Perim on the evening of the 5th. Next morning she went on towards Suez, where the Battalion disembarked on January 13th, and proceeded to Moascar Camp, near Ismailia, on the canal.

In Moascar Camp the Battalion remained for over two months, till the third week in March, while the Division was gradually

MOASCAR, MARCH, 1918

assembled. The camp was a good one, leave was open to Cairo and other parts of Egypt, and the time was a pleasant interlude between two periods of service in the front line. Much training was carried out, though the desert sand on which the camp stood made drill and movement anything but easy work.

While at Moascar the Battalion won the football championship of the 7th Division in a tournament which had been commenced in Mesopotamia.

On March 12th H.R.H. the Duke of Connaught visited the Battalion and decorated some of those who had been awarded honours in Mesopotamia. He particularly commended the smartness of the Guard of Honour. On March 16th The Black Watch and Seaforths held a Highland gathering. A week later the Division moved up to the front. The Battalion left Moascar and marched to Kantara in two stages, and there entrained for Ludd, where it arrived on March 27th. At Ludd steel helmets were issued to the Battalion for the first time.[1] Packs had already been issued at Moascar, in place of the great-coat straps used in Mesopotamia.

The Egyptian Expeditionary Force held at this time a line which can be most simply described as covering Jericho, Jerusalem and Jaffa. The defensive line was at distances varying from ten to twenty miles in advance of those points. The force was organized into three Corps, the Desert Mounted Corps on the right, which held the Jordan valley and Jericho; the XX Corps in the centre which held a line across the main Judean range, covering Jerusalem and the Jerusalem–Nablus road; and the XXI Corps on the left, which stretched from the foot-hills of the main range across the maritime plain to the sea in advance of Jaffa. It was to this last Corps that the 7th Division was assigned, to replace the 52nd Division which was to depart to the Western Front.

It had been the original intention to carry out an offensive in Palestine in the spring of 1918, and preparations to this end were in progress; but the success of the German attack on the Western Front in April changed the whole situation. The Egyptian Expeditionary Force sent to France two complete divisions, the 52nd and 74th, and in addition nine yeomanry regiments, five and a half heavy batteries and ten British battalions. The force had therefore to remain on the defensive till these troops could be replaced by the 7th and 3rd Indian Divisions from Mesopotamia, Indian cavalry from France and Indian battalions from India.

The 7th Division went into the line at the beginning of April on the extreme left, next to the sea. Thus the Battalion, in its third theatre of operations, found itself once more in a flat, low-lying terrain.

[1] A khaki cover was issued with the helmet to prevent its becoming unbearably hot in the strong sun of Palestine.

THE SECOND BATTALION THE BLACK WATCH

Though flat and open as a whole the coastal plain of Palestine is more broken and less uninviting than Mesopotamia. The narrow strip of sea beach is bounded by cliffs some 75 to 100 feet high, intersected at intervals by deep and narrow wadis which carry off the water in the rainy season but are dry all the summer. Above these cliffs runs a strip of sandhills varying from a few hundred yards to half a mile in width, and rising in places to a height of 150 feet above sea level. Inland from the sandhills the plain stretches for some ten to fifteen miles to the foothills; it is gently undulating and intersected with numerous small wadis. In rear of our lines towards Jaffa were cultivation and groves of oranges and other trees, but between the lines thick coarse grass and weeds had grown rank over the untilled land.

The rainy season was just coming to an end with occasional heavy showers, the " latter rains " of the Bible. The summer of Palestine is less oppressive than that of Mesopotamia, and the climate is on the whole good. Special precautions had been taken against malaria, the chief scourge of the country. To guard against risk of infection by mosquito bites orders were received to discontinue the wearing of the kilt during the summer. Long khaki drill trousers were issued and worn with a short puttee round the ankles. This dress was somewhat similar to the white trousers and short gaiter worn by the 42nd in Ashanti in 1874.

In the part of the line taken over by the 21st Brigade,[1] some five miles inland from the coast, the defences consisted of a series of small posts, some 3000 yards from the most advanced Turkish posts. Following its custom the Battalion at once started a policy of vigorous patrolling up to the enemy line. In one of these patrols, on April 7th, Captain Park received a severe wound in the thigh and his party was hard pressed by the enemy while bringing him in. Lance Corporal McMaster, the piper, one of the oldest soldiers in the Regiment, took charge of the patrol and gave a fine example of coolness and determination which was ably seconded by the remainder of the party. For his gallant behaviour on this occasion Lance Corporal McMaster subsequently received a decoration.

An advance of the line closer to the enemy was contemplated at this time, and all preparations had been made, but the operation was cancelled. On April 17th the Battalion went into Brigade reserve near an orange grove on the Auja River, where a quiet three weeks were spent. By arrangement with the owner two thousand oranges were bought daily at seven piastres (about 1s. 6d.) per hundred, and police sentries were posted to protect the grove from molestation.

[1] The other units in the Brigade were the 1st Guides Infantry, 20th Punjabis and 1/8th Gurkha Rifles.

ACTION OF ARSUF, JUNE 8TH, 1918

On May 8th the 21st Brigade was withdrawn to Divisional reserve, and the Battalion occupied a camp close to the sea, where it remained till the end of the month. Besides training, sports of every kind were organized during this period and the opportunity of sea bathing was much appreciated.

2.—*Action of Arsuf, June 8th,* 1918

On June 1st the Battalion went into the line again, this time on the extreme left next to the sea. Battalion Headquarters and the reserve company were at Arsuf on the coast, two companies were in the front line, while the fourth company held some support works about half a mile east of Battalion Headquarters. The two companies in the front line were about 1000 yards apart, the right company holding a post on a small knoll opposite two larger and higher features held by the enemy and known as " The Sisters," while the left company was on a ridge (known as Brown Ridge) overlooking the sea. This ridge had been captured from the enemy by the Leicestershire Regiment only two days before, and much work had to be done to make the trenches on it safe and habitable.

Between the right company and the enemy's main position lay a small under-feature just below the South Sister, which had received the name of Little Mary. It was soon discovered by a patrol that the enemy occupied Little Mary at night only, and accordingly a Lewis-gun section was sent forward at dawn to hold it as an observation post by day. The Turks promptly opened an extremely accurate shell fire on Little Mary; and as the section had orders not to hold on if to do so was likely to involve casualties, it withdrew. Unfortunately one man had already been severely wounded and could not be moved. Private Muir volunteered to remain behind with the wounded man till he could be brought in at dusk, and did so, giving him the contents of his water bottle though suffering severely himself from thirst. When dusk came, however, the Turks, who had all the advantages of observation and distance, reached and removed the wounded man before the rescue party could arrive. Private Muir, who remained with his comrade till the last possible moment and rejoined in an exhausted condition from thirst, later received the Military Medal.

Our position in this part of the line, overlooked by the enemy from their more commanding position, was thoroughly unsatisfactory, and the Division ordered an operation to improve the line and gain observation. As a preliminary, the Guides, who were to share with the Battalion the task of making the attack, took over the right sector of the front, relieving two Black Watch companies. The Battalion was then concentrated along the sea coast, between Brown Ridge and Arsuf.

The attack was ordered for the early morning of June 8th. Its objectives were, on the right, the two Sisters, to be taken by the Guides, and on the left, to be captured by The Black Watch, a line of high ground from Point 170 to the sea. The frontage to be taken and held by the Battalion was some 600 to 700 yards, and involved an advance of about half a mile over several lines of enemy trenches. Nos. 3 and 4 Companies were detailed for the attack, supported by " mopping up " parties from No. 2 Company, while No. 1 Company was in reserve. The strength of the Battalion actually present in the line was 20 officers and 614 other ranks.

The position of assembly for the attack was in a steep wadi (Cameron Creek) just in front of our defences on Brown Ridge. At 3.20 a.m., after a quiet night, the assaulting companies moved out and formed up in their assembly positions, No. 4 Company on the right in four waves, No. 3 Company on the left in two waves, with the mopping up parties of No. 2 Company following the waves as required. The attack commenced at 3.45 a.m. under a moving barrage and went entirely according to plan, both companies reaching their final objective up to time and with little loss. The enemy were completely surprised and put up a poor resistance; 4 officers and about 70 other ranks were taken prisoner and two machine guns and four automatic rifles captured. A bombing party under Lieutenant Crombie completely annihilated the enemy's beach post by dropping bombs on it from the cliff above. Consolidation then commenced, hampered by a heavy bombardment from the enemy when he realized the situation.

Meanwhile the Guides had also captured the two Sisters, but at 7 a.m. were partly dislodged by a heavy counter-attack, launched under cover of a severe bombardment. Simultaneously the Turks directed a bombing attack down a wadi (Doncaster Wadi) which was near the point of junction of The Black Watch and Guides. This was promptly countered by a bombing party from No. 4 Company, which drove the enemy some distance back from the wadi, and thus secured our own right flank and the left flank of the Guides. Further assistance to the Guides was immediately given by the reserve company, No. 1, which despatched two platoons under Lieutenant Paton to their help. These two platoons made a dashing counter-stroke on to the high ground which formed the left of the Guides' objective, and materially assisted them to regain their positions. The enemy then accepted the situation and made no further effort to recover the lost ground.

ACTION OF ARSUF, JUNE 8TH, 1918

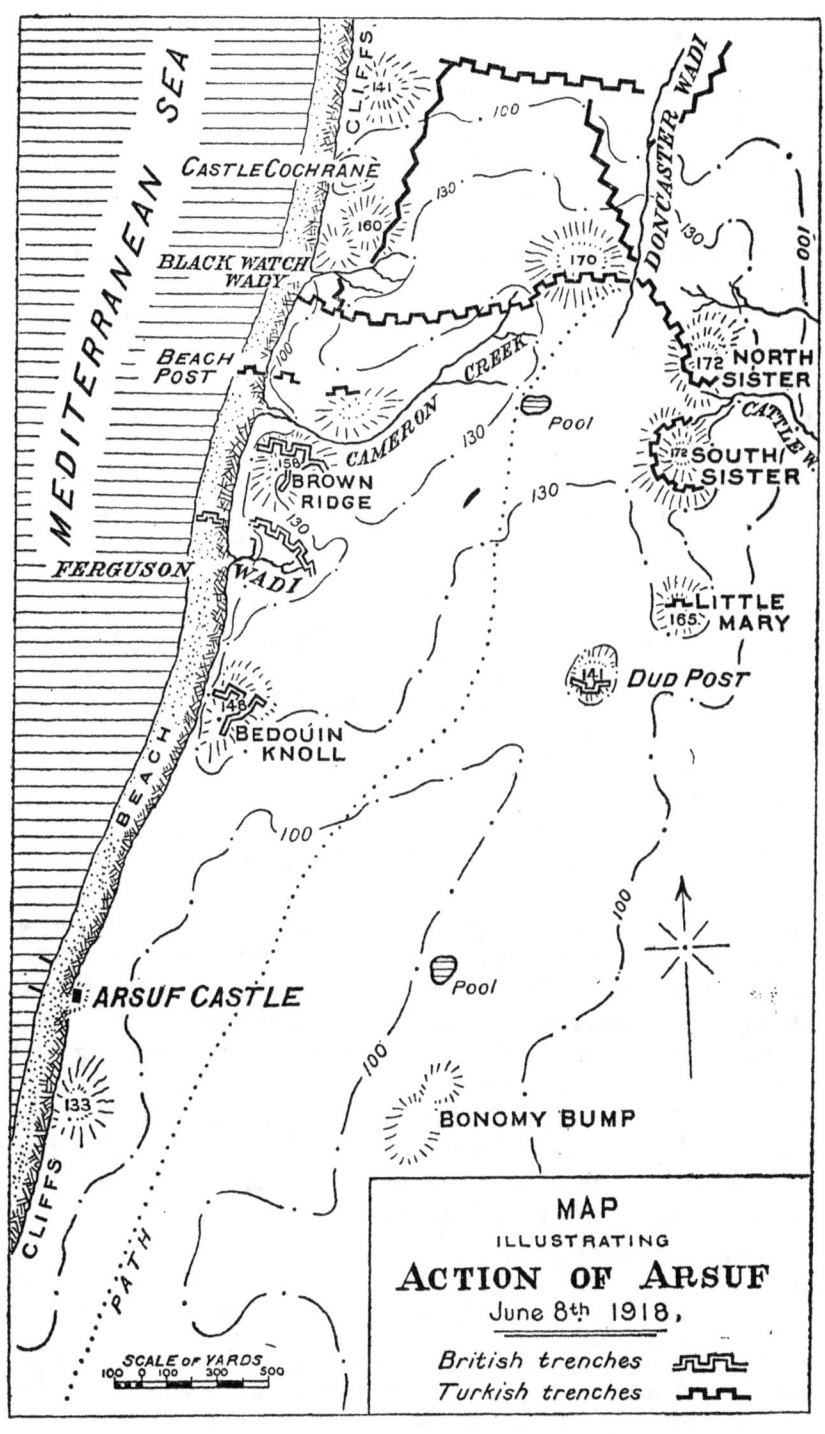

THE SECOND BATTALION THE BLACK WATCH

This brilliant little operation reflected great credit on the training and handling of the Battalion, and earned much commendation for the dash and skill with which it was executed. The promptitude with which the enemy counter-attack was met, and the help sent to the Guides, was a fine piece of work. The Commanding Officer of the Guides, Lieutenant Colonel Buist, came especially to see the Commanding Officer of the Battalion after the action, to express his appreciation of the work done by the two platoons of No. 1 Company. The total of prisoners was 110, of whom the majority were captured by The Black Watch; the enemy's total casualties were estimated at over 300. The losses of the Battalion were 9 officers (of whom 1 was killed and 1 died of wounds) and 58 other ranks (of whom 13 were killed). Captain W. A. Young, M.C., who died of his wounds, had been with the Battalion since September, 1915. A fine officer, of great personal courage, he had given many examples of gallant leading and had been twice wounded in Mesopotamia. The wounded included Major Cochrane, who was in command of the Battalion in the absence of Lieutenant Colonel Stewart, on leave in the United Kingdom; he was hit by a sniper late in the evening during a personal reconnaissance of the captured position. Captain R. D. Robertson, of the Gordons, who had been for some time attached to the Battalion, assumed command till Colonel Stewart's return a week or two later.

Lieutenant MacGregor was wounded early in the action and again in the evening of the 8th, but he did not leave the firing line till ordered to do so on the 9th, when he was sent to hospital. He subsequently received the Military Cross.

The work done by the medical officer, Captain Cameron, Royal Army Medical Corps, and the stretcher bearers, was, as usual, beyond all praise. Captain Cameron attended the wounded under heavy fire in the open and was himself hit on the 12th, though he did not leave his duty. One of the stretcher bearers, Private James, won a D.C.M. on the 10th for carrying in a wounded man under heavy fire. No. 7499 Lance Corporal Wilson, who served with the Battalion throughout the war, performed in this, as in every action in which the Battalion took part, most valuable service in the Regimental Aid Post. He, too, subsequently received the D.C.M.[1]

[1] "Teddy Falooral" was the name by which Lance Corporal Wilson was known throughout the Battalion. He was untiring. On the longest marches there he was, with a soldier's ordinary equipment, a medical haversack and two or three hurricane lanterns hanging from odd parts of his equipment. He was never "tidy," yet he was never tired; after the longest march "Teddy" would at once start his work and there he would sit half the day or night, doctoring sore feet, heedless of his own comfort or rest. In action he was the same: shelling never put "Teddy" out of step; he carried on, cool and methodical, careless of the

"THE RED HACKLE," JUNE, 1918

Major Cochrane received the D.S.O. for his leading of the Battalion in this action, and Lieutenant A. E. Blair the Military Cross. Sergeant J. Brodie was awarded a D.C.M. and Corporal Sharples, Lance Corporal Nicholson and Privates Smith, Gibson and Walker the Military Medal.

This action was the first since the granting of the Red Hackle to the Regiment in 1795, in which a Battalion of the Regiment went into action without this distinction in its head-dress. For a General Routine Order had been issued on June 4th, forbidding the wearing in the khaki helmet of any emblem not expressly authorized by the Dress Regulations to be so worn. Though a prescriptive right to wear the Red Hackle, won on the field of battle, in the head-dress on all occasions had existed since its first grant, and a circular letter issued by the Horse Guards in 1822 to every commanding officer in the army laid down that the Red Hackle was solely and exclusively a badge of honour for the Royal Highland Regiment—The Black Watch—it had not actually been inserted in the Dress Regulations that a Red Hackle could be worn in the khaki helmet. During the war, with that laxity in dress which the British Army always displays on service, other regiments had mounted, without any pretence of authority or claim, all kinds of emblems in the helmet, and it was to check this abuse that the General Routine Order was issued. Representations were at once made on behalf of the Regiment. Lieutenant Colonel Stewart, who was at home on sick leave, immediately interviewed the Colonel of the Regiment, General Sir John Maxwell. A short time afterwards, on June 28th, the following telegram was sent by the War Office to all fronts :—

" Battalions of Black Watch may wear Red Hackle in khaki
" helmet and tam-o'-shanter bonnets. Hackle to be provided
" regimentally."

Thus within a month the right to wear the Red Hackle was restored and confirmed for all time by the highest authority.

The Battalion remained in the front line for the rest of the month of June. The line was quickly consolidated and complete mastery over the enemy patrols and snipers established and maintained. The value to the Battalion of the system it established from the beginning of the war under Colonel Campbell, and continued under Colonels Harvey, Wauchope and Stewart, of having always a body of highly trained scouts and snipers at its disposal undoubtedly contributed greatly to its success in invariably main-

din and turmoil round him. He had served in the South African War and throughout the Great War, and never was a D.C.M. better earned.

"Teddy Falooral" died in Cologne when still serving with the Battalion, loved by every man as one who was always ready to give help in the hour of need.

taining its lines intact in defence, and frequently surprising the enemy in attack. It has been related how, in 1914, the offensive patrolling of the Battalion in the first line of trenches it occupied kept the enemy at a distance and saved it from much of the pressure and losses suffered on the rest of the front of the Indian Corps, and how, in 1916, the responsibility for the patrolling of the whole of the Brigade front was entrusted to the Battalion. In Palestine, too, its ascendancy gave the Battalion an inestimable moral advantage. It is to be hoped that the lesson will be remembered.

The enemy made one effort, on the 11th, to rush one of the new posts (Castle Cochrane), but left behind seven dead bodies, including two Germans. Thereafter the line was quiet, though an unlucky trench mortar shell, which landed in a dug-out, caused the death on the 27th of two subalterns, Second Lieutenants B. Quine and E. Ross.

One curious incident occurred during this tour. Lieutenant Haye found in the captured trenches a button stick with the regimental number and name of Private Mahon, who had been for a short time, in February, 1917, a prisoner in Turkish hands. Private Mahon rejoined the Battalion a few days later and identified his button stick, taken from him by his captors near Baghdad a year before.

On July 1st the Battalion was relieved by the 1/8th Gurkhas and withdrawn to Brigade reserve. The first fortnight of July was spent in Brigade reserve and the Battalion was then in Divisional reserve till August 12th, when it took over the Sisters section till August 28th. These two months were uneventful. The patrol work of the Battalion while in the Sisters section again earned the praise of the Divisional Commander, who wrote: " The information gained is most valuable; and the boldness and " initiative shown by the patrols and their success indicate a high " standard of training." The work of Lieutenant Henderson and Second Lieutenant Twentyman received special commendation.

On August 28th the Battalion went into reserve, and did not again go into the line till the great attack of September 19th, which was to destroy the Turkish army.

The Battalion had thus passed the summer under better conditions than in Mesopotamia. The heat had not been excessive and health was good. Incidentally, with the approach of cooler weather, the wearing of the kilt was resumed. Leave to Egypt and to a rest camp by the sea at El Arish had been open, and life was much more pleasant and less monotonous than in the two previous years. The Battalion reached the final of the Divisional football championship, but this time lost to the Seaforths after a replay. Casualties had been light and the Battalion was up to strength and in a high state of training for the coming operations.

CHAPTER VIII

SEPTEMBER, 1918, TO THE END OF THE WAR

1.—*The Battle of Megiddo, September 19th, 1918*

GENERAL ALLENBY's plan for the battle of September 19th was briefly as follows: the XXI Corps, which already comprised the 3rd and 7th Indian, the 54th and 75th Divisions, and was now strengthened by the addition of the 60th Division of the XX Corps, was to break the Turkish line on the coastal plain, and open a way for the Desert Mounted Corps, three divisions of cavalry, to pass through, gain the rear of the Turkish armies in the plain of Esdraelon, and there block all lines of retreat. The XXI Corps, after breaking the Turkish resistance in the plain, was to wheel to the right, drive the remnants of the enemy into the hills towards Tul Keram and Nablus, and, with the assistance of the XX Corps on the right, shepherd them into the arms of the cavalry. Nothing less than the complete destruction of the Turkish armies was thus hoped for. Like all great plans, it was a simple one. Its keystone was the secret concentration of an overwhelming force against the Turkish right. This was successfully accomplished by some able staff work and by the mastery which our Air Force gained over that of the enemy. One of the most remarkable features was the way in which the concentration of troops in the plain was concealed. The many orange groves north of Jaffa were used to hide troops; and for some time previous to the concentration the normal reserves were distributed in such a way that fresh troops could be accommodated without any increase of tentage or bivouacs being visible. Thus the Battalion while in reserve was quartered in two half-battalion camps; when the concentration took place, each of these camps was occupied by a whole battalion, and so the force in the area was doubled without any apparent change being noticeable from the air.

In the actual attack the 60th Division, from the XX Corps, was in the Coast sector, the 7th Division being on its right, with the 75th Division next. The objectives of the 7th Division on the 19th were, firstly, the enemy defences west of Tabsor, and secondly, with a swing north-east, the foothills about Et Taiyibeh.

The Battalion was lent to the 19th Brigade for the first phase of the attack, with the 1/8th Gurkhas in support. The remainder of the 21st Brigade was in reserve, and took no part in the initial assault.

On the portion of the front allotted to The Black Watch, the enemy's front line formed a large and pronounced salient. It was against the south face of this salient that the Battalion was directed; thus once the enemy's front line was passed, the defences of the west side of the salient, which were also in the area allotted to the Battalion, would be taken in flank. This involved the difficulty of a change of direction during the assault, a difficulty which was overcome by the use of compass bearings. The Turkish main position was in several lines, strongly entrenched and wired, and was covered by an outpost line some 1300 yards in advance, also wired, though not so strongly.

Several rehearsals of the attack were carried out, both by day and night, on ground well behind our lines, where the enemy trench system had been marked out with flags. Thus all ranks became acquainted with the general lie of the position they were to attack, and could find their way about it without difficulty. The general line of deployment had been fixed at about 500 yards from the enemy's main line. In The Black Watch sector it was 500 yards from the enemy outpost line, and some 1800 from his main line. For some days previous to the attack a strong line of standing patrols had been posted at night to prevent the Turks approaching the ground on which the attack was to form up. On the Battalion's front the enemy made no attempt to interfere with these patrols.

Early on the night of the 18th tapes were put down by a party under Lieutenant T. Gant, to mark the front of each company and platoon at the position of deployment; and guides led each company straight into their allotted stations.

The artillery barrage under which the attack was to be made was timed to move forward at the rate of 100 yards per minute, with a minute or two at each successive objective to allow the succeeding waves to come up. When the details of the assault were being elaborated some considered this rate too fast, but, as will be seen, it worked well, as far as the Battalion was concerned.

The following officers and warrant officers went into action with the Battalion, the remainder, in accordance with the practice at this stage of the war, remaining behind as a reinforcement:—

Headquarters

Lieutenant Colonel J. Stewart.
Captain N. Ritchie (Adjutant).
Lieut. T. A. Henderson, M.C.
Lieut. A. Crombie.
Captain W. M. Cameron, R.A.M.C.

No. 1 Company

Captain W. D. MacEwen. 2nd Lieut. D. Brown (R.S.F.)
2nd Lieut. A. Mackie (H.L.I.) C.S.M. Wilson.
    „   T. A. King.

BATTLE OF MEGIDDO, SEPTEMBER 19TH, 1918

No. 2 Company

Lieut. G. A. Boswell (Cameron Hrs.).
2nd Lieut. D. M. Murray (Gordons Hrs.).
2nd Lieut. W. A. Fairbairn (R. Scots).

No. 3 Company

Lieut. C. V. Hendry.
„ T. A. Mann.
2nd Lieut. J. J. Twentyman (H.L.I.).
2nd Lieut. J. M. Miller, D.C.M.

No. 4 Company

Lieut. J. MacGregor.
„ T. L. Smith.
2nd Lieut. W. C. Roy.
2nd Lieut. F. C. Swan (K.O.S.B.)
C.S.M. Nisbett.

(It will be noticed that no fewer than six other Scottish regiments were represented among the officers.)

The men went into action in shirt-sleeves, tunics being left behind. Sun helmets were also left and steel helmets worn. To lighten the weight, haversacks were not taken. Each man carried a bottle of water-sterilizing tablets.

Reveillé was sounded by the pipes ten minutes before midnight, and at ten minutes past one on the morning of the 19th the Battalion moved off. A mile from the position of deployment it halted and "A" echelon of the first line transport disengaged, while the companies went on in succession to their positions. It should be remarked that the 7th Division, as it would have to operate later in the roadless hills, had been equipped with pack transport.

All companies were in position by 4.15 a.m. The Battalion was deployed in eight waves, with two platoons in each, except in the second line, which consisted of one platoon, the remaining platoon being 150 yards in advance and on the left flank of the leading wave. It was the task of this platoon on reaching the enemy outpost line to proceed along its entire length and then rejoin the Battalion at its final objective. Each wave had its definite objective which it was to " mop up," then disengage to the left, re-form and follow on again in succession. Six extra Lewis guns had been issued a few days previous to the attack, and these were utilized as a battery. Their position at the commencement of the attack was immediately behind the right of the second wave, the wave that was detailed to deal with the enemy's front line. The orders to the commander of this Lewis-gun battery, Lieutenant Crombie, were to advance to the first objective just behind the second wave; assist in taking its objective if called upon; then to wait until the succeeding wave passed through, and accompany it to the second objective, and so on with the other waves. This system worked very well, and the extra guns gave great assistance. Two sections of the 125th Machine-gun company were also placed at the disposal of the Regiment; one section worked with the Lewis-gun battery and one with the seventh wave.

Zero hour was at 4.30 a.m. The ten to fifteen minutes which passed between the Battalion being reported in position and the commencement of the attack were quiet. From the number of Véry lights he put up the enemy appeared nervous, but only a few isolated shots passed harmlessly overhead; a little distance away a party of Turks was engaged in a nightly performance that was regular at some part of the line or another, that of hurling abuse or cajolements at their Mohammedan brethren in our Indian regiments; but to-night their audience was far larger, closer, and in a more critical mood than they suspected.

At Zero hour the bombardment began with a great roar, as if some button had been pressed which discharged every gun on the fifteen mile front of assault. The change from silence to pandemonium was startling, and with it the successive waves of the Battalion vanished menacingly into the darkness. Very little retaliating fire came from the enemy. It seemed as if they were stunned by the suddenness and volume of our fire, or too much alarmed and bewildered by the width of the attack to know what to do. What few shells came were scattered vaguely along the front; there was an entire absence of anything that could be called concentrated, controlled or directed artillery fire.

Of the actual assault the phrase " according to plan " for once in a way justified itself and practically sums up the whole story. The Turkish outpost line and each objective in turn was reached and dealt with according to the scheduled time-table of the barrage. The wire of the outpost line was found a formidable obstacle in places and had to be cut, as had also the wire of the front line, but thanks to careful organization this was accomplished without any confusion or delay. Any fire of the enemy was dealt with by Lewis guns. One enemy machine-gun post in the outpost line held up a portion of the assault for a few moments, till Sergeant May rushing forward with a Lewis gun, which he fired from the hip, caused the immediate surrender of the post. Sergeant May received the D.C.M. for his prompt courage.

In fact, the whole operation was executed with machine-like precision, and finally, exactly fifty minutes after Zero, the Reserve company and Battalion Headquarters arrived at the last objective,

BATTLE OF MEGIDDO, SEPTEMBER 19TH, 1918

roughly 5000 yards from the original starting point. A pace of 100 yards a minute had thus been maintained over a complicated maze of trenches, strongly garrisoned. The opposition was feeble after the first line was captured, the Turks, obviously shaken by the suddenness, pace and determination of the assault, surrendering freely.

The work of reorganization at once began, patrols being pushed out meanwhile to keep touch with the Gurkhas, who had passed through on their way to the second main objective.

By this time the enemy had been able to get a few heavy guns into action, but their fire was random and did no damage. The rapidity of the advance had prevented the telephone keeping up with the Regiment, but by seven o'clock the Brigade signallers appeared and communication was established. Between 7 and 8 a.m. all companies had rejoined Battalion Headquarters, having mopped up the areas allotted to them; and it was possible to ascertain the casualties and the number of prisoners and amount of material captured.

Only 2 men had been killed and no more than 2 officers and 19 men wounded, of whom 1 officer and 3 men were only slightly wounded and not evacuated. Two hundred and ninety-three prisoners had been taken, and one field gun, twelve machine guns and seven trench mortars captured. The number of prisoners above represents only those actually handed in to collecting stations by the Battalion, and only a small proportion of those who surrendered to it, who numbered well over a thousand; but so rapid was the advance that there was no time to deal with the majority of them and they were picked up by other units.

The accuracy of the barrage work of both artillery and machine guns was beyond praise; on the Battalion front the greater part of the barrage fire was arranged to come from a flank; although the companies were treading on the tail of the barrage the whole way, not one single casualty occurred from our own fire. To this accuracy and to the speed of the operation the lightness of our losses was due.

Soon after 8 a.m., when all companies had rejoined, the Battalion proceeded to clear the ground to the north as far as the Kh Ez Zerkiyeh marsh, some 4500 yards distant. No enemy was met with, but an enormous quantity of abandoned material was found. There was no time nor were there any facilities to collect this, but a report of its existence and position was sent in. A complete Turkish battery was seen, with all the personnel and horses lying dead round the guns, destroyed by a single shell. The Battalion then moved east and rejoined its own Brigade, the 21st. A halt of about an hour followed, till 11.45, when orders were received to move to Et Tireh, about seven miles distant. Prior to moving off, the men had the opportunity of refilling their water bottles at the Zerkiyeh Marsh. The water was almost black; but after the strenuous morning's work and with every prospect of an exhausting afternoon to come, the opportunity was eagerly seized.

After a trying march over sandy tracks, Et Tireh was reached about 4.30 p.m. With some difficulty the column passed through the village, which was crowded with guns, troops, and transport of neighbouring formations. After emerging on the east of the village the Battalion received orders to advance at once and attack El Medjel, a hill some two miles away, with a shrine and a few houses on top. The 20th Punjabis were at the same time sent off to the right, to co-operate with another battalion engaged against a village to the south of The Black Watch's objective.

The hill which the Battalion was to attack rose abruptly out of the plain, marking the change from the plain to the hill country. It was 700 feet high with a steep ascent, and was held by a small enemy force with machine guns or light automatic guns. The Battalion reached the foot of the hill at 5.30 p.m. after an advance over the flat open plain, but the actual ascent up the steep and rocky slope proved a hard task for tired men, and it was 6.30 before the objective was reached. The enemy did not wait for the assault, but retired down the eastern slopes, leaving behind one prisoner, an Austrian. The Adjutant, Captain Ritchie, did very fine work during the ascent of the hill, encouraging the tired men and carrying up a Lewis gun himself. Lieutenant Henderson and the scouts ably covered the advance, and the work they did on this and other occasions during the operations reflected great credit on them and on the training by Lieutenant Henderson.

The men were now completely exhausted, and many from thirst and fatigue had fallen behind during the climb up the hill. It was dark, and reorganization and the establishment of an outpost line took some time. Water was then the great need. The Austrian prisoner knew there was water somewhere in a ravine east of the hill, but could not give its exact location. Eventually two good wells were discovered by Private Woodward, one of the Regimental scouts. It was close on midnight before the Highlanders could settle down to rest, after twenty-four hours fighting and marching. There was, however, little rest for Battalion Headquarters, where messages were arriving and fresh dispositions for next day had to be made. The transport, owing to the roughness of the ground, was unable to reach the Battalion on El Medjel.

Next morning the Battalion moved at 5.45 a.m. and joined

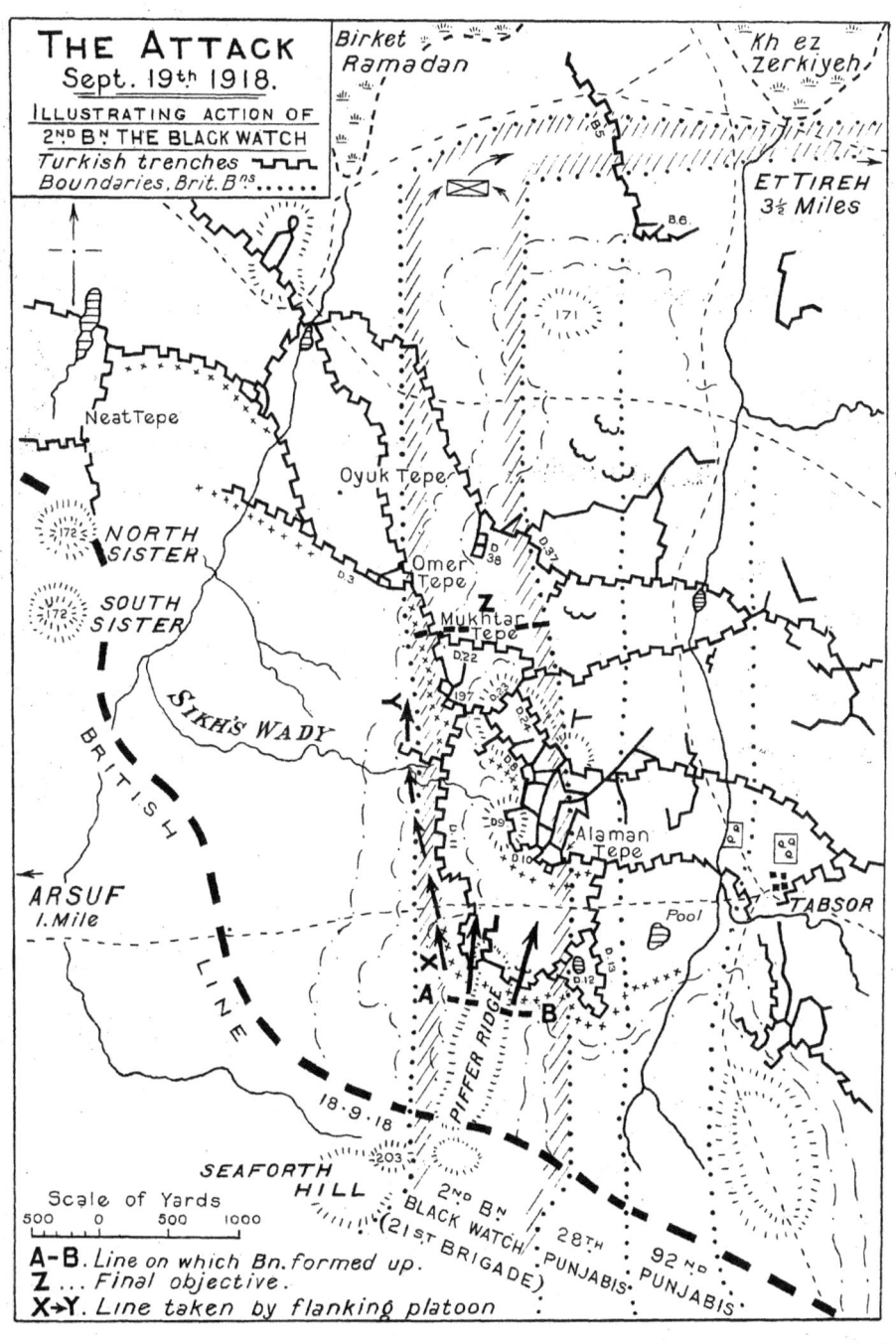

BATTLE OF MEGIDDO, SEPTEMBER 20TH, 1918

the remainder of the Brigade on a rough road to the south of the hill where they had spent the night. At 6.45 the whole column moved on into the hills, making north-east for Messudieh Junction, which was the 7th Division's objective. The task of the infantry was now to sweep the enemy into the arms of the cavalry who were already fast closing all lines of retreat of the Turkish armies.

On the way to the starting-point five more Austrians, wearing Red Cross brassards and armed with automatic pistols, were captured. These were doubtless some of the party which had opposed us the night before.

The road by Kefr Zibad and Beit Lid was a mere track, very stony and in places so narrow that the men had to march in file. At Kefr Zibad the road was congested with transport, and The Black Watch and Gurkhas halted for an hour and a half to water men and animals. The water was by no means good, but the men had had none since the previous night, and the animals none since the commencement of the attack on the 19th. Moving on again at about 1.30 p.m. the column came in sight of Beit Lid an hour and a half later. Here heavy firing was in progress, and it was learnt that another brigade of the Division, the 19th, was hotly engaged with an enemy rear-guard. When two miles short of the village the 21st Brigade received orders to disengage to the right and outflank the enemy from the east. Owing to the rough nature of the country this movement took time, and before the Guides, who led the advance, could make their presence felt, the village had been taken by direct assault. The two attacking battalions of the 19th Brigade—Seaforths and 125th Rifles—suffered somewhat severe casualties in the operation. The Black Watch was in reserve, but had one non-commissioned officer killed and one wounded by "overs." The non-commissioned officer, Lance Corporal A. Kelman, of Perth, was the last man of the Battalion to be killed in action during the war.

The 21st Brigade remained for the night in the positions it occupied at the end of the fight, the Guides on a hill they had reached on their outflanking movement, and the remainder of the Brigade in a wadi about 1½ miles south-east of Beit Lid. No rations or water reached the Brigade, nor could communication be established with Divisional Headquarters. The emergency ration was consumed. The transport was actually known to be within a mile or two, but so rough was the country that it was impossible to bring it up.

Next morning, the 21st, orders were received at 5 a.m. to resume the march on Messudieh, and ten minutes later the Battalion was on the move. It took nearly two hours to get out of the wadi and scale a steep hill to the north, Kh el Deir, where the

THE SECOND BATTALION THE BLACK WATCH

Guides had spent the night. Here a halt was made to fill water bottles. The march was continued at 8.30 a.m. and at 10 a.m. the Battalion went into bivouac about 1½ miles south of Messudieh Station.

By now the fate of the Turkish Seventh and Eighth Armies was sealed. The disorganized remnants, hemmed in a narrow space between our infantry and cavalry, surrendered during the next day or two. The Fourth Army, east of the Jordan, was also doomed, with its line of retreat already cut by the Arab forces under Feisal. Its annihilation followed shortly after. It was while at Messudieh that the troops of the 7th Division received the news which told them of the sweeping nature of the victory which their dash in the attack of September 19th and their determination and endurance on the two following days of hard marching in an almost waterless and trackless maze of hills had so worthily helped to win.

The following immediate awards were made to the Battalion:

M.C.	Captain N. M. Ritchie.
Bar to D.C.M.	Sergeant J. May.
	Private J. Morrison.
D.C.M.	Private W. Simpson.
	Lance Corporal G. McClunie.
	Sergeant F. Connell, M.M.
M.M.	Corporal T. Weir.
	Private J. Menzies.

2.—*Advance to Beirut and Tripoli*

The Turkish armies had been practically destroyed. It remained to gather the fruits of victory and occupy Syria. The mounted troops were already on the way to Damascus. It was decided to send the 7th Division to occupy Haifa and Acre, on which mounted troops were already moving, so as to have a force ready to move up the coast to Beirut in step with the cavalry advance along the plateau of the interior.

Moving from Messudieh in the afternoon of the 23rd, the Battalion reached Shuweike, north of Tul Keram, at 10.30 p.m. The march of sixteen miles revealed the appalling wreckage which our aeroplanes had caused amongst the retreating Turks on this road. Corpses of men and horses, and wrecked and abandoned transport of all kinds littered the pass through which the road ran. Night hid most of the horrors, but the atmosphere bore full evidence of what lay around.

From Shuweike the march to Haifa, which had been taken by the cavalry on the 23rd, after a brilliant little engagement, was completed in four stages, the intermediate halts being at Hudeira,

MARCHING THROUGH BEIRUT, OCTOBER, 1918

BEIRUT, OCTOBER, 1918

Zimmarin (both sites of Jewish colonies in which German Jews predominated) and Athlit, where stand the ruins of a Crusader castle. These marches, though not long, were very trying, the roads being mere sandy tracks, water scarce, and the heat sometimes approaching that of Mesopotamia.

At Haifa the Battalion spent four pleasant days, bivouacked close to the sea under the shadow of Mount Carmel, before resuming its march northwards. After such heavy and continuous marching it was not surprising that new boots and socks were required. These and other articles indented for at Haifa, were sent up by aeroplane and issued before the Battalion moved on.

On October 2nd the advance was resumed; the Battalion halted for two nights just east of Haifa railway station, and then moved on Beirut, the nightly halts being at Acre, Ras en Nakura, Ras el Ain, Khan Kamiye, Saida and Ed Damur. Beirut was reached on the 10th. By this time all ranks were accustomed to bad roads, and although the first two days were somewhat trying, few felt the long marches of the last three days, as the road was a great improvement on the sandy tracks of Palestine. It was during this march that signs were first noticed of a serious type of malaria which was responsible for many casualties in the Battalion later.

Bivouacked at Mar Rukos, "The Hill of Dancing," three miles south-east of Beirut, the Battalion remained for twelve days, during which it was called on to supply large working parties for unloading stores, cleaning up the streets of Beirut, and many other far from pleasant duties. The state of the city was terrible. It was no uncommon sight to see the dead bodies of little children starved to death lying uncared for and unnoticed in the streets; and the condition of the adult population was most miserable.

On October 13th the Battalion furnished a Guard of Honour, under Captain MacEwan, on the occasion of General Allenby's visit to Beirut.

During its stay near Beirut parties were employed in searching the surrounding countryside for arms. Many rifles and much ammunition was found, and a complete battery of field guns with limbers and ammunition was discovered about two miles from camp. With the battery was an Austrian artillery telescope, which was later presented to His Majesty the King, as Colonel-in-Chief of the Regiment.

Throughout October malaria had been taking heavy toll from the Battalion, and on the 19th influenza made its appearance, so it was with relief that orders were received for the march to Tripoli to commence on the 24th.

The road north ran through very different country from that which the Battalion had already traversed. The road, well metalled and with easy gradients, ran along the coast with the high hills of the Lebanon mountains rising abruptly from it, through a country almost void of cultivation, with the exception of a few olive groves and vineyards. On all sides the inhabitants welcomed the advancing troops, and many were the tales told of the completeness of the Turkish defeat.

After halting for successive nights at Junie, Jebeile, Batrun and Beshmezzin, the Battalion arrived at Medjelaya, three miles east of Tripoli, on the 28th, and moved on the following day to Ras el Lados, two miles N.E. of the town on the Homs road. Here, two days later, news was received that an armistice with Turkey had been signed.

By this time, malaria and influenza had taken such a hold that even the usual routine duties could only be carried out with the greatest difficulty. Since the battle on September 19th the Battalion had covered in twenty marching days 287 miles, half of which were over either sandy or rocky tracks. These marches were in pouring rain or oppressive heat; but with the exception of those, alas many, who fell victims to fever or influenza, not a man fell out; and it was a magnificent, though weak, Battalion that reached Ras el Lados on its last march of the " World War."

The announcement of the armistice with Turkey was received quietly, but on November 11th, when Germany took the same step, all realized that the war was over at last, and the rejoicings were somewhat more demonstrative.

3.—*After the War*

With the Armistice came many problems, chief of which was that of demobilization. Situated as it was in the north of Syria, the Battalion had little opportunity of gaining information regarding the progress of events further south. Nothing was known for some time as to how demobilization would be carried out, but the men realized that everything humanly possible was being done to expedite matters, and everyone did his utmost to tide over what was undoubtedly a trying period. Education schemes were set in motion; but these suffered very soon from the fact that the student class, from which the instructors were chosen, was the first to return to Scotland, and, excellent as was the idea, little came of it.

In November a large draft, over 500 men, arrived from India and Mesopotamia, supplemented later by others consisting of men who had been employed in various capacities in Egypt, Palestine and Syria, a few of whom had actually reached Aleppo.

The first draft of men for demobilization left the Battalion on November 24th, quickly followed by another, mainly of miners. Unfortunately shipping facilities proved inadequate, and

ALEXANDRIA, MAY, 1919

these men, with others similarly situated far from the port of embarkation, were delayed for some time, whilst those further south were more fortunate.

December passed without incident. Opportunities were given to officers and N.C.O.'s to visit Damascus and Baalbek; and many availed themselves of the chance. New Year was "seen in" by all ranks, the hour of midnight being struck by Acting Sergeant Major Parker, after which the pipers played in the New Year. The next day news reached the Battalion that it would move shortly to Beirut by road, No. 4 Company and baggage being sent by sea.

Starting on the 6th the Battalion reached Beirut on the 11th, where it was camped in the pine woods near the racecourse, and took over guards and duties from the 1st Battalion Seaforth Highlanders. Two days later, at short notice, the Battalion furnished a Guard of Honour, under Lieutenant Hendry, for General Allenby, who once again commented very favourably on its appearance and turnout. From January to the middle of March nothing worthy of record occurred. At various times drafts of men and officers left for Scotland whilst the remainder were employed on the usual routine duties of garrison life.

Advance orders for the move to Egypt reached the Battalion on March 15th. Men with only a few months' service remained in Beirut—the strength of this party being 9 officers and 171 other ranks—whilst the cadre and certain men due for demobilization (strength 18 officers and 479 other ranks) embarked on H.M.T. *Tagus* for Alexandria on the 24th. It was much regretted that a portion of the Battalion had to be left behind.

On reaching Alexandria, two days later, the Battalion proceeded to Mustapha, and camped within a stone's throw of the battlefield of Alexandria where, 118 years before, the Regiment had covered itself with glory under General Abercromby.

At this time all Egypt was in a state of civil unrest, and the Battalion found strong guards and picquets in many places. At Alexandria few actual disturbances took place; but the situation in Egypt was so grave that it was necessary to retain all available regular troops, and, in consequence, the departure of the cadre for Scotland was long delayed. Notwithstanding this, several parties of men overdue for demobilization were despatched, and by the end of May the strength of the Battalion had dwindled to 12 officers and about 200 other ranks.

In addition to the unrest amongst the civil population, serious trouble had arisen at Kantara and elsewhere amongst the men due for demobilization; the attitude of the Battalion towards this discontent cannot be passed over without record. Although approached by disaffected men of other formations on several occasions, and requested by them to send representatives to certain meetings, not one man of the Battalion complied. In fact, on one occasion a certain non-commissioned officer, who visited Mustapha with the view of persuading men to join the ranks of the disaffected, was chased out of the camp by men of The Black Watch armed with entrenching tool handles, and would undoubtedly have been badly injured had he been caught. Finally, such was the high state of discipline known to exist in the Battalion that on May 21st the Commanding Officer was directed to send a party consisting of 3 officers and 150 other ranks to Kantara, to arrest certain ringleaders who were to attend a meeting on the following day. The party arrived at Kantara, to find that news of their coming had preceded them; the meeting was not held, and no disturbance took place from that time onwards. A very high standard of discipline has ever been the boast of the Regiment, but at no period in its existence has it stood higher than it did in the 2nd Battalion in 1919; and it is well worth recording that although the men knew they were being retained in Egypt, partly by the action of certain disaffected units, they were as ready to do their duty, unpleasant as it was, as they had been in France, Mesopotamia and Palestine.[1]

Whilst at Mustapha a tug-of-war team, admirably coached and trained by Sergeant Major Parker, beat the Australian team in the final of a light-weight competition open to all Egypt, a performance all the more creditable in view of the fact that their opponents had a very large number of men from which to select, whereas The Black Watch team was chosen from 200 men. In a catch-weight competition The Black Watch lost to the Australians in the final.

On May 7th the Battalion was inspected by the Commander in-Chief, who expressed his admiration of its smartness. On June 3rd the cadre at last commenced its journey to Scotland; after a week at Port Said, it embarked at a strength of 9 officers and 62 other ranks on H.M.T. *Ellenger*. The route was by Taranto, thence by train across Italy and France to Boulogne. The cadre landed at Dover on June 24th, and proceeded to Perth next day. The Battalion had not been in the United Kingdom since it left for South Africa nearly twenty years previously, on October 21st, 1899.

In Perth the cadre received a great welcome, and on the 26th was entertained to luncheon by the Lord Provost and magistrates

---

[1] As a proof of the high reputation of the Battalion for discipline, it may be recorded that the Officer Commanding at Kantara, when asked during the most serious crisis of the disaffection in the demobilization camp what assistance he required, replied "A hundred men of The Black Watch or Seaforth Highlanders."

RETURN TO SCOTLAND

of the city, after a triumphal march through the leading thoroughfares.

The extraordinary welcome received at Perth was a symbol of the pride felt by their home city and by all Scotland at the record of the senior Highland regiment in the war. It had been true to its old fighting traditions. No higher praise than this can be given.

In this brief account of the doings of one of the battalions of the Regiment, some attempt has been made to show how the spirit of its old traditions was kept alive; and how that spirit, in its turn, reanimated the unit on the occasions when, after its own gallantry had reduced it to a small shattered remnant, it had to be reformed and rebuilt. The late war has added fresh traditions to the old ones, fresh flame to the spirit. Conditions of war change, but so long as the spirit remains undimmed, the future of this Battalion, and of the famous Regiment of which it forms a part, will be as glorious as its past.

NOTE TO CHAPTER VIII

The following officers and other ranks were serving with the 2nd Battalion on 4th August, 1914, and were still serving with it at the time of the Armistice, 11th November, 1918:—

Major and Quartermaster J. Anderson, D.C.M.
Lieut. B. Houston, M.C., D.C.M.
„ T. Kinnear.
„ T. Gant.
„ A. Muir.
„ J. Millar, D.C.M.
7083 R.Q.M.S. E. Hobbs.
8187 „ G. Cormack.
1543 C.S.M. A. Johnstone.
1471 „ J. Hutchison, D.C.M.
9359 C.Q.M.S. W. Wallace, D.C.M.
256 „ G. Morrison.
2037 „ S. Kelly.
6830 Sgt.-Piper J. Keith, D.C.M.
9640 Sgt.-Drummer J. Simpson, D.C.M.
7342 Sgt.-Cook J. Crawford.
1081 Sgt. J. Strachan, D.C.M.
1523 „ D. Yule, D.C.M.
947 „ D. Forrett.
655 „ R. Graham.
1993 „ J. Mitchell, D.C.M.
1414 „ R. Cowie.
7499 „ T. Wilson, D.C.M.
1443 „ D. Brown.
1193 „ D. Wilson.
204 „ A. Milligan, D.C.M.
1543 „ C. Easton, D.C.M.
1374 „ A. Waddell.
8358 Corpl.-Piper A. McLeod.
1774 Corpl. F. A. Powell.
974 „ P. Gilgallon.
8111 „ W. Foster, D.C.M.
875 „ A. McBeath.
679 Pte. W. Middleton.
843 „ W. Cooper.
911 „ P. Campbell.

THE SECOND BATTALION THE BLACK WATCH

1805	Pte.	A. Kelly.	1484	Pte.	R. Marshall.
274	,,	T. Leonard.	9300	,,	H. Andrews.
1284	,,	A. Proudfoot.	9221	,,	J. Davidson.
2064	,,	A. McLaren.	7423	,,	T. Lamont.
2121	,,	R. Ogilvie.	1171	Piper	T. Tallon.
1923	,,	G. Rae.	1998	,,	J. Jordan.
2024	,,	A. Smith.	2251	Drummer	A. Graham.
1785	,,	D. Watterson.	1468	,,	J. Hynie.

APPENDIX I

RECORD OF OFFICERS' SERVICE

THE SECOND BATTALION

Abbreviations.—"K."—Killed. "D. of W."—Died of Wounds. "W."—Wounded. "M."—Missing. "P. of W."—Prisoner of War. "S."—Evacuated Sick. "R."—Rejoined. "Reg."—Regular Army Commission. "M. in D."—Mentioned in Despatches.

Notes.—(*a*) For Officers commissioned from the Ranks, this record covers only the period of their service as Officers. (*b*) Where exact dates are not available, the month, where possible, has been entered.

Name	Rank on joining or commencement of campaign	Record	Actions at which present	Promotions and Regimental Appointments
Alexander, C. St. G.	2nd Lieut.	From 3rd B.W., 20.4.16. W., 22.4.16.	Sannaiyat, '16.	Nil.
Anderson, D. H.	2nd Lieut.	From 3rd B.W., 20.4.16. K., 22.4.16.	Sannaiyat, '16.	Nil.
Anderson, G. J.	2nd Lieut.	From 3rd B.W., 20.4.16. K., 22.4.16.	Sannaiyat, '16.	Nil.
Anderson, J.	Lt. & Qr.Mr.	From India with Bn. To Mesopotamia with Bn. S., 22.3.16. R., 9.4.16. Leave to U.K., 12.5.17 to 18.9.17. To Palestine with Bn.	Festubert, '14. Givenchy, '14. N. Chapelle, '15. Aubers Ridge, '15. Loos, '15. Shaikh Sa'ad, '16. Wadi River, '16. Hanna, '16. Sannaiyat, '16. Kut, '17. C. of Baghdad, '17. Mushaidie, '17. Istabulat, '17. Tekrit, '17. Arsuf, '18. Sharon, '18.	Q.M. to Bn. throughout the whole period of the war. Hon. Capt., 3.3.16. Major, 27.8.18.

295

Name	Rank on joining or commencement of campaign	Record	Actions at which present	Promotions and Regimental Appointments
Arthur, S.	2nd Lieut.	From U.K. (Reg.), 7.6.15. (Previous service in the ranks 20 yrs. 10 mths.) S., 20.8.15.	Nil.	Nil.
Bairstow, A. E.	2nd Lieut.	From U.K. (Reg.), 13.12.16. (Previous service as an Army Schoolmaster.) To Palestine with Bn. W., 8.6.18.	Kut, '17. C. of Baghdad, '17. Tekrit, '17. Arsuf, '18.	Nil.
Balfour-Melville, J. E.	2nd Lieut.	From 3rd B.W., 22.5.15. K., 25.9.15.	Loos, '15.	Nil.
Barstow, J. A.	2nd Lieut.	From 4th A. & S.H. for attachment, 2.6.15. W., 25.9.15. Transferred to B.W. as Regular Officer. R. in Mesopotamia, 22.8.16. S., 12.9.16. R., 28.9.16. W., 21.4.17. R., 3.6.17. Accidentally W., 22.11.17. R., 22.12.17. To Palestine with Bn. S., 29.10.18. R., 4.11.18. Subsequently S., and to U.K.	Loos, '15. Kut, '17. C. of Baghdad, '17. Mushaidie, '17. Istabulat, '17. Tekrit, '17. Arsuf, '18. Sharon, '18.	Lt., 1.7.17. A/Capt., 22.8.16 to end of war.
Blair, A. E.	2nd Lieut.	From 3rd B.W., 27.3.16. Leave to India, 17.5.17. R., 6.8.17. To Palestine with Bn. W., 8.6.18.	Hanna, '16. Sannaiyat, '16. Kut, '17. C. of Baghdad, '17. Mushaidie, '17. Istabulat, '17. Tekrit, '17. Arsuf, '18.	Lt., 1.7.17. Asst. Adjt., Aug., '16, to May, '17. A/Adjt., 8.12.17 to 19.12.17. A/Capt., 6.5.17 to 16.3.18; 23.4.18 to 26.5.18.

Name	Rank	Service	Battles	Honours
Blampied, H. J.	2nd Lieut.	From 11th B.W., 22.7.16. S., 31.10.16. R., 13.1.17. To Censor's Staff at Base, 27.1.17.	Nil.	Nil.
Bowie, H.	2nd Lieut.	From 3rd B.W., 7.10.15. (Previous service in the ranks 13 yrs. 6 mths.) To Mesopotamia with Bn. W., 7.1.16.	Shaikh Sa'ad, '16.	T/Lt., 12.10.15.
Boyd, A.	2nd Lieut.	From 6th B.W., 2.6.18. Attached to Brigade H.Q., 27.6.18.	Nil.	Nil.
Boyd, H. L. F.	Lieut.	From U.K. (Reg.), 12.5.15. S., 4.8.15. (Subsequently to 1st B.W. & K., 18.11.17.)	Nil.	Nil.
Broad, J. C. W.	2nd Lieut.	From 19th Canadians, 20.10.15. To Mesopotamia with Bn. W., 7.1.16.	Shaikh Sa'ad, '16.	Nil.
Brodie, E. M.	2nd Lieut.	From U.K. (Reg.), 5.6.15. S., 24.8.15.	Nil.	Nil.
Brown, G. J. R.	2nd Lieut.	From Service Bn. B.W., 11.4.17. W., 21.4.17. D. of W., 21.5.17.	Istabulat, '17.	Nil.
Browne, P. A.	2nd Lieut.	From 3rd B.W., 31.1.18. To Details, Kantara, 23.3.18.	Nil.	Nil.
Bruce, E.	2nd Lieut.	From 3rd B.W., 16. 4.16. S., 6.5.16. R., 12.9.16. S., 6.10.16. Died in Hospital, 17.11.16.	Sannaiyat, '16.	Nil.
Bruce, H. W.	2nd Lieut.	From 3rd B.W., 16.4.16. S., April, '16. R., 17.5.16. S., 18.5.16. R., 12.9.16. W., 6.11.16. R., 6.12.16. S., 17.1.17. R., 12.2.17. K., 17.2.17.	Sannaiyat, '16. Kut, '17.	Nil.

Name	Rank on joining or commencement of campaign	Record	Actions at which present	Promotions and Regimental Appointments
Buchan, J. I.	2nd Lieut.	Commissioned from ranks, 15.6.15. after 14 yrs. 7 mths. service. W., 25.9.15.	Loos, '15.	T/Capt., 6.8.15 to 25.9.15.
Buchanan, J. C. R.	2nd Lieut.	From 11th B.W., 9.6.17. To Palestine with Bn. To Trench Mortar Battery, 11.5.18.	Tekrit, '17.	Lt, 1.7.17.
Buchanan, K.	2nd Lieut.	From 3rd B.W., 7.10.15. To Mesopotamia with Bn. W., 7.1.16. R., 30.5.16. S., 28.6.16. R., 4.7.16. S., 12.8.16. R., 27.5.17. To Palestine with Bn. Attached Brigade Staff, 11.5.18. (Subsequently to Trench Mortar Battery.)	Shaikh Sa'ad, '16. Tekrit, 17.	Lt, 1.7.17.
Buist, K.	2nd Lieut.	From India with Bn. Left at Marseilles i/c Reinforcement. (Subsequently to 1st Bn. K., 15.1.15.)	Nil.	Nil.
Campbell, D.	Captain	From India with Bn. W.,21.11.14 R., 21.2.15. K., 18.5.15.	N. Chapelle, '15. Aubers Ridge, '15.	Nil.
Campbell, W. McL.	Lieut.-Col.	From India in command of Bn. S. and to U.K., 30.11.14.	Festubert, '14.	C.O. to 30.11.14.

Name	Rank	Service	Engagements	Notes
Cochrane, T. G. F.	2nd Lieut.	From Special R. of O., 11.3.15. W., 25.9.15. R., 13.10.15. To Mesopotamia with Bn. W., 7.1.16. R., 12.9.16. Leave to India, 8.6.17. R., 28.8.17. To Palestine with Bn. W., 8.6.18.	Aubers Ridge, '15. Loos, '15. Shaikh Sa'ad, '16. Kut, '17. C. of Baghdad, '17. Mushaidie, '17. Istabulat, '17. Tekrit, '17. Arsuf, '18.	T/Capt., 1.8.15. Lt., 18.2.15. Capt., 18.10.15. A/Major, 14.9.16 to 15.4.17 and 14.4.18 to 8.6.18. A/Lt.-Col. 8.5.18 to 14.5.18. 2nd-in-C., 12.9.16 to 14.4.17; 21.4.17 to 25.2.18; 30.3.18 to 31.3.18. C.O., 1.4.18 to 8.6.18.
Cocks, C. V. S.	2nd Lieut.	From 3rd B.W., 6.10.15. To Mesopotamia with Bn. 7.1.16.	Shaikh Sa'ad, '16.	Nil.
Cotterill, J. H.	2nd Lieut.	From 3rd B.W., 27.3.16. W., 22.4.16. R., 18.12.16. W., 14.3.17. D. of W., 15.3.17.	Hanna, '16. Sannaiyat, '16. Kut, '17. C. of Baghdad, '17. Mushaidie, '17.	Nil.
Cowie, T. McK.	2nd Lieut.	From 11th B.W., 2.12.16. W. & M., 16.2.17. Reported P. of W. Recaptured, 1.3.17. Subsequently to India.	Kut, '17.	Nil.
Cox, T. H. C.	Captain	From 3rd B.W., 2.3.18. S., 2.5.18. R., 26.5.18. S., 15.8.18. R., 24.8.18. S., 3.11.18.	Arsuf, '18. Sharon, '18.	Transport Officer, 4.3.18 to end of war.
Crombie, A.	2nd Lieut.	From 3rd B.W., 10.8.16. S., 6.3.17. R., 20.4.17. Leave to India, 16.6.17. R., 17.9.17. S., 27.11.17. R., 27.1.18. S., 10.10.18. R., 16.10.18.	Kut, '17. C. of Baghdad, '17. Istabulat, '17. Tekrit, '17. Arsuf, '18. Sharon, '18.	Lt., 1.7.17. A/Capt., June, 1918.

Name	Rank on joining or commencement of campaign	Record	Actions at which present	Promotions and Regimental Appointments
Cumming, A. B.	2nd Lieut.	From U.K. (Reg.), 22.10.15. To Mesopotamia with Bn. W., 7.1.16. R., 9.4.16. K., 22.4.16.	Shaikh Sa'ad, '16. Sannaiyat, '16.	M.G. Officer, Dec., '15 to 7.1.16.
Curdie, G.	2nd Lieut.	From U.K. (Reg.), 31.7.15. To Mesopotamia with Bn. W., 19.1.16.	Loos, '15. Shaikh Sa'ad, '16. Wadi River, '16.	A/Adjt., 7.1.16 to 19.1.16. T/Capt., 23.11.15 to 19.1.16.
Dawson, J.	2nd Lieut.	From 3rd B.W., 10. 8. 16. S., 1.9.16. R., 9.9.16. S., 20.9.16.	Nil.	Nil.
Denison, A. C.	Lieut.	From India with Bn. W., 10.3.15. R., 20.5.15. K., 25. 9. 15.	Festubert, '14. Givenchy, '14. N. Chapelle, '15. Loos, '15.	A/Capt., 1915.
Dougall, A. T.	2nd Lieut.	From 3rd B.W, 31.1.18. To Details, Kantara, 23.3.18.	Nil.	Nil.
Douglas, A.	2nd Lieut.	From 3rd B.W., 6.10.15. To Mesopotamia with Bn. W., 13.1.16. D. of W., 19.2.16.	Shaikh Sa'ad, '16. Wadi River, '16.	Nil.
Downie, A. T.	2nd Lieut.	From Service Bn. B.W., 15.6.17. S., 12.8.17. To Trench Mortar Battery, 16.11.17.	Nil.	Lt., 18.8.17.
Drumlanrig, F. A. K. D. (Viscount)	2nd Lieut.	From U.K. (Reg.), 17.6.15. S., 20.7.15.	Nil.	Nil.
Duffus, P. B.	Lieut.	From attachment to M.G. Corps (Reg. B.W.), 16.6.18. S., 4.11.18. R., after Armistice. To U.K. with Cadre.	Sharon, '18.	Asst. Adjt., June, '18 to end of war.

Dundas, R. H.	2nd Lieut.	From 3rd B.W., 6.10.15. To Mesopotamia with Bn. W., 21.1.16. R. from R.T.O. duties, 17.10.14. S., 13.11.14.	Shaikh Sa'ad, '16. Wadi River, '16. Hanna, '16.	Nil.
Durie, J. A.	Lieut.		Nil.	Nil.
Edye-Duff, J.	2nd Lieut.	From 3rd B.W., 27.1.18. To Details, Kantara, 23.3.18. R., 12.6.18. To R.A.F., 9.7.18.	Nil.	Lt., 23.2.18.
Egerton, P. G.	2nd Lieut.	From 3rd B.W., 21.3.15. W., 25.9.15. R., in Mesopotamia as a Captain, 27.7.17. To Trench Mortar Battery, 14.10.17. (Subsequently D. of W. received in Palestine.)	Aubers Ridge, '15. Loos, '15.	Lt., 1915. Capt., 8.3.16.
Eglinton, D. C.	2nd Lieut.	From Scottish Rifles (Temporary Commission), 26.3.15. W., 8.10.15.	Aubers Ridge, '15. Loos, '15.	Nil.
Forrester, H. F.	2nd Lieut.	From U.K. (Reg.), 27.3.16. W., & M. (presumed killed), 22.4.16.	Hanna, '16. Sannaiyat, '16.	Nil.
Forrester, R. E.	Captain	From India with Bn. W., 8.11.14 (K. with 1st Bn, 9.6.15.)	Nil.	Nil.
Gant, T.	2nd Lieut.	Commissioned from ranks, 16.2.17, after 9 yrs. 5 mths. service. W., 4.3.17. R., 26.4.17. To Palestine with Bn.	Kut, '17. C. of Baghdad, '17. Mushaidie, '17. Tekrit, '17. Arsuf, '18. Sharon, '18.	Lt., 6.8.18. A/Q.M., 12.5.17 to 18.9.17.
George, W.	2nd Lieut.	Commissioned from ranks, 4.12.14, after 11 yrs. 10 mths. service. K., 12.3.15.	Givenchy, '14. N. Chapelle, '15.	Nil.
Gillespie, T.	2nd Lieut.	From 3rd B.W., 1.12.16. K., 14.3.17.	Kut, '17. C. of Baghdad, '17. Mushaidiya, '17.	Nil.

Name	Rank on joining or commencement of campaign	Record	Actions at which present	Promotions and Regimental Appointments
Gilmour, C. D.	Lieut.	From U.K. (Reg.), 25.2.15. W. 10.3.15. R., 1.3.16. W., 22.4.16.	N. Chapelle, '15. Hanna, '16. Sanniayat, '16.	A/Adjt., 2.3.16 to 22.4.16.
Gilroy, A.	2nd Lieut.	From U.K. (Reg.), 21.10.16. S., 28.2.17. R., 6.3.17. W., 21.4.17.	Kut, '17. C. of Baghdad, '17. Mushaidie, '17. Istabulat, '17.	Lt., 1.1.17.
Gilroy, K. R.	Lieut.	From India with Bn. W. (slight), 5.11.14. K., 12.3.15.	Festubert, '14. Givenchy, '14. N. Chapelle, '15.	Nil.
Gordon, C. W. E.	Captain × 6 S Staffs	From a Territorial Adjutancy, 16.6.15. S., 1.8.15. R., 15.9.15. W., 25.9.15. (Subsequently K. in command of a brigade.) 123 Bde	Loos, '15.	Major, 1.9.15. 2nd-in-C., 6.9.15 to 25.9.15.
Gordon-Brown, D. S.	2nd Lieut.	From U.K. (Reg.), 26.4.16. W. (accidentally), 28.6.16.	Nil.	Nil.
Graham-Murray, R. T., The Hon.	Captain	From 3rd B.W., 27.3.16. To Staff in India, 28.3.16.	Nil.	Nil.
Graham-Scott, K.	2nd Lieut.	From U.K. (Reg.), 13.4.17. S., 3.10.17.	Istabulat, '17.	Lt., 16.2.17.
Grassie, J. T.	2nd Lieut.	From U.K. (Reg.), 1.3.16. Previous service in ranks 8 yrs. 1 mth W., 6.4.16.	Hanna, '16. Sanniayat, '16.	Nil.
Gray, J. M.	2nd Lieut.	From 6th B.W., 5.7.18. S., 27.9.18.	Nil.	Nil.

Name	Rank	Service	Battles	Notes
Grierson, W. G.	2nd Lieut.	From 11th B.W., 11.4.17. S., 15.4.17. R., 13.5.17. S., 30.5.17. R., 29.7.17. R., 27.1.18. To Base Depot, 27.12.17. R., 27.1.18. To Details, Kantara, 23.3.18.	Nil.	Lt., 29.7.17.
Grieve, A. MacL.	Captain	From 3rd B.W., 16.4.16. S., 27.4.16. R., 4.7.17. To Political Staff, June, '17. R., December, '17. To Base Depot, Basra, 27.12.17. R., 27.1.18. To 7th Div. Staff, February, '18.	Sannaiyat, '16.	Nil.
Haig, D.	2nd Lieut.	From 3rd B.W., 11.4.17. S., 6.5.17.	Istabulat, '17.	Nil.
Haldane, J. B. S.	Captain	From 3rd B.W., 14.12.16. W. (accidentally), 22.2.17.	Kut, '17.	Nil.
Hamilton-Johnston, D. C.	Lieut.	From India with Bn. W. (slight), 10.12.14. W., 3.3.15. R. as a Captain, 5.10.15. To Mesopotamia with Bn. W. & M. (presumed killed), 21.1.16.	Festubert, '14. Givenchy, '14. Shaikh Sa'ad, '16. Wadi River, '16. Hanna, '16.	A/Adjt., 6.10.15. to 7.1.16. T/Major, 7.1.16. to 21.1.16. A/C.O., 8.1.16 to 21.1.16.
Harvey, W. J. St. J.	Major	R. from Egyptian Army as Second-in-Command, November, 1914. Assumed Command of the Bn. vice Lieut.-Col. W. M. Campbell, 11.2.14. To Command of Dehra Dun Brigade, 6.9.15. (W. (Mesop.), 19.1.16. D. of W., 1.2.16.)	Givenchy, '14. N. Chapelle, '15. Aubers Ridge, '15.	2nd-in-C., Nov., 1914 to 31.11.14. C.O., 1.12.14 to 5.9.15.

Name	Rank on joining or commencement of campaign	Record	Actions at which present	Promotions and Regimental Appointments
Haye, R.	2nd Lieut.	From 3rd Bedfordshire Regt. for attachment, 28.4.17. Transferred to 3rd B.W., 14.8.17. S., 26.10.17. R., 30.11.17. To Palestine with Bn. S., 28.1.18. R., 24.2.18. Attached 21st Brigade H.Q. (from 11.5.18) during summer of 1918. S., 1.9.18.	Tekrit, '17.	Lt., 1.7.17.
Henderson, C. R. B.	Captain	From India with Bn. W., 11.11.14. R., 5.2.15. W., 19.4.15. R., 26.7.15. W., 25.9.15. R. in Mesopotamia as a Major, 9.2.16. S., 3.3.16. R. in Egypt, 22.2.18. S., 30.3.18.	N. Chapelle, '15. Loos, '15.	Adjt., to 25.9.15. A/C.O., 9.2.16. 2nd-in-C., 26.2.18 to 30.3.18.
Henderson, N. C.	2nd Lieut.	From U.K. (Reg.), 22.5.15. K., 25.9.15.	Loos, '15.	Nil.
Henderson, T. A.	2nd Lieut.	From 11th B.W., 7.10.15. To Mesopotamia with Bn. W., 7.1.16. R., 15.1.16. S., 21.6.16 R., 28.6.16. S., 12.9.16. R., 22.9.16. S., 6.4.17. R., 31.1.18. To U.K. on leave, 4.11.18.	Shaikh Sa'ad, '16. Hanna, '16.[1] Sannaiyat, '16. Kut, '17. Mushaidie, '17. Arsuf, '18. Sharon, '18.	Lt., 1.7.17.

[1] The only officer to go through this action unwounded.

Hendry, C. V.	2nd Lieut.	From 11th B.W., 22.7.16. S., 17.9.16. R., 7.11.17. To Base Depot, 27.12.17. R., 27.1.18.	Arsuf, '18. Sharon, '18.	Lt., 1.7.17.
Holland, B. T.	2nd Lieut.	From Artists' Rifles, 15.1.15. K., 10.3.15.	N. Chapelle, '15.	Nil.
Holt, A. V.	Lieut.	From U.K. (Reg.), 14.12.14. S., 31.1.15. R., 10.2.15. To Royal Flying Corps, 5.8.15.	Givenchy, '14. N. Chapelle, '15. Aubers Ridge, '15.	Capt., 30.1.15.
Houston, B. S.	2nd Lieut.	Commissioned from ranks, after 14 yrs. 5 mths. service, 15.2.17. S., 19.4.17. R., 14.5.17. To Palestine with Bn. Leave to U.K., 28.2.18. R., 21.5.18.	Kut, '17. C. of Baghdad, '17. Mushaidie, '17. Tekrit, '17. Arsuf, '18. Sharon, '18.	Lt., 16.8.18.
Hunter, S. L.	2nd Lieut.	From 11th B.W., 16.8.16. S., 24.8.16. R., 30.8.16. S., 4.10.16. R., 5.11.16. S., 22.12.16. To 3rd Echelon, 22.3.17.	Nil.	Nil.
Hunter, W. C.	2nd Lieut.	From 3rd B.W., 7.10.15. To Mesopotamia with Bn. W., 7.1.16.	Shaihk Sa'ad, '16.	Nil.
Hutchison, I. O.	2nd Lieut.	From Artists' Rifles, 15.1.15. To Mesopotamia with Bn. K., 7.1.16.	Aubers Ridge, '15. Loos, '15. Shaikh Sa'ad, '16.	Nil.
Inglis, J. N.	Lieut.	From India with Bn. S., 14.5.15. R. in Mesopotamia as a Captain, 1.3.16. K., 22.4.16.	Festubert, '14. Givenchy, '14. N. Chapelle, '15. Aubers Ridge, '15. Hanna, '16. Sannaiyat, '16.	A/Adjt., 11.11.14 to 4.2.15 and 20.4.15 to 14.5.15.

Name	Rank on joining or commencement of campaign	Record	Actions at which present	Promotions and Regimental Appointments
Jamieson, M.	2nd Lieut.	From 11th B.W., 14.12.16. S., 19.4.17. R., 18.5.17. S., 3.7.17. R., 24.7.17. To Palestine with Bn. S., 1.5.18. R., 12.6.18. W. (slight), 17.6.18. S., 10.8.18. R. 20.8.18. S., 5.11.18.	Kut, '17. C. of Baghdad, '17. Mushaidie, '17. Tekrit, '17. Sharon, '18.	Lt, 1.7.17.
Jeff, J.	2nd Lieut.	From 3rd B.W., 20.6.16. S., 28.6.16. R., 4.7.16. S., 21.7.16. R., 23.7.16. S., 13.12.16. R., 9.2.17. Leave to India, 25.5.17. R., 6.8.17. To Palestine with Bn. To U.K. with Cadre.	Kut, '17. C. of Baghdad, '17. Mushaidie, '17. Istabulat, '17. Tekrit, '17. Arsuf, '18. Sharon, '18.	Lt, 1.7.17. A/Capt., 8.6.18 to end of war. Signalling Officer during 1917.
Jessop, J. C.	2nd Lieut.	From 3rd B.W., 31.1.18. To Details, Kantara, 23.3.18.	Nil.	Nil.
Johnson, T.	2nd Lieut.	Commissioned from ranks, 5.4.15, after 14 yrs. 5 mths. service. W. (slight), 22.4.15. W. (slight), 19.5.15. S., 8.6.15.	Aubers Ridge, '15.	Nil.
Kay, W. B.	2nd Lieut.	From 11th B.W., 12.6.18. To Brigade H.Q., June, '18. Died in Hospital, 19.11.18	Sharon, '18.	Nil.
Kennedy, J.	2nd Lieut.	Commissioned from ranks, 4.12.14 after 14 yrs. 9 mths. service. To 5th B.W. as Adjutant, 23.4.15.	Givenchy, '14. N. Chapelle, '15.	Nil.

Name	Rank	Service	Engagements	Honours
King, J. A.	2nd Lieut.	Commissioned from ranks, 1.2.18, after 16 yrs. 6 mths. service. To U.K. with Cadre.	Arsuf, '18. Sharon, '18.	Nil.
Kinnear, T.	2nd Lieut.	Commissioned from ranks, 16.2.17, after 11 yrs. 6 mths. service. W. (accidentally), 22.2.17. R., 25.4.17. To Palestine with Bn. Leave to U.K., 28.2.18 to 17.5.18. W., 8.6.18.	Kut, '17. Tekrit, '17. Arsuf, '18.	Lt., 6.8.18. Bn. Transport Officer, 3.5.17 to 18.8.17.
Kirk, D. K.	Lieut.	From U.K. (Reg.), 6.10.15. S., 17.10.15.	Nil.	Nil.
Loudon, T.	2nd Lieut.	From 3rd B.W., 11.4.17. To Palestine with Bn. K., 8.6.18.	Istabulat, '17. Tekrit, '17. Arsuf, '18.	Lt., 5.3.18.
Lumsden, D.	2nd Lieut.	From 3rd B.W., 14.1.15. W. 6.5.15. (Subsequently to 1st Bn.)	N. Chapelle, '15.	Nil.
Lunn, B. H.	2nd Lieut.	From 11th B.W., 6.7.16. S., 24.7.16. R., August, '16. S., 30.11.16.	Nil.	Nil.
Lyell, T., M.C.	Captain	From 5th B.W., 1.5.18. To 7th Div. H.Q., 28.9.18.	Arsuf, '18. Sharon, '18.	Nil.
McArthur, D.	2nd Lieut.	From B.W., 11.4.17. D. of W., 21.4.17.	Istabulat, '17.	Nil.
McCall-McCowan, D.	2nd Lieut.	From 3rd B.W., 31.1.18. S., 18.6.18	Arsuf, '18.	Nil.
McConaghey, C. J.	2nd Lieut.	From U.K. (Reg.), 22.5.15. W., 25.9.15. R., 19.4.16. K., 22.4.16.	Loos, '15. Sannaiyat, '16.	Nil.

Name	Rank on joining or commencement of campaign	Record	Actions at which present	Promotions and Regimental Appointments
MacEwen, W. D.	Lieut.	From 3rd B.W. (attached to 1st H.L.I.), 3.3.16. W., 22.4.16. R., 12.9.16. S., 25.9.16. R., 9.6.17. To Palestine with Bn. To H.Q. 7th Div., 9.5.18. R., 30.8.18. To U.K. with Cadre.	Hanna, '16. Sannaiyat, '16. Tekrit, '17. Sharon, '18.	A/Capt., 20.7.17 to 2.3.18. Capt., Nov., '17.
Macfarlane, R.	Captain	From 3rd B.W., 26.4.16. W., 10.6.16. R., 1.12.16. S., 18.1.17. R., 9.2.17. W., 14.3.17. R., 16.3.17. K., 21.4.17.	Kut, '17. C. of Baghdad, '17. Mushaidie, '17. Istabulat, '17.	Nil.
Macfarlane-Grieve, R. W.	2nd Lieut.	From 3rd B.W., 6.10.15. To Mesopotamia with Bn. W., 7.1.16. R., 23.4.16. S., 15.6.16. R., 21.6.16. To M.G.C., 25.9.16. S., 18.10.16.	Shaikh Sa'ad, '16.	Bn. M.G. Officer, 19.8.16.
MacGregor, J.	2nd Lieut.	From Service Bn., B.W., 21.10.17. To Palestine with Bn. W., 8.6.18. R., 26.7.18.	Tekrit, '17. Arsuf, '18. Sharon '18.	Lt. 5.2.18.
McKenzie, G. M.	2nd Lieut.	From 3rd B.W., 20.6.16. S., 7.7.16. R., 17.7.16. S., 1.9.16. R., 9.10.16. To M.G. Corps, 26.10.16.	Nil.	Nil.

McLeod, G. C. S.	Captain	From India with Bn. W., 9.11.14. R., 22.3.15. W., 9.5.15. D. of W., 13.5.15.	Aubers Ridge, '15.	Nil.
MacLeod, I. B.	Lieut.	From India with Bn. K., 17.4.15.	Festubert, '14. Givenchy, '14. N. Chapelle, '15.	Lt., 9.9.14.
MacLeod, L.	2nd Lieut.	From Service Bn, B.W., 5.9.15. W. & P. of W., 25.9.15.	Loos, '15.	Nil.
McMicking, N.	Lieut.	From India with Bn. W., 11.3.15. (slight). To 6th Gordon Hrs. as Adjt., 5.5.15.	Festubert, '14. Givenchy, '14. N. Chapelle, '15.	Nil.
McWilliams, H.	2nd Lieut.	From Special R. of O., 22.5.15. W., 25.9.15. (Subsequently K. in France.)	Loos, '15.	Nil.
Mann, J. A.	2nd Lieut.	From 3rd B.W., 31.1.18 To U.K. with Cadre.	Arsuf, '18. Sharon, '18.	Nil.
Martin, A. W. D.	2nd Lieut.	From 3rd B.W., 31.1.18. To Details, Kantara, 23.3.18.	Nil.	Nil.
Miles, L. G.	2nd Lieut.	From Artists' Rifles, 15.1.15. S., 7.6.15.	N. Chapelle, '15. Aubers Ridge, '15.	Nil.
Miller, J. M.	2nd Lieut.	Commissioned from Ranks, 28.8.18, after 9 yrs. 10 mths. service. To U.K. with Cadre.	Sharon, '18.	Nil.
Miller-Stirling, E. G. B.	Lieut.	From 69th Punjabis, I.A., 22.7.16. S., 20.8.16. R., 19.10.16 D. of W., 15.3.17.	Kut, '17. C. of Baghdad, '17. Mushaidie, '17.	Nil.
Montgomerie, W. D.	2nd Lieut.	From 11th B.W., 15.6.17. To G.H.Q. as Cypher Officer, 22.8.17.	Nil.	Nil.

Name	Rank on joining or commencement of campaign	Record	Actions at which present	Promotions and Regimental Appointments
Moore, G. G.	2nd Lieut.	From Artists' Rifles, 15.1.15. W., 9.5.15. (Subsequently to 1st Bn. & R.F.C.)	N. Chapelle, '15. Aubers Ridge, '15.	Nil.
Morrison, R. S.	2nd Lieut.	From 3rd B.W., 5.10.15. To Mesopotamia with Bn. W., 7.1.16. D. of W., 8.1.16.	Shaikh Sa'ad, '16.	Nil.
Muir, A.	2nd Lieut.	Commissioned from ranks, 29.5.17, after 16 yrs. 9 mths. service. To Palestine with Bn. W., 8.6.18. R., winter of 1918. To U.K. with Cadre.	Tekrit, '17. Arsuf, '18.	Lt., 29.11.18.
Murray, H. F. F.	Captain	From India with Bn. W. 12.3.15.	Festubert, '14. Givenchy, '14. N. Chapelle, '15.	Nil.
Murray-Stewart, D.	2nd Lieut.	From 10th B.W., 14.12.16. S., 16.12.17. R., 27.1.18. S., 18.2.18. R., 28.2.18. To Details, Kantara, 23.3.18. R., 2.6.18. To R.A.F., 18.6.18.	Kut, '17. C. of Baghdad, '17. Mushaidie, '17. Istabulat, '17. Tekrit, '17. Arsuf, '18.	Lt., 1.7.17. A/Capt., 6.5.17 to 8.7.17; 27.10.17 to 16.12.17.
Orr-Ewing, H. E. D.	Lieut.	Left with Details in India. R., from U.K., 20. 3. 15. S., 14.5.15.	Aubers Ridge, '15.	T/Capt, 15.11.14 to 1.2.15. Capt., 2.2.15.

Name	Rank	Service	Battles	Remarks
Park, M. E.	Lieut.	From U.K. (Reg.), 25.1.15. To Mesopotamia with Bn. 7.1.16. R., 28.1.16. W., 10.4.16. R., 29.4.16. S., 25.3.17. R., 27.5.17. Leave to India, 2.6.17. R., 22.12.17. To Palestine with Bn. W., 7.4.18.	N. Chapelle, '15. Aubers Ridge, '15. Loos, '15. Shaikh Sa'ad, '16. Hanna, '16. Sannaiyat, '16. Kut, '17. C. of Baghdad, '17. Mushaidie, '17.	Transport Officer during part of 1915. A/Adjt., 13.5.15 to 26.7.15. T/Capt., 10.6.15. Capt., 2.3.16.
Paterson, J. C.	2nd Lieut.	From 3rd B.W., 17.10.15. S., 29.10.15. R., November, '15. To Mesopotamia with Bn. 7.1.16.	Shaikh Sa'ad, '16.	Nil.
Paton, G. D.	Lieut.	From 6th B.W., 2.6.18. S., 10.8.18. R., 31.8.18. S., 10.9.18.	Arsuf, 18.	Nil.
Peebles-Chaplin, C. J.	2nd Lieut.	From 3rd B.W., 22.5.15. W., 19.7.15.	Nil.	Nil.
Peel, T.	2nd Lieut.	From Service Bn, B.W., 11.4.17. D. of W., 21.4.17.	Istabulat, '17.	Nil.
Plunkett, H. A. T.	2nd Lieut.	From U.K. (Reg.), 13.3.15. To Mesopotamia with Bn. K., 7.1.16.	Aubers Ridge, '15. Loos, '15. Shaikh Sa'ad, '16.	Nil.
Porter, W.	2nd Lieut.	From 1/7th B.W., 27.1.18. Details, Kantara, 23.3.18.	Nil.	Nil.
Purvis, R. M.	2nd Lieut.	From 3rd B.W., 6.10.15. To Mesopotamia with Bn. 7.1.16. R., 9.4.16. W., 10.4.16. R. as a Captain, 6.2.17. D. of W., 14.3.17.	Shaikh Sa'ad, '16. Sannaiyat, '16. Kut, '17. C. of Baghdad, '17. Mushaidie, '17.	Nil.

Name	Rank on joining or commencement of campaign	Record	Actions at which present	Promotions and Regimental Appointments
Quine, A. H.	2nd Lieut.	From 3rd B.W., 11.4.17. W. & P. of W., 21.4.17.	Istabulat, '17.	Nil.
Quine, B. H.	2nd Lieut.	From 11th B.W., 22.7.16. S., 14.8.16. R., 2.6.18. K., 27.6.18.	Arsuf, '18.	Lt., 1.7.17.
Rawdon-Hastings, E. H.	2nd Lieut.	From U.K. (Reg.), 7.6.15. S., 7.9.15. D. in Hospital, 15.9.15.	Nil.	Nil.
Ritchie, J. C.	2nd Lieut.	From U.K. (Reg.), 12.4.17. S., 7.12.17. R., 23.12.17. To Palestine with Bn. S., 2.6.18.	Istabulat, '17. Tekrit, '17.	T/Lt., 25.5.17 to 1.7.17. Lt., 1.7.17. A/Capt., June, 1917 to 8.12.17. A/Adjt., 25.5.17 to 7.12.17.
Ritchie, N. M.	2nd Lieut.	From U.K. (Reg.), 1.3.16. S., 16.4.16. R., 23.4.16. S., 29.5.16. R., 2.6.16. S., 25.5.17. R., 19.12.17. To Palestine with Bn. To U.K. on leave, 12.10.18. R., after Armistice. To U.K. with Cadre.	Hanna, '16. Sannaiyat, '16. Kut, '17. C. of Baghdad, '17. Mushaidie, '17. Istabulat, '17. Arsuf, '18. Sharon, '18.	Lt., 2.10.15. T/Capt., 2.3.16 to 18.11.17. Capt., 19.11.17. A/Adjt., 22.4.16 to 4.1.17. Adjt., 5.1.17 to end of war.
Ritchie, R. C.	Lieut.	From 5th B.W., 14.6.18. S., 29.6.18.	Nil.	Nil.
Ross, E. N.	2nd Lieut.	From Service Bn, B.W., 22.6.17. S., 24.7.17. R., 31.1.18. To Details, Kantara, 23.3.18. R., 16.6.18. K., 27.6.18.	Nil	Nil.

Name	Rank	Service	Battles	Wounds/Honours
Roy, W. C.	2nd Lieut.	From 4th B.W., 2.6.18. S., 12.7.18. R., 20.7.18. S., 16.10.18.	Arsuf, '18. Sharon, '18.	Nil.
Ryrie, G.	2nd Lieut.	From 3rd B.W., 25.8.16. S., 12.9.16. R., 19.9.16. S., 3.11.16. R., 7.7.17. S., 7.12.17. R., 12.12.17. To Palestine with Bn. To Zeitoun as Instructor, 22.8.18.	Tekrit, '17.	Lt., 1.7.17. A/Adjt., Feb., to June, 1918.
Scobie, A.	2nd Lieut.	From Service Bn., B.W., 7.11.17. To Palestine with Bn. To 7th Div. H.Q., 28.1.18.	Nil.	Lt., 5.2.18.
Scotland, P. J.	2nd Lieut.	From 3rd B.W., 31.1.18. To Details, Kantara, 23.3.18.	Nil.	Nil.
Sinclair, A. K.	2nd Lieut.	From 11th B.W., 20.6.16. S., 28.6.16. R., 4.7.16. To M.G.C. 26.10.16. (Subsequently K., 5.12.16.)	Nil.	Nil.
Sinclair, R.	2nd Lieut.	Commissioned from ranks, 5.4.15, after 16 yrs. service. K., 9.5.15.	Aubers Ridge, '15.	Nil.
Skene, P. G. M.	Captain	From India with Bn. W., 5.11.14.	Nil.	Nil.
Smart, G. B.	2nd Lieut.	From 3rd B.W., 10.10.16. S., 16.10.16. R., 29.10.16. W., 14.3.17. R., 7.5.17. S., 15.10.17. R., 24.10.17. S., 30.10.17. R., 22.12.17 To Palestine with Bn. To Brigade H.Q., 16.5.18.	Kut, '17. C. of Baghdad, '17. Mushaidie, '17.	Lt., 1.7.17.

Name	Rank on joining or commencement of campaign	Record	Actions at which present	Promotions and Regimental Appointments
Smith, T. L.	2nd Lieut.	From Service Bn., B.W., 22.10.17. To Palestine with Bn. To Details, Kantara, 23.3.18. R., 20.5.18.	Tekrit, '17. Arsuf, '18. Sharon, '18.	Lt., 5.3.18.
Smythe, P. E.	2nd Lieut.	From 3rd B.W., 13.12.16. W., 21.4.17. R., 24.3.18. W., 8.6.18. R., 26.7.18. Died in Hospital, 30.11.18.	Kut, '17. C. of Baghdad, '17. Mushaidie, '17. Istabulat, '17. Arsuf, '18. Sharon, '18	Lt., 4.7.17.
Smythe, R. M.	2nd Lieut.	From 3rd B.W., 24.12.16. W., 14.3.17. R., 30.5.17 To Palestine with Bn. Leave to South Africa, 15.8.18. To U.K. with Cadre.	Kut, '17. C. of Baghdad, '17. Mushaidie, '17. Tekrit, '17. Arsuf, '18.	Lt., 1.7.17. A/Capt., 23.6.18.
Soutar, F. H.	2nd Lieut.	From 3rd B.W., 5.10.15. To Mesopotamia with Bn. K., 21.1.16.	Shaikh Sa'ad, '16. Wadi River, '16. Hanna, '16.	A/Adjt., 19.1.16 to 21.1.16.
Stewart, C. E.	Major	With Bn. from India. To command of 1st Bn. on arrival in France. (Subsequently K. as a Brigadier-General in France.)	Nil.	Nil.
Stewart, G. V.	2nd Lieut.	From 3rd B.W., 26.4.16. W., 14.3.17. R., 13.4.17. To R. F. C., 24.5.17.	Kut, '17. C. of Baghdad, '17. Mushaidie, '17. Istabulat, '17.	Nil.

Stewart, J.	Major	From U.K. (R. of O., B.W.), 13.4.17. Assumed command of Bn. vice Col. A. G. Wauchope, 21.4.17. To Palestine in command of Bn. S., 23.4.18. R., 13.5.18. To U.K. on leave, 23.5.18. R., 21.7.18. To U.K. with Cadre.	Istabulat, '17. Tekrit, '17. Sharon, '18.	A/Lt.-Col., 5.5.17 to end of war.
Stewart, K. A., The Hon.	2nd Lieut.	From U.K. (Reg.), 18.12.14. K. 9.5.15.	Givenchy, '14. N. Chapelle, '15. Aubers Ridge, '15.	Lt, 13.3.15.
Stewart, T. W.	2nd Lieut.	From 3rd B.W., 4.7.16. S., 14.7.16. R., 19.7.16. S., 9.11.16. R., 14.12.16. S., 17.1.17.	Nil.	Nil.
Stewart, W. D. MacL.	2nd Lieut.	From India with Bn. W., 18.5.15. (Subsequently K. with 1st Bn. in France.)	Festubert, '14. Givenchy, '14. N. Chapelle, '15. Aubers Ridge, '15.	Nil.
Stewart-Smith, D. C.	2nd Lieut.	From 3rd B.W., 22.5.15. W., 25.9.15. R., 4.12.15. To Mesopotamia with Bn. S., 21.2.16. R., 2.8.16. S., 18.8.16. (Subsequently to 1st Bn.)	Loos, '15. Shaikh Sa'ad, '16. Wadi River, '16.	Bn. Transport Officer, 10.1.16 to 23.1.16. A/Adjt., 24.1.16 to 21.2.16.
Strahan, C. E.	Captain	R., from R.T.O. Duties, October, '14. K., 27.11.14.	Festubert, '14.	Nil.
Sutherland, A. H. C.	Lieut.	R. at Rouen, October, '14. (From A.D.C. to C.-in-C., S. Africa.) S. 9.11.14. R., 26.3.15. W., 9.5.15.	Aubers Ridge, '15.	Nil.

315

Name	Rank on joining or commencement of campaign	Record	Actions at which present	Promotions and Regimental Appointments
Sutherland, H. H.	Major	With Bn. from India. W., 8.3.15. (Subseq'ntly to 1st Bn.)	Festubert, '14. Givenchy, '14. N. Chapelle, '15.	Nil.
Thorburn, M. M.	2nd Lieut.	From 3rd B.W., 28.5.15. S., 26.7.15. R., Aug. 15. To Mesopotamia with Bn. W., 21.1.16.	Loos, '15. Shaikh Sa'ad, '16. Wadi River, '16. Hanna, '16.	Bn. Transport Officer, Jan., '17 to 10/1/17.
Todd, J.	2nd Lieut.	From 3rd B.W., 5.10.15. To Mesopotamia i/c Bn. Transport. R., Bn. with Transport, 20.5.16. Leave to India, 17.5.17. R., 16.8.17. To Palestine with Bn. To U.K. for Med. Studies, 24.4.18.	Kut, '17. C. of Baghdad, '17. Mushaidie, '17. Istabulat, '17. Tekrit, '17.	Bn. Transport Officer, 18.10.15 to 3.5.17. A/Capt., 6.5.17 to 16.8.17, and 18.8.17 to 24.3.18.
Topping, J.	2nd Lieut.	From 3rd B.W., 31.1.18. To Details, Kantara, 23.3.18. (Subsequently to R.A.F. and reported M., 16.9.18.)	Nil.	Nil.
Walker, W. G.	2nd Lieut.	From 3rd B.W., 31.1.18. To Details, Kantara, 23.3.18.	Nil.	Nil.
Wauchope, A. G.	Major	With Bn. from India. W. (slight) 2.12.14. W., 21.12.14. R., 26.3.15. Assumed command of Bn. vice Lieut.-Col. W. J. St. J. Harvey, 6.9.15. In com-	Festubert, '14. Givenchy, '14. Aubers Ridge, '15. Loos, '15. Shaikh Sa'ad, '16. Kut, '17. C. of Baghdad, '17. Mushaidie, '17.	T/Lt.-Col., 6.9.15. 2nd-in-C., 26.3.15 to 5.9.15. C.O. 6.9.15 to 20.4.17.

Willett, L. H.	Captain	mand of Bn. to Mesopotamia. W., 7.1.16. R., 30.5.16. To command of 8th Brigade, 20.4.17.	Kut, '17. C. of Baghdad, '17. Mushaidie, '17. Istabulat, '17.	Nil.
Wilson, W.	2nd Lieut.	From 3rd B.W., 13.12.16. W., 21.4.17. Commissioned from ranks, 15.6.15, after 16 yrs. service. W., 25.9.15.	Loos, '15.	T/Capt., 8.9.15 to 25.9.15.
Woyka, A. G.	2nd Lieut.	From 11th B.W., 29.6.16. S., 22.7.16. R., 30.7.16. S., 22.12.16. R., 22.12.17. S., 23.12.17. R., 27.1.18. To Brigade H.Q., 1918. S., 21.10.18	Sharon, '18.	Lt, 1.7.17.
Yorston, K. MacQ.	2nd Lieut.	From 3rd B.W., 31.1.18. To Details, Kantara, 23.3.18. R., 5.7.18. To H.Q. 7th Div., 1.8.18.	Nil.	Nil.
Young, A. A.	2nd Lieut.	From 3rd B.W., 25.11.16. D. of W., 14.3.17.	Kut, '17. C. of Baghdad, '17. Mushaidie, '17.	Nil
Young, W. A.	2nd Lieut.	From 9th Royal Scots, 25.9.15. To Mesopotamia with Bn. W., 7.1.16. R., 9.4.16. S., 6.6.16. R., 13.6.16. S., 8.8.16. R., 13.8.16. W., 22.2.17. R., 14.5.17. Leave to India, 17.5.17. R., 11.8.17. To Palestine with Bn. W., 8.6.18. D. of W., 10.6.18.	Shaikh Sa'ad, '16. Sannaiyat, '16.[1] Kut, '17. Tekrit, '17. Arsuf, '18.	T/Lt., 8.7.16. Lt., 15.3.17. A/Capt., Oct., 1916, to 7.2.17. 29.4.18 to 8.6.18.

[1] This was the only B.W. Officer to return from the action of 22.4.16 unwounded. He had four bullet holes through his clothing.

ATTACHED OFFICERS

Name	Rank on joining or commencement of campaign	Record	Actions at which present	Promotions and Regimental Appointments
Black, D. N.	2nd Lieut.	From A.S.C., 4.9.18.	Sharon, '18.	Nil.
Boswell, G. A.	Lieut.	From 4th Cameron Hrs., 24.7.18. To U.K. with Cadre.	Sharon, '18.	Nil.
Brown, D.	2nd Lieut.	From R.S. Fusiliers, 8.9.18.	Sharon, '18.	Nil.
Brownlow, W. L.	2nd Lieut.	From 4th Northumberland Fusiliers, 10.4.15. K., 9.5.15.	Aubers Ridge, '15.	Nil.
Byrom, J. A.	2nd Lieut.	From 11th Argyll and Sutherland Hrs., 12.4.17. To 6th Bn. L.N. Lancs. Regt., 29.10.17.	Istabulat, '17.	Nil.
Bruce-Tomes, C.	2nd Lieut.	From 2nd London Scottish, 1.7.18. S., 1.9.18.	Nil.	Nil.
Cameron, W. M.	Lieut.	From R.A.M.C. as M.O. to Bn., 28.3.17. S., 21.9.17. R., 19.10.17. To Palestine with Bn. W. (slight), 12.6.18.	Istabulat, '17, Tekrit, '17. Arsuf, '18. Sharon, '18.	Medical Officer, 28.3.17 to end of war. T/Capt., 1917.
Campbell, P. C.	2nd Lieut.	From 4th Argyll & Sutherland Hrs., 11.3.15. S., 8.4.15.	N. Chapelle, 15.	Nil.
Collinson, W.	2nd Lieut.	From 11th Gordon Hrs., 25.4.17. To I Corps H.Q. as Cypher Officer, 5.5.17.	Nil.	Nil.
Crake, R. H.	Captain	From 1st K.O.S.B., 24.1.16. To Staff, 9.2.16.	Nil.	A/C.O., 24.1.16 to 9.2.16.

Name	Rank	Service	Battles	Honours
Dawson, G. F.	Captain	From India with Bn. as M.O. Relieved May, 1915.	Festubert, '14. Givenchy, '14. N. Chapelle, '15. Aubers Ridge, '15.	Nil.
Dixon, J. F. C.	2nd Lieut.	From 4th Argyll & Sutherland Hrs. 2.6.15. S., 19.7.15. R., 5,10.15. To Mesopotamia with Bn. W., 7.1.16. R., 15.1.16. W., 21.1.16. R., 30.6.16. S., 17.7.16. R., 25.7.16. S., 20.10.16. R., 8.11.17. To Palestine with Bn. To 1/5th A. & S.H., 7.2.18.	Shaikh Sa'ad, '16. Hanna, '16.	T/Lt., 8.7.16. Lt., 18.7.16.
Duncan, R. W.	Captain	From R.A.M.C. as M.O. to Bn., 4.7.15. To Mesopotamia with Bn. To Leicestershire Regt., 10.2.16. (Subsequently K., 10.3.16.)	Loos, '15. Shaikh Sa'ad, '16. Wadi River, '16. Hanna, '16.	Medical Officer 4.7.17 to 10.2.16.
Dunlop, A. G.	2nd Lieut.	From A.S.C., 2.8.18. To Political Staff, 11.11.18.	Sharon, '18.	Nil.
Fairbairn, W. A.	2nd Lieut.	From R. Scots, 8.9.18.	Sharon, '18.	Nil.
Gerard, C. E.	2nd Lieut.	From Gordon Hrs., 12.4.17. To Assessments Commission, Baghdad, summer, 1917.	Istabulat, '17.	Nil.
Gunlett, G. F.	Captain	From R.A.M.C. as M.O. to Bn., 24.3.17. To Fd. Amb. 28.3.17.	Nil.	Medical Officer, 24.3.17 to 28.3.17.
Halford, E. H. I.	Lieut.	From 1/4th Devon Regt, 2.8.16. S., 25.8.16.	Nil.	Nil.
Hunter, A. B.	2nd Lieut.	From 3/9th R. Scots, 17.6.18. S., 12.7.18. R., 20.7.18. S., 3.9.18.	Nil.	Nil.

Name	Rank on joining or commencement of campaign	Record	Actions at which present	Promotions and Regimental Appointments
Jackson, A. L.	2nd Lieut.	From A. & S.H., 25.9.17. To 6th L.N. Lancs. Regt., 30.10.17.	Nil.	Nil.
Johnstone, A. S.	2nd Lieut.	From 3rd Gordon Hrs., 22.6.17. To R.T.O., Samarrah, 7.7.17.	Nil.	Nil.
Lochead, F.	2nd Lieut.	From R.S. Fusiliers, 31.7.18. S., 2.9.18.	Nil.	Nil.
McDonald, W.	2nd Lieut.	From R.S. Fusiliers, 21.9.18.	Sharon, '18.	Nil.
Macfarlane, A.,	Rev.	From India with Bn. S., 18.4.15. R., 10.10.15. To Mesopotamia with Bn. S., 3.3.16. R., 10.3.16. S., 15.3.17. (Subseq'ntly apptd. chief Presbyterian Chaplain to Mesopotamian Force.)	Festubert, '14. Givenchy, '14. N. Chapelle, '15. Shaikh Sa'ad, '16. Wadi River, '16. Hanna, '16. Sannaiyat, '16. Kut, '17. C. of Baghdad, '17. Mushaidie, '17.	Chaplain to Bn.
Mackie, A.	2nd Lieut.	From H.L.I., 8.9.18. S., 23.10.18.	Sharon, '18.	Nil.
MacQueen, J.	Captain	From R.A.M.C. as M.O. to Bn., 18.7.16. S., 11.8.16. R., 13.8.16. Relieved, 25.3.17.	Kut, '17. C. of Baghdad, '17. Mushaidiya, '17.	Medical Officer, 18.7.16 to 25.3.17.
Maitland, W. E.	Lieut.	From 3rd Seaforth Hrs, 14.12.14. D. of W., 24.12.14.	Givenchy, '14.	Nil.
Marburg, C. L.	Lieut.	From 9th (Res.) R. Scots, 5.7.18. S., 18.7.18.	Nil.	Nil.
Murray, D. M.	2nd Lieut.	From Gordon Hrs., 31.7.18. S., 3.11.18.	Sharon, '18.	Nil.

Potts, G.	Captain	From R.A.M.C. as M.O. to Bn., 21.9.17. Relieved 20.10.17.	Nil.	Medical Officer, 21.9.17 to 20.10.17.
Reid, G. R. M.	2nd Lieut.	From 4th A. & S. H., 3.2.15. W., 9.5.15.	N. Chapelle, '15. Aubers Ridge, '15. Arsuf, '18.	Nil.
Robertson, R. D.	Captain	From 1st Gordon Hrs., 20.11.17. To Palestine with Bn. S., 11.2.17. R., 16.3.18. To S. Offs. School, Aug., '18. R., Oct., '18. To U.K. with Cadre.		2nd-in-C., 9.6.18 to end of war. A/C.O., 9.6.18 to 20.7.18. A/Major, 9.6.18 to end of war.
Russell, H. W.	Captain	From R.A.M.C. as M.O. to Bn., May, '15. To Fd. Ambulance, 4.7.15.	Nil.	Medical Officer, May, 1915 to 4.7.15.
Silver, A.	Rev.	Joined Bn., 13.5.17. To Palestine with Bn. S., 12.8.18. R., 7.9.18. To U.K. with Cadre.	Tekrit, '17. Arsuf, '18. Sharon, '18.	Chaplain to Bn. from 3.5.17 to end of war.
Simonet, K. W. L.	Captain	From 1st Yorks. Regt., 16.1.16. K., 21.1.16.	Hanna, '16.	Nil.
Skeat, S. S.	2nd Lieut.	From 3rd King's Own Royal Lancaster Regt., 23.4.15. S., 6.5.15.	Nil.	Nil.
Sotherby, L. F.	2nd Lieut.	From 3rd A. & S. H., 31.7.15. K., 25.9.15.	Loos, '15.	Nil.
Swan, F. C.	2nd Lieut.	From K.O.S.B., 8.9.18.	Sharon, '18.	Nil.
Symes, J. W.	Lieut.	From 1/4th Dorset Regt., February, '16. W., April, '16.	Hanna, '16. Sannaiyat, '16.	Nil.
Twentyman, J. J.	2nd Lieut.	From H.L.I., 2.8.18. W., 19.9.18.	Sharon, '18.	Nil.
Walker, R.	2nd Lieut.	From 11th A. & S. H., 12.4.17. K., 21.4.17.	Istabulat, '17.	Nil.

APPENDIX II

SUMMARY OF CASUALTIES. THE SECOND BATTALION

The discrepancy between these figures and those given by the war diaries is accounted for by the fact that, save in the case of regular battalions, the diaries seldom give a record of casualties other than those suffered in main actions.

OFFICERS, 1914–18

Year.	Killed. D. of Wounds. D. on Service.	Wounded.	Missing.	Total.	Year.
1914	2	7	0	9	1914
1915	15	25	1	41	1915
1916	14	28	0	42	1916
1917	11	14	1	26	1917
1918	4	13	0	17	1918
Totals:	46	87	2 (a)	135	

OTHER RANKS, 1914–18

1914	56	122	1	179	1914
1915	355	802	85	1242	1915
1916	398	689	176	1263	1916
1917	161	332	6	499	1917
1918	61	115	4	180	1918
Totals:	1031	2060	272 (b)	3363	

TOTAL: ALL RANKS

    1077   2147   274   3498

(a) Both wounded.
(b) Only 10 of these were ever reported as prisoners, the remainder (262) must be reckoned with the killed, the total of which is accordingly 1339.

APPENDIX III

Casualties—Officers

The Second Battalion

Name	Rank	Where Killed
Anderson, D. H.	2nd Lieut.	Sannaiyat, 22.4.16.
Anderson, G. J.	2nd Lieut.	Sannaiyat, 22.4.16.
Balfour-Melville, J. E.	2nd Lieut.	Loos, 25.9.15.
Brown, G. J. R.	2nd Lieut.	D. of W. received at Istabulat, 21.5.17.
Bruce, E.	2nd Lieut.	Died on service, 17.11.16.
Bruce, H. W.	2nd Lieut.	Sannaiyat, 17.2.17.
Campbell, D.	Captain	Aubers Ridge, 18.5.15.
Cotterill, J. H.	2nd Lieut.	Mushaidie, 15.3.17.
Cumming, A. B.	2nd Lieut.	Sannaiyat, 22.4.16.
Denison, A. C.	Captain	Loos, 25.9.15.
Douglas, A.	2nd Lieut.	D. of W. received at the Wadi, 19.2.16.
Forrester, H. F.	2nd Lieut.	Sannaiyat, 22.4.16.
George, W.	2nd Lieut.	N. Chapelle, 12.3.15.
Gillespie, T.	2nd Lieut.	Mushaidie, 14.3.17.
Gilroy, K. R.	Lieut.	N. Chapelle, 12.3.15.
Hamilton-Johnston, D. C.	Major	Hanna, 21.1.16.
Henderson, N. C.	2nd Lieut.	Loos, 25.9.15.
Holland, B. T.	2nd Lieut.	N. Chapelle, 10.3.15.
Hutchison, I. O.	2nd Lieut.	Shaikh Sa'ad, 7.1.16.
Inglis, J. N.	Captain	Sannaiyat, 22.4.16.
Loudon, T.	Lieut.	Arsuf, 3.6.18.
McArthur, D.	2nd Lieut.	Istabulat, 21.4.17.
McConaghey, C. J.	2nd Lieut.	Sannaiyat, 22.4.16.
Macfarlane, R.	Captain	Istabulat, 21.4.17.
MacLeod, G. C. S.	Captain	D. of W. received at Aubers Ridge, 13.5.15.
MacLeod, I. B.	Lieut.	Aubers Ridge, 17.4.15.
Miller-Stirling, E. G. B.	Lieut.	Mushaidie, 15.3.17.
Morrison, R. S.	2nd Lieut.	Shaikh Sa'ad, 8.1.16.
Peel, T.	2nd Lieut.	Istabulat, 21.4.17.
Plunkett, H. A. T.	2nd Lieut.	Shaikh Sa'ad, 7.1.16.
Purvis, R. M.	Lieut.	Mushaidie, 14.3.17.
Quine, B. H.	2nd Lieut.	Arsuf, 27.6.18.
Rawdon-Hastings, E. H.	2nd Lieut.	Died on service, 7.9.15.
Ross, E. N.	2nd Lieut.	Arsuf, 27.6.18.
Sinclair, R.	2nd Lieut.	Aubers Ridge, 9.5.15.
Soutar, F. H.	2nd Lieut.	Hanna, 21.1.16.
Stewart, K. A., The Hon.	2nd Lieut.	Aubers Ridge, 9.5.15.
Strachan, C. E.	Captain	Givenchy, 27.11.14.
Young, A. A.	2nd Lieut.	Mushaidie, 14.3.17.
Young, W. A.	Captain	D. of W. received at Arsuf, 10.6.18

THE SECOND BATTALION THE BLACK WATCH

Name	Rank	Where Killed
Attached.		
Brownlow, W. L.	2nd Lieut. N. Fusiliers.	Aubers Ridge, 9.5.15.
Maitland, W. E.	Lieut., Seaforth Hrs.	Givenchy, 24.12.14.
Simonet, K. W.	Captain, Yorks. Regt.	Hanna, 21.1.16.
Sotherby, L. F.	2nd Lieut., A. & S.Hrs.	Loos, 25.9.15.
Walker, R.	2nd Lieut., A. & S.Hrs.	Istabulat, 21.4.17.

APPENDIX IV

NOMINAL ROLL OF WARRANT OFFICERS, NON-COMMISSIONED OFFICERS AND MEN KILLED IN ACTION OR DIED OF WOUNDS OR DISEASE IN THE GREAT WAR, 1914–18

Abbreviations.—* Killed in action.　† Died of wounds.　§ Died.
¶ Died at sea.　‡ Died at home.

THE SECOND BATTALION

Abercrombie, J., Pte., S/7534	†10.5.15	Bannerman, J., Cpl., S/7305	§13.8.17
Adair, E., L/Cpl., S/10768	† 9.6.18	Barbour, A., Pte., 2278	* 9.5.15
Adam, J., Pte., S/15632	*21.4.17	Barbour, W. P., Pte., S/10576	*22.4.16
Adam, T., Pte., S/8647	*19.7.15	Barclay, T., Pte., 2687	†3.10.15
Adamson, W., Pte., 9797	† 1.8.15	Barnes, J., Pte., S/10023	*21.4.17
Aikman, R., Pte., 129	*20.4.15	Barnes, J., Pte., S/9034	*21.1.16
Aitchison, G., Pte., 3/2513	*18.5.15	Barnes, P. A., Pte., S/10656	*22.4.16
Aitchison, J., Pte., 435	* 9.5.15	Barrie, J., Sgt., 2084	*14.3.17
Aitken, D., Pte., S/19435	*14.3.17	Barrie, R. M., Pte., S/10469	*22.4.16
Aitken, J., Pte., 8179	* 9.5.15	Batchelor, C., Pte., S/13905	*21.4.17
Alexander, A., Pte., S/8119	*25.9.15	Bathgate, J., Pte., S/4158	*25.9.15
Allan, A., L/Cpl., S/3443	*13.5.15	Baxter, F., Pte., 1166	*21.1.16
Allan, J., Pte., S/6580	*25.9.15	Baxter, R., Pte., 3/3977	*13.5.15
Allan, M. J. G. T., L/Cpl., S/20003	†10.6.18	Bayne, J., Pte., 3/3694	*21.7.15
		Beattie, G., Pte., S/11800	*22.4.16
Allardice, J. F., Pte., S/14533	†10.11.17	Beattie, J. B., L/Cpl., 822	* 9.5.15
Allen, G., Pte., S/7004	†14.11.15	Beattie, J., Pte., 9852	§30.12.16
Allison, G., Pte., S/7956	*25.9.15	Beattie, L. R., L/Cpl., S/7158	* 7.1.16
Anderson, A., Pte., 3/2912	†13.5.15	Beattie, W., Pte., S/7943	*21.1.16
Anderson, D., L/Cpl., 332	† 3.10.15	Belcher, T., Pte., S/10113	*13.2.16
Anderson, J., Pte., 10	§ 9.11.18	Belderson, G., Pte., 2350	*30.8.15
Anderson, J., Pte., 791	*11.3.15	Bell, D., L/Cpl., S/7283	*22.4.16
Anderson, J., Pte., S/2920	†24.1.17	Bell, D., Pte., 3/3393	* 9.5.15
Anderson J., Pte., 948	†10.11.14	Bell, J. A., Pte., S/8696	* 7.1.16
Anderson, P., Pte., S/6763	*14.5.15	Bennett, D., Pte., 1549	§21.9.16
Anderson, S., Pte., 2019	†11.3.15	Bennett, J., L/Cpl., S/5142	*14.3.17
Arbuthnott, W., Sgt., 626	§15.10.17	Benson, W., Pte., S/13103	†22.4.17
Archer, J. S., Sgt., 72	*22.4.16	Benton, J. T., Pte., S/13949	†18.6.18
Armitage, G., L/Cpl., 3/3406	§15.8.16	Beveridge, J., Pte., 898	*22.4.16
Armstrong, T., Pte., S/8319	*21.1.16	Bewley, F., Pte., S/6436	†24.3.17
Atherton, W., Bdns., 9223	§ 6.3.15	Billington, G., Pte., S/3572	§ 1.7.16
		Birks, J., Pte., S/3350	†12.3.15
Baillie, J., Pte., S/7580	*22.4.16	Birse, A., L/Cpl., 1862	*21.1.16
Baillie, T., Pte., S/10545	* 5.12.16	Bissett, T., C.Q.M.S., 1859	*14.3.17
Bain, J., Pte., S/7164	* 9.5.15	Black, F., Pte., 3/1231	† 9.5.15
Bain, J., Pte., 3/3389	*21.1.16	Black, J., Pte., 3/2614	*22.4.16
Bain, J., Pte., S/13243	§28.6.16	Black, W., L/Cpl., 1517	†10.6.18
Bain, R., Pte., S/6249	*25.9.15	Black, W., Pte., S/5192	* 7.1.16
Baird, W. M. McG., Pte., S/13932		Blackie, J., Pte., 3/2719	* 9.5.15
	* 3.6.18	Blackledge, W., Pte., 6671	* 9.5.15
Ballantyne, W., Pte., S/7654	*16.4.15	Blackwood, J., Pte., 3/2891	* 9.5.15
Ballingall, W. B., Pte., S/10480		Blaik, D., Pte., S/20012	§13.8.17
	*13.1.16	Blyth, T. A., Pte., S/15829	†23.4.17
Banks, P., Pte., 1391	* 9.5.15	Boag, M., Pte., 3/2243	* 9.5.15
Bannerman, D. J., Pte., S/20010		Bogan, R., Pte., S/11533	*22.4.16
	¶15.4.17	Borland, J. M., Pte., S/5040	*11.7.15

325

THE SECOND BATTALION THE BLACK WATCH

Bothwell, W., Pte., S/3767 † 9.4.15
Bourne, H., Pte., S/6508 § 9.10.16
Bowman, H. D., Cpl., S/17481 *14.3.17
Bowman, R., Pte., S/7592 * 7.1.16
Boyd, G., Pte., S/7744 *30.9.15
Boyd, J. F., Pte., 3/2540 *25.9.15
Boyd, R., Pte., S/13227 §30.6.16
Bradie, J. T., Pte., S/8750 *21.1.16
Brady, P., Pte., 753 *10.3.15
Brash, W., Pte., S/7754 * 9.5.15
Brember, A., Pte., S/13458 *21.4.17
Bremner, W., Pte., S/8628 *25.9.15
Broadbent, J., Pte., S/12328 § 5.7.16
Broadbent, R. W., Pte., S/10047
§ 1.7.16
Brogden, J., Pte., S/8038 *25.9.15
Brockie, J., Pte., S/15547 §10.7.17
Brown, A. J., Pte., 268631 *26.8.18
Brown, A., Pte., S/17696 * 8.6.18
Brown, A., L/Cpl., 1207 * 7.1.16
Brown, C., L/Cpl., 1019 *30.8.15
Brown, D., Pte., 2063 *5.11.14
Brown, H., Pte., S/10230 *25.9.15
Brown, M., L/Cpl., S/13267 *10.10.15
Brown, P., Pte., S/7928 * 9.5.15
Brown, P., Pte., 3/2556 *12.3.15
Brown, R., L/Cpl., S/2876 †23.4.17
Brown, R., Pte., S/7967 *22.4.16
Brown, T., Cpl., 2545 *22.4.16
Bryden, D., L/Cpl., S/10118 * 8.6.18
Buchan, J., Pte., S/10641 *22.4.16
Buchan, R. R., Pte., 923 †18.7.15
Buchanan, J. G., Pte., S/13998 * 3.6.18
Buick, A., Pte., S/15666 §25.6.17
Buick, D., Pte., S/43025 §11.1.18
Bullion, G. C., Dmr., 2185 * 6.4.16
Bunce, A., L/Cpl., 9515 * 9.5.15
Burke, T., Pte., 3/3100 *21.4.17
Burness, G., Pte., 3/1791 * 7.1.16
Burnett, J., Pte., 1320 *5.11.14
Burnett, W. A., Pte., S/11835 *21.4.17
Burns, J., Pte., 868 † 9.3.15
Burns, W., Pte., S/7955 *25.9.15
Burry, J., Pte., 1850 * 9.5.15
Butterworth, M., Pte., 1671 *25.9.15

Caddow, T. F., Pte., 6818 *14.3.17
Cairney, J., L/Cpl., S/8713 §14.3.16
Cairns, G. A., L/Sgt., 6489 *29.11.14
Cairns, W. D., Pte., S/8496 *21.1.16
Calderwood, C., Pte., S/8060 *8.10.15
Cameron, A., Pte., 1208 *14.11.14
Cameron, P., Pte., 1759 §15.8.16
Campbell, A., Pte., 3/3360 * 9.5.15
Campbell, A., Pte., 1816 *25.9.15

Campbell, A., Pte., S/6723 * 9.5.15
Campbell, H. F., Pte., S/8257 *13.1.16
Campbell, J., Pte., S/10579 *22.4.16
Campbell, J., Pte., S/3569 *21.4.17
Campbell, N. McG., L/Cpl., 2451
* 7.1.16
Campbell, R. McF., Pte., 1692
*25.3.15
Campbell, W., L/Cpl, 13186 †15.3.17
Cannell, W. E., Pte., S/12162 †23.4.17
Carlyle, W., Pte., S/15657 *14.3.17
Carmichael, A., Pte., S/11726 *22.4.16
Carmichael, C., Pte., S/6070 * 9.5.15
Carmichael, R., L/Cpl., S/7056
† 9.1.16
Carnegie, W., Pte., 955 *24.3.15
Carnson, J. G., Pte., S/4235 *22.4.16
Carr, A., Pte., 682 *22.4 16
Carr, J., Pte., S/2955 §16.6.17
Carr, J., Pte., 9313 * 8.3.15
Carrigan, J., L/Cpl., 2119 †23.11.14
Carroll, E., Pte., 1392 * 25.9.15
Carroll, J., Pte., S/13191 §29.6.16
Carson, G., Pte., 14009 ¶13.1.17
Chalmers, J., Pte., S/4016 *16.6.15
Chapman, A., Pte., S/8912 *21.1.16
Chisholm, A., Pte., S/6710 * 9.5.15
Chisholm, J. W., Pte., S/18507
§10.10.17
Christie, A., Pte., 2139 *11.12.14
Christie, J., Pte., S/12519 §10.6.16
Christie, R., Pte., 2141 †12.3.15
Chrystal, W., A/Sgt., 3/2475 §19.6.16
Churchard, R. G., Pte., S/9850
*22.4.16
Clark, D., L/Cpl., 9714 *11.7.15
Clark, F., Pte., 1927 *5.11.14
Clark, J. G., Pte., 3/4229 §26.7.16
Clark, J., Pte., 3/2878 †20.5.16
Clark, J., Pte., S/3389 *22.4.16
Clark, J., Pte., 19426 *21.4.17
Clark, J. W., Pte., S/6707 *13.5.15
Clark, J. Pte., S/11193 *14.3.17
Clark, P., L/Cpl., 2136 †27.10.15
Clark, P., Pte., S/17785 §22.10.17
Clark, R., Pte., S/2632 *13.1.16
Clark, T. E., Pte., S/10563 *22.4.16
Clark, W., Pte., 2080 *10.3.15
Clink, R., Pte., 3/2522 †28.3.15
Clowe, T., Pte., 3/4246 § 7.7.16
Clyne, H., Pte., 3/7162 † 4.6.15
Cochrane, A. F., L/Cpl., S/8349
*14.3.17
Cockburn, C., Pte., S/20022 *22.6.18
Cockburn, W., Pte., S/7625 *25.9.15

APPENDIX IV

Combe, G., A/Cpl., S/6964	† 6.3.17	Daniel, J., L/Cpl., 1731	
Connelly, J., Pte., 3/2816	† 4.9.15	(D.C.M.)	† 6.6.15
Connelly, J., Pte., S/13192	§26.6.16	Davidson, G., C.S.M., 9437	* 7.1.16
Constable, T., Pte., 1492	* 9.5.15	Davidson, J., Pte., S/17470	§11.11.18
Cook, J., Pte., 1529	*25.9.15	Davidson, J., Cpl., S/8018	* 8.6.18
Cook, J., Pte., S/15613	†15.3.17	Davidson, T., Pte., S/13225	§ 2.7.16
Cook, J., Pte., S/18052	* 8.6.18	Davie, P., Pte., 9451	* 7.1.16
Cook, J., Pte., 3/2621	* 6.4.16	Davis, J. G., Piper, 1449	*25.9.15
Cooper, A., Pte., 436	†26.7.15	Davy, J. F., Pte., S/10072	†24.4.16
Cooper, D., L/Cpl., 1319	†30.1.16	Dawson, J., Pte., S/10567	*22.4.16
Corstorphine, A., Cpl., 1441	* 9.5.15	Dawson, W., Pte., S/4009	* 2.6.15
Cosh, R., Pte., 1990	*29.11.14	Denman, J., Pte., S/10194	*25.9.15
Cottle, T. E., Pte., S/10254	§ 7.7.16	Deuchar, A. B., Pte., S/18789	* 8.6.18
Coulter, D., Pte., 198	†15.12.14	Delvin, M., Pte., S/5062	*10.6.18
Coulter, J., Pte., S/3192	*18.5.15	Dewar, W. W., Pte., S/6689	†18.2.16
Coulter, J., Pte., S/7094	* 7.1.16	Diamond, J., Pte., S/3915	* 9.5.15
Cousins, W., Pte., 6393	† 5.10.15	Dick, J., Pte., S/10340	* 7.1.16
Cowie, A., L/Cpl., 1335	*21.4.17	Dick, W., Cpl., 7917	*25.9.15
Cowper, R., Pte., S/10012		Dickson, A., Pte., S/7346	*22.4.16
(D.C.M.)	§19.5.16	Dillon, H., Pte., 3/2571	*25.9.15
Cox, T., Pte., 2065	* 9.5.15	Dixon, J., Pte., S/5198	* 7.1.16
Coyne, W., Pte., S/15127	*21.4.17	Docherty, F., Pte., S/13137	§28.6.16
Craig, D, F., Pte., S/12623	*11.6.18	Docherty, J., Pte., 2142	*25.9.15
Craig, R., Pte., 1899	*14.3.17	Docherty, N., Pte., 1234	*21.1.16
Craigie, A., Pte., S/5414	§ 8.7.16	Dodds, J., L/Cpl., S/3807	* 8.6.18
Craigie, T., Pte., 345	*29.8.15	Doggett, E., L/Cpl., S/12202	*14.3.17
Cranston, T., Pte., S/8899	*13.1.16	Donaldson, A., Pte., S/7991	*1.11.15
Crawford, J., Pte., S/19436	*17.2.17	Donelly, T., Pte., 1846	*25.9.15
Crawley, D., Pte., S/5171	†30.3.15	Dougall, J., A/Cpl., S/9194	*21.1.16
Crerar, J., Pte., S/8417	*21.1.16	Douglas, W., Pte., 11571	§14.12.17
Crichton, A., Cpl., S/7994	*22.4.16	Dowie, A., Pte., S/3801	*25.9.15
Crick, C., Pte., S/15700	*14.3.17	Downie, A., Sgt., 828	† 5.5.16
Croally, F., Pte., S/12049	§ 6.8.17	Downie, J., Pte., 3/2519	* 7.1.16
Cross, G., Pte., S/13956	*14.3.17	Drysdale, G., Pte., S/7595	* 6.4.16
Cross, W., Pte., S/12096	*21.4.17	Duff, H., Sgt., 687	* 9.5.15
Crowe, A., Sgt., 1761	*25.9.15	Duff, J., Pte., S/13982	§ 8.7.16
Crowe, C., Pte., S/7072	*11.3.15	Duff, T., Pte., S/8002	*25.9.15
Culbert, T., Pte., S/3180	* 9.5.15	Duffy, F., Pte., S/7590	* 9.5.15
Cumming, G., Cpl., S/7032	* 4.4.16	Duffy, H., Pte., 3/2496	*22.4.16
Cunningham, J., L/Cpl., 2355	†16.3.17	Duke, D., L/Cpl., 1714	*22.4.16
Cunningham, T., Pte., 3/2569	*22.4.16	Dunbar, E., Pte., 3/7229	§ 3.7.16
Currie, W., Pte., S/9562	*22.4.16	Duncan, D., Pte., 1110	§ 1.3.16
Cuthbert, D. G., Pte., 3/4222		Duncan, D., Cpl., 1757	*30.8.15
(D.C.M.)	*21.1.16	Duncan, J., Pte., 2133	* 9.5.15
		Duncan, R. S., A/C.S.M., 6976	
Dair, P. R., L/Cpl., S/16233	*14.3.17		* 9.5.15
Dakers, G. A., A/Cpl., 116	*22.4.16	Dunleavy, A., Pte., 3/2872	*21.1.16
Dalgleish, J., Pte., 1295	*10.3.15	Dunsmore, J., Pte., S/6808	*22.4.16
Dalgleish, J., Pte., S/8550	*25.9.15		
Dallas, A. Y., L/Cpl., S/10677	*17.6.18	Eadie, W., Pte., 1379	*10.3.15
Dalton, J. R., Pte., S/10564	*21.4.17	Easton, J., Sgt., 1179	*25.9.15
Daly, C., Pte., 666	* 9.5.15	Egerton, A. N., Dmr., 128	* 9.5.15
Dalziel, A., Pte., S/7104	*21.1.16	Eglin, J. K., L/Cpl., S/17483	*14.3.17
Dand, H., Pte., 3/2312	†24.4.16	Elliot, J. D., Pte., S/8856	†22.4.16
Dand, J., Pte., 1174	†12.4.15	Ellis, D., L/Cpl., 1769	†10.10.15

THE SECOND BATTALION THE BLACK WATCH

Emerson, W., L/Cpl., S/11773	* 8.6.18	Gemmell, J., Pte., S/15537	*21.4.17
		Gibb, F., Pte., 2701	*22.4.16
Ettrick, A., Pte., 3/3755	†24.4.16	Gibb, J., A/Cpl., 578	*21.1.16
Evans, B., Pte., S/4004	†27.4.16	Gibb, W., Pte., 2381	†22.1.16
Ewan, A. H., Cpl., 1428	* 9.5.15	Gibson, A. G., L/Cpl., 10240	*21.4.17
Ewing, J., Pte., 597	§17.11.14	Gibson, A., Pte., 8551	*21.4.17
		Gibson, G., Pte., S/15640	§21.7.17
Fairfull, J., Pte., S/8874	*21.1.16	Gibson, J., Pte., 94 (M.M.)	†19.11.18
Fairlie, A., A/L/Cpl., S/11321	§13.7.18	Gibson, J., Pte., 1502	† 9.11.14
Ferguson, A., L/Cpl., 1949	†27.9.15	Gibson, J., L/Cpl., S/7009	* 9.8.16
Ferguson, J. R., Pte., S/8709	†14.1.16	Gibson, W., Pte., S/8353	* 4.10.15
Ferguson, R., Pte., S/10622	†10.6.18	Gilfillan, J., Pte., 3/2633	†12.4.15
Ferguson, W., Pte., S/7622	§3.10.16	Gilfillan, T., Pte., S/17494	*21.4.17
Fettes, J., Pte., S/4874	§20.7.16	Gillespie, A., Pte., S/5039	* 9.5.15
Findlay, D., Sgt., 1780 (V.C.)	*21.1.16	Gillespie, W., Pte., S/7757	*22.4.16
		Gillies, J., Cpl., S/4093	†22.4.16
Findlay, D., Pte., 3/2703	* 9.5.15	Gingan, J., L/Cpl., 1936	*25.9.15
Finlayson, G. R., L/Sgt., 9864	*12.11.14	Glancy, P., Pte., 3/3074	*21.1.16
		Glass, S., L/Cpl., 2167	* 9.5.15
Fisher, J., Pte., S/7038	*18.5.15	Glen, P. C., Pte., S/16082	† 9.5.17
Fleming, A., Pte., S/3934	†25.4.16	Golden, E., Cpl., 2188	† 6.5.15
Fleming, D., Pte., S/8888	§ 2.8.16	Goodwin, W., Pte., 2114	* 9.5.15
Fleming, J., Pte., 2075	*25.3.15	Gordon, J., Sgt., 606 (D.C.M.)	*25.9.15
Fleming, J., Pte., S/3971	* 9.5.15	Gordon, J., Pte., 1233	* 4.3.15
Fleming, J., Pte., S/7027	†9.10.15	Gorrie, C., Cpl., 1808	† 2.9.15
Fleming, W., Pte., S/8638	*22.4.16	Gouge, F., Pte., S/10560	*22.4.16
Flynn, A., Pte., S/14016	§12.7.16	Gow, D., Pte., 1189	*11.3.15
Forbes, D. C., Sgt., 523	* 9.5.15	Gow, W., Cpl., 3/2160	*20.4.16
Forbes, G., Pte., 3/3590	*22.4.16	Graham, A., Pte., S/10477	*21.4.17
Forbes, J., Sgt., 566	* 9.5.15	Graham, A. H., Pte., S/17055	* 8.6.18
Forbes, J., Pte., 3/3198	†12.4.16	Graham, J., Pte., 8539	* 5.11.14
Forbes, W. R., L/Cpl., S/13131	§20.7.16	Graham, N., Pte., 1001	* 9.5.15
		Graham, R., Pte., S/4221	*21.4.17
Ford, A., Pte., S/8540	*26.10.15	Graham, W., Pte., S/7996	* 7.1.16
Ford, W. T., Pte., S/10581	*22.4.16	Graham, W., Pte., S/21389	§3.11.18
Forrest, G., L/Sgt., 646	§ 4.8.16	Grant, J., Pte., S/7135	* 9.5.15
Foster, G., Pte., S/3811	.26.3.15	Grant, W., Pte., 3/4032	*13.5.15
Foster, T., L/Cpl., 2331	* 9.5.15	Granville, D., Pte., S/19746	§31.10.18
Frail, E., Pte., 3/2855	*14.3.15	Gratten, J., L/Cpl., 957	*25.9.15
Frame, W., Pte., 2122	†30.11.14	Gray, C., Pte., S/16041	†26.4.17
Fraser, D., L/Sgt., 1882	*25.9.15	Gray, J., Pte., 10475	*21.1.16
Fraser, M., Pte., 3/9643	*22.4.16	Gray, J., A/Cpl., 8399	*25.9.15
Fraser, T., Pte., S/8705	* 7.1.16	Green, H., Cpl., 3/8960	*22.4.16
		Greenwood, H., Pte., 11613	*14.3.17
		Gregory, R., Pte., S/13995	*14.3.17
Gair, M., A/Cpl., 166	*21.1.16	Greig, J., Pte., S/17497	†15.3.17
Galbraith, J., Pte., S/11333	*14.10.16	Grimley, M., Pte., 1331	* 5.11.14
Galloway, D., Dmr., 1797	*12.11.14	Grimmond, W. V., L/Cpl., 2277	*22.4.16
Galloway, J., Piper, 1871	* 8.10.15		
Galloway, T., Pte., S/11866	*21.4.17	Guest, H., L/Cpl., 2124	*25.9.15
Gardiner, W., Pte., 3/3585	†22.7.15		
Garland, P., Pte., 3/2282 (D.C.M.)	*21.1.16	Haig, T., Pte., 9352	* 9.5.15
		Haig, W., L/Cpl., S/10496	* 7.1.16
Gay, R. M., Pte., S/15105	§26.12.16	Hall, J., Pte., 1666	†13.11.14
Geddes, J. H., Pte., S/8413	§20.10.18	Hallam, W., Pte., 10439	†14.4.17

APPENDIX IV

Halter, J., Pte., S/10281 *11.6.18
Hamilton, D., Sgt., 1591 * 7.1.16
Hamilton, D., Pte., S/10671 *22.4.16
Hamilton, D., L/Cpl., S/8452 †21.1.16
Hamilton, J., Pte., S/8594 *22.4.16
Hannan, W., Pte., 3/2826 *25.9.15
Hanton, W., Sgt., 1062 § 6.7.16
Hanvey, T., Pte., S/14626 †23.4.17
Hardie, P. C., L/Cpl., S/10539 *22.4.16
Harker, A., Pte., S/10285 †16.1.16
Harkins, J., A/Cpl., S/11147 *22.4.16
Harkness, H., Pte., S/13121 * 8.6.18
Harkness, R., Pte., 3/4151 *24.4.16
Harley, D., Pte., S/8062 *22.4.16
Harley, W., Pte., 9862 *17.5.15
Harman, S., Pte., 3/3471 *22.4.16
Harper, J. P., Pte., 10333 †25.10.15
Harris, A., Pte., 10222 *14.3.17
Hastie, J., Pte., 8420 †12.6.15
Haxton, R., Pte., 7593 *13.5.15
Haxton, R., L/Cpl., S/7648 †30.10.15
Hay, A., Pte., 3/3012 *14.3.17
Hay, J., Pte., S/7019 *21.4.17
Hay, J., Pte., 9385 *18.5.15
Hay, J., L/Cpl., 429 * 9.6.15
Hay, J., Pte., S/17500 § 4.11.18
Hayes, G., Pte., S/11673 *16.6.16
Hazeldean, G., Pte., 981 *21.1.16
Healy, O., Pte., S/11173 † 5.6.16
Henderson, J., Pte., 3/2616 † 4.7.17
Henderson, S., Pte., S/10330 *25.9.15
Henderson, T., Sgt., 1701 * 7.1.16
Henderson, W., Pte., S/10644 *22.4.16
Henderson, W., Pte., S/17697 §2.10.18
Henderson, W., Pte., S/20045 ¶15.4.17
Herd, G., A/L/Cpl., 829 †13.5.15
Herd, J., Pte., 2201 *9.11.14
Herd, W., L/Cpl., 1751 † 6.8.15
Heron, R. J., Pte., 949 †24.4.15
Hewitt, J. G., Pte., S/11776 †14.3.17
Higgins, J., Pte., 3/2893 *25.9.15
Hiley, P., Pte., S/11259 †29.4.16
Hill, G. W., Pte., 569 † 5.6.15
Hilton, R., Pte., S/13167 §19.7.16
Hogg, J., Pte., 598 *21.1.16
Hoggan, H., Pte., 9698 † 9.12.14
Holmes, D., Pte., S/3061 *25.9.15
Holmes, S. B., Pte., S/10170 *21.1.16
Honeyman, J. D., Sgt., 9652 * 8.10.15
Hopton, J., Pte., 19673 §13.11.17
Horsburgh, T. M., Pte., S/8133 *25.9.15
Howard, A. F., Pte., S/10271 § 9.7.16
Howard, H. E., Pte., 2152 *25.9.15

Hughes, D., Pte., 5880 *25.9.15
Hughes, H. G., Pte., 1491 †12.11.14
Hughes, J., A/Cpl., 8458 *21.1.16
Hughes, P., Pte., S/6652 *22.4.16
Hughes, W., A/Cpl., 1856 *21.1.16
Humm, T., Sgt., 9260 (D.C.M.) *21.1.16
Hunter, T., Pte., S/8000 *29.10.15
Hush, J. D., L/Cpl., 601 *25.9.15
Hutcheon, J., Pte., 2604 * 9.5.15
Hutchieson, G., Pte., 3/2483 * 7.1.16
Hutchison, J., L/Cpl., S/11307 *14.3.17
Hutchison, R., Cpl., 781 (D.C.M.) *21.4.17
Hutton, A., Pte., S/11532 *21.4.17
Hutton, D., Pte., 1053 §21.11.14
Hyslop, J., Pte., 823 * 3.6.15

Inglis, F. W., Pte., S/10638 *22.4.16
Inglis, J., L/Sgt., 1060 * 7.1.16
Ireland, A., Pte., S/10338 *21.1.16
Ireland, J., Pte., S/21437 §13.10.18
Irvine, R., Pte., S/10029 * 28.1.16

James, G., Pte., S/10161 *21.1.16
Jamieson, W., Pte., S/12435 *21.4.17
Jennings, R., Pte., S/15888 *14.3.17
Jensen, F., Pte., 1696 †24.5.15
Jessop, A., C.Q.M.S., 8408 * 7.1.16
Johnson, S., Pte., S/4252 § 4.7.16
Johnstone, A., Pte., S/12395 *21.4.17
Johnstone, B., Pte., S/12215 §31.8.17
Johnstone, G., L/Cpl., 158 * 9.5.15
Johnstone, G. B., Sgt., 896 *22.4.16
Johnstone, J., Pte., 1579 * 9.5.15
Johnstone, J., Sgt., 8517 * 8.3.15
Johnstone, J. G., L/Cpl., 1747 *8.10.15
Jones, G., Pte., S/6711 * 7.1.16
Joyce, M., Pte., 3/2815 †15.3.15

Kay, A. D., L/Cpl., S/10652 †24.5.17
Kay, J., Pte., 3/3241 * 9.5.15
Keddie, A., A/Sgt., 2029 *21.1.16
Keir, J., L/Cpl., S/12475 *22.4.16
Kelly, E., Pte., 9702 * 4.7.15
Kelly, J., Pte., S/5030 †10.5.15
Kelly, P., A/Sgt., 1408 *17.5.15
Kelly, W. M., Pte., 1943 †15.3.15
Kelman, A., L/Cpl., S/18461 †21.9.18
Kenny, E., Pte., S/10299 *14.3.17
Keppie, R., Pte., S/13183 §29.3.17
Kerwin, J., Pte., 1891 *13.1.16
Kidd, T., Pte., S/7080 †13.5.15

329

THE SECOND BATTALION THE BLACK WATCH

Kidd, W., Pte., S/20049	* 8.6.18	Macdonald, J. K., Pte., 1326	*11.3.15
Kilgour, D. B., Pte., S/8252	*21.1.16	Macdonald, R., Pte., S/8534 (D.C.M.)	*22.4.16
Kilmartin, P., Pte., 3/2466	*25.9.15		
King, J., Pte., S/13989	§ 4.3.17	Macfarlane, J. D., Pte., S/18520	† 3.6.18
Kinnear, J., Pte., 2210	* 9.5.15		
Kirk, J., Pte., 895	†21.11.14	Macfarlane, T., Pte., 1038	* 7.1.16
Kirkham, W., Pte., S/11758	*22.4.16	Mackay, A., Pte., S/7548	*14.3.17
Kirkland, J. A., Pte., S/12433	§24.7.16	Mackay, D., Pte., 1317	†16.3.15
Knight, J., Pte., 13179	§20.8.16	Mackenzie, C., Pte., 1633	* 2.6.15
Kydd, D., Pte., 6745	*23.4.15	Mackie, J., A/L/Cpl., S/3954	*20.9.18
Kyle, J. K., Pte., S/10347	§ 1.11.18	Mackie, W., Pte., 4218	†24.4.16
		MacKnight, J., L/Cpl., 2718	† 7.1.16
Laben, T., Pte., S/11562	† 4.5.16	Maclure, E., Pte., S/6958	*21.1.16
Laing, J., Pte., 1770	* 9.5.15	Macrae, J., Pte., 1305	†30.1.16
Laing, J., Sgt., 3/8540	* 9.5.15	McAulay, D., Pte., 815	†19.5.15
Lamb, J., Pte., S/8918	*22.4.16	McAulay, G., Pte., 814	*21.1.16
Lamb, T., Pte., S/7508	* 7.1.16	McBean, R., L/Cpl., 2117	† 8.2.16
Lamond, A., Pte., S/7122	†25.1.16	McBride, G., Pte., 1084	*21.1.16
Lamond, C., L/Cpl., 1868	† 7.11.14	McBurnie, A., Pte., 69	†16.1.16
Lang, W., Pte., S/10621	*22.4.16	McCallum, J. B., Pte., S/14994	*21.4.17
Latto, L. R. J., L/Cpl., S/12321	†23.4.17		
		McCann, E., Pte., 2234	*12.3.15
Lauchlin, W., Pte., S/9501	*22.4.16	McCann, I., Pte., 9537	* 5.11.15
Law, D., Pte., S/10147	*21.1.16	McCann, J. W., L/Cpl., 6695	§ 2.9.18
Law, G., Pte., S/11669	*21.4.17	McCarey, A., Pte., S/13122	§19.6.18
Lawrie, R., C.S.M., 8561	*25.9.15	McCarthy, A., Pte., S/11966	*22.4.16
Lawson, J., Pte., S/15068	*21.4.17	McClive, R., Pte., 3/2509	†30.3.15
Lawson, R., Pte., S/13170	*21.4.17	McClusky, H., Pte., 2300	*12.12.14
Leach, R., Pte., S/10337	*21.1.16	McComb, A., Pte., S/3984	*21.1.16
Lees, J., Sgt., S/3342	*14.3.17	McConnell, D., Pte., S/8037	*18.4.15
Leggate, J., Pte., S/6969	* 9.5.15	McConville, G., Pte., 9661	* 7.1.16
Leishman, R., L/Cpl., 9906	*25.9.15	McCormac, J., Pte., 3/2382	*25.9.15
Lennox, S., Pte., S/13144	§22/.16	McCormick, J., Pte., S/7926	*22.4.16
Leslie, R., Pte., S/6690	*25.9.15	McCormick, T., Pte., 3/2850	*9.5.15
Lewis, J., Pte., S/10599	§ 8.8.16	McCraw, D., Pte., S/12238	*11.12.16
Liddle, G., Pte., S/8785	*21.4.17	McCurrach, W., Pte., 1695	† 1.10.15
Lightfoot, A., Pte., 10030	*25.9.15	McCutcheon, T. C., Sgt., S/9544	*22.4.16
Lindsay, R., Pte., 8235	*22.4.16		
Linton, H., Pte., S/7741	*29.8.15	McDonagh, A., L/Cpl., 952	†14.7.15
Lirone, P., A/Cpl., 3/1300	* 9.5.15	McDonald, A. V., L/Cpl., 2055	†13.5.15
Little, J., L/Cpl., S/11175	*22.4.16		
Livingstone, D., L/Cpl., 6836	†9.12.14	McDonald, H., Pte., 1357	†25.4.15
Logan, R., Pte., 1524	* 6.3.15	McDonald, T., Pte., 3/2765	*10.3.15
Lomas, C., Pte., 9901	* 8.10.15	McDonald, T., Pte., 5008	* 9.5.15
Lonie, J., Pte., 3/2597	* 9.5.15	McDonald, W. Pte., 3/3551	*14.3.17
Love, J., Pte., 3/3926	*13.10.15	McDougall, A., Pte., S/13148	§28.6.16
Low, C., L/Cpl., 3/2520	* 7.1.16	McDougall, H., Pte., S/7635	*13.5.15
Low, C., Pte., S/9504	*22.4.16	McDougall, J., Pte., S/4006	†28.10.15
Low, J., Pte., 3/2504	§ 4.12.17	McDougall, J., Pte., S/5230	†17.2.17
Low, W., Pte., S/10568	*22.4.16	McDougall, J., Pte., 3/2746	* 9.5.15
Lugton, J., Sgt., 8175	†15.3.17	McEwan, P., Pte., 2017	* 4.11.14
Lynch, J., Pte., 622	* 7.1.16	McFarlane, D., L/Cpl., S/10482	* 7.1.16
MacDonald, A., Sgt., S/8444	*21.1.16	McGarry, R., Pte., 3/2679	†11.2.15
Macdonald, J. A., Pte., 2294	*25.9.15	McGhie, W., Pte., S/13223	*21.4.17

APPENDIX IV

McGill, G., Pte., 1915 *23.4.15
McGinley, P., Pte., 3/4251 §27.6.16
McGlenon, J. P., Pte., S/10135 *22.4.16
McGregor, A., L/Cpl., 2820 *12.8.15
McGregor, A., Pte., 3/4223 †22.4.16
McGregor, G., Sgt., 2145 † 7.12.16
McGregor, R., Pte., S/17448 †18.7.17
McGuire, B., Pte., 2715 * 9.5.15
McGuire, J., Pte., S/7379 *19.9.18
McHugh, J., Pte., S/13145 §28.6.16
McInearney, R., Pte., 3/2646 * 9.5.15
McInroy, D., L/Cpl., 2323 *29.10.14
McIntosh, J., Pte., 58 † 6.9.15
McKay, H., Pte., S/16353 *14.3.17
McKay, J. A., L/Cpl., S/10598 *22.4.16
McKay, W., Pte., S/15866 *14.3.17
McKenzie, H., Pte., S/7128 † 5.2.16
McKenzie, J., Pte., S/10442 *21.1.16
McKenzie, W., L/Cpl., 780 †12.5.15
McKenzie, W., L/Cpl., 931 *30.6.15
McKillop, S., Pte., S/8316 * 7.1.16
McKinnie, W., Pte., S/7507 * 7.1.16
McLachlan, D., L/Cpl., 1614 *12.3.15
McLachlan, J. D., L/Cpl., S/7545 * 9.5.15
McLaren, A., Pte., S/8024 §29.5.16
McLaren, B., Pte., S/7062 *18.5.15
McLaren, J. A., Pte., 2058 * 2.6.15
McLaren, J. J., Pte., S/10662 *22.4.16
McLaren, T., Pte., 741 * 9.5.15
McLauchlan, A., Pte., 3/3591 *10.3.15
McLauchlan, P., Pte., S/7563 *25.9.15
McLaughlan, J., L/Cpl., S/7616 *21.1.16
McLaughlan, R., A/Sgt., S/7088 *13.1.16
McLean, D., Pte., S/10566 *14.3.17
McLean, J., Pte., S/11305 *13.4.16
McLean, R. H., Pte., 1889 *22.4.16
McLeod, J., Pte., S/15069 *14.3.17
McLeod, W., Pte., 4940 * 9.5.15
McMahon, M., Pte., S/8192 *22.4.16
McMeechan, R., Pte., S/11709 §27.6.16
McMillan, C., Pte., S/13913 § 3.7.16
McMillan, H., Pte., 3/2742 †21.12.16
McMillan, J., Pte., S/6981 *25.8.15
McMillan, J., Pte., S/13181 †17.6.18
McNab, A., Pte., 939 *21.12.14
McNab, A., Pte., 2706 *25.9.15
McNaughton, R., Pte., S/11958 *21.4.17
McNaughton, W. H., Pte., S/8110 * 2.6.15

McNee, P., A/Cpl., 941 (D.C.M.) †23.1.16
McNee, W., Pte., S/3500 *22.4.16
McNeil, W., Pte., S/11889 §22.7.17
McPhail, A., Pte., 1925 *30.10.14
McPhee, D., L/Cpl., S/8571 * 7.1.16
McPhee, R., Pte., 3/1755 †24.4.16
McPherson, T., Pte., S/7748 * 7.1.16
McPherson, W., Sgt., 1588 * 8.6.18
McQuarrie, N., Pte., 3/2585 *22.4.16
McQueen, R., Pte., S/8017 * 9.5.15
McRae, C., L/Cpl., S/7097 * 7.1.16
McRoberts, D., Pte., 3/2749 *12.3.15
McSkimming, P., L/Cpl., 16303 *11.2.17
Mack, W., L/Cpl., 1418 *22.4.16
Madill, R., Sgt., 1472 (D.C.M.) * 7.1.16
Mailer, A., Pte., 3/4144 * 7.1.16
Maitland, M., Pte., S/17644 §24.10.17
Malcolm, W., L/Cpl., S/10537 *22.4.16
Mallett, S., Pte., 281 * 2.6.15
Manby, A. G., Pte., 1831 †16.1.16
Mann, A. C., Pte., S/7743 *14.3.17
Mann, C. A., Pte., S/6973 *25.9.15
Marshall, A., Pte., S/2903 †22.4.16
Marshall, A., Pte., S/5064 *25.9.15
Marshall, D., Pte., S/2635 (M.M.) *22.4.16
Marshall, G., Pte., S/4379 *22.4.16
Marshall, H., Pte., 1643 †5.12.14
Marshall, T., A/Sgt., 2316 *21.1.16
Martin, T., Pte., 3/3287 *25.9.15
Mathers, D., Pte., S/11891 *14.3.17
Matheson, D. J., Pte., 3/2008 §18.6.16
Matheson, P., Pte., S/7574 *21.1.16
Mathieson, W., Pte., S/3686 *8.10.15
Maver, R. C., L/Cpl., 203107 §24.8.18
Mawhinnie, R., Pte., 8437 *11.3.15
Mechie, J., Pte., 8271 *25.9.15
Meek, G., Pte., 2205 * 9.5.15
Meldrum, C., Pte., 7849 * 8.2.15
Melrose, J., Cpl., 599 * 9.5.15
Menelaws, G. W., Pte., S/7753 * 7.1.16
Menzies, J., L/Cpl., 3/2941 *21.1.16
Menzies, J., Pte., S/17148 §15.10.17
Millar, E. F., Bdns., 79 (M.M.) †20.4.17
Millar, J., Pte., S/10323 * 7.1.16
Millar, S., Pte., 1603 *2.12.14
Millar, T., Pte., S/11723 §21.7.17
Miller, W., Pte., 266185 ¶27.10.18
Mills, W. A., Pte., S/11540 †14.7.16

THE SECOND BATTALION THE BLACK WATCH

Milne, A., Pte., 797	*21.4.17	Nicol, J., Pte., 2151	* 9.5.15
Milne, D., L/Cpl., 1825	*13.5.15	Nicol, J., Pte., S/11769	† 1.6.16
Milne, J., Pte., 1847	*29.11.14	Nicol, M., Pte., 1445	*27.11.14
Milne, R. A., L/Cpl., 1596	*7.2.15	Nicol, W., Pte., S/13149	§11.11.18
Mitchell, G., L/Cpl., 3/2564	*13.1.16	Niven, N., Pte., S/11369	*22.4.16
Mitchell, J., Pte., S/2786	†1.11.15	Noakes, G. V., A/Cpl., 431	§18.6.17
Mitchell, J., L/Cpl., S/7936	†21.1.16	Noble, W. W., L/Cpl., 1619	*14.3.17
Mitchell, T., Pte., 1370	*27.11.14	Nugent, J., Pte., 3/2482	* 9.5.15
Mitchell, W., Pte., S/8688	*21.1.16		
Moncrieff, D., A/Cpl., S/7430	§13.1.16	O'Donell, J., L/Cpl., 2125	* 9.5.15
Moncur, A., Pte., S/7738	* 7.1.16	O'Donell, J., Pte., 3/2584	*21.4.17
Montgomery, H., Pte., S/7697		O'Donnell, J., L/Cpl., 1050	* 9.5.15
	*22.4.16	O'Donnell, N., Pte., S/10574	*22.4.16
Moodie, J. S., Pte., 1120	*19.4.15	O'Neill, J., Pte., 3/2457	* 9.5.15
Moore, D., Pte., 583	*10.3.15	O'Neill, H., Sgt., 3/8805	†17.5.15
Moran, J., L/Cpl., 567	*25.9.15	Ogilvie, C. E., Pte., S/16020	†25.4.17
Morgan, G., Pte., S/11286	*22.4.16	Oliphant, J., Pte., S/8715	§17.8.16
Morgan, J., L/Cpl., 1678	* 1.8.15	Ormston, T., Pte., S/8494	*21.1.16
Morgan, W., Pte., S/7138	*25.9.15	Orr, J., Pte., 3/9207	* 7.1.16
Morris, R., Pte., S/19721	¶24.8.17	Orr, W., Pte., 1935	* 9.5.15
Morrison, D., Pte., S/3346	*22.4.16	Oswald, W. S., C.S.M., 887	*21.1.16
Morrison, F., Pte., 2675	†15.3.17		
Morrison, S., Pte., 8166	*22.4.16	Page, W., Pte., 3/3507	*25/9/15
Morrison, T., Pte., 1947	† 6.4.16	Palmer, D., C.S.M., S/7771	*21.4.17
Morrison, W., Pte., S/12531	§22.9.16	Paton, D., Pte., S/10428	* 8.6.18
Mowat, J., L/Cpl., 2096	§25.10.18	Paton, J., Pte., 489	†31.1.16
Mowat, S., Pte., 3/2508	*21.1.16	Paton, J., Pte., 1802	*21.1.16
Muir, W., A/Sgt., 384	†15.5.15	Patterson, A., Pte., S/22364	†19.9.18
Mulholland, J., L/Sgt., 1020	* 7.1.16	Patterson, A., Pte., S/19822	§21.6.18
Munro, W., Pte., 3/2623	*13.4.15	Patterson, A., Pte., 3078	* 9.5.15
Murdoch, D. MacP., Sgt., 9383		Pattullo, H., Pte., S/7081	*13.5.15
	*21.4.17	Paul, M., Pte., S/10586	*22.4.16
Murphy, M., Pte., S/4059	†16.4.15	Paul, P., Pte., S/10374	* 7.1.16
Murphy, W., Pte., 8390	§20.4.17	Peat, J. C., L/Cpl., 1275	*25.9.15
Murray, J., Pte., S/20056	¶15.4.17	Penman, J., L/Cpl., 102	*25.9.15
Murray, J., Pte., 7278	†17.6.18	Penman, J., A/L/Cpl., S/8798	§6.11.18
Murray, R., A/Cpl., 1921	*21.1.16	Perris, T. T., Pte., S/19705	§7.11.17
Murray, T. S., Sgt., 133,	* 7.1.16	Phee, L., Pte., 2745	† 7.1.16
Myles, J., Pte., 2187	*25.9.15	✗Philp, J., Pte., 3/2541 ✗	* 9.5.15 ✗ BROTH
Myles, T. G., L/Cpl., 1876	*4.11.14	Philp, W., Pte., S/7140	*10.7.15
		Plain, H., L/Cpl., 13177	*14.3.17
Nairn, A., L/Cpl., 8020	† 4.2.16	Pollock, D. E., Pte., 10501	*21.1.16
Neeley, R., L/Cpl., S/6979	*25.9.15	Porter, D., Pte., S/19445	†21.4.17
Neil, G., Pte., 2130	*25.9.15	Porter, J., Pte., S/12474	§14.7.16
Neill, D. F., A/Sgt., 1642	*22.4.16	Pratt, J., Pte., S/12217	*29.6.18
Neilson, G., Pte., S/19311	*21.4.17	Pratt, R., Cpl., 672	* 7.1.16
Neilson, J., Pte., 1384	* 9.5.15	Preston, J., Pte., S/11537	§12.10.16
Nelson, D. W., Pte., 2206	*18.5.15	Priest, R., Pte., 1481	†13.5.15
Nelson, W., Pte., S/13260	†14.3.17	Pringle, J., Pte., S/8006	†23.5.16
Ness, G., Pte., 3/2506	†13.6.15	Proudfoot, R. W., C.S.M., 7912	
Newton, R. F., A/Sgt., S/10207			*21.1.16
	*21.1.16	Purdie, J., Pte., S/7531	*17.5.15
Nicholson, J., Pte., 2271	*11.3.15		
Nicholson, T., Pte., S/8005	* 7.1.16	Rae, A., Pte., S/7427	† 8.1.16
Nicol, D., Pte., S/3916	* 9.5.15	Rae, J., Pte., 1860	†13.5.15

APPENDIX IV

Rae, J., Pte., S/7729 * 9.5.15
Rae, J. D., Pte., S/8255 *25.9.15
Ramage, J., Pte., 3/2744 * 3.2.15
Ramsay, D., L/Cpl., 10488 § 2.5.16
Ramsay, J., Pte., S/8082 *22.4.16
Ramsay, J., L/Cpl., S/10536 *22.4.16
Rattray, C., Pte., S/17512 §7.12.16
Rattray, W., Pte., 2267 *10.3.15
Reddie, J., Pte., S/13233 § 2.7.16
Reid, T., Pte., S/9231 *22.4.16
Reilly, J., Pte., 1790 †22.11.14
Reilly, P., L/Cpl., S/10634 *14.3.17
Rennie, S., Pte., S/7120 *21.1.16
Reoch, A., Pte., 1426 * 7.1.16
Reynolds, P., Pte., 1702 †25.3.15
Richardson, D., L/Cpl., S/3358
    (D.C.M.) †25.4.16
Rigby, J., Pte., 6152 *8.10.15
Ritchie, A., Pte., S/19753 §13.8.17
Ritchie, J., L/Cpl., 9531 *25.9.15
Roberts, H., Pte., S/10527 §14.7.16
Robertson, A., Pte., 883 ¶19.7.16
Robertson, A., Pte., 1493 *10.3.15
Robertson, A., Pte., 3/3081 *25.9.15
Robertson, A., L/Cpl., S/10429 *7.1.16
Robertson, A., Pte., S/12115 §18.7.16
Robertson, A., Pte., 3/2647 †15.1.16
Robertson, C., Pte., S/10116 †14.8.15
Robertson, F., Pte., 3/3917 *22.4.16
Robertson, G., Pte., 1513 §27.1.16
Robertson, J., Pte., 1338 *13.5.15
Robertson, J., Pte., 2243
    (D.C.M.) * 8.6.18
Robertson, J., Pte., 2646 *26.10.15
Robertson, J., Pte., S/11762 * 8.6.18
Robertson, J. McG., Pte., 2634 *18.4.15
Robertson, N., Pte., 659 *21.1.16
Robertson, P., Pte., 2218 *29.11.14
Robertson, P., Cpl., S/8390 * 7.1.16
Robertson, R., Pte., S/8185 *25.9.15
Robertson, W. A., Pte., 1946 * 9.5.15
Robson, J., L/Cpl., S/13207 *20.4.17
Rodger, J., Pte., S/16088 *14.3.17
Rodgers, A., Pte., S/8730 †17.1.16
Rodgers, H., Pte., S/6962 † 6.9.16
Rogerson, A., Pte., S/6415 *22.4.16
Rooke, H. G., Pte., 8169 * 7.1.16
Ross, E. M., Pte., S/13154 §20.7.16
Ross, J., Pte., S/1006 * 7.1.16
Russell, A. L., Pte., S/10122 †10.10.15
Russell, J., Pte., S/11751 *22.4.16
Russell, S., Pte., S/8040 §21.6.16

Sanderson, J., Pte., S/3892 §29/6/16
Sanderson, J., Pte., S/19316 *21.4.17

Scott, D., Pte., 3/3084 * 9.5.15
Scott, F., Pte., 8183 †22.4.16
Scott, T., Pte., S/5658 †26.4.16
Scott, W., Pte., S/17007 *11.6.18
Seath, J., Pte., S/22455 §10.11.18
Selkirk, J. A., L/Cpl., S/13160 §29.6.16
Shand, D., A/Cpl., 1605 *21.1.16
Shand, R., Pte., 372 *12.7.15
Shannon, J., Pte., S/7479 †19.1.16
Shaw, J., Pte., 634 *21.1.16
Sheach, T., L/Cpl., 9356 †9.11.14
Shelvin, J., Pte., 3/4221 *25.9.15
Shepherd, J., Pte., 1467 *7.12.14
Sherran, F., Pte., 20 5.2.15
Sherriff, J., Pte., S/6709 §27.5.16
Sherry, J., Pte., 3/2467 *10.7.15
Shiells, A., Pte., S/8254 *25.9.15
Shirra, J., L/Cpl., S/4484 *21.4.17
Sherret, D., Pte., S/10404 *8.10.15
Short, J., Pte., 3/2558 *10.3.15
Sim, D., Pte., 3/3970 *21.1.16
Simpson, A., L/Cpl., 1433 † 6.7.15
Simpson, A., Pte., 1950 †10.5.15
Simpson, D. M., Pte., S/16333
    §28.7.17
Simpson, D. R., A/Cpl., 2511 *14.3.17
Simpson, D. S., Pte., 736 *25.9.15
Simpson, T., Pte., S/13325 †14.3.17
Sims, J., L/Cpl., 10489 * 7.1.16
Sinclair, J., Pte., S/3708 *22.4.16
Small, D., L/Cpl., S/16651 *22.4.16
Small J., Pte., 755 * 9.5.15
Small, W., Pte., 556 *12.3.15
Smeaton, J., Pte., S/17121 †19.9.18
Smith, A., Pte., S/13111 *14.3.17
Smith, A., Pte., S/11557 *22.4.16
Smith, A., Pte., S/8682 *25.9.15
Smith, C., Pte., 3/2901 * 7.1.16
Smith, D. G., Pte., S/11535 †22.4.16
Smith, D., Pte., 3/3911 * 7.1.16
Smith, E., Pte., S/10592 *22.4.16
Smith, E., Pte., S/11753 *22.4.16
Smith, G., Pte., S/8330 * 7.1.16
Smith, J., Pte., 1452 *14.3.17
Smith, J., Pte., S/11570 *22.4.16
Smith, J., Pte., S/8867 * 7.1.16
Smith, R. G., L/Cpl., S/7103 * 9.5.15
Smith, W., Pte., 9432 *13.5.15
Souter, E. A., Pte., S/19755 §13.8.17
Speed, R., Cpl., 1884 *21.4.17
Spriggs, W. G., L/Cpl., S/7658
    *21.1.16
Stafford, F., Pte., S/6259 *22.4.16
Stevenson, G., Pte., 3/2674 * 7.1.16
Stewart, A., Pte., S/22140 §17.10.18

333

THE SECOND BATTALION THE BLACK WATCH

Stewart, D., Pte., S/22273	§7.11.18	Thomson, J., Pte., S/8057	*21.1.16
Stewart, J., Pte., S/7633	*25.9.15	Thomson J., Pte., 2272	†22.12.14
Stewart, J., Pte., S/11390	*22.4.16	Thomson, P., Pte., S/8880	*21.1.16
Stewart, J., Pte., S/11572	*22.4.16	Tierney, T., Pte., 3/2003	*23.6.16
Stewart, J., Pte., S/7730	†22.6.16	Tolland, P., Pte., 3/3614	
Stewart, J., Pte., S/8765	*18.6.16	(D.C.M.)	§14.6.15
Stewart, M., Pte., S/7538	*14.3.17	Torrance, G., L/Cpl., 1459	†22.4.16
Stewart, R., L/Cpl., 9950	* 9.5.15	Torrance, J., Pte., 1548	*25.9.15
Stewart, W., Pte., S/8266	† 8.1.16	Torrie, D., L/Cpl., 1240	*4.11.14
Stewart, W., Pte., S/20081	¶15.4.17	Trory, A. J., Pte., S/8356	† 7.9.16
Stewart, W. L., Pte., 1641	§14.10.14	Tuckerman, A. R., Pte., S/12494	
Stirling, S., Pte., 2474	* 9.5.15		*14.3.17
Strachan, C., Pte., 1828		Turner, C. W., Pte., S/9952	*14.3.17
(D.C.M.)	* 9.5.15		
Strachan, J., Pte., S/3380	*22.4.16	Ure, P. B., Pte., 1748	*14.4.15
Strachan, P., Pte., 1612	*21.11.14	Urquhart, D., Pte., S/7399	†20.4.16
Strachan, W., Pte., 1730	*2.12.14		
Strachan, W., Pte., 1732	*5.12.14	Vallance, D., Pte., 2663	*8.10.15
Stuart, J., Pte., S/6213	*22.4.16	Vanbieck, A., Pte., S/7621	*21.1.16
Studholme, J., Pte., S/11869	*22.4.16	Vessie, G., L/Cpl., 2131	*11.3.15
Sturrock, C., Pte., S/15059	§7.11.18		
Sturrock, J., Pte., 1232	†20.5.15	Waddell, D., Pte., 1651	*23.11.14
Styles, S., Pte., S/11607	*22.4.16	Waddell, L. C. F., Pte., S/10185	
Summers, A., Pte., 9528	*11.3.15		*25.9.15
Surgenor, T., Pte., S/10591	§15.7.16	Waldie, S., Pte., 2181	*16.4.15
Sutherland, A., A/Sgt., 3/3244		Walker, H. H., Pte., 3/4216	*25.9.15
	*10.3.15	Walker, J., Pte., S/10639	†27.4.16
Sutherland, W., Pte., 3/3505	*11.5.15	Walker, J., Pte., S/4076	*22.4.16
Suttie, D., Pte., S/8122	*25.9.15	Wallace, C., Pte., 1627	*27.11.14
Suttie, J., Pte., S/8329	* 6.3.16	Wallace, G., L/Cpl., 471	*12.3.15
Swan, T., L/Cpl., 484	*5.12.14	Wallace, J., Pte., 3/1909	§20.7.18
Swan, T., L/Cpl., 3/3854	†21.1.16	Wallace, J., L/Cpl., S/11631	*14.3.17
Swanston, A., Pte., S/12512	†24.2.17	Wallace, R., Pte., S/7643	§20.7.16
Sweeney, N., Pte., S/13234	§21.7.16	Wallace, W., Pte., S/18545	†5.10.18
		Wann, J., Piper, 9908	†13.3.15
Tait, A., Pte., S/8630	*25.9.15	Ward, C., L/Cpl., 2664	* 9.5.15
Tait, F., Pte., S/13176	§23.6.16	Ward, T., Pte., S/3459	* 9.5.15
Tallon, F., Pte., 1205	*5.12.14	Warden, G., Sgt., 8052	§26.5.17
Tarbet, J., Pte., S/7560	*22.4.16	Waterson, D., Pte., 8060	*21.12.14
Tarditto, W., Pte., 1986	†5.12.14	Watson, W., Pte., S/10633	*5.11.16
Taylor, J., Pte., 1141	*11.3.15	Watt, G. M., Pte., S/13717	¶22.4.17
Taylor, J., Pte., 3/3477	* 9.5.15	Watt, J., Pte., S/15080	*14.3.17
Taylor, J., Pte., S/7496	*25.9.15	Watt, J. Y., Drmr., 2750	§10.7.18
Taylor, W. H., L/Cpl., S/6757		Watt, R., Pte., S/8100	* 9.5.15
	*21.1.16	Watt, T., Pte., 2705	†17.5.15
Tennant, R., Pte., S/15121	§.1.7.17	Weatherhead, F., Pte., S/10291	
Thomson, E. F., L/Cpl., S/9728			*25.9.15
	†15.3.17	Webster, W., Pte., 3/4057	*28.3.15
Thomson, J., A/Cpl., 1542	*25.9.15	Weir, T., L.Cpl., S/6405	*13.3.16
Thomson, E., Pte., S/16323	†20.5.17	Welsh, J., Pte., 3/2112	†11.4.17
Thomson, C. G. R., Pte., S/9563		Welsh, P., Pte., 3/3362	† 3.5.16
	*22.4.16	Welsh, P., Pte., 10155	† 7.1.16
Thomson, D., Pte., 1365	*16.5.15	West, W. B., Pte., S/7078	*21.7.15
Thomson, J., Pte., 1970	* 9.5.15	Westrop, W. G., Pte., 10242	*21.1.16
Thomson, J., Pte., 3/3095	*11.3.15	Whannell, A., Pte., 1346	* 7.1.16

APPENDIX IV

White, D., Pte., S/8932 *21.1.16
White, E. C., Sgt., 9944 †31.10.14
White, J., Sgt., 1509 *25.9.15
White, J., Pte., S/7077 † 8.3.15
Whyte, J., Pte., S/7957 *21.1.16
Whyte, R., L/Cpl., 773 *6.11.16
Whyte, R., Pte., 2772 § 2.8.16
Wildgoose, H. E., A/L/Cpl., 262
  * 9.5.15
Wilkie, A., C.S.M., 7908 *22.4.16
Wilkins, E., Pte., S/6733 *21.1.16
Wilkins, F. L., L/Cpl., 7100 * 7.1.16
Wilkinson, J., Pte., S/19456 *21.4.17
Williams, C., Pte., 9217 †12.11.14
Williams, C., L/Cpl., S/10654 †24.4.16
Williams, R., Pte., S/7606 §13.12.17
Williamson, J., Pte., S/7925 † 2.8.15
Williamson, M., Cpl., 473 *5.12.14
Williamson, T., Pte., S/9339 *20.4.17
Wilson, A., Pte., 3/2521 †11.3.15
Wilson, A., Pte., 9461 †20.5.15
Wilson, A., Pte., S/7449 *11.4.15
Wilson, C., Pte., S/11731 *22.4.16
Wilson, G., Pte., S/7159 * 7.1.16
Wilson, H., Pte., S/4239 *22.4.16
Wilson, J., Pte., S/8428 * 7.1.16
Wilson, J., Pte., S/10674 *22.4.16

Wilson, J., Pte., S/10668 *22.4.16
Wilson, R., Pte., 1989 *21.1.16
Wilson, R., Pte., 3/3874 * 6.4.16
Wilson, R., Pte., S/10278 * 7.1.16
Wilson, T., Pte., S/9159 †24.4.16
Wilson, T. G., Pte., S/10532 †15.3.17
Wilson, W., Pte., 2116 * 9.5.15
Winter, D., Pte., S/8202 *21.4.17
Winters, C., Pte., S/14517 *21.4.17
Winters, T., Pte., 1098 *27.11.14
Wiseman, J., Pte., S/15853 *14.3.17
Wiseman, L. A., Cpl., 19450 *21.4.17
Wood, C., L/Cpl., S/10540 *22.4.16
Worthington, H., Pte., S/7902
  *21.1.16
Wotherspoon, R., Pte., S/8744
  *21.1.16
Wright, W., Pte., 148 *25.9.15
Wyllie, J., Pte., S/10648 *22.4.16

Young, F., Pte., S/8051 * 2.8.15
Young, G. W., L/Cpl., 3/4055
  * 9.5.15
Young, J. R., L/Cpl., S/7207 † 5.3.16
Younghusband, R., Pte., S/12437
  § 5.7.16
Yule, N., Pte., S/6806 *19.4.15

APPENDIX V

HONOURS AND AWARDS

The Second Battalion

PROMOTIONS

Brevet Colonel
Lieutenant Colonel A. G. Wauchope, D.S.O.

Brevet Lieut.-Colonel
Major W. St. J. Harvey.
Major A. G. Wauchope, D.S.O.

Major
Capt. and Quartermaster J. Anderson, D.C.M.

Hon. Captain
Lieut. and Quartermaster J. Anderson, D.C.M.

BRITISH DECORATIONS

Victoria Cross
L/Corpl. D. Finlay.   Pte. C. Melvin.

C.M.G.
Lieutenant Colonel (Brevet Col.) A. G. Wauchope, D.S.O.

D.S.O.
2nd Lieut. J. I. Buchan.
Capt. (A/Major) T. G. F. Cochrane.
2nd Lieut. J. T. Grassie.
Lieut. M. E. Park.
Lieut. N. M. Ritchie.
Lieut.-Col. J. Stewart.
Major H. H. Sutherland.

M.C.
2nd Lieut. J. A. Barstow.
Lieut. A. E. Blair.
2nd Lieut. J. F. C. Dixon (A. & S. attached).
Capt. C. D. Gilmour.
2nd Lieut. T. A. Henderson.
2nd Lieut. B. Houston, D.C.M.
Lieut. J. N. Inglis.
2nd Lieut. J. Kennedy.
Lieut. W. D. MacEwen.
Capt. R. Macfarlane.
Lieut. J. McGregor.
Lieut. N. McMicking.
2nd Lieut. J. C. Ritchie.
Capt. N. M. Ritchie, D.S.O.
2nd Lieut. M. M. Thorburn.
2nd Lieut. W. A. Young.
R.S.M. J. Johnstone.
A/R.S.M. A. Smart.

Bar to Distinguished Conduct Medal
Sgt. C. Easton.
Sgt. W. Logan.
A/Sgt. T. May.
Sgt. G. Mitchell.

APPENDIX V

2ND BAR TO DISTINGUISHED CONDUCT MEDAL

Sgt. W. Logan.   Sgt. G. Mitchell.

DISTINGUISHED CONDUCT MEDAL

Sgt. J. Anderson.
Corpl. J. Armstrong.
Corpl. D. Bell.
Pte. G. Beveridge.
Sgt. Blyth.
Pte. P. Brady.
A/Sgt. J. Brodie.
Pte. J. Clark.
Sgt. F. Connell.
L/Corpl. R. Cowper.
Pte. T. Cuthbert.
Pte. J. Daniel.
Sgt. J. Drummond.
A/Sgt. C. Easton.
Pte. R. Fawcett.
Sgt. P. Fenton.
L/Corpl. W. Field.
Pte. J. Finlayson.
Pte. W. Foster.
Pte. P. Garland.
Corpl. J. Gordon.
C.S.M. B. Houston.
Sgt. T. Humm.
Sgt. J. Hutchison.
Corpl. R. Hutchison.
Pte. T. James.
Sgt.-Piper J. Keith.
C.S.M. J. Kennedy.
A/Sgt. W. Logan.
Pte. R. Madill.
Pte. W. Mahon.
Corpl. J. Martin.
Pte. J. Marshall.
Corpl. G. McCabe.

Pte. G. McClure.
Piper A. McDonald.
Pte. R. McDonald.
Pte. J. McIntosh.
Pte. G. McLeod.
L/Corpl. P. McNee.
Sgt. A. Mercer.
A/Sgt. D. Miller.
C.S.M. J. Miller.
Sgt. A. Milligan.
Pte. G. Mitchell.
Pte. R. Pearson.
Sgt. A. Pratt.
Sgt. G. Rennie.
L/Corpl. F. Robertson.
Pte. J. Robertson.
Sgt.-Drmr. J. Simpson.
Pte. W. Simpson.
Pte. M. Stark
Pte. D. Stewart.
Pte. J. Stewart.
Pte. C. Strachan.
Sgt. H. Strachan.
Sgt. J. Strachan.
L/Corpl. T. Swan.
Pte. V. Thompson.
Pte. P. Tolland.
Corpl. A. Venters.
A/C.S.M. W. Wallace.
Pte. W. Watters.
A/Sgt. T. Wilson.
C.S.M. W. Wilson.
Sgt. D. Yule.

BAR TO MILITARY MEDAL

Pte. J. Morrison.

MILITARY MEDAL

L/Corpl. W. Blakey.
Pte. F. Bogle.
A/Sgt. F. Connell.
Pte. J. Gibson.
Pte. A. Manzie.
Pte. E. Miller.
L/Corpl. J. Morrison.

Pte. A. Nicol.
L/Corpl. J. G. Nicholson.
A/Corpl. N. Sharples.
Pte. J. Smith
Pte. J. Walker.
Corpl. J. Weir.

THE SECOND BATTALION THE BLACK WATCH

Meritorious Service Medal
A/Sgt. H. Graham.
R.Q.M.S. E. Hobbs.
R.S.M. J. Johnstone.
C.Q.M.S. G. Morrison.
O.R/Q.M.S. J. E. Niven.
C.S.M. A. Smart.
L/Corpl. T. Wilson.

FOREIGN DECORATIONS

Legion of Honour—Croix d'Officier (French)
Major A. G. Wauchope, D.S.O.

Silver Medal (Italian)
Capt. M. E. Park, D.S.O.

St. Vladimir (Russian)
2nd Lieut. T. A. Henderson, M.C.

Cross of St. George, 3rd Class (Russian)
Pte. R. Craig.   A/C.S.M. T. Gant.

Cross of St. George, 4th Class (Russian)
L/Corpl. T. Humm.
Sgt. R. Linton.
Sgt. W. Logan.
L/Sgt. J. Minninch.
Pte. G. McLellon.
Pte. C. Tennant.

Cross of Karageorge, 1st Class, with Crossed Swords (Serbian)
Sgt. J. Lees.   Sgt. G. Mitchell.

Gold Medal (Serbian)
Pte. A. Gibb.   Pte. C. Reid.

Panama Medal
Corpl. D. McMaster.

Mentioned in Dispatches
Major J. Anderson, D.C.M.
Capt. J. A. Barstow, M.C.
Lieut. A. E. Blair, M.C.
2nd Lieut. J. I. Buchan, D.S.O.
Major T. G. F. Cochrane, D.S.O. (3).
2nd Lieut. A. B. Cumming.
Capt. A. C. Denison.
2nd Lieut. J. C. F. Dixon, M.C.

APPENDIX V

Mentioned in Despatches (contd.)

2nd Lieut. R. H. Dundas.
2nd Lieut. H. F. Forrester.
Capt. C. D. Gilmour, M.C.
2nd Lieut. J. T. Grassie, D.S.O.
Capt. D. C. Hamilton-Johnston.
Lieut.-Colonel W. St. J. Harvey (2).
2nd Lieut. T. A. Henderson, M.C.
2nd Lieut. I. O. Hutchison.
Capt. J. N. Inglis, M.C. (2).
Lieut. J. Jeff.
2nd Lieut. J. Kennedy.
Lieut. W. D. McEwen, M.C.
Capt. N. McMicking, D.S.O., M.C.
Capt. H. F. F. Murray.
Capt. M. E. Park, D.S.O. (2).
2nd Lieut. J. C. Paterson.
Lieut. G. D. Paton.
Capt. N. M. Ritchie, D.S.O., M.C.
2nd Lieut. F. H. Soutar.
Lieut.-Colonel J. Stewart, D.S.O. (3)
Major H. H. Sutherland, D.S.O.
Colonel A. G. Wauchope, C.M.G., C.I.E., D.S.O. (4).
Lieut. W. A. Young, M.C. (2)

Pte. G. Beveridge.
Pte. W. Burns.
L/Corpl. D. Cameron.
Pte. J. Campbell.
Pte. G. Clark.
Sgt. W. Clark.
Sgt. R. Cowie.
Pte. J. Daniels.
Pte. A. Fairfull.
C.S.M. T. Gant.
L/Corpl. R. George.
Corpl. H. Graham (2).
Sgt. J. Hainey.
Pte. T. Hedley.
A/C.Q.M.S. W. Hill.
Corpl. W. Hobbs.
Sgt. T. Humm.
Pte. J. Hunter.
Corpl. R. Hutchison.
R.S.M. J. Johnstone.
A/C.Q.M.S. S. Kelly.
L/Corpl. W. Kivlin.
Sgt. W. Logan (2).
Pte. R. Madill.
Pte. W. Mahon.

Pte. Y. McArdell.
Pte. J. McIntosh.
Pte. J. Menzies.
Sgt. J. Minninch.
Sgt. G. Mitchell (2).
Pte. A. Nicholl.
Q.M.S. J. Niven.
Sgt. J. Pert.
Pte. J. Port.
C.S.M. A. Proudfoot.
Pte. G. Radford.
Pte. W. Simpson.
Pte. W. Sinclair.
A/R.S.M. A. Smart.
Pte. M. Stark.
Pte. G. Stevens.
Pte. D. Stewart.
Pte. J. Stewart.
L/Corpl. T. Swan.
Pte. W. Thomson.
L/Corpl. A. Venters.
A/C.S.M. W. Wallace.
Pte. W. Watters.
Sgt. D. Yule.

APPENDIX VI

List of Actions and Operations

The Second Battalion

1914. Arrived in France from India. 12th October.
Trench warfare. Givenchy, La Quinque Rue, Festubert. October–November.
Defence of Festubert. 23rd–24th November.
Defence of Givenchy. 20th–21st December.

1915. Trench warfare. Rue de l'Epinette Area and Rue du Bois. January–March.

BATTLE OF NEUVE CHAPELLE. (Rue du Bois, Port Arthur, Crescent and Orchard.) 10th–13th March.
Trench warfare. Neuve Chapelle Area. March–April.

BATTLE OF AUBERS RIDGE. (Rue du Bois.) 9th May.
Trench warfare. Rue du Bois, Rue de Bacquerot. May–September.

BATTLES OF LOOS. (Action of Piètre.) (Moulin de Piètre.) 25th September.
Trench warfare. Givenchy, Rue du Bois. October–December.
Left France. 5th December. Transhipped at Basrah. 31st December.

1916. Arrived Amarah. 5th January.

ACTION OF SHAIKH SA'AD. (First attempt to relieve Kut.) 7th January.

ACTION OF THE WADI. (First attempt to relieve Kut.) 13th–14th January.

FIRST ATTACK ON HANNA. (First attempt to relieve Kut.) 21st January.
Trench warfare. Orah, Hanna. March.

FIRST ATTACK ON SANNAIYAT. (Third attempt to relieve Kut.) 6th April.

SECOND ATTACK ON SANNAIYAT. (Third attempt to relieve Kut.) 21st–22nd April.
Trench warfare. Sannaiyat lines. April–December.

1917. Trench warfare. Sannaiyat, Hanna Picquet Line, The Narrows. January–February.

BATTLE OF KUT, 1917. (Capture of Sannaiyat.) 17th–24th February.

PURSUIT TO AND OCCUPATION OF BAGHDAD. 24th February–11th March.

APPENDIX VI

ACTION OF MUSHAIDIE. (Operations for the consolidation of Baghdad.) 14th March.

ACTION OF ISTABULAT. (With subsequent occupation of Samarrah. (Operations for the consolidation of Baghdad.) 21st–24th April.
Holding and consolidating position on the left of the Tigris. (Bait al Khalifa.) May–October.

ACTION OF TEKRIT. 5th November.
Advance to Tekrit. (Daur, 3rd November. Tekrit, 5th November.)

1918. Left Mesopotamia. 1st January.
Arrived Egypt. (Suez.) 13th January.
Holding advanced posts. Palestine. (Sarona Area, White Ruin Garden.) April–May.

ACTION OF ARSUF. 8th June.
Holding advanced posts. (Arsuf Area.) June–September.

BATTLE OF SHARON. (The Battles of Megiddo.) 19th September.

ADVANCE THROUGH PALESTINE AND SYRIA. September–October.

APPENDIX VII

Roll of "Other Ranks" appointed to Commissions during the Great War

The Second Battalion

Regtl. No.	Rank and Name.	Date of Commission	Corps to which Appointed.
7740	A/R.S.M. Kennedy, J.	4.12.14	The Black Watch
9468	C.S.M. George, W.	4.12.14	,, ,,
7990	C.S.M. Johnson, T.	5.4.15	,, ,,
7234	Sgt. Sinclair, R.	5.4.15	,, ,,
8490	C.Q.M.S. Bowie, H.	10.6.15	,, ,,
8012	C.S.M. Buchan, J. I.	15.6.15	,, ,,
7282	C.S.M. Wilson, W.	15.6.15	,, ,,
7144	Sgt. Mercer, A.	17.9.15	,, ,,
271	C.S.M. Kinnear, T.	31.1.17	,, ,,
976	C.S.M. Gant, T.	31.1.17	,, ,,
9284	C.S.M. Houston, B.	13.2.17	,, ,,
1271	Sgt. Leishman, A.	11.3.17	,, ,,
459	Sgt. Ritchie, T.	24.5.17	,, ,,
7911	A/R.S.M. Muir, A.	30.5.17	,, ,,
7201	C.Q.M.S. McLean, K.	24.9.17	,, ,,
8313	Sgt. King, J. A.	1.2.18	,, ,,
1920	Cpl. Brown, R.	15.2.18	,, ,,
1431	C.S.M. Miller, J. M.	20.8.18	,, ,,

All the above received commissions in the 2nd Battalion.

In addition to the above, 7912 Company Sergeant Major R. Proudfoot and S/8444 Sergeant A. McDonald were killed in action before the commission they were to receive could be gazetted; and 6761 Regimental Sergeant Major A. Smart gave up a commission to become Regimental Sergeant Major of the Battalion.

Commissions were also won by the following who were originally with the Battalion, but were appointed to other regiments:

Regtl. No.	Rank and Name.	Date of Commission	Corps to which Appointed.
574	Sgt. Shand, A.	4.12.14	
9363	Sgt. Sladen, W.	15.6.15	Cameron Highlanders.
762	C.Q.M.S. McDonald, P.	1.5.16	,, ,,
9097	L/Cpl. Anderson, J. F.	8.6.16	Indian Marine.
1727	Sgt. Forbes, A.	27.4.17	Highland Lt. Infantry.
216	Sgt. Reddy, W. G.	6.7.17	Cameron Highlanders.
8196	L/Cpl. Hall, H.	28.7.17	Royal Engineers.
S/12331	L/Cpl. Hill-Murray, S.	29.8.17	1st Seaforth Hrs.
8359	L/Cpl. Turnbull, D.	4.11.17	Indian Army.
S/12332	L/Cpl. Hill-Murray, N. I. G.	30.4.18	1st Seaforth Hrs.

THE THIRD (SPECIAL RESERVE) BATTALION

THE BLACK WATCH MEMORIAL HOME, DUNALISTAIR, NEAR DUNDEE

THE THIRD (SPECIAL RESERVE) BATTALION

AUGUST, 1914—AUGUST, 1919

THE Royal Perthshire Militia Regiment of Foot was originally embodied at Perth in 1798. The 3rd (Special Reserve) Battalion, The Black Watch, is the lineal descendant of this Regiment, no break occurring during the eighty years which passed before it was officially given the title of the 3rd Militia Battalion The Black Watch.

In view of the services rendered by this Battalion during the last war, it is interesting to recall that during the Peninsular war the Battalion then carried out a similar duty. The Battalion was embodied as part of a force held ready to repel invasion, and 700 men passed from the Perthshire Militia and were enrolled in the line. In the Crimean war the Battalion was again embodied, and during the period of embodiment 143 men passed into the line.

Again, in the South African war, the Battalion was embodied for twelve months, and 163 Militia Reservists were sent to join the 2nd Battalion The Black Watch in South Africa. During the last war the Battalion was embodied for five years, was trained and held ready to help to repel any invasion, and sent out some 1200 officers and 20,000 other ranks to reinforce the Battalions of The Black Watch in various theatres of war.

The 3rd (Special Reserve) Battalion mobilized at Perth on the 8th of August, 1914, and entrained that evening, over 1200 strong, for its war station at Nigg, Ross-shire. The following officers accompanied the Battalion:

    Lieutenant Colonel R. C. Campbell-Preston, Commanding Officer.
    Major J. G. H. Hamilton, D.S.O., Second-in-Command.
    Major A. H. O. Dennistoun.
    Captain C. H. Graham-Stirling.
    Captain the Honourable A. D. Murray.
    Captain Sir Edward Stewart-Richardson, Bart.
    Captain the Honourable R. Graham Murray.
    Captain K. J. Campbell.
    Captain P. L. Moubray.
    Captain C. C. West.
    Captain C. Boddam Whetham.
    Captain D. F. Campbell, D.S.O.
    Captain A. E. Parker.
    Lieutenant A. V. Holt.
    Lieutenant T. H. C. Cox.
    Lieutenant C. L. Bowes-Lyon.

THE THIRD (SPECIAL RESERVE) BATTALION

Lieutenant A. W. Tate.
Lieutenant N. Graham.
Lieutenant T. H. C. Thistle.
Lieutenant D. Lumsden.
Lieutenant R. S. S. Maxwell.
Second Lieutenant D. Cooke.
Second Lieutenant A. J. D. Murray-Graham.
Captain and Adjutant, R. A. Bulloch.
Medical Officer, Captain J. M. Bowie.

The mobilization station for the Battalion had been originally Devonport. It was changed in 1912 to Dover, and on mobilization orders were received for the Battalion to join the Brigade which was being formed under the command of Colonel H. K. Jackson, D.S.O., for the defence of Cromarty.

The battalions forming the Brigade were:

3rd The Black Watch and 3rd Scottish Rifles stationed at Nigg for the defence of the north Sutor Fort.

3rd Seaforth Highlanders stationed at Cromarty to defend the south Sutor Fort.

3rd Cameron Highlanders at Invergordon for guards over Naval oil tanks.

It was thought that the enemy might attempt a landing either at Balintore, with the north Sutor or Invergordon as its objective, or near Fortrose on the Moray Firth to attack the south Sutor. The Naval authorities had originally undertaken the defence of Cromarty, but on mobilization this responsibility was taken over by the War Office. The Battalion arrived at Nigg early on Sunday morning the 9th, and encamped on a shoulder of Nigg Hill. The 4th Battalion Seaforth Highlanders had been there for three days and had begun to put the place into a state of defence. This battalion left in the afternoon of the 9th to join the Highland Division of Territorials at Bedford, and was one of the first Territorial Divisions to arrive in France.

The first duty of the Battalion was to put Nigg Hill into a sound state of defence. Large working parties assembled each morning, and in a short time an elaborate system of trenches was dug, with barbed wire entanglements.

In spite of the fact that the fleet was daily searching the North Sea for the enemy, the possibility of an attempted landing at Balintore, a small fishing village with a good landing two miles north of the camp, was generally accepted. The outpost line on the hill was furnished each night by one company, another company being told off as inlying picket in camp. There were also guards and pickets at Balintore with examining posts on all main roads, and by day a section with an officer was posted on the

ENCAMPED AT NIGG, 1914

hill in telephonic communication with the camp, in order to prevent the enemy capturing the hill and north Sutor Fort, and thereby bottling up the fleet in Cromarty Bay. These precautions, however, only lasted a short time, and by the end of October all guards and pickets, with the exception of those at Balintore, were withdrawn, the trenches and barbed wire being still kept in a good state of repair.

In view of an early call for reinforcements, training of reservists was started at once. Orders were received for the first draft of 1 officer and 93 men, who left for France on the 26th of August, under Lieutenant A. V. Holt.

Lieutenant R. D. Nolan took out the second draft on the 30th of August, and Lieutenant C. Bowes-Lyon the third, on the 11th of September, both drafts being of 1 officer and 93 men. On the 19th of September, Captain Sir Edward Stewart-Richardson and Lieutenant Nigel Graham left with 186 men. Following the casualties on the Aisne, orders were received on September the 20th for a large number of junior officers (several having just left Sandhurst) to proceed to France to be posted to different Highland regiments, and by the middle of October almost every trained officer below the rank of Major, and *all* trained men available had left for France.

Of the officers who left for France with the first few drafts, the 3rd Battalion suffered very heavily, Captains D. F. Campbell, D.S.O., A. E. Parker, P. L. Moubray, C. Boddam Whetham, Lieutenants A. C. R. McNaughton, R. D. Nolan, C. L. Bowes-Lyon and Second Lieutenant Neil McNeill being killed, while Sir Edward Stewart-Richardson died in London from wounds received at the battle of the Aisne.

Although large numbers had left as reinforcements in the first few weeks, the strength of the Battalion had increased, both in officers and men. Large drafts of ex-soldiers and untrained men arrived daily from Perth. A vast amount of equipment and stores were also forwarded from the ordnance depot.

At this time the Battalion was without the services of a regular quartermaster. Captain J. Linning, who had been in ill health for some time, had been left behind at Perth. The work, however, at the Depot proved too much for his state of health, and he died early in September, an irreparable loss to the Battalion. Lieutenant C. W. McClellan was promoted quartermaster from the 1st Battalion, and arrived from France early in October. He soon put the quartermaster's department in order.

The Battalion was under canvas until the end of November, by which time an energetic contractor had erected almost a tin town for the two battalions stationed at Nigg. The men got into their huts several weeks before the officers, but by Christmas

THE THIRD (SPECIAL RESERVE) BATTALION

Day the whole Battalion was comfortably housed in a good hutted camp.

Training greatly improved by the move into huts. The Battalion, however, suffered from the want of trained officers and non-commissioned officers, owing to the heavy reinforcements sent out. This want was in time filled by the return of wounded officers and non-commissioned officers, who, while they were with the Battalion previous to returning to the front, were an enormous help in the development of training for modern war.

The first instruction in bomb throwing was given by Major A. G. Wauchope, D.S.O., in February, 1915. He was only a short time at Nigg, but was looked on as a fully qualified instructor, having been slightly wounded in France by both hand and rifle grenades. Up to the end of the year the class of recruit was not good, but after the New Year the improvement was very marked.

The Battalion was formed on the basis of nine companies. The ranks of six of these were filled with recruits; two others were filled with Expeditionary Force men, who only remained a few weeks with the Battalion, and one company was maintained for employed and Home Service men. Recruits undergoing the last three weeks of their training and all fit Expeditionary Force men were formed into a Training Company and given a special course of instruction. This company was invariably commanded by a returned Expeditionary Force officer doing duty for the time with the Battalion. Among the many who commanded the Training Company mention should be made of the following officers:

> Major F. G. Chalmer, D.S.O.
> Captain R. E. Forrester. (Killed.)
> Captain G. B. Rowan Hamilton, D.S.O., M.C.
> Captain D. C. Hamilton Johnston. (Killed.)
> Captain J. N. Inglis. (Killed.)
> Captain H. L. F. Boyd. (Killed.)
> Captain L. F. Hay.
> Captain D. Cooke. (Killed.)
> Captain J. E. M. Richard.
> Lieutenant T. Johnson. (Killed.)
> Lieutenant H. Bowie.

The work of the Battalion in a short time became one of routine, training recruits and sending out drafts. A weekly return was sent in showing the number of men available for reinforcements and generally the whole number was called for. Captain C. Kennard from the 10th Battalion was appointed Draft Conducting Officer, and as the strength of the Battalion increased

TRAINING AT NIGG, 1915

to over 2000, and drafts in large numbers were being sent out every week, Colonel H. A. Barker was also posted for the same duty.

As the fighting developed into trench warfare the training became more intensive. A syllabus of work was brought out by the War Office for a course of twelve weeks' training, and for the average recruit this was found sufficient. Specialist officers paid periodical visits of inspection, each specialist being convinced that *his* speciality only could win the war, be it bombing, bayonet fighting, musketry or physical drill. The Commanding Officer had to satisfy each and every specialist officer, to preserve his temper and maintain a well-balanced system of training. In these, as in other duties, Colonel Campbell-Preston was singularly successful. Elaborate Bayonet Fighting Courses were erected, a rifle range was made in close proximity to the camp, and systems of trenches dug representing a front line with communicating and support trenches in which the bombers practised daily.

Before proceeding overseas each draft was inspected by the G.O.C. Cromarty Defences. Colonel H. K. Jackson only commanded for a short time. He left for France at the end of September, 1914, and was succeeded by Major General W. C. Hunter Blair, C.B. Early in 1916 he was followed by Major General Sir Walter Lindsay, K.C.B., D.S.O., who had command until May, 1917, when the late Major General Sir Reginald Curtis, K.C.M.G., C.B., was given command.

Brigadier General D. A. Macfarlane, C.B., D.S.O., Inspector of Infantry, Scottish Command, also paid periodical visits to the Battalion and was of the greatest help and assistance to the Commanding Officer.

All drafts for France left direct for Etaples, an eighteen miles' march from Boulogne, which served as a test of the fitness of the men on arriving in France. While there, waiting to be sent to their units, the men were put through the famous " Bull ring " and tested in all branches of their training. Reports were sent on each draft by the O.C. Infantry Base Depot. Only on one occasion was an adverse report (and that in very moderate language) sent on a draft from the Battalion, which speaks well for the standard of the training carried out.

Drafts, before proceeding overseas, were entertained by the Managers of the Y.M.C.A. hut in camp. The Battalion had its own Regimental Institute and Coffee Shop, but there was plenty of room for two huts. Miss Gunn, who was in charge of the Y.M.C.A. hut, and her able assistants, did all in their power to add to the comfort of the men, while Mr. David Kay, the representative from Y.M.C.A. headquarters, was the most

THE THIRD (SPECIAL RESERVE) BATTALION

popular man in camp on account of his unfailing cheerfulness and initiative in organizing entertainments and treats for the men.

On the 9th of May, 1915, the 1st and 2nd Battalions suffered very heavy casualties, and large drafts were called for, but during the remainder of that summer the reinforcements sent out were not very heavy; consequently the strength of the Battalion increased greatly, the number of officers with it being out of all proportion to the accommodation provided. There was, however, a large exodus, both in officers and men after the Battle of Loos, as many as 50 officers and 500 men leaving during the fortnight following that battle. The 11th Battalion, which was at Tain at that time in the Reserve Brigade for the 9th and 15th Divisions, also sent out large reinforcements. This Battalion was formed at Nigg under Lieutenant Colonel J. MacRae-Gilstrap on the 31st of October, 1914—the 3rd Battalion supplying staff sergeants and a certain number of men.

Two days' field exercises took place that summer, the Tain Brigade attacking the Cromarty Brigade, which had taken up a position to the north of Balintore—the battalions bivouacing out in almost perfect weather, a pleasant change and greatly appreciated by all ranks.

On the 30th of September, Major R. A. Bulloch was relieved of the Adjutancy, and joined the Staff in France. He had been Adjutant of the Battalion since January, 1913, and since mobilization the work had largely fallen on his shoulders. Much of the efficiency of the Battalion was due to him and consequently his departure was greatly felt by all ranks. Fortunately a most capable and efficient successor was secured for the Battalion in the late Major R. E. Anstruther, M.C., who carried on the good work begun by Major Bulloch.

Early in 1916 the General Staff was fully prepared for a strong enemy landing on the coast of Fife, with the Forth Bridge and Rosyth Dockyard as its objectives. A defensive position had been selected and prepared which would be held by troops stationed in Fife and the Lothians. The Cromarty Brigade received orders for reinforcing this line, and as it would arrive probably several hours after the fighting had commenced, orders were to be received at Perth as to which sector of the line the Brigade was to hold.

The battalions were to proceed as strong as possible, leaving a small garrison behind for the defence of Cromarty. All recruits in the early stage of training, who were able to fire a rifle, were to be included, and a weekly return was sent in of the numbers available. Six hours were given for the Battalion to entrain on receipt of orders, and all transport was to be impressed locally.

SUMMER AT NIGG, 1917

Major R. E. Anstruther, in spite of a very severe wound, was passed fit for active service in May, and on the 2nd of June, 1916, was posted to the 8th Battalion. Lieutenant McC. Christison acted as Adjutant until the 8th of August, when Captain J. L. Rennie was appointed. He remained Adjutant until November 8th, 1917, when Lieutenant McC. Christison, who had been Acting Assistant Adjutant for the last fifteen months, took over from Captain Rennie and remained Adjutant until demobilized on May 13th, 1919.

In May, 1917, Field Marshal Lord French made a three days' inspection of the Scottish Command. In one day he visited both Montrose and Aberdeen and travelled through the night to Nigg. At 9 a.m. on the next day he arrived in camp and spent an hour watching the Battalion training. On leaving, he informed the Commanding Officer that he was extremely pleased with all he had seen.

In the early summer of 1917 it was thought advisable that those in charge of the training at home should have an opportunity of witnessing how the training in France was being carried out behind the lines. Representatives from each training centre were ordered to visit the Third Army School at Auxy-le-Château. Major General Sir Reginald Curtis and the Commanding Officer were detailed from Cromarty Command by Headquarters, Edinburgh. The party consisting of seven Major Generals, over fifty Brigadier Generals and about one hundred and fifty Lieutenant Colonels and Staff Officers left London on Friday morning the 28th of June and returned the following Monday, spending Saturday and Sunday at the School.

Lord Byng, Commanding the Third Army, visited the School on Saturday morning and in a short address mentioned, among other points, that he thought too much attention was being given at home to bombing. In the last fighting, he said, while commanding the Canadian Corps, he had seen men with their rifles slung over their shoulders, throwing bombs at the enemy retiring in the open 150 yards distant.

Demonstrations were given of an attack, first by a company and then by a battalion organized in self-contained platoons, consisting of Lewis gunners, rifle grenadiers, bombers, riflemen and moppers up. This form of platoon organization was new at this time, and the Commanding Officer organized certain platoons on these lines on his return to Nigg, with good results.

On the evening of the 5th of November, 1917, orders were received by telephone from Headquarters, Edinburgh, through Brigade Office, for the Commanding Officer to be prepared to move 300 men at short notice, each man to carry one blanket and

THE THIRD (SPECIAL RESERVE) BATTALION

300 rounds. Orders arrived next day to the effect that the Battalion was to move in a few days to Ireland.

Since the rebellion on Easter Monday, 1916, the Sinn Fein movement had greatly developed, and one source of anxiety was the loss of many rifles from the reserve battalions of Irish regiments stationed in that country. Many cases were discovered of recruits deserting after a few weeks' service, with their equipment and arms, later to be arrested in civilian clothes. Consequently it was decided to relieve all the Irish battalions stationed in Ireland by Scottish and English battalions.

On the 9th of November, Headquarters and half the Battalion left Nigg at 8 p.m. and arrived at Holyhead the next afternoon. They remained there overnight and crossed next day to Dublin. Orders were received there for the Battalion to proceed to Aghada on Queenstown Harbour. Cork was reached that evening and Queenstown early the following morning. The Battalion was then taken over in barges to Aghada.

The remainder of the Battalion, with the heavy baggage, arrived a fortnight later, under Major C. H. Graham-Stirling, who handed over the camp at Nigg to the Officer Commanding the 3rd Connaught Rangers.

The training of the Battalion suffered to a certain extent by the change from Nigg to Aghada. At the former there was plenty of open ground for exercising the troops in extended order and for manœuvres, while in the three years the Battalion had remained there, elaborate systems of trenches had been dug, and excellent Bayonet Fighting Courses erected; also there was a rifle range in close proximity to the camp. There was nothing like this at Aghada. Recruits had to fire their musketry course at Youghal, thirty miles away by rail, and as the country was enclosed and cultivated, the training grounds were confined to a couple of fields. The hutted camp, too, was in a bad state of repair, as it had been unoccupied since the 3rd Munster Fusiliers had left it twelve months previously. All ranks felt the change, and the effect of being in the midst of an unsympathetic population seemed to depress the men. Consequently crimes of absence without leave and overstaying passes increased considerably.

The Battalion was directly under the G.O.C. at Cork, Major General Beauchamp Doran, C.B., D.S.O., who visited the camp shortly after its arrival there. He impressed on all officers the necessity of taking every precaution against the theft or loss of rifles. Owing, however, to the hostile attitude of the Highlanders towards the natives of the country, there was very little chance of any traffic in arms taking place. Every care was, however, taken to prevent thieving, extra sentries being posted throughout the camp after dark, and chains for the rifles pro-

AT THE CURRAGH, 1918

cured from the Ordnance, similar to those supplied on the Indian Frontier.

It was a relief to all when orders were received to move to the Curragh. This took place on the 24th of March, 1918, the Battalion being quartered in Rath Camp, a hutted camp on the road to Kildare. The troops at the Curragh were composed almost entirely of Reserve Cavalry Regiments with a few dismounted Yeomanry.

There was a marked improvement in the training after leaving Aghada; every facility was available at the Curragh, and the Battalion benefited greatly in consequence.

Early in the year the Sinn Fein movement became very much stronger; this was partly due to the retreat of the Allied troops in France in the month of March. The authorities were fully alive to the situation. Two thousand Yeomanry converted into cyclists, arriving from Scotland and England, were formed into a mobile brigade, ready to move to any part of the country at a few hours' notice. The Battalion was posted to this Brigade, which was exercised once a week. This somewhat interfered with the training of the recruits, but had a good effect on the men, especially those who had been in France and who were only too anxious to fight the Sinn Feiner, whom they considered as much an enemy as the German. One of the chief duties of the Battalion was guarding a portion of the main line from Dublin to Cork, 4 officers and 200 men being detailed for this work.

At this time the strength of the Battalion reached its highest point, about 2500, a fine lot of ploughmen arriving from Perthshire and Forfarshire. The ploughman, next to the miner, was generally considered about the best recruit. He seemed sometimes to be slow to learn, but behaved well and after a few weeks' training quickly developed into a smart soldier.

On May 7th, after thirty-four years' service with the 3rd Battalion, and after commanding it for the past six years, Lieutenant Colonel R. C. Campbell-Preston gave up the command of the Battalion in order to take over that of a Labour Group in France. Colonel Campbell-Preston had done excellent work during a most difficult time, his sound sense and devotion to The Black Watch had been of the greatest service to the Regiment, and his departure was deeply regretted by all ranks. Lieutenant Colonel A. H. O. Dennistoun, who had been commanding the depot battalion of the 15th Division in France for the last eighteen months, now succeeded to the command of the Battalion.

When the casualties in France, caused by the heavy fighting in the spring had been replaced, the demand for reinforcements decreased considerably, the chief work of the Battalion being to

THE THIRD (SPECIAL RESERVE) BATTALION

hold itself in readiness to deal with any trouble caused by the Sinn Feiners.

Brigade sports were held in July, at which The Black Watch came out top, winning such events as wiring, signalling, bayonet fighting and relay race, as well as several individual races. The Battalion sports were also a great success.

Armistice Day found the Battalion still in the highest state of efficiency and good order and with a large number of fully trained recruits and returned Expeditionary Force men available for reinforcements. Altogether about 1200 officers and 20,000 other ranks had been sent out as reinforcements to the fighting battalions of The Black Watch to all theatres of war: to France for the 1st, 4th, 5th, 6th, 7th, 8th and 9th Battalions; to Mesopotamia for the 2nd Battalion; to the Balkans for the 10th Battalion; to Egypt and Palestine for the 13th and 14th Battalions. Very many officers and men went out more than once; some had gone out three or four times.

The Battalion moved into Kean Barracks on the 9th of December, and remained there till the 3rd of March, 1919, when it returned to Scotland and was quartered at Haddington. At Haddington, the work, in addition to demobilization, was chiefly gardening and education. Colonel Dennistoun was demobilized on May 13th and handed over command to Lieutenant Colonel Gervase Thorpe, C.M.G., D.S.O., of the Argyll and Sutherland Highlanders.

Lieutenant McC. Christison, the Adjutant, left the same day on demobilization; very severely wounded at the first Battle of Ypres while serving with the London Scottish, he joined The Black Watch at Nigg on the 4th of August, 1915. Not being fit for active service again, he was appointed Assistant Adjutant early in 1916, and Adjutant, 9th November, 1917. During these years he gave up his entire time to his work, never sparing himself for a moment. His one thought was for the efficiency of the Battalion and the credit of The Black Watch, thus proving himself a most worthy successor to the former Adjutants, Lieutenant Colonel R. A. Bulloch, D.S.O., and the late Major R. E. Anstruther, M.C. The Quartermaster, Captain C. W. McClellan, had also been indefatigable in his work, both in looking after the comfort and feeding of the men, and in the clothing and equipment of the drafts. Both Adjutant and Quartermaster were ably backed up by Sergeant Major J. Adamson and Orderly Room Clerk, Company Sergeant Major E. J. Johnstone, to whom the greatest credit is due for their good work during the four strenuous years of the war.

The Battalion details were taken over by the 2nd Battalion on August 8th, and the cadre returned to the Depot on 20th

RETURN TO SCOTLAND, 1919

August, just five years after the Battalion had marched out for its first war station at Nigg.

The departure of Colonel Campbell-Preston, in the spring of 1918, was much felt throughout the Battalion. The death of Sir Edward Stewart-Richardson has already been mentioned. In addition to these the Battalion during the war lost the services of several other experienced officers. In 1916 Major the Hon R. Graham Murray was ordered to join the 2nd Battalion in Mesopotamia. After serving for a short period with this Battalion he received a Staff appointment in India where he was employed until the end of the war. Another great loss was suffered by the posting of Major the Hon. A. D. Murray to the 1st Battalion in France, where he served for nearly a year and commanded the First Line Details and Transport. He will always be gratefully remembered by those in the trenches for whose welfare he did so much good service. Another loss was experienced in 1916 when Major Dennistoun was appointed to the 9th Battalion The Black Watch. Later on Major Dennistoun was given command of a battalion of Gordon Highlanders, with which he did very good service. At the end of the war Major Dennistoun took over command of the 3rd Battalion on the departure of Colonel Campbell-Preston.

The 3rd Battalion had not been called on to bear the strain of battle, nor to support the hardships of war, as had the fighting battalions of the Regiment. But the great majority of officers and men in the various theatres of war had been first trained in the 3rd Battalion, and while serving with it had been impressed with the traditions of The Black Watch.

The 3rd Battalion, and especially its Staff, may justly claim to have had some share in developing the brave spirit and feeling of comradeship that distinguished all battalions of The Black Watch throughout the Great War.

APPENDIX

Casualty List

Abbreviations.—‡ Died at home.   § Died at sea.

Third Reserve Battalion

Baxter, J., Pte., S/26596	‡27.7.18	McDonald, A., L/Cpl., 23245	‡15.9.17
Beveridge, J., Pte., S/26821	‡12.10.18	McFarlane, G., A/Cpl., 3/3143	
Bowman, J., Pte., S/15707	‡29.4.17		‡14.11.14
Bradley, T., Pte., S/5035	‡9.2.15	McNealy, T. H., Pte., 3/1897	‡19.8.16
Buchanan, J., Pte., 3/3227	‡3.9.14	Matthews, G., Pte., S/11150	‡13.12.15
		Murdoch, R., Pte., S/15028	‡22.10.18
Cameron, D., Pte., S/2591	‡ 7.10.14		
Child, J., Pte., S/11910	‡21.11.15	Nixon, J. G., Pte., S/23344	§10.10.18
Crombie, D., Pte., S/8125	‡21.2.15	Nelson, H., Pte., 10114	‡ 6.7.15
Dalziel, D., Pte., 7047	‡25.10.17	Patullo, A., Pte., S/18044	‡12.3.17
Duncan, W., Pte., S/14572	§10.10.18	Peters, C., Pte., S/21917	‡ 8.1.18
		Poole, A., Pte., S/20929	‡28.11.17
Edwards, A., Pte., S/26397	‡16.10.18	Purdhan, A., L/Cpl., 268615	‡11.5.17
Gifford, R., Pte., S/11932	‡ 1.7.17	Robertson, J., Sgt., 3/4033	‡10.10.18
Holt, F., Pte., S/11935	‡29.11.15		
Hynd, J., Pte., S/26416	‡10.10.18	Short, J., Pte., 3/4061	‡20.2.15
		Smith, T., A/Sgt., 3/2785	‡ 4.4.18
Jenkinson, J., Pte., S/8827	‡22.5.15	Smith, W., Pte., 3/1802	‡30.12.14
		Stewart, W., Pte., 7771	‡19.8.17
Kidd, A., Sgt., 9208	‡26.10.16	Sutherland, K., Pte., S/21913	‡ 8.9.17
Lawson, G. C., Pte., S/26337	‡13.10.18	White, E., Pte., S/9891	‡26.3.16
Lockhart, J., Sgt., S/9622	‡ 7.8.18	Wilkie, J., Pte., 3/8991	‡10.11.15

The Black Watch Depot

Adams, J., C.S.M., S/8195	‡11.11.16	McLeod, W., Pte., 17860	‡ 7.7.17
Cameron, J., Pte., S/16838	‡25.11.16	Paton, W., L/Sgt., 3/3939	‡31.10.14
Clark, P., Pte., S/7148	‡24.4.16		
Coleshill, R. G., Pte., S/20144		Robinson, C. C., Sgt., S/3957	‡ 2.12.16
	‡ 1.4.17		
Crawford, T., Pte., S/14775	‡23.12.16	Torley, P., Pte., 3/2818	‡13.1.17
Cuthbert, T. H., Pte., S/11292			
	‡16.7.15	Wallace, A., Pte., 7059	‡10.4.15

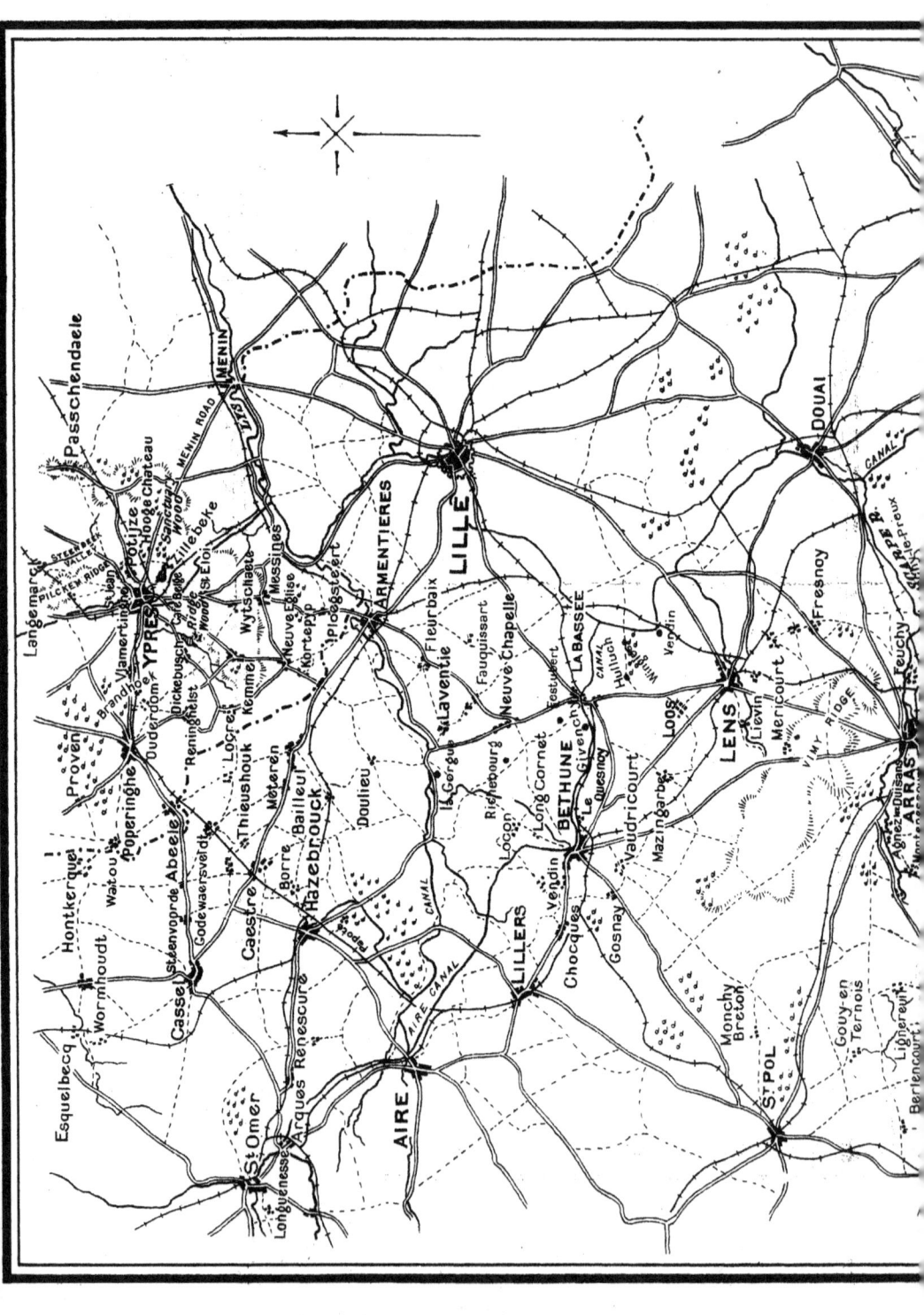

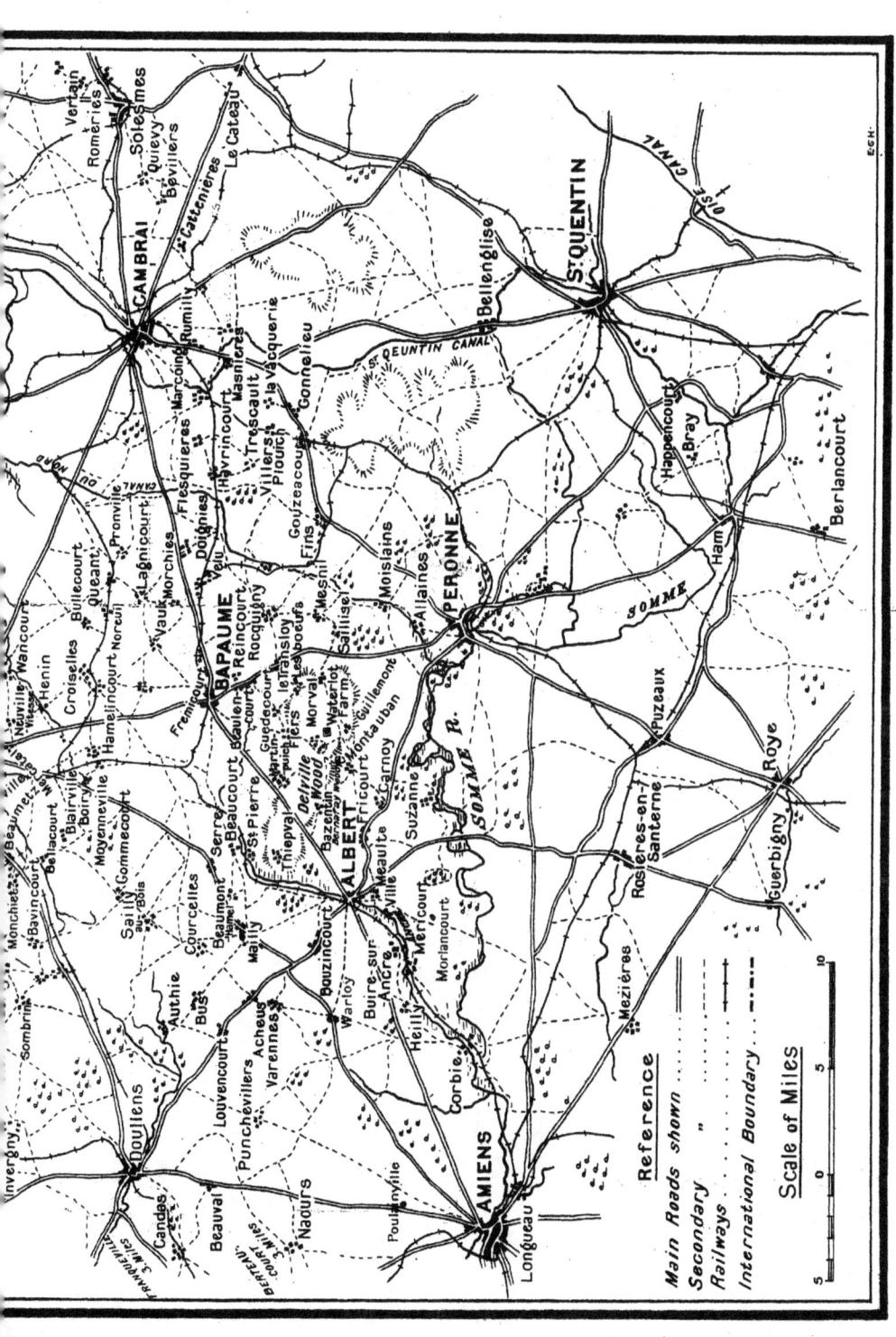

INDEX

The Roman numerals (I), (II), (III), after the entry, indicate
the Battalion to which the entry refers

Actions and Operations, List of
    1st Battalion, 154–5
    2nd Battalion, 340–1
Adam, 2nd Lieut. J. N., 104 (I)
Adamson, Sergt. Major J., 354 (III)
Addison, 2nd Lieut. W., 86 (I)
Aghada, 352–3 (III)
Aisne, Battle of the, 11 *sqq.*, 349 (I)
Alexander, 2nd Lieut. R., 48, 104 (I)
Alexandria, 291 (II)
Ali-el-Gharbi, 204, 207, 209 (II)
Allan, 2nd Lieut. J. G., 104 (I)
Allan, Lieut. W. D., 2, 104 (I)
Allen, Sergeant, 205 (II)
Allenby, General Sir Edmund, 271, 281, 289, 291, 292
"Allez-vous-en," 3, 103 (I)
Amarah, 203, 207 (II)
Amery, Captain, H. F. S., 3, 14, 19, 20, 104 (I)
Anderson, Private, 38 (I)
Anderson, Sergeant, 241 (II)
Anderson, Lieut. Gen. C. A., 161
Anderson, 2nd Lieut. D. H., 230 (II)
Anderson, Lieutenant F., 2, 7, 14, 22, 23, Major, A/Lieut. Colonel, 90, 103, 105 (I)
Anderson, 2nd Lieut. F. J., 105 (I)
Anderson, 2nd Lieut. G. J., 230 (II)
Anderson, Lieut. J., Quartermaster, 162, 205, 222, 240, Captain, 258, 266, 271, Major, 293 (II)
Anderson, 2nd Lieut. J., 105 (I)
Anderson, Lieut. R. C., Captain, 46, 62, 105 (I)
Anderson, 2nd Lieut. T. B., 105 (I)
Anderson, Sergeant W., 204, 250 (II)
Andrews, Private H., 294 (II)
Anstruther, Lieutenant R. E., 3, 14, 32 (I), Major, 350, 351, 354 (III)
Antwerp, Fall of, 16
Arabs, Characteristics of, in Mesopotamia, 203, 206–7, 226, 236
Arbuthnott, Lieut. R. K., 79, Captain, 85, 89 (I)

Ardennes, Boar-hunt, 101 (I)
Armitt, Piper, 194 (II)
Arms, *see* Dress, *and* Rifles
Army of Occupation, 102–3 (I)
Armytage, 2nd Lieut. E. O., 105 (I)
Arsuf, Battle of, 275 *sqq.* (II)
Aubers Ridge, Battle of, 34 *sqq.* (I), 166, 176, 181, 184 (II)
Auchy, Brick-stacks of, fight for, 29 (I)
Auxi-le-Chateau, 351
Aylmer, General, 204, 208, 221, 223 *n*

Bacon, Admiral Sir Reginald, 68
Baghdad, 203–4, 243, 258, 268
    Advance on, 248 *sqq.* (II)
Bailleul 16 (I)
Bain, Sergeant J., 66 (I)
Bairstow, 2nd Lieut. A. E., 272 (II)
Balfour-Melville, Lieut. J. E., 186, 193, 194 (II)
Balkans, the, 10th Battalion in, reinforcements for, 354 (III)
Ballantyne, 2nd Lieut. A., 48 (I)
Balmain, 2nd Lieut. W., 83, 87, 89 (I)
Banks, Corpl., 195 (II)
"Bantams, the," 55
Barclay, Sergeant, 61 (I)
Bareilly, 161, 163 (II)
Bareilly Brigade, *see under* Brigades
Barker, Colonel H. A., 349 (III)
Barstow, Lieut. J. A., 186, 193, Captain, 238, 258, 266, 272 (II)
Basrah, 200, 203, 207, 208, 268 (II)
Bawi, 249 (II)
Baxter, 2nd Lieut. D., 93 (I)
Beaulne Ridge, 13 (I)
Beirut, 288–9, 291 (II)
Belgians, T. M. the King and Queen of the, 67
Bellot, 10 (I)
Bennett, Sergeant Major, 86 (I)
Bertrand, M., Interpreter, 165 (II)

INDEX

Bisset, Company Sergt. Major, 258 (II)
Black Watch, Battalions
    1st, 1 *sqq.*, 164, 182, 199 *n.*
    2nd, 161 *sqq.*
        Names of those serving throughout the War, 100 (I), 293 (II)
        Strength of, on departure from India, 163, at Loos, 186, on leaving France, 199 *n.*, after Shaikh Sa'ad, 213, after Hanna, 220, on re-formation, 233, at end of 1916, 242, at action of Arsuf, 276
    3rd, 345 *sqq.*
    4th (T.F.), 176, 185, 189, 190, 195, 196
    8th, 41, 351
    9th, 355
    10th, 348
    13th, 354
    14th, 354
Blair, Lieut. A. E., 258, 266, Captain, 272, 279 (II)
Blair, 2nd Lieutenant P. E. A., 2 (I)
Blair, Major General W. C. Hunter, 349
Blyth, Corpl., 206 (II)
Bogle, Pte., 247 (II)
Bombers, Battalion, 191, 193, 206, 264 (II)
Bombs (Grenades), 32, 170–1, 173, 192, 202, 218–9, 348
Boswell, Lieut. G. A. (Cameron Highlanders), 283
Bowes-Lyon, Lieut. C. L. C., 15, 17 (I), 345, 347 (III)
Bowie, Lieut. H., 206 (II), 348 (III)
Bowie, Captain J. M., 346 (III)
Boyd, Captain H. L. F., 71 (I), 348 (III)
Boyd, 2nd Lieutenant N. J. L., 2, 14 (I)
Boyd, Pte., 169 (II)
Brezet, Gabriel, Interpreter, 165 (II)
Brigades
    Bareilly, 161, 164, 167, 176, 181, 183–5, 188 *n.*, 192–3

Brigades
    Dehra Dun, 172, 181, 183–4, 188 *n.*
    Garhwal, 183, 185–6, 192–3
    8th, 262
    9th, 217
    19th, 208, 210–11, 213–14, 222, 224–8, 247, 254, 262, 266–7, 281, 286
    21st, 208–10, 212, 214, 225, 227–8, 243, 245–9, 252–3, 262, 267, 274–5, 281, 286
    28th, 208–10, 214–15, 225–6, 248, 250, 252–3, 262, 267
    35th, 208–12, 214, 216
    38th, 224
    39th, 224
    40th, 224
    60th, 185, 188–9, 191
British ex-Prisoners-of-War, 101–2
Broad, Lieut. J. C. W., 206 (II)
Brodie, Captain (Cameron Highlanders), 22, 23
Brodie, Corpl., 206, Sergt., 279 (II)
Brown, Pte., 196 (II)
Brown, 2nd Lieut. D. (R.S.F.), 282
Brown, Sergeant D., 293 (II)
Brown, 2nd Lieut. G. J. R., 266 (II)
Brown, 2nd Lieut. I. D., 48 *n.* (I)
Brown Ridge, Palestine, 275–6 (II)
Brownlow, Lieut. W. L., 182 (II)
Buchan, Sergeant J. I., 184 *n*, Captain, 186 *sqq.*, 193–4 (II)
Buchanan, Lieut. J. C. R., 206, 271 (II)
Buchanan, 2nd Lieut. K., 272 (II)
Buffs, The (1/5 Bn.), 212, 217–19
Buist, Lieut. K., 24 (I), 163, 164 (II)
Buist, Lieut. Colonel (The Guides), 278
Bulloch, Captain R. A., 346, Major, 350, 354 (III)
Burnett, Company Sergeant Major, 162 *n.*, 163 (II)
Burns, Company Sergeant Major A., 3 (I)
Burton, Lieut. G. S. M., 87, Captain, 97 (I)
Butler, Brigadier General R., 31

INDEX

Byng, General Lord, 351
Byrom, 2nd Lieut. (A. and S.H.), 266

Cambrin Sector, 89 (I)
Cameron, Captain Moore (R.A.M.C.), 266, 268, 272, 278, 282 (II)
Cameron Highlanders and Black Watch (I), 66 n.
Campbell, Captain D., 46 (I)
Campbell, Captain D., 163, 183 (II)
Campbell, Captain D. F., 345, 347 (III)
Campbell, Captain K. J., 345 (III)
Campbell, 2nd Lieutenant P. K., 2, 14 (I)
Campbell, Pte. P., 293 (II)
Campbell, Lieut. Colonel W. McL., 14, 60, 162, 164, 171, 279 (II)
Campbell-Preston, Lieut.-Colonel R. C., 234, 345, 349, 353, 355 (III)
Capper, General, 48
Carrie, Private W., 237 (II)
Casualties, all ranks
  1st Bn., 130 *sqq.*; Summary, 149
  2nd Bn., 326 *sqq.*; Summary, 322
  163 n.
  Arsuf, 278
  Istabulat, 266
  Loos, 193
  May 9th, 182
  Mushaidie, 257
  Neuve Chapelle, 179
  Sannaiyat, 226, 231
  Shaikh Sa'ad, 213
  Sharon, 257
  Total in France, 199
  Umm-el-Hanna, 220
Cavan, General the Earl of, 64
Cerny, ridge by, 12, 13 (I)
Chalmer, Lieutenant F. G., 2, 10, 18 (I), Major, 348 (III)
Chemin des Dames, 11 *sqq.* (I)
Chivy Valley, 13 (I)

Chocolat Menier Corner, 33 & *n.*, 34, 35, 61 (I)
Christie, 2nd Lieut., 98 (I)
Christison, Lieut. McC., 351, 354 (III)
Clark, Corporal, 195 (II)
Clark, Pte., 195 (II)
Clarke, Pte., 100 (I)
Climate, in
  France, 166, 172, 199
  Mesopotamia, 234–5, 250
  Palestine, 274, 289, 290
Clothing, *see* Dress
Cobbe, General A. S., 243
Cochrane, Captain T. G. F., 186, 193–4, 205, 238–9, Major 258, 266, 267, 271, 278–9 (II)
Cocks, 2nd Lieut. C. V. S., 206 (II)
Colquhoun, Captain P. H. L. C., 66, 71, 92 (I)
Commissions conferred on Other Ranks during the War
  1st Bn., 156–7
  2nd Bn., 342
Connaught, H.R.H., the Duke of, 273
Connaught Rangers, 176
Connell, Sergeant F., 288 (II)
Contalmaison Wood 57 (I)
Cook, Captain R., 91 (I)
Cooke, Captain Dennis, 46, 75, 81, 86, 89 (I), 346, 348 (III)
Coope, Pte. W., 293 (II)
Coppinger, Captain C. J., R.A.M.C., 2 (I)
Cormack, Company Q. M. Sergeant, 205, 272, 293 (II)
Corps, Indian, 165, 172, 180, 183–4, 196
  Desert Mounted, 273, 281
  I., in France, 172, 182
  II., in Mesopotamia, 243, 249
  III., 243, 248–9, 259
  IV., 181
  XX., 273 281
  XXI., 273, 281
Cotterill, 2nd Lieut. T. H., 258 (II)
Courchamps, 11 (I)

359

INDEX

Cowie, Sergeant, R., 293 (II)
Cowie, 2nd Lieut. T. McK., 247 (II)
Cowie, Corporal, W., 205 (II)
Cox, Lieut. T. H. C., 345 (III)
Crake, Captain R. H. (K.O.S.B.), 231, 232
Crawford, Sergeant Cook J., 205, 236, 293 (II)
Crebar, Pte., 195 (II)
Crichton, Piper, 218 (II)
Crimean War, 345 (III)
Cromarty, 346, 349, 350 (III)
Crombie, Lieut. A., 266, 276, 282-3 (II)
Crow, Captain (1st Northamptonshire), 21
Crowe, Sergeant, 194-5 (II)
Ctesiphon, Battle of, 204, 249 (II)
Culpin, Corporal, 20 (I)
Culross, Pte. W., 100 (I)
Cumming, Lieut. A. B., 205, 213 (II)
Cumming, Lieut. L. R., 2, 14 (I)
Cunningham, Lieut. R. C., 195
Curdie 2nd Lieut. G., 186, 192 n., Lieut., 206, 217 (II)
Curragh, the, 353 (III)
Curtis, Major General Sir Reginald, 349, 351

Dalglish, Captain C. A. de G., 2, 10 (I)
Dahra Bend, 244, 245, 249 (II)
Davidson, Company Sergeant Major, 186, 205 (II)
Davidson, Pte. J., 294 (II)
Dawson Capt. (R.A.M.C.), 161 (II)
Dehra Dun Brigade, *see under* Brigades
Denison, Lieut. A. C., 162, 168, 179, Capt., 186-7, 193 (II)
Denniston, Lieut. J. E., 60 (I)
Dennistoun, Major A. H. O., 345, Lieut. Colonel, 353, 354, 355 (III)
Dewar, Corporal, 21 (I)
Diala River, 249 (II)
Dickinson, Lieut., 59 (I)
Dingwall, Pte. D., 100 (I)

Discipline, high standard of, 163, 199, 291-2 (II)
Divisions—
  Lahore (3rd Indian), 161, 166, 176, 179, 184, 207-8, 222, 234, 243, 273, 281
  Meerut (7th Indian), 161, 166, 183, 185, 188 n., 207-9, 214, 221-2, 225-6, 234, 243, 249-51, 259, 273, 281, 283, 287-8
  6th Indian, 204, 223
  13th, 223-6, 243
  14th, 243
  20th, 185
  52nd, 273
  54th, 281
  60th, 281
  74th, 273
  75th, 281
Dixon, Lieut., 205, 219 (II)
Dixon, Lieut. J. F. C. (A. and S.H.), 272
Dogras, 41st, *see* Indian Army Units
"Dolly," 67
Don, 2nd Lieutenant R. G., 2, 14 (I)
Doran, Major General Beauchamp, 352
Dormer, Company Q. M. Sergeant, 272 (II)
Double Crassier, the, 51 *sqq.* (I)
Douglas, 2nd Lieut. A., 205 216 (II)
Dress, 174, 200-2, 234, 267 *sqq.*, 273-4, 279-80, 283 (II)
Drummond, Captain the Hon. M. C. A., 2, 10 (I)
Drummond, Sergeant, 178 (II)
Du Cane, General, 64
Dujail River, 259-67 (II)
Dujailah Redoubt, Battle of, 223 (II)
Duke, Pte. D., 100 (I)
Duncan, Captain (R.A.M.C.), 185, 205, 216 (II)
Duncan, Captain A. G., 75 (I)
Dundas, 2nd Lieut. R. H., 206, 219 (II)
Durie, Lieut. J. A., 162 n., 163

INDEX

Easton, L/Corpl. C., 195, Sergeant, 239, 261, 293 (II)
Easton, Sergeant, J., 194 (II)
Eden, Lieut. Colonel S. H., 90 (I)
Edwards, Lieut. W. H. C., 30–1 (I)
Egerton, 2nd Lieut. P. G., 186, 193 (II)
Eglinton, 2nd Lieut. D. C., 186 (II)
Egypt, 13th Bn. in, reinforcements for, 354 (III)
Elephanta, ss., 164 (II)
El Medjel, 286 (II)
Elliott, Pte. R., 100 (I)
Equipment (*see also* Dress), 162, 201–2, 270, 273 (II)
Erskine-Bolst, Lieut., 46 (I)
Étaples, 349 (III)
Evans, Major (A/Lieut. Colonel) L. P., V.C., 76, 90

Fairbairn, 2nd Lieut. W. A. (R. Scots), 283
Falahiyeh, 224–6 (II)
Fane, Major General V. B., 243, 247
Feiling, Capt. H. St. L., 61, 62 (I)
Ferguson, Lieut., G. W., 66, 88 (I)
Ferguson, Private, 195 (II)
Fenton, Sergeant, 178 (II)
Festubert, 170, 196 (II)
Fife Coast defence, 350 (III)
Findlay, L/Corpl. David, V.C., 182, Sergeant, 205, 219, 220 (II)
FitzClarence, General, 20, 23, 24
Flers, 60, attack on, 61 (I)
Foch, General, 9
Football, 102–3 (I), 273, 280 (II)
Forbes, Pte. J., 100 (I)
Forrester, 2nd Lieut. H. F., 229–30 (II)
Forrester, Captain R. E., 41 (I), 163, 168 (II), 348 (III)
Forrett, Sergeant D., 293 (II)
Forsyth, Sergeant, 66 (I)
Fortune, Lieut. V. M., 2, 201, Captain, 12, 20, 21, 23, Major, 60, Lieut. Colonel, 74–5, 75–6, 149, 150
Foster, Corporal W., 293 (II)

Fourmoy Alley, attack on, 92 (I)
Fournier, General, 4
Fowler, Lieutenant W., 2, Captain, 74, 75, Major, 100, 103 (I)
France, Battalions in, reinforcements for, 354 (III)
Fraser, 2nd Lieut. A., 48 (I)
French, F. M. Sir J. D., C.-in-C., 5, 15, 24–5, 34, 49 (I) 351 (III)
Fyall, Lieut. R. K., 97 (I)

Games, *see* Football, *and* Highland Games
Gant, Sergeant T., 194, 206, Company Sergeant Major, 238, 2nd Lieut., 258, 272, 282, 293 (II)
Gardiner, Pte. J., 100 (I)
Gardner, Private, 22 (I)
Garhwal Brigade, *see under* Brigades
Garrity, Sergeant, 205 (II)
Gartside, Major L. G., 2nd H.L.I., 74 (I)
Gas, use of, at Loos, 186, 192 (II)
George, Company Sergt. Major, 162, 2nd Lieut., 171, 177 (II)
George V, His Majesty, 1, 24, 49, 289
George, Pte., 37 (I)
Gerard, 2nd Lieut. (Gordons), 266
"German Jimmy," 8 (I)
Gibson, Pte., 279 (II)
Gilgallon, Corporal, 293 (II)
Gillespie, Lieut. T., 255, 258 (II)
Gilmour, Lieut. C. D., 179, 230 (II)
Gilroy, 2nd Lieut. A., 258, 266 (II)
Gilroy, Lieut. K. R., 163–4, 179 (II)
Givenchy, 27 *sqq.*, 81 *sqq.*, 166, 196 *sqq.*
Godfrey, Lieut. W. H., 59 (I)
Gordon, Major C. W. E., 185, 193 (II)
Gordon, L/Corpl. J., 178 (II)
Gorringe, General, 233 *n.*
Graham, Drummer A., 294 (II)

INDEX

Graham, Lieut. Nigel, 346, 347 (III)
Graham, Sergeant R., 293 (II)
Graham-Murray, Captain Hon. R. T., 345, 355 (III later II)
Graham-Scott, 2nd Lieut. K., 266 (II)
Grant, 2nd Lieut., 99 (I)
Grant-Duff, Lieutenant Colonel A., 1, 2, 10, 13, 14, 19, 24, 25-6, 60 (I), 165
Grassie, 2nd Lieut. J. T., 226 (II)
Gray, Company Sergeant Major (later 2nd Lieutenant), A., 3, 23, 37 (I)
Green, Captain W., 2, 12, 13, 14, 30, 31, 38, Brigadier-General, 90, Lieut. Colonel, 103 (I)
Green, Lieut. Colonel W. E. (9th Liverpools), 44
Grenades, *see* Bombs
Guides, The, *see* Indian Army Units
Gunn, Miss, Y. M. C. A., 349
Gunn, Lieut. Marcus S., 57, 59 (I)
Gunn, 2nd Lieut., 46 (I)
Gurkhas, *see* Indian Army Units
Gyle, 2nd Lieut. C. W., 97 (I)

Hackle, the Red, right of The Black Watch to wear confirmed, 279
Haddington, 354 (III)
Hadow, Lieut. Colonel R. W., 64 (VIII)
Hai River, 244-5 (II)
Haifa, 288-9 (II)
Haig, Lieut. General Sir Douglas, 7, 40, C.-in-C., 62, 97
Haig, 2nd Lieut. D., 266 (II)
Haking, Major General R., 40
Haldane, Lieutenant J. B. S., 33 (I), Captain, 245 (II)
Hamilton, Major J. G. H., 42, 51, 60, Lieut. Colonel, 103 (I), 345 (III)
Hamilton, Sergeant, 206 (II)
Hamilton-Johnston, Lieut. D. C., 162, 177, 179, 192, Captain, 204, 213-14, 216, Major 217, 219 (II), 348 (III)

Hanlon, Corporal, 67 (I)
Hanna, Assault on, 216 (II)
Hart, Sergeant P., 32 (I)
Harvey, Major W. St. J., 167, 171, Lieut. Colonel, 176, 181, Brigadier General, 184, 221, 279 (II)
Hay, Corporal, 61 (I)
Hay, Lieut. L. F., 15, 17, Captain, 46 (I), 348 (III)
Haye, 2nd Lieut. R. J., 272, 280 (II)
Hayes, 2nd Lieut. H. V., 48 (I)
Henderson, Capt. C. R. B., 161, 180, 185, 198, Major, 222 (II)
Henderson, 2nd Lieut. N. C., 186, 189, 193-4 (II)
Henderson, 2nd Lieut. T. A., 205, 219-20, 222, 258, 280, 282, 286 (II)
Henderson, Sergeant, 197 *n.*, 206 (II)
Hendry, Lieut. C. V., 282, 291 (II)
Herts Keep, 83 *sqq.* (I)
Higginbotham, Lieut. I. K., 81 (I)
Highland Battalion (Black Watch and Seaforths), 161, 221 *sqq.*
Highland Games, 240, 273
Highland Light Infantry, 171-2
High Wood, attack on, 59 (I)
Hindenburg Line, the, Storming of, 93 *sqq.* (I)
Hobbs, Corporal L., 100 (I)
Hobbs, Regtl. Quartermaster Sergeant E., 162 *n.*, 205, 271, 293 (II)
Hohenzollern Redoubt, Action of, 43, 46 *sqq.* (I)
Holland, 2nd Lieut. B. T., 177, 179 (II)
Holt, Lieut. A. V., 11, 14, 345, 347 (I formerly III)
Home, 2nd Lieut. R. G., 48 (I)
Honeyman, Company Sergeant Major, 197 *n.*
Honours and Awards, lists of
  1st Battalion, 149 *sqq.*
  2nd Battalion, 288, 336 *sqq.*
Hore-Ruthven, Captain M., 15, 17, Lieut. Colonel, 90 (I)

362

INDEX

Houchin, 48, 49 (I)
Houston, Company Sergeant Major B. S., 186, 194, 200, 206, 238, 2nd Lieut., 250, 258, 293 (II)
Houston, Lieut. Colonel (58th Rifles), 179, 189
Houthulst Forest Front, 72 *sqq*. (I)
Hume, Lieut. R. M., 89 (I)
Humm, Sergeant, 213 *n*., 261 (II)
Hunter, Lieut., 206 (II)
Husband, Lieut. P. L., 61 (I)
Hussars, 14th, 251 *n*.
Hutchison, Corpl., 247 (II)
Hutchison, 2nd Lieut. I. O., 186, 189 *sqq*. 205 (II)
Hutchison, 2nd Lieut. R. H., 48 (I)
Hutchison, Sergeant, 198, 205, Company Sergeant Major, 267, 272, 292 (II)
Hynie, Drummer, 294 (II)

Indian Army Units—
 Bhopal Infantry, 9th, 209, 214, 243, 254, 256, 262, 265
 Cavalry, 4th, 178
 Dogras, 37th, 216
 Dogras, 41st, 161, 209, 214, 216–18, 221
 Garhwal Rifles, 170, 177
 Guides, The, 274–6, 287–8
 Gurkha Rifles, 2nd., 181
  2/3, 187
  1/8, 243, 246, 254, 256, 262, 265, 274, 281, 285, 287
  2/8, 161, 167, 169, 187, 190
 Jats, 6th, 209, 212–14, 216–17, 219, 221
 Punjabis, 20th, 243, 246, 262, 274, 286
  28th, 261–2
  33rd, 185, 189–90
  69th, 185, 188, 190
  92nd, 226
 Rifles, 56th, 225–6
  58th, 161, 169, 179, 185, 188–90
  125th, 226, 229, 287
 97th Infantry, 217, 221

Inglis, Lieut. J. N., 163, 164, 168, 178, Captain, 222, 229, 230 (II), 348 (III)
Intermediate Trench, attack on, 58 (I)
Invergordon, 346 (III)
Inverness Copse, 20 (I)
Ireland, 352 *sqq*. (III)
Iron, attack near, 6 (I)
Istabulat, 257
 Battle of, 258 *sqq*. (II)

Jacob, General Sir Claude, 75
Jacobs, Lieut. T. C., 83 (I)
Jackson, Colonel H. K., 346, 349 (III)
Jackson, Private, 22 (I)
Jaffa, 273, 281 (II)
Jalland, Lieut. H. H., 97 (I)
James, Lieut. (Welch Regt.), 30
James, Pte., 278 (II)
Jameson, Lieut., 89 (I)
Jamieson, 2nd Lieut. M., 258, 272 (II)
Jeff, 2nd Lieut. J., 258, 266, 272 (II)
Jericho, 273 (II)
Jerusalem, 273 (II)
Jessop, Company Q. M. Sergeant, 205 (II)
Joffre, General, 4, 9, 15, Marshal, 91
Johnson, Company Sergeant Major, 162 *n*., 2nd Lieut, 180 (II), 348 (III)
Johnston, L/Corpl. D., 100 (I)
Johnston, Pte. W., 100 (I)
Johnston, Sergeant, 177 (II)
Johnstone, Company Sergeant Major A., 272, 293 (II)
Johnstone, Company Sergeant Major E. J., 354 (III)
Johnstone, Regtl. Sergt. Major J., 162, 205, 222, 232, 245 (II)
Jones, Pte. B., 100 (I)
Jordan, Piper J., 294 (II)

Kaidiri Bend, 244–5 (II)
Kay, D., Y.M.C.A., 351 (III)
Keillor, Sergeant J., 100 (I)
Keith, Pipe Major J., 205, 239, 293 (II)

INDEX

Kelly, Company Q. M. Sergeant, 272, 293 (II)
Kelly, Pte. A., 293 (II)
Kelman, L/Corpl. A., 287 (II)
Kennard, Captain C., 348 (III)
Kennedy, Company Sergeant Major J., 162 n., 163, 167, 2nd Lieut. 171 (II)
Kiddie, Sergeant, 205 (II)
Kilgour, Lieut. A., 86, 89 (I)
Kilt, see Dress
Kinfauns Castle, s.s., 268, 271–2 (II)
King, Private, 61–2 (I)
King, 2nd Lieut. J. A., 282 (II)
King's Royal Rifle Corps, 2nd Bn., Thanks from, 39 (I)
Kinnear, Company Q. M. Sergeant T., 206, Company Sergeant Major, 238, 2nd Lieut., 272, 293 (II)
Kirkcaldy, Lieut., 89 (I)
Kortekeer Cabaret, 17, 72 (I)
Krook, Captain A. D. Campbell, 13, 18 (I)
Kut, 203–4, 207 sqq., 214, 223, 227, 230–1, 244 (II)

La Bassée, 165–6, 184 (II)
Lahore Division, see under Divisions
Lake, General Sir Percy, 223, 232
Lamb, 2nd Lieut. C. W., 48 (I)
Lamont, Pte. T., 294 (II)
La Valentine, Camp, 164 (II)
La Vallée Mulatre, Attacks on, 96–7 sqq. (I)
Lawrie, Company Sergeant Major, 186 (II)
Lawson, Regtl. Q. M. Sergeant A. S., later 2nd Lieut., 2, 20, 21, 23 (I)
Lees, Sergeant, 194, 205 (II)
Leicestershire Regt., 1st Bn., 161, 164, 177, 187, 216 n., 275
Leonard, Pte. T., 293 (II)
Le Plantin, 167, 196 (II)
Lewis Guns, 238, 270, 283
Lillers, 162, 172, 199 n.
Lindsay, Company Q. M. Sergeant R., 3 (I)

Lindsay, Major General Sir Walter, 351
Linning, Captain J., 347 (III)
Logan, Sergeant, 241 (II)
London Regt., 3rd Bn., 177, 182
Loos, Battle of, 43 sqq. (I), 184 sqq. (II)
   Reserves sent out after, 350 (III)
Loudon, 2nd Lieut. T., 266, 272 (II)
Low, Pte. R., 100 (I)
Lumsden, Lieut. D., 346 (III)
Lyle, Lieut. T. B., 37, 97 (I)
Lynch, Pte., 195 (II)

McAndrew, Company Q.M. Sergt. A., later 2nd Lieut., 2 (I)
McAra, Company Q. M. Sergeant, 162 (II)
McArthur, 2nd Lieut. D., 266 (II)
MacBean, Major General F., 161
McBeath, Corporal A., 293 (II)
McClellan, Lieut. C. W., 347, Captain, 354 (III)
McClunie, L/Corpl. G., 288 (II)
McConaghey, 2nd Lieut. C. J., 193 (II)
McCurrach, Pte. F., 100 (I)
McDiarmid, Pte. J., 100 (I)
Macdonald, Sergeant A., 182 n., 195, 200, 205, 219, 220, 241–2 (II)
Macdonald, Pte. R., 195 (II)
McDonald, Piper, 195 (II)
Macdougall, 2nd Lieut., 58 (I)
McEwan, Lieut. Colonel D., 22 (I)
McEwen, Captain W. D., 272, 282, 289 (II)
Macfarlane, Rev. A., 162, 222, 240, 258 (II)
Macfarlane, Brigadier General D. A., 351
Macfarlane, Captain R., 238, 258, 266 (II)
McFarlane, L/Corpl. F., 100 (I)
Macfarlane-Grieve, Lieut., 61 (I), 205 (II)
MacGregor, 2nd Lieut. J., 272, 278, Lieut., 283 (II)
McGregor, Pte., 195 (II)

INDEX

McHattie, Pte., 194 (II)
McInroy, Pte., 167 n. (II)
McIntosh, Pte., 169 (II)
McJade, Pte. J., 100 (I)
MacKay, Lieut., 85, 89 (I)
Mackie, 2nd Lieut. A. (H.L.I.), 282
McKinnon, Pte., 195 (II)
McKinnon, Pte. A., 100 (I)
Mackintosh, L/Corpl., 237 (II)
McLaren, Pte. A., 293 (II)
McLaren, Pte. W., 195 (II)
McLaughlan, L/Corpl., 195 (II)
McLeod, Corporal Piper A., 239, 293 (II)
McLeod, Captain G. C. S., 162, 181-2 (II)
McLeod, L/Corpl. D., 28 & n. (I)
McLeod, Lieut. I. B., 163, 188 (II)
MacLeod, 2nd Lieut. L., 186 (II)
McMaster, Corporal Piper D., 205, 239, 274 (II)
McMicking, Lieut. N., 163, 169, 179 (II)
MacMillan, 2nd Lieut., 62 (I)
MacNaughton, Lieutenant, 8, 13 (I), 347 (III)
McNeill, Lieut. M., 20, 22, 23 (I)
McNeill, 2nd Lieut. Neil, 347 (III)
McNicholl, Sergeant, 205 (II)
Macpherson, Lieut. R. S., 58 (I)
Macqueen, Captain, R.A.M.C., 258 (II)
Macrae, Captain (Seaforths), 222
MacRae, 2nd Lieutenant K. S., 3, 17 (I)
MacRae-Gilstrap, Lieut. Colonel J., 350
McVey, Sergeant, 7 (I)
McWilliams, 2nd Lieut., 186, 193 (II)
Maddill, Sergeant, 206 (II)
Mahon, Pte., 280 (II)
Maitland, 2nd Lieut. W. E., 192 (II)
Malcolm, Sergeant, 206 (II)
Mametz Wood, 60, 62 (I)
Mann, 2nd Lieut. T. A., 282 (II)
Manoury, General, 9
Marching Feats, 209, 249, 250, 268 n., 289, 290 (II)

Marindin, Major General A. H., 103 (I)
Marne, Battle of the, 9 sqq., 34 (I)
Maroc Sector, 51 sqq. (I)
Marseilles, 164-5, 199 (II)
Marshall, Captain, 97 (I)
Marshall, General, 243, 248, 249
Marshall, Pte. R., 294 (II)
Martin, Corpl., 194 (II)
Martin, Pte. R., 100 (I)
Maubeuge, 4, 5
Maude, General Sir Stanley, 200, 203, 243 sqq., 250, 268
Maxse, Brigadier General F. I., 1 n., 23 n.
Maxwell, Gen. Sir John, 208 n., 279
Maxwell, Lieut. R. S. S., 346 (III)
May, Sergeant, 284, 288 (II)
Medallion, the Wauchope, 269
Median Wall, 259 (II)
Medical Stores, shortage, in Mesopotamia, 214
Meerut Division, see under Divisions
Megiddo, Battle of, 281 sqq. (II)
Melvin, Pte. C., V.C., 265 (II)
Menelaws, Pte., 195 (II)
Menin road, 17 sqq. (I)
Menzies, Lieut. D. Murray, 48 n., 57, (I)
Menzies, Pte. J., 288 (II)
Mercer, 2nd Lieut. A., 47-8 (I)
Merrylees, Lieut., 48 (I)
Mesopotamia, Description of, 203, 207
2nd Battalion in, Reinforcements for, 354 (III)
Messines, Battle of, 64 sqq., (I)
Messudieh, 288 (II)
Methven, Sergeant, 206 (II)
Middleton, Pte. W., 293 (II)
Millar, Coy. Q. M. Sergt. J., 2 (I)
Miller, Lieut. D. A., 58 (I)
Miller, Coy. Sergeant Major J., 225, 258, 267, 2nd Lieut., 283 (II)
Miller-Stirling, Lieut. E. G. B., 258 (II)

365

INDEX

Milligan, Pioneer Sergeant, 205, Company Sergeant Major, 272, 293 (II)
Mitchell, Sergeant J., 194, 206, 218, 219, 227, 293 (II)
Mitchell, Private J., 21, 23, 100 (I)
Mitchell, Armourer Staff Sergeant W. (R.A.O.C.), 100
Moascar Camp, 272-3
Moat Farm, 83 sqq. (I)
Mobilization, 162
Moir, 2nd Lieut. J. M., 46 (I)
Monro, Lieutenant General Sir Charles, 40
Mons, Retreat from, 5 sqq., 63, 75 (I)
Mons Star, 75 (I)
Montgomery, Major General Sir Archibald, 94
Moore Cameron, Captain, see Cameron
Morrison, G., Orderly Room Sergeant, 205, 293
Morrison, Lieutenant, 205
Morrison, Private J., 288
Moubray, Captain P. L., 15, 18 (I), 345, 347 (III)
Moulin De Piètre, 187-93
Muguet Wood, 92 (I)
Muir, Company Sergeant Major, 162 n., 163, 258, 267, 2nd Lieutenant, 272, 293
Muir, Major J. B., 195
Muir, Private, 275
Munro, 2nd Lieut. D. L., 58 (I)
Murphy, Private, 236
Murray, Capt. the Hon. A. D., 345, 355 (III, later I)
Murray, General Sir Archibald, 103
Murray, 2nd Lieut. D. M. (Gordon Highlanders), 283
Murray, Captain H. F. F., 163, 179
Murray, 2nd Lieut. J. C., 48 n. (I)
Murray, Major J. T. C., 2, 14, 19, 32 (I)
Murray-Graham, 2nd Lieut. A. J. D., 346 (III)

Murray-Stewart, 2nd Lieut. D., 258, 266 (II)
Mushaidie, Battle of, 251 sqq. (II)
Mustapha, 291 (II)

Neuve Chapelle, Battle of, 176 sqq. (II)
New Zealand Division, 61, 62
Nicholson, L/Corpl., 279 (II)
Nigg, Reserve Battalion trained at, 234, 345 sqq. (III)
Niven, Quartermaster Sergeant J., 162, 204 (II)
Nixon, General Sir John, 204, 208, 223 n.
Nœux-les-Mines, 90-1 (I)
Nolan, Lieut. R. P. D., 15, 20, 347 (I from III)
Nonne Boschen Wood, 22-3 (I)
Norfolk Regiment, 221
Norie, Brigadier General C. E., 161, 193, 209, 243

Officers, Lists of, all Battalions
  1st, 2-3, 104 sqq.
  2nd, 162-3, 185-6, 204-6, 258, 266, 271-2, 282-3, 295 sqq.
  3rd, 345-6
Ogilvie, Pte., 195, 294 (II)
Organization, 162, 185 n., 195, 243 (II)
Orleans, 165-6 (II)
Orr-Ewing, Lieut. H. E. D., 163 (II)
Oswald, Sergeant, 205 (II)

Packard, Major (R.A.), 6
Paissy, 11 (I)
Palestine,
  description of, 273-4
  14th Bn. in, reinforcements for, 356 (III)
Palmer, Sergt., 206, Company Sergt. Major, 258, 267 (II)
Paradis, 179 (II)
Park, Captain M. E., 186, 187, 190, 191, 194, 197, 204-5, 227, 238, 241, 258, 272, 274 (II)
Parker, Captain A. E., 345, 347 (III)

INDEX

Parker, Regtl. Quartermaster Sergeant, 162 n., Acting Sergeant Major, 291–2 (II)
Passchendaele, first and second battles at, 16, 69–70 (I)
Paterson, Major P. J. (R.A.), 169
Paterson, 2nd Lieut., 206 (II)
Paton, Lieut. G. D., 276 (II)
Paton, 2nd Lieut. J. L., 48 (I)
Peacock, Pte., 195 (II)
Peebles, Brigadier General, 222
Peel, 2nd Lieut. T., 266 (II)
Picquet House, 170, 172–3 (II)
Pilckem, 17 (I)
Pipers
    1st Battalion, 28 & n., 37, 42, 98
    2nd Battalion, 194, 232–3, 239
Plunkett, 2nd Lieut. H. A. T., 186, 205 (II)
Poincaré, President, 91
Polson, 2nd Lieutenant G. W., 3, 14 (I)
Polygon Wood, 22 (I)
    "Black Watch Corner," 23
Ponsonby, Colonel (Coldstream), 13
Powell, Corpl. F. A., 293 (II)
Pratt, L/Corpl., 195, Corpl. 205, 219 (II)
Preston, 2nd Lieut. H. S., 59 (I)
Prince, Captain (North Lancashire), 21
Proudfoot, Coy. Quartermaster Sergt., 163, Coy. Sergeant Major, 205, 220, 241 (II)
Proudfoot, Pte. A., 293 (II)
Pryde, Pte., 195 (II)
Pullar, Lieut. J. L., 195
Punjabis, see Indian Army Units
Purvis, Lieut. R. M., 206, 227, Captain, 238, 258 (II)

Quine, 2nd Lieut. A. H., 266 (II)
Quine, 2nd Lieut. B. H., 280 (II)

Rae, Pte. G., 294 (II)
Raids, 66 (I), 168, 170, 173 (II)
Ramage, Lieut. W., 71 (I)
Ramsay, Lieut. R., 79, 89 (I)
Rations, in
    France, 77 (I)
    Mesopotamia, 235, 236 n. (II)
Rawlinson, Lieut. General Sir Henry, 49
Raynes, Major (B. Columbia Regt.), 88, 89
Reddie, Major A. J. (2nd South Wales Borderers), 28
Redpath, Corpl., 20, Sergt, 22 (I)
Rees, Major H. C. (2nd Welch Regt.), 30
Rennie, 2nd Lieut. J. L., 2, Lieut., 19, 20 (I), Captain, 351 (III)
Rennie, Sergeant P., 100 (I)
Renton, Company Q.M. Sergeant J. R., 3 (I)
Richard, Captain J. E. M., 348 (III)
Richmond, 2nd Lieut. G. M., 32 (I)
Ridgeway, Lieut. Colonel (33rd Punjabis), 189
Rifle Brigade (12th), 189 sqq.
Rifles (58th), see Indian Army Units
Rifles, new pattern issued, 165, jamming of, by mud, 173, 229 (II)
Ripley, Corpl., V.C., 38, 182 (I)
Ritchie, Lieut. J. C., 264, 266, 272 (II)
Ritchie, Captain N. M., 238, 258, 266, 271, 282, 286, 288 (II)
Ritchie, 2nd Lieut, 46 (I)
Robb, L/Corpl., 195 (II)
Robertson, Major F. M. B., 37 (I)
Robertson, Sergeant J., 83 (I)
Robertson, Lieut. J. W. H., 75, 83, 91 (I)
Robertson, Captain R. D. (Gordon Highlanders), 272, 278
Robertson, Coy. Sergeant Major, 162 n., 186 (II)
Rodman, Corporal, 205 (II)
Roisdorf, 102–3 (I)
Rollo, 2nd Lieut. J. E. H., 2 (I)
Rose, Lieut. Colonel Hugh, 62
Ross, 2nd Lieut. E. N., 280 (II)
Rosyth Dockyard, 350 (III)
Rowan-Hamilton, Lieut. G. B., 2, 22, 23 (I), Captain, 348 (III)

INDEX

Roy, Private, 21 (I)
Roy, 2nd Lieut. W. C., 283 (II)
Royal George, s.s., 199, 200 (II)
Royal Highlanders of Canada, granted the right to wear the Red Hackle, 70
Royal Munster Fusiliers, 2nd Bn., loss of, 6, reformation of, 40 & n.
Royal Sussex Regt., 2nd Bn., thanks of, 39 (I)
Russell-Brown, Major C. (R.E.), 22 (I)
Rutherford, Sgt. P., 100 (I)
Rynie, 2nd Lieut. G., 272 (II)

Sablon, 10 (I)
St. Quentin Canal, 93
  Crossing of, 94 (I)
Samarrah, Capture of, 267 (II)
Sambre-Oise Canal, 6–7 (I)
Sannaiyat, Battles of, 224 *sqq*.
  trenches at, 234, 240, 244, 248
Scobie, 2nd Lieut. A., 272 (II)
Scotsmen, percentage of in The Black Watch, 3, 163 *n*.
Scott, Company Sergt. Major C., 2, 57, Regtl. Sergt. Major, 75, 100 (I)
Scott, 2nd Lieutenant J. G., 37 (I)
Scott, 2nd Lieutenant J. M. 58 (I)
Scouts, 74 (I), 179, 196, 239, 240, 241, 279, 280 (II)
Seaforth Highlanders, 1st Bn., 161, 168, 172, 177, 195, 198, 204, 213, 221–2, 225, 232–3, 240, 247–8, 256, 273, 280, 287, 291, 292 *n*.
Sempill, Lieut. Colonel Lord, 41 (I)
Senior, L/Corpl. H., 100 (I)
Shaikh Sa'ad, 203, 209
  Battle of 210 *sqq*. (II)
  Railway from, 244
Shand, 2nd Lieut. A., 37 (I)
Sharples, Corporal, 179 (II)
Shumran, 209, 245, 248 (II)
Signallers, 164 *n*., 178 *n*., 208, 213 *n*., 239, 255 (II)
Silver, Rev. A., 272 (II)
Simonet, Captain (1st Dorsets), 219

Simpson, Piper D., 194 (II)
Simpson, Pte. W., 288 (II)
Simpson, Sergeant Drummer, 205, 293 (II)
Sinclair, Lieut. (A/Captain) J. G., 75, 82, 84, 89 (I)
Sinclair, Sergeant R., 172, 2nd Lieut., 180, 182 (II)
Sinn Fein movement, 352–3 (III)
Sisters, The, 275–6 (II)
Skene, Captain P. G. M., 32 (I), 163 (II)
Skey, Lieut. C. H., 58 (I)
Sladen, Sergeant, 184 *n*. (II)
Smart, Regtl. Sergeant Major A., 2 (I), Sergeant, 205, Regtl. Sergeant Major, 238, 245, 258, 271 (II)
Smart, 2nd Lieut. G. B., 258, 272 (II)
Smith, 2nd Lieut., 97 (I)
Smith, Pte. A., (20024), 294 (II)
Smith, 2nd Lieut. D., 79 (I)
Smith, 2nd Lieut. H. H., 93 (I)
Smith, Pte., 279 (II)
Smith, 2nd Lieut. T. L., 272 (II)
Smythe, 2nd Lieut. P. E., 258, 266 (II)
Smythe, 2nd Lieut. R. M., 258, 272 (II)
Snipers, 196–7, 279 (II)
Somme, Battle of the, 56 *sqq*. (I)
Sotheby, 2nd Lieut., 186, 193–4 (II)
Soutar, 2nd Lieut. F. H., 205, 219 (II)
South African War, 345
Southey, Brigadier General W. M., 161, 183
Special Reserve Officers attached to 1st Bn., 36
Spence, Pte. P., 100 (I)
Sprot, Lieut. J. W. L., 20, 22, 23 (I)
Stephen, Lieut. J. C., 85, 89 (I)
Stevenson, Lieut. P., 195 (1/4)
Stewart, Pte., 169 (II)
Stewart, L/Corpl., 173 *n*. (II)
Stewart, Sergeant (42nd Canadian Bn.), 70
Stewart, Lieut., 83 (I)

INDEX

Stewart, Lieut. Colonel C. E., 19, 22, 23, 31, 32, 37, 42, 51, 60, 83 (I), Major, 162, 165, 230 (II)
Stewart, 2nd Lieut. G. V., 258, 266 (II)
Stewart, Major J., 262, A/Lieut. Colonel, 266, 271, 278-9, 282 (II)
Stewart, Lieut. Hon. K. A., 182 (II)
Stewart, 2nd Lieut. M., 162 (II)
Stewart Lieut. W. D. Mc.L., 48 n., 61 (I)
Stewart Murray, Major Lord George, 2, 13, 14, 103 (I)
Stewart-Richardson, Capt. Sir E., 15 (I), 345, 347, 355 (III)
Stewart-Smith, Lieut. D. C., 85, 87, 88, 89 (I), 186, 193, 205, 220 (II)
Stirling, Captain C. H. Graham-, 345, Major, 352
Stirton, Pte., 195 (II)
Strachan, Corporal, 194, Sergeant, 293 (II)
Strahan, Captain C. E., 162 & n., 170 (II)
Strength, *see under* Black Watch
Stretcher Bearers, 71 (I), 195, 213, 226-7, 239, 247, 261 (II)
Strickland, Lieut. Colonel E. D., 28, Major General, 68, 75, 96, 99 (I)
Stuart, Sergeant, 205 (II)
Stubbs, Captain J. W. C. (R.A.M.C.), 52 (I)
Sucrerie, the, 12 (I)
Sutherland, Major A., 90
Sutherland, Lieut. A. H. C., 163, 181 (II)
Sutherland, Major H. H., 163, 177 (II)
Sutor Fort, 346 (III)
Suwada, 248-9 (II)
Suwaikiya Marsh, 214, 216, 224, 240, 244 (II)
Swan, 2nd Lieut. (K.O.S.B.), 283
Swan, L/Corpl., 31 (I)
Swan, Pte., 169 (II)
Swan, Sergeant, 31 (I)

Tabsor, 281 (II)
Tain, 350 (III)
Talana Hill (France), Captured, 96 (I)
Tallon, Piper, 294 (II)
Tarleton, Lieut. Colonel, 90 (I)
Tate, Lieut. A. W., 346 (III)
Tekrit, 268 (II)
Templeton, Lieut. A. A., 58 (I)
Thistle, Lieut. T. H. C., 346 (III)
Thompson, Captain (A. & S.H.), 24
Thompson, Corpl. V., 178 (II)
Thomson, Pte., R., 100 (I)
Thomson, Lieut. Col. W. M. (1st Seaforth), 196, 221-2, 232
Thorburn, Lieut., M.M., 206, 218 (II)
Thornton, Brigadier General, 88
Thorpe, Lieut. Col. Gervase, (III)
Todd, Lieut. J., 204, 250, 258, 266, 271 (II)
Townshend, General Sir Charles, 204, 208, 216, 221, 223, 227, 249
Transport, Battalion, 165, 204, 250, 253, 287
Tripoli, 289, 290 (II)
Twentyman, 2nd Lieut. J. J., 280, 283 (II)

Umm-el-Hanna, 214 *sqq.*, 224
Ure, Corporal W., 100 (I)
Urquhart, Captain E. F. M., 15, 17 (I)
Urquhart, 2nd Lieut., 58 (I)

Valentine, Lieut. B. G., 84, 99 (I)
Vendresse, 12 (I)
Venters, Pte., 169 (II)
Villers-Cottérêts, 8 (I)
Vox Farm, Attack on, 71 (I)

Waddell, Sergeant A., 293 (II)
Wadi, Battle of the, 214 *sqq.* (II)
Wales, H.R.H. the Prince of, 40 (I)
Walker, Lieut. Colonel, 189, 196 (IV)
Walker, Pte., 299 (II)
Walker, 2nd Lieut. R. (A. & S.H.), 266

INDEX

Wallace, 2nd Lieutenant J., 37 (I)
Wallace, Company Quartermaster Sergeant, 206 (II)
Wallace Sergeant, 168 (II)
Wanliss, Company Sergt. Major (later Lieutenant) A., 2, 37 (I)
War Book, The, 26
Wassigny, Capture of, 97 *sqq.* (I)
Watson, Sergeant, 62 *n.*, Company Sergeant Major, 206 (II)
Watterson, Pte. D., 294 (II)
Wauchope, Captain A. G., 163, Major, 169, 172, 179, 181, 182 *n.*, 184, 185, 187 *sqq.*, 195, Lieut. Colonel, 196, 204, 211, 213, 230, 232-3, 235-6, 238, 240-1, 246, 248, 256 *sqq.*, 262, 269, 279 (II), Major, 348 (III)
Wauchope Medallion, the, 269 (II)
Weir, Corpl. T., 288 (II)
Wells, 2nd Lieut. J. R., 59 (I)
West, Captain C. C., 20, 23 (I), 345 (III)
West Riding Regt., 166
Whetham, Captain C. Boddam, 345, 347 (III)
Whyte, 2nd Lieut., 46 (I)
Whytock, Sergeant, 194, 206 (II)
Wilkie, Company Sergeant Major, 230 (II)
Willcocks, Lieut. General Sir James, 165
Willett, Captain L. H., 238, 258 (II)
Wilson, Colonel (1/8 Gurkhas), 293 *n.*

Wilson, Company Quartermaster Sergeant D., 272, 293 (II)
Wilson, Lieut., 97, 99 (I)
Wilson, Lieut. E. H. H. J., 2, 10 (I)
Wilson, Sergeant G., 206, Company Sergeant Major, 272, 282 (II)
Wilson, L/Corpl. T., 278, Sergeant, 293 (II)
Wilson, Sergeant W., 171-2, 2nd Lieut., 184 *n.*, Captain, 186, 193-4 (II)
Winchester Road, 185-6, 191 (II)
Woodward, Pte., 286 (II)
Wynn, L/Corpl., 195 (II)

Youghal, 352 (III)
Young, 2nd Lieut. A. A., 258 (II)
Young, 2nd Lieut. J. S., 48, 74 (I)
Young, Pte. T., 100 (I)
Young, Lieut. W. A., 206, Captain, 238, 248, 272, 278 (II)
Younger, Pte., 195 (II)
Younghusband, General, 207, 209, 214
Y.M.C.A. in
 France, 198, 349
 Mesopotamia, 237
Ypres, 1st Battle of, 15 *sqq.* (I), 348 (III)
Ypres Salient, the, 16
Yule, Sergeant, 205, 239 (II)

Zandvoorde - Gheluvelt Road, 18 *sqq.* (I)
Zeebrugge, Attack on, 68 *sqq.* (I)
Zelobes, 170 (II)

NOTES

NOTES

NOTES

NOTES

NOTES

NOTES

NOTES

NOTES

NOTES

NOTES